Lecture Notes in Computer Science 1755

Edited by G. Goos, J. Hartmanis and J. van Leeuwen

Springer

Berlin
Heidelberg
New York
Barcelona
Hong Kong
London
Milan
Paris
Singapore
Tokyo

Dines Bjørner   Manfred Broy
Alexandre V. Zamulin (Eds.)

Perspectives of System Informatics

Third International
Andrei Ershov Memorial Conference, PSI'99
Akademgorodok, Novosibirsk, Russia
July 6-9, 1999
Proceedings

Series Editors

Gerhard Goos, Karlsruhe University, Germany
Juris Hartmanis, Cornell University, NY, USA
Jan van Leeuwen, Utrecht University, The Netherlands

Volume Editors

Dines Bjørner
Technical University of Denmark, Department of Information Technology
Bldg. 344, 2800 Lyngby, Denmark
E-mail: db@it.dtu.dk

Manfred Broy
Technical University of Munich, Computer Science Department
Arcisstr. 21, 80290 Munich, Germany
E-mail: broy@informatik.tu-muenchen.de

Alexandre V. Zamulin
A.P. Ershov Institute of Informatics Systems
av. Ac. Lavrentyev 6, Novosibirsk 630090, Russia
E-mail: zam@iis.nsk.su

Cataloging-in-Publication data applied for

Die Deutsche Bibliothek - CIP-Einheitsaufnahme

Perspectives of system informatics : proceedings / Third International
Andrei Ershov Memorial Conference, PSI '99, Akademgorodok,
Novosibirsk, Russia, July 6 - 9, 1999. Dines Bjørner ... (ed.). -
Berlin ; Heidelberg ; New York ; Barcelona ; Hong Kong ; London ;
Milan ; Paris ; Singapore ; Tokyo : Springer, 2000
(Lecture notes in computer science ; Vol. 1755)
ISBN 3-540-67102-1

CR Subject Classification (1998): F.3, D.3, D.1, D.2, I.2

ISSN 0302-9743
ISBN 3-540-67102-1 Springer-Verlag Berlin Heidelberg New York

Typesetting: Camera-ready by author
SPIN: 10719596 06/3142 – 5 4 3 2 1 0 Printed on acid-free paper

Preface

This volume comprises the papers presented at the Third International Andrei Ershov Memorial Conference "Perspectives of System Informatics", Akademgorodok (Novosibirsk, Russia), July 6–9, 1999. The main goal of the conference was to give an overview of research directions which are decisive for the growth of major areas of research activities in system informatics.

The conference was the third one in the line. The first and second international conferences "Perspectives of System Informatics" were held in Novosibirsk, Akademgorodok, in May, 1991, and June, 1996, respectively. Both conferences gathered a wide spectrum of specialists and were undoubtedly very successful.

The third conference included many of the subjects of the second conference, such as theoretical computer science, programming methodology, new information technologies, and the promising field of artificial intelligence — as important components of system informatics. The style of the second conference was preserved to a certain extent in that there were a considerable number of invited papers in addition to the contributed papers. However, posters were replaced by short talks mainly given by young researchers.

This time 73 papers were submitted to the conference by researchers from all continents. Each paper was reviewed by three experts, at least two of them from the same or a closely related discipline as the authors. The reviewers generally provided high quality assessments of the papers and often gave extensive comments to the authors for the possible improvement of the presentations. As a result, the program committee selected 27 high quality papers as regular talks and 17 papers as short talks. A broad range of "hot" topics in system informatics were covered by eight invited talks given by prominent computer scientists from different countries.

The conference, like the previous ones, was dedicated to the memory of A. P. Ershov, the real and recognized leader in Soviet (and Russian) informatics.

The late Academician Andrei P. Ershov was a man for all seasons. He commanded universal respect and received affection all over the world. His view of programming was both a human one and a scientific one. At Akademgorodok he created a unique group of scientists — some now in far away regions of the world: a good example of "technology transfer", although perhaps not one that too many people in Russia are happy about.

Many of his disciples and colleagues continue to work in the directions initiated or stimulated by him, at the A. P. Ershov Institute of Informatics Systems. The institute was the main organizer of the three conferences.

We are glad to express our gratitude to all the persons and organizations who contributed to the conference — to the sponsors for their moral, financial, and organizational support, and to the members of the local organizing committee for their mutual efforts towards the success of this event. We are especially grateful to N. Cheremnykh for her selfless labour when preparing the conference.

October, 1999

D. Bjørner,
M. Broy,
A. Zamulin

Organization

Conference Chair: Alexander Marchuk (Novosibirsk, Russia)

Program Committee Co-chairs: Dines Bjørner (Lyngby, Denmark)
Manfred Broy (Munich, Germany)
Alexandre Zamulin (Novosibirsk, Russia)

Program Committee:

Janis Barzdins (Latvia)
Frédéric Benhamou (France)
Christian Boitet (France)
Mikhail Bulyonkov (Russia)
Piotr Dembinski (Poland)
Alexander Dikovsky (France)
Victor Ivannikov (Russia)
Philippe Jorrand (France)
Leonid Kalinichenko (Russia)
Alexander Kleschev (Russia)
Vadim Kotov (USA)
Reino Kurki-Suonio (Finland)
Alexander Letichevski (Ukraine)
Eduard Ljubimsky (Russia)
Rudiger Loos (Germany)
Bernhard Möller (Germany)
Hanspeter Mössenböck (Austria)
Valery Nepomniaschy (Russia)
Gennady Osipov (Russia)
Jaan Penjam (Estonia)
Peter Pepper (Germany)
Igor Pottosin (Russia)
Wolfgang Reisig (Germany)
Dieter Rombach (Germany)
Dean Rosenzweig (Croatia)
Viktor Sabelfeld (Germany)
Vladimir Sazonov (Russia)
David Schmidt (USA)
Sibylle Schupp (USA)
Valery Sokolov (Russia)
Nicolas Spyratos (France)
Alexander Tomilin (Russia)
Enn Tyugu (Sweden)
Andrei Voronkov (Sweden)
Tatyana Yakhno (Russia)
Zhou Chaochen (Macau)

Additional Referees

P. A. Abdulla
I. Anureev
C. Bunse
K. Čerāns
Dang Van Hung
T. Ehm
S. Gaissaryan
A. Godlevskiy
M. Gorbunov-Posadov
T. Jen
M. Korovina
G. Kucherov
S. Krivoi
K. Lellahi
F. Moller
O. Müller
A. Mycroft
J. Philipps
K. Podnieks
A. Sabelfeld
U. Sarkans
K. Schneider
W. Schwerin
N. Shilov
T. Stauner
M. Tudruj
M. Valiev
D. von Oheimb
J. Winkovski
Xu Qiwen

Conference Secretary

Natalia Cheremnykh (Novosibirsk, Russia)

Local Organizing Committee

Sergei Kuznetsov	Vladimir Detushev	Anna Shelukhina
Gennady Alexeev	Olga Drobyshevich	Irina Zanina
Alexander Bystrov	Vera Ivanova	
Tatyana Churina	Vladimir Sergeev	

Sponsors

Support from the following institutions is gratefully acknowledged:

- Russian Foundation for Basic Research
- Office of Naval Research, USA
- Nortel Networks, Canada
- Relativity Technologies, Inc, USA
- UN University's International Institute for Software Technology, Macau

Table of Contents

Algebraic Specifications

Specifications with States

Partial Evaluation and Supercompilation

Concurrency and Parallelism

Logic and Processes

Languages and Software

Database Programming

Object-Oriented Programming

Constraint Programming

Model & Program Checking

Artificial Intelligence

The Common Framework Initiative for Algebraic Specification and Development of Software*

Donald Sannella

Laboratory for Foundations of Computer Science
University of Edinburgh, UK
dts@dcs.ed.ac.uk, www.dcs.ed.ac.uk/~dts/

Abstract. The Common Framework Initiative (CoFI) is an open international collaboration which aims to provide a common framework for algebraic specification and development of software. The central element of the Common Framework is a specification language called CASL for formal specification of functional requirements and modular software design which subsumes many previous algebraic specification languages. This paper is a brief summary of past and present work on CoFI.

1 Introduction

Algebraic specification is one of the most extensively-developed approaches in the formal methods area. The most fundamental assumption underlying algebraic specification is that programs are modelled as *many-sorted algebras* consisting of a collection of sets of data values together with functions over those sets. This level of abstraction is commensurate with the view that the correctness of the input/output behaviour of a program takes precedence over all its other properties. Another common element is that specifications of programs consist mainly of logical *axioms*, usually in a logical system in which equality has a prominent role, describing the properties that the functions are required to satisfy. This *property-oriented* approach is in contrast to so-called *model-oriented* specifications in frameworks like VDM which consist of a simple realization of the required behaviour. Confusingly — because the theoretical basis of algebraic specification is largely in terms of constructions on algebraic models — it is at the same time much more model-oriented than approaches such as those based on type theory (see e.g. [NPS90]), where the emphasis is almost entirely on syntax and formal systems of rules while semantic models are absent or regarded as of secondary importance.

The past 25 years has seen a great deal of research on the theory and practice of algebraic specification. Overviews of this material include [Wir90], [BKLOS91], [LEW96], [ST97], [AKK99] and [ST??]. Developments on the foundational side have been balanced by work on applications, but despite a number of success stories, industrial adoption has so far been limited. The proliferation of

* This research was supported by the ESPRIT-funded CoFI Working Group.

D. Bjørner, M. Broy, A. Zamulin (Eds.): PSI'99, LNCS 1755, pp. 1–9, 2000.

algebraic specification languages is seen as a significant obstacle to the dissemination and use of these techniques. Despite extensive past collaboration between the main research groups involved and a high degree of agreement concerning the basic concepts, the field has given the appearance of being extremely fragmented, with no *de facto* standard specification language, let alone an international standard. Moreover, although many tools supporting the use of algebraic techniques have been developed in the academic community, none of them has gained wide acceptance, at least partly because of their isolated usability: each tool uses a different specification language.

Since late 1995, work has been underway in an attempt to remedy this situation. The *Common Framework Initiative* (abbreviated CoFI) is an open international collaboration which aims to provide a common framework for algebraic specification and development of software. The Common Framework is intended to be attractive to researchers in the field as a common basis for their work, and to ultimately become attractive for use in industry. The central element of the Common Framework is a specification language called CASL (the Common Algebraic Specification Language), intended for formal specification of functional requirements and modular software design and subsuming many previous specification languages. Development of prototyping and verification tools for CASL will lead to them being interoperable, i.e. capable of being used in combination rather than in isolation.

Most effort to date has concentrated on the design of CASL, which concluded in late 1998. Even though the intention was to base the design on a critical selection of concepts and constructs from existing specification languages, it was not easy to reach a consensus on a coherent language design. A great deal of careful consideration was given to the effect that the constructs available in the language would have on such aspects as the methodology for formal development of modular software from specifications and the ease of constructing appropriate support tools. A complete formal semantics for CASL was produced in parallel with the later stages of the language design, and the desire for a relatively straightforward semantics was one factor in the choice between various alternatives in the design. Work on CoFI has been an activity of IFIP WG 1.3 and the design of CASL has been approved by this group.

This paper is a brief summary of work in CoFI with pointers to information available elsewhere. CASL is given special prominence since it is the main concrete product of CoFI so far. A more extensive description of the rationale behind CoFI and CASL may be found in [Mos97] and [Mos99].

2 CASL

CASL represents a consolidation of past work on the design of algebraic specification languages. With a few minor exceptions, all its features are present in some form in other languages but there is no language that comes close to subsuming it. Designing a language with this particular novel collection of features required solutions to a number of subtle problems in the interaction between features.

It soon became clear that no single language could suit all purposes. On one hand, sophisticated features are required to deal with specific programming paradigms and special applications. On the other, important methods for prototyping and reasoning about specifications only work in the *absence* of certain features: for instance, term rewriting requires specifications with equational or conditional equational axioms.

CASL is therefore the heart of a *family* of languages. Some tools will make use of well-delineated *sub-languages* of CASL obtained by syntactic or semantic restrictions, while *extensions* of CASL will be defined to support various paradigms and applications. The design of CASL took account of some of the planned extensions, particularly one that involves higher-order functions [MHK98], and this had an important impact on decisions concerning matters like concrete syntax.

CASL consists of the following major parts or "layers": basic specifications; structured specifications; architectural specifications; specification libraries. A detailed description of the features of CASL may be found in [Mos99] and the complete language definition is in [CoFI98]. Here we just give a quick overview and a couple of simple examples in the hope that this will give a feeling for what CASL is like. Further examples may be found in the appendices of [CoFI98]. Since features of various existing specification languages have found their way into CASL in some form, there are of course many interesting relationships with other languages. It is not the purpose of this paper to detail these so many relevant references are omitted.

A CASL basic specification denotes a class of *many-sorted partial first-order structures*: algebras where the functions are partial or total, and where also predicates are allowed. These are classified by *signatures*, which list sort names, partial and total function names, and predicate names, together with profiles of functions and predicates. The sorts are partially ordered by a subsort inclusion relation, which is interpreted as embedding rather than set-theoretic inclusion, and is required to commute with overloaded functions. A CASL basic specification includes *declarations* to introduce components of signatures and *axioms* to give properties of structures that are to be considered as *models* of a specification. Axioms are written in first-order logic (so, with quantifiers and the usual logical connectives) built over atomic formulae which include strong and existential equalities, definedness formulae and predicate applications, with generation constraints added as special, non-first-order sentences. The interpretation of formulae is as in classical two-valued first-order logic, in contrast to some frameworks that accommodate partial functions. Concise syntax is provided for specifications of "datatypes" with constructor and selector functions.

Here is an example of a basic specification:

free types $\mathit{Nat} ::= \mathit{0} \mid$ **sort** Pos;
$\qquad\qquad\quad \mathit{Pos} ::= \mathit{suc}(\mathit{pre} : \mathit{Nat})$
op $\quad \mathit{pre} : \mathit{Nat} \to ?\ \mathit{Nat}$
axioms
$\qquad \neg \mathit{def}\ \mathit{pre}(\mathit{0})$;
$\qquad \forall n : \mathit{Nat} \bullet \mathit{pre}(\mathit{suc}(n)) = n$

```
pred even__ : Nat
var  n : Nat
 •   even 0
 •   even suc(n) ⇔ ¬even n
```

The remaining features of CASL do not depend on the details of the features for basic specifications, so this part of the design is orthogonal to the rest. An important consequence of this is that sub-languages and extensions of CASL can be defined by restricting or extending the language of basic specifications (under certain conditions) without the need to reconsider or change the rest of the language.

CASL provides ways of building complex specifications out of simpler ones (the simplest ones being basic specifications) by means of various *specification-building operations.* These include translation, hiding, union, and both free and loose forms of extension. A structured specification denotes a class of many-sorted partial first-order structures, as with basic specifications. Thus the structure of a specification is *not* reflected in its models: it is used only to present the specification in a modular style. Structured specifications may be named and a named specification may be *generic*, meaning that it declares some *parameters* that need to be *instantiated* when it is used. Instantiation is a matter of providing an appropriate *argument specification* together with a *fitting morphism* from the parameter to the argument specification. Fitting may also be accomplished by the use of named *views* between specifications. Generic specifications correspond to what is known in other specification languages as (*pushout-style*) *parametrized specifications.*

Here is an example of a generic specification (referencing a specification named PARTIAL_ORDER, which is assumed to declare the sort *Elem* and the predicate __ ≤ __):

```
spec LIST_WITH_ORDER [PARTIAL_ORDER] =
   free type List[Elem] ::= nil | cons(hd :?Elem; tl :?List[Elem])
then
   local
        op  insert : Elem × List[Elem] → List[Elem];
        vars x, y : Elem; l : List[Elem]
        axioms insert(x, nil) = cons(x, nil);
               x ≤ y ⇒ insert(x, cons(y, l)) = cons(x, insert(y, l));
               ¬(x ≤ y) ⇒ insert(x, cons(y, l)) = cons(y, insert(x, l))
   within
        pred order[__ ≤ __] : List[Elem] × List[Elem]
        vars x : Elem; l : List[Elem]
        axioms order[__ ≤ __](nil) = nil;
               order[__ ≤ __](cons(x, l)) = insert(x, order[__ ≤ __](l))
end
```

Architectural specifications in CASL are for describing the modular structure of software, in constrast to structured specifications where the structure is only for presentation purposes. Architectural specifications are probably the most novel aspect of CASL; they are not entirely new, but they have no counterpart in most algebraic specification languages. An architectural specification consists of a list of *unit declarations*, indicating the component modules required with specifications for each of them, together with a *unit term* that describes the way in which these modules are to be combined. (There is an unfortunate potential for confusion here: in CASL, the term "architecture" refers to the "implementation" modular structure of the system rather than to the "interaction" relationships between modules in the sense of [AG97].) Units are normally functions which map structures to structures, where the specification of the unit specifies properties that the argument structure is required to satisfy as well as properties that are guaranteed of the result. These functions are required to be *persistent*, meaning that the argument structure is preserved intact in the result structure. This corresponds to the fact that a software module must use its imports as supplied without altering them.

Here is a simple example of an architectural specification (referencing ordinary specifications named LIST, CHAR, and NAT, assumed to declare the sorts *Elem* and *List*[*Elem*], *Char*, and *Nat*, respectively):

arch spec CN_LIST =
units
C : CHAR ;
N : NAT ;
F : ELEM $\rightarrow$ LIST[ELEM]
result $F[C$ **fit** $Elem \mapsto Char]$ **and** $F[N$ **fit** $Elem \mapsto Nat]$

More about architectural specifications, including further examples, may be found in [BST99].

Libraries in CASL are collections of named specifications. A specification can refer to an item in a library by giving its name and the location of the library that contains it. CASL includes direct support for establishing distributed libraries on the Internet with version control.

3 Semantics

The formal semantics of CASL, which is complete but whose presentation still requires some work, is in [CoFI99]. The semantics is divided into the same parts as the language definition (basic specifications, structured specifications, etc.) but in each part there is also a split into *static semantics* and *model semantics*.

The static semantics checks well-formedness of phrases and produces a "syntactic" object as result, failing to produce any result for ill-formed phrases. For example, for a basic specification the static semantics yields a *theory presentation* containing the sorts, function symbols, predicate symbols and axioms that belong to the specification. (Actually it yields an *enrichment*: when a basic specification is used to extend an existing specification it may refer to existing sorts, functions and predicates.) A phrase may be ill-formed because it makes reference to non-existent identifiers or because it contains a sub-phrase that fails to type check. The *model semantics* provides the corresponding model-theoretic part of the semantics, and is intended to be applied only to phrases that are well-formed according to the static semantics. For a basic specification, the model semantics yields a class of models. A statically well-formed phrase may still be ill-formed according to the model semantics: for example, if a generic specification is instantiated with an argument specification that has an appropriate signature but which has models that fail to satisfy the axioms in the parameter specification, then the result is undefined. The judgements of the static and model semantics are defined inductively by means of rules in the style of Natural Semantics.

The orthogonality of basic specifications in CASL with respect to the rest of the language is reflected in the semantics by the use of a variant of the notion of institution [GB92] called an *institution with symbols* [Mos98]. (For readers who are unfamiliar with the notion of institution, it corresponds roughly to "logical system appropriate for writing specifications".) The semantics of basic specifications is regarded as defining a particular institution with symbols, and the rest of the semantics is based on an arbitrary institution with symbols.

The semantics provides a basis for the development of a proof system for CASL. As usual, at least three levels are needed: proving consequences of sets of axioms; proving consequences of structured specifications; and finally, proving the refinement relation between structured specifications. The semantics of CASL gives a reference point for checking the soundness of each of the proposed proof systems and for studying their completeness.

4 Methodology

The original motivation for work on algebraic specification was to enable the stepwise development of correct software systems from specifications with verified refinement steps. CASL provides good support for the production of specifications both of the problem to be solved and of components of the solution, but it does not incorporate a specific notion of refinement. Architectural specifications go some way towards relating different stages of development but they do not provide the full answer. Other methodological issues concern the "endpoints" of the software development process: how the original specification is obtained in the first place (requirements engineering), and how the transition is made from CASL to a given programming language. Finally, the usual issues in programming methodology are relevant here, for instance: verification versus testing; software reuse and specification reuse; software reverse engineering; software evolution.

CASL has been designed to accommodate multiple methodologies. Various existing methodologies and styles of use of algebraic specifications have been considered during the design of CASL to avoid unnecessary difficulties for users who are accustomed to a certain way of doing things. For the sake of concreteness, the present author prefers the methodology espoused in [ST97], and work on adapting this methodology to CASL has begun.

5 Support Tools

Tool activity initially focussed on the concrete syntax of CASL to provide feedback to the language design since the exact details of the concrete syntax can have major repercussions for parsing. CASL offers a flexible syntax with *mixfix* notation for application of functions and predicates to arguments, which requires relatively advanced parsing methods. ASF+SDF was used to prototype the CASL syntax in the course of its design, and several other parsers have been developed concurrently. Also available is a LaTeX package for uniform formatting of CASL specifications with easy conversion to HTML format. ATerms [BKO98] have been chosen as the common interchange format for CoFI tools. This provides a tree representation for various objects (programs, specifications, abstract syntax trees, proofs) and annotations to store computed results so that one tool can conveniently pass information to another. Work is underway on a format for annotations and on a list of specific kinds of annotations.

At present, the principal focus of tools work in CoFI is on adapting tools that already exist for use with CASL. Existing rewrite engines such as in OBJ, ASF+SDF and ELAN should provide a good basis for prototyping (parts of) CASL specifications. For verification tools, we plan to reuse existing proof tools for specific subsets of CASL: equational, conditional, full first-order logic with total functions, total functions with subsorts, partial functions, etc. The integration of proof tools such as SPIKE, EXPANDER and others will provide the potential to perform proofs by induction, observational proofs, termination proofs, etc. One system on which development is already well-advanced is HOL-CASL [MKK98] which provides static analysis of CASL specifications and theorem proving via an encoding into the Isabelle/HOL theorem prover [Pau94]. Another is INKA 5.0 [AHMS99] which provides theorem proving for a sub-language of CASL that excludes partial functions.

6 Specification of Reactive Systems

An area of particular interest for applications is that of reactive, concurrent, distributed and real-time systems. There is considerable past work in algebraic specification that tackles systems of this kind, but nonetheless the application of CASL to such systems in speculative and preliminary in comparison with the rest of CoFI. The aim here is to propose and develop one or more extensions of CASL to deal with systems of this kind, and to study methods for developing software from such specifications. Extensions in three main categories are currently being considered:

- Combination of formalisms for concurrency (e.g. CCS, Petri nets, CSP) with CASL for handling classical (static) data structures;
- Formalisms built over CASL, where processes are treated as special dynamic data; and
- Approaches where CASL is used for coding at the meta-level some formalism for concurrency, as an aid to reasoning.

Work in this area begun only after the design of CASL was complete and so it is still in its early stages.

7 Invitation

CoFI is an open collaboration, and new participants are welcome to join at any time. Anybody who wishes to contribute is warmly invited to visit the CoFI web site at `http://www.brics.dk/Projects/CoFI/` where all CoFI documentation, design notes, minutes of past meetings etc. are freely available. Announcements of general interest to CoFI participants are broadcast on the low-volume mailing list `cofi-list@brics.dk` and each task group has its own mailing list; see the CoFI web site for subscription instructions. All of these mailing lists are moderated. Funding from the European Commission is available until September 2000 to cover travel to CoFI meetings although there are strict rules concerning eligibility, see `http://www.dcs.ed.ac.uk/home/dts/CoFI-WG/`.

Acknowledgements. Many thanks to all the participants of CoFI, and in particular to the coordinators of the various CoFI Task Groups: Bernd Krieg-Brückner (Language Design); Andrzej Tarlecki (Semantics); Michel Bidoit (Methodology); Hélène Kirchner (Tools); Egidio Astesiano (Reactive Systems); and especially Peter Mosses (External Relations) who started CoFI and acted as overall coordinator until mid-1998.

References

[AG97] R. Allen and D. Garlan. A formal basis for architectural connection. *ACM Transactions on Software Engineering and Methodology*, July 1997.

[AKK99] E. Astesiano, H.-J. Kreowski and B. Krieg-Brückner (eds.). *Algebraic Foundations of Systems Specification.* Springer (1999).

[AHMS99] S. Autexier, D. Hutter, H. Mantel and A. Schairer. Inka 5.0: a logic voyager. *Proc. 16th Intl. Conference on Automated Deduction*, Trento. Springer LNAI 1632, 207–211 (1999).

[BKLOS91] M. Bidoit, H.-J. Kreowski, P. Lescanne, F. Orejas and D. Sannella (eds.). *Algebraic System Specification and Development: A Survey and Annotated Bibliography.* Springer LNCS 501 (1991).

[BST99] M. Bidoit, D. Sannella and A. Tarlecki. Architectural specifications in CASL. *Proc. 7th Intl. Conference on Algebraic Methodology and Software Technology*, Manaus, Brazil. Springer LNCS 1548, 341–357 (1999).

[BKO98] M. van den Brand, P. Klint and P. Olivier. ATerms: exchanging data between heterogeneous tools for CASL. CoFI Note T-3, `http://www.brics.dk/Projects/CoFI/Notes/T-3/` (1998).

[CoFI98] CoFI Task Group on Language Design. CASL – The CoFI algebraic specification language – Summary (version 1.0). `http://www.brics.dk/Projects/CoFI/Documents/CASL/Summary/` (1998).

[CoFI99] CoFI Task Group on Semantics. CASL – The CoFI algebraic specification language – Semantics (version 1.0). CoFI Note S-9, `http://www.brics.dk/Projects/CoFI/Notes/S-9/` (1999).

[GB92] J. Goguen and R. Burstall. Institutions: abstract model theory for specification and programming. *Journal of the Assoc. for Computing Machinery* 39:95–146 (1992).

[Mos98] T. Mossakowski. Institution-independent semantics for CASL-in-the-large. CoFI Note S-8, `http://www.brics.dk/Projects/CoFI/Notes/S-8/` (1998).

[MHK98] T. Mossakowski, A. Haxthausen and B. Krieg-Brückner. Subsorted partial higher-order logic as an extension of CASL. CoFI Note L-10, `http://www.brics.dk/Projects/CoFI/Notes/L-10/` (1998).

[MKK98] T. Mossakowski, Kolyang and B. Krieg-Brückner. Static semantic analysis and theorem proving for CASL. *Recent Trends in Algebraic Development Techniques: Selected Papers from WADT'97*, Tarquinia. Springer LNCS 1376, 333–348 (1998).

[LEW96] J. Loeckx, H.-D. Ehrich and M. Wolf. *Specification of Abstract Data Types*. Wiley (1996).

[Mos97] P. Mosses. CoFI: the common framework initiative for algebraic specification and development. *Proc. 7th Intl. Joint Conf. on Theory and Practice of Software Development*, Lille. Springer LNCS 1214, 115–137 (1997).

[Mos99] P. Mosses. CASL: a guided tour of its design. *Recent Trends in Algebraic Development Techniques: Selected Papers from WADT'98*, Lisbon. Springer LNCS 1589, 216–240 (1999).

[NPS90] B. Nordström, K. Petersson and J. Smith. *Programming in Martin-Löf's Type Theory: An Introduction.* Oxford Univ. Press (1990).

[Pau94] L. Paulson. *Isabelle: A Generic Theorem Prover.* Springer LNCS 828 (1994).

[ST97] D. Sannella and A. Tarlecki. Essential concepts of algebraic specification and program development. *Formal Aspects of Computing* 9:229–269 (1997).

[ST??] D. Sannella and A. Tarlecki. *Foundations of Algebraic Specifications and Formal Program Development.* Cambridge Univ. Press, to appear.

[Wir90] M. Wirsing. Algebraic specification. *Handbook of Theoretical Computer Science* (J. van Leeuwen, ed.). North-Holland (1990).

A Logical Approach to Specification of Hybrid Systems

Margarita V. Korovina[1] and Oleg V. Kudinov[2]

[1] A. P. Ershov Institute of Informatics Systems
Acad. Lavrent'ev pr., 6, Novosibirsk, Russia,
rita@ssc.nsu.ru
[2] Institute of Mathematics
University pr., 4, Novosibirsk, Russia
kud@math.nsc.ru

Abstract. The main subject of our investigation is behaviour of the continuous components of hybrid systems. By a hybrid system we mean a network of digital and analog devices interacting at discrete times. A first-order logical formalization of hybrid systems is proposed in which the trajectories of the continuous components are presented by majorant-computable functionals.

1 Introduction

In the recent time, attention to the problems of exact mathematical formalization of complex systems such as hybrid systems is constantly raised. By a hybrid system we mean a network of digital and analog devices interacting at discrete times. An important characteristic of hybrid systems is that they incorporate both continuous components, usually called plants, as well as digital components, i.e. digital computers, sensors and actuators controlled by programs. These programs are designed to select, control, and supervise the behaviours of the continuous components. Modelling, design, and investigation of behaviours of hybrid systems have recently become active areas of research in computer science (for example see [7,10,11,15,16,19]). We use the models of hybrid systems proposed by Nerode, Kohn in [19].

A hybrid system is a system which consists of a continuous plant that is disturbed by external world and controlled by a program implemented on a sequential automaton. The control program reads sensor data, a sensor function of state of the plant sampled at discrete times, computes the next control law, and imposes it on the plant. The plant will continue using this control law until the next such intervention.

A representation of external world is an input data of the plant. The control automaton has input data (the set of sensor measurements) and the output data (the set of control laws). The control automaton is modelled by three units. The first unit is a converter which converts each measurement into input symbols of the internal control automaton. The internal control automaton, in practice,

D. Bjørner, M. Broy, A. Zamulin (Eds.): PSI'99, LNCS 1755, pp. 10–16, 2000.

is a finite state automaton with finite input and output alphabets. The second unit is the internal control automaton, which has a symbolic representation of a measurement as input and produces a symbolic representation of the next control law to be imposed on the plant as output. The third unit is a converter which converts these output symbols representing control laws into the actual control laws imposed on the plant. The plant interacts with the external world and the control automata at times t_i, where the time sequence $\{t_i\}$ satisfies realizability requirements.

The main subject of our investigation is behaviour of the continuous components. In [19], the set of all possible trajectories of the plant was called as a performance specification. We propose a first-order logical formalization of hybrid systems in which the trajectories of the continuous components (the performance specification) are presented by majorant-computable functionals. The following properties are the main characteristic properties of our approach.

1. An information about the external world is represented by a majorant-computable real-valued function. In nontrivial cases for proper behaviour our system should analyse some complicated external information at every moment when such information can be processed. In general case, we can't represent this information by several real numbers because the laws of behaviours of the external world may be unknown in advance. Note that an external information should be measured so, in some sense, it is computable. According this reasons we present an external information by a majorant-computable real-valued function.

2. The plant is given by a real-valued functional. At the moment of interaction, using the law computed by the discrete device, the plant transforms external function to a real value which is the output for the plant. So the theory of majorant-computable functionals is adequate mathematical tool for a formalization of the mentioned phenomena. Although the differential operator is not used as a basic one, this formalization is compatible with representation of the plant by an ordinary differential equation (see [13,20]). Really, if there exists some method for approximate computing of the solution to the differential equation that is based on difference operators like the Galerkin method, then such solution can be described by a computable functional (see [13,20]).

3. The trajectories of plants are described by computable functionals. So the trajectories are exactly characterized in logical terms (via Σ-formulas). Thus, the proposition is proved which connects the trajectory of a plant with validity of two Σ-formulas in the basic model.

2 Basic Notions

To construct a formalization of hybrid systems we introduce a basic model and recall the notions of majorant-computability of real-valued functions and functionals. To specify complicated systems such as hybrid systems we extend the real numbers $\mathbb{R}$ by adding the list superstructure $L(\mathbb{R})$, the set of finite sequences (words), A^*, of elements of A, where A is a finite alphabet, together with the predicates P_{a_i} for each elements a_i of A, and appropriate operations for working with elements of $L(\mathbb{R})$ and A^*.

We consider the many-sorted model $\mathbf{M} =< \mathrm{HW}(\mathbb{R}), \mathrm{A}^* >$ with the following sorts:

1. $\mathrm{HW}(\mathbb{R}) = \langle \mathbb{R}; L(\mathbb{R}), \mathrm{cons}, \in_l, [] \rangle$, where $\mathbb{R} =< \mathbb{R}, 0, 1, +, \cdot, \leq >$ is the standard model of the reals, denoted also by $\mathbb{R}$; the set $L(\mathbb{R})$ is constructed by induction:
   (a) $L_0(\mathbb{R}) = \mathbb{R}$;
   (b) L_{i+1}=the set of finite ordered sequences (lists) of elements of $\mathbb{R} \cup L_i(\mathbb{R})$;
   (c) $L(\mathbb{R}) = \bigcup_{i \in \omega} L_i(\mathbb{R})$.
   (d) $\sigma_{\mathrm{HW}(\mathbb{R})} = \{0, 1, +, \cdot, \leq\} \cup \{\mathrm{cons}, \in, []\}$, where cons,$\in$, [] (empty list) are defined in standard way (see [8]).

   At first this structure was proposed by Backus in [1], now, it is rather well studied in [2,5,8]. This structure enables us to define the natural numbers, to code, and to store information via formulas.
2. $A^* =< A^*, \sigma_{A^*} >$ is the set of finite sequences (words) of elements of A, where $A = \{a_1, \ldots, a_n\}$ is a finite alphabet. The elements of the language $\sigma_{A^*} = \{P_{a_1}, \ldots, P_{a_n}, =, \in, \mathrm{conc}, ()\}$ are defined in standard way (see [23]).
3. $\sigma_{\mathbf{M}} = \sigma_{\mathrm{HW}(\mathbb{R})} \cup \sigma_{A^*} \cup \{*\}$, where $*$ are defined in the following way:
   (a) $* : A^* \times \mathrm{HW}(\mathbb{R}) \to \mathrm{HW}(\mathbb{R})$,
   (b) $(a_{i_1}, \ldots, a_{i_k}) * [x_1, \ldots, x_n] = [y_1, \ldots, y_m]$, where $m = \min(i_k, n)$ and

$$y_j = \begin{cases} x_j & \text{if } a_{i_j} = a_1, \\ 0 & \text{otherwise} . \end{cases}$$

The variables of $\sigma_{\mathbf{M}}$ subject to the following conventions: $a, b, c, d, \ldots$ range over $\mathbb{R}$, $l_1, l_2, \ldots$ range over $L(\mathbb{R})$, $x, y, z, \ldots$ range over $\mathbb{R} \cup L(\mathbb{R})$, $a_1, \ldots a_n$ range over A, $\alpha, \beta, \gamma, w, \ldots$ range over A^*. This notation gives us easy way to assert that something holds of real numbers, of lists, or of words.

The notions of a term and an atomic formula in the languages $\sigma_{\mathrm{HW}(\mathbb{R})}$ and σ_{A^*} are given in a standard manner.

The set of atomic formulas in $\sigma_{\mathbf{M}}$ is the union of the sets of atomic formulas in $\sigma_{\mathrm{HW}(\mathbb{R})}$, σ_{A^*}, and the set of formulas of the type $w * l_i = l_j$. The set of *Δ_0-formulas* in $\sigma_{\mathbf{M}}$ is the closure of the set of atomic formulas in $\sigma_{\mathbf{M}}$ under $\wedge, \vee, \neg, \exists x \in l, \forall x \in l, \exists a \in w$ and $\forall a \in w$. The set of *Σ-formulas* in $\sigma_{\mathbf{M}}$ is the closure of the set of Δ_0-formulas under $\wedge, \vee, \exists x \in l, \forall x \in l, \exists a \in w, \forall a \in w$, and $\exists$. We define *Π-formulas* as negations of Σ-formulas.

We use definability as one of the basic conceptions. Montague [17] proposed to consider computability from the point of view of definability. Later, many authors among them Ershov [5], Moschovakis [18] paid attention to properties of this approach applied to various basic models.

Definition 1. *1. A set $B \subseteq \mathrm{HW}(\mathbb{R}) \times (A^*)^n$ is Σ-definable if there exists a Σ-formula $\Phi(x)$ such that $x \in B \leftrightarrow \mathbf{M} \models \Phi(x)$. 2. A function f is Σ-definable if its graph is Σ-definable*

In a similar way, we define the notions of *Π-definable functions* and *sets*. The class of *Δ-definable functions* (*sets*) is the intersection of the class Σ-definable functions (sets) and the class of Π-definable functions (sets). Properties of Σ-, Π-, Δ- definable sets and functions were investigated in [5,8,12]. Note only that Δ-definable sets are analogies of recursive sets on the natural numbers.

We will use majorant-computable functions and functionals to formalize information about external world and plants. Let us recall the notion of computability for real-valued functions and functional proposed and investigated in [12,13]. A real-valued function (functionals) is said to be *majorant-computable* if we can construct a special kind of nonterminating process computing approximations closer and closer to the result.

Definition 2. *A function* $f : \mathbb{R}^n \to \mathbb{R}$ *is called majorant-computable if there exist an effective sequence of Σ-formulas* $\{\Phi_s(\mathbf{x}, y)\}_{s\in\omega}$ *and an effective sequence of Π-formulas* $\{G_s(\mathbf{x}, y)\}_{s\in\omega}$ *such that the following conditions hold.*

1. *For all* $s \in \omega$, $\mathbf{x} \in \mathbb{R}^n$, *the formulas* Φ_s *and* G_s *define the same nonempty interval* $< \alpha_s, \beta_s >$.
2. *For all* $\mathbf{x} \in \mathbb{R}^n$, *the sequence* $\{< \alpha_s, \beta_s >\}_{s\in\omega}$ *decreases monotonically, i.e.,* $< \alpha_{s+1}, \beta_{s+1} > \subseteq < \alpha_s, \beta_s >$ *for* $s \in \omega$;
3. *For all* $\mathbf{x} \in \mathrm{dom}(f)$, $f(\mathbf{x}) = y \leftrightarrow \bigcap_{s\in\omega} < \alpha_s, \beta_s > = \{y\}$ *holds.*

For formalization of information about external world we will use the following set. $\mathcal{F} = \{f | f$ is a majorant–computable total real-valued function$\}$.
An important property of a total real-valued function, which will be used below, is that the function is majorant-computable if and only if its epigraph and ordinate set are Σ-definable (i.e. effective sets).

Definition 3. *Let* g_1 *be Gödel numbering of a set* A_1, g_2 *be Gödel numbering of a set* A_2. *A procedure* $h : A_1 \to A_2$ *is said to be effective procedure if there exists recursive function* ξ *such that the following diagram is commutative*

$$\begin{array}{ccc} N & \xrightarrow{\xi} & N \\ g_1 \downarrow & & g_2 \downarrow \\ A_1 & \xrightarrow{h} & A_2 \end{array} .$$

Denote the set of Σ-formulas by $\mathbf{\Sigma}$ and the set of Π-formulas $\mathbf{\Pi}$.

Definition 4. *A set* $R \subseteq \mathbb{R}^{n+1} \times \mathcal{F}$ *is said to be Σ-definable by an effective procedure* $\varphi : \mathbf{\Sigma} \times \mathbf{\Sigma} \to \mathbf{\Sigma}$ *if for each majorant–computable function* f *and for Σ–formulas* $A(\mathbf{x}, y)$, $B(\mathbf{x}, y)$ *with the following conditions:*
$f(\mathbf{x}) = y \leftrightarrow A(\mathbf{x}, \cdot) < y < B(\mathbf{x}, \cdot)$ *and* $\{z \mid A(\mathbf{x}, z)\} \cup \{z \mid B(\mathbf{x}, z)\} = \mathbb{R} \setminus \{y\}$
the following proposition holds $\mathbf{M} \models R(\mathbf{x}, y, f) \leftrightarrow \mathbf{M} \models \varphi(A, B)(\mathbf{x}, \mathbf{y})$.

In a similar way, we define the notion of *Π-definable functional by an effective procedure* $\psi : \mathbf{\Sigma} \times \mathbf{\Sigma} \to \mathbf{\Pi}$.

Definition 5. *A functional $F : \mathbb{R}^n \times \mathcal{F} \to \mathbb{R}$ is called majorant–computable if there exists effective sequence of sets $\{R_s\}_{s\in\omega}$, where each element R_s is Σ-definable by an effective procedure φ_s and Π-definable by an effective procedure ψ_s, such that the following properties hold:*

1. *For all $s \in \omega$, the set $R_s(\mathbf{x}, \cdot, f)$ is a nonempty interval;*
2. *For all $\mathbf{x} \in \mathbb{R}^n$ and $f \in \mathcal{F}$, the sequence $\{R_s(\mathbf{x}, \cdot, f)\}_{s\in\omega}$ decreases monotonically;*
3. *For all $(\mathbf{x}, f) \in \mathrm{dom}(F)$, $F(\mathbf{x}, f) = y \leftrightarrow \bigcap_{s\in\omega} R_s(\mathbf{x}, \cdot, f) = \{y\}$ holds.*

3 Specifications of Hybrid Systems

Let us consider hybrid systems of the type considered in Introduction. A *specification* of the hybrid system $\mathbf{SHS} = \langle TS, \mathcal{F}, Conv1, A, Conv2, I\rangle$ consists of:

- $TS = \{t_i\}_{i\in\omega}$. It is an effective sequence of real numbers. The real numbers t_i are the times of communication of the external world and the hybrid system, and the plant and the control automata. The time sequence $\{t_i\}_{i\in\omega}$ satisfies the realizability requirements:
  1. For every i, $t_i \geq 0$;
  2. $t_0 < t_1 < \ldots < t_i \ldots$;
  3. The differences $t_{i+1} - t_i$ have positive lower bounds.
- $\mathcal{F} : \mathrm{HW}(\mathbb{R}) \times \mathcal{F} \to \mathbb{R}$. It is a majorant-computable functional. The behaviour of the plant is modelled by this functional.
- $Conv1 : \mathbb{N} \times \mathbf{\Sigma}^2 \to A^*$. It is an effective procedure. At the time of communication this procedure converts the number of time interval, measurements presented by two Σ-formulas into finite words which are input words of the internal control automata.
- $A : A^* \to A^*$. It is a Σ-definable function. The internal control automata, in practice, is a finite state automata with finite input and finite output alphabets. So, it is naturally modelled by Σ-definable function (see [5,8,12]) which has a symbolic representation of measurements as input and produces a symbolic representation of the next control law as output.
- $Conv2 : A^* \to \mathrm{HW}(\mathbb{R})$. It is a Σ-definable function. This function converts finite words representing control laws into control laws imposed on the plant.
- $I \subset A^* \cup \mathrm{HW}(\mathbb{R})$. It is a finite set of initial conditions.

Theorem 1. *Suppose a hybrid system is specified as above. Then the trajectory of the hybrid system is defined by a majorant-computable functional.*

Proof. Let $\mathbf{SHS} = \langle TS, \mathcal{F}, Conv1, A, Conv2, I\rangle$ be a specification of the hybrid system. We consider behaviour of the hybrid system in terms of our specification on $[t_i, t_{i+1}]$. Let $\mathcal{F}(t_i, z, f) = y_i$, where z_i represents the recent control law , and y_i is the state of the plant at the time t_i.

At the moment t_i Converter 1 gets measurements of recent states of the plant as input. By properties of majorant-computable functionals, these measurements can be presented by two Σ-formulas which code methods of computations of measurements. These representations are compatible with real measurements. Indeed, using different approaches to process some external signals from the plant, Converter 1 may transform it to different results. This note is taken into account in our formalization of Converter 1 . Thus, $Conv1$ is a Σ-definable function and its arguments are the methods of computations of measurements. The meaning of the function $Conv1$ is an input word w_1 of the digital automaton which is presented by A. By w_1 the function A computes new control law w_2 and $Conv2$ transforms it to $\acute{z}$.

The plant transforms new information about external world presented by $\acute{f}$ to recent states of the plant according to the control law $\acute{z}$, i.e., $y = \mathcal{F}(t, \acute{z}, \acute{f})$ for $t \in [t_i, t_{i+1}]$. The theorem states that there exists a majorant-computable functional F such that $y(t) = F(t, f)$.

By Definition, $\mathcal{F}(t, z, f)$ is majorant-computable functional. Denote the initial time by t_0 and the initial position of the plan by y_0. Let f be a majorant-computable function, and O be its ordinate set, E be its epigraph. By the properties of majorant-computable functionals (see [13,14]) there exist two effective procedures h_1, h_2 such that

$$F(\mathbf{x}, f) = y \leftrightarrow h_1(O, E)(\mathbf{x}, \cdot) < y < h_2(O, E)(\mathbf{x}, \cdot) \text{ and}$$
$$\{z \mid h_1(O, E)(\mathbf{x}, z)\} \cup \{z \mid h_2(O, E)(\mathbf{x}, z)\} = \mathbb{R} \setminus \{y\}$$

Denote $\Phi_0^+ \rightleftharpoons (y > y_0)$, $\Phi_0^- \rightleftharpoons (y < y_0)$. For $t \in [t_0, t_1]$ put:

$$\phi_1(O, E)(t, y) \leftrightarrow \exists w_1 \exists w_2 \exists a[Conv1(1, \Phi_0^+, \Phi_0^-) = w_1 \wedge A(w_1) = w_2 \wedge Conv2(w_2, a) \wedge h_1(O, E)(t, a, y)],$$
$$\phi_2(O, E)(t, y) \leftrightarrow \exists w_1 \exists w_2 \exists a[Conv1(1, \Phi_0^+, \Phi_0^-) = w_1 \wedge A(w_1) = w_2 \wedge Conv2(w_2, a) \wedge h_2(O, E)(t, a, y)].$$

In the same way we can construct the procedure ϕ_1, ϕ_2 for each interval $[t_i, t_{i+1}]$. Put

$$F(t, f) = y \leftrightarrow \phi_1(O, E)(t, \cdot) < y < \phi_2(O, E)(t, \cdot) \text{ and}$$
$$\{z \mid \phi_1(O, E)(t, z)\} \cup \{z \mid \phi_2(O, E)(t, z)\} = \mathbb{R} \setminus \{y\}$$

By constructions, the functional F is majorant-computable and defines the trajectory of the hybrid system with **SHS** specification. □

This paper has presented the description of trajectories in terms of majorant-computable functionals which can be constructed by the specifications **SHS** of hybrid systems. The preliminary results suggest possible directions for future applications to study real hybrid systems.

References

1. J. Backus, Can Programming be Liberated from the von Neumann Style, A Functional Style and its Algebra of Programs, , Comm. of the ACM, V. 21, N 8, 1978, pages 613–642.

2. J. Barwise, Admissible sets and structures, Berlin, Springer–Verlag, 1975.
3. L. Blum and M. Shub and S. Smale, On a theory of computation and complexity over the reals:NP-completeness, recursive functions and universal machines, Bull. Amer. Math. Soc., (N.S.), v. 21, no. 1, 1989, pages 1–46.
4. A. Edalat, P. Sünderhauf, A domain-theoretic approach to computability on the real line, Theoretical Computer Science. To appear.
5. Yu. L. Ershov, Definability and computability, Plenum, New York, 1996.
6. H. Freedman and K. Ko, Computational complexity of real functions, Theoret. Comput. Sci. , v. 20, 1982, pages 323–352.
7. A Logical for specification of Continuous System, LNCS N 1386, 1998, pages 143–159.
8. S.S. Goncharov, D.I. Sviridenko, Σ-programming, Vychislitel'nye Sistemy, Novosibirsk, v. 107, 1985, pages 3–29.
9. A. Grzegorczyk, On the definitions of computable real continuous functions, Fund. Math., N 44, 1957, pages 61–71.
10. T.A. Henzinger, Z. Manna, A. Pnueli, Towards refining Temporal Specifications into Hybrid Systems, LNCS N 736, 1993, pages 36–60.
11. T.A. Henzinger, V. Rusu, Reachability Verification for Hybrid Automata, LNCS N 1386, 1998, pages 190–205.
12. M. Korovina, Generalized computability of real functions, Siberian Advance of Mathematics, v. 2, N 4, 1992, pages 1–18.
13. M. Korovina, O. Kudinov, A New Approach to Computability over the Reals, SibAM, v. 8, N 3, 1998, pages 59–73.
14. M. Korovina, O. Kudinov, Characteristic Properties of Majorant-Computability over the Reals, Proc. of CSL'98, LNCS, to appear.
15. C. Livadas, N.A. Lynch, Formal verification of Safety-Critical hybrid systems, LNCS N 1386, 1998, pages 253–273.
16. Z. Manna, A. Pnueli, Verifying Hybrid Systems, LNCS N 736, 1993, pages 4–36.
17. R. Montague, Recursion theory as a branch of model theory, Proc. of the third international congr. on Logic, Methodology and the Philos. of Sc., 1967, Amsterdam, 1968, pages 63–86.
18. Y. N. Moschovakis, Abstract first order computability, Trans. Amer. Math. Soc., v. 138, 1969, pages 427–464.
19. A. Nerode, W. Kohn Models for Hybrid Systems: Automata, Topologies, Controllability, Observability, LNCS N 736, 1993, pages 317–357.
20. M. B. Pour-El, J. I. Richards, Computability in Analysis and Physics, Springer-Verlag, 1988.
21. D. Scott, Outline of a mathematical theory of computation, In 4th Annual Princeton Conference on Information Sciences and Systems, 1970, pages 169–176.
22. V. Stoltenberg-Hansen and J. V. Tucker, Effective algebras, Handbook of Logic in computer Science, v. 4, Clarendon Press, 1995, pages 375–526.
23. B.A. Trakhtenbrot, Yu.Barzdin, Finite automata: Behaviour and Syntheses, North-Holland, 1973.

Algebraic Imperative Specifications

Marie-Claude Gaudel[1] and Alexandre Zamulin[2]

[1] L.R.I., URA CNRS 410
Université de Paris-Sud et CNRS, Bât. 490
91405 Orsay-cedex, France
fax 33 1 69 15 65 86, mcg@lri.fr
[2] A.P. Ershov Institute of Informatics Systems
Siberian Division of Russian Academy of Sciences
Novosibirsk 630090
fax: +7 3832 323494, zam@iis.nsk.su

Abstract. Algebraic imperative specifications (AIS) are specifications with implicit state represented by an algebra and with a number of transition rules indicating state transformations. They are designed for the formal definition of complex dynamic systems.
Two approaches to algebraic imperative specifications have been developed in parallel during the last decade: Abstract State Machines (ASMs), initially known as *evolving algebras*, and Algebraic Specifications with Implicit State (AS-IS). Moreover typed versions of ASM have been developed which have incorporated some aspects of AS-IS.
This survey paper provides a guided tour of these imperative approaches of specification based on the state-as-algebra paradigm, and sketches a synthesis of two of them, under the name of dynamic systems with implicit state.

1 Introduction

Algebraic imperative specifications (AIS) are specifications with implicit state represented by an algebra and with a number of transition rules indicating state transformations. They are designed for the formal definition of complex dynamic systems.

It is a fact that a complex system to be implemented in some programming language usually possesses static and dynamic features. The static features are represented by a number of data types involved and a number of functions defined over them. The dynamic features are represented by a number of states the system can be in and a number of operations (procedures, modifiers) transforming the states.

Conventional algebraic specifications [12,13,38] have proved to be an elegant and effective way of defining the static aspects of such a system. Using this technique, one can define a number of data types (sets with corresponding operations) and functions just by providing a signature (i.e., the names of sorts, and the names of operations accompanied by their profiles) and a set of axioms limiting the set of possible models. These data types and operations can be further used in the system specification.

D. Bjørner, M. Broy, A. Zamulin (Eds.): PSI'99, LNCS 1755, pp. 17–39, 2000.

However, algebraic specifications are less convenient in defining the dynamic aspects of a system. In this case, the state has to be defined in some way (for example, as a complex data type) and its instances have to be explicitly used as arguments and/or results in operations transforming one state into another. As a result, the specification becomes very clumsy: it is difficult both to write and read.

In parallel with algebraic specifications, a number of methods involving the notion of built-in state have been suggested which avoid the above-mentioned problem of the explicit state. The most well-known of them are VDM [31] and Z [36,37]. (See [35] for a good review.) One of the latest developments in the field is B [1]. The main idea of each of these methods is that all the operations transforming the state can be characterized by observing their effect on a number of variables (variables are understood here in the same way they are understood in programming languages) representing components of the system's state. Therefore, the variable value before the operation and after its execution is taken into account and a relation between these two values is specified. It is done by a logical formula relating pre-operation and post-operation values of one or more variables in Z, by giving two formulas specifying the condition to be satisfied by the variables before the operation (pre-condition) and the condition to be satisfied by them after the operation execution (post-condition) in VDM, and by substitution rules in B. For this purpose, special decoration is normally proposed for indicating variable values before the operation and after it (hooks for pre-operation values in VDM and primes for post-operation values in Z).

A common feature of the three methods is their use of a fixed number of basic types and type constructors for the representation of application data. The usual basic types are integers (with their subsets) and scalars given by enumerations. The usual type constructors are set constructor, tuple constructor and several kinds of function constructors. VDM restricts the set of function constructors to finite maps (i.e., partial functions with a finite domain) and offers a sequence constructor in addition. Z allows the definitions of binary relations in addition, and B does not possess a tuple constructor.

Another common feature of these methods is that some parts of the semantics of some basic notions remain informal. For example, the formal definition of "a simple and powerful specification language closely similar to the Z notation" in [36] does not explain the notion of state intensively used in its informal semantics. There, a not-producing-result operation is said to transform the state while its formal specification just sets some relations among primed and non-primed names in a model of the signature induced by the operation specification. In VDM and B such notions as *state*, *variable*, and *operation* are also introduced informally: it is assumed that they are well understood by those who write specifications and those who read them.

However, if we say "constant" instead of "variable", we can regard the state as an algebra with a number of defined constants and functions, and we can regard primed and non-primed (or hooked and non-hooked) names as denotations of the same constant name in two different algebras. In this case, we can say that a formula relates values associated with a given constant name in two algebras, and an operation updating the state can be defined as an algebra transformation. Moreover, if we specify the state as an algebra, we can delete the limitations on the sets of data types involved. In the specification of a particular application, those data types are defined which are practically needed in the application. All the power of the algebraic specifications can be used in this case.

The introduction of the notion of algebra update as a transition from one state to another naturally leads us to such form of specification which explicitly indicates in which way a constant (a function in the general case) is updated in the process of algebra transformation. No decoration of names is needed in this case. In parallel with imperative languages, we call this kind of specifications *algebraic imperative specifications (AIS)*. The word *algebraic* emphasizes the algebraic nature of the state; the word *imperative* suggests an analogy with imperative languages.

AIS may be used for describing algorithms: every step of an algorithm can be regarded as a transition from one state to another simulated at the most appropriate abstraction level. Imperative specifications may be also used for describing, in an abstract and non algorithmic way, dynamic features of a system: each state transforming operation is described in terms of some complex algebra updates.

Finally, it is generally accepted that the ease (or difficulty) of the implementation of a specification heavily depends on its structure and complexity. Since the majority of the programs are written in imperative languages, there is much more chance that a specification will be read and implemented by a programmer if it is imperative. This feature relates AIS to some other specification languages which could also be called imperative but not algebraic [1,6].

Two approaches to algebraic imperative specifications have been developed in parallel during the last decade: Abstract State Machines (ASMs), initially known as *evolving algebras* [28,29], and Algebraic Specifications with Implicit State (AS-IS) [8,33]. The main features of AS-IS are presented in the next section. Basic notions of ASM and its typed versions are described in Section 3. Dynamic systems with implicit state combining some features of the both approaches are presented in Section 4. Some related work, all based on the state-as-algebra idea, is discussed in Section 5 and some conclusions are given in Section 6.

2 Algebraic Specifications with Implicit State

The origins of this approach go back to the 1980's, to some work on compiler construction from some formal semantics of the source and target languages [14,15]. There, the semantics of imperative languages was modeled by state transformations, where the states were many-sorted-algebras. In the area of programming language semantics, other approaches generally model states as functions, which, roughly, go from some kinds of names into some kinds of values, the domain and co-domain of these state functions being unions of sets. Such approaches become clumsy when values of complex data types have to be stored and modified: some operations on names must mimic the operations on the data types (such as accesses to components and constructors) and adequate commutativity properties must be maintained when modifying the state. In [14], it was shown how to use many sorted algebras as models of such states, based on the classical idea that data types are algebras. Some extensions were invented to take into account the notion of variables, assignments being modeled as transformations of algebras. The advantage of such a framework for compiler specification is that the representation of the source data types by some target data types can be proved using the techniques developed for algebraic specifications [15].

Some years later, this first approach served as the inspiration for AS-IS, Algebraic Specifications with Implicit State. The motivation for the design of AS-IS was a case study on the formal specification of the embedded safety part of an automatic subway pilot [9,10]. The specified system was a classical control-command loop, where the body of the loop receives some inputs, performs some computations, and returns some outputs. Inputs come from some sensors or some ground controller. Outputs are alarms, commands, or messages to the ground controller. The first formal specification was written in a pure algebraic style, using the PLUSS specification language [16]. It turned out that the state of the system was characterized by 54 values of various types (abscissa, speed, next train, tables, ...). Most of these values were liable to be updated during some cycles of the loop. As a consequence, the specification contained 54 observer operations of the state, i.e. operations of profile $state \times \ldots \longrightarrow s$, where s is a sort different from *state*, and 54 update operations, i.e. operations of profile $state \times \ldots \times s \longrightarrow state$. A long and uninteresting axiomatization of these 108 operations was needed. In order to shorten the specification, a predefined notion of record, similar to the one in VDM, was introduced in the specification language. However, it was still boring and redundant to have states as parameters everywhere. This has led to the introduction of a concept of implicit state in the algebraic specification language. Of course, such a notion must not be limited to the special case of a record. Actually, it must be possible to specify any kind of data structure, at different abstraction levels, and any evolution concerning the implicit state.

Another, more complex, case study was then performed [17], namely the Steam-Boiler Control Problem. It has led to some addition to the formalism, in order to avoid too algorithmic specifications of complex evolutions of the system. The most recent version of AS-IS is presented in [32].

An AS-IS specification is based on a classical algebraic specification which describes the data types to be used by the system. This part is clearly isolated in the specification and its meaning is stable, whatever modification of the state is specified[1]. The evolving parts of the implicit state are specified as *access functions* whose results depend on the implicit state.

Example. In a subway example, there may be the following access functions which correspond to the section of the railway where the train is currently located, and a table where the speed limit for each section is stored.

[1] This implies that the carriers remain invariant.

$CurrentSection : \longrightarrow Section$
$LocalSpeedLimit : Section \longrightarrow Speed$
where the *Section* and *Speed* types are specified in the data type part.

The evolutions of the implicit state are described by *modifications* of the access functions.

Example. When the train progresses, one may have
$CurrentSection := next(CurrentSection)$
or when the weather conditions change
$\forall s : Section, LocalSpeedLimit(s) := LocalSpeedLimit(s) - 10$

Let Σ be the signature of the data types, Ax their axioms, and Σ_{ac} the part of the signature corresponding to the names and profiles of the access functions. A state is any $< \Sigma \cup \Sigma_{ac}, Ax >$-algebra. A modification is a mapping from the $< \Sigma \cup \Sigma_{ac}, Ax >$-algebras into themselves where the interpretation of some access functions of the resulting algebra are different from their interpretations in the source one. The example modifications above are called *elementary* since each of them involves one access function only.

In addition to the *elementary accesses*, such as the ones above, which characterize the implicit state, there are *dependent accesses* which are related by some property to the other accesses.

Example. One may define
$CurrentSpeedLimit : \longrightarrow Speed$
$CurrentSpeedLimit = min(LocalSpeedLimit(CurrentSection), \ldots)$

Among the design choices of AS-IS, it was decided to keep the specified behaviors deterministic. In order to ensure this, the dependent accesses must be defined by a set of axioms which is sufficiently complete with respect to the elementary accesses and data types. Thus an AS-IS specification includes, in addition to the specification of some data types with signature Σ satisfying some axioms Ax, some elementary access functions whose names and profiles are given in a sub-signature Σ_{eac}, some dependent access functions specified by a sub-signature Σ_{dac} and some axioms Ax_{ac}. Let $\Sigma' = \Sigma \cup \Sigma_{eac} \cup \Sigma_{dac}$. Then a state is any $< \Sigma', Ax \cup Ax_{ac} >$- algebra.

The semantics of elementary modifications is based on restrictions and extensions of the state algebras. First, all the dependent accesses are forgotten. Then, if *ac* is the name of an elementary access being modified, the algebra is extended by the new elementary access *ac'*, with the same profile as *ac*, which is different from *ac* for the values of the arguments specified in the modification (see below) and the same everywhere else. Then *ac* is forgotten, *ac'* is renamed *ac*, and the algebra is extended to include the dependent accesses and satisfy the corresponding axioms.

In an AS-IS specification, as soon as an elementary access $ac : s_1 \times \ldots \times s_n \longrightarrow s$ is declared, it is possible to write *elementary modifiers* of the form

$$\forall x_1 : s'_1, \ldots, x_p : s'_p, [ac(\pi_1, \ldots, \pi_n) := R(\pi_1, \ldots, \pi_n)]$$

where the π_i are terms of $T_{\Sigma'}(\{x_1, \ldots, x_p\})$, of sort s_i, which play a role similar to patterns in functional programming, and $R(\pi_1, \ldots, \pi_n)$ is a term built with

the constants of Σ', the π_i, and the operations of Σ'. Such a modifier induces the modification of the result of ac for all the values matching the patterns, i. e., if A is the original state and B the modified one, we have:
$\forall v_1, \ldots, v_n$ in $A_{s_1} \times \ldots \times A_{s_n}$
- if there exists an assignment α of the x_i into A_{s_i}, such that
$\overline{\alpha}(\pi_1) = v_1, \ldots, \overline{\alpha}(\pi_n) = v_n$, then $ac^B(v_1, \ldots, v_n) = R(\overline{\alpha}(\pi_1), \ldots, \overline{\alpha}(\pi_n))$
- otherwise
$ac^B(v_1, \ldots, v_n) = ac^A(v_1, \ldots, v_n)$.

In the above example a quantified elementary modifier is used to specify a global change of the local speed limits.

There is a conditional version of such modifiers, with the same restriction on the form of the conditions as on the result : they must involve the π_i only.

$\forall y_1, \ldots, y_p$ **cases**
ϕ_1 **then** $ac(\pi_1^1, \ldots, \pi_n^1) := R^1 | \ldots | \ \phi_m$ **then** $ac(\pi_1^m, \ldots, \pi_n^m) := R^m$
end cases

The restrictions on the form of the conditions and results ensure that only one result is specified for each item of the domain of the elementary access being modified. Counter-examples justifying these restrictions are given in [19].

Elementary accesses can be used to specify *defined modifiers*. Defined modifiers are specified by compositions of elementary modifiers and defined modifiers. The compositions are

- *Conditional composition* of the following form:
  begin ϕ_1 **then** $Em_1| \ldots | \ \phi_p$ **then** Em_p **end**
  indicating that a modification expression Em_i is chosen if its condition ϕ_i is valid. If several conditions ϕ_i are valid, the modification expression with the smallest index is chosen.
  Note: This form of modification is different from the conditional elementary modifier in two ways: the Em_i are any modification expressions and there are no universally quantified variables.
- *Sequential composition*, $m_1; m_2$, meaning that the execution of m_1 is followed by that of m_2.
- *Casually independent composition*, m_1 **and** m_2, indicating any sequential composition of m_1 and m_2. The order of execution of m_1 and m_2 is unimportant.
- *Simultaneous composition*, $m_1 \bullet m_2$, where the modifications specified by m_1 and m_2 are applied to the same state. If m_1 and m_2 specify a modification of the same access function, they must change it at different points; otherwise, only the modification m_1 is taken into account.

This list does not aim at being minimal. Actually, some constructs overlap in some cases. It aims to provide a convenient way of specifying complex state modifications, without worrying about details such as intermediate results or order of execution when they are not relevant to the specification.

Thus defined modifiers are declared with a profile which states the sorts of their arguments, and their effect on the state is described by a modification expression.

Example.
$switchSpeedLimits : Speed$
$switchSpeedLimits(\Delta s) = \forall s : Section,$
$[LocalSpeedLimit(s) := LocalSpeedLimit(s) - \Delta s]$

Defined modifiers and access functions may be exported by a system specification. When using a system specification, only the exported features can be mentioned. This ensures some encapsulation of the implicit state.

An AS-IS specification also contains a set of axioms Ax_{init} which specifies possible initial states of the specified system. The *behaviors of the system* are sequences of exported instantiated modifiers, i. e. exported defined modifiers with ground terms as arguments, or elementary modifiers of exported accesses with parameters either quantified or instantiated by ground terms. A *reachable state of the system* is either an initial state, or the resulting state of an exported instantiated modifier applied to a reachable state.

An example of a system specification is given below. It is a drastic (and thus unrealistic) simplification of the specification presented in [10].

The specified system can *progress*, with a measured speed, during an interval of time Δt, or the speed limits of the sections can be changed via the *switchSpeedLimits* modification, or an emergency stop can occur.

The *progress* modification is the most complex one. It checks that the speed limit is respected. If it is not, an emergency stop occurs, and if it is, the system deals with a possible section change, chooses an acceleration which depends on the current speed (this choice is not specified here), and computes the next position of the train.

system $TRAIN$ **export** *progress, emergencyStop, switchSpeedLimits*
use $UNITS$, % *defines the sorts Abscissa, Speed, and Acceleration*
% *and some constants of these sorts*
$SECTION$ % *defines the Section sort*
elementary accesses
$CurrentSection : \longrightarrow Section,$
$LocalSpeedLimit : Section \longrightarrow Speed,$
$MeasuredSpeed : \longrightarrow Speed,$
$CurrentAbscissa : \longrightarrow Abscissa,$
$CurrentAcceleration : \longrightarrow Acceleration$
accesses
$CurrentSpeedLimit : \longrightarrow Speed,$
accesses axioms
$CurrentSpeedLimit = min(LocalSpeedLimit(CurrentSection), \ldots)$
Init
$CurrentSection = section0,\ LocalSpeedLimit(s) = speedlim0,$
$MeasuredSpeed = speed0,\ CurrentAbscissa = 0,$
$CurrentAcceleration = acc0,$
modifiers %*declaration of some defined modifiers*
$progress\ :\ Speed,$
$emergencyStop,$

$switchSpeedLimits \; : \; Speed,$
$sectionChange,$
$accelerationChoice,$
modifiers definitions
$progress(s) =$
$MeasuredSpeed := s$ **and** $CurrentAbscissa := NextAbscissa$;
begin
$CurrentAbscissa > length(CurrentSection)$ **then** $sectionChange$
end ;
begin
$MeasuredSpeed > CurrentSpeedLimit$ **then** $emergencyStop$ |
$MeasuredSpeed \leq CurrentSpeedLimit$ **then**
$accelerationChoice$;
$NextAbscissa := CurrentAbscissa +$
$(CurrentSpeed + CurrentAcceleration \times \Delta t) \times \Delta t; \ldots$
end
$switchSpeedLimits(\Delta s) = \forall s : Section,$
$[LocalSpeedLimit(s) := LocalSpeedLimit(s) - \Delta s]$
$sectionChange =$
$CurrentSection := next(CurrentSection) \bullet$
$CurrentAbscissa := CurrentAbscissa - length(CurrentSection)$
% *NB : it is much more complex in reality ...*
$accelerationChoice = \ldots$
$emergencyStop = \ldots$
end system

3 Abstract State Machines

3.1 Gurevich Abstract State Machines

Abstract State Machines (ASMs), originally known as *evolving algebras*, have been proposed by Gurevich [25] as a framework for the formal definition of the operational semantics of programming languages. During the last decade many real-life programming languages and many complex algorithms including communication protocols and hardware designs have been defined as ASMs (the first complete description of the evolving algebra approach is contained in [28], the annotated bibliography of the majority of papers in the field can be found in [5], for the most recent developments look at *http://www.eecs.umich.edu/gasm/*).

The success of the approach can be attributed to two reasons: (1) sound mathematical background and (2) imperative specification style. The imperative nature of evolving algebras has led to the introduction of a new term for them, *Abstract State Machines* (the terms *Gurevich Abstract State Machines* or just *Gurevich Machines* are also in use). The latest version of ASM is described in [29] which is used as the main reference source in this section.

ASMs are based on the notion of a universal algebraic structure consisting of a set, a number of functions, and a number of relations. Such a structure serves for the representation of the *state*. The underlying set is called a *super-universe* and can be subdivided into *universes* by means of unary relations. A universe serves to model a data type (in fact, the set of data type values).

There are a number of transition rules indicating in which way a state can be converted into another state of the same signature. Normally, this is done by a slight change of a function. For this reason, functions can be either *static* or *dynamic*. A static function never changes, a change of a dynamic function produces a new state. Another means of state modification is changing the number of elements in the underlying set (importing new elements).

Only total functions are used in Gurevich ASM. A distinguished super-universe element *undef* is used to convert a partial function into a total one. Thus, every r-ary function f is defined on every r-tuple $\overline{a}$ of elements of the super-universe, but they say that f is undefined at an $\overline{a}$ if $f(\overline{a}) = undef$; the set of tuples $\overline{a}$ with $f(\overline{a}) \neq undef$ is called the *domain* of f.

The other two distinguished super-universe elements are *true* and *false*. The interpretation of an r-ary predicate (relation name) U, defined on the whole super-universe, with values in $\{true,\ false\}$ is viewed as a set of r-tuples $\overline{a}$ such that $U(\overline{a}) = true$. If relation U is unary, it can be viewed as a universe.

The vocabulary (signature) of any ASM contains the names of the above three distinguished elements, the name of the universe *Boole* defined as $\{true,\ false\}$, the names of the usual Boolean operations interpreted conventionally, and the equality sign interpreted as the identity relation on the super-universe. All the functions corresponding to the above names are static.

Example. The vocabulary for oriented trees contains a unary predicate *Nodes* and unary function names *Parent*, *FirstChild*, and *NextSibling*. An oriented tree with n nodes gives rise to a state with $n + 3$ elements: in addition to n nodes, the super-universe contains the obligatory elements $true$, $false$, *undef*. The universe *Nodes* contains the n nodes.

For the interpretation of transition rules, the notions of location, update, and update set are introduced. A *location* in a state A is a pair $l = (f, \overline{a})$, where f is a function name of arity r and $\overline{a}$ is an r-tuple of elements of A. In the case that f is nullary, $(f, ())$ is abbreviated to f.

Example. Assume that we have an oriented tree and let a be a node, then some locations are $(Parent, a)$, $(FirstChild, a)$, $(NextSibling, a)$

An update in a state A is a pair $\alpha = (l, b)$, where $l = (f, \overline{a})$ is a location in A and b is an element of A. To update the state A using α ("to fire α at A"), it is necessary to "put b into the location l", i.e. convert A into a new algebra B so that $f^B(\overline{a}) = b$. The other locations remain intact.

Example. Assume again that we have an oriented tree and let a, b be any two nodes, then some updates are $((Parent, a), b), ((FirstChild, b), a)$.

An *update set* over a state A is a set of updates of A. An update set γ is consistent if no two updates in γ clash, i.e. there are no two (l_1, b_1) and (l_2, b_2) such that $l_1 = l_2$ but $b_1 \neq b_2$. To update the state A using a consistent γ, it is necessary to "fire all its updates simultaneously". The state does not change if the update set is inconsistent.

The main transition rule (or simply "rule" in the sequel) called *update rule* has the following form:

$f(\overline{s}) := t,$

where f is the name of a function of arity r, $\overline{s}$ is a tuple $(s_1, ..., s_r)$ of terms, and t is a term. The interpretation of this rule in a state A causes an update $\alpha = ((f, \overline{a}), t^A)$, where $\overline{a} = (s_1^A, ..., s_r^A)$.

Example. Assume that c and p are terms denoting two nodes of an oriented tree. Then the transition rule

$parent(s) := p$

interpreted in a state A by the update $((parent, s^A), p^A)$ will transform A in B so that $parent^B(s^A) = p^A$ and the other locations remain intact.

A *conditional rule* having the form

if g **then** R_1 **else** R_2 **endif**, where g is a Boolean term and R_1, R_2 are rules, causes the execution of either R_1 or R_2 depending on whether g is true or false.

Another basic rule is a *block* constructed as follows:

do in-parallel $R_1, ..., R_n$ **enddo**,

where $R_1, ..., R_n$ are rules. The block rule is interpreted by an update set consisting of updates produced by interpretations of $R_1, ..., R_n$. The state does not change of course if the update set is inconsistent.

The last basic rule is an *import* rule having the following form:

import v $R(v)$ **endimport**,

where v is an identifier and $R(v)$ is a rule using this identifier as a free variable. The interpretation of this rule in a state A causes the extension of its basic set (super-universe) with a new element a and the subsequent interpretation of R with v bound to a. It is supposed that different imports produce different reserve elements. For example, the interpretation of the block

do in-parallel
  import v $Parent(v) := c$ **endimport**
  import v $Parent(v) := c$ **endimport**
enddo

creates two children of node c.

There are several extensions of the set of basic rules. A *try* rule of the form

try R_1 **else** R_2 **endif**

permits some form of exception handling, i.e., the rule R_2 is executed only if R_1 is inconsistent.

A nondeterministic *choose* rule of the form

choose $v : g(v)$ $R(v)$ **endchoose**,

where v is an indentifier, and $g(v)$ and $R(v)$ are, respectively, a Boolean term and a rule both using v as a free variable, causes the execution of R only for some one element of the superuniverse satisfying g. This means that, if there are several superuniverse elements such that g evaluates to true for v bound to any of them, then nondeterministically one of them is chosen and R is executed with v bound to this element.

Finally, a *do-forall* rule of the form

do forall $v : g(v) \quad R(v)$ **enddo**

causes the executon of R for any superuniverse element bound to v and satisfying g. In this way the quantification of elementary modifiers and conditional elementary modifiers of AS-IS is generalised to any transition rule.

Several abbreviation conventions introduce some syntactic sugar permitting to flatten enclosed conditional rules and omit the "else" part when it is not necessary, to import several elements in an import rule, combine try and block rules, etc.

It is important to note that, in contrast to AS-IS described in the previous section, no effort is made to ensure that any two function updates do not update the same function at the same point, all possible inconsistences are resolved at the level of update set as described above. That's why the quantification can be applied here to any transition rule.

To conclude this short review of GASM, we reproduce (using the syntax described) the specification of a stack machine given in [26].

The stack machine computes expressions given in reverse Polish notation, or RPN. It is supposed that the RPN expression is given in the form of a list where each entry denotes a number or an operation. The stack machine reads one entry of the list at a time. If the entry denotes a number, it is pushed onto the stack. If the entry denotes an operation, the machine pops two items from the stack, applies the operation and pushes the result onto the stack. At the beginning, the stack is empty. It is supposed that the desired ASM has universes *Data* for the set of numbers and *Oper* for the set of bynary operations on *Data*. $Arg1$ and $Arg2$ are distinguished elements of *Data*. To handle operations in *Oper*, the ASM has a ternary function *Apply* such that $Apply(f, x, y) = f(x, y)$ for all f in *Oper* and all x, y in *Data*.

To handle the input, the ASM has a universe *List* of all lists composed of data and operations. The basic functions $Head$ and $Tail$ have a usual meaning. If L is a list, then $Head(L)$ is the first element of L and $Tail(L)$ is the remaining list. F is a distinguished list initially containing the input. Finally, the ASM has a universe *Stack* of all stacks of data with the usual operations *Push*, *Pop*, and *Top*. S is a distinguished stack initially empty. With these explanations, the specification of the algorithm looks as follows:

if $Data(Head(F)) = true$ **then**
  do in-parallel $S := Push(Head(F), S)$
      $F := Tail(F)$
  enddo,
endif

if $Oper(Head(F)) = true$ **then**
  if $Arg1 = undef$ **then**
      do in-parallel

```
            Arg1 := Top(S) % Arg1 is defined now
            S := Pop(S)
        enddo
    elseif Arg2 = undef then
        do in-parallel
            Arg2 := Top(S) % Arg2 is defined now
            S := Pop(S)
        enddo
    else
        do in-parallel
            S := Push(Apply(Head(F), Arg1, Arg2), S)
            F := Tail(F)
            Arg1 := undef % Arg1 is undefined now
            Arg2 := undef % Arg2 is undefined now
        enddo
    endif
```

3.2 Typed Abstract State Machines

The above example clearly indicates some shortcomings of Gurevich ASMs. The first of them is the absence of a formal definition of the static part of the state. Therefore, it is defined in plain words (universes *Data*, *Stack*, *List*, and *Oper*, operations *Head*, *Tail*, etc.). This is typical of ASM. When writing a specification, one can write the signature of any function operating with values of one or more universes. One cannot, however, define formally the semantics of a static function or a sufficiently large set of values of a particular universe. It is assumed that the behavior of all static functions is either well known or defined by some external tools; in the majority of cases, the same refers to universes (one can make sure of this, looking at the definition of C [27] where almost all static functions and universes are defined in plain words).

The second shortcoming is the actual absence of a type system: one cannot construct arbitrary data types and functions with a well-defined semantics and either one has to use a small number of well-known data types like Boolean, Integer, etc. or one has to define informally needed data types and functions. The results of this shortcoming are well-known: neither an appropriate structuring of the data of an application nor type checking of a specification is possible. At the same time, a big specification like a big program is error-prone and type checking helps to detect many errors at the earliest state of the specification development. For example, the following error could be done in the above specification:

$S := Tail(F)$

Unfortunately, no formal tool is able to detect this error, and it can be only debugged with the use of a concrete input in the process of its interpretation if an interpreter is developed.

For these reasons several attempts have been done to introduce typing in ASMs. The first proposal is described in [39] and its modification in [40]. An

Oberon compiler is fully specified with the use of the method [41]. A distinguished feature of the approach is the actual proposal of a specification mechanism incorporating the advantages of both many-sorted algebraic specifications and ASMs. The main idea behind the choice of basic specification constructs has been to use the notions most familiar to the programming community. Another task has been avoidance of any other logic except the first-order many-sorted logic which is most familiar to the computer scientists.

As a result, universes are replaced with data types for which the semantics can be formally defined by means of algebraic equations. The mechanism provides means for defining both concrete data types and type constructors (generic, or parameterized data types). Some popular data types and type constructors are built-in (these are enumeration type, record type and union type constructors). Data type operations are defined together with the corresponding sort in a so called *data type specification.* In addition, independent static functions (i.e. functions not attributed to particular data types) can be specified with the use of data type operations.

The set of transition rules proposed in the approach is mainly based on the set of basic rules of [28]. There is, however, an important difference in the treatment of the assignment of an undefined value to a location. There cannot be a single *undef* value for all data types. To simplify the specification of data types, no one of them is equipped with its own *undef* value. Partial functions are used instead, and a definedness predicate, D, is introduced. For each term t, the predication $D(t)$ holds in a given algebra A if t is defined in it and does not hold otherwise. In an update rule

$f(t_1, ..., t_n) := undef$

undef is just a keyword indicating that $f(t_1, ..., t_n)$ becomes undefined.

For the interpretation of such a construction, another algebra update, β is introduced in addition to α described above. An update β is just a location. To update the state A using β, it is necessary to convert A into a new algebra B so that the content of the location is undefined. The other locations remain intact.

The other main additions are sequence constructor and a tagcase constructor resembling, respectively, a compound statement and a tagcase statement of some programming languages. The need for a *sequential rule* constructor has arisen in several practical applications and is noted in [4,22]. They are also part of AS-IS, as described in the Section 2. The *tagcase rule* constructor is needed when union types are used. It has the following form:

tagcase u **of** $T_1 : R_1,\ T_2 : R_2,\ .\ .\ .\ ,\ T_k : R_k$ **endtag**

where u is a term of type $Union(T_1, T_2, ..., T_n)$, $R_1, R_2, ..., R_k$ are rules, and $k <= n$. In the interpretaion of the rule, the component type of u is compared with $T_1, ...T_k$. If the component type is T_i, then R_i is executed regarding u as a term of type T_i. Thus, the tagcase constructor permits us to manipulate a union type value as a value of the type needed (this facility is not provided by the conditional constructor).

To demonstrate the facilities of the approach, we rewrite the previous example of a stack machine. Notation: the data type signature is enclosed in square brackets, the axioms are enclosed in curly brackets, the symbol "@" inside the data type signature denotes the type being specified.

```
type Oper = ('+', '-', '*', '/'); % enumeration type
type Doper = Union(Nat, Oper); %union type

type Stack(T: TYPE) = spec
 [empty: @;
 push: T, @ ⟶ @;
 pop: @ ⟶ @;
 top: @ ⟶ T];
 {axioms are conventional}

type List(T: TYPE) = spec
 [empty: @;
  append: T, @ ⟶ @;
  head: @ ⟶ T;
  length: @ ⟶ Nat;
  tail: @ ⟶ @;
  has: @, T ⟶ Boolean;
  is_empty: @ ⟶ Boolean]
 {axioms are conventional}

dynamic const S: Stack(Nat) = empty; initially empty stack
dynamic const Arg1, Arg2: Nat; % initially undefined constants
dynamic const F: List(Doper); % initialized by a demon

tagcase head(F) of
 Nat: do in-parallel S := push(head(F), S), F := tail( F) enddo,
 Oper:
     if ¬D(Arg1) then % if Arg1 is undefined
       do in-parallel Arg1 := top(S), S := pop(S) enddo
     elseif ¬D(Arg2) then % if Arg2 is undefined
       do in-parallel Arg2 := top(S), S := pop(S) enddo
     else
       do in-parallel S := push(apply(head(F), Arg1, Arg2), S),
                F := tail(F),
                Arg1 := undef, % Arg1 is undefined now
                Arg2 := undef % Arg2 is undefined now
       enddo
     endif
endtag
```

Note that all the operations used in the example are now formally defined in contrast to the previous version of the example. Moreover, a type checker can easily detect an error like the previous one and even one like the following one (which cannot be detected if a conditional rule were used):

```
tagcase head(F) of
 Oper: do in-parallel S := push(head(F), S), F := tail(F) enddo,
        ...
```

The other innovations of the approach are dependent functions and procedures (defined modifiers) resembling the corresponding constructs of AS-IS. However, their semantics, as it is defined in [43], is quite different. It will be explained in the next section.

There is no import rule, of course. In a typed environment where each algebra element is denoted by (at least one) ground term, it would be strange to manipulate unreachable elements in addition. Some technique of the specification of the operations as dynamic functions could help to solve the problem, but these complications do not seem necessary. Structures like sets or lists can be used to achieve the goal.

Another proposal for typed ASMs is contained in [11]. In contrast to the approach discussed above, this approach does not confine the user to the algebraic style of defining data types. Only general guidelines of a simple type system introducing parametric polymorphism as suggested in [34] are given. The interpretation of data type is also left abstract. The only requirement is that every closed type is interpreted as a set. The set of rules is borrowed from [29] with the exception of the import rule which, of course, is not needed in a typed environment. There is no construct corresponding to dependent function or defined modifier of AS-IS.

Object-oriented ASMs as a kind of typed ASMs are introduced in [42]. In addition to a number of data types, such an ASM uses a number of *object types*. While a data type defines a set of values and a set of operations, an object type defines a set of object behaviors. An object possesses a unique identifier and a number of methods subdivided in attributes (correspond to dynamic functions), observers (correspond to dependent functions) and mutators (correspond to modifiers). The tuple of attribute values defines the object's state.

For a given object type, different system's states can possess different numbers of objects with different object's states. An object's state can be updated with the use of a mutator. For creating new objects of type T, the import rule of Gurevich ASMs in the form $new(T)$ is reinvented. Note that this reinvention does not violate the term generation principle mentioned above since there is no basic term generating an object identifier (remember that an object type defines a set of object behaviors rather than a set of object identifiers!).

Object types are specified with the use of transition rules. Here is a example of it (method profiles and method calls are written like in object-oriented programming languages, the other notation is like that one used in data type specifications, two parts of an axiom are related by the symbol "=="):

class Rectangle = **spec**
[**mutator** default_rectangle; % *setting a default rectangle's state*
 create: Nat, Nat; % *setting a new rectangle's state*

attribute length, width: Nat; % *rectangle attributes definig the state*
observer area: Nat; % *computing a rectangle's area*
equal: Rectangle ⟶ Boolean; % *comparison of rectangles for equality*]
{**forall** r, r1: Rectangle, x, y: Nat.
r.default_rectangle == **do in-parallel** r.length := 0, r.width := 0 **enddo**;
r.create(x, y) == **do in-parallel** r.length := x, r.width := y **enddo**;
r.area == r.length * r.width;
r.equal(r1) == r.length = r1.length & r.width = r1.width};

Note the specification methodology: each mutator is defined in terms of a transition rule setting values of object's attributes, and each observer is defined by a conventional axiom.

Another version of Object-oriented ASMs permitting late binding of methods is described in [44].

4 Dynamic Systems with Implicit State

4.1 Notion of Dynamic System

The convergence of the works on AS-IS and typed ASM has eventually led to the notion of dynamic systems which is based on the state-as-algebra concept and formalizes state updates as operations on algebras [20,43].

Let Σ be a "static" signature introducing a number of data types, Σ_{eac} a signature of elementary access functions, Σ_{ac} a signature of dependent access functions, and Σ_{mod} a signature of modifiers. Then a dynamic system, $D(A)$, of signature $< \Sigma, \Sigma_{eac}, \Sigma_{ac}, \Sigma_{mod} >$, where A is a Σ-algebra, is defined as a 3-uple with:
- *carrier* $|D(A)|$ which is a set of $(\Sigma \cup \Sigma_{eac})$-algebras with the same Σ-algebra A,
- some set of *dependent access functions* with names and profiles defined in Σ_{ac},
- some set of *defined modifiers* with names and profiles defined in Σ_{mod}.

A dependent access function name $ac : s_1, ..., s_n \rightarrow s$ is interpreted in a dynamic system $D(A)$ by a map $ac^{D(A)}$ associating with each $D(A)$-algebra A' (i.e., an algebra belonging to the carrier of $D(A)$) a function $ac^{D(A)}(A') : A'_{s1} \times ... \times A'_{sn} \rightarrow A'_s$.

The operation associated with a defined modifier of Σ_{mod} is a transformation of a $D(A)$-algebra into another $D(A)$-algebra.

4.2 Specification of a Dynamic System

Let $DS < (\Sigma, Ax), (\Sigma_{eac}, Ax_{Init}), (\Sigma_{ac}, Ax_{ac}, \Sigma_{mod}, Def_{mod}) >$ be a dynamic system specification. It has three levels:

1. The first level is a classical algebraic specification $< \Sigma, Ax >$ (cf. [12,38]) which defines the data types used in the system. Semantics of this specification is given by the specification language used. The approach is relatively

independent of a particular specification language. It is only required that the semantics of a specification is a class of algebras.

2. The second level defines those aspects of the system's state which are likely to change and the initial states. It includes:
   - A signature, Σ_{eac}, which does not introduce new sorts. It defines the the names and profiles of *elementary access functions.* A model of the specification $< \Sigma \cup \Sigma_{eac}, Ax >$ is a state. In the sequel, Σ' stands for $\Sigma \cup \Sigma_{eac}$.
   - A set of axioms, Ax_{Init}, characterizing the admissible initial states, i. e. stating the initial properties of the system.
3. The third level defines some dependent access functions and possible evolutions of the system's states. Two parts are distinguished here.
   - A specification of *dependent access functions* $< \Sigma_{ac}, Ax_{ac} >$. It does not introduce new sorts and uses the elementary access functions and the operations of Σ. The form of this specification is the same as in AS-IS. However, the semantics is different (see the preceding subsection) in order to simplify the semantics of state updates.
     A $D(A)$-algebra A' can be extended into an algebra A'' of signature $\Sigma'' = \Sigma' \cup \Sigma_{ac}$ satisfying Ax_{ac}. Such an algebra is called an *extended state.* The extended state corresponding to the state A' is denoted by $Ext_{\Sigma''}(A')$ in the sequel. Given a Σ'-algebra A' and its extended state A'', any ground term of $T_{\Sigma''}$ corresponds to a value in A' since the specification of A'' does not introduce new sorts and is sufficiently complete with respect to the specification of A' (cf. Section 2). Thus, the notion of the value of a ground Σ''-term in a $D(A)$-algebra A' can be used.
   - A definition of *defined modifiers,* $< \Sigma_{mod}, Def_{mod} >$. The form of this specification is the same as in Section 2.
     As sketched above, a modifier name $mod : s_1, ..., s_n$ from Σ_{mod} is interpreted in a dynamic system $D(A)$ by a map $mod^{D(A)}$ associating a $D(A)$-algebra B with each pair $< A', < v_1, ..., v_n >>$, where A' is a $D(A)$-algebra and v_i is an element of A'_{s_i}; this map must satisfy the corresponding definition from Def_{mod} as stated in [20].
     This approach gives a semantics of modifications themselves, independently of their applications. Moreover, the fact that the dependent accesses are no more part of the state makes the semantics of elementary updates much simpler [20].

4.3 States and Behaviors of the System

The notions of state and behavior introduced in Section 2 are redefined below for dynamic systems.

Let $DS = < (\Sigma, Ax), (\Sigma_{eac}, Ax_{Init}), (\Sigma_{ac}, Ax_{ac}, \Sigma_{mod}, Def_{mod}) >$ be a specification of a dynamic system, and let $\Sigma' = \Sigma \cup \Sigma_{eac}$.

System's state. As already mentioned, a state of the system, defined by the specification DS is a Σ'-algebra satisfying the axioms Ax.

It is important that each change of state preserves the data types used. This leads to the partitioning of $< \Sigma', Ax >$-algebras into subsets, $state_A(\Sigma', Ax)$, consisting of algebras sharing the same interpretation of the data types. Since $< \Sigma', Ax >$ is just an extension of the specification $< \Sigma, Ax >$ with some operation names, we have :

$$(\cup state_A(\Sigma', Ax))_{A \in Alg(\Sigma, Ax)} = Alg(\Sigma', Ax)$$

Initial states. A subset of this set of models represents possible initial states of the system being specified. It corresponds to an enrichment of the specification $< \Sigma', Ax >$ with Ax_{Init}, thus:

$$state_{Init}(DS) = \{A' \in Alg(\Sigma', Ax >) | A' \models Ax_{Init}\}$$

Behavior of the system. A behavior is a sequence of updates which are produced by the invocations of some modifiers. Several sequences of states $(e_0, e_1, e_2, ...)$ correspond to a behavior $(m_0, m_1, m_2, ...)$ depending on the choice of the initial state:

- the initial state e_0 belongs to $state_{Init}(DS)$;
- each e_{i+1} is the result of the application of the modifier m_i to e_i ($e_{i+1} = [\![m]\!]e_i$).

The semantics of updates as it is defined in [20] guarantees that if e_0 belongs to a dynamic system $D(A)$, then any e_i also belongs to $D(A)$ (the state changes, but the data types do not change).

As AS-IS, this formalism is deterministic for two reasons: the semantics of elementary modifiers and, therefore, of all modifiers ensures that one[2] and only one state (up to isomorphism) is associated with the application of a modifier to a state; besides the specification of dependent access functions, $< \Sigma_{ac}, Ax_{ac} >$, is sufficiently complete with respect to $< \Sigma \cup \Sigma_{eac}, Ax >$. Thus, only one sequence of states starting with a given initial state is associated with a behavior.

Reachable states. The set of reachable states, $REACH(DS)$ is the set of states which can be obtained by a sequence of updates corresponding to the invocations of some modifiers of Σ_{mod}, starting from an initial state.

Thus, the set $REACH(DS)$ is recursively defined in the following way:

- $state_{Init}(DS) \subset REACH(DS)$
- $\forall m \in \Sigma_{mod}, \forall t_1 \in (T_{\Sigma''})_{s_1} \ldots t_n \in (T_{\Sigma''})_{s_n}, \forall A' \in REACH(DS)$, $[\![m(t_1, ..., t_n)]\!]A' \in REACH(DS)$.

[2] provided that the validity/invalidity of the conditions in conditional updates is always defined

5 Related Works

One of the first specification languages with states represented by algebras is COLD-K [18], the kernel language of the COLD family of specification languages. It possesses many of the features mentioned above, e.g. dynamic (elementary access) functions, dependent (access) functions and procedures (modifiers). Procedures are considered as relations on states. For the specification purposes some imperative constructions (sequential composition expressions and repetition expressions) are used. However, it is still mainly axiomatic specification language using pre- and post-conditions resembling those of VDM.

The idea of implicit state in terms of a new mathematical structure, *d-oid*, is given by Astesiano and Zucca [2]. A d-oid, like the dynamic system described above, is a set of algebras (states) called instant structures, set of dynamic operations (transformations of instant structures with a possible result of a definite sort) and a tracking map indicating relationships between instant structures. Dynamic operations in a d-oid serve as counterparts of dependent access functions and modifiers in AS-IS and the tracking map provides a very abstract way of identifying components of different instant structures (there is no notion of tracking map in the above definition of dynamic system since each algebra of the same signature is by definition a mapping of the same set of names to a semantics universe). The approach in question deals only with models and does not address the issue of specifying the class of such behaviors, which is the purpose of imperative specifications.

Dynamic types as a modified version of d-oid are further investigated in [45]. Although no direct definition of a dynamic abstract type is given in that paper, it has contributed by formal definitions of a static framework and of a dynamic framework with a corresponding logical formalism over a given static framework. It seems that the formalism can be used as a basis of an imperative specification language.

Another similar approach is the "Concurrent State Transformation on Abstract Data Types" presented in [23]. It also uses the idea of implicit state which is modeled as partial algebra that extends a fixed partial algebra considered as a static data type. All functions are given at the same level. Dynamic functions are considered totally undefined in the static data type. A state on a given partial algebra is a free extension of this algebra, specified by a set of function entries. Invariant relations between dynamic operations are given by axioms at the static level. Transitions between states are specified by conditional replacement rules indicating the function entries that should be added/removed when the condition is valid.

There are some restrictions on the partial equational specifications for the static data types, the admissible partial algebras and states, and the replacement rules in order to have the same structural properties as the algebraic specification logic. The most severe of them is the restriction of replacement rules only to redefinitions of so called contents functions corresponding to the mappings of variables to their values in programming languages. This leads to severe restrictions on the use of the formalism (one cannot define and update an arbitrary dynamic function).

In a slightly revised form the formalism is used in [24] for the definition of algebra transformation systems and their compositions.

Algebra updating operations are interpreted as relations between algebras in [3], and these relations are specified by the usual algebraic specification technique. To make the difference between the original and updated values of the same function (constant), one has to decorate its name in a formula. This leads to the necessity of having two signatures (one for the original algebra and one for the resulting algebra) and signature morphisms for establishing the correspondence between decorated and non-decorated versions of the same name and writing formulae in the discriminated union of the signatures. From some examples of the paper, it seems that this can lead to rather complex specifications.

Finally, the specification language Troll [30] should be mentioned. It is oriented on the specification of static and dynamic properties of objects where a method (event) is specified by means of evaluation rules resembling equations on attribute values. Although the semantics of Troll is given rather informally, there is a strong mathematical foundation of its dialect, Troll *light* [21], with the use of data algebras, attribute algebras and event algebras. An attribute algebra represents a state. A relation constructed on two sets of attribute algebras and a set of event algebra, called *object community*, formalizes a transition from one attribute algebra to another when a particular event algebra takes place.

6 Conclusion

This survey paper provides a guided tour of several imperative approaches of specification based on the state-as-algebra paradigm. Section 4 sketches a synthesis of two of them, under the name of dynamic systems with implicit state.

Some of these approaches differ in significant way. This is an indication of the generality of the paradigm. In AS-IS, the aim is to specify the dynamic evolutions of the specified systems in a high level and non algorithmic way. In ASM, the goal is to provide a way of describing algorithms in an abstract way. Moreover, the problem of multiple inconsistent updates is considered very differently in both approaches, as mentioned in Section 3.1.

One of the advantages of these approaches to formal specification is a better understandability for people familiar with imperative programming. AIS use a simple syntax which can be read as a form of high level code.

Another advantage is their generality. AIS have been shown to be useful in such wide variety of domains as sequential, parallel and distributed systems with either finite-state or infinite domains.

A current weakness of these approaches is the lack of formal calculus to perform proofs. It is very likely that a calculus based on the concept of substitution, in the line of Abrial's calculus for B [1] could be developed. It is the subject of some future work.

References

1. J. R. Abrial. *The B book - Assigning programs to meanings.* Cambridge University Press, 1996.
2. E. Astesiano and E. Zucca. D-oids: a Model for Dynamic Data Types. *Mathematical Structures in Computer Science*, 5(2), June 1995, 257-282.
3. H. Baumeister. Relations as Abstract Data Types: An Institution to Specify Relations between Algebras. *TAPSOFT'95*, LNCS, vol. 915, Springer Verlag, pp. 756-771.
4. E. Boerger and D. Rosenzweig. The WAM-Definition and Compiler Correctness. *Logic Programming: Formal Methods and Practical Applications*, North-Holland Series in Computer Science and Artificial Intelligence, 1994.
5. E. Boerger, J. Huggins. Commented ASM Bibliography. *Formal Specification Column (H. Erhig, ed.), EATCS Bulletin*, vol. 64, February 1998, pp. 105-127.
6. K.M. Chandy and J. Misra. *Parallel Program Design: a foundation.* Addison-Wesley, 1988.
7. Dauchy P., Développement et exploitation d'une spécification algébrique du logiciel embarqué d'un métro. Thèse de Docteur en Sciences de l'Université de Paris-Sud, Orsay, July 1992.
8. P. Dauchy and M.C. Gaudel. *Algebraic Specifications with Implicit State.* Tech. report No 887, Laboratoire de Recherche en Informatique, Univ. Paris-Sud, 1994.
9. Dauchy P., Marre B., Test data selection from algebraic specifications : application to an automatic subway module. *3rd European Software Engineering Conference, ESEC'91*, LNCS, vol. 550, 1991, pp. 80-100.
10. Dauchy P., Gaudel M.-C., Marre B., Using Algebraic Specifications in Software Testing : a case study on the software of an automatic subway. *Journal of Systems and Software*, vol. 21, no 3, June 1993, pp. 229-244.
11. G. Del Castillo, Y. Gurevich, and K. Stroetmann. Typed Abstract State Machines. Submitted to *Journal of Universal Computer Science*, available from http://www.eecs.umich.edu/gasm/), 1998.
12. H. Ehrig, B. Mahr. *Fundamentals of Algebraic Specifications 1, Equations and Initial Semantics.* EATCS Monographs on Theoretical Computer Science, vol. 6, Springer, Berlin, 1985.
13. H. Ehrig, B. Mahr. *Fundamentals of Algebraic Specifications 2.* EATCS Monographs on Theoretical Computer Science, vol. 21, Springer, Berlin, 1990.
14. Gaudel M.-C., Génération et Preuve de Compilateurs basées sur une Sémantique Formelle des Langages de Programmation, Thèse d'état, INPL (Nancy, France), 1980.
15. Gaudel M.-C., Correctness Proof of Programming Language Translations. *Formal Description of Programming Concepts-II*, D. Bjorner ed., North-Holland, 1983, pp.25-43.
16. Gaudel M-C., Structuring and Modularizing Algebraic Specifications: the PLUSS specification language, evolutions and perspectives *9th Annual Symposium on Theoretical Aspects of Computer Science (STACS'92)*, Cachan, feb. 1992, LNCS, vol. 577, pp. 3-18.
17. Marie-Claude Gaudel, Pierre Dauchy, Carole Khoury, A Formal Specification of the Steam-Boiler Control Problem by Algebraic Specifications with Implicit State. *Formal Methods for Industrial Applications: specifying and programming the Steam Boiler Control*, LNCS, vol. 1165, Springer Verlag, 1996, pp. 233-264.

18. H.B.M. Jonkers. An Introduction to COLD-K. *Algebraic Methods: Theory, Tools and Applications*, LNCS, vol. 394, 1989, pp. 139-205.
19. Gaudel, M.-C., Khoury, C. and Zamulin, A., Dynamic systems with implicit state, Rapport interne no 1172, Laboratoire de Recherche en Informatique, May 1998.
20. M.-C. Gaudel, C. Khoury, A. Zamulin. Dynamic systems with implicit state. *Fundamental Approaches to Software Engineering*, LNCS, vol. 1577, 1999, pp.114-128.
21. M. Gogolla & R. Herzig. An Algebraic Semantics for the Object Specification Language TROLL *light*. *Recent Trends in Data Type Specifications*, LNCS, vol. 906, pp. 290-306, 1994.
22. R. Groenboom and R. Renardel de Lavalette. Reasoning about Dynamic Features in Specification Languages. *Workshop in Semantics of Specification Languages*, Springer Verlag, 1994, pp. 340-355.
23. M. Grosse-Rhode. Concurrent State Transformation On Abstract data Types. *Recent Trends in Data Type Specifications*, LNCS, vol. 1130, pp. 222-236, 1995.
24. M. Grosse-Rhode. Algebra Transformation Systems And Their Composition. *Fundamental Approaches to Software Engineering*, LNCS, vol. 1382, pp. 107-122, 1998.
25. Y. Gurevich. Logic and the Challenge of Computer Science. *Trends in Theoretical Computer Sciience*, Computer Science Pres, ed. E. Boerger, 1988, pp. 1-57.
26. Y. Gurevich. Evolving Algebras: An Attempt to Discover Semantics. *Current Trends in Theoretical Computer Science*, World Scientific, 1993, pp. 266-292.
27. Y. Gurevich and J. Huggins. The semantics of the C programming language. *Computer Science Logic*, LNCS, vol. 702, 1993, pp. 274-309.
28. Y. Gurevich. Evolving Algebras 1993: Lipary Guide. *Specification and Validation Methods*, Oxford University Press, 1995, pp. 9-36.
29. Y. Gurevich. *May 1997 Draft of the ASM Guide*. Available electronically from http://www.eecs.umich.edu/gasm/.
30. T. Hartmann, G. Saake, R. Jungclaus, P. Hartel, and J. Kush. Revised Version of the Modeling Language TROLL. Technishe Universitaet Braunschweig, Informatik-Berichte 94-03, 1994.
31. C. B. Jones. *Systematic Software Development using VDM*. Prentice Hall, 1990.
32. Carole Khoury, Définition d'une approche orientée-objet de la spécification algébrique des systèmes informatiques. Thèse de Docteur en Sciences de l'Université de Paris-Sud, Orsay, March 1999.
33. C. Khoury, M.C. Gaudel and P. Dauchy. *AS-IS*. Tech. report No 1119, Laboratoire de Recherche en Informatique, Univ. Paris-Sud, 1997.
34. R. Milner. A Theory of Type Polymorphism in Programming. *Journal of Computer and System Sciences*, 1978.
35. B. Monahan and R. Shaw. Model-Based Specifications. *Software Engineer's Reference Book*, chapter 21, Butterworth-Heineman, 1991.
36. J. M. Spivey. *Understanding Z. A specification language and its formal semantics*. Cambridge University Press, 1988.
37. J. M. Spivey. *The Z Notation. A Reference Manual*. Prentice Hall, 1989.
38. M. Wirsing. Algebraic Specifications. *Handbook of Theoretical Computer Science*, Elsevier Science Publishers B.V., 1990, pp. 665-788.
39. A.V.Zamulin. *Typed Gurevich Machines*. Institute of Informatics Systems, Preprint No 36, Novosibirsk, 1996 (ftp://xsite.iis.nsk.su/pub/articles/tgm.ps.gz).
40. A.V.Zamulin. Typed Gurevich Machines Revisited. *Joint NCC&ISS Bull., Comp. Science*, 7 (1997), pp. 95-121 (available electronically from http://www.eecs.umich.edu/gasm/).

41. A.V. Zamulin. *Specification of an Oberon Compiler by means of a Typed Gurevich Machine.* Institute of Informatics Systems of the Siberian Division of the Russian Academy of Sciences, Report No. 589. 3945009.00007-01, Novosibirsk, 1997 (available electronically from http://www.eecs.umich.edu/gasm/).
42. A.V. Zamulin. Object-Oriented Abstract State Machines. *Proc. Int. Workshop on Abstract State Machines*, Magderburg, Germany, September 21-22, 1998, pp 1-21.
43. A.V. Zamulin. Dynamic System Specification by Typed Gurevich Machines. *Proc. Int. Conf. on Systems Science*, Wroclaw, Poland, September 15-18, 1998.
44. A.V. Zamulin. Object-Oriented Specification by Typed Gurevich Machines. *Joint NCC&ISS Bull., Comp. Science*, 8 (1998), pp. 77-103.
45. E. Zucca. *From Static to Dynamic Data Types. Mathematical Foundations of Computer Science*, LNCS, vol. 1113, 1996, pp. 579-590.

Enhanced Control Flow Graphs in Montages

Matthias Anlauff[1], Philipp W. Kutter[2], and Alfonso Pierantonio[3]

[1] GMD FIRST, D-12489 Berlin
ma@first.gmd.de
[2] Federal Institute of Technology, CH-8092 Zürich
kutter@tik.ee.ethz.ch
[3] Università di L'Aquila, I-67100 L'Aquila
alfonso@univaq.it

Abstract. A semi-visual framework for the specification of syntax and semantics of imperative programming languages, called Montages, was proposed in an earlier work by the authors. The primary aim of this formalism is to assist in recording the decisions taken by the designer during the language design process. The associated tool Gem-Mex allows the designer to maintain the specification and to inspect the semantics to verify whether the design decisions have been properly formalized. Experience with full-scale case studies on Oberon, Java, and domain specific languages showed the close relationship to *Finite State Machines* (FSMs). This paper gives a new definition of Montages based on FSMs. It confers to the formalism enhanced pragmatic qualities, such as writability, extensibility, readability, and, in general, ease of maintenance.

1 Introduction

The aim of Montages is to document formally the decisions taken during the design process of realistic programming languages. Syntax, static and dynamic semantics are given in a uniform and coherent way by means of semi-visual descriptions. The static aspects of a language are diagrammatic descriptions of control flow graphs, and the overall specifications are similar in structure, length, and complexity to those found in common language manuals.

The departure point for our work has been the formal specification of the C language [10][1], which showed how the state-based formalism Abstract State Machines [8, 9, 13] (ASMs), formerly called Evolving Algebras, is well-suited for the formal description of the dynamic behavior of full-blown practical languages. In essence, ASMs constitute a formalism in which a state is updated in discrete time steps. Unlike most state-based systems, the state is given by an algebra that is a collection of functions and universes. The state transitions are given by rules that update functions pointwise and extend universes with new elements. The model presented in [10] describes the dynamic semantics of the C language by presuming on an explicit representation of *control and data flow as a graph*. This

[1] Historically the C case-study was preceded by work on Pascal [8], and other languages, see [5] for a commented bibliography on ASM case studies.

D. Bjørner, M. Broy, A. Zamulin (Eds.): PSI'99, LNCS 1755, pp. 40–53, 2000.

represents a major limitation for such a model, since the control and data flow graph is a crucial part of the specification. Therefore, we developed Montages which extend the approach in [10] by introducing a mapping which describes how to obtain the control and data flow graph starting from the abstract syntax tree.

The formulation of Montages [17] was strongly influenced by some case studies [16, 18] where the object–oriented language Oberon [26] has been specified. Montages have been used also in other case studies, such as the specification of the Java [25] language, the front-end for correct compiler construction [11], and the design and prototyping of a domain-specific languages in an industrial context [19]. The experience showed that the underlying model for the dynamic semantics, namely the specification of a control flow graph including conditional control flow and data flow arrows and its close relationship to the well known concept of *Finite State Machines*, shortens the learning curve considerably. In this paper a new FSM based definition of Montages is given. Complete references, documentation and tools can be obtained via [4].

2 Montages

In our formalism, the specification of a language consists of several components. As depicted in Fig. 1, the language specification is partitioned into three parts.

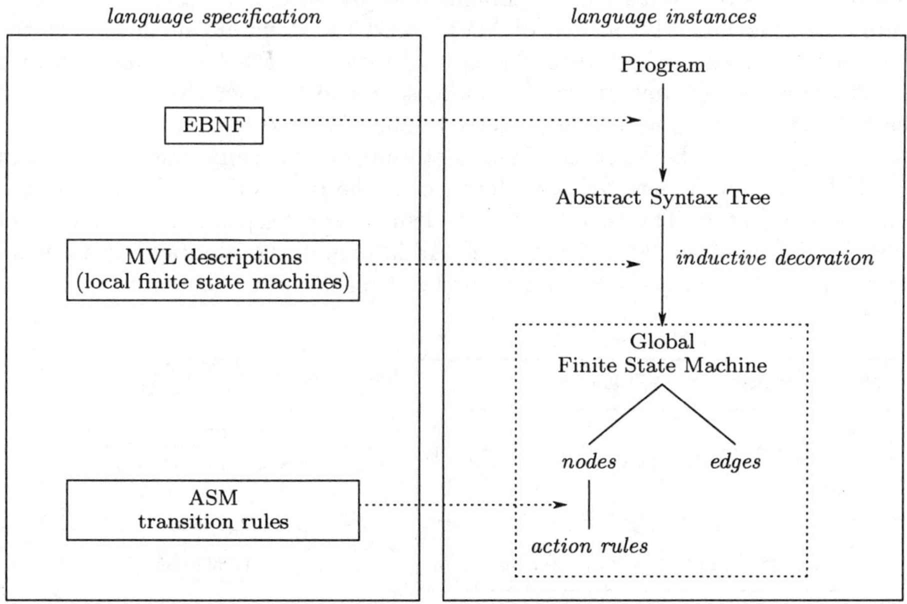

Fig. 1. Relationship between language specification and instances

1. The EBNF production rules are used for the context-free syntax of the specified language L, and they allow to generate a parser for programs of L. Furthermore, the rules define in a canonical way the signature of abstract syntax trees (ASTs) and how the parsed programs are mapped into an AST. Section 2.1 contains the details of this mapping. In Fig. 1 the dotted arrow from the EBNF rules indicates that this information is provided from the Montage language specification.
2. The next part of the specification is given using the *Montage Visual Language* (MVL). MVL has been explicitly devised to extend EBNF rules to finite state machines (FSM). A MVL description associated to an EBNF rule defines basically a *local* finite state machine and contains information how this FSM is plugged into the *global* FSM via an inductive decoration of the abstract syntax trees. To this end, each node is decorated with a copy of the finite state machine fragment given by its Montage. The reference to descendents in the AST defines an inductive construction of a global structured FSM. In Section 2.2 we define how this construction works exactly.
3. Finally, any state of the FSM may be associated with an Abstract State Machine (ASM) rule. This *action rule* is fired when the corresponding state is reached. As shown in Fig. 1, the specification of these rules is the third part of a language specification.

The complete language specification is structured in specification modules, called Montages. Each Montage is a "BNF-extension-to-semantics" in the sense that it specifies the context-free grammar rule (by means of EBNF), the (local) finite state machine (by means of MVL), and the dynamic semantics of the construct (by means of ASMs). The special form of EBNF rules allowed in a specification and the definition of Montages lead to the fact that each node in the abstract syntax tree belongs exactly to one Montage.

As an example the Montage for a nonterminal with name Sum is shown in Fig. 2. The topmost parts of this Montages is the production rule defining the context-free syntax. The remaining part defines static aspects of the construct given by means of an MVL description. Additionally, the Montage contains an action rule, which is evaluated when the FSM reaches the *add* state.

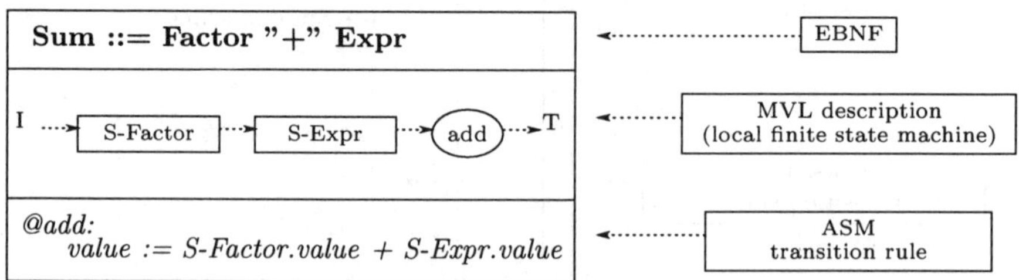

Fig. 2. Montage components

The definition of Montages usually contains a fourth section which is devoted to the specification of static analysis and semantics. After working with fixed traversal orders and non-local attributions, we found that Reference Attribute Grammars [12] are most suited for our purpose, since they do not restrict the use of non-local references. The result of the attribution can be used to define firing conditions and actions in the FSM.

The use of attribute grammars for static analysis and semantics is a standard technique. In [12] it is shown how reference attribute grammars define static properties of an object oriented languages in a simple and concise way. Further [22] uses a corresponding functional system in combination with ASMs and shows how to describe static and dynamic aspects of full-blown languages. In contrast to these works, Montages has an elaborated visual formalism for the specification of sequential control flow by means of FSMs. These aspects are going to be presented in the next sections.

2.1 From Syntax to AST

In this section, the first step in Fig. 1 is described. As a result of this step we get the abstract syntax tree of the specified program. But we also compose the Montages corresponding to the different constructs of the language. This composition of the partial specifications is done based on the structure of the AST.

EBNF rules. The syntax of the specified language is given by the collection of all EBNF rules. Without loss of generality, we assume that the rules are given in one of the two following forms:

$$A ::= B\ C\ D \tag{1}$$
$$E\ =\ F \mid G \mid H \tag{2}$$

The first form defines that A has the components B, C, and D whereas the second form defines that E is one of the alternatives F, G, or H. Rules of the first form are called *characteristic productions* and rules of the second form are called *synonym productions.* We guarantee that each non-terminal symbol appears in exactly one rule as the left-hand-side. Non-terminal symbols appearing on the left of the first form of rules are called *characteristic symbols* and those appearing on the left of synonym productions are called *synonym symbols.*

Composition of Montages. Each characteristic symbol and certain terminal symbols define a *Montage*. A Montage is considered to be a *class*[2] whose instances are associated to the corresponding nodes in the abstract syntax tree.

[2] In this context we consider class to be a special kind of abstract data type, having attributes and methods (actions) and, most important for us, where the notion of sub-typing and inheritance are predefined in the usual way.

Symbols in the right-hand side of a characteristic EBNF rule are called *(direct) components* of the Montage, and symbols which are reachable as components of components are called *indirect components.* In order to access descendants of a given node in the abstract syntax tree, statically defined attributes are provided. Such attributes are called *selectors* and they are unambiguously defined by the EBNF rule. In the above given rule, the B, C, and D components of an A instance can be retrieved by the selectors S-B, S-C, and S-D. In Fig. 3 a possible representation of the A-Montage as class and an abstract syntax tree (AST) with two instances of A and their components are depicted.

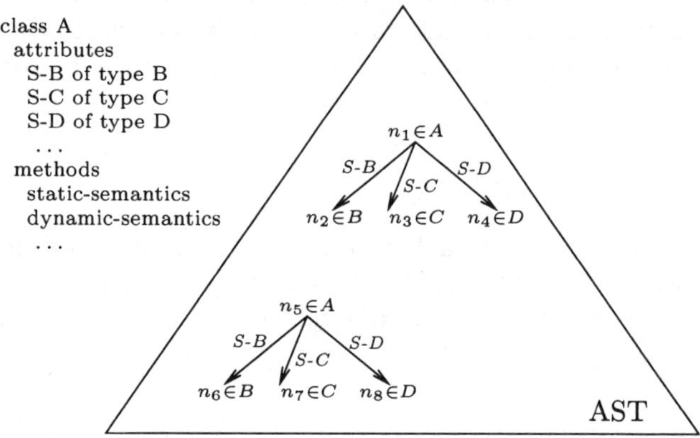

Fig. 3. Montage class A, instances in the AST, selectors S-B, S-C, S-D

Synonym rules introduce *synonym classes* and define subtype relations. The symbols on the right-hand-side of a synonym rule can be further synonym classes or Montage classes. Each class on the right-hand-side is a subtype of the introduced synonym class. Thus, each instance of one of the classes on the right-hand side is an instance of the synonym class on the left-hand-side, e.g. in the given example, all F-, G-, and H-instances are E-instances as well. In the AST, each inner node is an an instance of arbitrarily many (possibly zero) synonym classes and of exactly one Montage.

Terminals, e.g. identifiers or numbers, do not correspond to Montages. The micro-syntax can be accessed using an attribute *Name* from the corresponding leaf node. The described treatment of characteristic and synonym productions allows for an automatic generation of AST from the concrete syntax given by EBNF, see also the work in [21].

Induced structures. Inside a Montage class, the term *self* denotes the current instance of the class. Using the selectors, and knowledge about the AST, we can build paths w.r.t. to self. For instance, the path *self.S-B.S-H.S-J* denotes a node of class J, which can be reached by following the selectors S-B, S-H, and then S-J, see Fig. 4. The use of such a path in a Montage definition imposes a number of constraints on the other EBNF rules of the language. The example *self.S-B.S-H.S-J* requires that there is a B component in the Montage containing the path. Further, every subtype of B must have an H component, and every subtype of H must have an J component. In other words, the path *self.S-B.S-H.S-J* must exist in all possible ASTs.

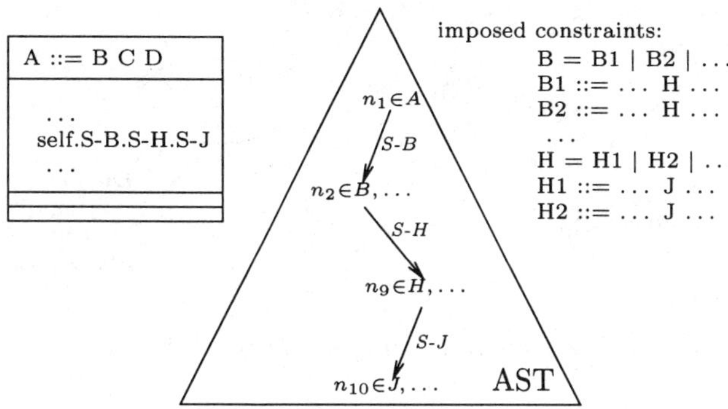

Fig. 4. Montage A using path self.S-B.S-H.S-J, situation in AST, and constraints on EBNF rules of B, H

Example. As a running example we give a small language $\mathcal{S}$. The expressions in this language potentially have side effects and must be evaluated from left to right. The atomic factors are integer constants and variables of type integer. The start symbol of the EBNF is Expr, and the remaining rules are

Expr	=	Sum | Factor
Sum	::=	Factor "+" Expr
Factor	=	Variable | Constant
Variable	::=	Ident
Constant	::=	Digits

The following term is an $\mathcal{S}$-program:

```
2 + x + 1
```

As a result of the generation of the AST we obtain the structure represented in Fig. 5. In particular, the nodes from 1 to 8 represent instances of the Montage classes and the edges point to the successors of a particular node. The edges are labeled with the selector functions which can be used in the Montage corresponding to the source node to access the Montage corresponding to the target node. The nodes themselves show the class hierarchy starting from the synonym class and ending with the Montage class. The leaf nodes contain the definition of the attribute Name, i.e. the micro-syntax.

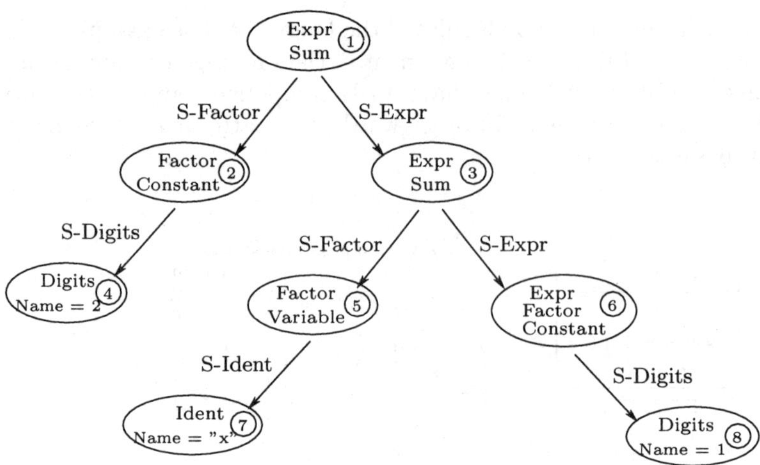

Fig. 5. The abstract syntax tree and composition of Montages for `2 + x + 1`

2.2 From AST to Control Flow Graphs

According to Fig. 1, the next step in building the data structure for the dynamic execution is the inductive decoration of the AST with a number of finite state machines. Again, this process is described rather informally here.

As we have seen in Fig. 2, the second part of a Montage contains the necessary specifications given in form of the *Montage Visual Language* (MVL). The Montages for the productions Variable and Constant are given in Fig. 6. Two kinds of information are represented in the second part of a Montage: (a) the local state machine to be associated to the node of the AST and (b) information on the embedding of this local state machine. Using our running example, Fig. 7 just represents the MVL sections of the Montages as they are associated to the corresponding nodes of the abstract syntax tree. The hierarchical state transition graph resulting from the inductive decoration is shown in Fig. 8 for the running example.

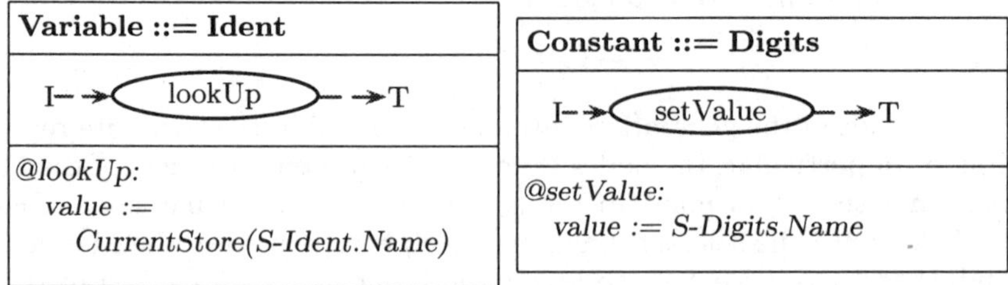

Fig. 6. The Montages for the language $\mathcal{S}$

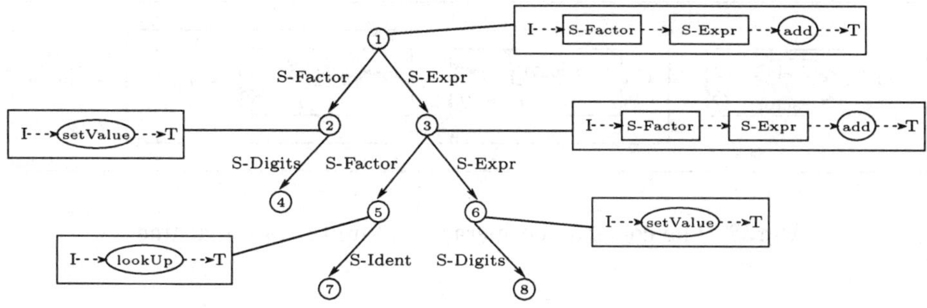

Fig. 7. The finite state machines belonging to the nodes

Montage Visual Language. Now, the elements of the MVL and their semantics can be described as follows:

- There are two kinds of nodes. The oval nodes represent states in the generated finite state machine. These states are associated to the AST node corresponding to the Montages. The oval nodes are labeled with an attribute. It serves to identify the state, for example if it is the target of a state transition or if it points to a dynamic action rule.
- The rectangular nodes or boxes represent symbols in the right hand side of the EBNF rule and are called direct components of a Montages, see Section 2.1. They are labeled with the corresponding selector function. Boxes may contain other boxes which represent indirect components. This way, paths in the AST are represented graphically.
- The dotted arrows are called control arrows. They correspond to edges in the hierarchical state transition graph of the generated finite state machine. Their source or target can be any box or oval. In addition, their source or target can be either the symbol I (I stands for initial) or T (T stands for terminal), respectively. In a Montage, at most one symbol of each, I and T, is allowed. If the I symbol is omitted, the states of the Montage can only be reached using a jump, if the T symbol is omitted, the Montages can only be left using a jump.
- As in other state machine formalisms (such as Harel's StateCharts), predicates can be associated to control arrows. They are simply terms in the underlying ASM formalism and are evaluated after executing the action rule associated to the source node. Predicates must not be associated to control arrows with source I.
- There are additional notations not used in this paper — for example data flow edges representing the mutual access of data between Montages and box structures representing lists in an effective way. Moreover, in this section of a Montage, one may specify further action rules to be performed in the static analysis phase, for example building up data structures necessary for the static and dynamic semantics.

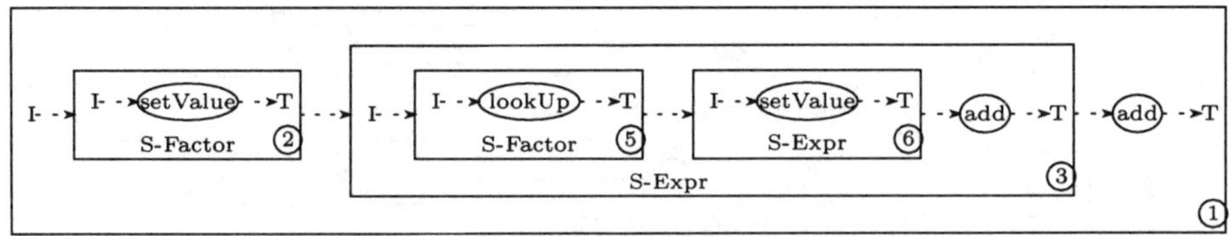

Fig. 8. The constructed hierarchical finite state machine

It remains to show how the hierarchical finite state machine, for example Fig. 8 is built and how its dynamic semantic is defined.

Hierarchical FSM. Building the hierarchical FSM is particularly simple. The boxes in the MVL are references to the corresponding local state transition graphs. Remember that nested boxes correspond to paths in the AST. Therefore, there are references to children only, i.e. to other state transition graphs along the edges of the AST. After resolving the references, a representation as in Fig. 8 is obtained.

The obtained hierarchical FSM gives the dynamic semantics of the parsed program. Direct execution of the hierarchical FSM is possible. Like in State-Charts a hierarchical state is entered at its initial state. This state is marked with an I-arrow. If a final state (marked with a T-arrow) is reached, the hierarchy is followed upwards.

Flat FSM. Alternatively, the FSM can be flattened. For this purpose the arrows from I and to the T symbols define two unary functions, *Initial* and *Terminal* denoting for each node in the AST the first, respectively last state that is visited. According to the semantics of hierarchical FSMs, the inductive definition of these functions is given over the FSM states and the boxes representing instances of Montages.

For each state s in the finite state machines,

$$s.Initial = s \tag{3}$$

$$s.Terminal = s \tag{4}$$

and for each instance n of a Montage N whose MVL-graph has an edge from I to a component denoted by path *tgt*,

$$n.Initial = n.tgt.Initial$$

and for each instance m of a Montage M whose MVL-graph has an edge from a component denoted by path *src* to T,

$$m.Terminal = m.src.Terminal$$

Using these definitions, the structured FSM is flattened by replacing each edge e from s to t with an edge from $s.Terminal$ to $t.Initial$. After this replacement the boxes are not related to the FSM anymore. Nevertheless, the information of the AST nodes related to source, target, and definition of an arrow are needed for the evaluation of advanced features usable in the the firing conditions.

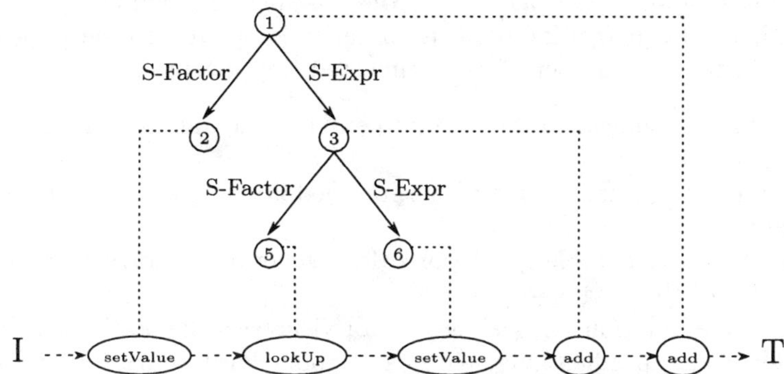

Fig. 9. The flat finite state machine and its relation to the AST

Applying the replacement to the running example results in the flat state machine of Fig. 9. In the same figure the dotted lines denote the relation of a state to its corresponding Montage instance, which is accessible as *self.* The relation of edges to the instances corresponding to source, target and definition is not given, since our example has no interesting conditions.

Given the flat FSM as in Fig. 9, we can track the behavior given by the actions in Figs. 2 and 6. The initial state is the leftmost *setValue* state. Its rule updates the additional attribute *value* with the constant stored in the field *Name* of the digits-token. After the action rule is executed, the firing conditions of outgoing arrows are evaluated. In our example there is only one arrow with the default condition *true* exists. Visiting the states sequentially the action rules are executed one after another. The most interesting is the *add* action. It accesses the values of its arguments using the selectors *S-Factor*, *S-Expr* and defines its own *value* field to be the sum of the arguments.

Assuming that *CurrentStore* maps x to 4, the execution of the flat or structured finite state machine sets the value of node two to the constant 2, sets the value of node five to the current store at x, sets the value of node six to 1, sets the value of node three to the sum of 4 and 1, and finally sets the value of node one to the sum of 2 and 5.

3 Gem-Mex: The Development Environment for Montages

The development environment for Montages is given by the Gem-Mex tool [2, 3]. The intended use of the tool Gem-Mex is, on one hand to allow the designer to 'debug' her/his semantics descriptions by empirical testing of whether the intended decisions have been properly formalized; on the other hand, to automatically generate a correct (prototype) implementation of programming languages from the description, including visualization and debugging facilities.

Gem-Mex is a system which assists the designer in a number of activities related with the language life cycle, from early design to routine programmer usage. It consists of a number of interconnected components

- a specialized graphical editor allows to enter and manipulate Montages in a convenient way;
- frames for the documentation of the specified languages are generated automatically;
- the Montages executable generator (Mex) generates a correct and efficient interpreter of the language;
- the generic animation and debugger tool visualizes the static and dynamic behavior of the specified language at a symbolic level; source programs written in the specified language and user-defined data structures can be animated and inspected in a visual environment.

3.1 Generation of Language Interpreters

Using the formal semantics description given by the set of Montages and a number of ADTs, the Gem-Mex system generates an interpreter for the specified language. The core of the Gem-Mex system is *Aslan* [1], which stands for *A*bstract *S*tate Machine *Lan*guage and provides a fully-fledged implementation of the ASM approach. Aslan can also be used as a stand-alone, general purpose ASM implementation. The process of generating an executable interpreter consists of two phases:

- The Montages containing the language definition are transformed to an intermediate format and then translated to an ASM formalization according to the rules presented in the previous Sections.
- The resulting ASM formalization is processed by the Aslan compiler generating an executable version of the formalization, which represents an interpreter implementing the formal semantics description of the specified language.

Using Aslan as the core of the Gem-Mex system provides the user the possibility to exploit the full power of the ASM framework to enrich the graphical ASM macros provided by Montages with additional formalization code.

3.2 Generation of Visual Programming Environments

Besides pure language interpreters, the Gem-Mex system is able to generate visual programming environments for the generated ASM formalization of the programming language semantics[3]. This is done by providing a generic debugging and animation component which can be accessed by the generated executable. During the translation process of the Montages/ASM code special instructions are inserted that provide the information being necessary to visualize the execution of the formalization. In particular, the visual environment can be used to debug the specification, animate the execution of it, and generate documents representing snapshots of the visualization of data structures during the execution. The debugging features include stepwise execution, textual representation of ASM data structures, definition of break points, interactive term evaluation, and re-play of executions.

3.3 Library of Programming Language Features

A concept for providing libraries of programming language features is currently under development. With this concept it shall be possible to reuse features of programming languages that have already been specified in other Montages. Examples for this kind of features are arithmetic expressions, recursive function call, exception handling, parameter passing techniques, standard control features etc. The designer of a new language can then import such a feature and customize it according to his or her needs. The customization may range from the substitution of keywords up to the selection among a set of variants for a certain feature, like different kinds of inheritance in object-oriented languages, for example. In the Verifix project [11], a number of reusable Montages has been defined with the intention to reuse not only the Montages but as well an associated construction scheme for correct compilers.

4 Related Work

Denotational semantics has been regarded as the most promising approach for the semantic description of programming languages. But its problems with the pragmatics have been discovered already in case studies of the scale of Pascal and C [23]. Moreover domain definitions often need to be changed when extending the language with unforeseen constructs, for instance a change from the direct style to the continuation style when adding *gotos* [20].

Other well known meta–languages for specifying languages are Natural Semantics [14], ASF+SDF [24], and Action Semantics [20]. For somebody knowing mathematical logic, Natural Semantics are pretty intuitive and we used it for the dynamic semantics of Oberon [15]. Although we succeeded due to the excellent tool support by Centaur [7], the result was much longer and more complex than the Montages counterpart given in [18], since one has to carry around all the state information in the case of Natural Semantics. Similar problems exist if ASF+SDF is applied to imperative languages. Action Semantics solves these

[3] This feature is again available to all kind of ASM formalizations implemented in Aslan not only to those generated from a Montages language specification

problems by providing standard solutions to the main concepts used in programming languages. Unfortunately the set of standard solutions is not easily extendible.

Using ASMs for dynamic semantics, the work in [22] defines a framework comparable to ours. For the static part, it proposes *occurrence algebras* which integrate term algebras and context free grammars by providing terms for all nodes of all possible derivation trees. This allows such an approach to define all static aspects of the language in a functional algebraic system. Since reference attribute grammars [12] correspond to occurrence algebras the static aspects of our formalisms are almost identical to those in [22].

None of the discussed approaches uses visual descriptions of control flow and none of them supports structuring of all specification aspects in a vertical way, e.g. in self–contained modules for each language construct. This way of structuring is novel with respect to existing frameworks, as far as we know. In combination with refinements of involved semantic functions, and renaming of the vocabulary, it allows to reuse large parts of language specifications directly in other specifications. Programming language specifications can be presented as a series of sub-languages, each reusing its predecessor and extending it with new features. This specification structure has been used in ASM case studies [6, 10] and was adapted to the Montages case study of Oberon [18]. Our experience with Montages shows, that such sub-languages are useful, working languages, that can be executed, tested, and explained to the user in order to facilitate understanding of the whole language. The design and prototyping of a language is much more productive if such a stepwise development and testing is possible.

Acknowledgments

We would like to thank S. Chakraborty, C. Denzler, B. Di Franco, W. Shen, L. Thiele, and C. Wallace for collaboration in the Montages project. Furthermore we thank G. Goos, A. Heberle, W. Löwe, and W. Zimmermann for the helpful discussions on the topic.

References

[1] M. Anlauff. The Aslan Language Manual. Part of the Aslan distribution.

[2] M Anlauff, P. W. Kutter, and A. Pierantonio. Formal Aspects of and Development Environments for Montages. In M. Sellink, editor, *2nd Int. Workshop on the Theory and Practice of Alg. Spec.*, Workshops in Computing. Springer, 1997.

[3] M. Anlauff, P. W. Kutter, and A. Pierantonio. The Gem-Mex Tool Homepage. `http://www.first.gmd.de/~ma/gem/`, 1997.

[4] M. Anlauff, P. W. Kutter, and A. Pierantonio. The Montages Project Web Page. http://www.tik.ee.ethz.ch/~montages, 1997.

[5] E. Börger and J. Huggins. Abstract state machines 1988 – 1998: Commented ASM bibliography. In H. Ehrig, editor, *EATCS Bulletin, Formal Specification Column*, number 64, pages 105 – 127. EATCS, February 1998.

[6] E. Börger and D. Rosenzweig. A Mathematical Definition of Full Prolog. In *Science of Computer Programming*, volume 24, pages 249–286. North-Holland, 1994.

[7] P. Borra, D. Clement, T. Despeyroux, J. Incerpi, G. Kahn, B. Lang, and V. Pascual. CENTAUR: The system. Technical Report 777, INRIA, Sophia Antipolis, 1987.

[8] Y. Gurevich. Logic and the Challenge of Computer Science. In E. Börger, editor, *Theory and Practice of Software Engineering*, pages 1–57. CS Press, 1988.

[9] Y. Gurevich. Evolving Algebras 1993: Lipari Guide. In E. Börger, editor, *Specification and Validation Methods*. Oxford University Press, 1995.

[10] Y. Gurevich and J. K. Huggins. *The Semantics of the C Programming Language*, volume 702 of *LNCS*, pages 274–308. Springer, 1993.

[11] A Heberle, W. Löwe, and M. Trapp. Safe reuse of source to intermediate language compilations. 9th Int. Symposium on Software Reliability Engineering, 1998. http://chillarege.com/issre/fastabstracts/98417.html.

[12] G. Hedin. Reference attribute grammars. In *Second Workshop on Attribute Grammars and Their Applications*, pages 153 – 172, 1999.

[13] J. Huggins. Abstract State Machines Web Page http://www.eecs.umich.edu/gasm.

[14] G. Kahn. Natural Semantics. In *Proceedings of the Symp. on Theoretical Aspects of Computer Science, Passau, Germany*, 1987.

[15] P. W. Kutter. Executable Specification of Oberon Using Natural Semantics. Term Work, ETH Zürich, implementation on the Centaur System [7], 1996.

[16] P. W. Kutter and F. Haussmann. Dynamic Semantics of the Programming Language Oberon. Term work, ETH Zürich, July 1995. A revised version appeared as technical report of Institut TIK, ETH, number 27, 1997.

[17] P. W. Kutter and A. Pierantonio. Montages: Specifications of Realistic Programming Languages. *JUCS, Springer*, 3(5):416–442, 1997.

[18] P. W. Kutter and A. Pierantonio. The Formal Specification of Oberon. *JUCS, Springer*, 3(5):443–503, 1997.

[19] P. W. Kutter, D. Schweizer, and L. Thiele. Integrating Formal Domain-Specific Language Design in the Software Life Cycle. In *Current Trends in Applied Formal Methods*, LNCS. Springer, October 1998.

[20] P. D. Mosses. Theory and Practice of Action Semantics. In *MFCS'96, 21st International Symposium*, volume 1113 of *LNCS*, pages 37–61. Springer Verlag, 1996.

[21] M. Odersky. *A New Approach to Formal Language Definition and its Application to Oberon.* PhD thesis, ETH Zürich, 1989.

[22] A. Poetzsch-Heffter. Prototyping realistic programming languages based on formal specifications. *Acta Informatica*, 34:737–772, 1997. 1997.

[23] D. A. Schmidt. *Denotational Semantics: A Methodology for Language Development.* Allyn & Bacon, 1986.

[24] A. van Deursen, J. Heering, and P. Klint, editors. *Language Prototyping – An Algebraic Approach*, volume 5 of *AMAST Series in Computing.* World Scientific, 1996.

[25] C. Wallace. The Semantics of the Java Programming Language: Preliminary Version. Technical Report CSE-TR-355-97, University of Michigan EECS Department Technical Report, 1997.

[26] N. Wirth. The Programming Language Oberon. *Software - Practice and Experience*, 18(7):671 – 690, 1988.

Abstract State Machines for the Composition of Architectural Styles

Asuman Sünbül*

Technische Universität Berlin
Computergestützte Informationssysteme (CIS)
Sekr.E-N7, Einsteinufer 17,
D-10587 Berlin, Germany
+49-30-31479463
asu@cs.tu-berlin.de

Abstract. Software architecture is widely recognized as one of the most fundamental concepts in software engineering, because of the fact, that today's software systems are assembled from components with different characteristics: for example heterogenous, legacy or distributed systems. At the software architecture level, designers combine subsystems into complete systems using different techniques, e.g. "Architecture Description Languages" (ADLs). There exists a number of ADLs, each of which is specialized for one or more architectural styles. They are designed by different research groups with different goals in mind corresponding to their mental model on how software architecture can be expressed in the most efficient and elegant way. As a result, ADLs are not compatible with each other, so that it is difficult to present a homogeneous view of the software architecture of a system assembled from different components. This paper presents an approach how architectural styles can be combined using a concept of ADL-interchange.

1 Introduction

The complexity of many of today's software developments makes it often not reasonable to fix a certain architectural style for the design process of the whole software system. The need for multiple styles can come from either the problem domain or the subparts used to construct the system. Imagine, while designing a mobile phone network station, there are several architectural styles, that need to be combined. For example for receiving signals from the mobile phone the architect may choose a streaming pipe-and-filter style to handle the constant flow of repetitive data. For processing signals may be an event-based style is chosen. For interacting with the user, an event-based style *"plus"* a pipe-and-filter style is chosen. For that part of the subsystem which is responsible for the collection of independent components or special customer service queries, a repository-based approach is chosen.

* This research was supported by the German Research Society, Berlin-Brandenburg Graduate School in Distributed Information Systems (DFG grant no. GRK 316)

D. Bjørner, M. Broy, A. Zamulin (Eds.): PSI'99, LNCS 1755, pp. 54–61, 2000.

Problem statement: These high level descriptions and the *"plus"* between these styles sound attractive on paper, but while composing different architectural styles, architects may rely on ad hoc methods in trusting their own personal experiences. Current practice tackles the component composition problem on the technical layer using e. g. scripting, broker, RPC, event channels or similar approaches. These approaches have strong emphasis on solving technical interaction problems. The realization of the overall problem specification is covered by these low-level problems.

Architecture Description Languages (ADLs) belong to the high-level approaches. ADLs are intended to describe the system structure and behavior at a sufficiently abstract level dealing with large and complex systems [6]. A lot of work has been done in this research area, e.g. Aesop[10], Unicon[11], ControlH[9], MetaH[5], Rapide[14], Darwin[15], Π[19], UNAS[18], Wright[1], GenVoca[4].

But the heterogeneity of today's software systems forces to use different components described in different ADLs. This leads to the situation, that the ADLs become nearly unuseful, because each ADL operates in a stand alone fashion, they are not interoperable. In large or heterogenous systems many of these common aspects of architectural design support are re-implemented afresh. This means a lot of unnecessary work, which is probably one of the reasons for the often discussed question [6] in software architecture, why ADLs are only taken as early life-cycle specification languages. A main reason for this interoperability is especially the underlying semantics of the architectural descriptions. For instance, the notion of a component in ADL A could be a different one as the component notion in ADL B.

In the following, we will discuss two aspects: how to use different ADLs in a large software system and how to perform the composition task on the architectural level. The basic idea is, that there exists an interchange level between the different architectural description means. Therefore we introduce a *service layer* as a platform and common service representation layer for the component composition (see Figure 1): The system description S and the components $C_1, \ldots, C_n$ are mapped to corresponding ASM descriptions $S', C'_1 \ldots, C'_n$ which must be consistent with their unmapped versions. This mapping can be done by using standard techniques, like language translation, or the definition of adaptors and wrappers. Finally, as the most challenging task, we transform the overall system specification S' step by step in such a way that it finally contains explicit references to the interfaces of the existing components $C'_1 \ldots, C'_n$. An example of this kind of transformation is the use of refinement techniques in formal description methods [3]. The result of these stepwise transformations represents the composition specification of the system. We will call this final specification S^+ in order to emphasize that it realizes the "sum" of the components. Finally, we can now analyze the resulting specification S^+ aiming at the identification of *new components* X that need to be developed besides the existing ones. As a side-effect, the specification of these newly identified components can then automatically be obtained from the specification S^+ and developed accordingly.

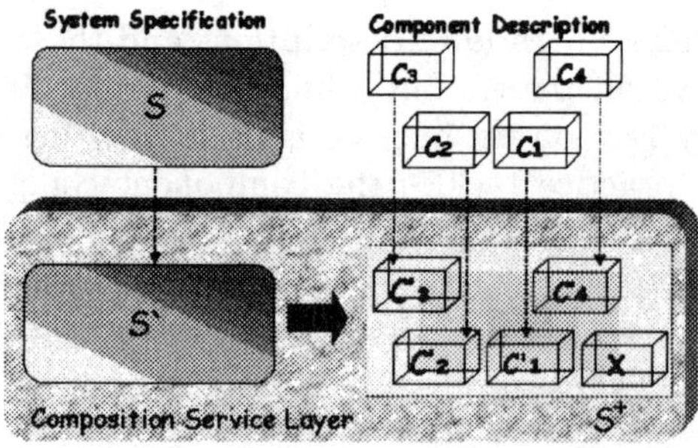

Fig. 1. Service layer for the composition of components

2 Why Mapping Architectural Descriptions to *Service Layer Representation*?

We argue, that the combination of different ADLs during the design of a system is useful at least because of the following reasons:

- If an architectural description problem is best solved by a certain ADL A, then the use of this A is the most natural thing even if for other parts of the system A is not appropriate, and therefore other ADLs are used.
- Developers often have individual favorites for describing the architecture of software. If a developer has the freedom to choose the ADL that he or she wants – if it is appropriate for the description of the problem – than his or her productivity is much higher than if he or she is forced to use an ADL that is fixed by the project policy. Often these "favorite" ADLs are none of the well known languages from literature, but individually designed "languages" the semantics of which is normally given by an implicit agreement among the members of a developer team.

Therefore, what is needed is the possibility to combine different ADLs so that

- for different portions and/or aspects of the software architecture the ADLs that **fits best** can be used and
- the resulting combined architectural description is **semantically consistent** w.r.t. the underlying models of the ADLs.

A promising way to solve this problem is to provide a concept for an interchange of ADLs. In principle, there exist the following alternatives for an interchange between different ADLs:

Defining a union language subsuming all the capabilities of the existing languages. This approach seems to be unrealistic because of the manifold characteristics of existing ADLs. There cannot be "the universal ADL language" that masters every requirement and every domain specific using of ADL.

Defining an intersection language that incorporates the features being contained in each of the ADLs.

Defining a service "interchange" providing services to describe and composition problems based on architectural descriptions.

The former two alternatives imply that the use of existing ADLs would be restricted, because they would be at least partially replaced by a new ADL. The experience gathered for the "old" ADLs will be lost and users are forced to learn a new language. The advantage of the third approach is, that existing ADLs can be used as they are, because the interchange is not done on the language level but on a basic semantic description level. Thus, the latter approach is much more promising, because there is no need to convince people in present and in future to use a "better" approach for their architectural description. For the same reason, the third alternative applies also for the integration of the architecture of legacy systems.

2.1 What Are the Problems Concerning ADL Interchange?

The combination of ADL A and B is less complicated, if A and B are designed to describe different aspects of the software. For example, if the static structures of the system is described in ADL A, and the dynamic behavior is encoded in ADL B, then the combination of these two descriptions should be easier. The situation looks quite different, if A and B are "competing" ADLs being designed for similar purposes. In this case, it is very important to carefully analyze the underlying semantics of A and B, so that a combination is possible and the consistency can be checked.

Therefore, an interplay of ADLs can only be achieved, if the semantics of each of them is unambiguously defined. Only with these descriptions it is possible to formulate propositions being valid for the combined architectural description.

As a consequence, there must be one single description language for formulating the underlying semantics of each of the ADLs. Thus, great care must be taken in selecting the right one, which must meet at least the following requirements:

- Due to the fact that ADLs are manifold, the formal description language must be universal in that sense, that it is possible to describe the feature of existing ADLs. Especially, the language must be able to express static structures as well as dynamic behavior.
- In order to be able to make statements about certain properties of the combined architectural description (e.g. consistency, liveness) the description language must have a well-defined mathematical basis.
- If during the process of combining ADLs is turns out, that aspects being important for the interplay of the ADLs are not expressible by any of the participating ADLs, the description language should as well be usable as an alternative ADL in order to insert missing parts in the architectural description.
- The previous item implies, that the description language must be intelligible for people involved in the software architecture.

- Due to the fact, that ADLs often describe large and complex software system, the underlying description language must be scalable.
- From a practical point of view, the description language should have a notion of execution, so that support tools can directly generate code that implements the interchange level.

The *Abstract State Machine* approach [12] seems to be a promising candidate for being used to describe software architecture models and the semantics of ADLs:

- Abstract State Machines (ASM) is an universal, mathematically well-founded method which is capable of the description of static structures as well as dynamic behavior of system.
- ASMs provide the possibility to choose appropriate levels of abstraction according to the problem that should be described. This feature is also important with respect to scalability.
- ASM have been used for many different problem areas. In the context of this work, the use of ASMs in describing the semantics of programming languages (e.g. [13]) and computer architecture (e.g. [7]) provides an excellent basis for the task of describing software architectures.
- ASM can as well be executed; there exist several tools that generate executable versions of the ASM specification.

The aim of this approach is neither the development of a new architecture definition language, nor a prescription of a common vocabulary, nor the generation of "architectural theorems". The aim is to form a basis for the combination of ADLs by using existing work and building a low level concept that can directly be used to implement the interchange of ADLs.

3 Scenario: Description of the Composition

We assume in the following, that we're working within the service layer. It serves as a platform for the architectural description and component composition. It abstracts from architectural styles that have been used to originally describe the components. However, the translation from the original description to the representation used in the service layer must be carried out in a way, that no semantic information gets lost The format of component description used in the service layer is very similar to the Π ([19]) component model, containing the services being provided and required by a component and additionally the specification of the functionality and dynamic behavior of the component in ASM-notation.

For the following description we revisit the example of Section 1. The following composition problem is described as an example: the "processing signals" component needs information from the "data management" component in order to decide whether a phone connection can be established or not, because of potentially existing limitations contained in the contract of a customer of the phone company. In order to combine these two models, we translate each of them into an ASM formalization. The union of these formalizations then forms the interchange level where the architectural composition can actually be performed.

As pointed out in the previous section we use ASMs for this purpose. At the first step, the architectural descriptions of the example mentioned in Section 1 are automatically translated into an ASM description using techniques like Montages [2]. The ASM formalization of the data structures of the "processing signal" component is given as follows:

```
universes
   ConnectionData
   Process = {Receive,Connection,
             Timer,Disconnection}
   ProcessState = {active,passive}
functions
   state: Process->ProcessState
   CurrentConnection: ->ConnectionData
   Connection Process: -> Process
relation
   access_check: ConnectionData->Boolean
```

For the "data management" component, the following relation is needed for describing the composition:

```
relation
  checkAccess:ConnectionData->Boolean
```

Using this data structures, the composition of the two components can be specified as follows:

```
if state(ConnectionProcess) = active then
  if not access_check(CurrentConnection)
  then
    access_check(CurrentConnection):=
             checkAccess(CurrentConnection)
  elseif access_check(CurrentConnection) then
    !ConnectionProcessRules
  else
    error := "no access granted"
    state(ConnectionProcess) := passive
  endif
endif
```

In the next steps, these abstract description must be stepwise refined until a layer is reached where concrete system access based on the technical description if the interface can be modeled. These refinement steps are omitted in this example.

4 Related Work

Currently, the only effort that has been undertaken to build an interchange of ADLs is the Acme approach [16] which is still under development. Acme is a software architecture description language that aims at providing a common interchange format for software architecture, so that different tools for architecture description languages can be integrated. The main difference between the approach presented in this work and Acme can be described as follows: Acme's goal is the convergence of all ADL related research activities into the Acme framework and tries to form an interchange between ADLs on the language level. Our approach retains existing ADLs by pushing the interchange activities on a lower level, the semantic description level of these ADLs.

5 Conclusion

Based on the fact that architectural design fragments using different architectural description means often need to be combined into larger architectures this paper presents a concept how to compose different architectural styles. This will be achieved by providing an **interchange level** for architectural composition. This work is focusing on ADLs and provides basic concepts for the composition based on ADLs. In contrast to existing approaches for combining ADLs, the idea presented here does not build on a consensus between ADL developers in present and future, because neither a superset nor an intersection of existing ADLs need to be introduced. Following our approach, the composition keeps the freedom of choosing the architectural description means, that is most suitable for the actual problem. The choice of an ADL is not restricted by the needs of the composition task.

References

1. Allen, R., and Garlan, D. Formalizing architectural connection. In *Proceedings of the 16th International Conference on Software Engineering* (May 1994), pp. 71–80.
2. Anlauff, M., Kutter, P., and Pierantonio, A. Formal Aspects of and Development Environments for Montages. In *2nd International Workshop on the Theory and Practice of Algebraic Specifications* (Amsterdam, 1997), M. Sellink, Ed., Workshops in Computing, Springer.
3. Anlauff, M., and Sünbül, A. Component based software engineering for telecommunication software. In *SCI/ISAS Conference, Orlando,Florida* (1999). (to appear).
4. Batory, D. Intelligent components and software generators. Tech. Rep. 97-06, Department of Computer Sciences, University of Texas at Austin, April 1997. Invited presentation to the Software Quality Institute Symposium on Software Reliability.
5. Binns, P., and Vestal, S. Formal real-time architecture specification and analysis. In *Tenth IEEE Workshop on Real-Time Operating Systems and Software* (New York, NY, May 1993).
6. Boehm, B. W., Garlan, D., Kramer, J., Kruchten, P., Luckham, D., Salasin, J., and Wolf, A. L. ICSE98 Panel: Are new-generation architecture description languages useful. In *ICSE98* (1998).

7. Börger, E., and Mazzanti, S. A Practical Method for Rigorously Controllable Hardware Design. In *ZUM'97: The Z Formal Specification Notation*, J. Bowen, M. Hinchey, and D. Till, Eds., vol. 1212 of *LNCS*. Springer, 1996, pp. 151–187.
8. Ciancarini, P., and Mascolo, C. Analyzing and refining an architectural style. In *ZUM '97: The Z Formal Specification Notation, 10th International Conference of Z Users* (Reading, UK, April 1997), J. Bowen, M. Hinchey, and D. Till, Eds., vol. 1212 of *LNCS*.
9. Englehart, M., and Jackson, M. ControlH: A fourth generation language for real-time GN&C applications. In *Proceedings of the CACSD* (Tucson, AZ, March 1994).
10. Garlan, D., Allen, R., and Ockerbloom, J. Exploiting style in architectural design environments. In *Proceedings of SIGSOFT '94: The Second ACM SIGSOFT symposium on the Foundations of Software Engineering* (Dec. 1995), ACM Press, pp. 179–185.
11. Garlan, D., and Shaw, M. *Software Architecture: Perspectives On An Emerging Discipline.* Prentice Hall, 1995.
12. Gurevich, Y. Evolving Algebras 1993: Lipari Guide. In *Specification and Validation Methods*, E. Börger, Ed. Oxford University Press, 1995, pp. 9–36.
13. Gurevich, Y., and Huggins, J. The Semantics of the C Programming Language. In *Computer Science Logic*, E. Börger, H. Kleine Büning, G. Jäger, S. Martini, and M. M. Richter, Eds., vol. 702 of *LNCS*. Springer, 1993, pp. 274–309.
14. Luckham, D., Augustine, L., Kenney, J., Veera, J., Bryan, D., and Mann, W. Specification and analysis of system architecture using rapide. In *IEEE Transactions on Software Engineering, Special Issue on Software Architecture* (Apr. 1995), vol. 21(4), pp. 336–355.
15. Magee, J., Dulay, N., Eisenbach, S., and Kramer, J. Specifying distributed software architectures. In *Proceedings of 5th European Software Engineering Conference (ESEC 95)* (1995).
16. Monroe, R. T., Garlan, D., and Wile, D. ACME Straw Manual. Tech. rep., Carnegie Mellon University, Pittsburgh, Nov. 1997. Version 0.1.1.
17. Potter, B., Sinclair, J., and Till, D. *An Introduction to Formal Specification and Z.* Prentice Hall, 1991.
18. Royce, W., and Royce, W. Software architecture: Integrating process and technology. *TRW Space and Defense* (1991).
19. Schumann, H., and Goedicke, M. Component-oriented software development with Π. ISST-Berichte 21/94, ISST, Sept. 1994.

The Essence of Program Transformation by Partial Evaluation and Driving*

Neil D. Jones

DIKU, University of Copenhagen
Universitetsparken 1, DK-2100 Copenhagen, Denmark
neil@diku.dk

Abstract. An abstract framework is developed to describe program transformation by *specializing* a given program to a restricted set of inputs. Particular cases include partial evaluation [19] and Turchin's more powerful "driving" transformation [33]. Such automatic program speedups have been seen to give quite significant speedups in practical applications.
This paper's aims are similar to those of [18]: better to understand the fundamental mathematical phenomena that make such speedups possible. The current paper is more complete than [18], since it precisely formulates correctness of code generation; and more powerful, since it includes program optimizations not achievable by simple partial evaluation. Moreover, for the first time it puts Turchin's driving methodology on a solid semantic foundation which is not tied to any particular programming language or data structure.

This paper is dedicated to Satoru Takasu with thanks for good advice early in my career on how to do research, and for insight into how to see the essential part of a new problem.

1 Introduction

1.1 History

Automatic program specialization evolved independently at several different times and places [13,31,33,5,11,20]. In recent years partial evaluation has received much attention ([19,6], and several conferences), and work has been done on other automatic transformations including Wadler's well-known *deforestation* [37,7,26].

Many of these active research themes were anticipated in the 1970's by Valentin Turchin in Moscow [29,30] in his research on *supercompilation* (= supervised computation and compilation), and experiments were made with implementations. Examples include program optimization both by deforestation and by partial evaluation; the use and significance of self-application for generating

* This work was supported in part by the Danish Natural Science Research Council (DART project) and by an Esprit Basic Research Action (Semantique).

D. Bjørner, M. Broy, A. Zamulin (Eds.): PSI'99, LNCS 1755, pp. 62–79, 2000.

compilers and other program generators; and the use of grammars as a tool in program transformation [31,32,17]. Recent works on driving and supercompilation include [33,14,15,27,24,22,1,36].

1.2 Goals

The purpose of this paper is to formulate the essential concepts of supercompilation in an abstract and language-independent way. For simplicity we treat only imperative programs, and intentionally do not make explicit the nature of either commands or the store, except as needed for examples.

At the core of supercompilation is the program transformation called *driving* (Russian "progonka"). In principle driving is stronger than both deforestation and partial evaluation [27,37,12,19], and an example will be given to show this (the pattern matching example at the end of the paper). On the other hand, driving has taken longer to come into practical use than either deforestation or partial evaluation, for several reasons.

First, the greater strength of driving makes it correspondingly harder to tame; cause and effect are less easily understood than in deforestation and partial evaluation, and in fact it is only in the latter case that self-application has been achieved on practical applications. Second, the first papers were in Russian, and they and later ones used a computer language Refal[1] unfamiliar to western readers. Finally, the presentation style of the supercompilation papers is unfamiliar, using examples and sketches of algorithms rather than mathematical formulations of the basic ideas, and avoiding even set theory for philosophical reasons [34].

We hope the abstract framework will lead to greater practical exploitation of the principles underlying supercompilation (stronger program transformations, more automatic systems, new languages), and a better understanding in principle of the difficult problem of ensuring termination of program transformation.

1.3 Preliminary Definitions

First, a quite abstract definition of an imperative program is given, as a state transition system. In our opinion the essence of the "driving" concept is more clearly exposed at this level. Later, a more intuitive flow chart formalism will be used for examples, and to clarify the problem of code generation.

Definition 1. *An* abstract program *is a quadruple* $\pi = (P, S, \rightarrow, p_0)$ *where* $p_0 \in P$ *and* $\rightarrow \subseteq (P \times S) \times (P \times S)$. *Terminology:* P *is the set of* program points, S *is the set of* stores, $\rightarrow$ *is the* transition relation, *and* p_0 *is the* initial program point. *We write* $\rightarrow$ *in infix notation, e.g.* $(p, s) \rightarrow (p', s')$ *instead of* $((p, s), (p', s')) \in \rightarrow$. *A* state *is a pair* $(p, s) \in P \times S$.

[1] Refal is essentially a language of Markov algorithms extended with variablesand two kinds of brackets to create tree structures. A program is a sequence of rewrite rules, used to transform data in the form of associative and possibly nested symbol strings. In contrast with most pattern matching languages, most general unifiers do not always exist.

A store such as $[\mathtt{X}\mapsto \mathtt{1:2:[]}, \mathtt{Y}\mapsto \mathtt{2:(4:5):[]}]$ usually maps program variables to their values. A program point may be a flow chart node, or can be thought of as a label in a program.

Definition 2. *$p \in P$ is* transient *if $(p, s_1) \to (p', s')$ and $(p, s_2) \to (p'', s'')$ imply $p' = p''$, i.e. there is at most one p' with $(p, \_) \to (p', \_)$. State (p, s) is* terminal *if $(p, s) \to (p', s')$ holds for no (p', s'). The abstract program π is* deterministic *if for all states (p, s), $(p, s) \to (p', s')$ and $(p, s) \to (p'', s'')$ imply $p' = p''$ and $s' = s''$.*

Definition 3. *A* computation *(from $s_0 \in S$) is a finite or infinite sequence*

$$(p_0, s_0) \to (p_1, s_1) \to (p_2, s_2) \to \ldots$$

Notation: subsets of S will be indicated by overlines, so $\overline{s} \subseteq S$. Given this, and defining $\to^*$ to be the reflexive transitive closure of $\to$, the input/output relation *that π defines on $\overline{s}_0 \subseteq S$ is*

$$IO(\pi, \overline{s}_0) = \{(s_0, s_t) \mid s_0 \in \overline{s}_0, (p_0, s_0) \to^* (p_t, s_t), \ \text{ and } (p_t, s_t) \ \text{ is terminal}\}$$

More concretely, programs can be given by flow charts whose edges are labeled by commands. These are interpreted by a *command semantics*:

$$\mathcal{C}[\![\_]\!] : Command \to (S \overset{partial}{\longrightarrow} S)$$

where *Command* and S are unspecified sets (but $S =$ the set of stores as above).

Definition 4. *A* flow chart *is a rooted, edge-labeled directed graph $F = (P, E, p_0)$ where $p_0 \in P$ and $E \subseteq P \times Command \times P$ (the* edges *of F). We write $p \overset{C}{\Rightarrow} p'$ whenever $(p, C, p') \in E$.*

If $p \overset{C}{\Rightarrow} p'$ then C denotes a store transformation, e.g. C could be an assignment statement changing a variable's value. The formulation includes tests too: the domain of partial function $\mathcal{C}[\![C]\!]$ is the set of stores which cause transition from program point p to p'. For example, command "`if odd(X) goto`" might label that edge, corresponding to "`p: if odd(X) then goto p'`" in concrete syntax.

Definition 5. *The* program denoted by F *is $\pi^F = (P, S, \to, p_0)$, where*

$$(p, s) \to (p', s') \text{ if and only if } s' = \mathcal{C}[\![C]\!]s \text{ for some } p \overset{C}{\Rightarrow} p'$$

2 Driven Programs, without Store Transformations

A major use of driving (and partial evaluation) is for *program specialization.* For simplicity we begin with a rather weak form of driving that does not modify the store, and give a stronger version in the next section.

Given partial information about a program's inputs (represented by a subset $\overline{s}_0 \subseteq S$ of all possible stores), driving transforms program π into another program π_d that is equivalent to π on any initial store $s_0 \in \overline{s}_0$. The goal is efficiency: once π_d has been constructed, local optimizations of transition chain compression and reduced code generation can yield a much faster program than π, as seen in [18,19] and many others.

A useful principle is to begin by saying *what* is to be done, as simply as possible, before giving constructions and algorithms saying *how* it can be accomplished. We thus first define what it means for a program π_d to be a "driven" form of program π, and defer the question of how to perform driving to Section 4.

Intuitively π_d is an "exploded" form of π in which any of π's program points p may have several annotated versions $(p, \overline{s}_1), (p, \overline{s}_2), \ldots$. Each $\overline{s}_i$ is a set of stores, required always to contain the current store in any computation by π_d.

Computations by π_d (state sequences) will be in a one-to-one correspondence with those of π, so nothing may seem to have been gained (and something lost, since π_d may be bigger than π). However, if control ever reaches an annotated program point $(p, \overline{s})$ in π_d, then the current runtime store *must lie in* $\overline{s}$. For example, $\overline{s}$ could be the set of all stores such that the value of variable X is always even.

This information is *the source of all improvements gained by partial evaluation or driving.* Its use is to optimize π_d by generating equivalent but more efficient code exploiting the information given by $\overline{s}$. In particular some computations may be elided altogether, since their effect can be achieved by using the $\overline{s}$ at transformation time; and knowledge of $\overline{s}$ often allows a much more economical representation of the stores $s \in \overline{s}$.

2.1 Abstract Formulation

The following is, in our opinion, the *essential core of the driving concept*:

Definition 6. *Given program* $\pi = (P, S, \rightarrow, p_0)$*, program* $\pi_d = (P_d, S, \rightarrow_d, (p_0, \overline{s}_0))$ *is an* $\overline{s}_0$-driven form *of* π *if* $P_d \subseteq P \times \mathcal{P}(S)$ *and* π_d *satisfies the following conditions.*

1. $((p, \overline{s}), s) \rightarrow_d ((p', \overline{s}'), s')$ *and* $s \in \overline{s}$ *imply* $(p, s) \rightarrow (p', s')$. soundness
2. $(p, \overline{s}) \in P_d$, $(p, s) \rightarrow (p', s')$, *and* $s \in \overline{s}$ *imply that there exists* $\overline{s}'$ *such that* $((p, \overline{s}), s) \rightarrow_d ((p', \overline{s}'), s')$ completeness
3. $((p, \overline{s}), s) \rightarrow_d ((p', \overline{s}'), s')$ *and* $s \in \overline{s}$ *imply* $s' \in \overline{s}'$ invariance *of* $s \in \overline{s}$.

To begin with, $P_d \subseteq P \times \mathcal{P}(S)$, so a program point of π_d is a pair $(p, \overline{s})$ where $\overline{s} \subseteq S$ is a set of stores. The *soundness* condition says that π_d can do *only* the store transformations that π can do. The *completeness* condition says that for any driven program point $(p, \overline{s})$ of π_d, any store transformation that π can do from p on stores $s \in \overline{s}$ can also be done by π_d.

Programs may in principle be infinite, but in practice we are only interested in finite ones.

The Significance of Store Sets. The invariance of $s \in \overline{s}$ in a transition $((p, \overline{s}), s) \rightarrow_d ((p', \overline{s}'), s')$ expresses a form of *information propagation* carried out at program transformation time [14,15].

One can think of a store set as a predicate describing variable value relationships, e.g. "X is even" or "$X = Y + 1 \wedge Z < Y$". Store sets could thus be manipulated in the form of logical formulas.

This view has much in common with regarding statements as forward or backward *predicate transformers*, as used by Dijkstra and many others for proving programs correct [10]. Further, a store set $\overline{s}$ that annotates a program point p corresponds to an *invariant*, i.e. a relationship among variable values that holds whenever control reaches point $(p, \overline{s})$ in the transformed program.

Instead of formulas, one could describe store sets using a set of *abstract values* Σ, using for example a function $\gamma : \Sigma \rightarrow \mathcal{P}(S)$ that maps an abstract value $\sigma \in \Sigma$ to the store set it denotes. In logic γ is called an *interpretation*, and Turchin uses the term *configuration* for such a store set description [33].

This idea is a cornerstone of abstract interpretation, where γ is called a *concretization function* [9,2,16]. Our approach can thus be described as *program specialization by abstract interpretation.* The abstract values are constructed "on the fly" during program transformation to create new specialized program points. This is in contrast to most abstract interpretations, which iterate until the abstract values associated with the *original program*'s program points reach their collective least fixpoint.

Lemma 1. *If π_d is an $\overline{s}_0$-driven form of π, then for any $s_0 \in \overline{s}_0$ there is a computation*

$$(p_0, s_0) \rightarrow (p_1, s_1) \rightarrow (p_2, s_2) \rightarrow \dots$$

if and only if there is a computation

$$((p_0, \overline{s}_0), s_0) \rightarrow ((p_1, \overline{s}_1), s_1) \rightarrow ((p_2, \overline{s}_2), s_2) \rightarrow \dots$$

Proof. "If" follows from soundness, "only if" by completeness and invariance of $s \in \overline{s}$.

Corollary 1. $IO(\pi, \overline{s}_0) = IO(\pi_d, \overline{s}_0)$

Program Specialization by Driving. Informally, program π is transformed as follows:

1. Given π and an initial set of stores $\overline{s}_0$ to which π is to be specialized, construct a driven program π_d. In practice, π will be given in flow chart or other concrete syntactic form, and finite descriptions of store sets will be used.
2. Improve π_d by and removing unreachable branches, and by compressing sequences of transient transitions

$$((p, \overline{s}), s) \rightarrow ((p', \overline{s'}), s') \rightarrow \dots \rightarrow ((p'', \overline{s''}), s'')$$

into single-step transitions

$$((p,\overline{s}),s) \rightarrow ((p'',\overline{s''}),s'')$$

3. If $\pi = \pi^F$ where F is a given flow chart, then F_d is constructed and improved in the same way: by compressing transitions, and generating appropriately simplified commands as edge labels.

The idea is that knowing a store set $\overline{s}$ gives contextual information used to transform π_d to make it run faster. Conditions for correct code generation will be given after we discuss the choice of store sets and the use of alternative store representations in Section 3.

2.2 Extreme and Intermediate Cases

In spite of the close correspondence between the computations of π and π_d, there is a wide latitude in the choice of π_d. Different choices will lead to different degrees of optimization. For practical use we need intermediate cases for which π_d has finitely many program points, and its store sets $\overline{s}$ are small enough (i.e. precise enough) to allow significant code optimization.

We will see a pattern-matching example where a program with two inputs of size m, n that runs in time $a \cdot m \cdot n$ can, by specializing to a fixed first input, be transformed into one running in time $b \cdot n$ where b is independent of m.

One extreme case is to choose every $\overline{s}$ to be equal to S. In this case π_d is identical to π, so no speedup is gained. Another extreme is to define π_d to contain $((p,\overline{s}),s) \rightarrow_d ((p',\{s'\}),s')$ whenever $(p,s) \rightarrow (p',s')$, $s \in \overline{s}$, and $(p,\overline{s}) \in P_d$. In this case π_d amounts to a totally unfolded version containing all possible computations on inputs from $\overline{s}_0$.

State Set Choice and Code Generation. The extreme just described will nearly always give infinite programs. It is not at all natural for code generation, as it deals with states one at a time.

In flow chart form, a test amounts to two different transitions $p \overset{C1}{\Rightarrow} p'$ and $p \overset{C2}{\Rightarrow} p''$ from the same p. A more interesting extreme can be obtained from the following principle: *the driven program should contain no tests that are not present in the original program.* The essence of this can be described without flow charts as follows.

Definition 7. π_d requires no new tests *if whenever* π *contains* $(p,s) \rightarrow (p',s')$, $s \in \overline{s}$, *and* π_d *contains* $((p,\overline{s}),s) \rightarrow_d ((p',\overline{s}'),s')$, *then*

$$\overline{s}' \supseteq \{s_2 \mid \exists s_1 \in \overline{s} \textit{ such that } (p,s_1) \rightarrow (p',s_2) \text{ is in } \pi\}$$

This defines the new store set $\overline{s}'$ to be *inclusive*, meaning that it contains every store reachable from any store in $\overline{s}$ by π transitions from p to p'. The target store set $\overline{s}'$ of a driven transition $((p,\overline{s}),s) \rightarrow_d ((p',\overline{s}'),s')$ includes not only the target s' of s, but also the targets of all its "siblings" $s_1 \in \overline{s}$ that go from p to p'.

For deterministic programs, this amounts to requiring that π_d can only perform tests that are also performed by π. This is a reasonable restriction for code generation purposes, but is by no means necessary: if one somehow knows that the value of a given variable x must lie in a finite set $X = \{a, b, \ldots, k\}$, new tests could be generated to select specialized commands for each case of $x \in X$.

Even though these new tests may seem unnecessary since they were not present in the original program, one often gains efficiency because the value of x will be known exactly in each of the specialized commands, leading to smaller subsequent code. See the discussion on "bounded static variation" in [19].

An $\overline{s}_0$-driven form of π can always be obtained by choosing equality rather than set containment for $\overline{s}'$, and choosing π_d to contain the smallest set of program points including $(p_0, \overline{s}_0)$ and closed under the definition above. This extreme preserves all possible information about the computation subject to the inclusiveness condition. It can be used in principle to produce a "most completely optimized" version of the given program, but suffers from two practical problems:

First, this $\overline{s}_0$-driven π_d will very often contain infinitely many specialized program points $(p, \overline{s})$. Second, its transition relation may not be computable.

Generalization. It is a subtle problem in practice to guarantee that the transformed program both is finite and is more efficient than the original program. A solution in practice is not to work with the mathematically defined and usually infinite store sets above, but rather to use finite descriptions of perhaps larger sets $\overline{s}'' \supseteq \overline{s}'$ that can be manipulated by computable operations.

Finiteness of the transformed program can be achieved by choosing describable store sets that are larger than $\overline{s}'$ but which are still small enough to allow significant optimizations.

Turchin uses the term *configuration* for such a store set description, and *generalization* for the problem of choosing configurations to yield both finiteness and efficiency [33,35].

2.3 Driven Flow Charts

We now reformulate the former abstract definition for flow charts. For now we leave commands unchanged, as Section 3 will discuss store modifications and code generation together.

Definition 8. *Given flow chart $F = (P, E, p_0)$ and $\overline{s}_0 \subseteq S$, $F_d = (P_d, E_d, (p_0, \overline{s}_0))$ is an $\overline{s}_0$-*driven form *of F if $P_d \subseteq P \times \mathcal{P}(S)$ and F_d satisfies the following conditions.*

1. *$(p, \overline{s}) \stackrel{C}{\Rightarrow} (p', \overline{s}')$ in F_d implies $p \stackrel{C}{\Rightarrow} p'$ in F* soundness.
2. *$(p, \overline{s}) \in P_d$, $\overline{s} \neq \{\}$, and $p \stackrel{C}{\Rightarrow} p'$ in F imply that $(p, \overline{s}) \stackrel{C}{\Rightarrow} (p', \overline{s}')$ in F_d for some $\overline{s}'$* completeness.

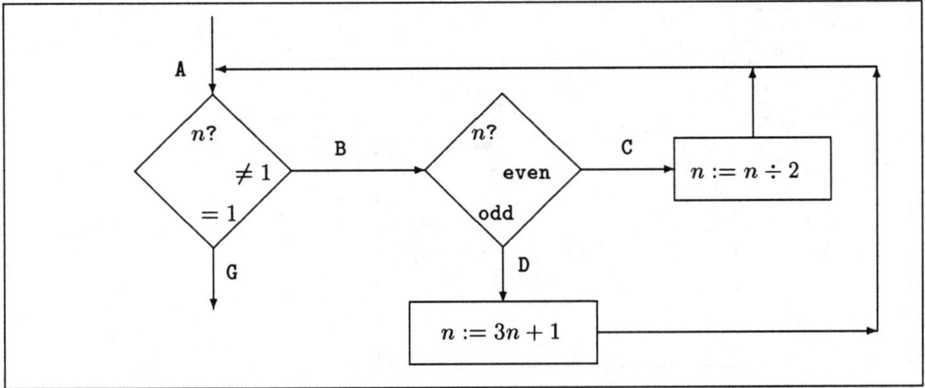

Fig. 1. Diagram of a simple flow chart program

3. $(p, \overline{s}) \stackrel{C}{\Rightarrow} (p', \overline{s}')$ *in* F_d *and* $s \in \overline{s}$ *and* $s' = \mathcal{C}[\![C]\!]s$ *is defined imply* $s' \in \overline{s}'$ invariance *of* $s \in \overline{s}$.

Theorem 1. *If* F_d *is an* $\overline{s}_0$*-driven form of* F*, then* π^{F_d} *is an* $\overline{s}_0$*-driven form of* π.

Proof. This is easily verified from Definitions 5 and 8, as the latter is entirely parallel to Definition 6.

2.4 An Example

Collatz' problem in number theory amounts to determining whether the following program terminates for all positive n. To our knowledge it is still unsolved.

A: **while** $n \neq 1$ **do**
  B: **if** n even
    then (C: $n := n \div 2$;)
    else (D: $n := 3 * n + 1$;)
  fi
  od
G:

Its flow chart equivalent is $F = (P, E, 0)$ where $P = \{A, B, C, D, G\}$ and edge set E is given by the diagram in Figure 1. The program has only one variable n, so a store set is essentially a set of values.

We use just four store sets:

$$\begin{aligned} Even &= \{[n \mapsto x] \mid x \in \{0, 2, 4, \ldots\}\} \\ Odd &= \{[n \mapsto x] \mid x \in \{1, 3, 5, \ldots\}\} \\ \top &= \{[n \mapsto x] \mid x \in \mathcal{N}\} \\ \bot &= \{\} \end{aligned}$$

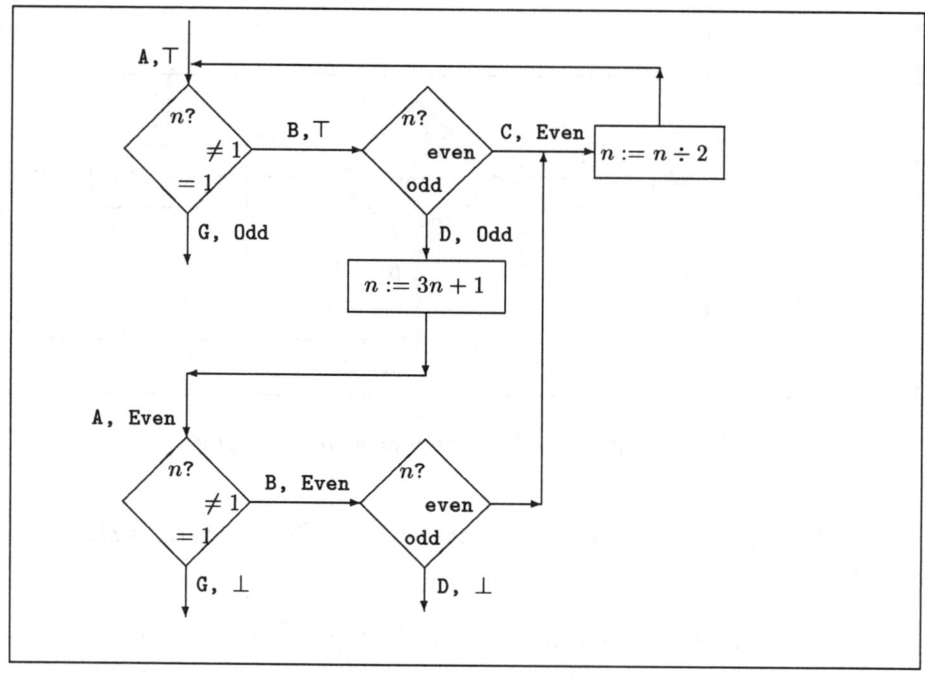

Fig. 2. A driven version of the same program

The flow chart F_d of Figure 2 is a driven version of F. Specialized program points $(D, \perp)$ and $(G, \perp)$ are unreachable since they have empty store sets. The driven version, though larger, contains two transient transitions, from (A, Even) and (B, Even). Transition compression redirects the branch from (D, Odd) to $(C, Even)$ to give a somewhat better program, faster in that two tests are avoided whenever n becomes odd.

3 Driven Programs, with Store Transformations

According to Definition 6, a driven program π_d has exactly the same stores as π. As a consequence the only real optimizations that can occur are from collapsing transient transition chains, and little computational optimisation occurs. We now revise this definition, "retyping" the store to obtain more powerful transformations such as those of partial evaluation by projections [19,18,21] or arity raising [25].

3.1 Abstract Formulation

From now on S_d will denote the set of possible stores in driven program π_d. Given the knowledge that $s \in \overline{s}$, a store s of π can often be represented in the driven program π_d by a simpler store $s_d \in S_d$. For example, if

$$\overline{s} = \{ [\mathtt{X} \mapsto 1,\ \mathtt{Y} \mapsto y,\ \mathtt{Z} \mapsto 3] \mid y \in \mathcal{N}\}$$

then $s \in \overline{s}$ at π_d program point $(p, \overline{s})$ can be represented by the value of Y alone since X, Z are known from context. In practice, $\overline{s}$ will be described finitely, e.g. by an abstract value σ in description set Σ:

$$\sigma = [\mathtt{X} \mapsto 1,\ \mathtt{Y} \mapsto \top,\ \mathtt{Z} \mapsto 3].$$

together with concretization function (or interpretation) $\gamma : \Sigma \to \mathcal{P}(S)$. To formalize this abstractly, we assume given a function

$$\Delta : \mathcal{P}(S) \times S_d \stackrel{partial}{\longrightarrow} S$$

satisfying the following two properties (note that Δ is written in infix notation.):

1. $\overline{s}\Delta s_d \in \overline{s}$ whenever $\overline{s} \subseteq S$, $s_d \in S_d$, and $\overline{s}\Delta s_d$ is defined; and
2. $\overline{s}_0 \Delta s_d = \overline{s}_1 \Delta s'_d = s$ implies $s_d = s'_d$

One can think of Δ as a reconstruction function to build s from store set $\overline{s}$ and a driven store s_d. For example, if $\overline{s}$ is as above and if s_d is, say, $[Y \mapsto 5]$ then we would have $\overline{s}\Delta s_d = [X \mapsto 1, Y \mapsto 5, Z \mapsto 3]$.

The restriction $\overline{s}\Delta s_d \in \overline{s}$ says that s_d can only represent a store in the current $\overline{s}$. The second restriction says that Δ is injective in its second argument.

The previous formulation without store transformations is expressible by putting $S = S_d$, and letting $\overline{s}\Delta s_d = s_d$ when $s_d = s_d \in \overline{s}$, with $\overline{s}\Delta s_d$ undefined otherwise.

We will see that allowing alternative representations of the driven stores enables much stronger program optimizations. The new Definition 6 is as follows. The essential idea is that a transition

$$(p, s) \to (p', s') \quad = \quad (p, \overline{s}\Delta s_d) \to (p', \overline{s}'\Delta s'_d)$$

is transformed, by a kind of reassociation, into a specialized transition of form

$$((p, \overline{s}), s_d) \to_d ((p', \overline{s}'), s'_d)$$

Definition 9. *Program* $\pi_d = (P_d, S_d, \to_d, (p_0, \overline{s}_0))$ *is an* $\overline{s}_0$-driven form *of* $\pi = (P, S, \to, p_0)$ *in case* $P_d \subseteq P \times \mathcal{P}(S)$ *and* π_d *satisfies the following conditions.*

1. $((p, \overline{s}), s_d) \to_d ((p', \overline{s}'), s'_d)$ *implies* $s = \overline{s}\Delta s_d$ *and* $s' = \overline{s}'\Delta s'_d$ *for some* s, s', *and* $(p, s) \to (p', s')$. soundness
2. $(p, \overline{s}) \in P_d$, $s \in \overline{s}$, *and* $(p, s) \to (p', s')$ *imply there are* $s_d, s'_d, \overline{s}'$ *such that* $s = \overline{s}\Delta s_d$, $s' = \overline{s}'\Delta s'_d$, *and* $((p, \overline{s}), s_d) \to_d ((p', \overline{s}'), s'_d)$. completeness
3. $((p, \overline{s}), s_d) \to_d ((p', \overline{s}'), s'_d)$ *imply* $\overline{s}'\Delta s'_d \in \overline{s}'$ invariance *of* $s \in \overline{s}$

Condition 3 is actually redundant, as it follows from 1 and the requirement on Δ.

Lemma 2. *If π_d is an $\overline{s}_0$-driven form of π, then for any computation*

$$(p_0, s_0) \rightarrow (p_1, s_1) \rightarrow (p_2, s_2) \rightarrow \ldots$$

with $s_0 = \overline{s}_0 \Delta s_{0d}$ there is a computation

$$((p_0, \overline{s}_0), s_{d0}) \rightarrow_d ((p_1, \overline{s}_1), s_{d1}) \rightarrow_d ((p_2, \overline{s}_2), s_{d2}) \rightarrow_d \ldots$$

with $s_i = \overline{s}_i \Delta s_{di}$ for all i. Further, for any such π_d computation with $s_0 = \overline{s}_0 \Delta s_{d0}$, there is a corresponding π computation with $s_i = \overline{s}_i \Delta s_{di}$ for all i.

The first part follows from initialization and completeness, and the second by soundness and invariance. The corollary on equivalent input/output behaviour requires a modification.

Corollary 2. *If every $s_0 \in \overline{s}_0$ equals $\overline{s}_0 \Delta s_{0d}$ for some s_{0d}, then $IO(\pi, \overline{s}_0) =$*

$$\{(\overline{s}_0 \Delta s_{0d}, \overline{s} \Delta s_d) \mid \overline{s}_0 \Delta s_{0d} \in \overline{s}_0 \text{ and } (((p_0, \overline{s}_0), s_{0d}), ((p, \overline{s}), s_d)) \in IO(\pi_d, \overline{s}_{0d})\}$$

3.2 Correctness of Code in Driven Flow Charts

We now redefine driven flow charts to allow different code in F_d than in F. Commands labeling edges of F_d will be given subscript d. Their semantic function is:

$$\mathcal{C}_d[\![\_]\!] : Command_d \rightarrow (S_d \stackrel{partial}{\longrightarrow} S_d)$$

The following rather technical definition can be intuitively understood as saying that for each paired $p \stackrel{C}{\Rightarrow} p'$ and $(p, \overline{s}) \stackrel{C_d}{\Rightarrow} (p', \overline{s}')$, the diagram corresponding to equation

$$\mathcal{C}[\![C]\!](\overline{s} \Delta s_d) = \overline{s}' \Delta (\mathcal{C}_d[\![C_d]\!] s_d)$$

commutes, provided that various of its subexpressions are defined.

$$\begin{array}{ccc} S_d & \xrightarrow{\mathcal{C}_d[\![C_d]\!]} & S_d \\ \overline{s}\Delta\_ \downarrow & & \downarrow \overline{s}'\Delta\_ \\ S & \xrightarrow{\mathcal{C}[\![C]\!]} & S \end{array}$$

Definition 10. *Given flow chart $F = (P, E, p_0)$ and $\overline{s}_0 \subseteq S$, $F_d = (P_d, E_d, (p_0, \overline{s}_0))$ is an $\overline{s}_0$-driven form of F if $P_d \subseteq P \times \mathcal{P}(S)$ and F_d satisfies the following conditions.*

1. *For each* $(p, \overline{s}) \stackrel{C_d}{\Rightarrow} (p', \overline{s}') \in E_d$ *there exists* $p \stackrel{C}{\Rightarrow} p' \in E$ *such that* $s = \overline{s} \Delta s_d$ *and* $s' = \mathcal{C}[\![C]\!]s$ *are defined if and only if* $s'_d = \mathcal{C}_d[\![C_d]\!]s_d$ *and* $s' = \overline{s}' \Delta s'_d$ *are defined* soundness
2. *If* $p \stackrel{C}{\Rightarrow} p'$, $(p, \overline{s}) \in P_d$, *and both* $s = \overline{s} \Delta s_d$ *and* $s' = \mathcal{C}[\![C]\!]s$ *are defined, then* F_d *has an edge* $(p, \overline{s}) \stackrel{C_d}{\Rightarrow} (p', \overline{s}')$ *such that* $s' = \overline{s}' \Delta(\mathcal{C}_d[\![C_d]\!]s_d)$ completeness
3. $(p, \overline{s}) \stackrel{C_d}{\Rightarrow} (p', \overline{s}')$, $p \stackrel{C}{\Rightarrow} p'$, *and both* $s = \overline{s} \Delta s_d$ *and* $s' = \mathcal{C}[\![C]\!]s$ *are defined imply* $\mathcal{C}_d[\![C_d]\!]s_d \in \overline{s}'$ invariance *of* $s \in \overline{s}$.

Theorem 2. *If* F_d *is an* $\overline{s}_0$*-driven form of* F, *then* π^{F_d} *is an* $\overline{s}_0$*-driven form of* π^F.

Proof. This is easily verified from Definitions 5 and 10, as the latter is entirely parallel to Definition 9.

3.3 Partial Evaluation by Projections

Suppose there is a way to decompose or factor a store s into static and dynamic parts without loss of information (a basic idea in [18,19]). A *data division* is a triple of functions ($stat : S \to S_s, dyn : S \to S_d, pair : S_s \times S_d \to S$). The ability to decompose and recompose without information loss can be expressed by three equations:

$$\begin{aligned} pair(stat(s), dyn(s)) &= s \\ stat(pair(v_s, v_d)) &= v_s \\ dyn(pair(v_s, v_d)) &= v_d \end{aligned}$$

An Example. For example, a division could be given (as in [18,19]) by an $S-D$ vector, for instance SDD specifies the division of $S = \mathcal{N}^3$ into $\mathcal{N} \times \mathcal{N}^2$ where $pair(n, (x, a)) = (n, x, a)$, $stat(n, x, a) = n$, and $dyn(n, x, a) = (x, a)$. Using this, the program

$$\begin{aligned} f(n, x) &= g(n, x, 1) \\ g(n, x, a) &= \textbf{if } n = 0 \textbf{ then } a \textbf{ else } g(n-1, x, x * a) \end{aligned}$$

can be specialized with respect to known $n = 2$ to yield:

$$\begin{aligned} f_2(x) &= g_2(x, 1) \\ g_2(x, a) &= g_1(x, x * a) \\ g_1(x, a) &= g_0(x, x * a) \\ g_0(x, a) &= 1 \end{aligned}$$

which by transition compression can be further reduced to

$$f_2(x) = x * x$$

Relationship between Driving and Projections. This method can be interpreted in current terms as specialization by using store sets that are equivalence classes with respect to static projections, i.e. every store set is of the following form for some $v_s \in S_s$:

$$\overline{s}_{v_s} = \{s \mid stat(s) = v_s\}$$

Store reconstruction can be expressed by defining: $\overline{s}_{v_s} \Delta v_d = pair(v_s, v_d)$. A specialized program π_d in [18,19] only contains transitions of form

$$((p, stat(s)), dyn(s)) \rightarrow ((p', stat(s')), dyn(s'))$$

where π contains $(p, s) \rightarrow (p', s')$. This corresponds to our soundness condition. The set "poly" in [18,19]) is constructed so if $(p_0, s_0) \rightarrow^* (p, s)$ by π for some $s_0 \in \overline{s}_0$, then poly and so π_d contains a specialized program point $(p, stat(s))$, ensuring completeness. Invariance of $s \in \overline{s}$ is immediate since every specialized state is of the form $((p, \overline{s}_{v_s}), v_d)$, and

$$\overline{s}_{v_s} \Delta v_d = pair(v_s, v_d) \in \{s \mid stat(s) = v_s\}$$

since $stat(pair(v_s, v_d)) = v_s$. The following definition is central in [18,19]:

Definition 11. *Function stat* : $S \rightarrow S_d$ *is* congruent *if for any* π *transitions* $(p, s) \rightarrow (p', s')$ *and* $(p, s_1) \rightarrow (p', s'_1)$, *if* $stat(s) = stat(s_1)$, *then* $stat(s') = stat(s'_1)$.

This is essentially the "no new tests" requirement of Definition 7.

4 An Algorithm for Driving

The driving algorithm of Figure 3 manipulates store descriptions $\sigma \in \Sigma$, rather than store sets. For the x^n example above, Σ is the set of all store descriptions σ of the form

$$\sigma = [n \mapsto u, x \mapsto \top, a \mapsto \top]$$

where $u \in \mathcal{N}$. We assume given a *concretization function* $\gamma : \Sigma \rightarrow \mathcal{P}(S)$ defining their meanings, and that the test "is $\gamma\sigma = \{\}$?" is computable, i.e. that we can recognize a description of the empty set of stores.

In addition we assume given a *store set update* function

$$\mathcal{S} : Command \times \Sigma \rightarrow \Sigma$$

and a *code generation* function

$$\mathcal{G} : Command \times \Sigma \rightarrow Command_d$$

```
read F = (P, E, p0);
read σ0;
Pending := {(p0, σ0)};                      (* Unprocessed program points *)
SeenBefore := {};                           (* Already processed pgm. points *)
Pd := {(p0, σ0)};                           (* Initial program points *)
Ed := {};                                   (* Initial edge set *)
while ∃(p, σ) ∈ Pending do                  (* Choose an unprocessed point *)
  Pending := Pending \ {(p, σ)};
  SeenBefore := SeenBefore ∪ {(p, σ)};
  forall p =C=> p' ∈ E do                   (* Scan all transitions from p *)
    σ' := S(σ, C);                          (* Update store set description *)
    if γσ' ≠ {} then                        (* Generate code if nontrivial *)
      Pd := Pd ∪ {(p', σ')};
      if (p', σ') ∉ SeenBefore then add (p', σ') to Pending;
      Cd := G(σ, C);                        (* Generate code *)
      Add edge (p, σ) =Cd=> (p', σ') to Ed; (* Extend flow chart by one edge *)
Fd := (Pd, Ed, (p0, σ0));
```

Fig. 3. An algorithm for driving

Correctness Criterion. For any $C \in \mathit{Command}, \sigma \in \Sigma, s_d \in S_d$, let $\sigma' = \mathcal{S}(C, \sigma)$ and $C_d = \mathcal{G}(C, \sigma)$. Definition 10 requires

$$\mathcal{C}[\![C]\!](\gamma\sigma \Delta s_d) = (\gamma\sigma')\Delta(\mathcal{C}_d[\![C_d]\!]s_d)$$

under certain conditions (where $t = t'$ means both are defined and the values are equal):

1. $s = (\gamma\sigma)\Delta s_d$ and $s'_d = \mathcal{C}_d[\![C_d]\!]s_d$ imply $\mathcal{C}[\![C]\!]s = (\gamma\sigma')\Delta s'_d$ *soundness*
2. $s' = \mathcal{C}[\![C]\!]s$ and $s = (\gamma\sigma)\Delta s_d$ imply $s' = (\gamma\sigma')\Delta(\mathcal{C}_d[\![C_d]\!]s_d)$ *completeness*
3. $s = (\gamma\sigma)\Delta s_d \in \gamma\sigma$ implies $\mathcal{C}_d[\![C_d]\!]s_d \in \gamma\sigma'$ *invariance* of $s \in \overline{s}$.

4.1 Example: Pattern Matching in Strings

A way to test a program transformation method's power is to see whether it can derive certain well-known efficient programs from equivalent naive and inefficient programs. One of the most popular of such tests is to generate, from a naive pattern matcher and a fixed pattern, an efficient pattern matcher as produced by the Knuth-Morris-Pratt algorithm. We shall call this *the KMP test* [27].

First we give a program for string pattern matching.

$$
\begin{array}{ll}
match\ p\ s & = loop\ p\ s\ p\ s \\
\\
loop\ []\ ss\ op\ os & = True \\
loop\ (p : pp)\ []\ op\ os & = False \\
loop\ (p : pp)\ (s : ss)\ op\ os & = \mathbf{if}\ p = s\ \mathbf{then}\ loop\ pp\ ss\ op\ os\ \mathbf{else}\ next\ op\ os \\
\\
next\ op\ [] & = False \\
next\ op\ (s : ss) & = loop\ op\ ss\ op\ ss
\end{array}
$$

For conciseness in exposition, we specify the store sets that are encountered while driving *match AAB u* by means of terms containing free variables. These are assumed to range over all possible data values. Given this, the result of driving can be described by the configuration graph seen in the Figure ending this paper (where some intermediate configurations have been left out). More details can be seen in [27].

The program generated is:

$$
\begin{array}{ll}
f\ u & = f_{AAB}\ u \\
\\
f_{AAB}\ [] & = False \\
f_{AAB}\ (s : ss) & = g\ s\ ss \\
\\
g\ s\ ss & = \mathbf{if}\ A = s\ \mathbf{then}\ f_{AB}\ ss\ \mathbf{else}\ f_{AAB}\ ss \\
\\
f_{AB}\ [] & = False \\
f_{AB}\ (s : ss) & = h\ s\ ss \\
\\
h\ s\ ss & = \mathbf{if}\ A = s\ \mathbf{then}\ f_B\ ss\ \mathbf{else}\ g\ ss \\
\\
f_B\ [] & = False \\
f_B\ (s : ss) & = \mathbf{if}\ A = s\ \mathbf{then}\ g\ s\ ss\ \mathbf{else} \\
 & \quad\ \mathbf{if}\ B = s\ \mathbf{then}\ true\ \mathbf{else}\ h\ s\ ss
\end{array}
$$

This is in essence a KMP pattern matcher, so driving passes the KMP test. It is interesting to note that driving has transformed a program running in time $O(m \cdot n)$ into one running in time $O(n)$, where m is the length of the pattern and n is the length of the subject string.

Using configurations as above can result in some redundant tests, because we only propagate positive information (what term describes the negative outcome of a test?). However this problem can easily be overcome by using both positive and negative environments, see [15].

Partial evaluators of which we know (other than the supecompiler) cannot achieve this effect without nontrivial human rewriting of the matching program.

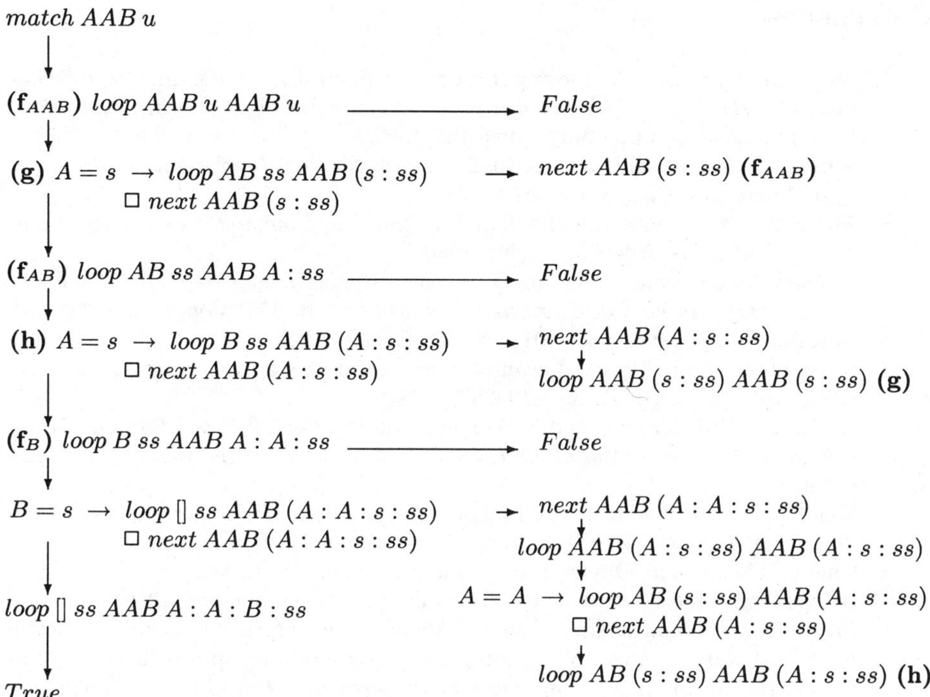

4.2 Finiteness and Generalization

Σ is usually an infinite set, causing the risk of generating infinitely many different configurations while driving. Turchin uses the term *generalization* for the problem of choosing configurations to yield both finiteness and efficiency [33,35].

The idea is to choose elements $\sigma' = \mathcal{S}(\sigma, C)$ which are "large enough" to ensure finiteness of the transformed program, but are still small enough to allow significant optimizations. This may require one to *ignore some information* that is available at transformation time, i.e. to choose descriptions of larger and so less precise store sets than would be possible on the basis of the current σ and C.

How to achieve termination without overgeneralization is not yet fully understood. Turchin advocates an online technique, using the computational history of the driving process to guide the choices of new σ' [35]. It is as yet unclear whether self-application for practical compiler generation can be achieved in this way, or whether some form of preprocessing will be needed. If offline preprocessing is needed, it will certainly be rather different from "binding-time analysis" as used in partial evaluation [19].

Acknowledgement

Many useful comments on this paper were made by Patrick Cousot, Robert Glück, Andrei Klimov, Sergei Romanenko, Morten Heine Sørensen, Carolyn Talcott, and Valentin Turchin.

References

1. Sergei M. Abramov, Metacomputation and program testing. In: *1st International Workshop on Automated and Algorithmic Debugging.* (Linköping, Sweden). pp. 121-135, Linköping University 1993.
2. Samson Abramsky and Chris Hankin, editors. *Abstract Interpretation of Declarative Languages.* Ellis Horwood, 1987.
3. Alfred V. Aho, Ravi Sethi, and Jeffrey D. Ullman. *Compilers: Principles, Techniques, and Tools.* Addison-Wesley, 1986.
4. Lennart Augustsson, Compiling lazy pattern-matching. *Conference on Functional Programming and Computer Architecture*, ed. J.-P. Jouannoud. Lecture Notes in Computer Science 201, Springer-Verlag, 1985.
5. L. Beckman et al. A partial evaluator, and its use as a programming tool. *Artificial Intelligence*, 7(4), pp. 319–357, 1976.
6. D. Bjørner, A.P. Ershov, and N.D. Jones, editors. *Partial Evaluation and Mixed Computation. Proceedings of the IFIP TC2 Workshop.* North-Holland, 1988. 625 pages.
7. Wei-Ngan Chin, Safe fusion of functional expressions II: further improvements. *Journal of Functional Programming.* To appear in 1994.
8. Charles Consel and Olivier Danvy, Partial evaluation of pattern matching in strings. *Information Processing Letters*, 30, pp. 79–86, January 1989.
9. Patrick Cousot and Radhia Cousot, Abstract interpretation: a unified lattice model for static analysis of programs by construction or approximation of fixpoints. In *Fourth ACM Symposium on Principles on Programming Languages*, pp. 238–252, New York: ACM Press, 1977.
10. Edsger W. Dijkstra. *A Discipline of Programming.* Prentice-Hall, 1976.
11. Andrei P. Ershov. Mixed computation: Potential applications and problems for study. *Theoretical Computer Science*, 18, pp. 41–67, 1982.
12. Alex B. Ferguson and Philip Wadler, When will deforestation stop? *Glasgow Workshop on Functional Programming*, August 1988.
13. Yoshihiko Futamura and Kenroku Nogi, Generalized partial computation. In *Partial Evaluation and Mixed Computation,* Eds. A. P. Ershov, D. Bjørner and N. D. Jones, North-Holland, 1988.
14. Robert Glück and Valentin F. Turchin, Application of metasystem transition to function inversion and transformation. *Proceedings of the ISSAC '90*, pp. 286-287, ACM Press,1990.
15. Robert Glück and Andrei V. Klimov, Occam's razor in metacomputation: the notion of a perfect process tree. In *Static analysis Proceedings*, eds. P. Cousot, M. Falaschi, G. Filé, G. Rauzy. Lecture Notes in Computer Science 724, pp. 112-123, Springer-Verlag, 1993.
16. Neil D. Jones and Flemming Nielson, Abstract interpretation: a semantics-based tool for program analysis, 122 pages. In *Handbook of Logic in Computer Science*, Oxford University Press to appear in 1994.
17. Neil D. Jones, Flow analysis of lazy higher-order functional programs. In *Abstract Interpretation of Declarative Languages*, pp. 103-122. Ellis Horwood, 1987.
18. Neil D. Jones, Automatic program specialization: A re-examination from basic principles, in D. Bjørner, A.P. Ershov, and N.D. Jones (eds.), *Partial Evaluation and Mixed Computation*, pp. 225–282, Amsterdam: North-Holland, 1988.
19. Neil D. Jones, Carsten Gomard and Peter Sestoft. *Partial Evaluation and Automatic Program Generation.* Prentice Hall International, 425 pp., 1993.

20. Stephen S. Kleene, *Introduction to Metamathematics.* Van Nostrand, 1952, 550 pp.
21. John Launchbury, *Projection Factorisations in Partial Evaluation.* Cambridge: Cambridge University Press, 1991.
22. Andrei V. Klimov and Sergei Romanenko, A metaevaluator for the language Refal: basic concepts and examples. Keldysh Institute of Applied Mathematics, Academy of Sciences of the USSR, Moscow. Preprint No. 71, 1987 (in Russian).
23. Donald E. Knuth, James H. Morris, and Vaughan R. Pratt, Fast pattern matching in strings, *SIAM Journal of Computation*, 6(2), pp. 323–350, 1977.
24. Alexander Y. Romanenko, The generation of inverse functions in Refal, in D. Bjørner, A.P. Ershov, and N.D. Jones (eds.), *Partial Evaluation and Mixed Computation*, pp. 427-444, Amsterdam: North-Holland, 1988.
25. Sergei A. Romanenko, A compiler generator produced by a self-applicable specializer can have a surprisingly natural and understandable structure. In D. Bjørner, A.P. Ershov, and N.D. Jones (eds.), *Partial Evaluation and Mixed Computation*, pp. 445–463, Amsterdam: North-Holland, 1988.
26. Morten Heine Sørensen, *A grammar-based data flow analysis to stop deforestation.Colloquium on Trees and Algebra in Programming (CAAP)*, edinburgh, Scotland. Lecture Notes in Computer Science, Springer-Verlag, to appear in 1994.
27. Morten Heine Sørensen, Robert Glück and Neil D. Jones, Towards unifying partial evaluation, deforestation, supercompilation, and GPC. *European Symposium on Programming (ESOP).* Lecture Notes in Computer Science, Springer-Verlag, to appear in 1994.
28. Akihiko Takano, Generalized partial computation for a lazy functional language. *Symposium on Partial Evaluation and Semantics-Based Program Manipulation*, eds. Neil D. Jones and Paul Hudak, ACM Press, 1991.
29. Valentin F. Turchin, Equivalent transformations of recursive functions defined in Refal. In: *Teorija Jazykov i Metody Programmirovanija* (Proceedings of the Symposium on the Theory of Languages and Programming Methods). (Kiev-Alushta, USSR). pp. 31-42, 1972 (in Russian).
30. Valentin F. Turchin, Equivalent transformations of Refal programs. In: *Avtomatizirovannaja Sistema upravlenija stroitel'stvom.* Trudy CNIPIASS, 6, pp. 36-68, 1974 (in Russian).
31. Valentin F. Turchin, *The Language Refal, the Theory of Compilation and Metasystem Analysis.* Courant Computer Science Report 20, 245 pages, 1980.
32. Valentin F. Turchin, Semantic definitions in Refal and automatic production of compilers. *Semantics-Directed Compiler Generation*, Aarhus, Denmark. Lecture Notes in Computer Science, Springer-Verlag, pp. 441-474, vol. 94, 1980.
33. Valentin F. Turchin, The concept of a supercompiler. *ACM Transactions on Programming Languages and Systems*, 8(3), pp. 292–325, July 1986.
34. Turchin V. F., A constructive interpretation of the full set theory. In: *The Journal of Symbolic Logic*, 52(1): 172-201, 1987.
35. Valentin F. Turchin, The algorithm of generalization in the supercompiler. In D. Bjørner, A.P. Ershov, and N.D. Jones (eds.), *Partial Evaluation and Mixed Computation*, pp. 531-549, Amsterdam: North-Holland, 1988.
36. Valentin F. Turchin, Function transformation with metasystem transitions. *Journal of Functional Programming*, 3(3), pp. 283–313, July 1993.
37. Philip L. Wadler, Deforestation: transforming programs to eliminate trees. European Symposium On Programming (ESOP). Lecture Notes in Computer Science 300, pp. 344-358, Nancy, France, Springer-Verlag, 1988.

Binding-Time Analysis in Partial Evaluation: One Size Does *Not* Fit All

Niels H. Christensen, Robert Glück, and Søren Laursen

DIKU, Department of Computer Science
University of Copenhagen, Universitetsparken 1
DK-2100 Copenhagen, Denmark
{mrnc,glueck,scrooge}@diku.dk

Abstract. Existing partial evaluators usually fix the strategy for binding-time analysis. But a single strategy cannot fulfill all goals without leading to compromises regarding precision, termination, and code explosion in partial evaluators. Our goal is to improve the usability of partial evaluator systems by developing an adaptive approach that can accommodate a variety of different strategies ranging from maximally polyvariant to entirely uniform analysis, and thereby make offline specialization more practical in a realistic setting. The core of the analysis has been implemented in FSpec, an offline partial evaluator for a subset of Fortran 77.

1 Introduction

Partial evaluation of imperative programs was pioneered by Ershov and his group [13,7]; later Jones et al. [21] introduced binding-time analysis (BTA) to achieve self-application of a partial evaluator. This offline approach to partial evaluation has been studied intensively since then.

However, not much attention has been paid to the properties of the binding-time analysis in offline partial evaluation (notable exceptions are [11,23,8,6]). This is surprising because the annotations a BTA produces, *guide the specialization process* of an offline partial evaluator and, thus, control the quality of the program transformation. The choice of the annotation strategy is therefore the *most decisive factor* in the design of an offline partial evaluator.

Existing offline partial evaluators *fix* a particular binding-time strategy (e.g., [3,9,12,22]). None of them allow the partial evaluator to function with different levels of precision, and all systems implement different strategies based on decisions taken on pragmatic grounds. The growing importance of non-trivial applications with varying specialization goals (e.g. interpreter specialization vs. software maintenance) motivated us to examine a more flexible approach to binding-time analysis for imperative languages. Our goal is to improve the usability of partial evaluation systems by developing an analysis framework that allows an easy adaptation and control of different binding-time strategies within the same specialization system.

D. Bjørner, M. Broy, A. Zamulin (Eds.): PSI'99, LNCS 1755, pp. 80–92, 2000.

Program	Source code	Res. code (unif. BTA)	Res. code (poly. BTA)

Monitor
`Upd = FALSE`
`Val = 100`
`OutVal = 0`
`CurVal` *is dynamic*
	1
	`...`
	`10: IF Upd=TRUE THEN`
	`11:    Val:=CurVal;`
	`12: ENDIF;`
	`13: OutVal:=f(Val);`
	`14: OUTPUT OutVal;`
	`...`
		1A
		`...`
		`10: Val:=100;`
		`11: OutVal:=f(Val);`
		`12: OUTPUT OutVal;`
		`...`
			1B
			`...`
			`10: OUTPUT 5;`
			`...`

Affine
`a = 2`
`b = 5`
`x` *is dynamic*
`count` *is dynamic*
	2
	`...`
	`10: IF a>0 THEN`
	`11:    p(x);`
	`12:    GOTO 10;`
	`13: ENDIF;`
	`...`
	`100: PROCEDURE p(y):`
	`101: a:=a-1;`
	`102: b:=b+y;`
	`103: count:=count+1;`
	`104: RETURN;`
		2A
		`...`
		`10: b:=5;`
		`11: p(x);`
		`12: p(x);`
		`...`
		`100: PROCEDURE p(y):`
		`101: b:=b+y;`
		`102: count:=count+1;`
		`103: RETURN;`
			2B
			`...`
			`10: p1(x);`
			`11: p2(x);`
			`...`
			`100: PROCEDURE p1(y):`
			`101: b:=5+y;`
			`102: count:=count+1;`
			`103: RETURN;`
			`104: PROCEDURE p2(y):`
			`105: b:=b+y;`
			`106: count:=count+1;`
			`107: RETURN;`

Fig. 1. Problem source: One BTA is *not* best for all source programs

In this paper we examine the design space of binding-time strategies and develop a framework to formalize different strategies that allows a partial evaluator to function with different levels of granularity. We claim that it is expressive enough to cover all existing strategies and allows the design and comparison of new strategies. The core of the analysis engine is implemented for FSpec, an offline partial evaluator for a subset of Fortran 77 [22]. We assume familiarity with the basic notions of offline partial evaluation, e.g. [19, Part II].

2 Problem Source: One Size Does *Not* Fit All

In existing partial evaluators, the strategy of the binding-time analysis (BTA), and thus its precision, is fixed at design-time; in essence assuming 'One Size Fits All'. The most popular strategy for BTA, due to its conceptual simplicity, is to annotate programs using uniform divisions [19]. In this case *one* division is valid for *all* program points. A polyvariant BTA allows *each* program point to be annotated with *one or more* divisions.

Figure 1 shows two pieces of source programs and for each the result of two different specializations: One directed by a *uniform BTA* (column A) and one directed by a *polyvariant BTA* (column B). We assume *polyvariant program point specialization* [7,19] (a program point in the source program may be specialized wrt. different static stores). Program *Monitor* updates variable `Val` depending on the value of flag `Upd` (we assume that function `f` has no side effects and that `f(100)` = `5`). Program *Affine* repeatedly calls procedure `p`. Variables `a`, `b` and `count` are global.

For *Monitor*, the polyvariant BTA (1B) clearly achieves the best specialization because result `5` is computed at specialization time. The uniform BTA (1A) must consider `Val` dynamic and can therefore not allow the call of `f` to be computed at specialization time. For *Affine*, the uniform BTA (2A) seems to provide a better specialization. The polyvariant BTA (2B) recognizes that the value of b is sometimes static (in the first round of the loop) and creates an extra instance of procedure p. This leads to undesirable duplication of code (which is more dramatic for larger programs). Almost all existing partial evaluators, such as C-Mix [3] and FSpec [22], give (1A,2A); Tempo [12] gives (1A,2B).

To conclude, the uniform BTA is preferable for *Affine* and the polyvariant BTA is preferable for *Monitor*. A partial evaluator that is confined to one of the two strategies, A or B, may not be suitable for the task at hand. In such a case the user has to resort to *rewriting the source program* to influence the specialization. This is why we are looking for a more elegant and flexible solution to BTA.

3 Binding-Time Analysis and Maximal Polyvariance

First, we give a quite abstract definition of a programming language as a state transition system. Then, we give a formalization of binding-time analyses and define maximal polyvariance.

3.1 Preliminary Definitions

We consider only first-order deterministic programming languages, and assume that any program has a set of *program points*. Examples include labels in a flow chart language and function names in a functional language. Their essential characteristics is that computation proceeds sequentially from program point to program point by execution of a series of *commands*, each of which updates a program *state*. These states are usually described by a pair consisting of a *program point* and a *store*. The meaning of each command is then a state transformation computing the effect of the command on a state. We assume a small steps semantics (i.e., the execution of each command terminates).

Definition 1. *A* programming language *is a tuple* $L = (\mathcal{P}, \mathcal{C}, \mathcal{S}, [\![\cdot]\!])$, *where* $[\![\cdot]\!] : \mathcal{C} \to \mathcal{S} \to \mathcal{P} \times \mathcal{S}$ *is a partial function. Terminology:* $\mathcal{P}$ *is the set of* program points, $\mathcal{C}$ *is the set of* commands, $\mathcal{S}$ *is the set of* stores, *and* $[\![\cdot]\!]$ *is the* semantics *of* L. *A* state *is a pair* $(p, \sigma) \in \mathcal{P} \times \mathcal{S}$.

Definition 2. *Let* L *be a programming language, then an* L-program *is a partial mapping* $P : \mathcal{P} \to \mathcal{C}$, *where* $\mathcal{P}$ *is the set of program points of* L *and* $\mathcal{C}$ *is the set of commands of* L. *We assume each* L*-program* P *has the property that* $\forall \sigma \in \mathcal{S}. \forall p \in \text{dom}(P) : [\![P(p)]\!]\sigma = (p', \sigma')$ *implies* $p' \in \text{dom}(P)$, *if defined. Notation: The* initial program point *of a program* P *is denoted by* p_0.

Definition 3. *Let* P *be an* L*-program, define* computation step *as transition relation* $\to \subseteq (\mathcal{P}, \mathcal{S}) \times (\mathcal{P}, \mathcal{S})$ *such that* $(p, \sigma) \to (p', \sigma')$ *iff* $[\![P(p)]\!]\sigma = (p', \sigma')$ *is defined. A* computation *(from* $\sigma_0 \in S$*) is a finite or infinite sequence*

$$(p_0, \sigma_0) \to (p_1, \sigma_1) \to \ldots$$

From now on we look at programming languages where the store is modelled by a finite function $\sigma = [x_1 \mapsto v_1, \ldots, x_n \mapsto v_n]$ which maps variables $x \in \mathcal{X}$ to values $v \in \mathcal{V}$. We assume there are only finitely many variables in any given program. Notation $\sigma(x_i)$ denotes value v_i in σ. More complicated store models exist and can be handled in our framework (e.g., including locations for modelling pointers and aliasing), but are omitted for simplicity.

3.2 Abstract Formulation of Binding-Time Analysis

The main feature of offline partial evaluation [19] is that program specialization proceeds in two steps: a *binding-time analysis* (BTA) followed by a *specialization phase.* First, the source program is analyzed over a domain consisting of two abstract values, S and D, where S (static) represents a value known at specialization time, D (dynamic) represents a value that may be unknown at specialization time (such a classification of the variables is often called a *division*). Second, the source program is specialized wrt. known values following the static/dynamic annotations made by the BTA.

The BTA associates with each program point one or more *binding-time stores* where each binding-time store maps variables to binding-time values. We limit ourselves to a finite description of binding-time values.

Definition 4. *A* binding-time value *is a value* $b \in \mathcal{B}$ *where* $\mathcal{B} = \{S, D\}$. *A* binding-time store $\beta : \mathcal{X} \to \mathcal{B}$ *maps variables to binding-time values. A* binding-time semantics $[\![\cdot]\!]_{bta} : \mathcal{C} \to (\mathcal{X} \to \mathcal{B}) \to (\mathcal{X} \to \mathcal{B})$ *maps a command and a binding-time store to a binding-time store. A* binding-time state *is a pair* (p, β), *where* p *is a program point and* β *is a binding-time store. Notation* $\sigma|_{\beta:S}$ *denotes a store restricted to variables mapped to* S *in* β.

Defining binding-time stores as a map from variables to binding-time values does not exclude data structures, such as arrays or records, where the size of the structure is fixed at compile time. For example, fields of a record can be treated as an individual variables. Often a single variable is used to represent the binding-time value of the whole array.

Definition 5. *Let* P *be an* L*-program, define* binding-time step *as transition relation* $\overset{bta}{\to} \subseteq (\mathcal{P}, \mathcal{B}) \times (\mathcal{P}, \mathcal{B})$ *such that* $(p, \beta) \overset{bta}{\to} (p', \beta')$ *iff*

$$[\![P(p)]\!]_{bta}\beta = \beta' \;\wedge\; \exists \sigma, \sigma'.(p, \sigma) \to (p', \sigma')$$

We expect $[\![\cdot]\!]_{bta}$ to be a realization of the *congruence rules* of language L [19]. Given $[\![P(p)]\!]_{bta}\beta = \beta'$, we expect that for any transition $(p, \sigma) \to (p', \sigma')$, the values of the variables classified as S in β' must be computable from the values of the variables classified as S in β. This congruence requirement is captured more formally by the following definition.

Definition 6. *A binding-time semantics* $[\![\cdot]\!]_{bta}$ *is* congruent *iff for every program* P, *any variable* $x \in \mathcal{X}$, *any transition* $(p, \beta) \overset{bta}{\to} (p', \beta')$, *and any two stores* σ, σ' *such that* $[\![P(p)]\!]\sigma = (p', \sigma_1)$ *and* $[\![P(p)]\!]\sigma' = (p', \sigma_2)$ *we have*

$$\sigma|_{\beta:S} = \sigma'|_{\beta:S} \wedge \beta'(x) = S \Rightarrow \sigma_1(x) = \sigma_2(x)$$

3.3 Maximally Polyvariant Binding-Time States

The task of a BTA is, given an L-program P and a bt-state (p_0, β_0) of P, to compute a *set of bt-states* (denoted by *Ann*). This set is always finite because a program has finitely many variables and there are finitely many bt-values. To keep our discussion language-independent, we shall clearly separate the set of bt-states from the syntactic annotation of a source program.

We wish to specify a soundness condition for an annotation, intuitively stating that a specializer should be able to partially evaluate the source program using the annotation. The definition must thus be relative to the specializer. We let the properties of this specialiser be reflected by a corresponding binding-time semantics (which thus represents the needs of the specializer).

Definition 7. *A set of bt-states is called an* annotation. *An annotation, Ann, is sound iff the initial bt-state $(p_0, \beta_0) \in Ann$ and for all $(p_j, \beta_j) \in Ann$ we have*

- *There is a $(p_i, \beta_i) \in Ann$ and a bt-store β'_j such that $(p_i, \beta_i) \overset{bta}{\rightarrow} (p_j, \beta'_j)$ and $\beta'^{-1}_j(D) \subseteq \beta^{-1}_j(D)$.*
- *For all $p_k \in \{p \in \mathcal{P} \mid \exists \sigma, \sigma' : (p_j, \sigma) \rightarrow (p, \sigma')\}$ there is a $(p_k, \beta_k) \in Ann$ and a binding-time store β'_k such that $(p_j, \beta_j) \overset{bta}{\rightarrow} (p_k, \beta'_k)$ and $\beta'^{-1}_k(D) \subseteq \beta^{-1}_k(D)$.*

Definition 8. *Let P be an L-program and let β_0 be an initial bt-store, then polymax(P, β_0) denotes the set of bt-states defined by*

$$\textit{polymax}(P, \beta_0) \overset{\text{def}}{=} \{(p, \beta) \mid (p_0, \beta_0) \overset{bta}{\rightarrow}{}^{*} (p, \beta)\}$$

Clearly, this set is sound. We call it the maximally polyvariant *annotation.*

We have not discussed how to model procedures and calls. This is possible but requires non-trivial extensions of the store model (e.g. locations) which we shall not describe here.

4 Dimensions of Binding-Time Analysis

Programs can be annotated in many ways. A binding-time strategy for realistic applications has to accommodate three important, but—unfortunately—often conflicting transformation goals:

1. **Increasing staticness** by more precise analysis.
2. **Taming code explosion** by reducing the amount of polyvariance at specialization time.
3. **Ensuring termination** of the specialization process by dynamizing operations that lead to infinite transformations.

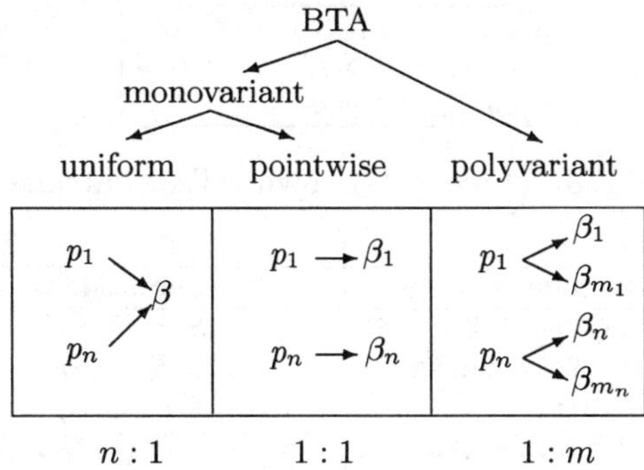

Fig. 2. Granularity of binding-time analysis

A uniform BTA computes *one* division that is valid for *all* program points (illustrated in Fig. 2). For small programs this assumption is reasonable, but not for larger applications because of the non-locality of binding-time effects, a problem with flow-insensitive analyses known from the design of optimizing compilers. For example, a uniform BTA carries the dynamization of a variable in one region to all other regions of a program, even though the variable may serve locally distinct purposes in each region.

Pointwise and *polyvariant* analyses are flow-sensitive. They allow each program point to be annotated with *one or more* local divisions (Fig. 2). This can significantly improve staticness in programs and avoid the need for manual binding-time improvements. For example, the BTA of Tempo [17] computes pointwise divisions for basic blocks and polyvariant divisions on the procedure level.

Increased staticness in a program does not always come for free. *Non-termination* of the specialization process and *code explosion* of the generated programs are some of the risks one faces. In particular, static values that vary without bound, lead to infinite specialization (for each static store encountered at a program point, a specialized version is produced by the specialization phase). Termination can be ensured by dynamizing such static variables. Strategies for ensuring termination without being overly conservative are a topic of current research [5,14].

5 Strategy Language

Informally, a BTA strategy is a guiding principle for annotation. Known strategies include uniform analysis and pointwise analysis. Our aim is to specify a high-level 'strategy language' which may be used to control a binding-time analysis. The ambition is that the language be simple while offering a large design space allowing to compare the relative strength of different BTA strategies.

Formally, we define a strategy to be a criterion for being *well-formed* (wrt. the strategy). For instance, an annotation is well-formed wrt. the uniform BTA

$$\begin{array}{|ll|}\hline \mathcal{S}_{uniform} & \equiv \beta'(x) = D \\ \mathcal{S}_{pointwise} & \equiv \mathcal{S}_{uniform} \wedge p = p' \\ \mathcal{S}_{polymax} & \equiv \mathit{False} \\ \hline\end{array}$$

Fig. 3. Three well-known BTA strategies

Source code	Annotations
`10: IF Upd=TRUE THEN`	$\langle S, S, D, S\rangle$
`11:     Val:=CurVal;`	$\langle S, S, D, S\rangle$
`12: ENDIF;`	$\langle S, D, D, S\rangle$
`13: OutVal:=f(Val);`	$\langle S, S, D, S\rangle$ $\langle S, D, D, S\rangle$
`14: OUTPUT OutVal;`	$\langle S, S, D, S\rangle$ $\langle S, D, D, S\rangle$

Fig. 4. Polyvariant annotation of *Monitor*: $\langle \texttt{Upd}, \texttt{Val}, \texttt{CurVal}, \texttt{OutVal}\rangle$

strategy if and only if every variable has the same annotation in all bt-stores in the annotation. In this paper, all strategies are of the form

$$\boxed{\begin{array}{l}\forall x \in \mathcal{X}.\forall (p, \beta), (p', \beta') \in Ann : \\ \quad \mathcal{S}(x, p, p', \beta, \beta') \Rightarrow \beta(x) = D\end{array}}$$

where the predicate $\mathcal{S}$ can take many forms. We will identify a strategy with the predicate $\mathcal{S}$ that defines it. We implicitly assume that all annotations be sound. For convenience, we omit the parameters of a predicate, as in the definitions in Fig. 3. Regard the definition of $\mathcal{S}_{uniform}$. This predicate defines a strategy that allows only one annotation for each variable in the source program. The predicate is so simple that it does not need to refer to p or p'.

To see what this strategy means, consider the *Monitor* program. A polyvariant annotation is given in Fig. 4. This annotation is not well-formed wrt. $\mathcal{S}_{uniform}$ since `Val` has more than one annotation. More formally, choosing

$$x = \texttt{Val};\ (p, \beta) = (13, \langle S, S, D, S\rangle);\ (p', \beta') = (13, \langle S, D, D, S\rangle)$$

we evidently get a counterexample to $\mathcal{S}_{uniform}$. We say that x and (p, β) form a *violation* of the strategy. Of course, if an annotation is not well-formed wrt. some strategy $\mathcal{S}$, a violation of $\mathcal{S}$ must exist.

A natural annotation that *does* satisfy the uniformity constraint is the set $\{(p, \langle S, D, D, S\rangle) \mid p \in \{10, 11, 12, 13, 14\}\}$, which is also the one that we would expect as output of a uniform BTA. Note, however, that classifying *all* variables dynamic at *all* program points is an annotation that is also (trivially) well-formed wrt. $\mathcal{S}_{uniform}$. This annotation will be well-formed wrt. any strategy.

Another example of a well-known strategy is $\mathcal{S}_{pointwise}$ which is also defined in Fig. 3. It is obtained by applying the uniform strategy to individual program points, merging bt-stores only if different ones occur at a single point in the program. This strategy forces a monovariant (but not necessarily uniform) annotation of all variables. Finally, as we have implicitly required all annotations to be sound, we get a maximally polyvariant strategy by adding no further requirements.

BTA Classification Formulating the BTA strategies in our language allows us to study their relative strengths formally. Recall the overall classification of BTA strategies given in Figure 2. Most systems (e.g. C-Mix [3] and FSpec [22]) use some BTA strategy, $\mathcal{S}$, which is no stronger than the pure, uniform strategy in the sense that $\mathcal{S} \Rightarrow \mathcal{S}_{uniform}$, i.e. these systems detect no more staticness than one does with the pure, uniform strategy. For several systems biimplication does not hold because some variables are generalized in order to ensure termination of the specializer.

The Tempo system has a non-uniform BTA strategy, $\mathcal{S}_{Tempo}$, that allows a limited amount of polyvariance[1]. Among $\mathcal{S}_{uniform}$ and $\mathcal{S}_{Tempo}$ neither left- or right-implication holds; Tempo is non-uniform, but it forces generalization of static variables defined under dynamic control.

The strategy $\mathcal{S}_{polymax}$ is trivially stronger than all other strategies. Note that what we compare is *precision*, which is *not* a universal measure of quality. We argue that for some source programs the user needs a precise analysis, for other source programs a less precise analysis is better.

6 Simple Construction of Well-Formed Annotations

In this section, we take a small detour to sketch one way of implementing a BTA algorithm that is able to realize any strategy as described above. The algorithm builds upon a maximally polyvariant BTA as defined in Section 3. The authors have implemented a maximally polyvariant `PolyMax` function [10] for a non-trivial subset of Fortran — the subset of the FSpec partial evaluator [22].

We assume to have a command $dyn_{p,x}$ in the source language, for which

$$\begin{aligned} [\![dyn_{p,x}]\!]\sigma &= (\sigma, p) \\ [\![dyn_{p,x}]\!]_{\mathrm{BTA}}\beta &= \beta[x \mapsto D] \end{aligned}$$

Also, we assume that for any program P we have $dom(P) \neq \mathcal{P}$ so that we may choose a *new* program point $p_{new} \in \mathcal{P} \setminus dom(P)$.

Our algorithm can be seen in Figure 5. The basic idea is to start out with a maximal annotation, then remove strategy violations one at a time until none are left. Violations are removed by inserting *dyn* commands in the source program where generalization is needed. A maximally polyvariant BTA should be used in step 1 to get maximal preciseness within the constraints defined by the strategy.

Termination of the algorithm is guaranteed by the fact that *Ann* will be strictly increasing its dynamicity during each iteration. Well-formedness (wrt. the input strategy) of the final result should be evident. We do not claim this algorithm to be efficient, it merely serves to illustrate how a strategy chosen at specialization-time can be used to control the result of partial evaluation.

[1] In Tempo, the annotated program may contain several copies of each function – one for each bt-store it is called with. But within one copy, a statement can have only one annotation.

Given source program, P, and a strategy, $\mathcal{S}$:

1. Compute Ann:=`PolyMax`(P).
2. If Ann is well-formed wrt. $\mathcal{S}$ then stop, outputting Ann; else goto 3.
3. Pick $x \in X$ and $(p_{vio}, \beta) \in Ann$ that form a violation of $\mathcal{S}$.
4. Choose a new program point p_{new}, set

$$P := P[p_{vio} \mapsto dyn_{p_{new},x}; p_{new} \mapsto P(p_{vio})]$$

5. Goto 1.

Fig. 5. Algorithm implementing BTA parameterized by strategy

7 An Example Strategy

To illustrate our method, we show a new strategy that can be modeled in our framework. It is characterized by separate treatment of different language constructs, e.g. conditionals, loops and procedures.

The idea is to minimize code explosion in the residual program while being robust wrt. procedure inlining[2], a feature that is not currently achieved by any system implementing polyvariant procedure calls for an imperative language. We also wish to allow polyvariance elsewhere as long as it can only lead to code explosion in the annotated program – not the residual program. Towards this end, we decree that loop entry points may only be annotated polyvariantly if the test-expression (i.e. the loop condition) is static, in which case only one branch will be chosen by the specializer (leaving the other branch as dead code in the annotated program). We denote by $\mathcal{P}_{loopentry}$ the set of program points that constitute loop entries. The new strategy is defined by

$$\mathcal{S}_{example} \equiv \; p \in \mathcal{P}_{loopentry} \wedge \beta(test(p)) = D \wedge \mathcal{S}_{pointwise}$$

Here, the term $\beta(test(p))$ is a shorthand for stating that the test expression of the loop starting at p is dynamic in β. The above strategy will not always prevent code explosion, and it does not guarantee termination of the specialization phase. However, it demonstrates that reasonable heuristics can be simple to phrase.

An example where this strategy turns out to be useful is shown in Fig. 6. The source program is a fragment of an interpreter for a Fortran-like language with one local and one global scope. Beside the input expression, the position of the global scope in the store is also statically known. However, the store itself and the position of the local scope in the store are dynamic.

The reader may convince himself that a uniform BTA will not achieve satisfactory specialization in this example. As demonstrated [8] in a similar case, the return value of `eval` will be considered dynamic, disallowing full evaluation of $2+3$. On the other hand, using a maximally polyvariant BTA, we run into a different problem. In the `WHILE`-loop of procedure `lookup`, there is a possibility

[2] That is, treating both procedure entry and exit fully polyvariantly.

Source code

```
PROCEDURE eval(E):
 CASE E.op:
   'cnst: RETURN E.val;
   'var : RETURN lookup(E.id);
   '+   : RETURN eval(E.Lexp)+
                 eval(E.Rexp);
   ...
PROCEDURE lookup(Id):
COMMON GlobS,LocS,St;
INTEGER Cur;
 Cur:=LocS;
 WHILE (St[Cur].id≠Id) DO
   IF (St[Cur]='end)
   THEN Cur:=GlobS;
   ELSE Cur:=Cur+1;
 ENDWHILE
 RETURN St[Cur].val;
END;
```

Residual code of `eval((2+3)+x)`

```
(* E = (2+3)+x               *)
(* GlobS = 0                 *)
(* LocS and St are dynamic. *)

...
COMMON LocS,St;
INTEGER Cur;
 Cur:=LocS;
 WHILE (St[Cur].id≠'x) DO
   IF (St[Cur]='end)
   THEN Cur:=0;
   ELSE Cur:=Cur+1;
 ENDWHILE
RETURN 5+St[Cur].val;
```

Fig. 6. Specialization of an interpreter fragment using the example strategy

of variable `Cur` turning static (by assigning to it the value of `GlobS`). This possibility will be explored by the specializer. However, since `Cur` increases under dynamic control, specialization will run into an infinite loop.

Now consider our example strategy. Because of the polyvariant procedure annotation, $(2+3)$ can be completely evaluated. Since the (dynamically controlled) `WHILE`-loop must be annotated monovariantly, `Cur` will always be considered dynamic and we avoid infinite specialization. Thus, we avoid both problems and obtain useful residual code.

8 Related Work

Binding-time analysis for partial evaluation was first developed in the context of functional languages [20] and was later carried over to imperative languages [16,1]. Analyses for imperative languages are usually more complex due to the different storage model, side-effects, aliasing of variables and pointer manipulations [2,17]. Binding-time analyses for object-oriented languages are still under development. A multi-level binding-time analysis [15] analyses source programs over an abstract domain representing two or more stages of computation.

Regardless of the source language or the type of analysis, all existing offline partial evaluators fix one particular binding-time strategy for program specialization (e.g., [3,9,12,22]). The most popular strategy, due to its conceptual simplicity, it to annotate programs using a uniform binding-time analysis [19]. The use of a flow-sensitive binding-time analysis for partial evaluation was pioneered in Tempo [17,18].

Few attempts have been made to examine the impact of different annotation strategies on the quality of the residual programs and the specialization process. Notable exceptions are [11,6] who developed a polyvariant BTA for a higher-order applicative language, and [23] who implemented a polyvariant BTA for the Similix partial evaluator. An alternative approach was suggested in [8] where polyvariance is achieved by instrumenting programs with explicit bt-values and performing partial evaluation in two passes; [24] used the interpretive approach to the same effect. These works deal with higher-order functional languages.

Strategies for guaranteeing termination of the specialization process without being overly conservative are a topics of current research [5,14]. These strategies ensure termination by controlling the degree of polyvariance at specialization time by dynamizing appropriate variables. A speed-up analysis that predicts the relative speedup of residual programs obtained using a uniform annotation was studied in [4].

9 Conclusion

Our goal was to develop the foundations for an adaptive approach to binding-time analysis which is flexible and powerful enough to study the impact of binding-time strategies in a realistic context. We advocate that partial evaluation systems be built that allow flexibility in the BTA instead of hard-coding a single strategy on pragmatic grounds. We showed that different BTA strategies drastically influence of the quality of generated programs. The strategy language we developed allows us to catalog and design different BTA strategies.

References

1. L. O. Andersen. C program specialization (revised version). DIKU Report 92/14, DIKU, University of Copenhagen, 1992.
2. L. O. Andersen. Binding-time analysis and the taming of C pointers. In *Proc. of ACM Symposium on Partial Evaluation and Semantics-Based Program Manipulation, PEPM'93*, 1993.
3. L. O. Andersen. Program analysis and specialization for the C programming language. DIKU Report 94/19, Department of Computer Science, University of Copenhagen, 1994.
4. L. O. Andersen and C. K. Gomard. Speedup analysis in partial evaluation: preliminary results. In *Proceedings of the Workshop on Partial Evaluation and Semantics-Based Program Manipulation*, pages 1–7, San Francisco, California, 1992. Yale University, Dept. of Computer Science.
5. P. H. Andersen and C. K. Holst. Termination analysis for offline partial evaluation of a higher order functional language. In R. Cousot and D. Schmidt, editors, *Static Analysis*, volume 1145 of *Lecture Notes in Computer Science*, pages 67–82, Aachen, Germany, 1996. Springer-Verlag.
6. J. M. Ashley and C. Consel. Fixpoint computation for polyvariant static analyses of higher-order applicative programs. *ACM TOPLAS*, 16(5):1431–1448, 1994.

7. M. A. Bulyonkov. Polyvariant mixed computation for analyzer programs. *Acta Informatica*, 21:473–484, 1984.
8. M. A. Bulyonkov. Extracting polyvariant binding time analysis from polyvariant specializer. In *Proceedings of the Symposium on Partial Evaluation and Semantics-Based Program Manipulation*, pages 59–65, Copenhagen, Denmark, 1993. ACM Press.
9. M. A. Bulyonkov and D. V. Kochetov. Practical aspects of specialization of Algol-like programs. In O. Danvy, R. Glück, and P. Thiemann, editors, *Partial Evaluation. Proceedings*, volume 1110 of *Lecture Notes in Computer Science*, pages 17–32, Dagstuhl Castle, Germany, 1996. Springer-Verlag.
10. N. H. Christensen and S. Laursen. Partial evaluation of an imperative language. DIKU Student Report 98-7-3, DIKU, Dept. of Computer Science, University of Copenhagen, 1998.
11. C. Consel. Polyvariant binding-time analysis for applicative languages. In *ACM SIGPLAN Workshop on Partial Evaluation and Semantics-Based program Manipulation*, pages 66–77. ACM Press, 1993.
12. C. Consel and F. Nöel. A general approach for run-time specialization and its application to C. In *Conference Record of the Twenty Third Symposium on Principles of Programming Languages*, pages 145–156, St. Petersburg Beach, Florida, 1996. ACM Press.
13. A. P. Ershov and V. E. Itkin. Correctness of mixed computation in Algol-like programs. In J. Gruska, editor, *Mathematical Foundations of Computer Science 1977*, volume 53 of *Lecture Notes in Computer Science*, pages 59–77, Tatranská Lomnica, 1977. Springer-Verlag.
14. A. J. Glenstrup and N. D. Jones. BTA algorithms to ensure termination of off-line partial evaluation. In D. Bjørner, M. Broy, and I. V. Pottosin, editors, *Perspectives of System Informatics. Proceedings*, volume 1181 of *Lecture Notes in Computer Science*, pages 273–284, Novosibirsk, Russia, 1996. Springer-Verlag.
15. R. Glück and J. Jørgensen. Fast binding-time analysis for multi-level specialization. In D. Bjørner, M. Broy, and I. V. Pottosin, editors, *Perspectives of System Informatics. Proceedings*, volume 1181 of *Lecture Notes in Computer Science*, pages 261–272, Novosibirsk, Russia, 1996. Springer-Verlag.
16. C. K. Gomard and N. D. Jones. Compiler generation by partial evaluation: a case study. *Structured Programming*, 12:123–144, 1991.
17. L. Hornof, C. Consel, and J. Noyé. Effective specialization of realistic programs via use sensitivity. In P. Van Hentenryck, editor, *Static Analysis. Proceedings*, volume 1302 of *Lecture Notes in Computer Science*, pages 293–314, Paris, France, 1997. Springer-Verlag.
18. L. Hornof and J. Noyé. Accurate binding-time analysis for imperative languages: flow, context, and return sensitivity. In *Proceedings of the Symposium on Partial Evaluation and Semantics-Based Program Manipulation*, pages 63–73, Amsterdam, The Netherlands, 1997. ACM Press.
19. N. D. Jones, C. K. Gomard, and P. Sestoft. *Partial Evaluation and Automatic Program Generation*. Prentice-Hall, 1993.
20. N. D. Jones, P. Sestoft, and H. Søndergaard. An experiment in partial evaluation: the generation of a compiler generator. In J.-P. Jouannaud, editor, *Rewriting Techniques and Applications*, volume 202 of *Lecture Notes in Computer Science*, pages 124–140. Springer-Verlag, 1985.

21. N. D. Jones, P. Sestoft, and H. Søndergaard. Mix: a self-applicable partial evaluator for experiments in compiler generation. *LISP and Symbolic Computation*, 2(1):9–50, 1989.
22. P. Kleinrubatscher, A. Kriegshaber, R. Zöchling, and R. Glück. Fortran program specialization. *SIGPLAN Notices*, 30(4):61–70, 1995.
23. B. Rytz and M. Gengler. A polyvariant binding time analysis. In *Proceedings of the Workshop on Partial Evaluation and Semantics-Based Program Manipulation*, pages 21–28, San Francisco, California, 1992. Yale University, Dept. of Computer Science.
24. P. Thiemann and M. Sperber. Polyvariant expansion and compiler generators. In D. Bjørner, M. Broy, and I. V. Pottosin, editors, *Perspectives of System Informatics. Proceedings*, volume 1181, pages 285–296, Novosibirsk, Russia, 1996. Springer-Verlag.

Abstraction-Based Partial Deduction for Solving Inverse Problems – A Transformational Approach to Software Verification
(Extended Abstract)

Robert Glück[1] and Michael Leuschel[2]

[1] DIKU, Department of Computer Science,
University of Copenhagen, DK-2100 Copenhagen, Denmark
glueck@diku.dk

[2] Department of Electronics and Computer Science
University of Southampton, Southampton SO17 1BJ, UK
mal@ecs.soton.ac.uk

Abstract. We present an approach to software verification by program inversion, exploiting recent progress in the field of automatic program transformation, partial deduction and abstract interpretation. Abstraction-based partial deduction can work on infinite state spaces and produce finite representations of infinite solution sets. We illustrate the potential of this approach for infinite model checking of safety properties.

1 Introduction

Modern computing applications increasingly require software and hardware systems that are extremely reliable. Unfortunately, current validation techniques are often unable to provide high levels of assurance of correctness either due to the size and complexity of these systems, or because of fundamental limitations in reasoning about a given system. This paper examines the latter point showing that *abstraction-based partial deduction* can serve as a powerful analytical tool. This has several advantages in comparison with, e.g., standard logic programming. Among others, abstraction-based partial deduction has the ability to form recursively defined answers and can be used for program verification.

We apply the inversion capabilities of abstraction-based partial deduction to other languages using interpretive definitions. This means that a wide class of different verification tasks can be analyzed in a common framework using a set of uniform transformation techniques. We examine the potential for infinite model checking, and support our claims by several computer experiments.

2 Inversion, Partial Deduction, and Interpreters

Inversion. While direct computation is the calculation of the output of a program for a given input, *inverse computation* is the calculation of the possible

D. Bjørner, M. Broy, A. Zamulin (Eds.): PSI'99, LNCS 1755, pp. 93–100, 2000.

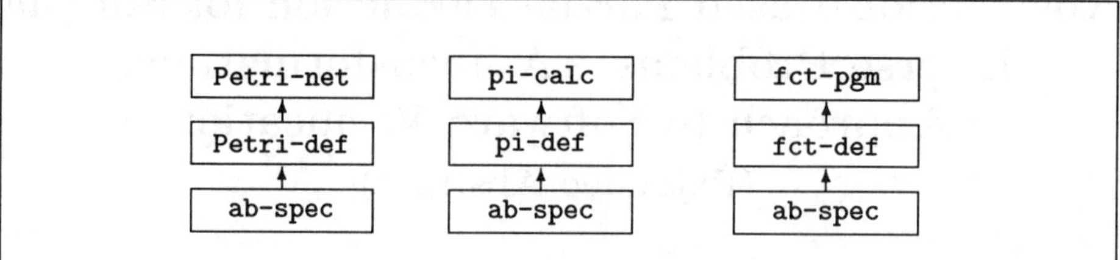

Fig. 1. Abstraction-based partial deduction `ab-spec` applied to Petri-nets, π-calculus, and functional programs via interpretive language definitions

input of a program for a given output. Consider the familiar *append* program, it can be run forwards (to concatenate two lists) and backwards (to split a list into sublists). Advances in this direction have been made in logic programming, based on solutions emerging from logic and proof theory.

However, inversion problems are not restricted to logic languages. Reasoning about the correctness of, say, a software specification, one may need to verify whether and how a critical state can be reached from any *earlier* state. This analysis requires inverse computation. The key idea is this: to show that a given system satisfies a given specification—representing a safety property—start with the bad states violating the specification, work *backwards* and show that no initial state leads to such a bad state.

Abstraction-Based Partial Deduction. The relationship between *abstract interpretation* and *program specialisation* has been observed and several formal frameworks have been developed [6,10,9]. *Abstraction-based partial deduction* (APD) combines these two approaches and can thereby solve specialisation and analysis tasks which are outside the reach of either method alone [12,11]. It was shown that program specialisation combined with abstract interpretation can vastly improve the power of both techniques (e.g., going beyond regular approximations or set-based analysis) [12].

Interpreters. Language-independence can be achieved through the *interpretive approach* [18,7,1]: an interpreter serves as mediator between a (domain-specific) language and the language for which the program transformer is defined. Efficient implementations can be obtained by removing the interpretive overhead using program specialisation (a notable example are the Futamura projections). Work on porting inverse computation to new languages includes the inversion of imperative programs by treating their relational semantics as logic programs [15] and applying the Universal Resolving Algorithm to interpreters written in a functional language [1].

Our Approach. The approach we will pursue in this paper is twofold. First, we apply the power of APD to inverse computation tasks. Instead of enumerating a list of substitutions, as in logic programming, we produce a *new logic program* which can be viewed as model of the original program instantiated to the given query. The transformation will (hopefully) derive a much simpler program (such as `p :- fail`), but APD has also the ability to form recursively defined programs.

Second, we use the interpretive approach to achieve language-independence. APD is implemented for a logic language, but we can apply its inversion capabilities to different language paradigms, such as Petri-nets and the π-calculus, via interpreters without having to write tools for each language (see Fig. 1).

To put these ideas to a trial, we use the ECCE logic program specialiser [12,13]—employing *advanced control techniques* such as characteristic trees to guide the specialisation process—coupled with an *abstract interpretation technique.* (A more detailed technical account is beyond the scope of this extended abstract; the interested reader will find a complete description in [12,13].) This APD-system does not yet implement the full power of [12,11], but it will turn out to be sufficiently powerful for our purposes.

3 Advanced Inversion Tasks for Logic Programs

To illustrate three questions about a software requirement specification relying on solving inversion problems, let us consider a familiar example: exponentiation of natural numbers ($z = x^y$).

1. *Existence of solution?* Given output state z (e.g. $z = 3$), does there exist an input state x, y with $y > 1$ that gives raise to z? *Answer:* state $z = 3$ can never be reached. Observe that here we are not interested in the values of x, y, we just want to know whether such values exist. We will call such a setting *inversion checking.*
2. *Finiteness of solution?* Given output state z (e.g. $z = 4$), is there a finite number of input states x, y that can give raise to z? *Answer:* only two states ($x = 4, y = 1$ and $x = 2, y = 2$) lead to $z = 4$.
3. *Finite description of infinite solution?* Given output state z (e.g. $z = 1$), can an infinite set of input states be described in a finite form? *Answer:* any input state with $y = 0$ leads to $z = 1$, regardless of x.

Example 1. All three questions from above can be answered with APD. Consider a logic program encoding exponentiation of natural numbers where numbers are represented by terms of type $\tau = 0 \mid s(\tau)$.

```
exp(Base,0,s(0)).
exp(Base,s(Exp),Res) :- exp(Base,Exp,BE),mul(BE,Base,Res).
mul(0,X,0).
mul(s(X),Y,Z) :- mul(X,Y,XY),plus(XY,Y,Z).
plus(0,X,X).
plus(s(X),Y,s(Z)) :- plus(X,Y,Z).
```

1. *Existence of solution.* Inverting the program for $x^y = 3, y > 1$, that is by specialising `exp/2` wrt. goal `exp(X,s(s(Y)),s(s(s(0))))`, produces an empty program: no solution exists.
2. *Finiteness of solution.* Inverting $x^y = 4$, that is by specialising `exp/2` wrt. goal `exp(X,Y,s(s(s(s(0)))))`, produces a program in which the two solutions $x = 4, y = 1$ and $x = 2, y = 2$ are explicit:

```
exp__1(s(s(s(s(0)))),s(0)).
exp__1(s(s(0)),s(s(0))).
```

3. *Finite representation of infinite solution.* Finally, inverting $x^y = 1$ can be solved by specialising `exp/2` wrt. goal `exp(X,Y,s(0))`. The result is a recursive program: infinitely many solutions were found (x^0 and 1^y for any x, y) and described in a *finite* way.[1] This finite description is possible in our approach, but not in conventional logic programming, because APD generates (recursive) programs instead of enumerating an (infinite) list of answers.

```
exp__1(X1,0).
exp__1(s(0),s(X1)) :- exp_conj__2(X1).
exp_conj__2(0).
exp_conj__2(s(X1)) :- exp_conj__3(X1).
exp_conj__3(0).
exp_conj__3(s(X1)) :- exp_conj__3(X1).
```

Example 2. As a more practical application, take the following program which allows to determine whether a list has an even number of elements (`pairl/1`) and to delete from a list an element contained in the list (`del/3`).

```
pairl([]).
pairl([A|X]):- oddl(X).        del(X,[X|T],T).
oddl([A|X]):- pairl(X).        del(X,[Y|T],[Y|DT]):- X\=Y,del(X,T,DT).
```

One might want to verify the property that deleting an element from a pair list will not result in a pair list. This can be translated into requiring that the following predicate always fails: `error(X,L) :- pairl(L),del(X,L,DL),pairl(DL).` which *can* be deduced by our APD-system: `error__1(X,L) :- fail.` To conclude, APD can invert programs in ways not possible with other approaches.

4 Case Study: Inversion and Infinite Model Checking

Recent years have seen considerable growth [5] in the application of model checking techniques [4,3] to the validation and verification of correctness properties of hardware, and more recently software systems. The method is to model a hardware or software system as a finite, labelled transition system (LTS) which is then exhaustively explored to decide whether a given specification holds for all reachable states. One can even use tabling-based logic programming as an efficient means of performing explicit model checking [14].

However, many software systems cannot be modelled by a *finite* LTS (or similar system) and, as a consequence, there has been a lot of effort to enable *infinite model checking* (e.g., [17]). We argue that inverse computation in general, and our APD-technique in particular, has a lot to offer for this avenue of research:

[1] The residual program can be improved by better post-processing.

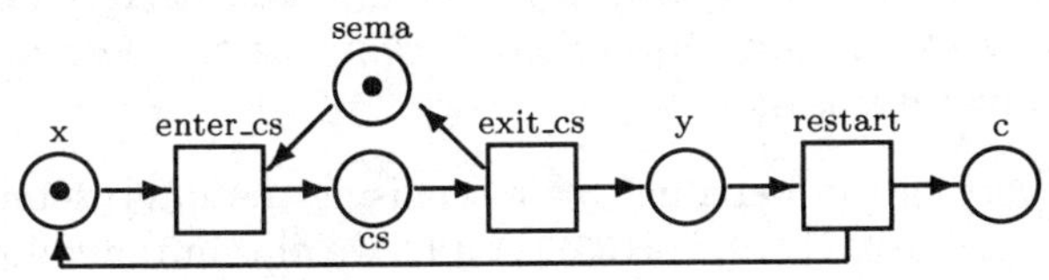


```
start(Trace,X,ReachableMarking) :-
        trace(Trace,[X,s(0),0,0,0],ReachableMarking).
trace([],Marking,Marking).
trace([Action|As],InMarking,OutMarking) :-
        trans(Action,InMarking,M1),trace(As,M1,OutMarking).
trans(enter_cs,[s(X),s(Sema),CritSec,Y,C],[X,Sema,s(CritSec),Y,C]).
trans(exit_cs,[X,Sema,s(CritSec),Y,C],[X,s(Sema),CritSec,s(Y),C]).
trans(restart,[X,Sema,CritSec,s(Y),C],[s(X),Sema,CritSec,Y,s(C)]).
```

Fig. 2. Petri net with a single semaphore and its encoding as logic program

- The system to be verified can be modelled as a program (possibly by means of an interpreter). This obviously includes finite LTS but also allows to express systems with an infinite number of states.
- Model checking of safety properties then amounts to *inversion checking*: we prove that a specification holds by showing that there exists no trace (the input argument) which leads to an invalid state.
- To be successful, infinite model checking requires refined abstractions (a key problem mentioned in [5]). The control of generalisation of APD provides just that (at least for the examples we treated so far). In essence, the *specialisation component of APD performs a symbolic traversal of the state space, thereby producing a finite representation of it, on which the abstract interpretation performs the verification of the specification.*

Consider the Petri net shown in Fig. 2. It models a single process which may enter a critical section (cs), the access to which is controlled by a semaphore (sema). The Petri net can be encoded directly as a logic program using an interpreter for Petri-nets `trace/3`, where the object-level Petri net is represented by `trans/3` facts. The `trace/3` predicate checks for enabled transitions and fires them.

The initial marking of `trace/3` can be seen in `start/3`: 1 token in the semaphore (sema), no tokens in the reset counter (c), no processes in the critical section (cs) and no processes in the final place (y). There may be `X` processes in the initial place (x). Again, numbers are represented by terms of type $\tau = \texttt{0} \mid \texttt{s(}\tau\texttt{)}$. More processes can be modelled if we increase the number of tokens in the initial place (x). Forward execution of the Petri net: given an initial value for `X` and a sequence of transitions `trace` determine the marking(s) that can be reached.

Let us now check a safety property of the given Petri net, namely that it is *impossible* to reach a marking where two processes are in their critical section at the same time. Clearly, this is an inversion task: given a marking where two processes are in the critical section, try to find a trace that leads to this state. More precisely we want to do *inversion checking*, as the desired outcome is to prove that *no* inverse exists.

Example 3. Inverting the Petri net by specialising the interpreter in Fig. 2 wrt. the query `start(Tr,s(0),[X,S,s(s(CS)),Y,C])` we obtain the following program:

```
start(Tr,s(0),[X3,X4,s(s(X5)),X6,X7]) :- fail.
```

This inversion task cannot be solved by PROLOG (or XSB-PROLOG [16] with tabling), even when adding moding or delay declarations. Due to the counter (c) we have to perform infinite model checking which in turn requires *abstraction* and *symbolic execution*. Both of these are provided by our APD approach.

Example 4. Similarly, one can prove the safety property *regardless* of the number of processes, i.e., for *any* number of tokens in the initial place (x). When we specialise the interpreter of Fig. 2 for the query `unsafe(X,s(0),0,0,0)` we get (after 2 iterations each of the specialisation and abstract interpretation components of ECCE): `start(Tr,Processes,[X3,X4,s(s(X5)),X6,X7]) :- fail.`

5 Porting to Other Languages and Paradigms

We can apply the power of our APD-approach, along with its capabilities for inversion and verification [8], to the π-calculus by writing an interpreter for it. We have also successfully ported inverse computation to a functional language via an interpreter (omitted from extended abstract). Apart from highlighting the power of our approach, these examples provide further computational evidence for the theoretical result [1] that inverse computation can applied to arbitrary languages via interpreters.

6 Conclusion and Assessment

We presented an approach to program inversion, exploiting progress in the field of automatic program transformation, partial deduction and abstract interpretation. We were able to port these inversion capabilities to other languages via interpretive definitions. We examined the potential for infinite model checking of safety properties, and supported our claims by computer experiments. We believe, by exploiting the connections between software verification and automatic program specialisation, one may be able to significantly extend the capabilities of analytical tools that inspect the input/output behaviour.

The emphasis was on novel ways of reasoning rather than efficiency and large scale applications. In principle, it is possible to extend our approach to verify larger, more complicated infinite systems.[2] As with all automatic specialisation

[2] Larger systems have been approached with related techniques as a processing phase [9]. However, their purpose is to reduce the state space rather than provide novel ways of reasoning. Another approach related to ours is [2].

tools, there are several points that need to be addressed: allow more generous unfolding and polyvariance (efficiency, both of the specialisation process and the specialised program, are less of an issue in model checking) to enable more precise residual programs and implement the full algorithm of [11] which allows for more fine grained abstraction and use BDD-like representations whenever possible. Currently we can only verify safety properties (i.e., no bad things happen) and not liveness properties (i.e., good things will eventually happen). The latter might be feasible by a more sophisticated support for the negation.

References

1. S.M. Abramov, R. Glück. Semantics modifiers: An approach to non-standard semantics of programming languages. In M. Sato, Y. Toyama (eds.), *International Symposium on Functional and Logic Programming*, 247–270. World Scientific, 1998.
2. M. Bruynooghe, H. Vandecasteele, A. de Waal. Detecting Unsolvable Queries for Definite Logic Programs. In C. Palamidessi, H. Glaser, K. Meinke (eds.) *Principles of Declarative Programming*, LNCS 1490, 118–133. Springer-Verlag, 1998.
3. R. Bryant. Symbolic boolean manipulation with ordered binary-decision diagrams. *ACM Computing Surveys*, 24(3):293–318, 1992.
4. E.M. Clarke, E.A. Emerson, A. Sistla. Automatic verification of finite-state concurrent systems using temp. logic specifications. *ACM TOPLAS*, 8(2):244–263, 1986.
5. E.M. Clarke, J.M. Wing. Formal methods: State of the art and future directions. *ACM Computing Surveys*, 28(4):626–643, 1996.
6. C. Consel, S.C. Khoo. Parameterized partial evaluation. *ACM TOPLAS*, 15(3):463–493, 1993.
7. R. Glück. On the generation of specializers. *Journal of Functional Programming*, 4(4):499–514, 1994.
8. P. Hartel, M. Butler, A. Currie, P. Henderson, M. Leuschel, A. Martin, A. Smith, U. Ultes-Nitsche, B. Walters. Questions and answers about ten formal methods. In S. Gnesi, D. Latella (eds.) *Formal Methods for Industrial Critical Systems*, pages 179–203. Trento, Italy, 1999.
9. J. Hatcliff, M. Dwyer, S. Laubach. Staging analysis using abstraction-based program specialization. In C. Palamidessi, H. Glaser, K. Meinke (eds.) *Principles of Declarative Programming*, LNCS 1490, 134–151. Springer-Verlag, 1998.
10. N.D. Jones. The essence of program transformation by partial evaluation and driving. In N.D. Jones, M. Hagiya, M. Sato (eds.) *Logic, Language and Computation*, LNCS 792, 206–224. Springer-Verlag, 1994.
11. M. Leuschel. Program specialisation and abstract interpretation reconciled. In J. Jaffar (ed.) *JICSLP'98*, 220–234. MIT Press, 1998.
12. M. Leuschel, D. De Schreye. Logic program specialisation: How to be more specific. In H. Kuchen, S. Swierstra (eds.) *Programming Languages: Implementations, Logics and Programs.*, LNCS 1140, 137–151. Springer-Verlag, 1996.
13. M. Leuschel, B. Martens, D. De Schreye. Controlling generalisation and polyvariance in partial deduction of normal logic programs. *ACM TOPLAS*, 20(1):208–258, 1998.
14. Y.S. Ramakrishna, C.R. Ramakrishnan, I.V. Ramakrishnan, S.A. Smolka, T. Swift, D.S. Warren. Efficient model checking using tabled resolution. In O. Grumberg (ed.) *Computer-Aided Verification*, LNCS 1254, 143–154. Springer-Verlag, 1997.
15. B.J. Ross. Running programs backwards: The logical inversion of imperative computation. *Formal Aspects of Computing*, 9:331–348, 1997.

16. K. Sagonas, T. Swift, D.S. Warren. XSB as an efficient deductive database engine. In *Intern. Conference on the Management of Data*, 442–453. ACM Press, 1994.
17. B. Steffen (ed.). *Tools and Algorithms for the Construction and Analysis of Systems*, LNCS 1384. Springer-Verlag, 1998.
18. V.F. Turchin. Program transformation with metasystem transitions. *Journal of Functional Programming*, 3(3):283–313, 1993.

Sonic Partial Deduction

Jonathan Martin and Michael Leuschel

Department of Electronics and Computer Science
University of Southampton, Southampton SO17 1BJ, UK
{jcm93r,mal}@ecs.soton.ac.uk

Abstract. The current state of the art for ensuring finite unfolding of logic programs consists of a number of online techniques where unfolding decisions are made at specialisation time. Introduction of a static termination analysis phase into a partial deduction algorithm permits unfolding decisions to be made offline, before the actual specialisation phase itself. This separation improves specialisation time and facilitates the automatic construction of compilers and compiler generators. The main contribution of this paper is how this separation may be achieved in the context of logic programming, while providing non-trivial support for partially static datastructures.
The paper establishes a solid link between the fields of static termination analysis and partial deduction enabling existing termination analyses to be used to ensure finiteness of the unfolding process. This is the first offline technique which allows arbitrarily partially instantiated goals to be sufficiently unfolded to achieve good specialisation results. Furthermore, it is demonstrated that an offline technique such as this one can be implemented very efficiently and, surprisingly, yield even better specialisation than a (pure) online technique. It is also, to our knowledge, the first offline approach which passes the KMP test (i.e., obtaining an efficient Knuth-Morris-Pratt pattern matcher by specialising a naive one).

1 Introduction

Control of partial deduction — a technique for the partial evaluation of pure logic programs — is divided into two levels. The local level guides the construction of individual SLDNF-trees while the global level manages the forest, determining which, and how many trees should be constructed. Each tree gives rise to a specialised predicate definition in the final program so the global control ensures a finite number of definitions are generated and also controls the amount of polyvariance. The local control on the other hand determines what each specialised definition will look like.

Techniques developed to ensure finite unfolding of logic programs [2, 22, 21] have been inspired by the various methods used to prove termination of rewrite systems [7, 6]. Whilst, by no means *ad hoc*, there is little direct relation between these techniques and those used for proving termination of logic programs (or even those of rewrite systems). This means that advances in the static termination analysis technology do not directly contribute to improving the control of partial deduction. This paper aims to bridge this gap.

D. Bjørner, M. Broy, A. Zamulin (Eds.): PSI'99, LNCS 1755, pp. 101–112, 2000.

Moreover, the control described in [2, 22, 21] as well as the more recent [27, 16, 15] are inherently online, meaning that they are much slower than offline approaches and that they are not based on a *global analysis* of the program's behaviour which enables control decisions to be taken before the actual specialisation phase itself.

Offline approaches to local control of partial deduction on the other hand [25, 11, 12, 3] have been very limited in other respects. Specifically, each atom in the body of a clause is marked as either *reducible* or *non-reducible*. Reducible atoms are *always* unfolded while non-reducible atoms on the other hand are *never* unfolded. Whilst this approach permits goals to be unfolded at normal execution speed, it can unduly restrict the amount of unfolding which takes place with a detrimental effect on the resulting specialised program. Another problem of [25, 12] is that it classifies *arguments* either as static (known at specialisation time) or dynamic (unknown at specialisation time). This division is too coarse, however, to allow refined unfolding of goals containing partially instantiated data where some parts of the structure are known and others unknown. Such goals are very common in logic programming, and the key issue which needs to be considered is termination. A partial solution to this problem has been presented in [3], but it still sticks with the limited unfolding mentioned above and can "only" handle a certain class of partially instantiated data (data bounded wrt some semi-linear norm).

A Sonic Approach. This paper proposes a flexible solution to the local termination problem for offline partial deduction of logic programs, encompassing the best of both worlds. Based on the cogen approach[1] for logic programs [12], the construction of a generating extension will be described which "compiles in" the local unfolding rule for a program and is capable of constructing maximally expanded SLDNF-trees of finite depth.

The technique builds directly on the work of [23] which describes a method for ensuring termination of logic programs with delay. The link here is that the residual goals of a deadlocked computation are the leaves of an incomplete SLD-tree. The basic idea is to use static analysis to derive relationships between the sizes of goals and the depths of derivations. This depth information is incorporated in a generating extension and is used to accurately control the unfolding process. At specialisation time the sizes of certain goals are computed and the maximum depth of subsequent derivations is fixed according to the relationships derived by the analysis. In this way, termination is ensured whilst allowing a flexible and generous amount of unfolding. Section 3 reviews the work of [23] and shows how it can be used directly to provide the basis of a generating extension which allows finite unfolding of bounded goals. A simple extension to the technique is described in Section 4 which also permits the safe unfolding of unbounded goals.

This is the *first* offline approach to partial deduction which is able to successfully unfold arbitrarily **partially instantiated** (i.e. unbounded) goals. In fact,

[1] Instead of trying to achieve a compiler generator (cogen) by self-application [8] one writes the cogen directly [26].

it is demonstrated that the method can, surprisingly, yield even better specialisation than (pure) online techniques. In particular, some problematic issues in unfolding, notably unfolding under a coroutining computation rule and the back propogation of instantiations [21], can be easily handled within the approach (for further details see [24]). Furthermore, it is the *first* offline approach which passes the **KMP test** (i.e., obtaining an efficient Knuth-Morris-Pratt pattern matcher by specialising a naive one), as demonstrated by the extensive experiments in Section 6.

An analysis which measures the depths of derivations may be termed a *sounding analysis*. Section 5 describes how such an analysis can be based on existing static termination analyses which compute level mappings and describes how the necessary depths may be obtained from these level mappings. Unfolding based on a sounding analysis then, is the basis of *sonic partial deduction.*

2 Preliminaries

Familiarity with the basic concepts of logic programming and partial deduction is assumed [19, 20]. A *level mapping* (resp. *norm*) is a mapping from ground atoms (resp. ground terms) to natural numbers. For an atom A and level mapping $|.|$, $A_{|.|}$ denotes the set $\{|A\theta| \mid A\theta \text{ is ground}\}$. An atom A is *(un)bounded* wrt $|.|$ if $A_{|.|}$ is (in)finite [4]. For this paper, the notion of level mapping is extended to non-ground atoms by defining for any atom A, $|A| = min(A_{|.|})$; and similarly for norms. The norm $|t|_{len}$ returns the length of the list t. A list t is rigid iff $|t|_{len} = |t\theta|_{len}$ for all θ. A clause $c : H \leftarrow A_1, \ldots, A_n$ is *recurrent* if for every grounding substitution θ for c, $|H\theta| > |A_i\theta|$ for all $i \in [1, n]$.

3 Unfolding Bounded Atoms

A fundamental problem in adapting techniques from the termination literature for use in controlling partial deduction is that the various analyses that have been proposed (see [4] for a survey) are designed to prove *full* termination for a given goal and program, in other words guaranteeing finiteness of the complete SLDNF-tree constructed for the goal. For example, consider the goal ← Flatten([x, y, z], w) and the program Flatten consisting of the clauses app_1, app_2, $flat_1$ and $flat_2$.

$flat_1$ Flatten([], []).
$flat_2$ Flatten([e|x], r) ← Append(e, y, r) ∧ Flatten(x, y).
app_1 Append([], x, x).
app_2 Append([u|x], y, [u|z]) ← Append(x, y, z).

A typical static termination analysis would (correctly) fail to deduce termination for this program and goal. Most analyses can infer that a goal of the form ← Flatten(x, y) will terminate if x is a rigid list of rigid lists, or if x is a rigid list and y is a rigid list. In the context of partial deduction however, such a condition for termination will usually be too strong. The problem is that the information relating to the goal, by the very nature of partial deduction, is often incomplete. For example, the goal ← Flatten([x, y, z], w), will not terminate but the program can be partially evaluated to produce the following specialised definition of Flatten/2.

Flatten([x, y, z], r) ← Append(x, r1, r) ∧ Append(y, r2, r1) ∧ Append(z, [], r2).

The scheme described in [23] transforms programs into *efficient* and *terminating* programs. It will for instance transform the non-terminating program Flatten into the following efficient, terminating program, by adding an extra depth parameter.

$flat^*$ Flatten(x, y) ← SetDepth_F(x, d) ∧ Flatten(x, y, d).

DELAY Flatten(_, _, d) UNTIL Ground(d).
$flat_1^*$ Flatten([], [], d) ← d ≥ 0.
$flat_2^*$ Flatten([e|x], r, d) ← d ≥ 0 ∧ Append(e, y, r) ∧ Flatten(x, y, d − 1).

app^* Append(x, y, z) ← SetDepth_A(x, z, d) ∧ Append(x, y, z, d).

DELAY Append(_, _, _, d) UNTIL Ground(d).
app_1^* Append([], x, x, d) ← d ≥ 0.
app_2^* Append([u|x], y, [u|z], d) ← d ≥ 0 ∧ Append(x, y, z, d − 1).

For now, assume that the (meta-level) predicate SetDepth_F(x, d) is defined such that it always succeeds instantiating the variable d to the length of the list x if this is found to be rigid,(i.e., $|x|_{len} = |x\theta|_{len}$ for every substitution θ), and leaving d unbound otherwise. Note that a call to Flatten/3 will proceed only if its third argument has been instantiated as a result of the call to SetDepth_F(x, d). The purpose of this last argument is to ensure finiteness of the subsequent computation. More precisely, d is an upper bound on the number of calls to the recursive clause $flat_2^*$ *in any successful derivation.* Thus by failing any derivation where the number of such calls has exceeded this bound (using the test d ≥ 0), termination is guaranteed without losing completeness. The predicate SetDepth_A/3 is defined in a similar way, but instantiates d to the minimum of the lengths of the lists x and z, delaying if both x and z are unbounded.

The main result of [23] guarantees that the above program will terminate for every goal (in some cases the program will deadlock). Moreover, given a goal of the form ← Flatten(x, y) where x is a rigid list of rigid lists or where x is a rigid list and y is a rigid list, the program does not deadlock and produces all solutions to such a goal. In other words, both termination and completeness of the program are guaranteed.

Since the program is terminating for all goals, it can be viewed as a means of constructing a finite (possibly incomplete) SLD-tree for any goal. As mentioned above, it is indeed capable of complete evaluation but a partial evaluation for bounded goals may also be obtained. Quite simply, the deadlocking goals of the computation are seen to be the leaf nodes of an incomplete SLD-tree.

For example, the goal ← Flatten([x, y, z], r) leads to deadlock with the residual goal ← Append(x, r1, r, d1) ∧ Append(y, r2, r1, d2) ∧ Append(z, [], r2, d3). Removing the depth bounds, this residue can be used to construct a partial evaluation of the original goal resulting in the specialised definition of Flatten/2 above.

The approach, thus far, is limited in that it can only handle bounded goals. For unbounded goals the unfolding will deadlock immediately and it is not possible, for example, to specialise ← Flatten([[], [a] | z], r) in a non-trivial way. This strong limitation will be overcome in the following sections.

The method proposed in [1] (and further developed in [21]) ensures the construction of a finite SLD-tree through the use of a measure function which associates with each node (goal) in the tree a weight from a well-founded set. Finiteness is ensured by imposing the condition that the weight of any goal is strictly less than the weight of its *direct covering ancestor*. This last notion is introduced to prevent the comparison of unrelated goals which could precipitate the end of the unfolding process. Consider the atoms Append([1], y, r, 1) and Append([2], y1, y, 1) appearing in the LD-tree for Flatten([[1],[2]], r,2) (see Figure 1 in the appendix). Any sensible measure function would assign exactly the same weight to each atom. But, if these weights were compared, unfolding would be prematurely halted after four steps. Hence, this comparison must be avoided and this is justified by the fact that the atoms occur in separate "sub-derivations." In the sonic approach, the above notions are dealt with implicitly. Figure 1 depicts the SLD-tree for the goal ← Flatten([[1], [2]], r, 2) using the transformed version of Flatten. The depth argument of each atom may be seen as a weight as described above. Note that the weight of any atom in a sub-derivation (except the first) is implicitly derived from the weight of its direct covering ancestor by the process of resolution. This conceptual simplicity eliminates the need to explicitly trace direct covering ancestors, improving performance of the specialisation process.

4 Unfolding Unbounded Atoms

The main problem with the above transformation is that it only allows the unfolding of bounded goals. Often, as mentioned in the introduction, to achieve good specialisation it is necessary to unfold *unbounded* atoms also. This is *especially true in a logic programming setting*, where partially instantiated goals occur very naturally even at runtime. This capability may be incorporated into the above scheme as follows. Although an atom may be unbounded, it may well have a *minimum* size. For example the length of the list [1,2,3|x] must be at least three regardless of how x may be instantiated. In fact, this minimum size is an accurate measure of the size of the part of the term which is partially instantiated and this may be used to determine an estimate of the number of unfolding steps necessary for this part of the term to be consumed in the specialisation process. For example, consider the Append/3 predicate and the goal ← Append([1,2,3|x], y, z). Given that the minimum size of the first argument is three it may be estimated that at least three unfolding steps must be performed. Now suppose that the number of unfolding steps is fixed at one plus the minimum (this will usually give exactly the required amount of specialisation). The transformed Flatten program may now be used to control the unfolding by simply calling ← Append([1,2,3|x], y, z, 3). The problem here, of course, is that completeness is lost, since the goal fails if x does not become instantiated to []. To remedy this, an extra clause is introduced to capture the leaf nodes of the SLD-tree. The Append/3 predicate would therefore be transformed into the following.

app_1^* Append([], x, x, d) ← d ≥ 0.
app_2^* Append([u|x], y, [u|z], d) ← d ≥ 0 ∧ Append(x, y, z, d − 1).
app_3^* Append(x, y, z, d) ← d < 0 ∧ Append(x, y, z, _).

The call to Append/4 in the clause app_3^* immediately suspends since the depth argument is uninstantiated. The clause is only selected when the derivation length has exceeded the approximated length and the effect is that a leaf node (residual goal) is generated precisely at that point. For this reason, such a clause is termed a *leaf generator* in the sequel. Now for the goal ← Append([1,2,3|x], y, z, 3) the following resultants are obtained.

Append([1,2,3], y, [1,2,3|y], 3) ←
Append([1,2,3,u|x'], y, [1,2,3,u|z'], 3) ← Append(x', y, z')

Observe that the partial input data has been completely consumed in the unfolding process. In fact, in this example, one more unfolding step has been performed than is actually required to obtain an "optimal" specialisation, but this is due to the fact that the goal has been unfolded non-deterministically. In some cases, this non-deterministic unfolding may actually be desirable, but this is an orthogonal issue to termination (this issue will be re-examined in Section 6).

Furthermore, note that the SetDepth predicates must now be redefined to assign depths to unbounded atoms. Also a predicate such as SetDepth_A(x, z, d) must be defined such that d gets instantiated to the *maximum* of the minimum lengths of the lists x and z to ensure a maximal amount of unfolding. Note that this maximum will always be finite.

5 Deriving Depth Bounds from Level Mappings

The above transformations rely on a sounding analysis to determine the depths of derivations or unfoldings. Such an analysis may be based on exisiting termination analyses which derive level mappings. To establish the link with the termination literature the *depth* argument in an atom during *unfolding* may simply be chosen to be the *level* of the atom with respect to some level mapping used in a termination proof. Whilst, in principle a depth bound for unfolding may be derived from any level mapping, in practice this can lead to excessive unfolding and, as a consequence, poor specialisation. (E.g., based on some termination analysis, an atom might have a *level* mapping of 15, diminishing by 5 on every recursive call. One could give the atom a *depth* of 15, but in this case the value of 3 would be much more appropriate, preventing over-eager unfolding.)

A number of techniques have been devised to obtain accurate depth bounds from fairly arbitrary level mappings derived from termination analyses. Space restrictions prohibit a detailed presentation here, but the techniques are extremely simple to apply and introduce minimal overhead (and sometimes none at all; for further details see [24]). It is important to note, however, that finiteness can always be guaranteed; the problems encoutered only relate to the quality of the specialisation and this is also dependent on the control of determinacy. Although this has been touched upon in [9] this is still a relatively unexplored area in the context of partial deduction. Many of the problems may disappear altogether with the right balance of bounded and determinate unfolding.

6 Experiments and Benchmarks

To gauge the efficiency and power of the sonic approach, a prototype implementation has been devised and integrated into the ECCE partial deduction system ([13, 14, 18]). The latter is responsible for the global control and code generation and calls the sonic prototype for the local control. A comparison has been made with ECCE under the default settings, i.e. with ECCE also providing the local control using its default unfolding rule (based on a determinate unfolding rule which uses the homeomorphic embedding relation $\trianglelefteq$ on covering ancestors to ensure termination). For the global control, both specialisers used conjunctive partial deduction ([17, 10, 5]) and characteristic trees ([18]).

All the benchmarks are taken from the DPPD library ([13]) and were run on a Power Macintosh G3 266 Mhz with Mac OS 8.1 using SICStus Prolog 3 #6 (Macintosh version 1.3). Tables 1 and 2 show respectively, the total specialisation times (without post-processing), and the time spent in unfolding during specialisation.[2] In Table 1 the times to produce the generating extensions for the sonic approach are not included, as this is still done by hand. It is possible to automate this process and one purpose of hand-coding the generating extensions was to gain some insight into how this could be best achieved. In any case, in situations where the same program is repeatedly respecialised, this time will become insignificant anyway. Due to the limited precision of the `statistics/2` predicate, the figures of "0 ms" in Table 2 should be interpreted as "less than 16 ms." (The runtimes for the residual programs appear in Table 3 in the appendix, which, for a more comprehensive comparison, also includes some results obtained by MIXTUS.)

The sonic prototype implements a more agressive unfolding rule than the default determinate unfolding rule of ECCE. This is at the expense of total transformation time (see Table 1), as it often leads to increased polyvariance, but consequently the speed of the residual code is often improved, as can be seen in

[2] Note that, because ECCE uses characteristic trees whereas the sonic prototype builds trace terms, running the latter involves some extra (in principle unnecessary) overhead.

Table 3.[3] Default ECCE settings more or less guarantee no slowdown, and this is reflected in Table 3, whereas the general lack of determincay control in the prototype sonic unfolding rule leads to two small slowdowns. There is plenty of room for improvement, however, on these preliminary results. For instance, the sonic approach is flexible enough to allow determinacy control to be incorporated within it.

All in all, the sonic approach provides extremely fast unfolding combined with very good specialisation capabilities. Observe that the sonic approach even *passes the KMP test*, and it is thus the first offline approach to our knowledge which does so.[4] If it were possible to extend the sonic approach to the global control as well, one would hopefully obtain an extremely efficient specialiser producing highly optimised residual code.

Table 1. Specialisation times (total w/o post-processing)

Benchmark	sonic + ECCE	ECCE
advisor	**17** ms	150 ms
applast	83 ms	**33** ms
doubleapp	50 ms	**34** ms
map.reduce	**33** ms	50 ms
map.rev	**50** ms	67 ms
match.kmp	300 ms	**166** ms
matchapp	**66** ms	83 ms
maxlength	**184** ms	200 ms
regexp.r1	**34** ms	400 ms
relative	**50** ms	166 ms
remove	**367** ms	400 ms
remove2	1049 ms	**216** ms
reverse	50 ms	50 ms
rev_acc_type	316 ms	**83** ms
rotateprune	**67** ms	183 ms
ssupply	**34** ms	100 ms
transpose	**50** ms	467 ms
upto.sum1	**33** ms	284 ms
upto.sum2	**50** ms	83 ms

7 Conclusion

The majority of termination analyses rely on the derivation of level mappings to prove termination. This paper has described how these level mappings may be

[3] A more agressive unfolding rule, in conjunctive partial deduction, did not lead to improved speed under compiled code of Prolog by BIM; see [14]. So, this also depends on the quality of the indexing generated by the compiler.

[4] One might argue that the global control is still online. Note, however, that for KMP no generalisation and thus no global control is actually needed.

Table 2. Specialisation times (unfolding)

Benchmark	sonic + ECCE	ECCE
advisor	0 ms	33 ms
applast	0 ms	16 ms
doubleapp	0 ms	0 ms
map.reduce	0 ms	17 ms
map.rev	0 ms	34 ms
match.kmp	0 ms	99 ms
matchapp	0 ms	33 ms
maxlength	0 ms	67 ms
regexp.r1	0 ms	383 ms
relative	0 ms	166 ms
remove	34 ms	201 ms
remove2	33 ms	50 ms
reverse	16 ms	33 ms
rev_acc_type	0 ms	32 ms
rotateprune	0 ms	99 ms
ssupply	0 ms	67 ms
transpose	16 ms	400 ms
upto.sum1	0 ms	168 ms
upto.sum2	0 ms	66 ms

used to obtain precise depth bounds for the control of unfolding during partial deduction. Thus, a solid link has been established between the fields of static termination analysis and partial deduction enabling existing and future termination analyses to be used to ensure finiteness of the unfolding process.

Furthermore, the paper has described now such depth bounds can be incorporated in generating extensions. The construction of these forms the foundation of any offline partial deduction method whether it is based on the self-application or the cogen approach. This is the first offline technique which allows arbitrarily partially instantiated goals to be sufficiently unfolded to achieve good specialisation results. The technique can, surprisingly, yield even better specialisation than a pure online technique (and thus the choice of an offline approach does not necessarily entail the sacrifice of unfolding potential). This is due to the availability of global information in the unfolding decision making process. It is also, to our knowledge, the first offline approach which passes the KMP test.

The framework admits elegant solutions to some problematic unfolding issues and these solutions are significantly less complex than their online counterparts. Of course, an online technique may still be able to make refined unfolding decisions based on the availabilty of concrete data. This strongly suggests that offline and online methods be combined to achieve maximal unfolding power. Another, possibly more challenging, avenue for further research is to extend the sonic approach for the global control, so that its advantages in terms of efficiency, termination, and specialisation power also apply at the global control level.

References

[1] M. Bruynooghe, D. De Schreye, and B. Martens. A general criterion for avoiding infinite unfolding during partial deduction of logic programs. In *Proceedings of ILPS'91*, pages 117–131. MIT Press, 1991.

[2] M. Bruynooghe, D. De Schreye, and B. Martens. A general criterion for avoiding infinite unfolding during partial deduction. *New Generation Computing*, 11(1):47–79, 1992.

[3] M. Bruynooghe, M. Leuschel, and K. Sagonas. A polyvariant binding-time analysis for off-line partial deduction. In C. Hankin, editor, *Proceedings of ESOP'98*, LNCS 1381, pages 27–41. Springer-Verlag, April 1998.

[4] D. De Schreye and S. Decorte. Termination of logic programs: The never-ending story. *The Journal of Logic Programming*, 19 & 20:199–260, May 1994.

[5] D. De Schreye, R. Glück, J. Jørgensen, M. Leuschel, B. Martens, and M. H. Sørensen. Conjunctive partial deduction: Foundations, control, algorithms and experiments. *The Journal of Logic Programming*, 41(2 & 3):231–277, 1999.

[6] N. Dershowitz. Termination of rewriting. *Journal of Symbolic Computation*, 3:69–116, 1987.

[7] N. Dershowitz and Z. Manna. Proving termination with multiset orderings. *Communications of the ACM*, 22(8):465–476, 1979.

[8] A. Ershov. On Futamura projections. *BIT (Japan)*, 12(14):4–5, 1982. In Japanese.

[9] J. Gallagher. Tutorial on specialisation of logic programs. In *Proceedings of PEPM'93*, pages 88–98. ACM Press, 1993.

[10] R. Glück, J. Jørgensen, B. Martens, and M. H. Sørensen. Controlling conjunctive partial deduction of definite logic programs. In H. Kuchen and S. Swierstra, editors, *Proceedings of PLILP'96*, LNCS 1140, pages 152–166, Aachen, Germany, September 1996. Springer-Verlag.

[11] C. A. Gurr. *A Self-Applicable Partial Evaluator for the Logic Programming Language Gödel.* PhD thesis, Dept. of Computer Science, University of Bristol, 1994.

[12] J. Jørgensen and M. Leuschel. Efficiently generating efficient generating extensions in Prolog. In O. Danvy, R. Glück, and P. Thiemann, editors, *Proceedings of the Dagstuhl Seminar on Partial Evaluation*, LNCS 1110, pages 238–262, 1996.

[13] M. Leuschel. The ECCE partial deduction system and the DPPD library of benchmarks. Obtainable via `http://www.cs.kuleuven.ac.be/~dtai`, 1996.

[14] M. Leuschel. *Advanced Techniques for Logic Program Specialisation.* PhD thesis, K.U. Leuven, May 1997. Accessible via `http://www.ecs.soton.ac.uk/~mal`.

[15] M. Leuschel. Improving homeomorphic embedding for online termination. In P. Flener, editor, *Proceedings of LOPSTR'98*, LNCS 1559, pages 199–218, Manchester, UK, June 1998. Springer-Verlag.

[16] M. Leuschel. On the power of homeomorphic embedding for online termination. In G. Levi, editor, *Proceedings of SAS'98*, LNCS 1503, pages 230–245, Pisa, Italy, September 1998. Springer-Verlag.

[17] M. Leuschel, D. De Schreye, and A. de Waal. A conceptual embedding of folding into partial deduction: Towards a maximal integration. In M. Maher, editor, *Proceedings of JICSLP'96*, pages 319–332, Bonn, Germany, September 1996. MIT Press.

[18] M. Leuschel, B. Martens, and D. De Schreye. Controlling generalisation and polyvariance in partial deduction of normal logic programs. *ACM Transactions on Programming Languages and Systems*, 20(1):208–258, January 1998.

[19] J. W. Lloyd. *Foundations of Logic Programming.* Springer-Verlag, 1987.

[20] J. W. Lloyd and J. C. Shepherdson. Partial evaluation in logic programming. *The Journal of Logic Programming*, 11(3& 4):217–242, 1991.

[21] B. Martens and D. De Schreye. Automatic finite unfolding using well-founded measures. *Journal of Logic Programming*, 28(2):89–146, 1996.

[22] B. Martens, D. De Schreye, and T. Horváth. Sound and complete partial deduction with unfolding based on well-founded measures. *Theoretical Comput. Sci.*, 122(1–2):97–117, 1994.

[23] J. Martin and A. King. Generating Efficient, Terminating Logic Programs. In *TAPSOFT'97*. Springer-Verlag, 1997.

[24] J. Martin and M. Leuschel. Sonic partial deduction. Technical Report DSSE-TR-99-3, Dept. of Electronics and Computer Science, University of Southampton, February 1999.

[25] T. Mogensen and A. Bondorf. Logimix: A self-applicable partial evaluator for Prolog. In K.-K. Lau and T. Clement, editors, *Proceedings of LOPSTR'92*, pages 214–227. Springer-Verlag, 1992.

[26] S. A. Romanenko. A compiler generator produced by a self-applicable specializer can have a surprisingly natural and understandable structure. In D. Bjørner, A. P. Ershov, and N. D. Jones, editors, *Partial Evaluation and Mixed Computation*, pages 445–463. North-Holland, 1988.

[27] M. H. Sørensen and R. Glück. An algorithm of generalization in positive supercompilation. In J. W. Lloyd, editor, *Proceedings of ILPS'95*, pages 465–479, Portland, USA, December 1995. MIT Press.

A Further Figures and Tables

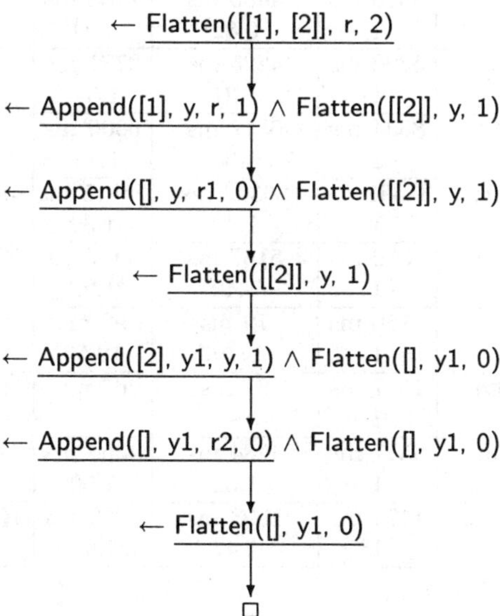

Fig. 1. Unfolding of ← Flatten([[1], [2]], r, 2)

Table 3. Speed of the residual programs (in ms, for a large number of queries, interpreted code) and Speedups

Benchmark	Original	sonic + ECCE	ECCE	MIXTUS
advisor	1541 ms	483 ms	426 ms	471 ms
	1	3.19	3.62	
applast	1563 ms	491 ms	471 ms	1250 ms
	1	3.18	3.32	
doubleapp	1138 ms	700 ms	600 ms	854 ms
	1	1.63	1.90	
map.reduce	541 ms	100 ms	117 ms	383 ms
	1	5.41	4.62	
map.rev	221 ms	71 ms	83 ms	138 ms
	1	3.11	2.66	
match.kmp	4162 ms	1812 ms	3166 ms	2521 ms
	1	2.30	1.31	
matchapp	1804 ms	771 ms	1525 ms	1375 ms
	1	2.34	1.18	
maxlength	217 ms	283 ms	208 ms	213 ms
	1	0.77	1.04	
regexp.r1	3067 ms	396 ms	604 ms	na
	1	7.74	5.08	
relative	9067 ms	17 ms	1487 ms	17 ms
	1	533.35	6.10	
remove	3650 ms	4466 ms	2783 ms	2916 ms
	1	0.82	1.31	
remove2	5792 ms	4225 ms	3771 ms	3017 ms
	1	1.37	1.54	
reverse	8534 ms	6317 ms	6900 ms	na
	1	1.35	1.24	
rev_acc_type	37391 ms	26302 ms	26815 ms	25671 ms
	1	1.42	1.39	
rotateprune	7350 ms	5167 ms	5967 ms	5967 ms
	1	1.42	1.23	
ssupply	1150 ms	79 ms	92 ms	92 ms
	1	14.56	12.50	
transpose	1567 ms	67 ms	67 ms	67 ms
	1	–	–	
upto.sum1	6517 ms	4284 ms	4350 ms	4716 ms
	1	1.52	1.50	
upto.sum2	1479 ms	1008 ms	1008 ms	1008 ms
	1	1.47	1.47	

On Perfect Supercompilation

Jens Peter Secher and Morten Heine Sørensen

Department of Computer Science, University of Copenhagen (DIKU)
Universitetsparken 1, DK-2100 Copenhagen Ø, Denmark
{jpsecher,rambo}@diku.dk

Abstract. We extend *positive supercompilation* to handle *negative* as well as positive information. This is done by instrumenting the underlying *unfold rules* with a small rewrite system that handles *constraints on terms*, thereby ensuring *perfect information propagation.* We illustrate this by transforming a naïvely specialised string matcher into an optimal one. The presented algorithm is guaranteed to *terminate* by means of *generalisation steps.*

1 Introduction

Turchin's supercompiler [21] is a program transformer for functional programs which performs optimisations beyond *partial evaluation* [9] and *deforestation* [23].

Positive supercompilation [7] is a variant of Turchin's supercompiler which was introduced in an attempt to study and explain the essentials of Turchin's supercompiler, how it achieves its effects, and its relation to other transformers. In particular, the language of the programs to be transformed by positive supercompilation is a typical first-order functional language — the one usually studied in deforestation — which is rather different from the language Refal, usually adopted in connection with Turchin's supercompiler.

For the sake of simplicity, the positive supercompiler was designed to maintain *positive information* only; that is, when the transformer reaches a conditional **if** $x == x'$ **then** t **else** t', the information that $x = x'$ is assumed to hold is taken into account when transforming t (by performing the substitution $\{x := x'\}$ on t). In contrast, the *negative information* that $x \neq x'$ must hold is discarded when transforming t' (since no substitution can represent this information!). In Turchin's supercompiler this negative information is maintained as a constraint when transforming t'. Consequently, Turchin's supercompiler can perform some optimisations beyond positive supercompilation.

In this paper we present an algorithm which we call *perfect supercompilation* — a term essentially adopted from [6] — which is similar to Turchin's supercompiler. The perfect supercompiler arises by extending the positive supercompiler to take negative information into account. Thus, we retain the typical first-order language as the language of programs to be transformed, and we adopt the style of presentation from positive supercompilation.

A main contribution of the extension is to develop techniques which manipulate constraints of a rather general form. Although running implementations

D. Bjørner, M. Broy, A. Zamulin (Eds.): PSI'99, LNCS 1755, pp. 113–127, 2000.

of Turchin's supercompiler use such techniques to some extent, the techniques have not been presented in the literature for Turchin's supercompiler as far as we know. The only exception is the paper by Glück and Klimov [6] which, however, handles constraints of a simpler form; for instance, our algorithm for *normalising* constraints has no counterpart in their technique. As another main contribution we generalise a technique for ensuring that positive supercompilation always terminates to the perfect supercompiler and prove that, indeed, perfect supercompilation terminates on all programs[1]. As far as we are aware, no version of Turchin's supercompiler maintaining negative information has been presented which in general is guaranteed to terminate.

The remainder of this paper is organised as follows. We first (Sect. 2) present a classical application of positive supercompilation (of transformers in general): the generation of an efficient specialised string pattern matcher from a general matcher and a known pattern. As is well-known, positive supercompilation generates specialised matchers containing redundant tests. We also show how these redundant tests are eliminated when one uses instead perfect supercompilation. We then (Sect. 3) present an overview of perfect supercompilation and (Sect. 4) an overview of the proof that perfect supercompilation always terminates. In Sect. 5 we conclude and compare to related work.

2 The Knuth-Morris-Pratt Example

In this paper we will only consider programs written in a first-order, functional language with pattern matching and conditionals. For simplicity, pattern-matching functions are allowed to match with non-nested patterns on one parameter only, and conditionals can only be used to test the equality of two values by means of the == operator. We will use the convention that function names are written *slanted*, variables are written in *italics*, and constructors are written in SMALL CAPS. We also use standard shorthand notation $[]$ and $h:t$ for the empty list and the list constructed from h and the tail t, respectively; we further use the usual notation $[h_1,\ldots,h_n]$.

Consider the following *general matcher* program which takes a pattern and a string as input and returns TRUE iff the pattern occurs as a substring in the string.

$$
\begin{array}{ll}
match(p,s) & = m(p,s,p,s) \\
m([],ss,op,os) & = \textsc{true} \\
m(p:pp,ss,op,os) & = x(p,pp,ss,op,os) \\
x(p,pp,[],op,os) & = \textsc{false} \\
x(p,pp,s:ss,op,os) & = \textbf{if } p{=}{=}s \textbf{ then } m(pp,ss,op,os) \textbf{ else } n(op,os) \\
n(op,s:ss) & = m(op,ss,op,ss)\ .
\end{array}
$$

[1] When termination is guaranteed we cannot guarantee perfect transformation, but the underlying unfolding scheme is still perfect in the sense that all information is propagated.

Although this example only compares variables to variables, our method can manipulate more general equalities and inequalities.

Now consider the following *naïvely specialised matcher* $match_{\text{AAB}}$ which matches the fixed pattern $[\text{A}, \text{A}, \text{B}]$ with a string u by calling *match*:

$$match_{\text{AAB}}(u) \;=\; match([\text{A}, \text{A}, \text{B}], u)\;.$$

Evaluation proceeds by comparing A to the first component of u, A to the second, and B to the third. If at some point the comparison fails, the process is restarted with the tail of u.

This strategy is not optimal. Suppose that after matching the two occurrences of A in the pattern with the first two occurrences of A in the string, the B in the pattern fails to match yet another A in the string. Then the process is restarted with the string's tail, even though it is known that the first two comparisons will succeed. Rather than performing these tests whose outcome is known, we should *skip* the first three occurrences of A in the original string and proceed directly to compare the B in the pattern with the fourth element of the original string. This is done in the *KMP specialised matcher:*

$$
\begin{array}{ll}
match_{\text{AAB}}(u) & = m_{\text{AAB}}(u)\\
m_{\text{AAB}}([\,]) & = \text{FALSE}\\
m_{\text{AAB}}(s\!:ss) & = \textbf{if } \text{A}{=}{=}s \textbf{ then } m_{\text{AB}}(ss) \textbf{ else } m_{\text{AAB}}(ss)\\
m_{\text{AB}}([\,]) & = \text{FALSE}\\
m_{\text{AB}}(s\!:ss) & = \textbf{if } \text{A}{=}{=}s \textbf{ then } m_{\text{B}}(ss) \textbf{ else } m_{\text{AAB}}(ss)\\
m_{\text{B}}([\,]) & = \text{FALSE}\\
m_{\text{B}}(s\!:ss) & = \textbf{if } \text{B}{=}{=}s \textbf{ then } \text{TRUE}\\
 & \qquad\qquad \textbf{else if } \text{A}{=}{=}s \textbf{ then } m_{\text{B}}(ss) \textbf{ else } m_{\text{AAB}}(ss)\;.
\end{array}
$$

After finding two As and a third symbol which is not a B in the string, this program checks (in m_{B}) whether the third symbol of the string is an A. If so, it continues immediately by comparing the next symbol of the string with the B in the pattern (by calling m_{B}), thereby avoiding repeated comparisons.

Can we get this program by application of *positive* supercompilation to the naïvely specialised matcher? The result of this application is depicted graphically as a *process tree* in Fig. 1 (it will be explained later why some nodes are emphasised). The root of the process tree is labelled by the initial term that is to be transformed (here, the naïvely specialised matcher). The children of a node α in the process tree represent possible unfoldings for the term in α; the edges are labelled with the assumptions made about free variables (e.g. $u = [\,]$). Each arc in the process tree can therefore be seen as one step of transformation. At the same time the whole tree can be viewed as a new program, where arcs with labels represent tests on the input, and the leaves represent final results or recursive calls.

Informally, a program can be extracted from a process tree by creating a new function definition for each node α that has labelled outgoing edges; the new function has as parameters the set of variables in α and a right-hand side

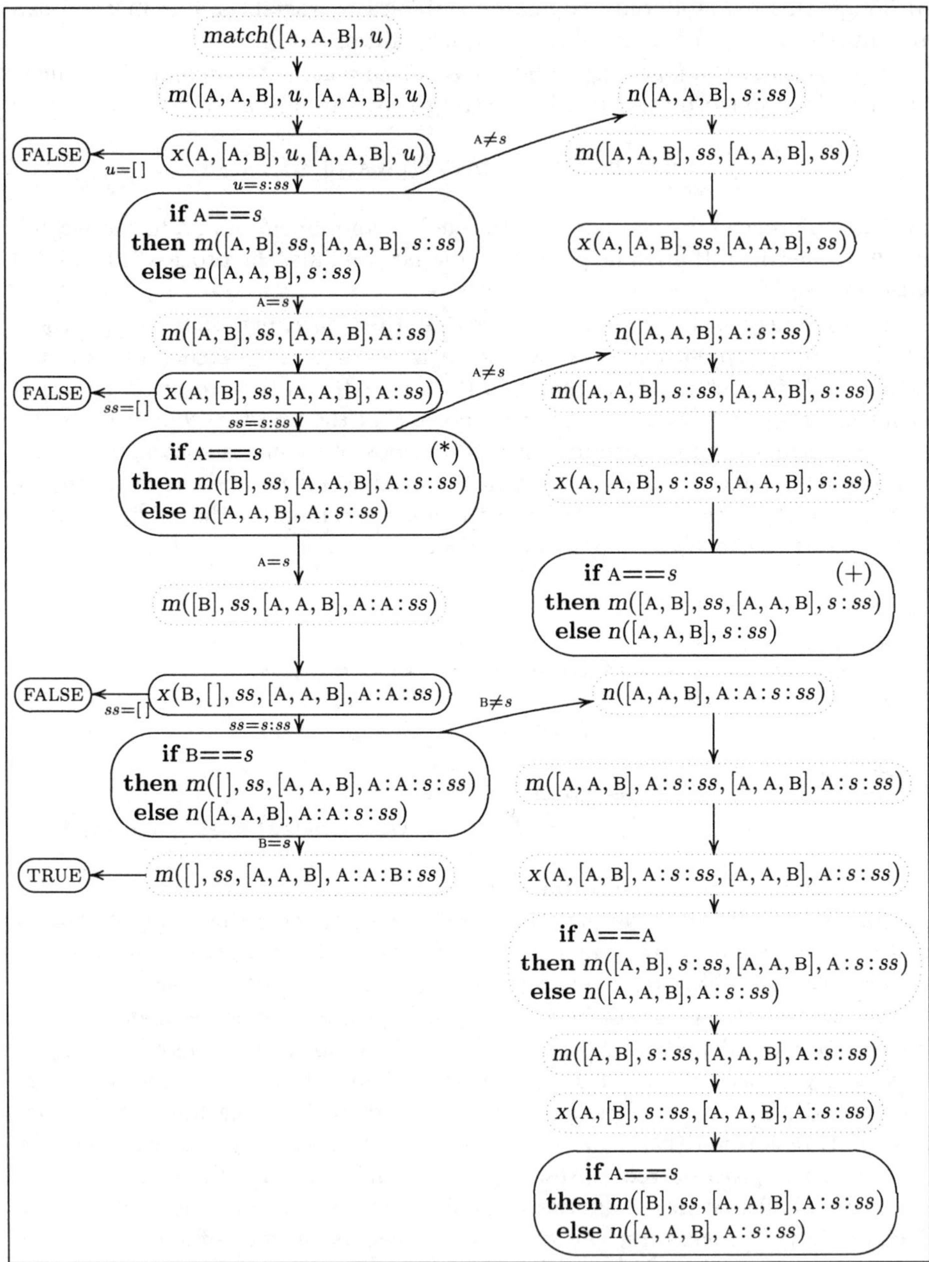

Fig. 1. Driving the naïvely specialised matcher. The children of a node α represent possible unfoldings for the term in α; the edges are labelled with the assumptions made

created from the children of α. In fact, the program corresponding to the tree in Fig. 1 is the following:

$$\begin{array}{ll}
m_{\text{AAB}}([\,]) & = \text{FALSE} \\
m_{\text{AAB}}(s\!:\!ss) & = \textbf{if } \text{A}{==}s \textbf{ then } m_{\text{AB}}(ss) \textbf{ else } n_{\text{AAB}}(ss, s) \\
m_{\text{AB}}([\,]) & = \text{FALSE} \\
m_{\text{AB}}(s\!:\!ss) & = \textbf{if } \text{A}{==}s \textbf{ then } m_{\text{B}}(ss) \textbf{ else } n_{\text{AB}}(ss, s) \\
m_{\text{B}}([\,]) & = \text{FALSE} \\
m_{\text{B}}(s\!:\!ss) & = \textbf{if } \text{B}{==}s \textbf{ then } \text{TRUE} \textbf{ else } n_{\text{B}}(ss, s) \\
n_{\text{AAB}}(ss, s) & = m_{\text{AAB}}(ss) \\
n_{\text{AB}}(ss, s) & = \textbf{if } \text{A}{==}s \textbf{ then } m_{\text{AB}}(ss) \textbf{ else } n_{\text{AAB}}(ss, s) \\
n_{\text{B}}(ss, s) & = \textbf{if } \text{A}{==}s \textbf{ then } m_{\text{B}}(ss) \textbf{ else } n_{\text{AB}}(ss, s)\ .
\end{array}$$

The term $m_{\text{AAB}}(u)$ in this program is more efficient than $match([\text{A}, \text{A}, \text{B}], u)$ in the original program. In fact, this is the desired KMP specialised matcher, except for the redundant test $\text{A}{==}s$ in n_{AB} (and the redundant argument in n_{AAB}). The reason for the redundant test $\text{A}{==}s$ is that positive supercompilation ignores negative information: when proceeding to the false branch of the conditional (from the original program)

$$\textbf{if } \text{A}{==}s \textbf{ then } m([\text{B}], ss, [\text{A}, \text{A}, \text{B}], \text{A}\!:\!s\!:\!ss) \textbf{ else } n([\text{A}, \text{A}, \text{B}], \text{A}\!:\!s\!:\!ss)\ , \qquad (*)$$

the information that $\text{A} \neq s$ holds is forgotten. Therefore, the test is repeated in the subsequent conditional

$$\textbf{if } \text{A}{==}s \textbf{ then } m([\text{A}, \text{B}], ss, [\text{A}, \text{A}, \text{B}], s\!:\!ss) \textbf{ else } n([\text{A}, \text{A}, \text{B}], s\!:\!ss)\ . \qquad (+)$$

In contrast, with perfect supercompilation, this information is maintained as a constraint, and can be used to decide that the conditional (+) has only one possible outcome. The tree would therefore continue below the node (+), and the resulting program would skip the superfluous test and have a recursive call back to the first branching node, $\text{X}(\text{A}, [\text{A}, \text{B}], u, [\text{A}, \text{A}, \text{B}], u)$; this is exactly the KMP specialised matcher.

3 Overview of Perfect Supercompilation

In this and the next section we will give an informal account of the supercompilation algorithm. For proofs, examples and in-depth treatment of the algorithm, see [15].

Despite the intended informality we will need the following definitions. Let x, y, z range over variables from the set X. Let c, f and g range over fixed arity constructor, function and pattern-matching-function names in the finite sets C, F and G, respectively. Let p range over patterns of the form $c(x_1, \ldots, x_n)$ and let t, u, s range over terms. By $\text{var}(t)$ we denote the variables in t, and we let θ range over substitutions, written $\{x_1 := t_1, \ldots, x_n := t_n\}$; application of substitutions is defined as usual and written prefix. Finally, we write $f(\ldots) \triangleq t$ to denote that function f is defined in the program under consideration.

Perfect supercompilation of a program is carried out in two phases. First, a model of the subject program is constructed in form of a *constrained process tree.* Second, a new program is extracted from the constrained process tree. A constrained process tree is similar to the tree in Fig. 1, but each node is labelled by a term *and* a set of *constraints.* From here on we will not distinguish between constrained and unconstrained process trees, and we will refer to some part of the label of a node α simply by saying "node α contains ... ".

The root of the process tree is labelled by the initial term that is to be transformed, together with an empty *constraint system.* The process tree is developed by repeated unfoldings of the terms in the leaves. The rules that govern the unfolding of terms have been constructed by extending the small-step semantics of the language by rules that speculatively execute tests that depend on variables. For each possible outcome of a test, a child is added and information about the test that has been conducted is appended to the current constraint system. The extended constraint system is then passed on to the child that resulted from the speculative execution. Our constraint systems (a subset of the ones defined in [2]) are restricted kinds of conjunctive normal forms of formulae of the form

$$\left(\bigwedge_{i=1}^{n} a_i = a'_i\right) \wedge \left(\bigwedge_{i=1}^{m} b_i \neq b'_i\right)$$

where a, b are terms that consist of variables and constructors only, *i.e.*

$$a, b ::= x \mid c(a_1, \ldots, a_n) \ .$$

The constraint systems are used to prune branches from the process tree: speculative execution of a test that results in a constraint system that cannot be *satisfied* will not produce a new child. For instance, consider the again the conditional (+); blindly unfolding this term would result in a node with two children:

$$\textbf{if}\ \text{A}{==}s\ \textbf{then}\ m([\text{A},\text{B}], ss, [\text{A},\text{A},\text{B}], s\!:\!ss)\ \textbf{else}\ n([\text{A},\text{A},\text{B}], s\!:\!ss)$$

$\text{A}=s$: $m([\text{A},\text{B}], ss, [\text{A},\text{A},\text{B}], s\!:\!ss)$ $\qquad$ $\text{A}\neq s$: $n([\text{A},\text{A},\text{B}], s\!:\!ss)$

But since we have inherited the constraint system $\text{A} \neq s$ from the conditional (*), the left child will not be produced because the resulting constraint system $\text{A} \neq s \wedge \text{A} = s$ is not satisfiable. More precisely, for a constraint system to be satisfiable, it must be possible to assign values to the variables in the system such that the constraints are satisfied. A constraint system is thus satisfiable iff there exists a substitution θ such that, for each equation $a = a'$, θa will be syntactically identical to $\theta a'$, and likewise, for each disequation $b \neq b'$, θb will be syntactically different from $\theta b'$. To decide the satisfiability of a constraint system R, we first apply a set of rewrite rules to bring R into a *normal form.* The core of these rewrite rules (a modified version of the ones presented in [2]) is shown in Fig. 2. Additional control on these rules ensure that non-deterministic,

$$
\begin{array}{rcll}
x = x & \hookrightarrow & \top & \\
x \neq x & \hookrightarrow & \bot & \\
\bullet \wedge \top & \hookrightarrow & \bullet & \\
\bullet \vee \bot & \hookrightarrow & \bullet & \\
\bullet \wedge \bot & \hookrightarrow & \bot & \\
\bullet \vee \top & \hookrightarrow & \top & \\
c(b_1,\ldots,b_n) = c'(a_1,\ldots,a_m) & \hookrightarrow & \bot & (c \neq c') \\
c(b_1,\ldots,b_n) \neq c'(a_1,\ldots,a_m) & \hookrightarrow & \top & (c \neq c') \\
c(b_1,\ldots,b_n) = c(a_1,\ldots,a_n) & \hookrightarrow & b_1 = a_1 \wedge \cdots \wedge b_n = a_n & \\
c(b_1,\ldots,b_n) \neq c(a_1,\ldots,a_n) & \hookrightarrow & b_1 \neq a_1 \vee \cdots \vee b_n \neq a_n & \\
x = a & \hookrightarrow & \bot & (x \in \mathrm{var}(a) \,\&\, a \notin X) \\
x \neq a & \hookrightarrow & \top & (x \in \mathrm{var}(a) \,\&\, a \notin X) \\
x = a \wedge \bullet & \hookrightarrow & x = a \wedge \bullet\{x{:=}a\} & (x \notin \mathrm{var}(a)) \\
x \neq a \vee \bullet & \hookrightarrow & x \neq a \vee \bullet\{x{:=}a\} & (x \notin \mathrm{var}(a))
\end{array}
$$

Fig. 2. Rewrite system for normalisation of constraint systems. $\bot$ represents an unsatisfiable element, $\top$ represents the trivially satisfiable element, and $\bullet$ stands for an arbitrary part of a formula

exhaustive application of the rewrite rules to any constraint system terminates and results in a constraint system in normal form. A constraint system in normal form is either $\bot$ (false), $\top$ (true), or of the form

$$\left(\bigwedge_{i=1}^{n} x_i = a_i\right) \wedge \bigwedge_{j=1}^{m}\left(\bigvee_{k=1}^{l} y_{j,k} \neq b_{j,k}\right) .$$

When no *type information* about the variables in a constraint system is present, a constraint system in normal form is satisfiable exactly when it is different from $\bot$. However, when it is known that a variable x can assume a *finite* set of values only, it is necessary to verify that there indeed exists a *value* which, when assigned to x, satisfies the constraint system. For instance, consider the constraint system

$$x \neq y \wedge y \neq z \wedge z \neq x$$

where all variables have boolean type. This system is in normal form and therefore appears to be satisfiable — but it is not possible to assign values FALSE or TRUE to the variables such that the system is satisfiable. When a constraint system R is in normal form, it is thus necessary to systematically try out all possible combinations of value assignments for variables with known, finitely-valued types. This is done by instantiating such variables in R, which possibly will call for further rewrite steps to take R into a normal form, and so on until there are no more finitely-valued variables left. If R now is different from $\bot$, R is satisfiable [15].

We can now show how constraint systems can be used to guide the construction of the process tree. Every term t in the process tree is associated with a constraint system R, denoted $\langle t, R \rangle$. The complete set of unfold rules is presented in Fig. 3. Rules (A)–(B), (D), (E)–(F)[2] and (G)–(J) correspond to normal evaluation with respect to the semantics of language[3]. Rules (C) and (E)–(F)[4] perform speculative execution of a term based on the information in the associated constraint system.

Rule (C) instantiates a free variable y to the pattern $c(y_1, \ldots, y_m)$ taken from the function definition (using fresh variables). This is achieved by appending the equation $y = c(y_1, \ldots, y_m)$ to the current constraint system. If the new constraint system is satisfiable, the function application can be unfolded. In the same manner, rules (E) and (F) handle conditional expressions where general equations and disequations can be appended to the constraint system. Rule (K) finally separates the resulting constraint system R into positive and negative information by normalising R: the positive information (of the form $\bigwedge x = a$) can be regarded as a substitution, which can then be separated from the normalised R; we denote this separation by $R' \cong (\theta \wedge R'')$. The positive information can then be propagated to the context by applying the substitution θ to the whole term[5].

Unfolding of a branch is stopped if the leaf in that branch is a value or if an ancestor node *covers* (explained below) all possible executions that can arise from the leaf. The latter case constitutes a *fold* operation which will eventually result in a recursive call in the derived program.

We say that a node covers another node if the terms of the two nodes are equal up to renaming of variables *and* the constraint system in the leaf is at least as restrictive as the one in its ancestor. Intuitively speaking, if these two conditions are met, any real computation performed by the leaf can also be performed by the ancestor; we can then safely produce a recursive call in the derived program. In [15] an algorithm is presented that gives a safe approximation to the question "is R more restrictive than R'?".

If we look at the process tree in Fig. 1, we will see that some parts of the tree are created by *deterministic unfolding*, *i.e.* they each consist of a single path. This is a good sign, since it means that the path represents local computations that will *always* be carried out when the program is in this particular state, regardless of the uninstantiated variables. We have thus precomputed these intermediate transitions once and for all — as done in partial evaluation — and we can omit the intermediate steps and simply remember the result.

---

[2] Without free variables in a and a'.

[3] The intended semantics of our language is evaluation to weak head normal form, except for comparison in conditionals where the terms to be compared are *fully* evaluated before the comparison is carried out. For simplicity, the unfolding rules are call-by-name which, unfortunately, can give rise to duplication of computation.

[4] With free variables in a or a'.

[5] The positive information is re-injected into the context because such re-injection neatly disposes of irrelevant information about variables that are no longer present.

$$\boxed{\langle t, R\rangle \mapsto \langle t', R'\rangle}$$

$$\text{(A)}\ \frac{f(x_1,\ldots,x_n) \triangleq t}{\langle f(t_1,\ldots,t_n), R\rangle \mapsto \langle \{x_1 := t_1,\ldots,x_n := t_n\}t, R\rangle}$$

$$\text{(B)}\ \frac{g(c(x_1,\ldots,x_m),x_{m+1},\ldots,x_n) \triangleq t}{\langle g(c(t_1,\ldots,t_m),t_{m+1},\ldots,t_n), R\rangle \mapsto \langle \{x_1 := t_1,\ldots,x_n := t_n\}t, R\rangle}$$

$$\text{(C)}\ \frac{g(p,x_1,\ldots,x_n) \triangleq t \qquad R' = R \wedge [x = p] \qquad \text{satisfiable}(R')}{\langle g(x,t_1,\ldots,t_n), R\rangle \mapsto \langle \{x_1 := t_1,\ldots,x_n := t_n\}t, R'\rangle}$$

$$\text{(D)}\ \frac{g(p,x_1,\ldots,x_n) \triangleq t \qquad \langle t, R\rangle \mapsto \langle t', R'\rangle}{\langle g(t,t_1,\ldots,t_n), R\rangle \mapsto \langle g(t',t_1,\ldots,t_n), R'\rangle}$$

$$\text{(E)}\ \frac{R' = R \wedge [a = a'] \qquad \text{satisfiable}(R')}{\langle \textbf{if}\ a{==}a'\ \textbf{then}\ t\ \textbf{else}\ t', R\rangle \mapsto \langle t, R'\rangle}$$

$$\text{(F)}\ \frac{R' = R \wedge [a \neq a'] \qquad \text{satisfiable}(R')}{\langle \textbf{if}\ a{==}a'\ \textbf{then}\ t\ \textbf{else}\ t', R\rangle \mapsto \langle t', R'\rangle}$$

$$\text{(G)}\ \frac{\langle t_1, R\rangle \mapsto\!\!\!\Rightarrow \langle t_1', R'\rangle}{\langle \textbf{if}\ t_1{==}t_2\ \textbf{then}\ t_3\ \textbf{else}\ t_4, R\rangle \mapsto \langle \textbf{if}\ t_1'{==}t_2\ \textbf{then}\ t_3\ \textbf{else}\ t_4, R'\rangle}$$

$$\text{(H)}\ \frac{\langle t_2, R\rangle \mapsto\!\!\!\Rightarrow \langle t_2', R'\rangle}{\langle \textbf{if}\ a{==}t_2\ \textbf{then}\ t_3\ \textbf{else}\ t_4, R\rangle \mapsto \langle \textbf{if}\ a{==}t_2'\ \textbf{then}\ t_3\ \textbf{else}\ t_4, R'\rangle}$$

$$\boxed{\langle t, R\rangle \mapsto\!\!\!\Rightarrow \langle t', R'\rangle}$$

$$\text{(I)}\ \frac{\langle t, R\rangle \mapsto \langle t', R'\rangle}{\langle t, R\rangle \mapsto\!\!\!\Rightarrow \langle t', R'\rangle}$$

$$\text{(J)}\ \frac{\langle t, R\rangle \mapsto\!\!\!\Rightarrow \langle t', R'\rangle}{\langle c(a_1,\ldots,a_{m-1},t,t_{m+1},\ldots,t_n), R\rangle \mapsto\!\!\!\Rightarrow \langle c(a_1,\ldots,a_{m-1},t',t_{m+1},\ldots,t_n), R'\rangle}$$

$$\boxed{\langle t, R\rangle \Rrightarrow \langle t', R'\rangle}$$

$$\text{(K)}\ \frac{\langle t, R\rangle \mapsto\!\!\!\Rightarrow \langle t', R'\rangle \qquad R' \cong (\theta \wedge R'')}{\langle t, R\rangle \Rrightarrow \langle \theta t', R''\rangle}$$

Fig. 3. Unfold rules with perfect information propagation

Creation of a process tree in the manner just described does not always terminate since infinite process trees can be produced. To keep the process trees finite, we ensure that no infinite branches are produced. It turns out that in every infinite branch, there must be a term that *homeomorphically embeds* an ancestor (this is known as Kruskal's Tree Theorem). The homeomorphic embedding relation $\trianglelefteq$ is the smallest relation on terms such that, for any symbol $h \in C \cup F \cup G \cup \{\textbf{ifthenelse}\}$,

$$\frac{}{x \trianglelefteq y} \qquad \frac{\exists i \in \{1,\ldots,n\} : t \trianglelefteq t'_i}{t \trianglelefteq h(t'_1,\ldots,t'_n)} \qquad \frac{\forall i \in \{1,\ldots,n\} : t_i \trianglelefteq t'_i}{h(t_1,\ldots,t_n) \trianglelefteq h(t'_1,\ldots,t'_n)} .$$

When a term t' in a leaf homeomorphically embeds a term t in an ancestor, there is thus a danger of producing an infinite branch. In such a situation, t or t' is split up by means of a *generalisation step.*

Definition 1 (Generalisation).

1. A term u is an *instance* of term t, denoted $u \geq t$, if there exists a substitution θ such that $\theta t = u$.
2. A generalisation of two terms t, u is a term s such that $t \geq s$ and $u \geq s$.
3. A *most specific generalisation* (msg) of two terms t, u is a generalisation s such that, for all generalisation s' of t, u, $s \geq s'$. (There exists exactly one msg of t, u modulo renaming). □

A generalisation step on a process tree calculates the msg of the terms t, t' in two nodes α, α'; the msg is then used to divide one of the nodes into subterms that can be unfolded independently:

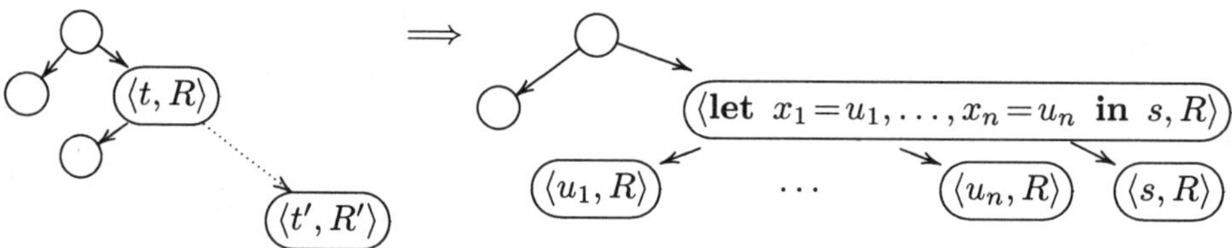

where s is the msg of t and t', and $t = s\{x_1 := u_1, \ldots, x_n := u_n\}$. Which of the nodes t, t' that is split up depends on how similar the nodes are (this will be made more precise below). The introduction of **let**-terms are merely for notational convenience; they will be unrolled in the derived program.

We can now sketch the full supercompilation algorithm. To ensure termination and, at the same time, provide reasonable specialisation, we partition the nodes in the process tree into three categories (in the lines of [18]):

1. nodes containing **let**-terms,
2. *global* nodes, and
3. *local* nodes.

Global nodes are those that represent speculative execution or final results (both of which must be present in the derived program). Local nodes are those nodes that are not global and does not contain **let**-terms. For example, in Fig. 1 the set of local nodes are indicated by dotted frames (there are no nodes containing **let**-terms since there is no need for generalisation in that particular example). This partitioning of the nodes is used to control the unfolding.

Definition 2 (Relevant ancestor). Let T be a process tree and let the set of *relevant ancestors* $\text{relanc}(T, \alpha)$ of a node α in T be defined thus:

$$\text{relanc}(T, \alpha) = \begin{cases} \emptyset, & \text{if } \alpha \text{ contains a } \textbf{let}\text{-term} \\ \text{all ancestors that are global,} & \text{if } \alpha \text{ is global} \\ \text{all local ancestors,} & \text{if } \alpha \text{ is local} \end{cases}$$

where the *local ancestors* to α is all ancestors that are local up to the first common ancestor that is global. □

For an example, consider the process tree in Fig. 1; the local node $x(\text{A}, [\text{B}], s\!:\!ss, [\text{A}, \text{A}, \text{B}], \text{A}\!:\!s\!:\!ss)$ near the bottom has as local ancestors all ancestors up to and including the node $n([\text{A}, \text{A}, \text{B}], \text{A}\!:\!\text{A}\!:\!s\!:\!ss)$.

Definition 3 (Drive). Let T be a process tree and α a node in T. Then

1. $T(\alpha)$ denotes the label of node α.
2. $T\{\alpha{:=}T'\}$ denotes a new tree that is identical to T except that the subtree rooted at α has been replaced by T'.
3. ϵ denotes the root node of a tree.
4. If $\{\langle t_1, R_1\rangle, \ldots, \langle t_n, R_n\rangle\} = \{\langle t, R\rangle \,|\, T(\alpha) \Rrightarrow \langle t, R\rangle\}$, then

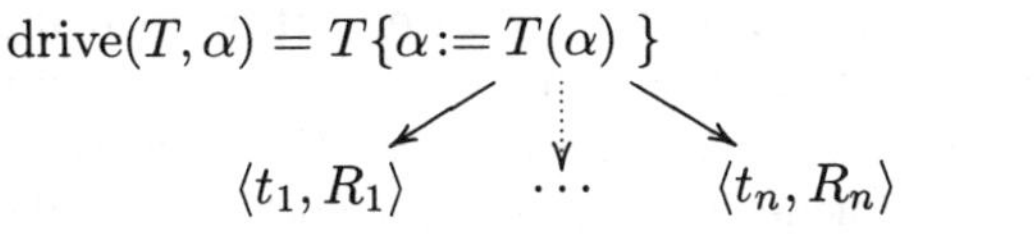

□

Definition 4 (Finished). A leaf α in a process tree T is *finished* if one of the following conditions is satisfied:

1. $T(\alpha) = \langle c(), \ldots\rangle$ for some constructor c.
2. $T(\alpha) = \langle x, \ldots\rangle$ for some variable x.
3. There is an ancestor α' to α such that (a) α, α' are global nodes, and (b) if $T(\alpha) = \langle t, R\rangle$ and $T(\alpha') = \langle t', R'\rangle$ then t is a renaming of t' and R' is at least as restrictive as R.

A tree T is said to be *finished* when all leaves are finished. □

With these definitions, we can sketch the supercompilation algorithm thus:

> **input** a term t
> **let** T consist of a single node labelled $\langle t, \top \rangle$
> **while** T is not finished **begin**
>   **let** $\alpha = \langle t, R \rangle$ be an unfinished leaf in T
>   **if** $\forall \alpha' = \langle t', R' \rangle \in \text{relanc}(T, \alpha) : t' \not\trianglelefteq t$ **then** $T = \text{drive}(T, \alpha)$
>   **else begin**
>   **let** $\alpha' = \langle t', R' \rangle \in \text{relanc}(T, \alpha)$ such that $t' \trianglelefteq t$
>   **if** R' is more restrictive than R **then** $T = T\{\alpha' := \langle t', \top \rangle\}$
>   **else if** $t \gtrsim t'$ **then** $T = T\{\alpha := \langle \text{generalise}(t, t'), R \rangle\}$
>   **else** $T = T\{\alpha' := \langle \text{generalise}(t', t), R' \rangle\}$
>   **end**
> **end**
> **output** T

The transformed program can be extracted from the process tree by examination of the global nodes (collecting the set of free variables) and the labels on the edges.

4 Overview of the Termination Proof

A language-independent framework for proving termination of *abstract program transformers* has been presented in [17], where sufficient conditions have been established for abstract program transformers to terminate. In this section we will give a very rough sketch of how this framework have been used to prove termination of our algorithm.

An abstract program transformer is a map from trees to trees, such that a single step of transformation is carried out by each application of the transformer. Termination then amounts to a certain form of convergence of the sequences of trees obtained by repeatedly applying the transformer.

For a transformer to fit the framework, it is sufficient to ensure that

1. the transformer converges, in the sense that for each transformation step, the difference between two consecutive trees lessens. More precisely, in the sequence of trees produced by the transformation, for any depth d there must be some point from which every two consecutive trees are identical down to depth d; and
2. the transformer maintains some invariant such that only finite trees are produced.

By induction on the depth of the trees produced, the former can be proved by the fact that the algorithm either

1. adds new leaves to a tree which trivially makes consecutive trees identical at an increasing depth, or

2. generalises a node, *i.e.* replaces a subtree by node containing a let-term (or a node containing the empty constraint system $\top$). Since generalisation only occurs on terms which are not let-terms (or contain non-empty constraint systems, respectively), a node can be generalised at most twice.

The latter is ensured because, in every proces tree,

1. a path that consists of let-terms only, must be finite since each let-term t will have subsets of t as children proper; thus the size of the nodes in such a path strictly decreases.
2. all other nodes are not allowed to homeomorphically embed an ancestors (except for finished nodes, but these are all leaves).

5 Conclusion and Related Work

We have presented an algorithm for a supercompiler for a first-order functional language that maintains positive as well as negative information. The algorithm is guaranteed to terminate on all programs, it is strong enough to pass the so-called KMP-test.

In [22], Turchin briefly describes how the latest version of his supercompiler utilises *contraction* and *restriction* patterns in driving Refal graphs, the underlying representation of Refal programs. It seems that the resolution of clashes between assignments and contractions/restrictions can achieve propagation of negative information that — to some extent — provides the power equivalent to what has been presented in the present paper, but the exact relationship is at present unclear to us.

In the field of partial evaluation, Consel and Danvy [3] have described how negative information can be incorporated into a naïvely specialised matcher, thereby achieving effects similar to those described in the present paper. This, however, is achieved by a non-trivial rewrite of the subject program before partial evaluation is applied, thus rendering full automation difficult.

In the case of Generalised Partial Computation [5], Takano has presented a transformation technique [19] that exceeds the power of both Turchin's supercompiler and perfect supercompilation. This extra power, however, stems from an unspecified theorem prover that needs to be fed the properties about primitive functions in the language, axioms for the data structures employed in the program under consideration, etc. In [20] the theorem prover is replaced by a congruence closure algorithm [14], which allows for the automatic generation of a KMP-matcher from a naïvely specialised algorithm when some properties about list structures are provided. In comparison to supercompilation, Generalised Partial Computation as formulated by Takano has no concept of generalisation and will therefore terminate only for a small class of programs.

When one abandons simple functional languages (as treated in the present paper) and considers logic programming and constraint logic programming, several accounts exist of equivalent transformation power, *e.g.* [16, 8, 10, 11]. In these frameworks, search and/or constraint solving facilities of the logic language provides the necessary machinery to avoid redundant computations. In this field, great efforts have been made to produce optimal specialisation, and at the same time to ensure termination, see *e.g.* [12, 13].

Acknowledgements. Thanks to Robert Glück, Neil D. Jones, Laura Lafave and Michael Leuschel for discussions and comments. Thanks to Peter Sestoft for many insightful comments to [15].

References

[1] ACM. *Proceeding of the ACM SIGPLAN Syposium on Partial Evaluation and Semantics-Based Program Manipulation*, volume 26(9) of *ACM SIGPLAN Notices*, New York, September 1991. ACM Press.

[2] Hubert Comon and Pierre Lescanne. Equational problems and disunification. *Journal of Symbolic Computation*, 7(3–4):371–425, March–April 1989.

[3] Charles Consel and Olivier Danvy. Partial evaluation of pattern matching in strings. *Information Processing Letters*, 30(2):79–86, 1989.

[4] O. Danvy, R. Glück, and P. Thiemann, editors. *Partial Evaluation*, volume 1110 of *Lecture Notes in Computer Science*. Springer-Verlag, 1996.

[5] Y. Futamura and K. Nogi. Generalized partial computation. In D. Bjørner, A.P. Ershov, and N.D. Jones, editors, *Partial Evaluation and Mixed Computation*, pages 133–151, Amsterdam, 1988. North-Holland.

[6] R. Glück and A.V. Klimov. Occam's razor in metacomputation: the notion of a perfect process tree. In P. Cousot, M. Falaschi, G. Filè, and G. Rauzy, editors, *Workshop on Static Analysis*, volume 724 of *Lecture Notes in Computer Science*, pages 112–123. Springer-Verlag, 1993.

[7] R. Glück and M.H. Sørensen. A roadmap to metacomputation by supercompilation. In Danvy et al. [4], pages 137–160.

[8] T.J. Hickey and D. Smith. Toward the partial evaluation of CLP languages. In *PEPM'91* [1], pages 43–51.

[9] N.D. Jones, C.K. Gomard, and P. Sestoft. *Partial Evaluation and Automatic Program Generation*. Prentice-Hall, 1993.

[10] L. Lafave and J. P. Gallagher. Partial evaluation of functional logic programs in rewriting-based languages. Technical Report CSTR-97-001, Department of Computer Science, University of Bristol, March 1997.

[11] L. Lafave and J. P. Gallagher. Extending the power of automatic constraint-based partial evaluators. *ACM Computing Surveys*, 30(3es), September 1998. Article 15.

[12] Michael Leuschel and Danny De Schreye. Constrained partial deduction and the preservation of characteristic trees. *New Generation Computing*, 1997.

[13] Michael Leuschel, Bern Martens, and Danny De Schreye. Controlling generalization and polyvariance in partial deduction of normal logic programs. *ACM Transactions on Programming Languages and Systems*, 20(1):208–258, January 1998.

[14] Greg Nelson and Derek C. Oppen. Fast decision procedures based on congruence closure. *Journal of the ACM*, 27(2):356–364, April 1980.

[15] J. P. Secher. Perfect supercompilation. Technical Report 99/01, Department of Computer Science, University of Copenhagen, 1999.

[16] D. Smith. Partial evaluation of pattern matching in constraint logic programming. In *PEPM'91* [1], pages 62–71.

[17] M.H.B. Sørensen. Convergence of program transformers in the metric space of trees. In J. Jeuring, editor, *Mathematics of Program Construction*, volume 1422 of *Lecture Notes in Computer Science*, pages 315–337. Springer-Verlag, 1998.

[18] M. H. Srensen and R. Glück. Introduction to supercompilation. In *DIKU Summer school on Partial Evaluation*, Lecture Notes in Computer Science. Springer-Verlag, to appear.

[19] A. Takano. Generalized partial computation for a lazy functional language. In *PEPM'91* [1], pages 1–11.

[20] A. Takano. Generalized partial computation using disunification to solve constraints. In M. Rusinowitch and J.L. Remy, editors, *Conditional Term Rewriting Systems. Proceedings*, volume 656 of *Lecture Notes in Computer Science*, pages 424–428. Springer-Verlag, 1993.

[21] V.F. Turchin. The concept of a supercompiler. *ACM Transactions on Programming Languages and Systems*, 8(3):292–325, 1986.

[22] V.F. Turchin. Metacomputation: Metasystem transition plus Supercompilation. In Danvy et al. [4], pages 481–510.

[23] P.L. Wadler. Deforestation: Transforming programs to eliminate intermediate trees. *Theoretical Computer Science*, 73:231–248, 1990.

Linear Time Self-Interpretation of the Pure Lambda Calculus

Torben Æ. Mogensen

DIKU, University of Copenhagen, Denmark
Universitetsparken 1, DK-2100 Copenhagen O, Denmark
phone: (+45) 35321404, fax: (+45) 35321401
torbenm@diku.dk

Abstract. We show that linear time self-interpretation of the pure untyped lambda calculus is possible. The present paper shows this result for reduction to weak head normal form under call-by-name, call-by-value and call-by-need.
We use operational semantics to define each reduction strategy. For each of these we show a simulation lemma that states that each inference step in the evaluation of a term by the operational semantics is simulated by a sequence of steps in evaluation of the self-interpreter applied to the term.
By assigning costs to the inference rules in the operational semantics, we can compare the cost of normal evaluation and self-interpretation. Three different cost-measures are used: number of beta-reductions, cost of a substitution-based implementation and cost of an environment-based implementation.
For call-by-need we use a non-deterministic semantics, which simplifies the proof considerably.

1 Program and Data Representation

In order to talk about self-interpretation of the pure lambda calculus, we must consider how to represent programs as data.

We will use the representation defined (for closed terms) in [5]:

$$\begin{array}{ll}\lceil M \rceil & \equiv \lambda a.\lambda b.\overline{M} \\ \multicolumn{2}{l}{where} \\ \overline{x} & \equiv x \\ \overline{P\ Q} & \equiv a\ \overline{P}\ \overline{Q} \\ \overline{\lambda x.P} & \equiv b\ \lambda x.\overline{P}\end{array}$$

where M has been renamed so the variables a and b do not occur anywhere. $\equiv$ is alpha-equivalence. We get an exceedingly simple self-interpreter:

$$selfint \equiv \lambda m.m\ I\ I$$

where $I \equiv \lambda x.x$. It is trivial to prove that $selfint\ \lceil M \rceil \twoheadrightarrow M$.

D. Bjørner, M. Broy, A. Zamulin (Eds.): PSI'99, LNCS 1755, pp. 128–142, 2000.

2 Linear Time Self-Interpretation Using Call-by-Name Reduction

Call-by-name evaluation can be described by the inference rules:

$$\rho \vdash \lambda x.M \Rightarrow (\lambda x.M,\, \rho) \qquad \mathit{(LAMBDA)}$$

$$\frac{\rho' \vdash M \Rightarrow W}{\rho \vdash x \Rightarrow W} \;\text{ where } \rho(x) = (M, \rho') \qquad \mathit{(VAR)}$$

$$\frac{\rho \vdash M \Rightarrow (\lambda x.M',\, \rho') \qquad \rho'[x \mapsto (N, \rho)] \vdash M' \Rightarrow W}{\rho \vdash M\ N \Rightarrow W} \qquad \mathit{(BETA)}$$

We can define various cost measures by assigning costs to uses of the inference rules in an evaluation tree. For example, we can count beta reductions by letting each use of the *(BETA)* rule count 1 and not charge anything for the other rules. But we can also define more fine-grained (and more realistic) cost measures by assigning different costs.

For lack of space, we omit showing how the inference rules can be used to derive the initial stages of self-interpretation of a closed term M. These stages, however, define the relation between the environments used in normal evaluation and in self-interpretation:

$$\begin{array}{ll}
\overline{[]} & = \rho_2 \\
\overline{\rho[x \mapsto (S, \rho')]} & = \overline{\rho}[x \mapsto (\overline{S}, \overline{\rho'})] \\
\text{where} & \\
\rho_2 & = [a \mapsto (I, \rho_1),\, b \mapsto (I, \rho_1)] \\
\rho_1 & = [m \mapsto (\lceil M \rceil, [])]
\end{array}$$

The empty environment is denoted $[]$. The M referred to in ρ_1 is the entire term being interpreted. Note that $|\overline{\rho}| = |\rho| + 2$. We need a *simulation lemma:*

Lemma 1. *If we from the call-by-name inference rules can derive the evaluation* $\rho \vdash N \Rightarrow (\lambda y.W,\, \rho')$ *then we can also derive the evaluation* $\overline{\rho} \vdash \overline{N} \Rightarrow (\lambda y.\overline{W},\, \overline{\rho'})$.,

which we prove in figure 1. We use in this (and the following proofs) a notation where "..." refers to an unspecified proof tree. This is to indicate where an induction step is used: If normal evaluation has a proof tree indicated by "...", we replace this in the simulation by a proof tree that by induction is assumed to exist. This proof tree is in the simulation also indicated by "...". Semantic variables (place holders) in the conclusion of a rule where the premise is "...", can be considered existentially quantified, like variables in the premise of an inference rule typically are.

By assigning costs to the inference rules, we can count the costs for normal evaluation and self-interpretation and hence prove linear-time self-interpretation.

We prove lemma 1 by induction over the the evaluation tree with N at its root:
$N = x$: Let $\rho(x) = (S,\ \rho'')$:

Normal evaluation: $\dfrac{\dfrac{\cdots}{\rho''\vdash S \Rightarrow (\lambda y.W,\ \rho')}}{\rho\vdash x \Rightarrow (\lambda y.W,\ \rho')}$ Self-interpretation: $\dfrac{\dfrac{\cdots}{\overline{\rho''}\vdash \overline{S} \Rightarrow (\lambda y.\overline{W},\ \overline{\rho'})}}{\overline{\rho}\vdash x \Rightarrow (\lambda y.\overline{W},\ \overline{\rho'})}$

$N = \lambda y.W$: $\rho\vdash N \Rightarrow (\lambda y.W,\ \rho)$ is a leaf tree. $\overline{N} = b\ (\lambda y.\overline{W})$, so we get

$$\dfrac{\dfrac{\rho_1\vdash I\Rightarrow(I,\rho_1)}{\overline{\rho}\vdash b\Rightarrow(\lambda z.z,\rho_1)} \qquad \dfrac{\overline{\rho}\vdash \lambda y.\overline{W}\Rightarrow(\lambda y.\overline{W},\overline{\rho})}{\rho_1[z\mapsto(\lambda y.\overline{W},\overline{\rho})]\vdash z\Rightarrow(\lambda y.\overline{W},\overline{\rho})}}{\overline{\rho}\vdash b\ (\lambda y.\overline{W})\Rightarrow(\lambda y.\overline{W},\overline{\rho})}$$

$N = N_1\ N_2$: The normal evaluation tree is

$$\dfrac{\dfrac{\cdots}{\rho\vdash N_1\Rightarrow(\lambda v.N_3,\ \rho'')}\qquad \dfrac{\cdots}{\rho''[v\mapsto(N_2,\rho)]\vdash N_3\Rightarrow(\lambda y.W,\ \rho')}}{\rho\vdash N_1\ N_2\Rightarrow(\lambda y.W,\ \rho')}$$

We have $\overline{N} = a\ \overline{N_1}\ \overline{N_2}$, so we get (by induction) the following tree for self-interpretation

$$\dfrac{\dfrac{\dfrac{\rho_1\vdash I\Rightarrow(I,\rho_1)}{\overline{\rho}\vdash a\Rightarrow(\lambda z.z,\rho_1)}\quad\dfrac{\dfrac{\cdots}{\overline{\rho}\vdash\overline{N_1}\Rightarrow(\lambda v.\overline{N_3},\ \overline{\rho''})}}{\rho_1[z\mapsto(\overline{N_1},\ \overline{\rho})]\vdash z\Rightarrow(\lambda v.\overline{N_3},\ \overline{\rho''})}}{\overline{\rho}\vdash a\ \overline{N_1}\Rightarrow(\lambda v.\overline{N_3},\ \overline{\rho''})}\qquad\dfrac{\cdots}{\overline{\rho''}[v\mapsto(\overline{N_2},\ \overline{\rho})]\vdash\overline{N_3}\Rightarrow(\lambda y.\overline{W},\ \overline{\rho'})}}{\overline{\rho}\vdash a\ \overline{N_1}\ \overline{N_2}\Rightarrow(\lambda y.\overline{W},\ \overline{\rho'})}$$

Fig. 1. Proof of lemma 1 □

We start by counting beta reductions. For this, we let each use of the *(BETA)* rule count 1 and the other rules count 0.

The (not shown) tree for the initial stages of self-interpretation uses the beta rule three times, so this tree has cost 3. For the remainder of the computations we use this lemma:

Lemma 2. *If derivation of* $\rho\vdash N \Rightarrow (\lambda y.W,\ \rho')$ *uses* n *beta-reductions, then derivation of* $\overline{\rho}\vdash\overline{N} \Rightarrow (\lambda y.\overline{W},\ \overline{\rho'})$ *uses* $3n+1$ *beta-reductions.*

The proof is done by induction over the structure of the evaluation tree, using the proof of lemma 1 as skeleton.

$N = x$: Neither normal evaluation nor the self-interpretation uses the *(BETA)* rule, so the result follows by induction on the subtree.

$N = \lambda y.W$: The normal evaluation tree has cost 0 while self-interpretation uses the *(BETA)* rule once. Since $3\cdot 0+1 = 1$, we are done.

$N = N_1\ N_2$: Assuming the subtrees have costs k_1 and k_2 respectively, the total cost of normal evaluation is $k_1 + k_2 + 1$. By induction, the cost for the subtrees for self-interpretation are $3k_1+1$ and $3k_2+1$ and the tree uses *(BETA)* twice, so the total cost is $3k_1 + 3k_2 + 4 = 3(k_1 + k_2 + 1) + 1$, which is what we want. □

By adding the cost for the initial states of self-interpretation, we get:

Theorem 1. *If a closed term M via the call-by-name semantics evaluates to a weak head normal form (WHNF) using n beta reductions, then selfint $\lceil M \rceil$ evaluates to a WHNF using $3n + 4$ beta reductions.*

2.1 A More Realistic Cost Measure

Just counting beta reductions is a fairly crude way of measuring the cost of reduction of lambda terms. In this section and the next we will study measures that emulate common methods for implementing functional languages.

The first of these is (simplified) graph rewriting. In graph rewriting, a beta-reduction is implemented by making a new copy of the body of the function and inserting the argument in place of the variables. This has a cost which is proportional to the size of the function that is applied. Hence, we will use a cost measure that for each use of the *(BETA)* rule has a cost equal to the size of the function $(\lambda x.M')$ that is applied. The other rules still count 0, as the use of environments and closures in the inference rules do not directly correspond to actions in graph rewriting. Instead, we will treat each closure (P, ρ) as the term obtained by substituting the free variables in P by the values bound to them in ρ, after the same has been done recursively to these values. More formally, we define the function *unfold* by:

$$\begin{aligned} &\mathit{unfold}(P, []) &&= P \\ &\mathit{unfold}(P, \rho[x \mapsto (Q, \rho')]) &&= \mathit{unfold}(P, \rho)[x \backslash \mathit{unfold}(Q, \rho')] \end{aligned}$$

We need a small lemma

Lemma 3. $\mathrm{unfold}(\overline{P}, \overline{\rho}) = \overline{\mathrm{unfold}(P, \rho)}[a \backslash I][b \backslash I]$.

We prove this by induction over the definition of *unfold*:
$\mathit{unfold}(P, []) = P$:

$$\begin{aligned} &\mathit{unfold}(\overline{P}, \overline{[]}) \\ &= \mathit{unfold}(\overline{P}, \rho_3) \\ &= \mathit{unfold}(\overline{P}, \rho_2)[b \backslash \mathit{unfold}(I, \rho_1)] \\ &= \mathit{unfold}(\overline{P}, \rho_2)[b \backslash I] \\ &= \mathit{unfold}(\overline{P}[a \backslash \mathit{unfold}(I, \rho_1)], [])[b \backslash I] \\ &= \overline{P}[a \backslash I][b \backslash I] \end{aligned}$$

$\mathit{unfold}(P, \rho[x \mapsto (Q, \rho')]) = \mathit{unfold}(P, \rho)[x \backslash \mathit{unfold}(Q, \rho'')]$:

$$
\begin{aligned}
&\mathit{unfold}(\overline{P}, \overline{\rho[x \mapsto (Q, \rho')]}) \\
&= \mathit{unfold}(\overline{P}, \overline{\rho}[x \mapsto (\overline{Q}, \overline{\rho'})]) \\
&\qquad\qquad\qquad\qquad \text{by definition of } \overline{\rho} \\
&= \mathit{unfold}(\overline{P}, \overline{\rho})[x \backslash \mathit{unfold}(\overline{Q}, \overline{\rho'})] \\
&\qquad\qquad\qquad\qquad \text{by definition of } \mathit{unfold} \\
&= \overline{\mathit{unfold}(P, \rho)}[a \backslash I][b \backslash I][x \backslash \overline{\mathit{unfold}(Q, rho')}[a \backslash I][b \backslash I]] \\
&\qquad\qquad\qquad\qquad \text{by induction} \\
&= \overline{\mathit{unfold}(P, \rho)}[x \backslash \overline{\mathit{unfold}(Q, rho')}][a \backslash I][b \backslash I] \\
&= \overline{\mathit{unfold}(P, \rho)[x \backslash \mathit{unfold}(Q, rho')]}[a \backslash I][b \backslash I]
\end{aligned}
$$

□

We count the size of a term as the number of nodes in the syntax tree, i.e. one for each variable occurrence plus one for each application and one for each abstraction. It is easy to see that the size of $\overline{P}[a \backslash I][b \backslash I]$ is strictly less than 4 times the size of P.

We first count the cost of the initial part of the tree to be $|selfint| = 8$ for the first beta reduction, $|\lceil M \rceil| < 3|M|$ for the second and the size of $\lambda b.\overline{M}$ with a replaced by I ($< 4|M|$) for the third, for a total cost less than $7|M| + 8$.

We now proceed with the lemma

Lemma 4. *If derivation of* $\rho \vdash N \Rightarrow (\lambda y.W,\ \rho')$ *has cost* c*, then derivation of* $\overline{\rho} \vdash \overline{N} \Rightarrow (\lambda y.\overline{W},\ \overline{\rho'})$ *has cost at most* $4c + 2$.

Again we prove this by induction following the structure of the proof for lemma 1.

$N = x$: Neither normal evaluation nor the self-interpretation uses the *(BETA)* rule, so the result follows by induction on the subtrees.

$N = \lambda y.W$: The normal evaluation tree has cost 0 while self-interpretation uses the *(BETA)* rule once. The applied function is $\lambda z.z$ which has size 2, so we have what we need.

$N = N_1\ N_2$: Assuming the subtrees have costs k_1 and k_2 respectively, the total cost of normal evaluation is $k_1 + k_2 + s$, where s is the size of $\mathit{unfold}(\lambda v.N_3,\ \rho'')$. By induction, the cost for the subtrees for self-interpretation are at most $4k_1 + 2$ and $4k_2 + 2$. The tree uses *(BETA)* twice, once for the function $\lambda z.z$ (size 2) and once for $\mathit{unfold}(\lambda v.\overline{N_3},\ \overline{\rho''}) = \lambda v.\overline{\mathit{unfold}(N_3,\ \rho'')}[a \backslash I][b \backslash I]$.

Since the size of $\overline{\mathit{unfold}(N_3,\ \rho'')}[a \backslash I][b \backslash I]$ is strictly less than 4 times the size of $\mathit{unfold}(N_3,\ \rho'')$, we have that the size of $\lambda v.\overline{\mathit{unfold}(N_3,\ \rho'')}[a \backslash I][b \backslash I]$ is at most $4|\mathit{unfold}(N_3,\ \rho'')| - 1 + 1 = 4(s-1)$. Hence, we have a total cost bounded by $4k_1 + 2 + 4k_2 + 2 + 2 + 4(s-1) \leq 4(k_1 + k_2 + s) + 2$, which is what we needed.

□

By combining lemma 4 with the start-up cost of $7|M| + 8$, we get the theorem

Theorem 2. *If a closed term* M *via the call-by-name semantics evaluates to a WHNF in cost* c*, selfint* $\lceil M \rceil$ *evaluates to a WHNF in cost at most* $4c + 7|M| + 10$.

The start-up cost proportional to the size of M is unavoidable, regardless of how lambda terms are represented and how the self-interpreter works. We required representations to be in normal form, so to perform any evaluation that depends on the representation, we will have to apply the representation to one or more arguments, which by our measure has a cost proportional to the size of the representation, which can not be less than linear in the size of the term.

2.2 Environment-Based Cost

Another common method for implementing call-by-name lambda calculus is using environments and closures, much as indicated by the inference rules. The cost measure used for an environment-based implementation depends on how the environments are implemented. Typical data structures for environments are linked lists and frames.

Using a linked list, a new variable is added to the front of the list at unit cost, but accessing a variable equires a walk down the linked list and hence has a cost that depends on the position of the variable in the environment. With the chosen interpreter, we can not get linear time self-interpretation if linked-list environments are used, as looking up the two specail variables a and b has a cost that depends on the size of the environment, which again depends on the size of the program.

If frames are used, a new extended copy of the environment is built every time a new variable is added to it. This has cost proportional to the size of the built environment, but accessing a variable in the environment is now using aconstant offset from the base of the frame, which is unit cost. We shall see below that we can get linear time self-interpretation when frames are used to represent environments.

Our cost measure now counts each use of the *(VAR)* or *(LAMBDA)* rule as 1 and each use of the *(BETA)* rule as the size of the new frame, i.e. $|\rho'| + 1$.

We first note that the cost of the initial part of the evaluation tree is 8. We then state and prove the following lemma:

Lemma 5. *If derivation of* $\rho \vdash N \Rightarrow (\lambda y.W, \rho')$ *has cost* c*, then derivation of* $\overline{\rho} \vdash \overline{N} \Rightarrow (\lambda y.\overline{W}, \overline{\rho'})$ *has cost at most* $8c$.

$N = x$: Both normal evaluation and self-interpretation use the *(VAR)* rule once, so if the cost of evaluating the contents of the variable is k, the total evaluation cost is $k+1$. By induction, self-interpretation of the contents costs at most $8k$, for a total self-interpretation cost of $8k+1$, which is less than the $8(k+1)$ limit.

$N = \lambda y.W$: The normal evaluation tree has cost 1, for a single use of the *(VAR)* rule. Self-interpretation uses *(VAR)* and *(LAMBDA)* twice each and the *(BETA)* rule once. The size of the expanded environment is 2, so we have a total cost of 6, which is less than 8 times the cost of normal evaluation.

$N = N_1\ N_2$: Assuming the subtrees have costs k_1 and k_2 respectively, the total cost of normal evaluation is $k_1 + k_2 + |\rho''| + 1$. By induction, the cost for the subtrees for self-interpretation are at most $8k_1$ and $8k_2$. The tree uses *(VAR)* twice, *(LAMBDA)* once and *(BETA)* twice, once for the function $\lambda z.z$ (where the size of the expanded environment is 2) and once for $(\lambda v.\overline{N_3},\, \overline{\rho''})$. Since $|\overline{\rho''}| = |\rho''| + 2$, the total cost is bounded by $8k_1 + 8k_2 + 2 + 1 + 2 + |\rho''| + 3 = 8k_1 + 8k_2 + |\rho''| + 8$, which is less than the budget of $8(k_1 + k_2 + |\rho''| + 1)$.

□

By adding the start-up cost of 8 to the cost found in lemma 5, we get:

Theorem 3. *If a closed term M evaluates to a WHNF in cost c (using the environment-based cost function), selfint $\lceil M \rceil$ evaluates to a WHNF in cost at most $8c + 8$.*

3 Linear Time Self-Interpretation Using Call-by-Value Reduction

We define call-by-value reduction by the inference rules

$$\rho \vdash \lambda x.M \Rightarrow (\lambda x.M,\, \rho) \quad (LAMBDA) \qquad\qquad \rho \vdash x \Rightarrow \rho(x) \quad (VARV)$$

$$\frac{\rho \vdash M \Rightarrow (\lambda x.M',\, \rho') \quad \rho \vdash N \Rightarrow V \quad \rho'[x \mapsto V] \vdash M' \Rightarrow W}{\rho \vdash M\ N \Rightarrow W} \quad (BETAV)$$

We again omit the derivation of the initial stages of self-interpretation. We will slightly change definition of $\overline{\rho}$ to reflect that variables are bound to values, *i.e.*, (closures of) terms in WHNF:

$$\begin{aligned} \overline{[]} &= \rho_3 \\ \overline{\rho[x \mapsto (\lambda x.P, \rho')]} &= \overline{\rho}[x \mapsto (\lambda x.\overline{P}, \overline{\rho'})] \end{aligned}$$

We first define a simulation lemma for call-by-value:

Lemma 6. *If we, using the call-by-value inference rules, can derive $\rho \vdash N \Rightarrow (\lambda y.W,\, \rho')$ then we can also derive $\overline{\rho} \vdash \overline{N} \Rightarrow (\lambda y.\overline{W},\, \overline{\rho'})$.*

which we prove in figure 2.

Again, we assign different costs to the rules to obtain linear-time self-interpretation results. We start by counting beta-reductions.

The initial part of the tree uses 3 beta reductions. For the remainder we use a lemma like the one for call-by-name:

Lemma 7. *If call-by-value derivation of $\rho \vdash N \Rightarrow (\lambda y.W,\, \rho')$ uses n beta-reductions, then call-by-value derivation of $\overline{\rho} \vdash \overline{N} \Rightarrow (\lambda y.\overline{W},\, \overline{\rho'})$ uses at most $4n + 1$ beta-reductions.*

We prove lemma 6 by induction over the evaluation tree with N at its root:
$N = x$:

Normal evaluation: $\rho \vdash x \Rightarrow (\lambda y.W,\ \rho')$ Self-interpretation: $\overline{\rho} \vdash x \Rightarrow (\lambda y.\overline{W},\ \overline{\rho'})$

$N = \lambda y.W$: $\rho \vdash N \Rightarrow (\lambda y.W,\ \rho)$ is a leaf tree. $\overline{N} = b\ (\lambda y.\overline{W})$, so we get

$$\frac{\overline{\rho} \vdash b \Rightarrow (\lambda z.z, \rho_1) \quad \rho_1[z \mapsto (\lambda y.\overline{W}, \overline{\rho})] \vdash z \Rightarrow (\lambda y.\overline{W}, \overline{\rho})}{\overline{\rho} \vdash b\ (\lambda y.\overline{W}) \Rightarrow (\lambda y.\overline{W}, \overline{\rho})}$$

$N = N_1\ N_2$: The normal evaluation tree is

$$\frac{\dfrac{\cdots}{\rho \vdash N_1 \Rightarrow (\lambda v.N_3, \rho'')} \quad \dfrac{\cdots}{\rho \vdash N_2 \Rightarrow (\lambda w.N_4, \rho''')} \quad \dfrac{\cdots}{\rho''[v \mapsto (\lambda w.N_4, \rho''')] \vdash N_3 \Rightarrow (\lambda y.W, \rho')}}{\rho \vdash N_1\ N_2 \Rightarrow (\lambda y.W, \rho')}$$

We have $\overline{N} = a\ \overline{N_1}\ \overline{N_2}$, so we get (by induction) the following tree for self-interpretation

$$\frac{(*) \quad \dfrac{\cdots}{\overline{\rho} \vdash \overline{N_2} \Rightarrow (\lambda w.\overline{N_4},\ \overline{\rho'''})} \quad \dfrac{\cdots}{\overline{\rho''}[v \mapsto (\lambda w.\overline{N_4},\ \overline{\rho'''})] \vdash \overline{N_3} \Rightarrow (\lambda y.\overline{W},\ \overline{\rho'})}}{\overline{\rho} \vdash a\ \overline{N_1}\ \overline{N_2} \Rightarrow (\lambda y.\overline{W},\ \overline{\rho'})}$$

where $(*)$ is the tree

$$\frac{\overline{\rho} \vdash a \Rightarrow (\lambda z.z, \rho_1) \quad \dfrac{\cdots}{\overline{\rho} \vdash \overline{N_1} \Rightarrow (\lambda v.\overline{N_3},\ \overline{\rho''})} \quad \rho_1[z \mapsto (\lambda v.\overline{N_3},\ \overline{\rho''})] \vdash z \Rightarrow (\lambda v.\overline{N_3},\ \overline{\rho''})}{\overline{\rho} \vdash a\ \overline{N_1} \Rightarrow (\lambda v.\overline{N_3},\ \overline{\rho''})}$$

□

Fig. 2. Proof of lemma 6

We will use the structure of lemma 6 for proving this.

$N = x$: Neither normal evaluation nor self-interpretation use beta reductions.

$N = \lambda y.W$: The normal evaluation tree uses 0 reductions while self-interpretation uses the *(BETA)* rule once, giving $4 \cdot 0 + 1$, as we needed.

$N = N_1\ N_2$: Assuming the subtrees use k_1, k_2 and k_3 beta reductions respectively, the total number of reductions in normal evaluation is $k_1 + k_2 + k_3 + 1$. By induction, the the subtrees for self-interpretation use at most $4k_1 + 1$, $4k_2 + 1$ and $4k_3 + 1$ reductions. The tree uses *(BETA)* twice, so the total reduction count is bounded by $4k_1 + 4k_2 + 4k_3 + 5 = 4(k_1 + k_2 + k_3 + 1) + 1$, which is what we want.

□

By adding the cost for the initial states of self-interpretation, we get:

Theorem 4. *If a closed term M evaluates to a WHNF using n call-by-value beta reductions, selfint $\lceil M \rceil$ evaluates to a WHNF using at most $4n + 4$ call-by-value beta reductions.*

3.1 Substitution-Based Cost

Again we want to base the cost of a beta reduction on the size of the function, and again we consider a value $(\lambda y.P, \rho)$ to represent the term *unfold*$(\lambda y.P, \rho)$.

We need a variant of lemma 3, using the new definition of $\overline{\rho}$. We do not get equality, as we did in lemma 3, as some terms T may be replaced by $(I\ T)$. We define $P \preceq Q$ to mean that some subterms T in P may be replaced by $(I\ T)$ in Q and use this in the definition of the new lemma. Note that size of P is no larger than the size of Q.

Lemma 8. $\text{unfold}(\lambda y.\overline{P}, \overline{\rho}) \preceq \lambda y.\overline{\text{unfold}(P, \rho)}[a\backslash I][b\backslash I]$,

where $P \preceq Q$ means that some subterms T in P may be replaced by $(I\ T)$ in Q. Hence, the size of P is no larger than the size of Q. We prove lemma 8 similarly to the way we proved lemma 3:

$\mathit{unfold}(\lambda y.P, []) = \lambda y.P$:

$$\begin{aligned}
&\mathit{unfold}(\lambda y.\overline{P}, \overline{[]})\\
&= \mathit{unfold}(\lambda y.\overline{P}, \rho_3)\\
&= \mathit{unfold}(\lambda y.\overline{P}, \rho_2)[b\backslash \mathit{unfold}(I, \rho_1)]\\
&= \mathit{unfold}(\lambda y.\overline{P}, \rho_2)[b\backslash I]\\
&= \mathit{unfold}(\lambda y.\overline{P}[a\backslash \mathit{unfold}(I, \rho_1)], [])[b\backslash I]\\
&= \lambda y.\overline{P}[a\backslash I][b\backslash I]
\end{aligned}$$

$\mathit{unfold}(\lambda y.P, \rho[x \mapsto (\lambda z.Q, \rho')]) = \mathit{unfold}(\lambda y.P, \rho)[x\backslash \mathit{unfold}(\lambda z.Q, \rho'')]$:

$$\begin{aligned}
&\mathit{unfold}(\lambda y.\overline{P}, \overline{\rho[x \mapsto (\lambda z.Q, \rho')]})\\
&= \mathit{unfold}(\lambda y.\overline{P}, \overline{\rho}[x \mapsto (\lambda z.\overline{Q}, \overline{\rho'})])\\
&\qquad\qquad\qquad\qquad \text{by definition of } \overline{\rho}\\
&= \mathit{unfold}(\lambda y.\overline{P}, \overline{\rho})[x\backslash \mathit{unfold}(\lambda z.\overline{Q}, \overline{\rho'})]\\
&\qquad\qquad\qquad\qquad \text{by definition of } \mathit{unfold}\\
&\preceq \lambda y.\overline{\mathit{unfold}(P, \rho)}[a\backslash I][b\backslash I][x\backslash \lambda z.\overline{\mathit{unfold}(Q, rho')}[a\backslash I][b\backslash I]]\\
&\qquad\qquad\qquad\qquad \text{by induction}\\
&= \lambda y.\overline{\mathit{unfold}(P, \rho)}[x\backslash \lambda z.\overline{\mathit{unfold}(Q, rho')]}[a\backslash I][b\backslash I]\\
&\preceq \lambda y.\overline{\mathit{unfold}(P, \rho)[x\backslash \mathit{unfold}(\lambda y.Q, rho')]}[a\backslash I][b\backslash I]
\end{aligned}$$

Since the size of $\overline{P}[a\backslash I][b\backslash I]$ is strictly less than 4 times the size of P, we see that $|\mathit{unfold}(\lambda y.\overline{P}, \overline{\rho})| \leq$
$|\lambda y.\overline{\mathit{unfold}(P, \rho)}[a\backslash I][b\backslash I]| < 1 + 4|\mathit{unfold}(P, \rho)|$.

□

We count the cost of the initial part of the tree to be at most $7|M| + 8$, just as for the call-by-name case. For the rest, we use the lemma

Lemma 9. *If call-by-value derivation of* $\rho \vdash N \Rightarrow (\lambda y.W,\ \rho')$ *has cost* c*, then call-by-value derivation of* $\overline{\rho} \vdash \overline{N} \Rightarrow (\lambda y.\overline{W},\ \overline{\rho'})$ *has cost at most* $5c + 2$.

Proof:

$N = x$: Both normal evaluation and self-interpretation has cost 0.

$N = \lambda y.W$: The normal evaluation tree has cost 0 while self-interpretation uses the *(BETA)* rule once for the term $\lambda z.z$, which has size 2, giving $5 \cdot 0 + 2$, as we needed.

$N = N_1\ N_2$: Assuming the subtrees have costs k_1, k_2 and k_3 respectively, the total cost of normal evaluation is $k_1 + k_2 + k_3 + s$, where s is the size of $\mathit{unfold}(\lambda v.N_3, \rho'')$. By induction, the cost for the subtrees for self-interpretation are at most $5k_1 + 2$, $5k_2 + 2$ and $5k_3 + 2$. The tree uses *(BETA)* twice, once for $\lambda z.z$, which has size 2 and once for $\mathit{unfold}(\lambda v.\overline{N_3}, \overline{\rho''})$, which is of size at most $4(s-1)$, so the total cost is bounded by $5k_1 + 5k_2 + 5k_3 + 8 + 4(s-1) \leq 5(k_1 + k_2 + k_3 + s) + 4 - s$. Since the smallest possible value for s is 2, we have what we want.

Combined with the initial cost of $7|M| + 8$, we get

Theorem 5. *If a closed term M evaluates by call-by-value to a WHNF in cost c, selfint $\lceil M \rceil$ evaluates by call-by-value to a WHNF in cost at most* $5c+7|M|+10$.

3.2 Environment-Based Cost

The environment-based cost measure is the same as for call-by-name. The cost of the initial section of the tree is 9. For the rest, the lemma

Lemma 10. *If call-by-value derivation of $\rho \vdash N \Rightarrow (\lambda y.W,\ \rho')$ has cost c, then call-by-value derivation of $\overline{\rho} \vdash \overline{N} \Rightarrow (\lambda y.\overline{W},\ \overline{\rho'})$ has cost at most $7c$.*

is used. We prove this as before

$N = x$: Both normal evaluation and self-interpretation has cost 1.

$N = \lambda y.W$: The normal evaluation tree has cost 1 while self-interpretation uses *(VAR)* twice and the *(BETA)* rule once for the term $\lambda z.z$, where the expanded environment is of size 2, giving a total cost of 4. This is well below the limit.

$N = N_1\ N_2$: Assuming the subtrees have costs k_1, k_2 and k_3 respectively, the total cost of normal evaluation is $k_1 + k_2 + k_3 + |\rho''| + 1$. By induction, the cost for the subtrees for self-interpretation are at most $7k_1$, $7k_2$ and $7k_3$. The tree uses *(VAR)* and *(BETA)* twice each, the latter once for $\lambda z.z$ (cost 2) and once for $(\lambda v.\overline{N_3}, \overline{\rho''})$, which has cost $|\overline{\rho''}| + 1 = |\rho''| + 3$, so the total cost is bounded by $7k_1 + 7k_2 + 7k_3 + |\rho''| + 7 \leq 7(k_1 + k_2 + k_3 + |\rho''| + 1)$, which is what we want.

Combined with the initial cost of 9, we get

Theorem 6. *If a closed term M evaluates by call-by-value to a WHNF in cost c (using environment-based cost), selfint $\lceil M \rceil$ evaluates by call-by-value to a WHNF in cost at most $7c + 9$.*

4 Call-by-Need Reduction

Describing call-by-need reduction by a set of inference rules is not as easy as for call-by-name or call-by-value. Typically, a store is threaded through the evaluation and used for updating closures. This is, however, rather complex, so we use a different approach: We make the semantics nondeterministic by adding an alternative application rule to the call-by-value semantics:

$$\frac{\rho \vdash M \Rightarrow (\lambda x.M',\, \rho') \quad \rho'[x \mapsto \bullet] \vdash M' \Rightarrow W}{\rho \vdash M\ N \Rightarrow W} \quad \textit{(DUMMY)}$$

The *(BETAV)* rule from teh call-by-value semantics evaluates the argument, the *(DUMMY)* rule doesn't but inserts a dummy value • in the environment instead of the value of the argument. There is no rule that allows • in computations, so choosing the latter application rule will only lead to an answer if the value is not needed.

These rules model both call-by-need, call-by-value and everything in-between. We can define a partial order on inference trees for the same expression by saying that a tree T_1 is less than a tree T_2 if T_2 uses the *(BETAV)* rule whenever T_1 does. The least tree in this ordering that computes a non-• result corresponds to call-by-need reduction to WHNF. Hence, we have moved parts of the operational behaviour of the language to the meta-level of the semantic rules, rather than in the rules themselves.

This characterization of call-by-need may not seem very operational. However, a process that builds a mininal evaluation tree may mimic traditional implementations of call-by-need: When an application is evaluated, the *(DUMMY)* rules is first used. If it later turns out that the argument is in fact needed (when a use of a • is attempted), the origin of the • is traced back to the offending *(DUMMY)* rule. This is then forcibly overwritten with a *(BETAV)* rule and the sub-tree for the argument constructed. When this is done, the • is replaced by the correct value and computation resumed at the place it was aborted. Hence, •'s play the rôle of suspensions and the replacement of a *(DUMMY)* rule by a *(BETAV)* rule corresponds to updating the suspension.

The initial part of self-interpretation for call-by-need is the same as for the call-by-value case, except that for simple terms, the variables a or b may not be needed and can hence be bound to • and the corresponding evaluations of their closures not occur. However, the cost of the initial portion will (by any reasonable cost measure) be no more than the cost of the call-by-value tree. We will use the same initial environments as for the call-by-value case, but extend the definition of $\overline{\rho}$ to handle variables that are bound to •.

$$\begin{aligned}
\overline{[]} &= \rho_3 \\
\overline{\rho[x \mapsto (\lambda x.P, \rho')]} &= \overline{\rho}[x \mapsto (\lambda x.\overline{P}, \overline{\rho'})] \\
\overline{\rho[x \mapsto \bullet]} &= \overline{\rho}[x \mapsto \bullet]
\end{aligned}$$

Like in the previous cases, we define a call-by-need simulation lemma:

Lemma 11. *If we using the call-by-need inference rules can derive* $\rho \vdash N \Rightarrow (\lambda y.W,\, \rho')$ *then we can also derive* $\overline{\rho} \vdash \overline{N} \Rightarrow (\lambda y.\overline{W},\, \overline{\rho'})$.

Which we prove in figure 3.

Since lemma 11 includes the cases where variables in the environment are bound to •, we conclude that, if normal evaluation does not need the value of a variable, then neither does the self-interpreter.

We prove lemma 11 by induction over the evaluation tree with N at its root. Only the case for the *(DUMMY)* rule differs from the proof of lemma 6, so we omit the rest.

$N = N_1\ N_2$: Using the *(DUMMY)* rule, the normal evaluation tree is

$$\frac{\dfrac{\cdots}{\rho \vdash N_1 \Rightarrow (\lambda v.N_3, \rho'')} \quad \dfrac{\cdots}{\rho''[v \mapsto \bullet] \vdash N_3 \Rightarrow (\lambda y.W, \rho')}}{\rho \vdash N_1\ N_2 \Rightarrow (\lambda y.W, \rho')}$$

Which (by induction) leads us to the following self-interpretation tree

$$\frac{(*) \quad \dfrac{\cdots}{\overline{\rho''}[v \mapsto \bullet] \vdash \overline{N_3} \Rightarrow (\lambda y.\overline{W}, \overline{\rho'})}}{\overline{\rho} \vdash a\ \overline{N_1}\ \overline{N_2} \Rightarrow (\lambda y.\overline{W}, \overline{\rho'})}$$

where $(*)$ is the tree

$$\frac{\overline{\rho} \vdash a \Rightarrow (\lambda z.z, \rho_1) \quad \dfrac{\cdots}{\overline{\rho} \vdash \overline{N_1} \Rightarrow (\lambda v.\overline{N_3}, \overline{\rho''})} \quad \rho_1[z \mapsto (\lambda v.\overline{N_3}, \overline{\rho''})] \vdash z \Rightarrow (\lambda v.\overline{N_3}, \overline{\rho''})}{\overline{\rho} \vdash a\ \overline{N_1} \Rightarrow (\lambda v.\overline{N_3}, \overline{\rho''})}$$

□

Fig. 3. Proof of lemma 11

We will in the proofs of linear-time self-interpretation also refer to the proofs for the call-by-value case except for the *(DUMMY)* case, as we use the same cost measures and the same constant factors.

We start by counting beta reductions. Our theorem is

Theorem 7. *If a closed term M via the call-by-need semantics evaluates to a WHNF using n call-by-need beta reductions, selfint $\lceil M \rceil$ evaluates to a WHNF using at most $4n + 4$ call-by-need beta reductions.*

The corresponding lemma proves simulation using $4n + 1$ steps, after the initial portion. We use the proof for lemma 7 with the addition of a case for the *(DUMMY)* rule: Normal evaluation uses $k_1 + k_3 + 1$ beta reductions, where k_1 and k_3 are the numbers of beta reductions required for N_1 and N_3. By induction, interpreting $\overline{N_1}$ and $\overline{N_3}$ costs at most $4k_1 + 1$ and $4k_2 + 1$. Additionally, 2 beta reductions are used, so the total cost is bounded by $4(k_1 + k_2 + 1)$, which is one less than our limit.

We can now go on to substitution-based cost. We assign the same cost to the *(DUMMY)* rule as to the *(BETAV)* rule: The size of the extended environment.

We extend the definition of *unfold* to handle $\bullet$:

$$\mathit{unfold}(P, \rho[x \mapsto \bullet]) \quad = \quad \mathit{unfold}(P, \rho)[x \backslash d]$$

where d is a free variable that does not occur anywhere else. It is easy to see that the same size limit as before applies: $|\mathit{unfold}(\lambda y.\overline{P}, \overline{\rho})| \leq 4|\mathit{unfold}(P, \rho)|$. Hence, we shall go directly to the theorem

Theorem 8. *If a closed term M evaluates by call-by-need to a WHNF in cost c, selfint $\lceil M \rceil$ evaluates by call-by-need to a WHNF in cost at most $5c + 7|M| + 10$.*

Again, we only state the case for the *(DUMMY)* rule and refer to lemma 9 for the rest: If normal evaluation has cost k_1 and k_3 for evaluation of N_1 and N_3, the total cost is k_1+k_2+s, where s is the size of $unfold(\lambda v.N_3, \rho'')$. For self-interpretation, interpretation of $\overline{N_1}$ and $\overline{N_3}$ have by induction costs bounded by $5k_1+2$ and $5k_3+2$. Additionally, we use *(BETAV)* once at cost 2 and *(DUMMY)* once at cost $|unfold(\lambda v.\overline{N_3}, \overline{\rho''})| \leq 4|unfold(N_3, \rho'')| = 4(s-1)$. This gives a total cost bounded by $5(k_1+k_2+s)-s+2$, which is well within our limit.

Environment-based cost is no bigger problem:

Theorem 9. *If a closed term M evaluates by call-by-need to a WHNF in cost c (using environment-based cost), selfint $\lceil M \rceil$ evaluates by call-by-need to a WHNF in cost at most $7c+9$.*

Again, we refer to the proof for the call-by-value case except for an additional case for the proof of lemma 10 to handle the *(DUMMY)* rule:

Normal evaluation uses the *(DUMMY)* rule at cost $|\rho''|+1$ plus the costs of evaluating N_1 and N_3, which we set at k_1 and k_2. Self-interpretation uses at most $7k_1$ and $7k_3$ to interpret $\overline{N_1}$ and $\overline{N_3}$. To this we add two uses of *(VARV)*, one use of *(BETAV)* at cost 2 and the use of *(DUMMY)* at cost $|\overline{\rho''}|+1 = |\rho''|+3$. This adds up to $7(k_1+k_3+|\rho''|+1)-6|\rho''|$, which is within our budget.

5 Conclusion and Future Work

We have proven that a simple self-interpreter for the pure lambda calculus can do self-interpretation in linear time, *i.e.* constant overhead. We proved this for reduction to weak head normal form using call-by-name, call-by-value and call-by-need using three different cost measures.

It would be interesting to extend the present work to include studies of self-interpretation cost for reduction to head normal form and full normal form. The author expects these to have linear-time self-interpretation too, but is not currently working on proving this.

Apart from being interesting in its own right, the result is a step towards proving the existence of a linear-time complexity hierarchy for the pure lambda calculus, along the lines of Jones' result for first-order functional and imperative languages [2]. The proof involves a self-interpreter that not only has constant overhead but also counts the amount of time (by some cost measure) it uses. If it can not finish within a set budget of time, the self-interpreter stops with a special error-value. This self-interpreter is then used in a diagonalization proof reminiscent of the classical halting-problem proof to show that a certain problem can be solved in time $o(kn)$ but not in time $o(n)$, where k is the interpretation overhead.

We are currently working on this and have sketched a proof for call-by-name reduction to WHNF. However, due to the resource counting the proof is about an order of magnitude harder than the proofs shown in this paper, so we are investigating ways to simplify the proofs.

This study has some relation to the work by Rose [7] on showing that there exist a linear-time hierarchy for CAM, an abstract machine used for implementing higher-order functional languages. This was proven by showing linear-time interpretations between CAM and the language used in Jones' paper. This method does not carry over to the lambda calculus, as such interpretations are not likely to exist, at least not for natural complexity measures for reduction in the lambda calculus.

Rose [6] goes on to attempt to characterize neccesary conditions for the existence of a linear-time hierarchy. It is stated that for a language to support a linear-time hierarchy, it may not allow constant-time access to a non-constant number of variables, locations, symbols or functions, where the constant is uniform over all programs. This would indicate that any cost measure for the lambda calculus that allow constant time access to variables (e.g. counting beta-reductions) contradics the existence of a linear-time hierarchy. However, the proof sketch mentioned above indicates that one such actually does exist. We will look further into this apparent contradiction in future work.

In [4], a different representation of lambda terms was used. It was based on higher-order abstract syntax, but used a standard-style representation where recursion over the syntax is not encoded in the term itself. Hence, the self-interpreter needed to use an explicitly coded fixed-point combinator, making it somewhat more complex than the one used in this paper. Redoing the proofs in this paper for that self-interpreter will be much more work duc to the larger size, but the same principles should apply and we expect a (much larger) constant overhead for this case as well.

The use of a nondeterministic operational semantics to encode call-by-need reduction made the proofs for this very simple. In our knowledge, this technique hasn't been used earlier, though a similar notion (repacing a term by $\bullet$) has been used to define neededness [1]. We expect it to be useful for proving other properties about call-by-need reduction.

Our discussion of different cost measures may seem similar to the discussions by *e.g.* Lawall and Mairson [3] on cost models for the lambda calculus. However, these models are meant to be independent of any particular implementation whereas the measures presented here try to mimic specific implementation methods.

References

[1] I. Durand and A. Middeldorp. Decidable call by need computations in term rewriting. In *CADE '97, Lecture Notes in Artificial Intelligence 1249*, pages 4–18. Springer-Verlag, 1997.

[2] N. D. Jones. Constant time factors *do* matter. In Steven Homer, editor, *STOC '93. Symposium on Theory of Computing*, pages 602–611. ACM Press, 1993.

[3] J. L. Lawall and H. G. Mairson. Optimality and inefficiency: What isn't a cost model of the lambda calculus. In R. Kent Dybvig, editor, *Proceedings of ICFP '95*, pages 92–101. ACM, ACM Press, 1996.

[4] T. Æ. Mogensen. Efficient self-interpretation in lambda calculus. *Functional Programming*, 2(3):345–364, July 1992.

[5] T. Æ. Mogensen. Self-applicable online partial evaluation of the pure lambda calculus. In William L. Scherlis, editor, *Proceedings of PEPM '95*, pages 39–44. ACM, ACM Press, 1995.

[6] Eva Rose. Characterizing computation models with a constant factor time hierachy. In B. Kapron, editor, *DIMACS Workshop On Computational Complexity and Programming Languages*, New Jersey, USA, July 1996. DIMACS, RUTCOR, Rutgers University.

[7] Eva Rose. Linear time hierachies for a functional language machine model. In Hanne Riis Nielson, editor, *Programming Languages and Systems – ESOP'96*, volume 1058 of *LNCS*, pages 311–325, Linköping, Sweden, Apr 1996. Linköping University, Springer-Verlag.

An Optimal Algorithm for Purging Regular Schemes

Denis L. Uvarov

A. P. Ershov Insitute of Informatics Systems,
Lavrent'ev pr., 6,
Novosibirsk, Russia
duvarov@hotmail.com

1 Regular Schemes

In the following, we assume that sets of *variables*, *basic statements*, and *selectors* are given. Let us choose subsets of arguments $A(s)$, results $R(s)$, and obligatory results $R'(s) \subseteq R(s)$ in the set of variables for each basic statement s. For each selector c, we choose the set of its arguments $A(c)$. The sets of results and obligatory results for selectors are considered to be empty. In addition, an *arity* $ar(c) \in \mathbf{N}$ is assigned to each selector c.

Regular schemes (hereafter, *schemes*) are directed ordered labeled graphs of a special kind. The set of schemes can be inductively described as follows.

1. The graph with the empty set of nodes and arcs is a scheme: this is an *empty scheme*. For any nonempty scheme S, we will indicate two distinguished nodes — the *input* and the *output*.

2. A graph without arcs with the single node v labeled by a basic statement s is a scheme: this scheme *corresponds* to the basic statement s and has node v as its input and output.

3. Let S_1 and S_2 be nonempty schemes. Connect the output of S_1 with the input of S_2 by a new arc. Let the input of S_1 be the input of graph S constructed in this way, and the output of S_2 be its output. Extend the order of S by the relation of the new arc with itself. Then, the graph S is a scheme: we will say that S is obtained from S_1 and S_2 by the *series union* and write it as $S = S_1 \circ S_2$.

4. Let B be a scheme, c be a selector, and $ar(c) = 2$. Consider two new nodes v and w — the input and the output of a new scheme S, respectively. Let us label w by the selector c and connect w and v by a new arc. Then, we act as follows. If B is nonempty, we connect v with the input of B by a new arc, and the output of B with w, by another new arc. If B is empty, we connect v and w by a new arc. For each new arc, we extend the order of S by the relation of this arc with itself. Graph S, constructed as described above, is a scheme: we will say that S is the *loop* with the *body* B and the *condition* c.

5. Let $B_1, \ldots, B_n$ be regular schemes, c be a selector, and $ar(c) = n$. Consider two new nodes v and w — the input and the output of a new scheme S, respectively. Let us label v by the selector c. Then, we act as follows. For each nonempty scheme B_i, we connect v with the input of B_i by a new arc, and the

D. Bjørner, M. Broy, A. Zamulin (Eds.): PSI'99, LNCS 1755, pp. 143–148, 2000.

output of B_i with w, by another new arc. For each empty scheme B_i, we connect v and w by a new arc. For each pair of new arcs with the common beginning and belonging to schemes B_i and B_j, respectively, extend the order of S by the relation between these arcs if $i \leq j$. Graph S constructed as described above is a scheme: we will say that S is the *hammock* with the selector c and the *branches* $B_1, \ldots, B_n$.

A scheme is called a *component* if it is nonempty and cannot be represented in a form of the series union of two nonempty schemes.

We now define the sets of arguments $A(S)$, results $R(S)$, and obligatory results $R'(S)$ for scheme S. A *path* in a regular scheme is a sequence $v_1e_1 \ldots v_{n-1}e_{n-1}v_n$, consisting of nodes $v_1, \ldots, v_n$ and arcs $e_1, \ldots, e_{n-1}$ in which the arc e_i leads from v_i to v_{i+1}. An *execution chain* in a regular scheme is a sequence of labels written down when going along a path from the input to the output. For an execution chain α, let us set $A(\alpha) = R(\alpha) = R'(\alpha) = \emptyset$, if α is empty, and $A(\alpha) = A(\alpha_1) \cup (A(\alpha_2) \backslash R'(\alpha_1))$, $R(\alpha) = R(\alpha_1) \cup R(\alpha_2)$, $R'(\alpha) = R'(\alpha_1) \cup R'(\alpha_2)$, if α can be represented as a concatenation of subchains α_1 and α_2 at least one of which is nonempty.

If S is empty, we set $A(S) = R(S) = R'(S) = \emptyset$. Now assume that S is nonempty. Let $EC(H)$ be the set of all execution chains of S. Then, $A(S) = \bigcup_{\alpha \in EC(S)} A(\alpha)$, $R(S) = \bigcup_{\alpha \in EC(S)} R(\alpha)$, and $R'(S) = \bigcap_{\alpha \in EC(S)} R'(\alpha)$.

Let T be a nonempty subscheme of S. Let us denote by $S[T/T']$ a scheme that is obtained from S as a result of the *change of T for T'*. If T' is the empty scheme, we will say that $S_{(T)} = S[T/T']$ is obtained from S by deleting subscheme T.

A *memory state* is either determined by the set of values of all variables or is an *invalid* state. An *interpretation* assigns a function of transformation of memory states to each basic statement; interpretation also assigns to each selector a function that generates a number of the branch to be chosen, depending on the memory state, or generates an error message. Once an interpretation is specified, it can be extended on the set of all regular schemes in a natural way. Two schemes are called *equivalent* if any interpretation assigns them identical functions.

A regular scheme S is called a *pseudoscheme* if the *parent* scheme $par(S)$ and the sets of *candidates for deletion* after the removal up or down, *u-dels*(S) and *d-dels*(S), are specified.

An execution chain α is called *irredundant* if it cannot be represented in the form of the concatenation of three subchains $\alpha = \alpha_1\alpha_2\alpha_3$, in such a way that $t \in R(\alpha_2)$, $t \in R'(\alpha_3)$, $t \notin A(\alpha_2)$, and $t \notin A(\alpha_3)$ for some variable t. A scheme S is irredundant if, for any of its arc, there exists an irredundant execution chain obtained from a path involving this arc. If a scheme is irredundant, any of its subscheme is also irredundant.

2 Removal from Loops and Hammocks

Let L be a subloop of a scheme S with a body $B = \underline{X} \circ X \circ \overline{X}$ and a condition c, where $\underline{X}$, X, $\overline{X}$ be regular schemes, and X be a component. If the *conditions of removal up* from L $A(\overline{X}) \cap R(X) = R(\overline{X}) \cap A(X) = R(\overline{X}) \cap R(X) \cap (A(\underline{X}) \cup (A(c) \setminus R'(\underline{X}))) = R(\overline{X}) \cap R(X) \setminus R'(\underline{X}) = A(X) \cap R(\overline{X} \circ X \circ \underline{X}) = \emptyset$, and either $(A(\overline{X} \circ \underline{X}) \cup (A(c) \setminus R'(\overline{X} \circ \underline{X}))) \cap R(\overline{X} \circ X \circ \underline{X}) = \emptyset$ or $R(X) \cap R''(\overline{X} \circ \underline{X}) = R(X) \cap R'(\overline{X} \circ \underline{X}) \cap (A(\overline{X} \circ \underline{X}) \cup (A(c) \setminus R'(\overline{X} \circ \underline{X}))) = \emptyset$, hold for X, the *removal up* of X from L consists in the substitution of scheme $X \circ L_{(X)}$ for subloop L. If the *conditions of removal down* from L $A(X) \cap R(\underline{X}) = R(X) \cap (A(\underline{X}) \cup (A(c) \setminus R'(\underline{X}))) = R(X) \cap R(\underline{X}) = R(X) \cap (A(\overline{X} \circ \underline{X}) \cup (A(c) \setminus R'(\overline{X} \circ \underline{X}))) = \emptyset$, and either $A(X) \cap R(\overline{X} \circ X \circ \underline{X}) = \emptyset$ or $(A(\overline{X} \circ \underline{X}) \cup (A(c) \setminus R'(\overline{X} \circ \underline{X}))) \cap R(\overline{X} \circ \underline{X}) = A(X) \cap R(X) \setminus R'(\overline{X} \circ \underline{X}) = \emptyset$, hold for X,. the *removal down* of X from L consists in the substitution of scheme $L_{(X)} \circ X$ for subloop L.

Let X and Y be linear subcomponents of B. We say that the removal up of Y *depends* on the removal up of X and write $X \rightarrow_u Y$, if X is arranged before Y in B, Y is not a pseudoscheme with $par(Y) = X$, and one of the intersections $A(X) \cap R(Y)$, $R(X) \cap A(Y)$, or $R(X) \cap R(Y)$ is not empty, or $X = Y$ and $A(Y) \cap R(Y) \neq \emptyset$, or X is arranged after Y in B and one of the intersections $A(Y) \cap R(X)$, or $R(Y) \cap R(X)$ is not empty. We say that the removal down of Y *depends* on the removal down of X and write $X \rightarrow_d Y$, if one of the following conditions X is arranged after Y in B, Y is not a pseudoscheme with $par(Y) = X$, and one of the intersections $A(Y) \cap R(X)$, $R(Y) \cap A(X)$, or $R(Y) \cap R(X)$ is not empty, or $X = Y$ and $A(Y) \cap R(Y) \neq \emptyset$, or X is arranged before Y in B and one of the intersections $R(X) \cap A(Y)$, $A(X) \cap R(Y)$, or $R'(X) \cap R(Y)$ is not empty. We say that the removal down of Y depends on the selector c and write $c \rightarrow_d Y$, if $A(c) \cap R(Y) \neq \emptyset$.

We define a *removal dependency graph* $\Delta(L)$ as follows. The set of nodes consists of the selector c and all the linear subcomponents of B. The set of arcs is divided in two nonoverlapping sets of *u-arcs* and *d-arcs*, in such a way that u-arc e connects nodes v and w if and only if $v \rightarrow_u w$, and d-arc e connects nodes v and w if and only if $v \rightarrow_d w$. Let $deg_u^+(v)$ be the number of u-arcs with the end node v, and $deg_d^+(v)$ be the number of d-arcs with the end node v.

Let H be a hammock with a selector c and branches $B_1, \ldots, B_n$. A *candidate chain for removal up* from H is a sequence $X = X_1, \ldots, X_n$ of mutually isomorphic schemes, such that X_i is a linear subcomponent of B_i and the number of linear subcomponents of B_i that are isomorphic to X_i and are arranged in B_i before X_i is the same for all i. Similarly, a *candidate chain for removal down* from H is a sequence $X = X_1, \ldots, X_n$ of mutually isomorphic schemes, such that X_i is a linear subcomponent of B_i and the number of linear subcomponents of B_i that are isomorphic to X_i and are arranged in B_i after X_i is the same for all i. Let us designate any of the schemes $X_1, \ldots, X_n$ as $Comm(X)$ and the hammock obtained from H by deleting all schemes $X_1, \ldots, X_n$ as $H_{(X)}$. Let X be a candidate chain for removal (up or down), and $\overline{X_i}$, $\underline{X_i}$, $i = 1 \ldots n$ be the subschemes of H such that $B_i = \underline{X_i} \circ X_i \circ \overline{X_i}$ for all i. If X is a candidate for removal up and the *conditions of removal up* from H $(A(c) \cup A(\overline{X_i})) \cap R(X_i) = R(\overline{X_i}) \cap A(X_i) = R(\overline{X_i}) \cap R(X_i) \cap A(\underline{X_i}) = R(\overline{X_i}) \cap R(X_i) \setminus R'(\underline{X_i}) = \emptyset$ for all i, hold for X, the *removal up* of chain X from H consists in the substitution of scheme $Comm(X) \circ H_{(X)}$ for hammock

H. Similarly, if X is a candidate for removal down and the *conditions of removal down* from H $A(X_i) \cap R(\underline{X_i}) = R(X_i) \cap A(\underline{X_i}) = R(X_i) \cap R(\underline{X_i}) = \emptyset$ for all i, hold for X, the *removal down* of chain X from H consists in the substitution of scheme $H_{(X)} \circ Comm(X)$ for hammock H.

Let X_i be a linear subcomponent of B_i, Y be a candidate for removal up from H. We say that the removal up of Y *depends* on X_i and write $X_i \rightarrow_u Y$, if X_i is arranged before Y_i in B_i, Y_i is not a pseudoscheme with $par(Y_i) = X_i$, and one of the intersections $A(Y_i) \cap R(X_i)$, $R(Y_i) \cap A(X_i)$, or $R(Y_i) \cap R(X_i)$ is not empty. Let X be a candidate for removal up from H. We say that the removal up of Y depends on the removal up of X and write $X \rightarrow_u Y$, if $X_i \rightarrow_u Y$ for all i. We say that the removal up of Y depends on the selector c and write $c \rightarrow_u Y$, if $A(c) \cap Comm(Y)) \neq \emptyset$. Similarly, let X_i be a linear subcomponent of B_i, Y be a candidate for removal down from H. We say that the removal down of Y depends on the removal down of X_i and write $X_i \rightarrow_d Y$, if X_i is arranged after Y_i in B_i, Y_i is not a pseudoscheme with $par(Y_i) = X_i$, and one of the intersections $A(Y_i) \cap R(X_i)$, $R(Y_i) \cap A(X_i)$, or $R(Y_i) \cap R(X_i)$. Let X be a candidate for removal down from H. We say that the removal down of Y depends on the removal down of X and write $X \rightarrow_d Y$, if $X_i \rightarrow_d Y$ for all i.

We define a *removal dependency graph* $\Delta(H)$ as follows. The set of nodes consists of the selector c, candidate chains for removal up or down from H, and all the linear subcomponents of $B_1, \ldots, B_n$ that do not belong to any of candidate chains. The set of arcs is divided into two nonoverlapping sets of *u-arcs* and *d-arcs* in such a way that u-arc e connects nodes v and w if and only if $v \rightarrow_u w$, and d-arc e connects nodes v and w if and only if $v \rightarrow_d w$. Let $deg_u^+(v)$ be the number of u-arcs with the end node v, and $deg_d^+(v)$ be the number of d-arcs with the end node v.

If $X = X_1, \ldots, X_n$ is a candidate chain for removal up or down, then a candidate chain $\hat{X}$ for removal in opposite direction is called *dual* to X if $X_i = \hat{X}_i$ for some i.

3 The Purging Algorithm

Algorithm.

Input: a regular scheme S.

Output: a regular scheme S'.

First, procedure 1 is applied to the input scheme S. It constructs a scheme S' and the set $\Pi(S')$. Then, each pseudoscheme $T \in \Pi(S')$ is transformed to an ordinary scheme (additional information is deleted) and all subschemes belonging to the set $u\text{-}dels(T)$ are deleted from S' in the process.

Procedure 1.

Input: a regular scheme S.

Outputs: a scheme S' and the set $\Pi(S')$.

1. If S is an empty scheme, or S corresponds to a basic statement, then return S and the set $\Pi(S) = \emptyset$. Otherwise, go to step 2.

2. If S is a loop, then go to step 3. If S is a hammock, then go to step 4. Otherwise, let $S = S_1 \circ \ldots \circ S_n$, $n \geq 2$. The procedure 1 is then applied to schemes $S_1, \ldots, S_n$. Let S'_1, $\Pi(S'_1)$, ..., S'_n, $\Pi(S'_n)$, respectively, be the outputs obtained. Then, return the scheme $S' = S'_1 \circ \ldots \circ S'_n$ and the set $\Pi(S') = \bigcup_{i \in [1:n]} \Pi(S'_i)$.

3. Let S be a loop with a body B and a condition c. The procedure 1 is then applied to the scheme B. Let B' and $\Pi(B')$ be the outputs obtained, and S' be the loop with the body B' and the condition c. The procedure 2 is then applied to the loop S' and to the set $\Pi(S') = \Pi(B')$. Let S'' be the output obtained. Then, return S'' and the set $\Pi(S'') = \emptyset$.

4. Let S be a hammock with a selector c and branches $B_1, \ldots, B_n$. The procedure 1 is then applied to schemes $B_1, \ldots, B_n$. Let B'_1, $\Pi(B'_1)$, ..., B'_n, $\Pi(B'_n)$, respectively, be the outputs obtained, and S' be the hammock with the selector c and branches $B'_1, \ldots, B'_n$. The procedure 3 is then applied to the hammock S' and to the set $\Pi(S') = \bigcup_{i \in [1:n]} \Pi(B'_i)$. Let S'' and $\Pi(S'')$ be the outputs obtained. Then, return S'' and the set $\Pi(S'')$.

Procedure 2.

Inputs: a loop L and the set $\Pi(L)$.

Output: a regular scheme L'.

1. Construct the graph $\Delta(L)$. Then, transform each pseudoscheme $T \in \Pi(L)$ to an ordinary scheme and delete from S' all subschemes that belong to set $d\text{-}dels(T)$. Set $M = N = \varepsilon$. Then, go to step 2.

2. If there exists at least one scheme X such that $deg^+_d(X) = 0$, select this scheme and go to step 3. Otherwise, go to step 4.

3. Delete the node X and all arcs that begin in X from $\Delta(L)$. Then, delete X from L, set $N = X \circ N$, and go to step 2.

4. If there exists at least one scheme X such that $deg^+_u(X) = 0$, select this scheme and go to step 5. Otherwise, go to step 6.

5. Delete from $\Delta(L)$ the node X and all arcs that begin in X. Then, delete X from L, set $M = M \circ X$, and go to step 2.

6. Recalculate $A(L)$, $R(L)$, and $R'(L)$. Then, return the scheme $M \circ L \circ N$.

Procedure 3.

Inputs: a hammock H and the set $\Pi(H)$.

Outputs: a scheme H' and the set $\Pi(H')$.

1. Construct the set Φ of all the candidate chains for removal up from H and the set Ψ, of all the candidate chains for removal down from H. Construct the graph $\Delta(H)$ and set $F = G = \varepsilon$. Then go to step 2.

2. If there exists at least one chain $X \in \Psi$ such that $deg^+_d(X) = 0$, select this chain, set $\Psi = \Psi \setminus \{X\}$, and go to step 3. Otherwise, go to step 6.

3. Delete from $\Delta(H)$ all arcs that begin from X. Set $G = Comm(X) \circ G$. If a dual chain for X exists, then go to step 4. Otherwise, go to step 5.

4. $\Omega = \Omega \cup \{(T, X)\}$. Go to step 2.

5. For each element X_i that is a pseudoscheme, delete from H all the schemes that belong to set $d\text{-}dels(X_i)$. Then, delete all elements of X from H. Return to step 2.

6. If there exists at least one chain $X \in \Phi$ such that $deg_u^+(X) = 0$, select this chain, set $\Phi = \Phi \setminus \{X\}$, and go to step 7. Otherwise, go to step 10.

7. Delete from $\Delta(H)$ all the arcs that begin from X. If X has no dual chain or if there is no pair of the $(T, \hat{X})$ form in set Ω, then go to step 8. Otherwise, go to step 9.

8. For each element X_i that is a pseudoscheme, delete from H all the schemes that belong to set $u\text{-}dels(X_i)$. Then, delete all elements of X from H. Set $F = F \circ Comm(X)$ and return to step 6.

9. Let $(T, \hat{X}) \in \Omega$. From T, construct a pseudoscheme for which $par(T) = H$, $f\text{-}dels(T) = \bigcup_{i=1}^{n} f\text{-}dels(X_i)$, and $b\text{-}dels(T) = \bigcup_{i=1}^{n} b\text{-}dels(X_i)$ (for the sake of convenience, we set $f\text{-}dels(X_i) = b\text{-}dels(X_i) = \{X_i\}$ if scheme X_i is not a pseudoscheme). Add T to set Π and delete from H all the elements of X and $\hat{X}$ that are pseudoschemes. Go to step 6.

10. Recalculate $A(H)$, $R(H)$, and $R'(H)$. In the process, we should take into account only those deletions that were really performed (ordinary schemes are not deleted when pseudoschemes are constructed). Then, return the scheme $H' = F \circ H \circ G$ and the set $\Pi(H') = \Pi$.

Theorem. The scheme that is obtained from the input scheme as a result of applying the algorithm described above can be obtained by applying transformations of removal from subloops and subhammocks.

The number of the nodes of a regular scheme S will be called its *size* and denoted by $|S|$. The *depth* $d(S)$ of a scheme S is the maximum length n of the sequences of the components $T_1, \ldots, T_n$ such that T_i is a proper subcomponent of C_{i+1} for all $i = 1, \ldots, n-1$. If there are no such sequences, we set $d(S) = 1$.

Theorem. The algorithm described above requires the time $O(d(S)|S|^2 time(m))$ and the storage $O(|S|^2 + space(m))$ to work with a scheme S. Here m is the number of variables, $time(m)$ is the upper bound of the time required for one operation ($\cap$, $\cup$, or $\setminus$) over subsets of the set of variables, and $space(m)$ is the upper bound of the memory needed to store one subset of the set of variables.

Theorem. Let S be an irredundant scheme without degenerate subloops, and let S' be a scheme obtained from S by applying the algorithm described above. Let S'' be any scheme obtained from S by applying transformations of removal from subloops and subhammocks. Then, the following statements are true.

1. Let l' be a number of transformations that must be applied to obtain S' from S, and let l'' be a number of transformations that must be applied to obtain S'' from S. Then, $l' \geq l''$.

2. $|S'| \leq |S''|$.

References

[1] Pottosin, I.V., Justification of Algorithms for Optimization of Programs, *Programmirovanie*, 1979, no. 2, pp. 3—13.

[2] Pottosin, I.V. and Yugrinova, O.V., Justification of Purging Transformations for Loops, *Programmirovanie*, 1980, no. 5, pp.8—16.

Polymorphism in OBJ–P

Martin Plümicke

Wilhelm-Schickard-Institut, Universität Tübingen, Sand 13
D-72076 Tübingen, Fax.: +49 7071 610399
pluemick@informatik.uni-tuebingen.de

Abstract. In this paper we present the functional programming language OBJ–P. OBJ–P is a polymorphic extension of OBJ–3. The main features are overloaded function symbols, set inclusion subtyping, and parametric polymorphic types.

Introduction

The functional programming language OBJ–3 (e.g. [GWM⁺93]) has two main features: overloading of function symbols and subtyping in the sense of set inclusion. There is also a powerful module system for OBJ–3. In OBJ–3 parameterized types are missing. There is sure the possibility to parameterize whole modules. But this is a not good solution, because if one type within a module has a parameter the whole module must be parameterized.
We extend OBJ–3 by parametric polymorphic types, which are well-known from SML [Mil97]. We call this extension OBJ–P. This means that OBJ–P allows both, parameterized types and parameterized modules. The combination leads to a powerful language which has enormous possibilities to reuse code and to overload function symbols; however, function evaluation remains unambiguous. Our overloading feature is more expressive than overloading in Haskell [PH⁺97]. These features (overloading and set inclusion subtyping) are very interesting in computer algebra, as in mathematics we deal with overloaded function names and with set hierarchies.
The semantic base of OBJ–3 is the theory of order-sorted algebras (e.g. [GM89]). Therefore, we generalize the theory to polymorphic order-sorted algebras. For our theory we extend the theory of Smolka [Smo88].

1 The Functional Programming Language OBJ–P

The types of OBJ–P programs are sorted type terms $T_\Theta(TV)$ over a finite rank alphabet Θ of type constructors and a set of type variables TV.

Definition 1. (**Type term ordering**) Let $T_\Theta(TV)$ be a set of type terms. Then $\leq$ is a *type term ordering* if $\leq$ is finite, from $\theta \leq \theta'$ follows $\mathsf{TVar}(\theta) = \mathsf{TVar}(\theta')$ (where TVar denotes the occurring type variables), and if $\theta \leq \theta'$ then θ is no type variable and θ' has the form $\Psi(a_1, \ldots, a_n)$, where $\Psi \in \Theta^{(n)}$ and $a_1, \ldots, a_n \in TV$. The ordering of the type terms in an OBJ–P program is defined as the closure $\leq^*$ of a declared type term ordering $\leq$ wrt. substitutions.

D. Bjørner, M. Broy, A. Zamulin (Eds.): PSI'99, LNCS 1755, pp. 149–154, 2000.

The function symbols of a program form a polymorphic order-sorted signature.

Definition 2. **(Polymorphic order-sorted signature)** A *polymorphic order-sorted signature* Σ_{os} is a triple $(T_\Theta(TV),\ \leq,\ F)$ where $T_\Theta(TV)$ is a set of type terms and F is a $(T_\Theta(TV)^* \times T_\Theta(TV))$-sorted family of function symbols, and $\leq$ is a type term ordering such that the function symbols satisfy the *monotonicity condition*: $f \in F^{(\theta_1 \dots \theta_n, \theta_0)} \cap F^{(\theta'_1 \dots \theta'_n, \theta'_0)}$ and $\sigma(\theta_i) \leq^* \theta'_i$ for all $1 \leqslant i \leqslant n$ implies $\sigma(\theta_0) \leq^* \theta'_0$.

[GM89] gives a regularity condition for order-sorted signatures. This condition guarantees that each term over a regular order-sorted signature has a least type. We generalized this regularity condition for polymorphic order-sorted signatures such that each term has a least principal type. [Plü99]
The semantics of OBJ–P programs is defined as polymorphic order-sorted algebras [Plü99], which is declared in OBJ–P programs by recursive equations over the signature.

Example 1. The OBJ–P program `MATRIX` declares a type term ordering, a polymorphic order-sorted signature, and a polymorphic order-sorted algebra.

```
obj MATRIX is
  *** Type term ordering declaration
  sorts Int nsVector(a) Vector(a) Matrix(a) .
  subsort nsVector(a) < Vector(a) .
  subsort Vector(nsVector(a)) < Matrix(a) .
  *** Signature declaration
  op scalar : a -> Vector(a) .
  op vec : a Vector(a) -> nsVector(a) .
  op + : Int Int -> Int .
  op + : Vector(Int) Vector(Int) -> Vector(Int) .
  op + : Matrix(Int) Matrix(Int) -> Matrix(Int) .
  *** Equation declaration
  vars s1 s2 : Int .
  vars v1 v2 : Vector(Int) .
  eq +(scalar(s1), scalar(s2)) = scalar(+(s1, s2)) .
  eq +(vec(s1, v1), vec(s2, v2)) = vec(+(s1, s2), +(v1, v2)) .
  vars vs1 vs2 : nsVector(Int) .
  vars vv1 vv2 : Vector(nsVector(Int)) .
  eq +(scalar(vs1), scalar(vs2)) = scalar(+(vs1, vs2)) .
  eq +(vec(vs1, vv1), vec(vs2, vv2)) = vec(+(vs1, vs2), +(vv1, vv2)) .
endo
```

The basic part of the declared infinite type term ordering is presented by following Hasse diagram:

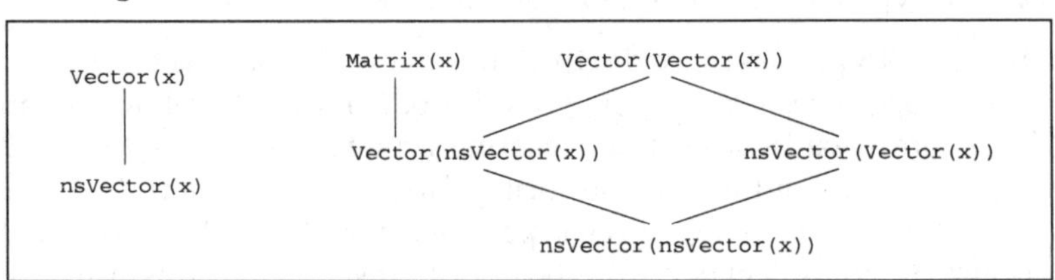

2 The Module System of OBJ–P

We present the powerful module system with an interesting example, which shows the enormous possibilities of overloading and set inclusion subtyping in connection with module hierarchies.
The module hierarchy presented in this example describes the sum of polynomials over rings. The parameters of this module are the ring over which the polynomials are defined and the sum over the ring elements, respectively. The appendant product function is presented in [Plü99].
The function symbol + is overloaded with the sum over the ring elements, the monomials, and the polynomials over the ring, respectively. There is a predefined module `Int`, which exports usual functions about numbers.

The Recursive Representation of Polynomials In the SACLIB [BCE+92] computer algebra library, polynomials are described in the recursive representation.
The OBJ–P sorts declaration in the OBJ–P module `Polynom` represents recursive polynomials over any ring.

```
module Polynom (nmPolynom(Ring), nrMonom(Ring),
                mono: Ring nzCard -> Monom(Ring),        *** exports
                poly: Monom(Ring) Polynom -> nmPolynom(Ring))
               [sorts Ring, Polynom] is                  *** parameters
  import Int .
  sorts Monom(a) nmPolynom(a) .
  subsorts Ring Monom(Ring) nmPolynom(Ring) < Polynom .
  op mono: Ring nzCard -> Monom(Ring) .
  op poly: Monom(Ring) Polynom -> nmPolynom(Ring) .
endm
```

In the module two type constructors `Monom` and `nmPolynom` are declared. The type `Monom(Ring)` stands for the set of monomials with exponents greater than 0 and `nmPolynom(Ring)` stands for the general polynomials (the non-monomial polynomials). Both types are parameterized by the module parameter `Ring` which stands for the type of the ring elements. The other module parameter is `Polynom`. It stands for the type of the union of all ring elements (`Ring`), all Monomials (`Monon(Ring)`), and all non-monomial polynomials (`nmPolynom(Ring)`). The exported sorts are `nmPolynom(Ring)` and `Momon(Ring)`, while the exported constructors (function symbols) are `mono` and `poly`.
A polynomial in this representation consists of a list of monomials with the list constructor `poly`. In this representation the names of the variables are unknown. Now we give an example. Let us consider a polynomial in two variables:

$$x_2^3 + (3x_1^3 + 2x_1 + 1)x_2^2 + (x_1^2 + x_1 + 1)x_2 + (x_1^2 + x_1 + 12).$$

For polynomials in two variables we must import the module `Polynom` twice:

```
import Polynom[Ring = Int, Polynom = Polynom1].
import Polynom[Ring = Polynom1, Polynom = Polynom2].
```

where `Polynom1` (stands for $Z[x_1]$) and `Polynom2` (stands for $Z[x_1][x_2]$) are new sorts, which are instantiated in the imported modules. Then, the above polynomial is represented by:

```
poly(mono(mono(1, 0), 3),
     poly(mono(poly(mono(3, 3), poly(mono(2, 1), 1)), 2),
          poly(mono(poly(mono(1, 2), poly(mono(1, 1), 1)), 1),
               poly(mono(1, 2), poly(mono(1, 1), 12)))))
```

It is an element of the ring $Z[x_1][x_2]$. Therefore, the type is `Polynom2`.
If we have a closer look at the representation (`poly(mono(1, 2), poly(mono(1, 1), 12))`) of the coefficient $(x_1^2 + x_1 + 12)$ (last line) we notice that its type is `Polynom1` instead of `Polynom2`. This is possible as the type `Polynom1` is a subtype of `Polynom2` induced by the subsort declaration `Ring < Polynom` in module `Polynom` through the second import. On the other hand, the type of the monomial x_2^3 (represented by `mono(mono(1, 0), 3)`) is `Monom(Monom(Int))` and not `Monom(Int)` as $Z[x_2]$ is not a subset of $Z[x_1][x_2]$.
The main difference to the usual recursive representation of polynomials is the following: A polynomial $p \in R[x_1]\dots[x_{n-1}]$ is usually represented in $R[x_1]\dots[x_n]$ as $p \cdot x_n^0$ and not as p like in our representation. This is only possible, because OBJ–P allows set inclusion subtyping and multiplied importation of one module with different parameter instantiations.

Sum of Polynomials

```
module PolynomSUM (+: Polynom Polynom -> Polynom) *** exports
                  [sorts Ring Polynom, op +: Ring Ring -> Ring] is
 import Int .                                      *** parameters
 import Polynom[Ring = Ring, Polynom = Polynom]. *** import where
                                                   *** the parameters
 op +: Polynom Polynom -> Polynom .                *** are instatiated

 vars coe1 coe2 re : Ring .
 vars exp1 exp2 : nzCard .
 vars p1 p2 : Polynom .
 var m : Monom(Ring) .
 eq +(mono(coe1, exp1), re) = poly(mono(coe1, exp1), re) .
 eq +(poly(m, p1), re) = poly(m, +(p1, re)) .
 eq +(mono(coe1, exp1), mono(coe2, exp2)) = ...
 eq +(poly(mono(coe1, exp1), p1), mono(coe2, exp2)) =
  if (exp1 > exp2) then poly(mono(coe1, exp1), +(p1, mono(coe2, exp2)))
  else
   if (exp2 > exp1) then poly(mono(coe2,exp2), poly(mono(coe1,exp1), p1))
   else poly(mono(+(coe1, coe2), exp1), p1) fi fi .

 eq +(poly(mono(coe1, exp1), p1), poly(mono(coe2, exp2), p2)) = ...
 eq +(p1, p2) = +(p2, p1) .
endm
```

In the module `PolynomSUM` there is a function call named by the overloaded function symbol `+` (underlined). This function call produces either a recursive call (depended on the argument type) or the call of the module parameter `+` function. This is an example for the overloading feature in OBJ–P.
The module `PolynomSUM` is a parameterized module similar to the module `Polynom`. Now we present different possibilities to import these two modules.

Polynomials over the Integer Numbers

```
module Int2PolynomSUM is
  sorts Polynom1 Polynom2 .
  import Int .
  import PolynomSUM [Ring = Int, Polynom = Polynom1,
                     + = +: Int Int -> Int] .
  import PolynomSUM [Ring = Polynom1, Polynom = Polynom2,
                     + = +: Polynom1 Polynom1 -> Polynom1] .
  op Main: Polynom2 Polynom2 -> Polynom2 .
  vars x y : Polynom2 .
  eq Main(x, y) = +(x, y) .
endm
```

The module `PolynomSUM` is imported twice. While in the first import the parameters of `PolynomSUM` are instantiated by `Int`, `Polynom1`, and `+: Int Int -> Int`, in the second import the parameters `Ring` and `+: Ring Ring -> Ring` are instantiated by the already imported types `Polynom1` and `+: Polynom1 Polynom1 -> Polynom1` and `Polynom` is instantiated by the additionally declared type `polynom2`. Finally, the function `Main` define the polynomial sum over the ring $Z[x_1][x_2]$.
We notice that the type `Polynom1` is the union of `Int`, `Monom(Int)`, and `nmPolynom(Int)` while `Polynom2` is the union of `Polynom1`, `Monom(Polynom1)`, and `nmPolynom(Polynom1)`. From this follows that the `Main` function is enormously overloaded. `Main` is applicable to integer numbers, to polynomials in the variable x_1 as well as to polynomials in the variables x_1 and x_2, and to the mixture of all these types. This is a very natural way to overload the sum function. In languages like Haskell [PH+97] this is impossible, as we have shown in [Plü99].

Polynomials over Z/n The ring over which the polynomials are defined is now Z/n. We assume that there is module `Zmodn`, which is parameterized by n and where the sum function of Z/n is exported.

```
module Zmod43PolynomSUM is
  import Int .
  import Zmodn [n = 4] as Zmod4 .     *** the identifiers id are used
                                      *** qualified as Zmod4.id
  sorts Polynom1, Polynom2, Polynom3 .

  import PolynomSUM [Ring = Card, Polynom = Polynom1, + = Zmod4.+: ...] .
  import PolynomSUM [Ring = Polynom1, Polynom = Polynom2, + = +: ...] .
  import PolynomSUM [Ring = Polynom2, Polynom = Polynom3, + = +: ...] .
  op Main: Polynom3 Polynom3 -> Polynom3 .
```

```
  vars x y : Polynom3 .
  eq Main(x, y) = +(x, y)
endm
```

The `Main` function defines the sum of polynomials over $Z/4[x_1][x_2][x_3]$.
This example shows the possibilities for reuse code in OBJ–P. It is possible to give a new sum function (in this example from module `Zmodn`) and assign them to the function parameter `+` in the module `PolynomSUM`, while the code of `PolynomSUM` is unchanged.

Summary The subtyping feature of OBJ–P allows to represent polynomials $p \in R[x_1] \dots [x_m]$ in the supertype $R[x_1] \dots [x_n]$, $(m < n)$ identical as in $R[x_1] \dots [x_m]$. This is not possible in other programming languages.
Furthermore, the subtyping feature enables the sum function to have only two arguments, instead of three (the third for the number of variables) as would usually be expected (cf. SACLIB [BCE+92]).
Additionally, because of the overloading feature of OBJ–P, there is the same function symbol for the sum function over ring elements, monomials, and polynomials, although these sets of elements are represented by different types.

3 Conclusion and Further Work

We have presented the programming language OBJ–P, which has the special features of overloaded function symbols, set inclusion subtyping, and parametric polymorphic types.
Additionally, in [Plü99] we have defined a type inference system and a corresponding type reconstruction algorithm, which allows us to omit the declarations of the function symbols and the variable declarations in OBJ–P programs.

References

[BCE+92] B. Buchberger, G. Collins, M. Encarnacón, H. Hong, J. Johnson, W. Krandick, A. Mandache, A. Neubacher, and H. Vielhaber. *SACLIB User's Guide (version 1.0)*, September 1992.

[GM89] J. A. Goguen and J. Meseguer. Order-sorted algebras I: Equational deduction for multiple inheritance, overloading, exceptions and partial operations. Technical report, SRI International, July 1989.

[GWM+93] J. A. Goguen, T. Winkler, J. Meseguer, K. Futatsugi, and J.-P. Jouannaud. *Introducing OBJ*, October 1993.

[Mil97] Robin Milner. *The definition of Standard ML (Revised).* MIT Press, Cambridge, Mass., 1997.

[PH+97] John Peterson, Kevin Hammond, et al. Report on the programming language Haskell, version 1.4, April 1997.

[Plü99] Martin Plümicke. OBJ–P *The Polymorphic Extension of* OBJ–3. PhD thesis, University of Tuebingen, WSI-99-4, 1999.

[Smo88] Gert Smolka. Logic programming with polymorphically order-sorted types. *Proc. First International Workshop on Algebraic and Logic Programming, Springer-Verlag*, LNCS 343:53–70, 1988. Gaussig, GDR.

Formal Modelling of Services for Getting a Better Understanding of the Feature Interaction Problem:

A Multi-view Approach

Paul Gibson[1] and Dominique Méry[2]

[1] NUI, Maynooth, Ireland
pgibson@cs.may.ie
[2] Université Henri Poincaré-Nancy 1 & LORIA UMR 7503 CNRS
Campus Scientifique, BP 239,
54506 Vandœuvre-lès-Nancy, (France)
mery@loria.fr

Abstract. We report results of a joint project with France Telecom on the modelling of telephone services (features) using formal methodologies such as OO ACT ONE, B and TLA$^+$. We show how we formalise the feature interaction problem in a multi-view model, and we examine issues such as animation, validation, proof and verification.

1 Introduction

In this section we briefly introduce the need for formal methods in software engineering, the use of formal methods to help resolve the feature interaction problem, and the particular formal methods we adopt in our mixed-semantic model.

1.1 Formality

Many software engineers do not acknowledge the value of formality. In 1993, a major study [13] concluded by stating: "*...formal methods, while still immature in certain important respects, are beginning to be used seriously and successfully by industry to design and develop computer systems ...*" We believe that formal methods are, five years later, *just about* ready for transfer to the industrial development of telephone features. Like all forms of engineering, one must always compromise between quality and cost. In telephone systems, it appears that the cost of resolving interactions between features at the implementation stage is now (or will soon be) greater than the cost of developing formal features requirements models and eliminating many of the potential interactions before implementation begins. Formal methods in this domain should be regarded as an investment for the future.
There are a wide and varied range of definitions of *formal method* which can be found in the majority of texts concerned with mathematical rigour in computer

D. Bjørner, M. Broy, A. Zamulin (Eds.): PSI'99, LNCS 1755, pp. 155–179, 2000.

science. The most common methods used for telephone feature specification are reviewed in [42]. For the purposes of this paper we propose the following definition: *A formal method is any technique concerned with the construction and/or analysis of mathematical models which aid the development of computer systems.* Formal methods are fundamentally concerned with *correctness*: the property that an abstract model fulfils a set of well defined *requirements*. In this paper, we are concerned with the construction of such requirements models.
A formal model of requirements is unambiguous — there is only one correct way to interpret the behaviour being defined. Although the model must still be mapped onto the real world (i.e. validated by the customer), this mapping is in essence more rigorous than in informal approaches. Building a formal model requires a better understanding of the problem domain and a better understanding of how the problem domain is viewed by the customer.
A major problem when using formal methods in software engineering is that much of the recent research places emphasis on analysis rather than synthesis. The means of constructing complex formal models is often overlooked in favour of techniques for analysing models.
Re-usable analysis techniques will automatically arise out of re-usable composition mechanisms. Formal method engineers need to learn techniques for building very large, complex systems. Such techniques have been followed, with various degrees of success, by programmers. In particular, object oriented programmers have evolved techniques which have been successfully transferred to the analysis and design phases of software engineering. Where better then to look for aid in the construction of large formal models?

1.2 Feature Interactions

A *feature interaction* is a situation in which system behaviour is specified as a composition of some set of features: each individual feature can meet its requirements in isolation but all features cannot meet their requirements when composed.
The problem of feature interaction is a major topic in telecommunications where formal methods have been usefully applied. There is no single technique which addresses all the aspects of the problem, but the most common approaches that have been used to tackle the problem, at the requirements stage, are: SDL [29, 30], LOTOS [18, 7, 17], state machine and rule based representation [19], and temporal logic[4, 3, 11], .

1.3 Our Formal Models

In our formal approach, interactions occur only when requirements of multiple features are *contradictory*. The complexity of understanding the problem is thus contained within a definition of *contradiction* in our semantic framework. We have argued that in most of the feature interaction examples found in published texts, there is no generally accepted standard formal definition of feature interaction[25, 43, 6, 9, 15]. In fact, most of the interactions which we studied correspond to incomplete and informal requirements models. In other words, if the features were modelled *better* then we would be able to better understand what is and what isn't an interaction.

LOTOS (Language Of Temporal Ordering Specifications), see [40, 28], is a wide spectrum language, which is suitable for specifying systems at various levels of abstraction. Consequently, it can be used at both ends of the software development spectrum. Its natural division into ADT part (based on ACT ONE [16]) and process algebra part (similar to CSP [26] and CCS [37]) is advantageous since it provides the flexibility of two different semantic models for expressing behaviour, whilst managing to integrate them in a relatively coherent fashion.

LOTOS provides an elegant way to specify services and to detect interaction among services; it allows the user to specify services in a compositional manner and it provides a set of tools such as LITE from the project LOTOSPHERE[1], to assist in service engineering. Questions regarding fairness cannot be easily expressed or solved in LOTOS: modeling fairness requires us to state properties on traces, or a scheduling policy, and LOTOS has not yet integrated fairness constraints.

We have used LOTOS in our project and compared the expressivity of different languages such as B, TLA^+ and OO ACT ONE LOTOS and on the availability of practical development environments for B and LOTOS. The style of specification plays a very important role and the approach of Gammelgaard [19] is automaton-oriented; their approach uses a specification language based on transition systems as predicates. The weakness of their solution relies on the partial view of details whereas a sound and semantically complete reasoning system is required. The solution using TLA [31, 24] borrows the initial idea from their model, but TLA has the advantage of a very carefully equipped proof system. Finally, as the temporal framework can be very expressive, we need a computer-aided proof environment and more generally applicable software environments based on these formalisms.

Blow et Al. [3] and Middelburg [36] investigate the use of temporal logic for specifying services; Blom uses a temporal logic integrating the reactive and the frame parts for services. Middelburg introduces a temporal logic of branching time and restricts its expressivity to obtain a TLA-like logic.

In fact, the integration of very different formalisms such as TLA, B and LOTOS is a way to improve service engineering. B is simple and a tool helps the user in developing specifications: we do not claim that B will solve the entire problem but it is very helpful in the building of requirements models for telecommunication services. As we emphasize B as a tool for developing services specifications using a theorem prover, another crucial element of B is its animator. Several problems are detected by animation which do not need to be resolved by the prover. We have experimented with B as a tool for service engineering, although it was not one of the original goals of the language. Another point is that B and TLA are very close, at least for the action part; we have studied the integration of B and

[1] (see http://wwwtios.cs.utwente.nl/lotos/)

TLA [35] to re-use the B tools for TLA and to extend the scope of B through temporal features.
Our paper is organized as follows. Section 2 describes our mixed model involving different aspects of the formal development. Section 3 introduces service requirements. Section 4 gives details on the way we model services in TLA$^+$; we explain how our mixed views can be checked to be coherent. Section 5 concludes our paper.

2 A Mixed Semantic Model

We have shown the need for a mixed semantic model when specifying telephone feature requirements [22]. Such a model is used to provide three different client views:

- An *object oriented* view which provides the operational semantics used during animation for validation, and the structuring mechanisms which are fundamental to our approach. This view is formalised using an object oriented style of specification in LOTOS [20].
- An *invariant* view which allows the client to describe abstract properties of a system (or component) which must *always* be true. This view is formalised using B and leads to the automatic detection of many interactions [33, 34].
- A *fairness* view which allows the client to describe properties of the system which must *eventually* be true even though they have no direct control over them. A temporal logic provides an ideal means of specifying and verifying such requirements [23].

2.1 Objects and Classes

Labelled state transition systems are often used to provide executable models during the analysis and requirements stages of software development [12, 14]. In particular, such models play a role in many of the object oriented analysis and design methods [5, 10]. However, a major problem with state models is that it can be difficult to provide a good decomposition of large, complex systems when the underlying state and state transitions are not fully understood. The object oriented paradigm provides a natural solution to this problem. By equating the notion of class with the state transition system model, and allowing the state of one class to be defined as a composition of states of other classes, we provide a means of specifying state transition models in a constructive fashion. Further, such an approach provides a more constructive means of testing actual behaviour with required behaviour.
This state based view forms the basis on which we build our feature animations and permits behaviour validation in a compositional manner. However, such operational models are not *good* for formal reasoning about feature requirements [44]: for this we need to consider specification of state invariants and fairness properties.

2.2 Invariants

Invariants are used to specify properties of a system which must *always* be true for reachable states. Within the object oriented framework we have three kinds of invariant:

- **Typing:** By stating that all objects are defined to be members of some class we are in fact specifying an invariant. These invariants are verified automatically by our object oriented tools.
- **Service requests:** Typing also permits us to state that objects in our system will only ever be asked to perform services that are part of their interfaces. These invariants are also verified automatically by the object oriented tools.
- **State Component Dependencies:** In a structured class we may wish to specify some property that depends on the state of two or more of the components, and which is invariant. This cannot be statically verified using the object oriented tools, but it can be treated through a dynamic analysis (model check). Unfortunately, such a model check cannot be guaranteed when we have a large (possibly infinite) number of states in our systems. For this reason we need to utilise a less operational framework. By translating our state invariant requirements into B, we have been able to statically verify our state component invariants.

2.3 Nondeterminism and Fairness

TLA is a temporal logic introduced by Lamport [31] and based on the action-as-relation principle. A system is considered as a set of actions, namely a logical disjunction of predicates relating values of variables before the activation of an action and values of variables after the activation of an action; a system is modeled as a set of traces over a set of states. The specifier may decide to ignore traces that do not satisfy a scheduling policy such as strong or weak fairness, and temporal operators such as $\Box$ (Always) or $\Diamond$ (Eventually) are combined to express these assumptions over the set of traces. Such fairness is important in feature specification and cannot be easily expressed using our state based semantics. The key is the need for nondeterminism in our requirements models. Without a temporal logic, nondeterminism in the features can be specified only at one level of abstraction: namely that of an internal choice of events. This can lead to many problems in development. For example, consider the specification of a shared database. This database must handle multiple, parallel requests from clients. The order in which these requests are processed is required to be nondeterministic. This is easily specified in our object model. However, the requirements are now refined to state that every request must be eventually served (this is a fairness requirement which we cannot directly express in our semantic framework). The only way this can be done is to *over-specify* the requirement by defining how this fairness is to be achieved (for example, by explicitly queueing the requests). This is bad because we are enforcing implementation decisions at the requirements level. With TLA we can express fairness requirements without having to say how these requirements are to be met.

2.4 Composition Mechanisms

Composition is primarily a question of re-use: given two already specified *components*, how can we create a new *component* from those given? A composition mechanism defines a creation mechanism which is reusable (i.e. can be applied to different sets of components). Clearly, we have to be more precise as to the meaning of a *component*. From the customer's point of view, and hence at the requirements level of abstraction, a component must be some piece of behaviour which can be validated independently. In other words, a component must be able to be seen as a model of behaviour in its own right. We give an overview of the composition techniques from each of our three different view points and argue that a user oriented view would be best during requirements capture:

(1) Object oriented composition in LOTOS:

LOTOS [8] is made up from an abstract data type part [32], and a process algebra part [26]. Clearly there are ways of composing behaviours in each of these models. However, the object oriented composition is at a higher level of abstraction. We do not compose with language operators; rather we compose using object oriented concepts.

(2) Invariant composition (in B):

B [1] is a model-oriented method providing a complete development process from abstract specification towards implementations through step-by-step refinement of abstract machines. An abstract machine describes data, operations and invariant preserved by every operation. Abstract machines are composed by conjunction of its invariants and combination of operations. The resulting abstract machine may either preserve the resulting invariant, or invalidate it. The violation of the invariant is interpreted as an interaction [34] and is in fact an interference between operations: it is a way to detect interaction among services specified as abstract machines. The main advantage of B is that it is supported by a powerful sofware environment, namely the Atelier B [39]. The B method [1] is itself a conceptual tool for specifying, refining and developing systems in a mathematical and rigorous, but simple way.

(3) Fairness composition (in TLA):

The composition of fairness assumptions in TLA is done at a high level of abstraction and is preserved through the composition process. A model for a TLA formula is an infinite trace of states, and a TLA specification is made up of three parts:

- the initial conditions, Init,
- the relation over variables, $\mathrm{Next}(x, x')$, and
- the fairness constraints, $\bigwedge_{A \in WFA} \mathrm{WF}_x(A) \wedge \bigwedge_{A \in SFA} \mathrm{SF}_x(A)$
  (we require that $A \Rightarrow \mathrm{Next}(x, x')$, for all A in WFA or SFA to ensure the machine-closure property).

Fairness constraints remove models or traces that do not satisfy them. A service is characterized by a set of flexible variables, initial conditions, a next relation over variables and fairness contraints. When combining two services, we increase the restrictions over traces but we extend the models by adding new variables. TLA provides an abstract way to state fairness assumptions but in our approach this unfriendly syntax is hidden from the customer. We encapsulate fairness within each object as a means of resolving nondeterminism due to internal state transitions. This is a simple yet powerful way for the fairness to be structured and re-used within our requirements models.

(4) Feature composition (user conceptualisation):
In an ideal world, feature composition would be done using concepts within the clients' conceptual model of their requirements. Clients cannot be expected to express themselves using formal language operators. This does not mean that they cannot express themselves formally. It is the role of the analyst to map the clients' composition concepts onto composition methods in the formal model. For now, we are forced to communicate through the object oriented models (which could be argued to be *client friendly*). In the future we hope to develop a modeling language based on client concepts rather than modeling language concepts.

3 Requirements for Features

3.1 Requirements Modeling: Customer Orientation

Requirements capture is the first step in the process of meeting customer needs. Building and analysing a model of customer needs, with the intention of passing the result of such a process to system designers, is the least well understood aspect of software engineering. The process is required to fulfil two very different needs: the customer must be convinced that requirements are completely understood and recorded, and the designer must be able to use the requirements to produce a structure around which an implementation can be developed and tested. In this paper, we concentrate on the customers' point of view, whilst noting that the object oriented approach does lend itself to meeting the designers' needs [21]. We advocate such a *customer oriented* approach since it is generally agreed that customer communication is the most important aspect of analysis [27, 38, 41].

The fundamental principle of requirements capture is the improvement of mutual understanding between customer and analyst, and the recording and validation of such an understanding in a structured model. The successful synthesis of a requirements model is dependent on being able to construct a system as the customer views the problem. [2, 25] illustrate this point with respect to feature models.

3.2 Feature Interaction: What's New?

We concentrate on the domain of telephone features, where the problem has been acknowledged for many years![6, 9]. Figure 1 illustrates the problem within the formal framework which we adopt throughout this paper. We note that the means by which features are composed is not specified.

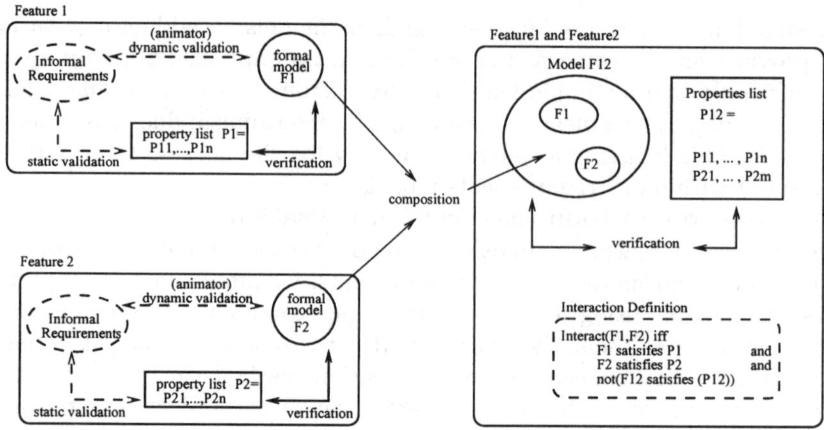

Fig. 1. Feature Interaction: A formalisation

Features are observable behaviour and are therefore a requirements specification problem [45]. Many feature interaction problems can be resolved through communication with the customer during requirements capture. Given a feature requirements specification which is not contradictory, interaction problems during the design and implementation will arise only through errors in the refinement process. Certainly the feature interaction problem is more prone to the introduction of such errors because of the highly concurrent and distributed nature of the underlying implementation domain, but this is for consideration *after* each individual feature's requirements have been modelled and validated. We have extended the work given in [25], where the composition of features was done in an ad-hoc fashion, by identifying and formalising re-usable composition mechanisms. The configuration of multiple features will be shown to depend on the way in which individual features are composed with POTS (plain old telephone service).

Features are requirements modules *and* the units of incrementation as systems evolve. A telecom system is a set of features. Having features as the incremental units of development is the source of our complexity. An understanding of feature composition helps us manage the four main sources of this complexity —

(1) State explosion:

Potential feature interactions increase exponentially with the number of features in the system and traditional model checking techniques cannot cope with the complexity. The fundamental problem is that analysis cannot be done compositionally. We argue that compositional (re-usable) analysis depends on having a formal understanding of the composition mechanisms. This is the main goal of this work.

(2) Chaotic Information Structure In Sequential Development Strategies:

The arbitrary sequential ordering of feature development is what drives the internal structure of the resulting system. As each new feature is added the feature must *potentially* include details of how it is to be configured with all the features already in the system. Consequently, to understand the behaviour of one feature, it is necessary to examine the specification of all the features in the system. All conceptual integrity is lost since the distribution of knowledge is *potentially* chaotic. At the moment this is certainly true. However, we believe that we can control the distribution of this *configuration knowledge* by containing it within a re-usable set of configuration mechanisms.

(3) Implicit Assumption Problem:
Already developed features often rely on assumptions which are no longer true when later features are conceived. Consequently, features may rely on contradictory (implicit) assumptions. This is a great source of interactions. We propose forcing the specifiers to formalise their (explicit) assumptions, by forcing them to use a certain set of configuration mechanisms.

(4) Independent Development:
Traditional approaches require a new feature developer to consider how the feature operates with all others already on the system. Consequently, we cannot concurrently develop new features: since how the new features work together will not be considered by either of the two independent feature developers. This problem is amplified if feature developers can configure features in any way that they wish.

4 Feature Interaction: An Incremental Development View

In figure 2, we take POTS as one requirement model. We note that to extend this base requirement with a new feature we must define a means of composing POTS with this feature, or, as illustrated in the diagram, use a previously defined mechanism. Unfortunately, for two different features there is no guarantee that we can use the same composition mechanism. Furthermore, for each composition we may require an additional restriction (called the composition invariant) on the way in which the parts are configured in order to gurantee that individual requirements are met.

Given such a composition technique we must now address the problem of integrating `Feature1` and `Feature2` in the same set of requirements. In figure 3, we see that an interaction occurs if the invariants introduced by the two features and/or the two composition mechanisms are contradictory. Properties are required to be preserved through the composition process; the multi-view approach allows us to integrate the view of invariants (using B) and the view of fairness (using TLA).

We note that there are many different ways in which we may wish to compose the three components. The four most obvious structures are:

- `Compose1(comp1(POTS,feature1), feature2)`, where we compose the `feature2` with the component which results from a composition between `POTS` and the `feature1`.

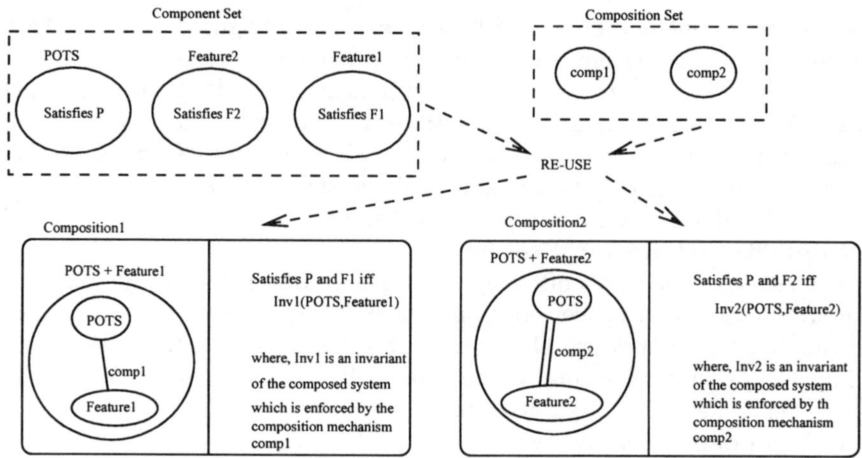

Fig. 2. Incrementing POTS

- `Compose2(comp2(POTS,feature2), feature1)`, where we compose the `feature1` with the component which results from a composition between `POTS` and the `feature2`.
- `Compose3(POTS, comp3(feature1,feature2))`, where we first compose the two features and then compose this new component with `POTS`.
- `Compose4(POTS, feature1, feature2)`, where we define a new composition mechanism which acts on all three components.

The feature composition problem is certainly difficult (even when there are only 2 features); now we argue that having formal requirements models makes it manageable, but we need to develop a methodology for composing features

4.1 Modelling Services

A service is an extension of POTS, - the basic service - , providing functionality to the customer for interacting with the switch and the billing system. The modeling of services is based on the view of services as processes altering a set of *calls*. The current state of a service is characterized by an invariant over calls. A call is a structure that manages and describes the current parameters as the caller, the callee, the call state, the paying party ... However, a call may be extended into another call by operations over calls such as fusion, completion etc. This means that calls are central concepts in our modelling but this makes the modelling more flexible. More generally, a call is a structure recording the current participants, the connection, the state, the billing. We use the TLA$^+$ syntax for writing service specifications, as follows:

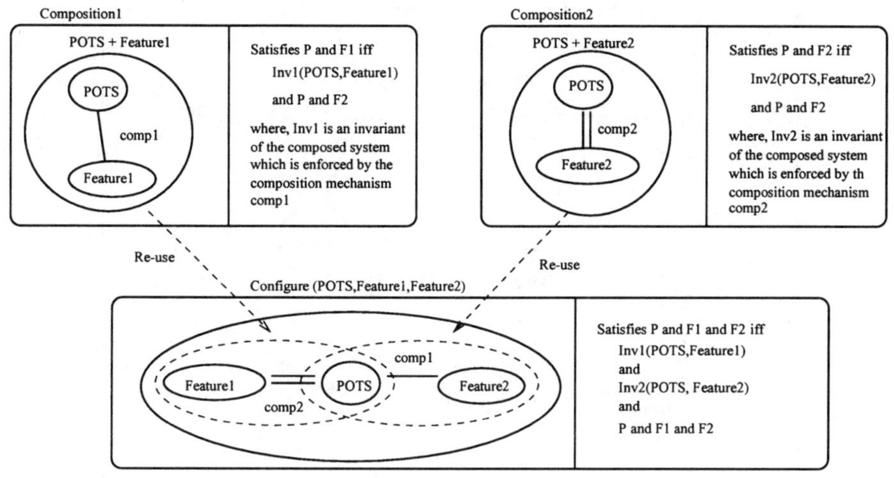

Fig. 3. Integrating Two Features

$COEF \triangleq 0..100$ used to define the percentage for contributing in the billing

$CALLS \triangleq$

$[party : \text{SUBSET } USERS,$
$linkcall : \text{SUBSET } (USERS \times USERS),$
$paycall : \text{SUBSET } \{USERS \times USERS \times USERS \times COEF \times TIME \times TIME)$

$com : \text{SUBSET } (USERS \times USERS),$
$state : CALLSTATES]$

Variables such as calls, phones, tones, messages, billings, services are typed according to the following typing invariant. We define it and operations or actions which have to preserve it.

$Typing\_Variables\_Invariant \triangleq$

$\wedge\ calls \in CALLS$
$\wedge\ phones \in [USERS \rightarrow PHONESTATES]$
$\wedge\ tones \in [USERS \rightarrow TONESTATES]$
$\wedge\ messages \in [USERS \rightarrow \text{SUBSET } STRING]$
$\wedge\ billings \in USERS \times COEF \times USERS \times COEF \times TIME \times TIME$
$\wedge\ services \in USERS \rightarrow \text{SUBSET } SERVICES$

Now, we can incrementally add new operations that are either activated by users or customers, or by the telecom systems. The basic service, called POTS, provides the following operations :

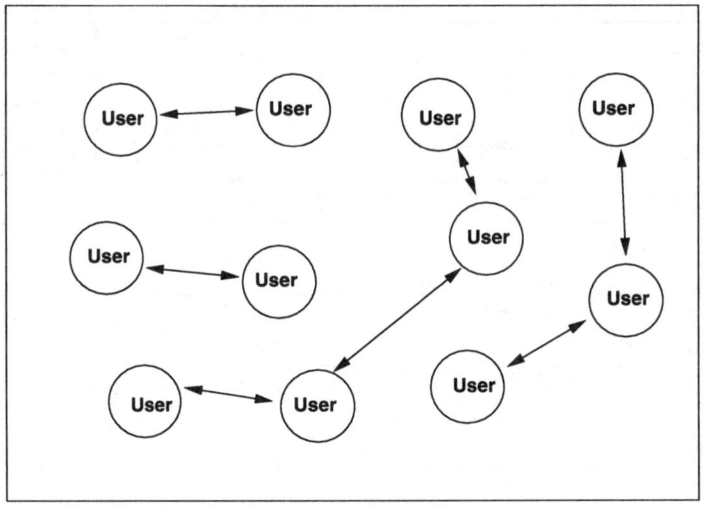

Fig. 4. View of services through calls

– off-hook

A user can off hook the phone because he/she wants to call somebody somebody else is calling him/her. The switch will reply either by sending a dialtone or by starting the communication.

$$
\begin{aligned}
&OFFHOOKCALLING(Xcaller) \triangleq \\
&\quad \wedge\ phones' = [phones\ !\text{EXCEPT}[Xcaller] = \text{"offhook"}] \\
&\quad \wedge\ tones' = [tones\ !\text{EXCEPT}[Xcaller] = \text{"notone"}] \\
&\quad \wedge\ \text{UNCHANGED}\ < tones, calls, messages, billings, t >
\end{aligned}
$$

Y wants to call somebody, namely X, in the call $Xcall$

$$
\begin{aligned}
&OFFHOOKRINGING(X, Y, Xcall) \triangleq \\
&\wedge\ Xcall \in calls \\
&\wedge\ \{X, Y\} \subseteq Xcall.party \\
&\wedge\ tones[X] = \text{"ringing"} \\
&\wedge\ tones[Y] = \text{"ringbacktone"} \\
&\wedge\ tones' = [[tones\ !\text{EXCEPT}[X] = \text{"notone"}]\ !\text{EXCEPT}[Y] = \text{"notone"}] \\
&\wedge phones[Xcalled] \neq \text{"offhook"} \Rightarrow phones' = [phones!\text{EXCEPT}[Xcaller] = \\
&\text{"offhook"}] \\
&\wedge\ phones[Xcalled] = \text{"offhook"} \Rightarrow phones' = phones \\
&\wedge\ \text{UNCHANGED}\ < calls, messages, billings, t, services >
\end{aligned}
$$

Xcalled is called by somebody else and Xcalled is ringing;
the operation is done by the user

- on-hook
- dial
- communication

We have added an event which is executed infinitly often to model the time, since we need to specify the starting point of a call and the ending point of a call, for instance.

$$TICTAC \triangleq \wedge t' = t + 1$$
$$\wedge \text{UNCHANGED} < tones, calls, messages, billings, phones, services >$$

The global system, called POTS, is operationally defined as a disjunction of relations over primed and unprimed variables (thanks to TLA).

we define the set of possible events of the basic system, called
POTS

$$\begin{aligned} EventsBasicSystem \triangleq\ & \cup\ OffHookCallingEvents \\ & \cup\ OffHookRingingEvents \\ & \cup\ OnHookFirstEvents \\ & \cup\ UpdateCallsEvents \\ & \cup\ FinalUpdateCallEvents \\ & \cup\ OnHookLastEvents \\ & \cup\ DialEvents \\ & \cup\ SendingToneDialevents \\ & \cup\ DialToneEvents \\ & \cup\ CommunicationOkEvents \\ & \cup\ CommunicationDownEvents \\ & \cup\ CommunicationBusyEvents \\ & \cup\ OnHookDownEvents \\ & \cup\ OnHookBusyEvents \\ & \cup\ Clean\_Down\_CallsEvents \\ & \cup\ Clean\_Busy\_CallsEvents \\ & \cup\ Clean\_Completed\_Calls \\ & \cup\ \{TICTAC\} \end{aligned}$$

Now we apply the 'Next' operator to obtain the next relation
for the operational semantics.

$$NextBasicSystem \triangleq Next(EventsBasicSystem)$$

TLA$^+$ requires that we specify the variables of the system.

$VarsBasicSystem \triangleq < messages, calls, phones, tones, billings, t, services >$

Finally, we assume that every event is executed under the weak fairness assumption.

$FairnessBasicSystem \triangleq WF(VarsBasicSystem, EventsBasicSsystem)$

We have defined an operator assigning a formula from a set of formulae; it allows us to get a simpler way to specify, since we have to give the set of possible events and to apply it on the current set of events. Now, the bare basic service is simply specified by the following formulae.

$$
\begin{array}{l}
InitBasicSystem \triangleq \\
\quad \wedge\ calls = \{\} \\
\quad \wedge\ \forall p \in USERS : phones[p] = \text{"onhook"} \\
\quad \wedge\ \forall p \in USERS : tones[p] = \text{"notone"} \\
\quad \wedge\ billing = \{\} \\
\quad \wedge\ \forall p \in USERS : messages[p] = \text{""} \\
\quad \wedge\ \forall p \in USERS : services[p] = \{\text{"basic"}\} \\
\quad \wedge\ t = 0
\end{array}
$$

$$
\begin{array}{l}
SpecificationBasicSystem \triangleq \\
\quad \wedge\ InitBasicSystem \\
\quad \wedge\ \Box[NextBasicSystem]\_\{VarsBasicSystem\} \\
\quad \wedge\ FairnessBasicSystem
\end{array}
$$

The basic system provides the user with the basic functionality required for calling somebody else. At this stage, a user 'X' can call only one user 'Y'; if we increase the calling possibilities, we add functionality related to a new service. Increasing the basic functionalities means that we allow the user additional operations; if N is the relation characterizing the current service, then a new functionality is obtained by adding another relation, namely F, as follows: N $\vee$ F. Composing is reduced to logical operations over relations on states, but we may have transformations to do on relations. The user view of the service is like a reactive system. The modules for POTS have a very restricted scope, since the functionality of each is very limited.

4.2 Adding a New Service

The user's view deals with operations such as subscribing, unsubscribing, paying, billing, and a service is generally characterized by at least two operations that enable or disable the service, when the user has subscribed; for instance the service, called CCBS, allows the user/subscriber to be informed, when another, whom he is calling and busy, becomes idle.

$$
\begin{aligned}
&CCBS\_activation(X) \triangleq \\
&\quad \land X \in USERS \\
&\quad \land X \notin CCBS\_sub \\
&\quad \land CCBS\_sub' = CCBS\_sub \cup \{X\} \\
&\quad \land CCBS\_heap' = [x \in DOM\ CCBS\_heap \cup \{X\} \\
&\qquad\qquad \mapsto \text{IF } x = X \text{ THEN } \{\} \text{ ELSE } CCBS\_heap[x]] \\
&\quad \land \text{UNCHANGED } < list\_of\_unchanged\_variables >
\end{aligned}
$$

$$
\begin{aligned}
&CCBS\_inhibition(X) \triangleq \\
&\quad \land X \in USERS \\
&\quad \land X \in CCBS\_sub \\
&\quad \land CCBS\_sub' = CCBS\_sub - \{X\} \\
&\quad \land CCBS\_heap' = [x \in DOM\ CCBS\_heap - \{X\} \mapsto CCBS\_heap[x]] \\
&\quad \land \text{UNCHANGED } < list\_of\_unchanged\_variables >
\end{aligned}
$$

We modify the basic service, by strengthening operations of the callee; moreover, CCBS is a very interesting service, since it requires the expression of a fairness constraint. A first step is to analyse what is shared by CCBS and POTS and what is private or local for CCBS. We introduce two variables that will manage the current subscribers of CCBS and the waiting users for re-calling somebody.

VARIABLES

$CCBS\_sub$,	set of users that have subscribed to CCBS
$CCBS\_heap$	function defining heaps

The typing invariant of CCBS declares the role of those variables.

$$
\begin{aligned}
INVARIANT\_CCBS \triangleq\ &\land CCBS\_sub \subseteq USERS \\
&\land CCBS\_heap \in [USERS \rightarrow \text{SUBSET } USERS]
\end{aligned}
$$

The next step is to define "side-effects" on events of the basic service. CCBS requires an event for dequeing recalls for users having subscribed to CCBS; we call it $CCBS\_Dequeue(X, Y, Xcall)$, and it requires a fairness assumption.

$$
\begin{aligned}
&CCBS\_Dequeue(X, Y, Xcall) \\
&\land tones[X] = \text{"notone"} \\
&\land phones[X] = \text{"onhook"} \\
&\land phones[Y] = \text{"onhook"} \\
&\land tones[Y] = \text{"notone"} \\
&\land X \in CCBS\_sub \\
&\land tones' = [[tones\ !\text{EXCEPT}[X] = \text{"ringing"}]!\text{EXCEPT}[Y] = \text{"ringing"}] \\
&\land Xcall.state = \text{"busyCCBS"} \\
&\land Xcall \in calls \cap CCBS\_heap[Y] \\
&\land \{X, Y\} \subseteq Xcall.party \\
&\land \text{LET } newcall = \text{CHOOSE } c\ .\ \land c \in calls \cap CCBS\_heap[Y] \\
&\qquad\qquad\qquad\qquad\qquad \land c.state = \text{"waiting"} \\
&\qquad\qquad\qquad\qquad\qquad \land c.com = Xcall.com
\end{aligned}
$$

$$
\begin{array}{l}
\qquad\qquad\qquad\qquad \wedge\ c.paycall\ =\ Xcall.paycall \\
\qquad\qquad\qquad\qquad \wedge\ c.linkcall\ =\ Xcall.linkcall \\
\quad \text{IN}\ \ \wedge\ calls'\ =\ calls - \{Xcall\} \cup \{newcall\} \\
\qquad\quad \wedge\ CCBS\_heap'\ =\ [CCBS\_heap\ !\text{EXCEPT}[Y]\ =\ @ - \{Xcall\}] \\
\wedge\ \text{UNCHANGED}\ < messages, phones, billings, calls, t, CCBS\_sub >
\end{array}
$$

Now, we modify two events in the specification of the basic service, namely the COMMUNICATION-BUSY, which manages calls when they are busy, and OFFHOOKRINGING, which manages when somebody is called and this phone is ringing. Hence, we modify events of the basic service and add new events.

$$
\begin{array}{l}
CBS\_COMMUNICATION\_BUSY(X, Y, Xcall)\ \triangleq \\
\wedge\ Xcall\ \in\ calls \\
\wedge\ Xcall.state\ =\ \text{"waiting"} \\
\wedge\ Xcall.party\ =\ \{X, Y\} \\
\wedge\ X\ \neq\ Y \\
\wedge\ \exists\, c\ \in\ calls\ : \\
\quad \wedge\ c\ \neq\ Xcall \\
\quad \wedge\ phones[Y]\ =\ \text{"offhook"} \\
\quad \wedge\ tones[Y]\ =\ \text{"talking"} \\
\quad \wedge\ Y\ \in\ c.party \\
\quad \wedge\ c.state\ =\ \text{"active"} \\
\quad \wedge\ X\ \notin\ c.party \\
\quad \wedge\ phones[X]\ =\ \text{"offhook"} \\
\quad \wedge\ tones[X] = \text{"dialling"} \\
\quad \wedge\ \text{LET}\ newcall\ \triangleq \\
\qquad\qquad \text{CHOOSE}\ c\ .\ \wedge\ c\ \in\ CALLS\ \setminus\ calls \\
\qquad\qquad\qquad\qquad \wedge\ c.state\ =\ \text{"busyCCBS"} \\
\qquad\qquad\qquad\qquad \wedge\ c.party\ =\ \{X, Y\} \\
\qquad\qquad\qquad\qquad \wedge\ c.com\ =\ \{\} \\
\qquad\qquad\qquad\qquad \wedge\ c.paycall\ =\ \{\} \\
\qquad\qquad\qquad\qquad \wedge\ c.linkcall\ =\ \{< X, Y >\} \\
\qquad \text{IN}\ \ \wedge\ calls'\ =\ calls - \{Xcall\} \cup \{newcall\} \\
\qquad\qquad \wedge\ CCBS\_heap'\ =\ [CCBS\_heap\ !\text{EXCEPT}[Y]\ =\ @ \cup \{newcall\}] \\
\qquad\qquad \wedge\ tones'\ =\ [tones\ !\text{EXCEPT}[X]\ =\ \text{"CCBStone"}] \\
\wedge\ \text{UNCHANGED}\ < phones, messages, billings, t, CCBS\_sub >
\end{array}
$$

$$
\begin{array}{l}
CCBS\_OFFHOOKRINGING(X, Y, Xcall)\ \triangleq \\
\wedge\ Xcall\ \in\ calls \\
\wedge\ \{X, Y\}\ \subseteq\ Xcall.party \\
\wedge\ \vee\ tones[X]\ =\ \text{"ringing"} \\
\quad \vee\ tones[Y]\ =\ \text{"ringing"} \\
\wedge\ < X, Y >\ Xcall.linkcall \\
\wedge\ X\ \in\ CCBS\_sub \\
\wedge\ phones[X] \neq \text{"offhook"}\ \Rightarrow\ \wedge\ phones'\ =\ [phones\ !\text{EXCEPT}[X]\ =\ \text{"offhook"}]
\end{array}
$$

$$\begin{array}{lll} & \wedge\ tones' & = [tones\ !\text{EXCEPT}[X] = \text{"notone"}] \\ \wedge\ phones[X] = \text{"offhook"} \Rightarrow & \wedge\ phones' & = [phones\ !\text{EXCEPT}[Y] = \text{"offhook"}] \\ & \wedge\ tones' & = [tones\ !\text{EXCEPT}[Y] = \text{"notone"}] \end{array}$$

$\wedge$ UNCHANGED $< calls, messages, billings, t, CCBS\_sub, CCBS\_heap >$

Now, events of CCBS are defined as follows:

$$\begin{aligned} & CCBS\_events \triangleq \\ & \quad \cup\ UNION_1(CCBS\_activation, USERS) \\ & \quad \cup\ UNION_1(CCBS\_inhibition, USERS) \\ & \quad \cup\ UNION_2(CCBS\_Dequeue, USERS, USERS, CALLS) \\ & \quad \cup\ UNION_2(CCBS\_OFFHOOKRINGING, USERS, USERS, CALLS) \end{aligned}$$

However, POTS is modified by the service CCBS, by restricting COMMUNICATION events when the called user is busy; in fact, it leads to an enqueueing of the busy called user. We define a restriction of the POTS service which is modified and then we define a way to instantiate a system, defined by a set of events.

$$\begin{aligned} & CCBS\_Restriction(System\} \triangleq \\ & \quad System - CommunicationBusyEvents \\ & \quad \cup\ UNION_3(CCBS\_COMMUNICATION\_BUSY, USERS, USERS, CALLS) \end{aligned}$$

$$CCBS\_instance(System) \triangleq CCBS\_Restriction(System\} \cup CCBS\_events$$

Properties of CCBS tells us that when somebody (X) calls somebody else (Y) and, if Y is busy, then when Y is put onhook, the system will recall X and Y. X and Y will ring together, when fairness constraints are ensured.

$$\begin{aligned} & CCBSPlusBSEvents \triangleq CCBS\_instance(EventsBasicSystem) \\ & SpecCCBSPlusBS \triangleq \\ & \quad \wedge\ InitBasicSystem \\ & \quad \wedge\ InitCCBS \\ & \quad \wedge\ \Box\ [Next(CCBSPlusBSEvents)]\_ < VarsBasicSystem, VarsCCBS > \\ & \quad \wedge\ WF(VarsCCBS \cup VarsBasicSystem, CCBSPlusBSEvents) \end{aligned}$$

THEOREM $SpecCCBSPlusBS \Rightarrow \Box\ INVARIANT\_CCBS$

---

if 'X' calls 'Y', while 'Y' is busy and 'X' has subscribed 'CCBS',

then eventually 'Y' is appended to the waiting heap for 'X'

THEOREM

$SpecCCBSPlusBS \Rightarrow$

$(\Box\ (Calling(X, Y) \wedge (X \in CCBS\_sub \wedge Busy(Y)) \leadsto (X \in CCBS\_heap[Y]))$

---

if 'X' is in the waiting heap of 'Y', and if 'Y' has subscribed CCBS,
while 'X' is infinitly often busy, then eventually 'X' and 'Y' will
ring both

THEOREM

$$SpecCCBSPlusBS \Rightarrow$$
$$(X \in CCBS\_heap[Y] \land \Box (Y \in CCBS\_sub) \land \Box \Diamond \neg Busy(X) \leadsto (RingingBoth(X,Y))$$

We have expressed the formal modelling of the basic service and of CCBS; now, we have to verify theorems and to validate the specifications.

4.3 Coordinating Views

Our model of services in TLA$^+$ can be verified and validated using the Atelier B toolkit. This means that we can verify invariants using a coding of our TLA specifications in B. Services can be viewed as abstract machines or as TLA$^+$ modules. The coordination of views means that properties that are observed in each model are not contradictory. Our model of services in TLA$^+$ can be verified and validated using the Atelier B toolkit, since our TLA$^+$ specifications are made up of imperative actions; these actions are written $x' = f(x)$ where $f(x)$ is an expression codable in B. Services in TLA$^+$ can be viewed as B abstract machines, but this leads us to forget fairness issues. However, it means that we do get a framework for animating and verifying the B view of a TLA$^+$ specification. It is clear that our approach is based on the use of a theorem prover but one can also use a model-checking-based tool.

4.4 Validation and Verification

We give a graphical representation of our formal models. The graphical syntax is informally explained and, where appropriate, we comment on how the formal meaning is captured using LOTOS, B and TLA. The semantics are clearly based on a state transition model and, as such, are easily communicated to the client through a process of animation.

We have specified a simple (POTS) client-oriented model of phone behaviour. This is sufficiently complex to illustrate the graphical syntax, in figure 5, being employed to communicate the formal semantics with the client.

The following aspects of the specification should be noted:

The header

The name of the class (`Phone`) being specified is given first in the header of the diagram. The other classes which are used in the specification of the new class are listed after the `USING` keyword: the `Phone` uses classes `signal` and `on-off`.

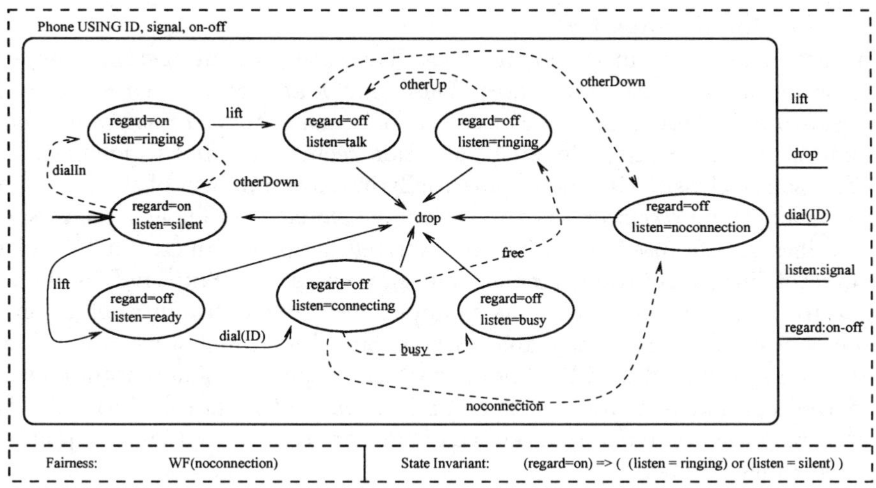

Fig. 5. The Phone

The interface

The interface to the class is represented by the connections at its boundary. Each connection corresponds to a service. In this case there are 5 services, namely: `lift`, `drop`, `dial`, `listen` and `regard`. `Lift`, `drop` and `dial` correspond to *transformer* services. When requested they result in a state transition. `Listen` and `regard` correspond to *accessor* services. When requested they return a value to the service requester. The type of the value returned is identified by a class name: `listen`, for example, returns a `signal` value. Services can be parameterised by a set of *input classes*: `dial`, for example, is parmeterised by an `ID` value. Services can be polymorphic on their input classes. In other words, a class can have two different services of the same name provided they can be distinguished by the types of their input parameters. The user of the class sees the class as a *black box*. The internal state of the class is encapsulated by its interface. The only access to state information is through the *accessors*. (There is one more type of service which is not illustrated by the `Phone`: the *dual* service is a combination of a *transformer* and an *accessor*: it returns a value *and* results in a state transition.)

Communication

Communication between an object *server* and its environment of *clients* is taken, unless otherwise specified, to be synchronous. This may lead to situations in which services are requested but are not enabled by the server. We note that *accessor* services are always enabled. *Duals* and *transformers* may not always be enabled: if a client requests a service which is not enabled then it is the client's responsibility to avoid a potential deadlock situation. One role of *fairness* in our models is to gurantee that services will be *eventually* enabled.

The operational semantics

There are eight states in the `Phone` class. Thus every `Phone` instance (object) must be in one of these eight states. These states are represented as nodes in the inside of the class boundary. For each state, each of the *accessor* values must be defined. To aid compositional specification techniques, and to facilitate the specification of classes with large (potentially infinite) numbers of states, we can define a class to be *structured* as a set of *component* classes. Then, these *internal* state values can be used to define the *external accessor* values. This provides a degree of implementation freedom and emphasises that *internal* details are hidden to the outside. In the `Phone` example, there is no *structure* definition as the number of states is manageable without one. The initial state of an object on creation is specified by a bold pointer which does not originate from another state. Hence, a `Phone` always starts `on` and `silent`. The state transitions which occur in response to an external service request are represented by solid pointers from old to new states.

Invariants

State invariant properties define restrictions on the possible sets of component values. For example, as it is shown in figure 5, we may require that when `onhook` the `Phone` *must* be `ringing` or `silent`. These properties are verified, for more complex cases, using B: by checking that all transitions are closed with respect to the invariant it is not necessary to examine every single reachable state (which we can do directly with the simple `Phone` model). Note that the state invariants specified in this way are explicit requirements of the client that must be respected by the model. A specification where the invariants are not true is said to be *contradictory.*

Nondeterminism

Nondeterminism is formalised as internal state transitions that may occur independent from external service requests. These are represented by (possibly labelled) dotted pointers from old to new states. For example, when `off` and `connecting` the `Phone` user has no control over whether the number they are trying is `busy, free` or if `noconnection` is possible. These three cases are specified using internal actions (labelled appropriately). The difference between internal and external actions specifies a *point-of-view* onto a class (and the objects of the class). In this paper, our models specify the `Phone` user's point of view (or abstraction). The way in which the telephone network interacts with the `Phone` is abstracted away from in the form of nondeterministic transitions. Certainly, it is necessary to specify other points of view when modelling the whole telephone network. Our modular approach lets us work with different abstractions and then helps us to integrate these abstractions into a complete specification. This is beyond the scope of this paper, which concentrates on user requirements.

Fairness

Liveness conditions can be specified on the nondeterministic events in the model. For example, we may require that when `off` and `connecting` the user does not wait forever for a state transition if they refuse to drop the phone. This must be specified in a separate TLA (temporal) clause. In figure 5, we specify *weak fairness* on the `noconnection` action.

(In)finite processes

A `Phone` is an *infinite* process. In later examples we specify finite behaviours which `EXIT` after some specific behaviour is fulfilled. A `Phone` is said to be of type `NOEXIT`.

A new feature: black list

The `Black List` feature has a similar function to originating call screening, but restricts incoming rather than outgoing calls. The idea is that you can store a list of numbers that you know you do not wish to talk with and then your phone does not ring when such numbers are the source of an incoming call. Our specification of this feature is illustrated in figure 6.

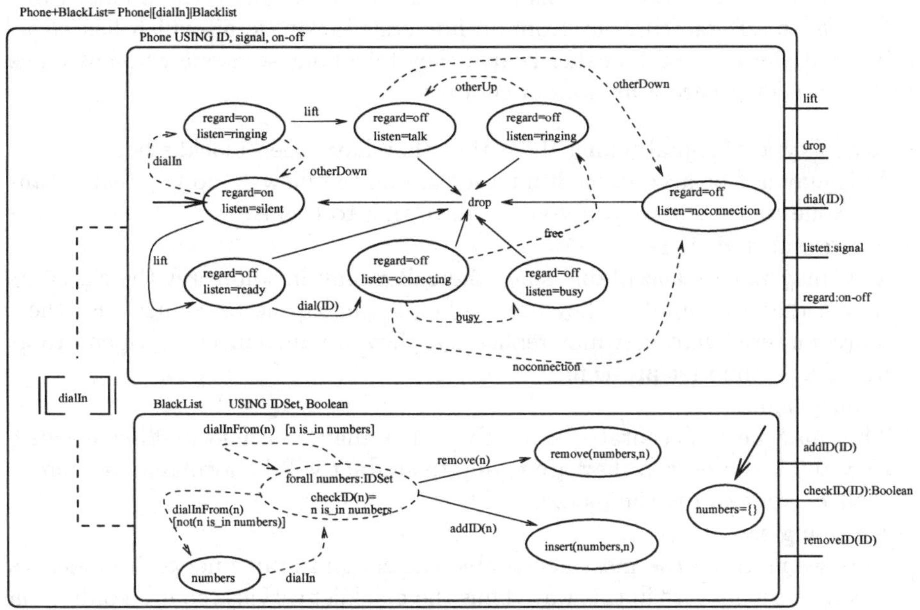

Fig. 6. Black list

Again, we have some comments to make with regard to this feature model:

Composition Re-Use

The composition is precisely that seen for a similar, better known, `CallerID` feature: there is internal synchronisation on the `dialIn` event and the system depends on an action refinement in the network to carry the new identification data using a `dialInFrom` action.

Phone refinement

Unlike `CallID`, not all `dialInFrom` actions result in a `dialIn` action: the blacklist filters out all incoming dials which are stored in the list of numbers in its state.

However, like `CallID`, from the point of view of the user the new system is a refinement of the old phone — the only difference is the resolution of some of the nondeterminism in the original phone model.

Weak fairness guarantees eventuality

We require *weak fairness* on the `dialIn` event in the `BlackList` component. In the `BlackList` component we see that after a `dialInFrom` event, the external services `removeID` and `addID` may not be enabled until a `dialIn` action is performed, in the case where the number is not black listed. However, weak fairness on `dialIn` guarantees that this transition will eventually occur. Thus, we guarantee that the telephone user will not be deadlocked if they wish to `add` or `remove` a number from the blacklist because of an incoming call.

Localisation

At first glance, this feature seems to be *local.* All other users of the telephone system can remain unaware of this particular feature at any given phone. However, we have abstracted away from an implementation detail which has *global* effect: what signal should a caller hear if they telephone someone who has black listed them? There are a number of choices:

- A new type of signal telling them that they have been blacklisted.
  This may not be acceptable from a social point of view — do you really want someone to know that you don't wish to talk to them.
- A noconnected signal.
  This may not be acceptable since the caller may misinterpret the signal as saying that the number they are dialling is impossible to connect. Furthermore, an intelligent user may realise *why* they are unconnected, which brings us back to the first problem.
- A busy signal.
  This may be unacceptable since the caller may continue dialling because they think the person they are trying to contact will be available as soon as their current call is completed.
- A ringing signal.
  This seems to be the most acceptable choice, and in our network model we specified the feature in this way. Thus the blacklist service required only *local* change to the telephone user which requested this service. All other users retain their original behaviour.

It is only through animation that a user can be expected to understand such choices and help the designers to resolve the nondeterminism.

5 Conclusion

The problem of telephone feature interaction is just a particular instance of a general problem in software engineering. The same problem occurs when we consider inheritance in object oriented systems, sharing data in distributed systems, multi-way synchronisation in systems of concurrent processes, etc... However, the problem is particularly difficult in telephone systems because features are the increments of development.

We have shown the importance of re-usable composition mechanisms. Although our work is targeted towards the client during requirements capture, we believe that the same models could be used during design and at the network level. We support the principle of developing re-usable analysis techniques based on re-usable synthesis mechanisms. The object oriented approach can be extended to include a classification of feature types and we hope to map this onto a formal algebra for feature development.

We have used a graphical notation for communicating with the customer. However, our graphics are based on formal notations of languages, which may be difficult for the customer to understand. This work was very helpful in studying the complementary nature of different formalims. Logical formalisms such as B or TLA are really suitable for logical analysis of services based on proof techniques. Animation is made easier by automata-based representations.

This work is dependent on the different view points and the different semantic models. The integration of these semantics and the development of user-oriented tools is the most important element of our current, and future work. Finally, the integration of refinement-based reasoning is an important point to develop, with experiments in other domains.

References

[1] J.-R. Abrial. *The B book - Assigning Programs to Meanings.* Cambridge University Press, 1996.

[2] J. Blom. Formalisation of requirements with emphasis on feature interaction detection. In *Feature Interactions In Telecommunications IV*, Montreal, Canada, June 1997. IOS Press.

[3] J. Blom, B. Johnsson, and L. Kempe. Automatic detection of feature interactions in temporal logic. In K. E. Cheng and T. Ohta, editors, *Feature Interactions in Telecommunications Systems*, pages 1–19. IOS Press, 1996. [9].

[4] J. Blom, B. Jonsson, and L. Kempe. Using temporal logic for modular specification of telephone services. In L. G. Bouma and H. Velthuijsen, editors, *Feature Interactions in Telecommunications Systems*, pages 197–216. IOS Press, 1994.

[5] G. Booch. *Object oriented design with applications.* Benjamin Cummings, 1991.

[6] L. G. Bouma and H. Velthuijsen, editors. *Feature Interactions in Telecommunications Systems.* IOS Press, 1994.

[7] R. Boumezbeur and L. Logrippo. Specifying telephone systems in LOTOS. *IEEE Communications Magazine*, 31(8):38–45, 1993.

[8] Ed. Brinksma, Giuseppe Scollo, and Chris Steenbergen. LOTOS specifications, their implementation and their tests. In *Sixth International Symposium on Protocol Testing, Specification and Verification*, Montreal, June 1986.

[9] K. E. Cheng and T. Ohta, editors. *Feature Interactions in Telecommunications Systems.* IOS Press, 1996.

[10] P. Coad and E. Yourdon. *Object oriented design.* Prentice-Hall (Yourdon Press), 1990.

[11] P. Combes and S. Pickin. Formalisation of a user view of network and services for feature interaction detection. In L. G. Bouma and H. Velthuijsen, editors, *Feature Interactions in Telecommunications Software System*, pages 120–135. IOS Press, 1994. [6].

[12] L. Constantine. Beyond the madness of methods: System structure methods and converging design. In *Software Development 1989*. Miller-Freeman, 1989.

[13] Dan Craigen, Susan Gerhart, and Ted Ralston. An international survey of industrial applications of formal methods. Nistgcr 93/626, U.S. Department of Commerce, Technology Administration, National Institute of Standards and Technology, Computer Systems Lab., Gaithersburg, MD 20899, 1993.

[14] Geoff Cutts. *Structured system analysis and design method.* Blackwell Scientific Publishers, 1991.

[15] P. Dini, R. Boutaba, and L. Logrippo, editors. *Feature Interactions in Telecommunications Newtworks IV*, Montreal, 1997. IOS Press.

[16] H. Ehrig and Mahr B. *Fundamentals of Algebraic Specification I.* Springer-Verlag, Berlin, 1985. EATCS Monographs on Theoretical Computer Science (6).

[17] M. Faci and L. Logrippo. Specifying features and analysing their interactions in a lotos environment. In L. G. Bouma and H. Velthuijsen, editors, *Feature Interactions in Telecommunications Software System*, pages 136–151. IOS Press, 1994. [6].

[18] M. Faci, L. Logrippo, and B. Stepien. Formal specification of telephone systems in lotos : constraint-oriented style approach. *Computer Networks and ISDN Systems*, 21:53–67, 1991.

[19] A. Gammelgaard and J. E. Kristensen. Interaction detection, a logical approach. In L. G. Bouma and H. Velthuijsen, editors, *Feature Interactions in Telecommunications Systems*, pages 178–196. IOS Press, 1994.

[20] J.-P. Gibson. *Formal Object Oriented Development of Software Systems Using LOTOS.* Tech. report CSM-114, Stirling University, August 1993.

[21] J.-P. Gibson. Formal object based design in LOTOS. Tr-113, University of Stirling, Computing Science Department, Stirling, Scotland, 1994.

[22] J.-P. Gibson. Feature Requirements Models: Understanding Interactions. In *Feature Interaction Workshop 1997, Montreal, Canada*, Feature Interaction Workshop. IOS Press, June 1997.

[23] J.-P. Gibson, B. Mermet, and D. Méry. Feature interactions: A mixed semantic model approach. In Gerard O'Regan and Sharon Flynn, editors, *1st Irish Workshop on Formal Methods*, Dublin, Ireland, July 1997. Irish Formal Methods Special Interest Group (IFMSIG), Springer Verlag. http://ewic.springer.co.uk/.

[24] J.-P. Gibson, B. Mermet, D. Méry, and Y. Mokhtari. Spécification de services dans une logique temporelle compositionnelle. Rapport de fin du lot1 du marché n^o96 1B CNET-CNRS-CRIN, Centre de Recherche en Informatique de Nancy, décembre 1996.

[25] J.-P. Gibson and D. Méry. A unifying framework for multi-semantic software development. In Max Mühlhäuser, editor, *Special Issues in Object-Oriented Programming.* Dpunkt, 1997.

[26] C.A.R Hoare. *Communicating Sequential Processes.* Prentice-Hall International, 1985.

[27] IEE. *Special Collection On Requirements Analysis.* IEE Transactions on Software Engineering, 1977.

[28] ISO. LOTOS — a formal description technique based on the temporal ordering of observed behaviour. Technical report, International Organisation for Standardisation IS 8807, 1988.

[29] B. Kelly, M. Crowther, and J. King. Feature interaction detection using sdl models. In *GLOBECOM. Communications: The Global Bridge. Conference Record*, pages 1857–61. IEEE, 1994.

[30] B. Kelly, M. Crowther, J. King, R. Masson, and J. Delapeyre. Service validation and testing. In K. E. Cheng and T. Ohta, editors, *Feature Interactions in Telecommunications Systems*, pages 173–184. IOS Press, 1996. [9].

[31] L. Lamport. A temporal logic of actions. *Transactions On Programming Languages and Systems*, 16(3):872–923, May 1994.

[32] B. Liskov and Zilles S. Programming with abstract data types. In *ACM SIGPLAN Notices*, volume 9, pages 50–59, 1974.

[33] B. Mermet and D. Méry. Incremental specification of telecommunication services. In M. Hinchey, editor, *First IEEE International Conference on Formal Engineering Methods (ICFEM)*, Hiroshima, November 1997. IEEE.

[34] B. Mermet and D. Méry. Safe combinations of services using b. In John McDermid, editor, *SAFECOMP97 The 16th International Conference on Computer Safety, Reliability and Security*, York, September 1997. Springer Verlag.

[35] D. Méry. Requirements for a temporal B : Assigning Temporal Meaning to Abstract Machines ... and to Abstract Systems. In A. Galloway and K. Taguchi, editors, *IFM'99 Integrated Formal Methods 1999*, Workshop In Computing Science, YORK, June 1999.

[36] C. A. Middleburg. A simple language for expressing properties of telecommunications services and features. Technical report PU-94-356, KPN Research, Network and Service Control department, 1994.

[37] R. Milner. *A Calculus of Communicating Systems.* Springer-Verlag, 1980.

[38] D. T. Ross. Structured analysis (SA): A language for communicating ideas. In *IEE Transactions on Software Engineering.* IEE, 1977.

[39] Steria Méditerrannée. *Atelier B, Version 3.2, Manuel de Référence du Langage B.* GEC Alsthom Transport and Steria Méditerrannée and SNCF and INRETS and RATP, 1997.

[40] Kenneth J. Turner. *Using Formal Description Techniques - An Introduction to ESTELLE, LOTOS and SDL.* John Wiley, New York, January 1993.

[41] K.J. Turner. SPLICE I: Specification using LOTOS for an interactive customer environment — phase 1. University of Stirling SPLICE Internal Technical Document, 1992.

[42] K.J.T. Turner. *Using FDTS: An Introduction To ESTELLE, LOTOS and SDL.* John Wiley and Sons, 1993.

[43] P. Zave. Feature interactions and formal specifications in telecommunications. *Computer*, August 1993.

[44] Pamela Zave. The operational versus the conventional approach to software development. *Comm. ACM*, 27:104–118, 1984.

[45] Pamela Zave. Feature interactions and formal specifications in telecommunications. *IEEE Computer Magazine*, pages 18–23, August 1993.

Serializability Preserving Extensions of Concurrency Control Protocols

Dmitri Chkliaev[1], Jozef Hooman[2], and Peter van der Stok[1]

[1] Dept. of Computing Science, Eindhoven University of Technology
P.O. Box 513, 5600 MB Eindhoven, The Netherlands
{dmitri,wsstok}@win.tue.nl

[2] Computing Science Institute, University of Nijmegen, The Netherlands
hooman@cs.kun.nl

Abstract. The verification system PVS is used to obtain mechanized support for the formal specification and verification of concurrency control protocols, concentrating on database applications. A method to verify conflict serializability has been formulated in PVS and proved to be sound and complete with the interactive proof checker of this tool. The method has been used to verify a few basic protocols. Next we present a systematic way to extend these protocols with new actions and control information. We show that if such an extension satisfies a few simple correctness conditions, the new protocol is serializable by construction.

1 Introduction

Concurrency control protocols [SKS97, Ull88], when applied to databases, manage the concurrent access to a database by multiple users or processes. Access is performed by means of transactions, consisting of a number of actions (such as reads and writes of data items). This access has to be both correct, i.e. always leaving the database in a consistent state, and efficient, i.e. providing a good overall performance. One of the most important correctness notions is serializability of transactions, which is the main topic of this paper.

It is prominently difficult to achieve both correctness and efficiency at the same time. The most popular database protocol, the Two Phase Locking protocol (2PL), is simple and ensures serializability. Although it became a commercial standard in the seventies, it has been criticized for low performance and the possibility of deadlock (see, for instance, [Tho93]). A number of more efficient database protocols has been suggested, often on top of basic protocols such as 2PL. Newly developed protocols are becoming increasingly complex, and their correctness becomes difficult to ensure. Specification and reasoning are often very informal, which easily leads to ambiguous specifications. All these factors make the understanding and the use of these new protocols difficult and they increase the danger of incorrect protocols.

To address this problem, observe that many database protocols can be modeled as variations of a few basic concurrency control protocols. Although these variations can be obtained in different ways, they can often be considered as

D. Bjørner, M. Broy, A. Zamulin (Eds.): PSI'99, LNCS 1755, pp. 180–193, 2000.

extensions of a basic protocol. An extension of a database protocol is a protocol, which includes more control information (such as timestamps and versions) and corresponding new actions.

The aim is to obtain the correctness of extensions from the correctness of a basic protocol. Here we focus on only one important correctness notion, namely serializability. An interleaved execution of a number of transactions is said to be *serializable*, if it has the same effect on a database as some *serial* execution of these transactions, i.e. an execution which has no interleaving between actions of different transactions. Deadlocks are assumed not to occur (as e.g. [Ull88]), since they do not influence serializability.

Given some set of basic concurrency control protocols, we propose to prove the correctness of extensions of these protocols, using the following strategy: a) Prove correctness (i.e. serializability) of the basic protocols. b) Derive the correctness of the extensions in a systematic way, using some assumptions on their construction. Ideally, this should be done in a structured way, using some mechanical support. The aim of our paper is to suggest a method to implement this strategy. Therefore, we address the following questions: 1) How to obtain mechanical support for specification and verification? 2) How to model concurrency control protocols? 3) How to formalize serializability? 4) How to verify serializability? 5) How to formalize protocol extensions and which conditions are needed to ensure their correctness?

1) Mechanical support. To get mechanical support, we use a higher-order interactive theorem prover, since notions like serializability are easily expressed in a property-oriented, assertional, way. To express general properties about these notions, that hold for all protocols, a higher-order logic is needed. Since we would like to use arbitrary data types and not restrict ourselves to finite state systems, completely automatic verification is not feasible. Although there are several verification systems that satisfy our requirements, we have chosen to use PVS [PVS], because it has a convenient specification language and is relatively easy to learn and to use.

The specification language of PVS is a strongly-typed higher-order logic. Specifications can be structured into a hierarchy of parameterized theories. There is a number of built-in theories and a mechanism for constructing abstract datatypes. The PVS system contains an interactive proof checker with, for instance, induction rules, automatic rewriting, and decision procedures for arithmetic. It allows users to construct proofs interactively, to discharge simple verification conditions automatically, and to check proofs mechanically.

2) Specification of protocols. To model a particular protocol in PVS, we define two types: 1) `Actions`, such as read and write, and possibly additional actions necessary for the adjustment of the control information 2) `States`, representing control information (locks, timestamps, etc.); and two predicates: 3) `Effect`, defining how a state is changed after applying a particular action 4) `Pre`, defining which actions are allowed in a particular state, and which are not.

3) Serializability notions. A *schedule* is a sequence of actions by transactions. Intuitively, a schedule is considered to be correct, if it is equivalent to some serial schedule. Serial schedules are those which have no interleaving between actions of different transactions. There are different ways to define equivalence of schedules. The most intuitively appealing one leads to the notions of view equivalence. Informally, two schedules are view equivalent iff each transaction in these schedules reads the values written by the same transaction. A schedule is said to be view serializable, if it is view equivalent to some serial schedule. Testing view serializability is NP-complete [Pap79], and therefore this notion is difficult to use in practice. Another form of schedule equivalence is conflict equivalence, leading to conflict serializability. Two schedules are conflict equivalent iff one of them can be transformed into the other by a sequence of swaps of non-conflicting actions. Testing conflict serializability has a quadratic complexity, and therefore the majority of existing database protocols ensures not just view serializability, but the stronger notion of conflict serializability.

We formalize the notions of conflict and view serializability, and prove, that any conflict serializable schedule is also view serializable. This relation is well known but has never been checked mechanically. In fact, there is no standard definition of view serializability in the literature. Here we combine the informal intuition of [SKS97] with the reads-from relation of [Vid91].

4) Method of verification. A traditional method for proving conflict serializability is based on *conflict graphs*. Our method is a modification of this traditional method and does not use any notions from graph theory. We believe that our method is logically more simple and straightforward, and therefore more appropriate for mechanical verification. This makes it possible to efficiently implement our method in PVS.

Our method is based on the notion of *conflict-preserving timestamps (CPT)*. We formulate a condition for schedules to be conflict serializable using an assignment of timestamps to transactions which orders conflicting transactions (two transactions are conflicting iff at least one of them contains a write to a common data item). We prove that this condition is necessary and sufficient. Hence, to show that a protocol ensures conflict serializability, we must prove that any schedule accepted by this protocol satisfies the condition. This implies then that the protocol indeed ensures conflict serializability, as well as the weaker notion of view serializability.

5) Extensions and correctness conditions. Suppose some basic protocol, for instance the 2PL protocol, has been proved correct. Adding more control information and more actions, we obtain various extensions of this protocol. We show that serializability of these extensions is ensured by four simple correctness conditions. The proof that these conditions lead to serializable protocols is far from trivial, but has to be done only once. By applying the resulting extension scheme, we easily obtain protocols that are serializable by construction.

As an example, we consider the 2PL protocol and several layered extensions. In the basic protocol, serializability is ensured by locking and unlocking data items. The first extension adds sequences of transactions, waiting for data items to become available (i.e., unlocked). The second extension gives priority to urgent transactions, resulting in a more realistic protocol. Since we formally verified the correctness of the 2PL protocol, a simple check of the four conditions leads to the correctness of these new protocols.

Structure of this paper. This paper is organized as follows. In section 2, we provide a general specification pattern and apply it to the specification of the 2PL protocol. In section 3, the notions of conflict and view serializability are formalized. We prove that conflict serializability implies view serializability. In section 4, our verification method is presented and its soundness and completeness are shown. The method has been applied to verify the 2PL protocol and the Timestamp Ordering protocol. In section 5, we formalize extensions of protocols and the restrictions on these extensions, needed to ensure their correctness. In section 6, we apply our method to specify and verify several layered extensions of the 2PL protocol. Section 7 contains some concluding remarks.

2 Specification of Protocols

We consider protocols in which transactions perform atomic actions on certain data items. Two basic actions are common for such database protocols: read and write, which are the only actions that concern the values of the data items. Additionally, there are usually other actions, necessary for the concurrency control. The set of actions of a database protocol is defined by type `ActionNames`, containing at least read and write actions (denoted as `R` and `W`). In the PVS notation (henceforth written in `typewriter` style):

```
R, W : ActionNames
```

The set of data items is defined by uninterpreted type `Variables`; the set of transactions is defined by type `Transactions`, representing the names of transactions. Moreover, we define a type `Actions` consisting of records with three fields, called `act`, `tr`, and `vari`, expressing that a particular action is performed by a transaction on a data item.

```
Actions : TYPE = [# act  : ActionNames, tr : Transactions,
                    vari : Variables #]
```

E.g., `(W, T, x)` represents a write action by transaction `T` on variable `x`.

Concurrency control protocols maintain a control part to determine which actions on data items are allowed and which are not allowed in a particular state of a database. E.g., the control part for lock-based protocols determines which data items are locked and in which mode (shared or exclusive). The control part for timestamp-based protocols contains information about timestamps of data items. In PVS, the control part for database protocols is defined by type `States`.

Each action causes certain changes in the control part. For example, for lock-based protocols, it may lock or unlock some data items. For timestamp-based protocols, this concerns the adjustment of read- and write-timestamps of some data items. Therefore, we define the initial value of the control part, i.e. the initial state, and how the control part is changed after every possible action. We also have to define which actions are allowed in a particular state, and which are not. E.g., a transaction cannot lock a data item in an exclusive mode if it is already locked by another transaction. Consequently, a database protocol is defined by the following steps:

1. Define type `ActionNames`, containing the atomic actions `R` and `W` and possibly some other atomic actions, responsible for the adjustment of control information.
2. Define type `States`, containing all control information essential for the definition of the protocol, and define the initial state `is`.
3. Define how a particular state is changed after applying a particular (allowed) action (e.g., a read or write of a data item) by means of the `Effect` predicate; a function with three arguments of types `States, Actions, States`, resp., and result of type `bool`. For states `s1` and `s2` and an action `a1`, we have `Effect(s1, a1, s2) = TRUE` iff `s2` is obtained from `s1` by applying `a1`.
4. Define which actions are allowed in a particular state by the `Pre` predicate. For a state `s1` and an action `a1` we have `Pre(s1, a1) = TRUE` iff `a1` is allowed in `s1`.

A finite execution is represented by a sequence r of the form $s_0 \stackrel{a_0}{\rightarrow} s_1 \stackrel{a_1}{\rightarrow} ... s_n \stackrel{a_n}{\rightarrow} s_{n+1}$. Here s_i $(0 \leq i \leq n+1)$ are states, and a_i $(0 \leq i \leq n)$ are actions. Infinite executions are represented by all finite approximations. Sequence r is a correct execution or *run* iff s_0 is the initial state, subsequent states are related by the `Effect` predicate, and actions are enabled, as expressed by the `Pre` predicate.

In PVS, a run `r` is formalized as a record with two fields: `StateSeq(r)` is a finite sequence of states, and `ActionSeq(r)` is a finite sequence of actions, where `StateSeq(r)` has one more element then `ActionSeq(r)`. For the example run above, we have `StateSeq(r) =` $s_0 s_1 ... s_n s_{n+1}$ and `ActionSeq(r) =` $a_0 a_1 ... a_n$.

A finite sequence of actions is called a *schedule*. For instance, `(W, T1, x)(W, T2, y)(R, T1, y)` represents an execution where first transaction `T1` writes a data item `x`, then transaction `T2` writes a data item `y`, and next `T1` reads `y`.

For a protocol, represented by `States`, `is`, `Actions`, `Effect` and `Pre`, and a run r of this protocol, we say that `ActionSeq(r)` is *a schedule, allowed by this protocol.* Given a definition by the four points mentioned above, we identify a protocol with the set of allowed schedules.

```
protocol : setof[Schedules] =
   { S : Schedules | EXISTS (r : Runs) : S = ActionSeq(r) }
```

2.1 Example of the Two Phase Locking Protocol

Informal description. The 2PL protocol (see, e.g., [SKS97]) requires that access to data items is done in a mutually exclusive manner; that is, while one transaction is accessing a data item, no other transaction can modify that data item. The most common method used to implement this requirement is to allow a transaction to access a data item only if it is currently holding a lock on that item. There are various modes in which a data item may be locked. The basic 2PL protocol, considered in this paper, has only two modes:

– **Shared**. If a transaction T has obtained a shared-mode lock on item x, then T can read, but cannot write, x.
– **Exclusive**. If a transaction T has obtained an exclusive-mode lock on item x, then T can both read and write x.

Let A and B represent arbitrary lock modes. Suppose that transaction T2 requests a lock of mode B on item x on which transaction T1 (T1 $\neq$ T2) currently holds a lock of mode A. If T2 can be granted a lock on x immediately, in spite of the presence of the mode A lock, then we say that mode B is *compatible* with mode A. In the 2PL protocol, shared mode is compatible with shared mode, but not with exclusive mode; exclusive mode is not compatible with both shared and exclusive modes.

To access a data item, transaction T must first lock that item in the corresponding mode. If the data item is already locked in an incompatible mode, the request to lock this item is rejected. The 2PL protocol requires that each transaction issues lock and unlock requests in two phases:

– **Growing phase.** A transaction may obtain locks, but may not release any lock.
– **Shrinking phase.** A transaction may release locks, but may not obtain any new locks.

Initially, a transaction is in the growing phase. The transaction acquires locks as needed. Once the transaction releases a lock, it enters the shrinking phase, and it can issue no more lock requests.

PVS implementation. We specify this protocol, following the four steps mentioned above. The Effect2PL predicate and the Pre2PL predicate are not shown here.

– ActionNames. In our model, locking is incorporated in read and write actions, and hence does not require a separate action. We only add an unlock action to unlock a data item which is locked in a shared or exclusive mode and a downgrade action which changes the mode of the lock from exclusive to shared.

```
ActionNames2PL : TYPE = { R, W, unlock, downgrade }
```

– We define States2PL by a record with three fields. xset and sset map each transaction to a set of data items which it locks in an exclusive and shared mode, respectively. shrinking is a set of transactions which already entered the shrinking phase and therefore cannot issue any new locks.

```
States2PL : TYPE =
   [# xset  : [Transactions -> setof[Variables] ],
      sset  : [Transactions -> setof[Variables] ],
      shrinking  : setof[Transactions] #]
```

In the initial state, is2PL, all the data items are unlocked and no transaction is shrinking.

3 View and Conflict Serializability

To define view serializability, we first define view equivalence between schedules, following [SKS97]. Consider two schedules `S1` and `S2`, where the same set of transactions participates in both schedules.

Definition 1. *The schedules* `S1` *and* `S2` *are* view equivalent *if the following three conditions are met:*

1. *For each data item x, if transaction* `T1` *reads the initial value of x in schedule* `S1` *then, in schedule* `S2`*, transaction* `T1` *must also read the initial value of x.*
2. *For each data item x, if transaction* `T1` *reads a value of x in schedule* `S1` *and the value was produced by transaction* `T2` *then, in schedule* `S2`*, transaction* `T1` *must also read the value of x that was produced by transaction* `T2`*.*
3. *For each data item x, the transaction* `T1` *(if any) that performs the last write action on x in schedule* `S1`*, must also perform the last write action on x in schedule* `S2`*.*

Conditions 1 and 2 ensure that each transaction reads the same values in both schedules and, therefore, performs the same computation. Condition 3, coupled with conditions 1 and 2, ensures that both schedules result in the same final system state.

The definition of view equivalence can be presented in a more formal way using the notion of a *reads-from* relation [Vid91]. We associate with each schedule `S` a reads-from relation `Reads_from(S)`, not shown here, relating a transaction that read a value of an item and the transaction that wrote this value. Then view equivalence can be defined as follows.

Definition 2. *(Equivalent to 1.) The schedules* `S1` *and* `S2` *are* view equivalent *if their reads-from relations are equal:*

```
view_equiv(S1, S2) : bool = (Reads_from(S1) = Reads_from(S2))
```

As we mentioned in introduction, a schedule is serial, in PVS represented by predicate `serial(S)`, if it has no interleaving between actions of different transactions. For instance, schedule `(W, T2, y)(W, T1, x)(R, T1, y)` is serial, because an action by `T2` precedes both actions by `T1`. Schedule `(W, T1, x) (W, T2, y)(R, T1, y)` is not serial, because two actions by `T1` are interleaved by an action by `T2`.

A schedule `S` belongs to the set of view serializable schedules, denoted by `View_serializable`, iff it is view equivalent to a serial schedule.

```
View_serializable : setof[Schedules] =
  { S | EXISTS S0 : serial(S0) AND view_equiv(S, S0) }
```

Next we explain the notion of conflict equivalence. Suppose `S` includes two consecutive actions `a1 = (A1, T1, x)` and `a2 = (A2, T2, y)`, where `A1` and `A2` belong to { `R, W` }. Thus `S = S1 a1 a2 S2` for some subschedules `S1` and `S2`. As explained in [SKS97], the order of `a1` and `a2` does not influence the result of computation if either x $\neq$ y or (x = y and A1 = A2 = R). If x = y and (A1 = W or A2 = W), then the order of a1 and a2 matters, i.e. changes the result of computation. Observe that T1 = T2 is allowed, assuming that actions of a transaction are partially ordered rather than totally ordered as in [SKS97].

Definition 3. *The actions* (A1, T1, x) *and* (A2, T2, y) *are* conflicting *iff* x = y *and (*A1 = W *or* A2 = W*).*

Definition 4. *The schedules* S1 *and* S2 *are* elementary equivalent *iff* S1 = S3 a1 a2 S4*,* S2 = S3 a2 a1 S4 *and the actions* a1 *and* a2 *are not conflicting.*

Definition 5. *The schedules* S1 *and* S2 *are* conflict equivalent*, denoted* conf_equiv(S1,S2) *iff there is a finite sequence of schedules* S_0, S_1,...S_k, k >= 0*, such that* S1 = S_0, S2 = S_k *and for all* i < k *the schedules* S_i *and* S_(i + 1) *are elementary equivalent.*

A schedule S belongs to the set of conflict serializable schedules, denoted by Conf_serializable, iff it is conflict equivalent to a serial schedule.

```
Conf_serializable : setof[Schedules] =
   { S | EXISTS S0 : serial(S0) AND conf_equiv(S, S0) }
```

Since swaps of nonconflicting actions do not change the result of computation, we can expect that they do not change the reads-from relation as well. Indeed, we have proved in PVS theorem ConfView, expressing that conflict equivalent schedules S1 and S2 are also view equivalent:

```
ConfView : THEOREM  Conf_equiv(S1, S2) IMPLIES View_equiv(S1, S2)
```

4 Our Method of Verification

We present a general method for mechanical verification of conflict serializability. Our approach is a modification of a traditional method for proving conflict serializability based on *conflict graphs.* We do not use graphs, but do need a notion of conflicting transactions which is defined as a *conflict relation.*

Definition 6. *A conflict relation* Conflict(S) *of a schedule* S *is defined as follows: a pair* (T1, T2) *belongs to* Conflict(S) *iff* T1 $\neq$ T2 *and*

- S *includes actions* a1 *and* a2 *by* T1 *and* T2 *respectively*
- a1 *precedes* a2 *in* S
- a1 *and* a2 *are conflicting.*

It is well-known (although not mechanically verified) that a schedule S is conflict serializable iff the relation Conflict(S), considered as a graph in which nodes are transactions, is acyclic. Our method does not use graph theory, but assigns timestamps to transactions, using an irreflexive order on timestamps. A time domain Time is some domain with a transitive, irreflexive order. For instance, the set of natural, rational or real numbers with the conventional order. A timestamp TS is a function from Transactions to Time.

Our method is based on the notion of *conflict-preserving timestamps (CPT).*

```
CPT(S, TS) : bool = FORALL T1, T2: Conflict(S)(T1, T2) IMPLIES
                                       TS(T1) < TS(T2)
```

Definition 7. *A timestamp* TS *is a* conflict-preserving timestamp (CPT) *with respect to schedule* S *iff* CPT(S, TS) = TRUE.

If a schedule S has a CPT then the transitive closure of Conflict(S) is irreflexive, because < is an irreflexive order on Time.

A schedule S belongs to the set of *ordered* schedules Ordered iff there is a timestamp TS which is conflict-preserving with respect to S.

```
Ordered : setof[Schedules] = { S | EXISTS TS : CPT(S, TS) }
```

We proved that any ordered schedule is conflict serializable, and any conflict serializable schedule is ordered. The proof has been constructed by means of the interactive proof checker of PVS and is technically fairly complicated.

```
OrdSerializable : THEOREM Ordered = Conf_serializable
```

Theorem OrdSerializable provides a basis for a sound and complete method for proving serializability. Given a particular protocol, we prove that each schedule allowed by this protocol is ordered, i.e. has a conflict-preserving timestamp. Thus, for a particular protocol, the aim is to prove the following theorem.

```
ProtocolOrdered : THEOREM subset?(protocol, Ordered)
```

After that, theorem OrdSerializable implies that protocol indeed ensures conflict serializability:

```
ProtocolCS : THEOREM subset?(protocol, Conf_serializable)
```

We successfully applied our method to the machine-checked verification of the Timestamp Ordering protocol and the 2PL protocol.

5 Extensions of (Serializable) Protocols

Although we have formulated in the previous section a complete method to prove conflict serializability, it is not always easy to find a conflict-preserving timestamp function for any schedule (and to prove that it actually is one). Observing that many protocols can be seen as extensions of a basic protocol (such as Timestamp Ordering or 2PL), we investigate how we can obtain serializability of an extension from serializability of a basic protocol. First we define the notion of an extension more precisely.

We say that protocol NewProt is an *extension* of protocol OldProt iff

- OldActionNames, the set of atomic actions of OldProt, is a subset of NewActionNames, the set of atomic actions of NewProt.

– NewStates, the control part of NewProt, is obtained from OldStates, the control part of OldProt, by adding a record ext of type Extension, representing the added control information:

```
NewStates : TYPE = [# old  : OldStates, ext : Extension #]
```

Our goal is to prove that if OldProt ensures conflict serializability and extension NewProt satisfies certain conditions, then NewProt also ensures conflict serializability. Below we derive the required conditions during the construction of the proof.

Let Conf_ser_Old and Conf_ser_New be instantiations of set of schedules Conf_serializable for schedules from OldProt and NewProt, respectively. Our aim is to prove the following theorem.

```
MainTheorem : THEOREM subset?(OldProt, Conf_ser_Old) IMPLIES
                      subset?(NewProt, Conf_ser_New)
```

Proof: Suppose OldProt ensures conflict serializability and schedule NewS is accepted by NewProt. The proof that NewS is conflict serializable consists of two steps.

Step 1 We prove that NewS is a *refinement* of some schedule OldS, accepted by OldProt, i.e. it is obtained from OldS by adding some actions. To construct OldS, we simply remove from NewS all added actions, i.e. all actions that do not occur in OldActionNames. The result is formally defined by function Extract(NewS). Note that we don't remove any read or write actions, because R and W belong to OldActionNames. The following theorem expresses that Extract(NewS) is accepted by OldProt.

```
ExtractOld : THEOREM NewProt(NewS) IMPLIES OldProt(Extract(NewS))
```

As we show below, the proof of this theorem reveals the required correctness conditions. Since OldProt is conflict serializable, theorem ExtractOld implies Conf_ser_Old(Extract(NewS)).

Step 2 If Extract(NewS) is conflict serializability, then also NewS:

```
ConfNewOld : THEOREM Conf_ser_Old(Extract(NewS)) IMPLIES
                     Conf_ser_New(NewS)
```

The proof of this theorem uses completeness of our verification method for conflict serializability. Since it implies Conf_ser_New(NewS), this completes the proof of theorem MainTheorem. **End Proof**

It remains to prove theorem ExtractOld and to derive the required correctness conditions.

Proof of theorem ExtractOld
Assume NewProt(NewS). Then there exists a run NewR = $s_0 \xrightarrow{a_0} s_1 \xrightarrow{a_1} \ldots s_n \xrightarrow{a_n} s_{n+1}$ of NewProt such that NewS = ActionSeq(NewR), i.e. NewS $= a_0 a_1 \ldots a_n$. Let

$a'_0a'_1...a'_k$ be the sequence obtained from $a_0a_1...a_n$ by removing all actions that are not in `OldActionNames`, i.e., `Extract(NewS)` $= a'_0a'_1...a'_k$.

To prove `OldProt(Extract(NewS))`, we construct a run $s'_0 \xrightarrow{a'_0} s'_1 \xrightarrow{a'_1} ... s'_k \xrightarrow{a'_k} s'_{k+1}$ of `OldProt`. This run is extracted from run `NewR` by the function `ExtractR` which removes from a run of `NewProt` any action that is not in `OldActionNames` and its successor state. Moreover, we take only the old part of the remaining states. Since `Extract` and `ExtractR` both remove the same actions (those with action names not in `OldActionNames`), observe that `ActionSeq(ExtractR(NewR))` = `Extract(ActionSeq(NewR))` = `Extract(NewS)` $= a'_0a'_1...a'_k$. Hence, it remains to prove that `OldR = ExtractR(NewR)` is a run of `OldProt`.

For any run `r`, let `last(r)` denote the last state of `r`. Instead of proving, that `ExtractR(NewR)` is a run in `OldProt`, it is more convenient to prove the following, stronger statement, consisting of two parts:

(i) `ExtractR(NewR)` is a run of `OldProt` and

(ii) `last(ExtractR(NewR)) = old(last(NewR))`.

The proof proceeds by induction on the length of `ActionSeq(NewR)`.

Basic Step Let `length(ActionSeq(NewR)) = 0`. Then `NewR = NewInitState` and, by definition of `ExtractR`, `ExtractR(NewR) = old(NewInitState)`. Hence, `ExtractR(NewR)` is a run if `old(NewInitState)` is equal to the initial state of `OldProt`. Then also **(ii)** is satisfied. This leads to the first condition.

Condition 1 `old(NewInitState) = OldInitState`

Induction Step Let `length(ActionSeq(NewR)) = m + 1`. Then `NewR =` `NewR1`$\xrightarrow{a}$`last(NewR)` for some run `NewR1`. We distinguish two cases.

act(a) $\notin$`OldActionNames` Then `ExtractR(NewR)` = `Extract(NewR1)`. For part **(i)**, recall that by the induction hypothesis `ExtractR(NewR1)`, and hence also `ExtractR(NewR)`, is a run of `OldProt`.

For **(ii)**, note that `last(ExtractR(NewR))` = `last(ExtractR(NewR1))` = `old(last(NewR1))`, using the induction hypothesis. To obtain `old(last(NewR1)) = old(last(NewR))`, we introduce a condition expressing that if we apply a newly added action `aa` to an extended state `es1`, then the `old` part of it should not change.

Condition 2
`NewEffect(es1, aa, es2) IMPLIES old(es1) = old(es2)`

act(a) $\in$`OldActionNames` By definition of `ExtractR`, we have in this case `ExtractR(NewR) = Extract(NewR1)`$\xrightarrow{a}$ `old(last(NewR))`.

By the induction hypothesis, part **(ii)**, we have

`last(Extract(NewR1)) = old(last(NewR1))`. (*)

To prove **(i)**, note that `ExtractR(NewR)` is a run of `OldProt` if the following two conditions are satisfied.

– a is allowed in the last state of `Extract(NewR1)`, that is, `OldPre(last(Extract(NewR1)),` a`) = TRUE`.
By (*), it remains to prove `OldPre(old(last(NewR1)),` a`) = TRUE`. Since a is allowed in the last state of `NewR1`, we have that `NewPre(last(NewR1),` a`) = TRUE`. Hence it is sufficient to require

that any old action `oa` which is allowed in an extended state `es` according to `NewPre`, is also allowed in the `old(es)` according to `OldPre`.

Condition 3 `NewPre(es, oa) IMPLIES OldPre(old(es), oa)`

– `old(last(NewR))` is obtained from `last(Extract(NewR1))` by applying a to it, i.e.
`OldEffect(last(Extract(NewR1)),`a`, old(last(NewR)))` = `TRUE`.
By (*), it remains to prove
`OldEffect(old(last(NewR1)),` a`,old(last(NewR))) = TRUE`.
Since `last(NewR)` is obtained from `last(NewR1)` by applying a to it, we have `NewEffect(last(NewR1),` a`,last(NewR)) = TRUE`. Hence it is sufficient to require, for any old action `oa`, that `NewEffect` must transform the `old` part of an extended state `es1` in the same way `OldEffect` does.

Condition 4 `NewEffect(es1, oa, es2) IMPLIES` `OldEffect(old(es1), oa, old(es2))`

This proves **(i)**. To prove **(ii)**, observe that by the definition of `ExtractR`, in this case
`last(ExtractR(NewR))` = `old(last(NewR))`.

This completes the induction step and also the proof of `ExtractOld`. **End Proof**

To implement extensions in PVS, we define a general PVS theory `ProtExtend`. As parameters, it has all types and predicates that are needed to define `OldProt` and `NewProt`. Theorem `MainTheorem`, which establishes the main result, is proved in `ProtExtend`. The conditions 1 through 4 mentioned above are added to this theory by including them as four *assumptions*. If any theory imports `ProtExtend` then a proof of these assumptions is required.

Given a conflict serializable protocol `OldProt` we can prove serializability of an extension `NewProt`, by importing theory `ProtExtend`. This requires a proof of the four assumptions. Once they have been proved, we can use `MainTheorem`, and obtain conflict serializability of `NewProt`.

6 Two Extensions of the 2PL Protocol

We have applied our method to the basic 2PL protocol, described in section 2. This protocol is extended in two steps, leading to a realistic protocol which is serializable by construction.

First extension — adding a sequence of waiting transactions. In the first step, we associate with each data item a sequence of transactions that are waiting for the permission to read or write this data item. If a transaction is not allowed to read or write a data item `x` immediately (because it is currently locked in an incompatible mode), the corresponding action is inserted into the sequence of x. After x becomes available, a postponed action from the sequence of x may be executed.

The operation of inserting an action into a sequence is modeled by *read-request actions* (Rrequest) and a *write-request actions* (Wrequest). The extension of the state consists of a function that maps each data item to a finite sequence, consisting of read- and write-requests performed by certain transactions; in an initial state all sequences are empty. A new effect predicate transforms the state in the same way Effect2PL does for old actions, it leaves the old part of the state unchanged for added actions, and includes an additional predicate to define how to insert and remove requests from the waiting sequences. A new precondition ensures that not only preconditions defined by Pre2PL are satisfied, but also some additional preconditions.

Second step — adding priorities to waiting transactions. We define a second-level extension of the 2PL protocol by extending the first-level extension above such that the processing of transactions depends on their *priorities*. A priority function PR assigns to each transaction T its priority PR(T) from the set of natural numbers.

We also introduce the notion of *urgent* transactions, which is important for real-time protocols. Assume given a natural number U. Transaction T is called *urgent with respect to* U, if PR(T) >= U. We define our protocol in a new theory, such that its set of parameters includes PR and U. Changing PR and U, we obtain different protocols. Therefore our theory actually defines a class of protocols.

This extension does not introduce any new control information or any new actions. Instead, it introduces some restrictions on the order, in which transactions are performed. The aim of these new restrictions is to ensure that "urgent" transactions obtain immediate access to data items, whereas that non-urgent transactions should be served on a first-in, first-out basis.

Suppose a data item x has a sequence xs. We define a predicate urgent_exist, which expresses that xs includes requests from urgent transactions. If urgent_exist(xs) = TRUE, then we must execute one of the urgent transactions with the highest priority MaxPriority(xs). Otherwise, we may execute the first-inserted request of the waiting sequence.

Correctness of the obtained extensions. After importing the theory ProtExtend with corresponding parameters for both protocols, it turned out to be very easy to prove that our four assumptions are satisfied for both protocols. Therefore our extensions indeed ensure conflict serializability.

Note that one may satisfy the conflict serializability condition by not allowing any schedule. Therefore, we additionally show that for every valid schedule in the initial protocol there is a representative in the extended protocol. For the first extension of the 2PL protocol presented above, it is easy to see that for every schedule S in the 2PL protocol there is a representative S' in the extension, which consists of the same actions. Let S' be a schedule where a transaction never tries to read or write a data item if it is not immediately available; then all sequences of requests are always empty and `S'` is indeed accepted by the extension. The same holds for the second extension of the 2PL protocol.

7 Concluding Remarks

We have presented a formal framework for the specification of concurrency control protocols and the verification of serializability, and successfully applied it to the verification of the 2PL protocol and the Timestamp Ordering protocol. Mechanical support has been obtained by formulating this framework in the language of the verification system PVS, and all proofs have been constructed by means of the interactive theorem prover of PVS.

Moreover, a systematic way to extend serializable concurrency control protocols has been developed. If such an extension satisfies four simple verification conditions, it is serializable by construction. This can be applied in a hierarchical way, thus complex protocols can be obtained by a sequence of extensions of a basic concurrency control protocol. An old, serializable, protocol can be extended to a new protocol by adding more control information to the state and introducing additional control actions. One has to define the new initial state, a new precondition for all actions and a new effect predicate which describes the state change after each action. Then the new protocol is serializable if the following conditions are satisfied.

1. Ignoring the added control part, the new initial state equals the old initial state.
2. A new action only affects the added part of the state; it does not change the original part of the state.
3. The new precondition of an old action implies its old precondition.
4. The new effect of an old action implies its old effect.

There are several directions for future work. We intend to investigate more protocols and develop more detailed strategies for their verification. We may also add timing, i.e. extend our method to real-time database protocols. Another possibility is to study not only serializability for databases, but also more general protocols and correctness notions such as atomicity of transactions.

References

[Pap79] C.H. Papadimitriou. The serializability of concurrent database updates. *Journal of the ACM*, 26(4):631–653, 1979.

[PVS] *PVS Specification and Verification System, http://pvs.csl.sri.com/.*

[SKS97] A. Silberschatz, H. F. Korth, and S. Sudarshan. *Database System Concepts.* The McGraw-Hill Companies, Inc., 1997.

[Tho93] A. Thomasian. Two-phase locking performance and its thrashing behavior. *ACM Transactions on Database Systems*, 18(4):579–625, 1993.

[Ull88] J. D. Ullman. *Principles of Database and Knowledge-Base Systems, Volume 1.* Computer Science Press, 1988.

[Vid91] K. Vidyasankar. Unified theory of database serializability. *Fundamenta Informaticae*, 14:147–183, 1991.

Platform Independent Approach for Detecting Shared Memory Parallelism

Yury V. Chelomin

Institute for Automation, Far Eastern Branch of Russian Academy of Sciences
5 Radio St., Vladivostok 690041, Russia
chelomin@yahoo.com

Abstract. This paper presents the platform independent approach to detecting shared memory parallelism. The brief overview of Automatic Parallelizing Expert Toolkit being developed and the description of basic concepts used by this toolkit are given.

1 Introduction

Known approaches to porting existing serial programs onto parallel platforms could be divided into two groups:

- using of automatically parallelizing compilers [1,2];
- adding to the source codes of serial program special directives, which explicitly specify the actions to be taken by the compiler and run-time system in order to execute the program in parallel.

Both of these approaches have some shortcomings.

Parallelizing compilers usually does not detect all the regions where parallelization is possible. Moreover, it could be uneasy task to determine rather compiler detect the parallelism or not, and why. Adding new parallelizing techniques to such compilers is up to vendor, so developer cannot rely on soon release of techniques needed. This approach also led to portability problems — different compilers can be significantly different in parallelization quality.

Explicit specification of all the necessary parallel regions may be even more complex task. Though the resulting program would probably work better this is not the case of program reuse — this approach is comparable to writing completely new code.

The way out from such situation could be found in using restructuring tools that automatically inserts parallelization directives into ordinary serial source code; the possibility of adding new parallelization techniques by tool's user should be present.

This approach has the following obvious advantages:

- the output of such tool is a meaningful source code thus developer understand clearly what parallelization has made;

D. Bjørner, M. Broy, A. Zamulin (Eds.): PSI'99, LNCS 1755, pp. 194–197, 2000.

- appearance of such directive sets as OpenMP API [3] solves a problem of cross-platform portability within a class of SMP platforms;
- the tool based on expert systems technology can explain all the parallelizing actions made;
- once an existing set of techniques does not satisfy a particular developer it is possible to expand this set with new ones.

It is clear that such tool needs powerful models of both the "parallel program" and the "parallelization technique". This paper presents these models targeted on implementation of Automatic Parallelizing Expert Toolkit (APET) and provides toolkit architecture overview.

2 Parallel Program and Execution Models

APET utilizes two models (the single at the same time) of parallel program:

- Extension of Model of Structured Program (MSP [4]), called Model of Parallel Program (MPP [5]). This model represents a parallel program in n-processor SMP-system as n serial programs with common data space and additional synchronization points, so-called barriers.
- Open-MP compliant Fork-Join Model, FJM. In this model program begins execution as a single thread of execution called master thread. The master thread executes as a serial region until the parallel construct creates a team of threads, which executes in parallel. Upon completion of parallel construct, the threads in the team synchronize at an implicit barrier, and only the master thread continues execution. Work sharing directives, nested parallelism and orphaning is permitted.

It is shown that for a great enough n the conformity between these models exists. The MPP is quite a simple model to operate, but APET's output in this model can be used only as an illustration of toolkit's actions. On the contrary, the FJM is much more complex; APET's output using this model can be interpreted as C or FORTRAN program with Open MP compliant extensions and than immediately be compiled under the most of the popular SMP-platforms.

3 Parallelizing Technique Model

Parallelizing technique in APET is represented in three parts:

- Condition — logical expression in terms of MPP or FJM. The Parallelizing technique is possible to apply if and only if this condition is true.
- Subset of variables defined in Condition. These variables are the parts of the program, which will change due to the given technique, so-called "Parallelization Region". Note that the value of these variables is one or more consequent operators and/or directives.
- Parallelizing Transformation — the set of expressions determining the new value of "Parallelization Region".

4 Overview of Automatic Parallelizing Expert Toolkit Architecture

APET's input is a model of serial program (MSP) obtained by specialized compiler from high-level languages and the knowledge base of parallelization techniques. The output is MPP or FJM model that represents the source program after all the parallelization techniques possible applied. Both of the models can be converted back into the high-level language (not necessary the same as the source) form. APET also provides an extensive report explaining which of the parallelization techniques were (or were not) applied and why (see figure 1).

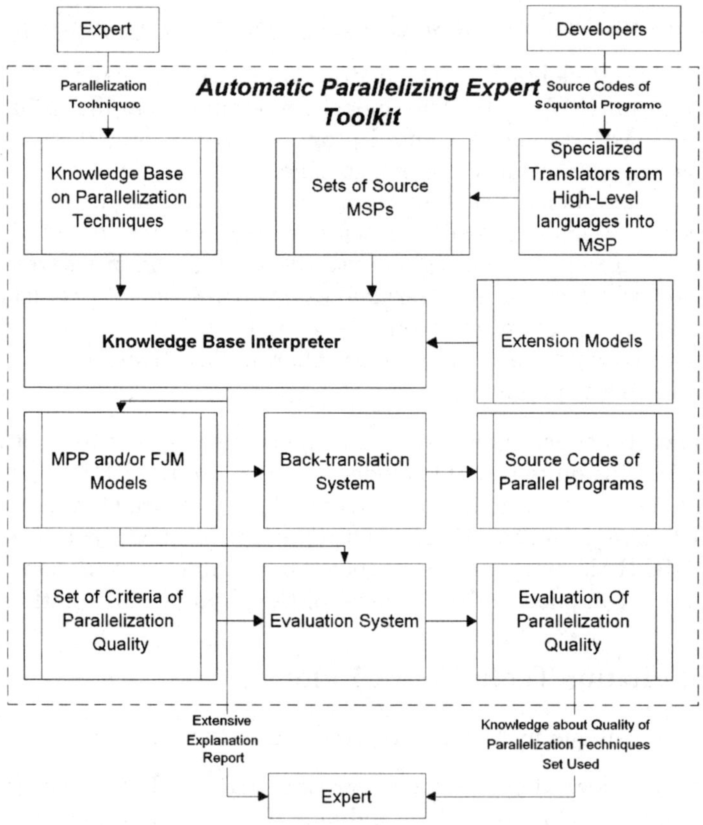

Fig. 1. APET's architecture diagram

It is also possible to define the set of criteria of parallelization quality to measure some static values of parallelization made by selected set of parallelization techniques.

References

1. William Blume, Ramon Doallo, Rudolf Eigenmann et al. Advanced Program Restructuring for High-Performance Computers with Polaris. Technical report 1473. University of Illinois at Urbana-Champaign, Center for Supercomputing Res. & Dev. January 1996.
2. Briang Armstrong, Seon Wook Kim, Insung Park, Michael Voss and Rudolf Eigenmann. Compiler-Based Tools for Analyzing Parallel Programs. Parallel Computing Journal, 1997.
3. Open MP C and C++ Application Program Interface. Document No. 004-2229-001. October 1998; Open MP Architecture Review Board. http://www.openmp.org.
4. Oleg A. Kupnevich, Margarita A. Knyazeva. Expert Toolkit for Simulating Program Optimization. Preprint. Institute for Automation, Vladivostok, 1997.
5. Yury V. Chelomin. Model of optimization process for shared memory parallel programs. Proceedings of E. Zolotov's workshop. Vladivostok, June 1998. (In Russian)

Hierarchical Cause-Effect Structures

A.P. Ustimenko

A. P. Ershov Institute of Informatics Systems,
Siberian Division, Russian Academy of Sciences,
630090 Novosibirsk, Russia,
apu@iis.nsk.su

Abstract. We suggested an extension of the class of cause-effect structures by semantics of hierarchy. As an example of hierarchical c-e structure we use a simulation of zero-testing operator. Relationships between classes of hierarchical c-e structures and hierarchical Petri Nets introduced by V.E. Kotov are investigated.

1 Introduction

In order to describe concurrent systems, L.Czaja has introduced in [1] cause-effect structures (CESs) which were inspired by condition/event Petri nets (PNs). CES can be defined as a triple (X, C, E) where X is the set of nodes, C and E are the cause and effect functions from X to the set of formal polynomials over X such that $x \in X$ occurs in $C(y)$ iff y occurs in $E(x)$. Each polynomial $C(x)(E(x))$ denotes a family of cause (effect) subsets of the node x. The operator $*$ combines nodes into subsets, and the operator $+$ combines subsets into families.

Unfortunately, practical expressiveness of CESs is not sufficient to use them in real-life applications. Some supplementary constructions, for instance, semantics of coloured tokens or hierarchy are necessary.

Note that the extension of CESs by coloured tokens has been received in [7]. In ordinary CESs a token or an active state of a node denotes presence of some resource. However this approach does not allow qualitative difference between resources functioning in CES to be discovered. Moreover, each node should not simultaneuosly have more than one token-resource. Sometimes it is important to differ resource qualitatively. This difference is represented by colours of tokens, and each node may have several differently coloured tokens.

This work is devoted to constructing a class of hierarchical CESs (HCESs) which improves compactness of the algebraic representation of CESs and enlarges their practical expressiveness.

Relationships between this new class and the class of hierarchical Petri nets (HPNs) introduced by V.E.Kotov in [3] are investigated. We prove that every HCES has behaviorally equivalent HPN.

There was an interesting open problem: in [4] Raczunas investigates converse mapping from PNs to CESs. He remarks that so called strong equivalence is not the case for converse mapping. We decided this problem in [6] by introducing extension of cause-effect structures – two-level CESs (TCESs). TCESs is

D. Bjørner, M. Broy, A. Zamulin (Eds.): PSI'99, LNCS 1755, pp. 198–207, 2000.

a convenient intermediate class between PNs and CESs, because it is strongly equivalent to the class of PNs and we can transform any TCES into structurally equivalent CES with the help of folding-transformation. On the other hand, each CES has a strongly equivalent TCES.

The problem of the converse mapping from HPNs to HCESs is decided with help of the class of two-lewel HCESs.

2 Preliminaries

2.1 Regular and Hierarchycal Petri Nets

The algebra of regular Petri nets (RPN) introduced in [2] is generated by the class of atomic nets with the use of the set of net operations.

An atomic net is a net of the following form:

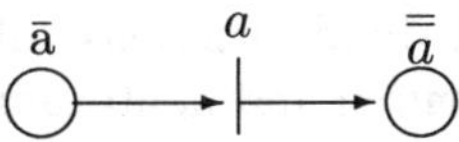

where is a transition symbol, ¯is a head net place, = is its tail place.

The concurrency operation (denoted by ",") is defined as a common graph union: it superposes one net on another.

If $N_1 = (P_1, T_1, F_1)$ and $N_2 = (P_2, T_2, F_2)$ then
$N = (N_1, N_2) = (P_1 \cup P_2, T_1 \cup T_2, F_1 \cup F_2)$

Let $h(N)$ denote the set of head places of a net N and l(N) be the set of tail places of N. By definition, $h(N) = h(N_1) \cup h(N_2)$ and $l(N) = l(N_1) \cup l(N_2)$.

Other net operations can be defined via the concurrency operation and an auxiliary merging operation. The latter merges two sets of places in a specific way. This involves two suboperations: 1) formation of a set of merged places, 2) replacement of two existing sets by a new set.

Given two sets of places X and Y *the forming operation* $\times$ results in the set Z of merged places:
$Z = X \times Y = \{x \cup y | x \in X, y \in Y\}$

The merging operation M merges two sets of places, X and Y, in a net $N = (P, T, F)$ and generates a new net $M(N, X \times Y) = (P', T', F')$, where

$P' = P - (X \cup Y) \cup (X \times Y), T' = T,$

$\forall p \in X \times Y : F'(p) = F(x) \cup F(y),$

where $p = x \cup y$.

The operation of iteration "*" merges the sets of head and tail places of the net if their intersection is empty:

$N' = *(N) = m(N, h(N) \times l(N))$

By definition, its sets of head and tail places are equal.

The precedence operation ";" joins two nets by merging the set of tail places of the first net with the set of head places of the second net. By definition, $h(N) = h(N_1)$ and $l(N) = l(N_2)$.

The alternative operation "∇" unites two nets by merging their sets of head places and their sets of tail places separately. By definition, $h(N) = h(N_1) \times h(N_2)$ and $l(N) = l(N_1) \times l(N_2)$.

Let E be a class of atomic nets, i.e. a class of transition symbols. A net formula in the algebra of RPN over basis E is defined as follows:

1) each symbol of E is a formula;

2) if A is a formula, then $*(A)$ is a formula;

3) if A and B are formulae, then (A, B), $(A; B)$ and $(A \nabla B)$ are formulae.

The class of hierarchical Petri nets (HPN) introduced in [3] is a generalization of the class of RPN and is used for modelling hierarchical systems.

To define HPN, we should divide the class of transition symbols into two nonintersecting subclasses: terminal and nonterminal symbols. Correspondingly, any transition can be simple or compound.

HPN is defined by a structural formula constructed from terminal and nonterminal symbols using the set of the (regular) net operations and an ordered set of nonterminal symbols' definitions.

Each such definition looks like $s : A$, where s is a nonterminal symbol, and A is a formula of HPN which is internal for this symbol.

We have two contextual restrictions:
1) Any symbol of a structural formula is terminal if it is not defined in this formula.
2) Each nonterminal symbol is defined only once and it can not join the right-hand part of its definition and all the following ones.

A compound transition may be in a passive or active (when its internal net is working) state. The begining and the end of a compound transition's work are momentary events.

On Fig.1 you can see HPN which allows us to check whether the place x has token. Thus, expressive power of the class of HPNs is greater than of the class of PNs.

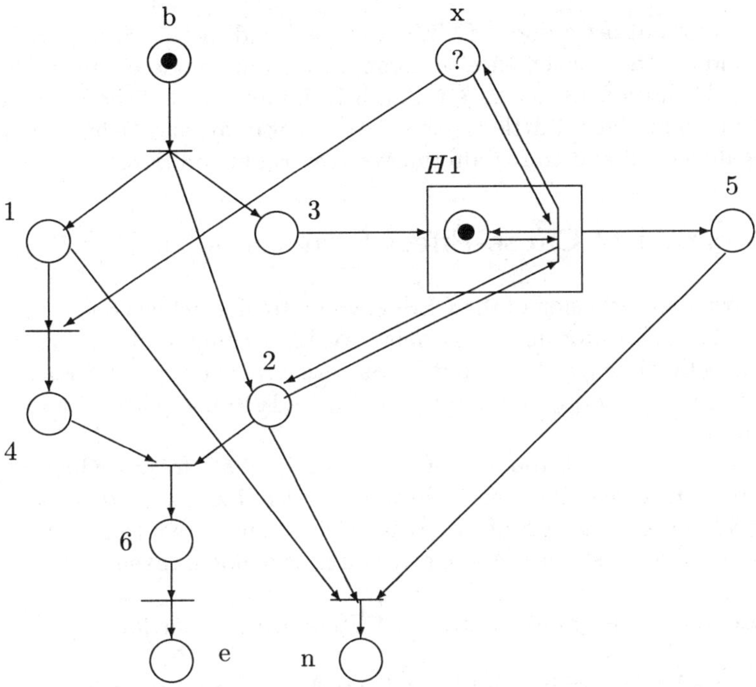

Fig. 1. Zero-testing operator

2.2 Cause-Effect Structures

Cause-effect structures are represented as directed graphs with an additional structure imposed on the set of nodes. These graphs, with operations + and $*$ corresponding to nondeterministic choice and parallelism, constitute a near-semi-ring where "near" means that distributivity of $*$ over + holds conditionally.

A CES is completely represented by the set of annotated nodes: each node x is subscribed by a formal polynomial $E(x)$ built of (names of) its successors and superscribed by a formal polynomial $C(x)$ built of its predecessors and may be either in an active or passive state. The active state of a node represents the presence of control in it.

If a node is active, then we try to move control from it simultaneously to all its successors which form a product in its lower (subscript) polynomial - if they are passive. Symmetrically, if a node is passive, then we try to move control to it simultaneously from all its predecessors which form a product of its upper (superscript) polynomial - if they are active (if no predecessors or successors exist then the upper or lower polynomial is θ, omitted sometimes). This rule renders complex - in general - interdependences between nodes in the aspect of a control flow: a group of nodes have to "negotiate" the possibility of changing their state with one another. Such groups of nodes will play a role similar to that of transitions in PNs. They are called firing components. The set of all firing components of the CES U is denoted by $FC[U]$.

All the formal definitions of CESs can be found in [1]. Moreover, for better understanding and convenience of comparison, we include all these definitions to Sect.3: Definitions 3.1, 3.2, 3.3, 3.6, 3.7, 3.8 and 3.10 without any changes; Definition 3.5 modifed a little for the case of hierarchy, and Definition 3.12 with additional (second and third) alternative groups of conditions.

3 Hierarchical Cause-Effect Structures

We construct an extension of the CESs class up to hierarchical one in the manner proposed by V.E.Kotov for Petri nets. We have compound transitions in the hierarchical Petri nets (HPNs), but CESs have only one type of vertices – nodes. The attempt to introduce compound nodes leads to complicated and unwieldy construction.

Our solution is to introduce compound or "global" tokens which appear on some directions of moving control between nodes. Each such token includes an inner CES. When a group of nodes is ready to move control jointly to their successors and at least one of them gives birth to a global token on this direction, then:
– this group of nodes move control to CES which is inner for appearing global token;
– the inner CES is working and when it reaches the final state it moves control to all successors of the original group of nodes.

In fact we have some subclass of hierarchycal or global firing components. This way allows us to preserve the style and the scheme of defining CESs. We add only a globalization function on the set of nodes, and extend semantics correspondingly.

Definition 1. *(3.1.) Let X be a set called a space of nodes and let θ be a symbol called neutral. The least set Y satisfying the following: $\theta \in Y, X \subseteq Y$, if $K \in Y$ and $L \in Y$ then $(K + L) \in Y$ and $(K * L) \in Y$, is a set of polynomials over X denoted by F[X].*

Definition 2. *(3.2.) We say that the algebraic system $A = (F[X], +, *, \theta)$ is a near-semi-ring of polynomials over X if the following axioms hold for all $K \in F[X], L \in F[X], M \in F[X], x \in X$:*

(+)	$\theta + K = K + \theta = K$	$(*)$	$\theta * K = K * \theta = K$
(++)	$K + K = K$	$(**)$	$x * x = x$
(+++)	$K + L = L + K$	$(***)$	$K * L = L * K$
(++++)	$K + (L + M) = (K + L) + M$	$(****)$	$K * (L * M) = (K * L) * M$
$(+*)$	$K * (L + M) = K * L + K * M$		

provided that either $L = M = \theta$ or $L \neq \theta$ and $M \neq \theta$

Definition 3. *(3.3.) Let X be a space of nodes and $(F[X], +, *, \theta)$ be a near-semi-ring of polynomials. A CES over X is a pair (C,E) of functions:*

$C : X \longrightarrow F[X]$ *(cause function)*
$E : X \longrightarrow F[X]$ *(effect function)*
such that x occurs in the polynomial $C(y)$ iff y occurs in $E(x)$ (then x is a cause of y and y is an effect of x). The set of all CES's over X is denoted by CE[X]. The CES is completely represented by the set of annotated nodes x.

Definition 4. *(3.4.) Let (C, E) is a CES over X, and let for each $x \in X$ its effect polynomial be transformed to the canonical form: $E(x) = \sum E_i(x)$, where each $E_i(x)$ is a monomial. The globalization function G prescribes some global token (i.e. a token which includes an inner CES or the neutral element θ) to each effect direction $E_i(x)$ of each node x. Then a hierarchical cause-effect structure is a triple of functions $(C(X), E(X), G(< X, E(X) >))$.*
The set of all HCESs over is denoted by $H[]$.

Remark 1. A token may be an ordinary "unfaced" resource denoted by θ. That is, if $G(< x, E_i(x) >) = \theta$ for some node x and direction $E_i(x)$, then it means that the token on this direction is non-compound, and moving of control runs without delay.

Definition 5. *(3.5.) Let us define the addition and multiplication of functions by the rules:*
$(C_1 + C_2)(x) = C_1(x) + C_2(x)$ *and* $(E_1 + E_2)(x) = E_1(x) + E_2(x)$,
$G(< x, E_i >) = G_i(< x, E_i >)$;
$(C_1 * C_2)(x) = C_1(x) * C_2(x)$ *and* $(E_1 * E_2)(x) = E_1(x) * E_2(x)$,
$G(< x, E_1 * E_2 >) = G_1(< x, E_1 >) + G_2(< x, E_2 >)$.
Then an algebra of HCESs is obtained as follows. Let $\theta : X \longrightarrow F[X]$ be a constant function $\theta(x) = \theta$, let, for brevity, the HCES (θ, θ) be denoted by θ, and let $+$ and $*$ on HCESs be defined by the following:

$({}_1, {}_1, G_1) + ({}_2, {}_2, G_2) = ({}_1 + {}_2, {}_1 + {}_2, G)$,
$({}_1, {}_1, G_1) * ({}_2, {}_2, G_2) = ({}_1 * {}_2, {}_1 * {}_2, G)$.

Obviously, if $U_i = (C_i, E_i, G_i) \in HCE[X](i = 1, 2)$, then $U_1 + U_2 \in HCE[X]$ and $U_1 * U_2 \in HCE[X]$.

Definition 6. *(3.6.) A CES U is decomposable iff there exist CESs V, W such that*
$\theta \neq V \neq U, \theta \neq W \neq U$ *and either* $U = V + W$ *or* $U = V * W$.

Definition 7. *(3.7.) Let U, V be CESs. V is a substructure of U iff $V + U = U$. Then we write $V \leq U$. $SUB[U] = \{V : V \leq U\}$. Easy checking ensures that $\leq$ is a partial order. The set of all minimal (wrt $\leq$) and $\neq \theta$ elements of SUB[U] is denoted by MIN[U].*

Definition 8. *(3.8.) For a CES U, let* $Q = (C_Q, E_Q)$ *be a minimal substructure of U such that for every node x in Q:*

(i) polynomials $C_Q(x), E_Q(x)$ *do not comprise '+',*

(ii) exactly one polynomial, either $C_Q(x)$ *or* $E_Q(x)$*, is* θ*.*

Then Q is called a firing component of U. $FC^1[U] = \{Q \in MIN[U] : (i), (ii)$ *hold*$\}$ *is the set of all firing components of the first level. We denote by* $^\bullet Q$ *(pre-set of Q) the set of nodes x in Q with* $C_Q(x) = \theta$*, and by* $Q^\bullet$ *(post-set of Q) the set of nodes x in Q with* $E_Q(x) = \theta$*.*

Definition 9. *(3.9.) If* $G(x) \neq \theta$ *for any node* $x \in^\bullet Q$*, then we say that a global firing component Q has an internal CES denoted by* $G(Q) = \sum_{x \in^\bullet Q} G(x)$*.*

Remark 2. Each internal CES has a set of its own firing components. Thus, there exist a union of sets of firing components over all internal CESs of the first level called a set of firing components of the second level, and so on. The full set of firing components of any HCES U (denoted by $FC[U]$) is a union of its sets of firing components of all levels.

Definition 10. *(3.10.) A state is a subset of the space of nodes X. A node x is active in the state s iff* $x \in s$ *and passive otherwise.*

Definition 11. *(3.11.) Let us define, for each global firing component Q, two supplementary subsets of its nodes: an initial state of its internal HCES* $G(Q)$ *denoted by* $S_0(G(Q))$ *and a terminal state of* $G(Q)$ *denoted by* $S_{end}(G(Q))$*.*

Definition 12. *(3.12.) For* $Q \in FC[U]$*, let* $[[Q]]$ *denote a binary relation on the set of all states:* $(s,t) \in [[Q]]$ *iff*

$^\bullet Q \subseteq s,\ G(Q) = \theta,\ Q^\bullet \cap s = \oslash,\ t = (s -^\bullet Q) \cup Q^\bullet$

or

$^\bullet Q \subseteq s,\ G(Q) \neq \theta,\ S_0(G(Q)) \cap s = \oslash,\ t = (s -^\bullet Q) \cup S_0(G(Q))$

or

$S_{end}(G(Q)) \subseteq s,\ Q^\bullet \cap s = \oslash,\ t = (s - S_{end}(G(Q))) \cup Q^\bullet$*.*

Semantics $[[U]]$ *of a HCES U is a union of relations:*

$$[[U]] = \bigcup_{Q \in FC[U]} [[Q]]$$

Remark 3. Firstly, in preserving the condition $Q^\bullet \cap s = \oslash$ and similar, we follow the tradition of defining semantics of CESs that requires the artificial safety. That is, each node must not have more than one token.

Secondly, alternative groups of conditions in Def.3.12 mean the following:
- if the firing component is not global, all nodes of its pre-set are active and all nodes of its post-set are passive (the requirement of safety), then control is moving from all nodes of its pre-set to all nodes of its post-set;
- if the firing component is global, all nodes of its pre-set are active and all nodes of the initial state of its internal HCES are passive (the requirement of safety), then control is moving into the internal HCES,"firing" all nodes from the initial state;
- if the internal HCES of the global firing component has reached the terminal state and all nodes of the post-set of this global firing component are passive, then control is moving to them.

On Fig.2 one can see a HCES which is equivalent in a sense to HPN on Fig.1:

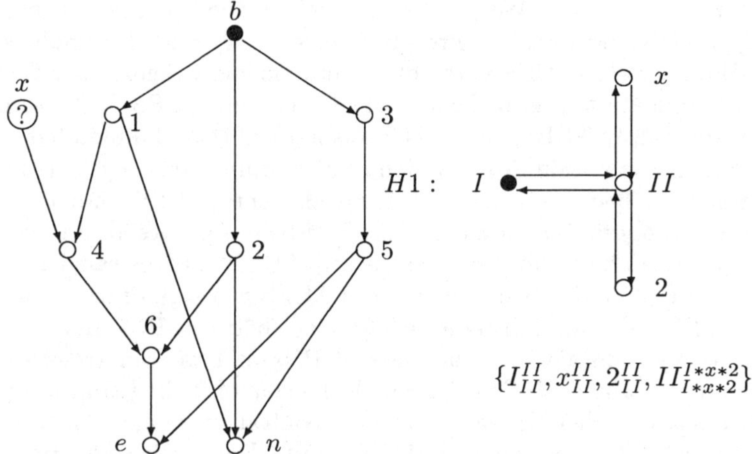

Fig. 2. Zero-testing operator

4 Relationships between HCESs and HPNs

There is an interesting question about relationships between CESs and PNs. In [4] Raczunas states that every CES has a strongly equivalent PN, i.e., two bijections exist: between the firing components of CES and transitions of PN, and between nodes of CES and places of PN; moreover, the bijections must preserve pre- and post-sets of firing components and transitions.

In [2] Kotov proved that each PN has a behaviorally equivalent regular PN, i.e., their sets of languages or traces of firing are equal. So we can formulate:

Theorem 1. *(1.) Each HCES has a behaviorally equivalent HPN.*

Sketch of a proof. In [4] Raczunas proves that each CES has strongly equivalent PN. But the only structural difference between CES and HCES is the globalization function which does not touch an external cover of HCES (the cover is a HCES in which all global firing components are substituted by simple ones). The last is an ordinary CES and so it has a strongly equivalent PN which is the cover of some HPN. But the cover of an internal HCES of any global firing component also is a CES and has a strongly equivalent PN which is internal for corresponding global transition of this cover-HPN, and so on. Finally, with the help of the regularization algorithm (see [2]), we construct a behaviorally equivalent HPN from given set of strongly equivalent external and internal PNs.

Raczunas investigates a converse mapping from PNs to CESs. He remarks that strong equivalence is not the case for the converse mapping.

We decided this problem in [6] by introducing an extension of cause-effect structures – two-level CESs (TCESs). Any CES is completely represented by the set of annotated nodes $\{x^{C(x)}_{E(x)}\}$ where E(x) and C(x) are polynomials with operations + and $*$. We propose to exclude the operation + from the formal polynomials and to call the resulting elementary CES (or unalternative CES – UCES) a two-level CES of the first syntactic level. Elementary CESs are united by the operation $\oplus$ into the set called a two-level CES of the second syntactic level, or simply TCES. Thus, TCES is a set of sets of annotated nodes.

So, the operation $\oplus$ is a union of sets of an upper level. It differs from the operation + because it does not merge elementary CESs into a set of annotated nodes. An operation $\otimes$ on the set of TCESs is a Cartesian product of sets of an upper level. The operation $\otimes$ on the set of UCESs is the same as operation $*$ on the set of CESs. In its canonical form TCES is a sum of its firing components.

TCESs is an usefull intermediate class between PNs and CESs, because it is strongly equivalent to the class of PNs and we can transform any TCES into structurally equivalent CES with the help of folding-transformation. On the other hand, each CES has a strongly equivalent TCES. Thus, there are only structural differences between TCESs and CESs, their semantics are the same. So the semantics of hierarchy is transferred to the class of TCES without essential changes. Thus, we have:

Theorem 2. *(2.) Each HPN has a strongly equivalent hierarchical TCES.*

Sketch of a proof. An algorithm of constructing of a strongly equivalent HCES is stage by stage:
1. we map the cover-net of given HPN in a strongly equivalent CES which is the cover-structure of the constructed HCES;
2. we map the cover-net of an internal HPN of each compound transition of the first level in a strongly equivalent CES which is the cover-structure of an internal HCES of corresponding global firing component;
3. and so on.

On the each stage we deal with mapping an ordinary PN in ordinary CES. But the algorithm of such mapping has constructed and proof of its correctness and fullness has made in [6].

5 Conclusion

This work is a continuation of the series of papers [5], [6], [7] devoted to constructing different extensions and generalization of the cause-effect structures. Moreover, the globalization function proposed in this work has more general and important meaning. It allows us to unite all these extensions into an universal model. That is, such function may prescribe internal CESs to one group of firing components, time restrictions to another one, and rules of token colour transformations to some other firing components. Thus, an important direction of future investigations is constracting a high-level class of CESs which will unite feasibilities and advantages of all above semantics and two-level representation.

Acknowledgements

The author thanks Dr. Valery Nepomniaschy for useful discussions.

This work is supported by the Grant of Presidium of Siberian Division of Russian Academy of Sciences.

References

1. **Czaja L.** Cause-effect structures// Inform. Process. Lett. **26** (1988) 313-319.
2. **Cherkasova L.A., Kotov V.E.** Structured nets// Lecture Notes in Computer Science **118** (Springer-Verlag, Berlin, 1981) 242-251.
3. **Kotov V.E.** An algebra for parallelism based on Petri nets// Lecture Notes in Computer Science **64** (Springer-Verlag, Berlin, 1978) 39-55.
4. **Raczunas M.** Remarks on the equivalence of c-e structures and Petri nets// Inform. Process. Lett. **45** (1993) 165-169.
5. **Ustimenko A.P.** Mapping of time cause-effect structures into time Petri nets// Cybernetics and system analysis **2** (Kiev, 1997) 44-54.
6. **Ustimenko A.P.** Algebra of two-level cause-effect structures// Inform. Process. Lett. **59** (1996) 325-330.
7. **Ustimenko A.P.** Coloured cause-effect structures// Inform. Process. Lett. **68** (1998) 219-225.

Some Decidability Results for Nested Petri Nets*

Irina A. Lomazova[1] and Philippe Schnoebelen[2]

[1] Program Systems Institute of the Russian Academy of Science
Pereslavl-Zalessky, 152140, Russia
irina@univ.botik.ru

[2] Lab. Specification & Verification, ENS de Cachan & CNRS UMR 8643
61, av. Pdt. Wilson, 94235 Cachan Cedex, France
phs@lsv.ens-cachan.fr

Abstract. *Nested Petri nets* are Petri nets using other Petri nets as tokens, thereby allowing easy description of hierarchical systems. Their nested structure makes some important verification problems undecidable (reachability, boundedness, ...) while some other problems remain decidable (termination, inevitability, ...).

1 Introduction

For modelling and analysis of distributed concurrent systems, there exists a large variety of formalisms based on Petri nets [Rei85, Jen92, Smi96, Lom97]. Among them, several approaches extend the Petri nets formalism by notions and structures inspired from object oriented programming [Sib94, Lak95, MW97, Val98]. Such extensions are helpful for modelling *hierarchical* multi-agent distributed systems.

While Sibertin-Blanc [Sib94], Lakos [Lak95], Moldt and Wienberg [MW97] consider systems with communicating coloured Petri nets, Valk [Val98] in his *object Petri nets* considers tokens as objects with a net structure. In his approach, the system net and object nets are elementary net systems, but an object is in some sense not located in one place (since Valk uses object Petri nets for solving specific fork-join situations in task planning systems), and this leads to a rather complex definition of the notion of states for object Petri nets.

Nested Petri nets. Here we study another Petri net model where tokens may be nets themselves: *nested* [1] *Petri nets* [Lom98]. Nested Petri nets are a convenient tool for modelling hierarchical multi-agent dynamic systems. The object nets in a nested Petri net have their own structure and behaviour, they may evolve and

* This work was mainly prepared during the stay of the first author at Lab. Specification & Verification in June-July 1998, and was partly supported by INTAS-RFBR (Grant 95-0378) and the Russian Fund for Basic Research (Project No. 96-01-01717)

[1] The word "nested" points to the analogy with nested sets, containing sets as their elements, which in turn may contain sets and so on. There may be any fixed number of levels in nested Petri nets. It is also possible to consider nested nets with unbounded depth, but we do not do this here.

D. Bjørner, M. Broy, A. Zamulin (Eds.): PSI'99, LNCS 1755, pp. 208–220, 2000.

disappear during the system lifetime, and their number is unlimited. A nested Petri net has four kinds of steps. A *transfer step* is a step in a system net, which can "move", "generate", or "remove" objects, but does not change their inner states. An *object-autonomous* step changes only an inner state in one object. There are also two kinds of synchronisation steps. *Horizontal synchronisation* means simultaneous firing of two object nets, situated in the same place of a system net. *Vertical synchronisation* means simultaneous firing of a system net together with some of its objects involved in this firing.

In this paper we show how some crucial verification problems remain decidable for nested Petri nets and some become undecidable. This shows that nested Petri nets are in some weaker than Turing machines and stronger than ordinary, "flat" Petri nets. The decidability results are mostly based on the theory of Well-Structured Transition Systems [Fin90, AČJY96, FS98].

The paper is organised as follows. In section 2 we start with a simple example of a two-level nested Petri net with ordinary Petri nets as tokens. Section 3 contains definitions of nested Petri nets. In Section 4 the expressive power of nested Petri nets and some other Petri nets models is compared. In Section 5 we prove that nested Petri nets are well-structured transition systems and deduce some decidability and undecidability properties. Section 6 gives some conclusions and directions for further research.

2 An Introductory Example

To give the reader an intuitive idea of nested Petri nets we start with a small example of a two-level nested Petri net *NPN* represented in Fig. 1. It models a set of workers receiving some tasks from time to time. A worker's behaviour is described by an object (element) net *EN*. *EN* is an elementary Petri net. When a task comes, a worker is to borrow a tool from the buffer of tools. A buffer of tools is represented by a system net *SN*. It is a high-level Petri net with tokens of three types: black dots, tools (unstructured dots of some color) and workers (represented by nets).

The number of workers involved in this system is unlimited. The set A of tools is fixed and initially represented in the place S_5. In our example A is finite (with N elements).

Arcs in the system net *SN* are further labeled by expressions (variables and constants in our example), as in high-level Petri nets. If no expression is ascribed, the arc is supposed to transfer a black dot. In our *NPN* example, the arc expression x is a variable for a worker (having a marked net *EN* as its value), y is a variable for a tool (a corresponding arc transfers a coloured dot for a tool), $\mathbf{W}_2$ is a constant for an element net *EN* with the marking $\{W_2\}$, i.e., having only one token in place W_2.

Some transitions are marked by labels t_1, t_2, t_3, t_4 in *EN* and $\overline{t_1}, \overline{t_2}, \overline{t_3}, \overline{t_4}$ in *SN*. They are used for synchronisation of transition firings in system and element nets. Thus transition marked by $\overline{t_2}$ in *SN* may only fire simultaneously with the

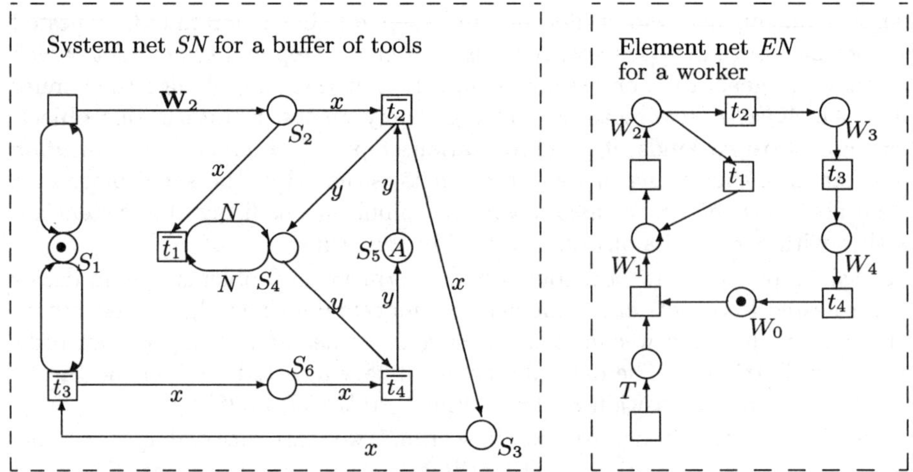

Fig. 1. *NPN*, a nested Petri net

firing of a transition marked by t_2 in the element net *EN* which is involved in firing $\overline{t_2}$ (i.e, which is transfered by it).

The substantive meaning of places in the element net *EN* is as follows: T — there is a task for the worker; W_0 — the worker is idle; W_1 — the worker has got a task; W_2 — the worker is applying for a tool; W_3 — the worker is busy with a task; W_3 — the worker finished a task.

In the system net *SN* places are: S_1 — a buffer of tools is open; S_2 — workers, applying for a tool; S_3 — workers with tools; S_4 — the number of borrowed tools; S_5 — tools available; S_6 — workers, returning tools.

In the initial marking represented in Fig. 1 the system net *SN* (modelling a buffer of tools) contains a black dot token in the place S_1 (meaning the buffer is open for workers) and the set A of N tools in the place S_5, a net *EN* for a worker contains a token in the place W_0 (a worker is idle) and T is empty, meaning there are no tasks for a worker. Note that initially there are no net tokens (workers) in *SN*, so the element net *EN* for a worker plays a role of type description.

To illustrate the behaviour of a nested Petri net we follow several possible steps of *NPN*. In the initial marking the unlabelled transition in *SN* may fire, putting a net token $\mathbf{W}_2$ (*EN* with marking $\{W_2\}$) into place S_2. This step creates an instance of *EN* in S_2. After that the transition marked by $\overline{t_2}$ in *SN* may fire synchronously with the transition marked by t_2 in the element net lying in S_2. After that the net *EN* with the marking $\{W_3\}$ will be situated in the place S_3, the set A in S_5 will be diminished by one token and the place S_4 gets one token. Then the transition marked by $\overline{t_4}$ in *SN* may fire synchronously with transition marked by t_4 in the element net lying in S_3. Continuation of this process may lead to a marking shown in Fig. 2, where there is one worker applying for a tool, two workers with tools and one worker has come to return a tool. Here A' designates the set A diminished by three tokens.

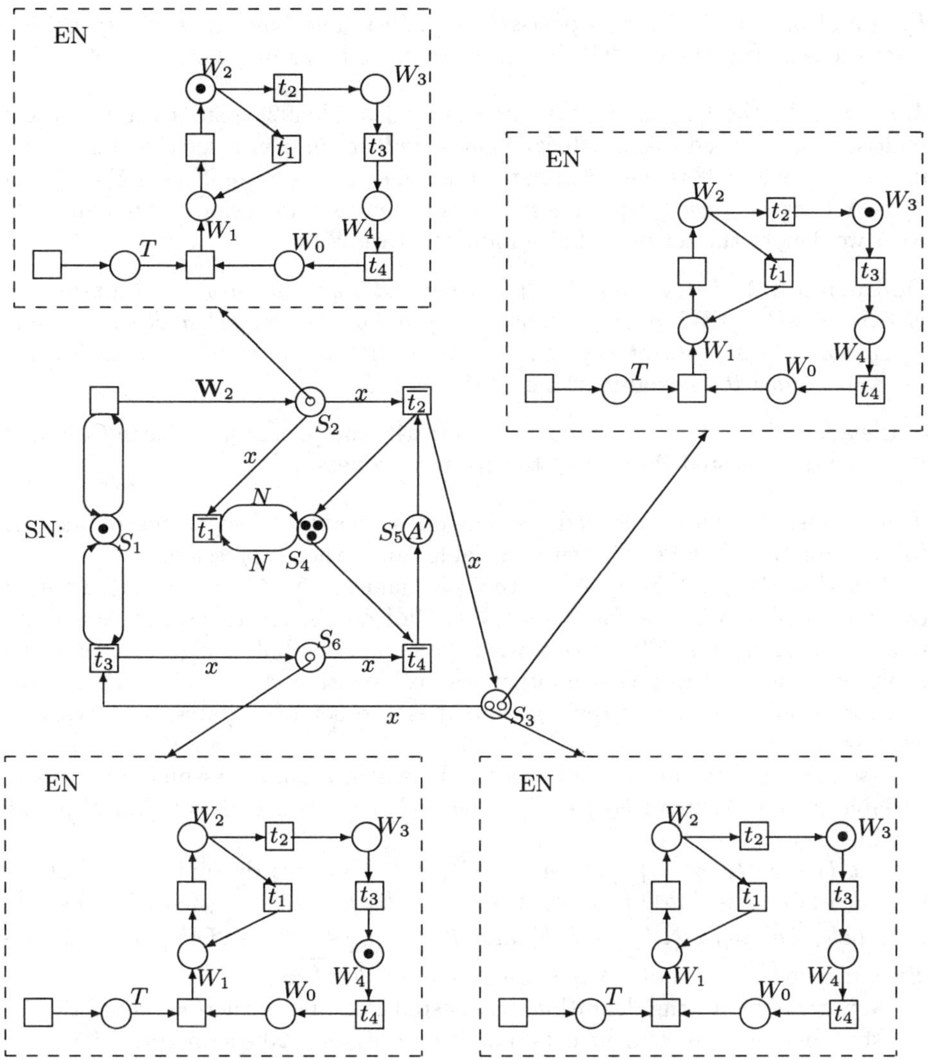

Fig. 2. An example of a reachable state for *NPN*

3 Nested Petri Nets

Definition 3.1. *Let P and T be disjoint sets and let $F \subseteq (P \times T) \cup (T \times P)$. Then $\mathcal{N} = (P, T, F)$ is a* net. *The elements of P, T and F are called* places, transitions *and* arcs *respectively.*

Pictorially, P-elements are represented by circles, T-elements by boxes, and the flow relation F by directed arcs. For $x \in P \cup T$ we write $^\bullet x$ for the pre-set

$\{y \mid yFx\}$ of x, and $x^\bullet$ for its post-set $\{y \mid xFy\}$. The *input arcs* of a transition t are those in $\{(x,t) \mid x \in {}^\bullet t\}$, its *output arcs* are those in $\{(t,x) \mid x \in t^\bullet\}$.

Markings. In the Coloured Petri nets formalism [Jen92], places carry marked multisets of coloured tokens. Recall that a *multiset* m over a set S is a mapping $m : S \to \mathbb{N}$, where $\mathbb{N}$ is the set of natural numbers. m is *finite* iff $\{s \in S \mid m(s) > 0\}$ is. We let $m \leq m'$ (resp. $m + m'$) denote multiset inclusion (resp. sum). By S_{MS} we denote the set of all finite multisets over S.

Definition 3.2. *Let $\mathcal{N} = (P,T,F)$ be a net and S an arbitrary set. A* marking *of $\mathcal{N}$ over S, also called an S-*marking*, is a function M from P to S_{MS} mapping every place to a multiset over S. A* marked net *is a net together with some marking, called the* initial marking *of this net.*

In the above definition tokens may be arbitrarily complex objects (as in Coloured Petri nets). In nested Petri nets, tokens may be nets.

Transitions. As with Coloured Petri nets, we want to keep track of moving tokens. For this we label arcs with variables and other expressions.

Let $V = \{v_1, \ldots\}$ be a set of *variable* names, and $C = \{c_1, \ldots\}$ a set of *constant* names. Write A for the set $V \cup C$ of *atoms*. An *expression* is a finite multiset of atoms (usually written with the binary symbol $+$: e.g., $v_1 + (c_2 + v_1)$ is an expression). *Expr*(A) is another way of denoting $A_{MS} = \{e, \ldots\}$, the set of expressions. For $e \in$ *Expr*(A), *Var*(e) is the set of variables occurring in expression e.

Assume any constant c denotes a fixed element c_S in S. Assume b maps any variable v to an element $b(v) \in S$. Then $b(e)$ denotes a multiset over S in the obvious way.

Let $Lab = \{l_1, l_2, \ldots\}$ and $Lab' = \{l^1, l^2, \ldots\}$ be two disjoint sets of labels. For each label $l \in Lab \cup Lab'$ we define an *adjacent* label $\overline{l}$, such that the sets Lab, Lab', $\overline{Lab} =_{\text{def}} \{\overline{l} \mid l \in Lab\}$ and $\overline{Lab'} =_{\text{def}} \{\overline{l'} \mid l' \in Lab'\}$ are pairwise disjoint. Let $\overline{\overline{l}} =_{\text{def}} l$ and $\mathcal{L} =_{\text{def}} Lab \cup Lab' \cup \overline{Lab} \cup \overline{Lab'}$.

Now we come to the definition of a nested Petri net structure, consisting of a system net, several element nets, labels on arcs, and labels on transitions.

Definition 3.3. *A* nested Petri net structure *Σ is an array of $k \geq 1$ nets $\mathcal{N}_1$, $\ldots$, $\mathcal{N}_k$, where $\mathcal{N}_1$ is a distinguished net, called a* system net, *and the $\mathcal{N}_i$'s, for $i = 2, \ldots, k$, are called* element nets.

In any $\mathcal{N}_i = (P_i, T_i, F_i)$ the input (resp. output) arcs from F_i are labeled by expressions $\mathcal{E}(p,t)$ (resp. $\mathcal{E}(t,p)$) from Expr(A). We require that there are no constants in input arc labels and no variable occurs twice in an input label $\mathcal{E}(p,t)$, or in two input labels for a same transition. (There is no restriction on the output labels.) Examples of forbidden arc inscriptions are shown in Fig. 3.

In any $\mathcal{N}_i$, the transitions may carry labels from $\mathcal{L}$ (possibly several labels).

Assume a given nested Petri net structure Σ and let markings in element nets $\mathcal{N}_2, \ldots, \mathcal{N}_k$ be considered over some *finite* sets $S_2, \ldots, S_k$ correspondingly and let $\mathcal{M}$ denote the set of all marked element nets of Σ.

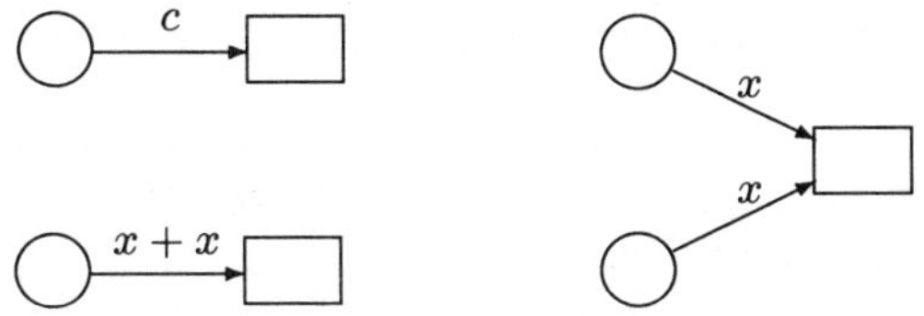

Fig. 3. Forbidden input arc inscriptions

Definition 3.4. *A* nested Petri net *(NP-net) is a nested Petri net structure Σ with each constant $c \in C$ interpreted as some marked element net from $\mathcal{M}$.*

By a marking *of a NP-net, we mean a marking of its system net over the set $\mathcal{M}$.*

A marked NP-net *is an NP-net together with some (initial) marking.*

Note that the definition of an NP-net depends on the sets $S_2, \ldots, S_k$ as parameters. If the S_i's are one-element sets, then the object nets are ordinary Petri nets with black dots as tokens, and a nested Petri net is just a system net with ordinary nets as tokens. If the S_i's are sets of coloured tokens, then a nested Petri net has Coloured Petri nets as tokens. If the S_i's are sets of marked nets, we get a three-levels (or more) structure, in which element nets are system nets with respect to the next level. It's clear that we can have as many levels as we like. And at last, if some of sets $S_2, S_3, \ldots, S_k$ contain the system net $\mathcal{N}_1$, as its element we get recursion, which is not considered here.

In NP-nets, firing a transition requires instantiating the variables in arc labels:

Definition 3.5. *Let $\mathcal{N}_i = (P_i, T_i, F_i)$ be a net in a nested net NPN.*

1. *A* binding *of a transition $t \in T_i$ is a function b mapping each variable $v \in V$ to a value $b(v)$ from the set $\mathcal{M} \cup S_2 \cup S_3 \cup \ldots \cup S_k$.*
2. *A* binded transition *is a pair $Y = (t, b)$, where t is a transition and b is a binding of t.*
3. *A binded transition $Y = (t, b)$ is* enabled *in a marking M of $\mathcal{N}_i$ iff $\forall p \in {}^\bullet t$: $b(\mathcal{E}(p, t)) \subseteq M(p)$.*
4. *An enabled binded transition $Y = (t, b)$ may fire in a marking M and yield a new marking M', written $M[Y\rangle M'$. For any $p \in P_i$, $M'(p) =_{def} M(p) - b(\mathcal{E}(p, t)) + b(\mathcal{E}(t, p))$.*
5. *For marked element nets (except black dot tokens), which serve as variable values in input arc expressions from $\mathcal{E}(t)$, we say, that they are* involved *in firing of t. (They are removed from input places and may be brought to output places of t).*

Now we come to defining a step in a NP-net.

Definition 3.6. *Let NPN be an NP-net. A step of NPN is either*

a transport step: *firing (through some appropriate binding) an unlabeled transition in the system net $\mathcal{N}_1$, not changing markings of element nets;*

an object-autonomous step: *firing an unlabeled transition in one of the element nets, while all element nets remain in the same places of the system net;*

an horizontal synchronisation step: *simultaneous firing of two transitions of two element nets lying in the same place w.r.t. the same binding, provided these two transitions are marked by two adjacent labels l and $\bar{l}$ from $Lab' \cup \overline{Lab'}$;*

a vertical synchronisation step: *simultaneous firing of a transition t marked by a label $l \in Lab \cup \overline{Lab}$ in the system net and transitions marked by the adjacent label $\bar{l}$ in element nets involved in firing of t.*

We say a marking M' is (directly) reachable from a marking M and write $M \to M'$, if there is a step in *NPN* leading from M to M'.

An execution of NP-net *NPN* is a sequence of markings $M_0 \to M_1 \to M_2 \ldots$ successively reachable from the initial marking M_0.

4 Nested Petri Nets and Other Petri Net Models

In this section we compare expressive power of nested Petri nets with some other Petri net models. First of all, since tokens in a system net may be just black dots, we immediately get

Proposition 4.1. *Ordinary Petri nets form a special case of nested Petri nets.*

Then we compare nested Petri nets with some extensions of ordinary Petri net model.

Petri nets with reset arcs [Cia94] extend the basic model with special "reset" arcs, which denote that firing of some transitions resets (empties) the corresponding places.

Theorem 4.2. *Petri nets with reset arcs can be simulated by nested Petri nets with ordinary Petri nets as object nets.*

Proof. The idea is to simulate the presence of n tokens in a place by one simple element net having n tokens. Then it is possible simulate the effect of a reset arc by removing this net token in one step, replacing it with $E0$, a constant net with zero tokens. Incrementations and decrementations of tokens in a place are simulated by incrementations and decrementations of tokens in the corresponding element nets. They are enforced by the synchronisation mechanism.

Fig. 4(a) shows a fragment of a Petri net with n tokens in a place p, incrementing (for p) arc (t_+, p) and decrementing arc (t_-, p). Fig. 4(b) represents a fragment of a NP-net, simulating it. Here n tokens in p are replaced by one net token *EN*, which has one place with n black dot tokens and two transitions marked by $\overline{l_+}$ and $\overline{l_-}$, which add or remove a token to/from p. These transitions fire synchronously with transitions t_+, or t_- respectively in a system net. Transition t_r in a system net removes a et token from p, thus emptying it. □

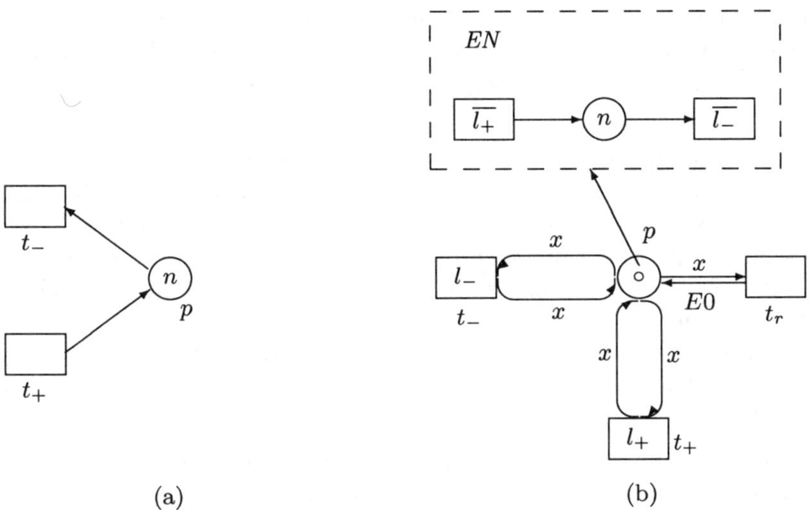

Fig. 4. Simulation of a reset arc

Since it is known [DFS98, DJS99] that Petri nets with reset arcs are more expressive than ordinary Petri nets, we immediately get the following

Theorem 4.3. *Nested Petri nets with ordinary Petri nets as object nets are more expressive than "flat" ordinary Petri nets.*

5 Decidability for Nested Petri Nets

In this section we discuss some issues of decidability for nested Petri nets. First, we briefly formulate some problems crucial for verification of Petri nets.

A net terminates if there exists no infinite execution (*Termination Problem*). A marking M' is reachable from M, if there exists a sequence of steps leading from M to M' (*Reachability Problem*). The reachability set of a net is the set of all markings reachable from the initial marking. A net is bounded if its reachability set is finite (*Boundedness Problem*). The *Control-State Maintainability Problem* is to decide, given an initial marking M and a finite set $Q = \{q_1, q_2, \ldots, q_m\}$ of markings, whether there exists a computation starting from M where all markings cover (are not less than w.r.t. some ordering) one of the q_i's. The dual problem, called the *Inevitability Problem*, is to decide whether all computations starting from M eventually visit a state not covering one of the q_i's, e.g. for Petri nets we can ask whether a given place will eventually be emptied.

Since NP-nets simulate Petri nets with reset arcs, problems undecidable for Petri nets with reset arcs are also undecidable for NP-nets.

Theorem 5.1. *1. Reachability is undecidable for nested Petri nets.*
2. Boundedness is undecidable for nested Petri nets.

Proof. Due to Theorem 4.2 nested Petri nets can simulate Petri nets with reset arcs, hence, validity of this two statements follows from undecidability of reachability [AK77] and boundedness [DFS98, DJS99] for Petri nets with reset arcs. □

To obtain decidability results we use the notion of well-structured transition system introduced in [Fin90, AČJY96]. Recall that a transition system is a pair $\mathcal{S} = \langle S, \to \rangle$ where S is an abstract set of states (or configurations) and $\to \subseteq S \times S$ is any transition relation. For a transition system $\mathcal{S} = \langle S, \to \rangle$ we write $Succ(s)$ for the set $\{s' \in S \mid s' \to s\}$ of immediate successors of s. $\mathcal{S}$ is finitely branching if all $Succ(s)$ are finite.

A well-structured transition system is a transition system with a compatible wqo: recall that a quasi-ordering (a qo) is any reflexive and transitive relation $\leq$ (over some set X).

Definition 5.2. *A* well-quasi-ordering *(a wqo) is any quasi-ordering $\leq$ such that, for any infinite sequence $x_0, x_1, x_2, \ldots,$ in X, there exist indexes $i < j$ with $x_i \leq x_j$.*

Note, that if $\leq$ is a wqo, then any infinite sequence contains an infinite increasing subsequence: $x_{i_0} \leq x_{i_1} \leq x_{i_2} \ldots$

Definition 5.3. *A well-structured transition system (a WSTS) is a transition system $\Sigma = \langle S, \to, \leq \rangle$ equipped with an ordering $\leq \subseteq S \times S$ between states such that*
– $\leq$ is a wqo, and
– $\leq$ is "compatible" with $\to$,
where "compatible" means that for all $s_1 \leq t_1$, and transition $s_1 \to s_2$, there exists a transition $t_1 \to t_2$, such that $s_2 \leq t_2$.

[FS98, FS97] introduce more liberal notions of compatibility:

A WSTS Σ has *transitive compatibility* if for all $s_1 \leq t_1$, and transition $s_1 \to s_2$, there exists a nonempty sequence $t_1 \to t_2 \to \ldots \to t_n$ with $s_2 \leq t_n$.

A WSTS Σ has *stuttering compatibility* if for all $s_1 \leq t_1$, and transition $s_1 \to s_2$, there exists a nonempty sequence $t_1 \to t_2 \to \ldots \to t_n$ with $s_2 \leq t_n$ and $s_1 \leq t_i$ for all $i < n$.

Now we define a wqo on the set of states of our NP-nets and show that they are WSTS.

Definition 5.4. *Let NPN be a nested Petri net, $\mathcal{M}_{MS}$ — the set of all its states.*

A quasi-ordering $\preceq$ on $\mathcal{M}_{MS}$ is defined as follows:
for $M_1, M_2 \in \mathcal{M}_{MS}$: $M_1 \preceq M_2$ iff for all $p \in P_{\mathcal{N}_1}$ there exists an injective function $\jmath_p : M_1(p) \to M_2(p)$, such that $\forall \langle \mathcal{N}_i, m \rangle \in M_1(p)$, for $s \in M_1(p)$: either $\jmath_p(s) = s$ or $s = \langle \mathcal{N}_i, m \rangle$ and $\jmath_p(\langle \mathcal{N}_i, m \rangle) = \langle \mathcal{N}_j, m' \rangle$ implies $m \preceq m'$.

Fig. 5 shows an example of two markings M_1, M_2 of some NP-net, ordered w.r.t. $\preceq$. Here the system net has three places p_1, p_2, p_3. The only element net has places q_1, q_2. In both markings the place p_1 is empty and the place p_2 contains one net token, but the marking of this net token in M_1 is included in the corresponding marking in M_2. The place p_3 in M_2 contains the same net token as in in M_1 plus one more net token. Thus, the relation $\preceq$ is a kind of a nested set inclusion.

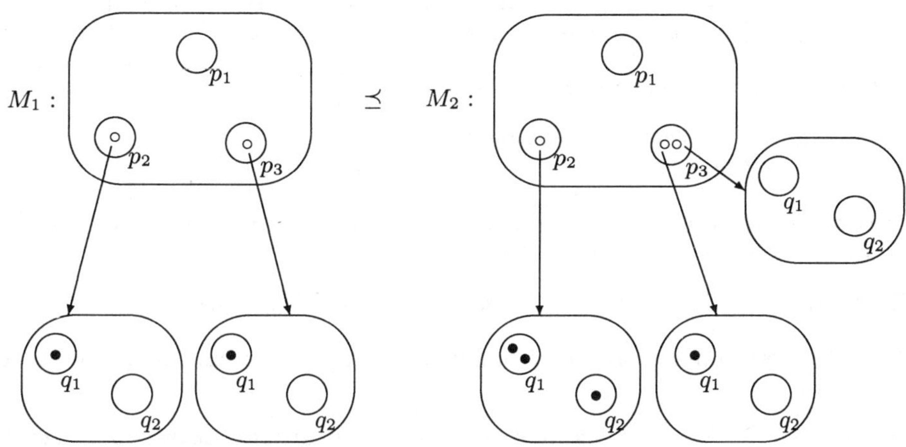

Fig. 5. An example of markings $M_1 \preceq M_2$

Proposition 5.5. *Let NPN be a nested Petri net, with $\mathcal{M}_{MS}$ the set of all its states, $\rightarrow$ the step relation on $\mathcal{M}_{MS}$, and $\preceq$ the quasi-ordering on $\mathcal{M}_{MS}$, defined above. Then $\langle \mathcal{M}_{MS}, \rightarrow, \preceq \rangle$ is a well-structured transition system.*

Proof. $\preceq$ is clearly a well quasi-ordering but we must show that it is compatible with the transition relation $\rightarrow$. We have four cases.

1. Let $M_1 \xrightarrow{t} M_1'$ be a transport step in a nested net via a transition t and let $M_1 \preceq M_2$. Then for every token $s \in M_1(p)$ transferred by t (with $p \in {}^\bullet t$) there exists an object $\jmath_p(s) \in M_2(p)$. Since due to the restriction on input expressions all objects are transferred independently and firing of t doesn't depend actually on object markings, the transition t is enabled also in M_2. It is easy to see, that if $M_2 \xrightarrow{t} M_2'$, then $M_1' \preceq M_2'$.
2. For an object-autonomous step compatibility is obvious.
3. A horizontal synchronisation step is a simultaneous execution of several object-autonomous steps. Its compatibility can be proved analogously to the previous case.
4. A vertical synchronisation step is a simultaneous execution of a transport and several object-autonomous steps. Its compatibility is not a direct implication from the two first cases, but it can be proved by combining previous proofs.

□

Note that if we would not restrict multiple occurrences of variables in input arc expressions, we would not have WSTS, as well as Object Petri nets of Valk are not WSTS.

It was proved in [FS97] that

- Termination is decidable for WSTS's with (1) transitive compatibility, (2) decidable $\leq$, and (3) effective *Succ*(s). (Theorem 4.6.)
- The control-state maintainability problem and the inevitability problem are decidable for WSTS's with (1) stuttering compatibility, (2) decidable $\leq$, and (3) effective *Succ*(s). (Theorem 4.8.)

It turns out that for NP-nets

Lemma 5.6. *(1). The qo $\preceq$ is decidable.*
(2). Succ is effective.

With the help of these statements we can obtain the following decidability results for NP-nets:

Theorem 5.7. *Termination is decidable for nested Petri nets.*

Proof. Follows from Proposition 5.5, Lemma 5.6 and Theorem 4.6 in [FS97]. □

Corollary 5.8. *Nested Petri nets are expressively strictly weaker than Turing machines.*

Proof. Since termination is not decidable for Turing machines. □

Theorem 5.9. *The control-state maintainability problem and the inevitability problem (w.r.t. $\preceq$) are decidable for nested Petri nets.*

Proof. Follows from Proposition 5.5, Lemma 5.6 and Theorem 4.8 in [FS97]. □

6 Concluding Remarks

Nested Petri nets are an extension of the Petri nets formalism which gives visual and clear dynamic hierarchical and modular structure of the system. The synchronization of hierarchical components is natural and powerful.

The structure of nested Petri nets gives a good intuition of its distributed behaviour. Though we have only defined here an interleaving semantics, it can be naturally generalised to simultaneous or independent firings. With two kinds of synchronisation: horizontal for cooperation of elements and vertical for coordination of system and its elements nested Petri nets formalism can be considered as a kind of generalisation of module Petri nets (see, e.g., [CP92, Lom97a]) and hierarchical Petri nets (e.g., [Jen92]) models.

Thus, nested Petri nets turns out to be a visual and expressive tool for modelling multi-agent distributed systems. At the same time, decidability of such important properties as termination gives ground for solving some verification problems for them. Being still less expressive than Turing machines, nested Petri nets preserve merits of Petri nets model.

Further research on nested Petri nets supposes investigation of recursive nested Petri nets, when a system net contains its own copy as its element (directly or via other elements) and decidability questions for them.

References

[AČJY96] P. A. Abdulla, K. Čerāns, B. Jonsson, and T. Yih-Kuen. General decidability theorems for infinite-state systems. In *Proc. 11th IEEE Symp. Logic in Computer Science (LICS'96), New Brunswick, NJ, USA, July 1996*, pages 313–321, 1996.

[AK77] T. Araki and T. Kasami. Some decision problems related to the reachability problem for Petri nets. *Theoretical Computer Science*, 3(1):85–104, 1977.

[CP92] S. Christensen and L. Petrucci. Towards a modular analysis of coloured petri nets. In *Proc. 13th Int. Conf. Application and Theory of Petri Nets, Sheffield, UK, June 1992*, volume 616 of *Lecture Notes in Computer Science*, pages 113–133. Springer, 1992.

[Cia94] G. Ciardo. Petri nets with marking-dependent arc cardinality: Properties and analysis. In *Proc. 15th Int. Conf. Application and Theory of Petri Nets, Zaragoza, Spain, June 1994*, volume 815 of *Lecture Notes in Computer Science*, pages 179–198. Springer, 1994.

[DFS98] C. Dufourd, A. Finkel, and Ph. Schnoebelen. Reset nets between decidability and undecidability. In *Proc. 25th Int. Coll. Automata, Languages, and Programming (ICALP'98), Aalborg, Denmark, July 1998*, volume 1443 of *Lecture Notes in Computer Science*, pages 103–115. Springer, 1998.

[DJS99] C. Dufourd, P. Jančar, and Ph. Schnoebelen. Boundedness of Reset P/T nets. In *Proc. 26th Int. Coll. Automata, Languages, and Programming (ICALP'99), Prague, Czech Republic, July 1999*, volume 1644 of *Lecture Notes in Computer Science*, pages 301–310. Springer, 1999.

[Fin90] A. Finkel. Reduction and covering of infinite reachability trees. *Information and Computation*, 89(2):144–179, 1990.

[FS97] A. Finkel and Ph. Schnoebelen. Well-structured transition systems everywhere ! Accepted for publication in Theor. Comp. Sci., October 1997.

[FS98] A. Finkel and Ph. Schnoebelen. Fundamental structures in well-structured infinite transition systems. In *Proc. 3rd Latin American Theoretical Informatics Symposium (LATIN'98), Campinas, Brazil, Apr. 1998*, volume 1380 of *Lecture Notes in Computer Science*, pages 102–118. Springer, 1998.

[Jen92] K. Jensen. *Coloured Petri Nets. Basic Concepts, Analysis Methods and Practical Use. Vol. 1, Basic Concepts.* EATCS Monographs on Theoretical Computer Science. Springer, 1992.

[Lak95] C. Lakos. From coloured Petri nets to object Petri nets. In *Proc. 16th Int. Conf. Application and Theory of Petri Nets, Turin, Italy, June 1995*, volume 935 of *Lecture Notes in Computer Science*, pages 278–297. Springer, 1995.

[Lom97] I. A. Lomazova. Multi-agent systems and In *Proc. Int. Workshop on Distributed Artificial Intelligence and Multi-Agent Systems (DAIMAS'97), St. Petersburg, Russia, June 1997*, pages 147–152, 1997.

[Lom97a] I. A. Lomazova On Proving Large Distributed Systems: Petri Net Modules Verification. In *Proc. 4th Int. Conf. Parallel Computing Technologies (PaCT'97), Yaroslavl, Russia, Sep. 1997*, volume 1277 of *Lecture Notes in Computer Science*, pages 70–75. Springer, 1997.

[Lom98] I. A. Lomazova. Modelling of multi-agent dynamic systems by nested Petri nets (in Russian), August 1998. In *Programmnye Sistemy: Teoreticheskie Osnovy i Prilozheniya,* pages 143–156, Moscow: Nauka, 1999.

[MW97] D. Moldt and F. Wienberg. Multi-agent-systems based on coloured Petri nets. In *Proc. 18th Int. Conf. Application and Theory of Petri Nets, Toulouse, France, June 1997*, volume 1248 of *Lecture Notes in Computer Science*, pages 82–101. Springer, 1997.

[Rei85] W. Reisig. *Petri Nets. An Introduction*, volume 4 of *EATCS Monographs on Theoretical Computer Science.* Springer, 1985.

[Sib94] C. Sibertin-Blanc. Cooperative nets. In *Proc. 15th Int. Conf. Application and Theory of Petri Nets, Zaragoza, Spain, June 1994*, volume 815 of *Lecture Notes in Computer Science*, pages 471–490. Springer, 1994.

[Smi96] E. Smith. A survey on high-level Petri-net theory. *EATCS Bull.*, 59:267–293, June 1996.

[Val98] R. Valk. Petri nets as token objects: An introduction to elementary object nets. In *Proc. 19th Int. Conf. Application and Theory of Petri Nets, Lisbon, Portugal, June 1998*, volume 1420 of *Lecture Notes in Computer Science*, pages 1–25. Springer, 1998.

Abstract Structures for Communication between Processes

Gabriel Ciobanu and Emanuel Florentin Olariu

Institute of Theoretical Computer Science, Romanian Academy
6600 Iaşi, Romania
gabriel@info.uaic.ro, oflorin@iit.tuiasi.ro

Abstract. This paper describes an algebraic structure which allows to define an abstract framework for communication in distributed systems. Using this structure we introduce an equivalence relation; the quotient induced by this equivalence relation preserves the initial algebraic structure. Our results represent a starting point in abstract investigation of the communication between processes, complementing the achievements of the process algebras.

1 Introduction

The aim of this paper is to find a class of structures as mathematical abstractions used for structural and dynamic aspects of communication between concurrent processes. We refer here just to the structural aspects of the communication between processes. In process algebra, processes are usually considered as terms. We treat a process by considering its internal structure which is only related with communication, namely its ports and communication symmetries. This work is somehow related to those of Milner [Mi] (flowgraphs, action structures) and Lafont [La] (interaction nets). The name–free approach presented here is similar to that of [Ho1, Ho2].

We describe how two processes can communicate each other by using communication handles. We consider mainly correspondences and maps of suitable handles used by communicating processes. The basic elements of our approach are the interface ports used by processes for interaction. We give a name–free presentation where the notion of symmetry plays an essential role. Communication between processes assume points of interaction called handles (ports). Each communication channel is determined by two points of interaction. Various concurrent algebras and calculi use names for communicating channels, i.e. they use names for the corresponding interaction points which determine the communication channels. This fact suggests that the semantics of processes depends on names. Here we "forget" names, but still keep their functionalities. The essence of the functionality of channel names is to determine multiple identities and to represent in an intelligible way how we relate the communication entities. Over the set of interaction points given by the communication channels, we define a permutation group. Each permutation represents an interchange of interaction

D. Bjørner, M. Broy, A. Zamulin (Eds.): PSI'99, LNCS 1755, pp. 221–227, 2000.

points which preserve the external communication capabilities of a process. In this way we introduce a communication structure which is based on the notions of process, communication channels, interaction points and permutations. These structures are designed to make easy the introduction of a suitable notion of congruence, and then a suitable notion of quotient. Our main result is that any two quotients are isomorphic.

2 Communication Structures and Correspondences

Definition 1. *A* communication structure *is given by the following elements:*

(i) a set $\mathcal{P}$ of processes – $p, q, s, \ldots$ range over $\mathcal{P}$;
(ii) every process $p \in \mathcal{P}$ has a set of handles (interaction points) $H(p)$;
(iii) for every process $p \in \mathcal{P}$, and for every subset $K \subseteq H(p)$, there exists a permutation subgroup S^p_K over K;
(iv) for every $H \subset H' \subseteq H(p)$ we have:
  (a) if $\rho \in S^p_{H'}$ and $\rho/_{H'\setminus H} = id_{H'\setminus H}$, then $\rho/_H \in S^p_H$,
  (b) S^p_H is a subgroup in $S^p_{H'}$ (we use the extension by identity on $H' \setminus H$).

The set $H(p)$ is the set of all communication points of a process p. The permutations of $S^p_{H(p)}$ describe the internal symmetry of p, which express the possibility to interchange the communication points without affecting the external communication between processes.

Definition 2. *Let $\mathcal{P}$ and $\mathcal{Q}$ be two communication structures; a* correspondence *between two processes $p \in \mathcal{P}$ and $q \in \mathcal{Q}$ is a triple $(S^p_H, \varphi, S^q_{H'})$, where $H \subseteq H(p)$, $H' \subseteq H(q)$, and $\varphi : S^p_H \to S^q_{H'}$ is a group morphism. We denote by $\partial(P, Q)$ the set of all correspondences between processes from $\mathcal{P}$ and $\mathcal{Q}$.*

3 Composing Correspondences. Maps

Definition 3. *Let $\mathcal{P}$, $\mathcal{Q}$ and $\mathcal{S}$ be three process structures. The composition of correspondences is a partial binary operation*

$$"\circ" : \partial(P, Q) \times \partial(Q, S) \longrightarrow \partial(P, S)$$

defined by

$$(S^p_H, \varphi, S^q_{H'}) \circ (S^q_{H'}, \varphi', S^s_{H''}) = (S^p_H, \varphi' \circ \varphi, S^s_{H''}),$$

where $p \in \mathcal{P}$, $q \in \mathcal{Q}$, $s \in \mathcal{S}$ and $H \subseteq H(p)$, $H' \subseteq H(q)$, $H'' \subseteq H(s)$.

Remark: It is not difficult to prove that the composition of correspondences is associative.

Definition 4. *If $\mathcal{P}$ and $\mathcal{Q}$ are two communication structures, a* map *from $\mathcal{P}$ to $\mathcal{Q}$ is a set of correspondences $\mathcal{F} \subseteq \partial(P, Q)$ such that for every process $p \in \mathcal{P}$ and every subset $H \subseteq H(p)$, there exists a unique correspondence $(S^p_H, \varphi, S^q_{H'}) \in \mathcal{F}$, where $q \in \mathcal{Q}$ and $H' \subseteq H(q)$. We denote this map by $\mathcal{F} : \mathcal{P} \longrightarrow \mathcal{Q}$.*

If $\mathcal{F} : \mathcal{P} \to \mathcal{Q}$, $\mathcal{F}' : \mathcal{Q} \to \mathcal{S}$ are two maps, then we define their composition $\mathcal{F}' \circ \mathcal{F} : P \to S$ as the set of all possible compositions of correspondences from $\mathcal{F}$ and $\mathcal{F}'$. The composition $\mathcal{F}' \circ \mathcal{F}$ is also a map.

Definition 5. *Let $\mathcal{P}$ be a communication structure.*

(i) identity map *over $\mathcal{P}$, $\mathbf{1}_{\mathcal{P}} : \mathcal{P} \to \mathcal{P}$, is the set $\{(S^p_H, id, S^p_H) : H \subseteq H(p)\}$.*
(ii) a map $\mathcal{F} : \mathcal{P} \to \mathcal{Q}$ is an isomorphism *if there exists another map $\mathcal{F}' : \mathcal{Q} \to \mathcal{P}$ such that $\mathcal{F} \circ \mathcal{F}' = \mathbf{1}_{\mathcal{Q}}$ and $\mathcal{F}' \circ \mathcal{F} = \mathbf{1}_{\mathcal{P}}$. In this case $\mathcal{F}'$ is the* inverse map *of $\mathcal{F}$, and it is denoted by $\mathcal{F}^{-1}$.*

4 p–Translations and p–Equivalences

Definition 6. *Let $\mathcal{P}$ be a communication structure.*

(i) for two given processes $p, q \in \mathcal{P}$, a translation *from p to q is a triple (H, δ, H'), where $H \subseteq H(p)$, $H' \subseteq H(q)$ and $\delta : H \to H'$ is a bijective function, denoted by $p_H \overset{\delta}{\longleftrightarrow} q_{H'}$ or, if it is possible, simply by δ.*
(ii) two translations $p_H \overset{\delta_1}{\longleftrightarrow} q_{H'}$ and $p_H \overset{\delta_2}{\longleftrightarrow} q_{H'}$ from p to q are equivalent *(and we denote this by $\delta_1 \sim \delta_2$) if we have two permutations $\rho \in S^p_H$ and $\rho' \in S^q_{H'}$ such that $\delta_1 = \rho' \circ \delta_2 \circ \rho$;*
(iii) a p–translation *$\mathfrak{R} : \mathcal{P} \longrightarrow \mathcal{P}$ over the communication structure $\mathcal{P}$ is a family $\mathfrak{R}$ of translations from $\mathcal{P}$ to $\mathcal{P}$ with the following properties:*
– for every translation $\delta \in \mathfrak{R}$, if $\delta \sim \delta'$, then $\delta' \in \mathfrak{R}$, and
– if $p_H \overset{\delta}{\longleftrightarrow} p_H \in \mathfrak{R}$, then $\delta \in S^p_H$.

The relation $\sim$ defined over translations is an equivalence relation.
We define the following operations over translations and p–translations:

(i) the *inverse* of a translation $p_H \overset{\delta}{\longleftrightarrow} q_{H'}$ is the translation $q_{H'} \overset{\delta^{-1}}{\longleftrightarrow} p_H$; the *inverse* of a p–translation $\mathfrak{R}$ is the set $\{\delta^{-1} : \delta \in \mathfrak{R}\}$ denoted by $\mathfrak{R}^{-1}$;

(ii) the *composition* of two translations $p_H \overset{\delta}{\longleftrightarrow} q_{H'}$ and $q_{H'} \overset{\delta'}{\longleftrightarrow} s_{H''}$ is the translation $p_H \overset{\delta' \circ \delta}{\longleftrightarrow} s_{H''}$; the *composition* of two p–translations $\mathfrak{R}_1$ and $\mathfrak{R}_2$ over the same communication structure is the family $\{\delta_1 \circ \delta_2 : \delta_1 \in \mathfrak{R}_1, \delta_2 \in \mathfrak{R}_2\}$ (whenever the composition $\delta_1 \circ \delta_2$ is possible), and it is denoted $\mathfrak{R}_1 \circ \mathfrak{R}_2$.

Lemma 1.

(i) the inverse of a p–translation is also a p–translation;
(ii) the composition of two p–translations over the same structure is a p–translation.

Proof. (i) Let $\mathfrak{R} : \mathcal{P} \longrightarrow \mathcal{P}$ be a p–translation, $\delta \in \mathfrak{R}$, and let η be a translation such that $\delta^{-1} \sim \eta$. If $p_H \overset{\delta}{\longleftrightarrow} q_{H'}$, then $q_{H'} \overset{\delta^{-1}}{\longleftrightarrow} p_H$, and $q_{H'} \overset{\eta}{\longleftrightarrow} p_H$; moreover, there exist two permutations $\rho \in S^p_H, \rho' \in S^q_{H'}$ such that $\rho \circ \delta^{-1} \circ \rho' = \eta$. As a consequence, we have $\delta \sim \eta^{-1}$, $\eta^{-1} \in \mathfrak{R}$, and $\eta \in \mathfrak{R}^{-1}$. The second condition of the p–translation definition is obviously satisfied by $\mathfrak{R}^{-1}$.

(ii) Let $\Re_1 : \mathcal{P} \longrightarrow \mathcal{P}$, $\Re_2 : \mathcal{P} \longrightarrow \mathcal{P}$ two p–translations, and two translations $p_H \overset{\delta}{\longleftrightarrow} q_{H'} \in \Re_1$, $q_{H'} \overset{\delta'}{\longleftrightarrow} s_{H''} \in \Re_2$. If $p_H \overset{\eta}{\longleftrightarrow} s_{H''}$ is a translation from p to s such that $\delta' \circ \delta \sim \eta$, then we can find two permutations $\rho \in S^p_H$ and $\rho' \in S^s_{H''}$ such that $\rho' \circ \delta' \circ \delta \circ \rho = \eta$. For every permutation $\sigma \in S^q_{H'}$ the above equality becomes $\eta = (\rho' \circ \delta' \circ \sigma) \circ (\sigma^{-1} \circ \delta \circ \rho)$. If we denote $\delta_2 = \rho' \circ \delta' \circ \sigma$, and $\delta_1 = \sigma^{-1} \circ \delta \circ \rho$, then we have $\delta_1 \in \Re_1$, $\delta_2 \in \Re_2$ and $\eta = \delta_2 \circ \delta_1 \in \Re_2 \circ \Re_1$.
The second condition from the definition of p–translations is easy to be verified.

Definition 7.

(i) the identity p–translation *over a communication structure $\mathcal{P}$, denoted by $id_{\mathcal{P}}$, is the family* $\{\ p_H \overset{\rho}{\longleftrightarrow} p_H : p \in \mathcal{P},\ H \subseteq H(p),\ \rho \in S^p_H\ \}$;

(ii) a p–equivalence *is a p–translation $\Re$ defined over a communication structure $\mathcal{P}$ which is reflexive ($id_{\mathcal{P}} \subseteq \Re$), symmetric ($\Re^{-1} \subseteq \Re$), and transitive ($\Re \circ \Re \subseteq \Re$).*

Remark: The used definition of the correspondences between two processes has the advantage that it does not require an equivalence relation like in [Ho1, Ho2]. The correspondences are not used to define translations and p–translations and this fact helps us to differentiate between maps and equivalences.

5 Quotient Structure. Isomorphism Theorem

In this section we define the quotient related to a *p*–equivalence, and we show that this quotient can get a communication structure which is unique up to an isomorphism. Let $\Re : \mathcal{P} \longrightarrow \mathcal{P}$ be a p–translation, and we consider the set $\wp = \{(p, H) : p \in \mathcal{P}, H \subseteq H(p)\}$; for the sake of simplicity, we use the notation p_H instead of (p, H). Then we define the binary relation $\approx_{\Re} \subseteq \wp \times \wp$ by $p_H \approx_{\Re} q_{H'}$ if and only if there exists a translation $p_H \overset{\delta}{\longleftrightarrow} q_{H'} \in \Re$.

Lemma 2. *$\approx_{\Re}$ is an equivalence relation over $\wp$ if and only if $\Re$ is a p–equivalence.*

Proof. $\approx_{\Re}$ is reflexive because $id_{\mathcal{P}} \subseteq \Re$. Symmetry comes from the fact that $\Re^{-1} \subseteq \Re$. For transitivity, let $p_H \overset{\delta}{\longleftrightarrow} q_{H'}$, and $q_{H'} \overset{\delta'}{\longleftrightarrow} r_{H''} \in \Re$; since $\Re \circ \Re \subseteq \Re$, then $p_H \overset{\delta' \circ \delta}{\longleftrightarrow} s_{H''} \in \Re$. For the other implication (i.e. *only if*) the proof is similar.

We will denote the quotient $\wp/_{\approx_{\Re}}$ by $\Re^{\approx}$, and the equivalence class of p_H by $[p_H]$. We choose a representative from every equivalence class and for each such family of representatives, we can build a communication structure on $\Re^{\approx}$ in the following way :

- the set of processes is the family of the all equivalence classes $[p_H]$;

- for every equivalence class $[p_H]$, p_H is the representative we have chosen above, and we define $H([p_H])$ as being the set H (which is included in $H(p)$);

- for every equivalence class $[p_H]$, and $K \subseteq H([p_H])$, the corresponding permutation group is S_K^p (which exists from our initial communication structure).

Theorem 1. *The structure defined above on $\Re^{\approx}$ is a communication structure.*

Proof. It is enough to verify only the condition (iv) of the communication structure definition. Let $[p_H]$ be an equivalence class; according to the above construction, for this class we have $H([p_H]) = H$. We consider $H' \subseteq H'' \subseteq H$. If $\rho \in S^p_{H''}$ with $\rho/_{H''\setminus H'} = id/_{H''\setminus H'}$, then $\rho/_{H'} \in S^p_{H'}$ – this relation comes from the original structure. On the other hand, $S^p_{H'} \leq S^p_{H''}$ (by extending the permutations) – this is valid by the definition of our initial communication structure $\mathcal{P}$.

According to the construction described above, two different representative choices can determine different structures on the quotient $\Re^{\approx}$. The following theorem shows the relationship between these structures.

Theorem 2. *Any two structures determined by different representative choices are isomorphic communication structures.*

Proof. Let $\{p_{iH} : i \in I\}$ and $\{q_{iH'} : i \in I\}$ two families of representatives selected from the equivalence classes such that $p_{iH} \approx_{\Re} q_{iH'}$, for every $i \in I$. We denote by $\Re^{\approx}$ and $\Re^{\approx'}$ the structures determined by these families of representatives. Since $p_{iH} \approx q_{iH'}$, we have a translation $p_{iH} \overset{\delta_i}{\longleftrightarrow} q_{iH'} \in \Re$, for every $i \in I$.

Let $H_1 \subseteq H([p_{iH}]) = H$ and $H'_1 = \delta_i(H_1)$. Consider now $\rho_1 \in S^{p_i}_{H_1}$; we extend ρ_1 on $H \setminus H_1$ by identity, and we obtain $\rho \in S^{p_i}_H$. On the other hand, $\delta_i^{-1} \in \Re$ – from the symmetry of $\Re$, and $\rho \in \Re$ – from the reflexivity of $\Re$. Now, from the transitivity of $\Re$, we have

$$\rho' = \delta_i \circ \rho \circ {\delta_i}^{-1} \in \Re.$$

This means $q_{iH'} \overset{\rho'}{\longleftrightarrow} q_{iH'} \in \Re$, which implies $\rho' \in S^{q_i}_{H'}$.

We show now that $\rho'/_{H'\setminus H'_1} = id_{H'\setminus H'_1}$. Let h be in $H' \setminus H'_1$; then ${\delta_i}^{-1}(h) \in H \setminus H_1$ and $\rho \circ {\delta_i}^{-1}(h) = {\delta_i}^{-1}(h)$; it follows that $\rho'(h) = h$ for every $h \in H' \setminus H'_1$. Therefore

$$\rho'_1 = \rho'/_{H'_1} \in S^{q_i}_{H'_1}.$$

In this way we can define ${\varphi_i}^{H_1} : S^{p_i}_{H_1} \longrightarrow S^{q_i}_{H'_1}$ by ${\varphi_i}^{H_1}(\rho_1) = {\rho'}_1$. In order to simplify our notation, we denote ${\varphi_i}^{H_1}$ by φ, and we prove that φ is a group morphism.

First of all it is easy to see that $\varphi(id_{H_1}) = id_{H_1'}$. Let $\rho_1, \pi_1 \in S_{H_1}^{p_i}$ be two permutations and $\rho, \pi \in S_H^{p_i}$ their corresponding extensions by identity on $H \setminus H_1$; we have $\sigma_1 = \rho_1 \circ \pi_1 \in S_{H_1}^{p_i}$, and $\sigma = \rho \circ \pi \in S_H^{p_i}$. Then we have

$$\rho' = \delta_i \circ \rho \circ {\delta_i}^{-1}, \quad \pi' = \delta_i \circ \pi \circ {\delta_i}^{-1} \in S_{H'}^{q_i}$$

$$\rho_1' = \rho'/_{H_1'}, \quad \pi_1' = \pi'/_{H_1'} \in S_{H_1'}^{q_i}.$$

If we consider $\sigma' = \delta_i \circ \sigma \circ {\delta_i}^{-1}$, then

$$\varphi(\rho_1 \circ \pi_1) = \varphi(\sigma_1) = \sigma_1' = \sigma'/_{H_1'}.$$

For every $h \in H_1'$ we have

$$\sigma'(h) = ((\delta_i \circ \rho \circ {\delta_i}^{-1}) \circ (\delta_i \circ \pi \circ {\delta_i}^{-1}))(h) = (\rho' \circ \pi')(h) =$$

$$\rho'(\pi_1'(h)) = \rho_1'(\pi_1'(h)) = (\rho_1' \circ \pi_1')(h).$$

In this way $\varphi(\rho_1 \circ \pi_1) = \varphi(\rho_1) \circ \varphi(\pi_1)$, i.e. φ is a group morphism.

Now we can define ${\psi_i}^{H_1'} : S_{H_1'}^{q_i} \longrightarrow S_{H_1}^{p_i}$; we use ψ as simplified notation of ${\psi_i}^{H_1'}$. For each permutation $\rho_1' \in S_{H_1'}^{q_i}$, we consider $\rho' \in S_{H'}^{q_i}$ – the usual extension to H'. Then we have $\rho = {\delta_i}^{-1} \circ \rho' \circ \delta_i \in S_H^{p_i}$, and we define

$$\psi(\rho_1') = \rho_1 = \rho/_{H_1}.$$

Following similar arguments as above, we can prove that ψ is a group morphism.

The family $\mathcal{F} = \{ \varphi_i^{H_1} : i \in I, H_1 \subseteq H \}$ is a map from $\Re^{\approx}$ to $\Re^{\approx'}$, and $\mathcal{F}' = \{ {\psi_i}^{H_1'} : i \in I, H_1' \subseteq H' \}$ is a map from $\Re^{\approx'}$ to $\Re^{\approx}$. $\mathcal{F}'$ is the inverse map of $\mathcal{F}$ since for every $i \in I$ we have

$${\varphi_i}^{H_1} \circ {\psi_i}^{H_1'} = id_{S_{H_1'}^{q_i}} \text{ and } {\psi_i}^{H_1'} \circ {\varphi_i}^{H_1} = id_{S_{H_1}^{p_i}}.$$

6 Conclusion

This paper is an attempt to define and study a formal framework for communication between processes of a distributed system. It introduces communication structures, an abstract notion which could lead to a complementary point of view to that of process algebras (CCS, ACP, π-calculus, action calculi etc).

Communication structures are essentially sets of processes. Each process is equipped with a set of interaction points called handles, and with a family of permutations over this set. The main contribution of the paper is the definition of an equivalence on communication structures, and the construction of the respective quotient structure, where an equivalence consists of suitable correspondences between sets of handles of processes.

References

[Ho1] K. Honda. Notes on P–Algebra(1); Process Structure. Proceedings TPPP'94, LNCS 907, pp.25-44, Springer Verlag, 1995.

[Ho2] K. Honda. Composing Processes, Proceedings POPL'96, Principles of Programming Languages, pp.344-357, ACM Press, 1996.

[Ku] A. Kurosh. *Cours d'algèbre supérieure* Ed. MIR, Moscou, 1980.

[La] Y. Lafont. Interaction Nets, Proceedings POPL'90, Principles of Programming Languages, pp.95-108, ACM Press, 1990.

[Mi] R. Milner. Action Structures and the π–calculus, In *Proof and Computation*, ed. H. Schwichtenberg, series F, pp.219-280, Springer Verlag, 1994.

Applying Temporal Logic to Analysis of Behavior of Cooperating Logic Programs*

Michael I. Dekhtyar[1], Alexander Ja. Dikovsky[2], and Mars K. Valiev[3]

[1] Dept. of CS, Tver State University
Tver, Russia, 170000,
Michael.Dekhtyar@tversu.ru
[2] Keldysh Institute for Applied Mathematics
Moscow, Russia, 125047,
dikovsky@spp.keldysh.ru
[3] Keldysh Institute for Applied Mathematics
Moscow, Russia, 125047,
valiev@spp.keldysh.ru

Abstract. We consider systems of cooperating logic programs which generalize dynamic deductive databases (DDDBs) from [1,2]. Some properties of the system behavior are defined which ensure an infinite steady life of the system. Decision problems for these properties of cooperating productional logic programs are investigated. It is shown that these problems are reducible to the satisfiability problem for the propositional temporal logic of branching time. It follows that stability problems for the cooperating productional logic programs are decidable with the exponential time complexity.

1 Introduction

In this paper we consider a logical approach to the mathematical analysis of the behavior of interactive discrete dynamic systems. A state of a dynamic system is represented by a data base state (*DB state*), i.e. a finite set of facts. The behavior of the system is determined by actions of a set of logical programs which update the DB states. These actions generate a set of possible trajectories of the system, i.e. sequences of DB states. Different requirements on the system behavior can be defined in terms of conditions which should be satisfied by the set of trajectories. Here we consider only one of interesting kinds of the behavior properties which are expressible in such terms, namely, the *stability* property of the system. Moreover, we limit our consideration by the case when the system $\mathcal{B}$ consists of $n+1$ (in general, nondeterministic) logic programs, a master MP and a set of slaves $SP =< SP_1, ..., SP_n >$, which work over a (finite dynamic) database $\mathcal{E}$, updating states of $\mathcal{E}$ in turn: on every odd step slave programs concurrently change the current database state, and on even steps the

* This work was sponsored by the Russian Fundamental Studies Foundation (Grants 97-01-00973 and 98-01- 00204).

D. Bjørner, M. Broy, A. Zamulin (Eds.): PSI'99, LNCS 1755, pp. 228–234, 2000.

master program updates the database state with the aim of restoring integrity constraints possibly violated by the slaves in the previous step. This notion of cooperating (symbiotic) logic programs generalizes the notion of dynamic deductive databases with external updates from [1,2].

The binary relation on the DB states induced by the updates executed by the set LP of logic programs $LP_1, ..., LP_n$ we denote by $\vdash_{LP}$ (with the aim to avoid some inessential complications we consider in this paper only systems LP defining total relations $\vdash_{LP}$, so below we can consider only infinite trajectories of the systems). Then local behavior of the system $\mathcal{B}$ in the current state $\mathcal{E}_0$ is described as one interaction of SP and MP applied to this state, i.e. as the sequence of two updates $\mathcal{E}_0 \vdash_{SP} \mathcal{E}'_1 \vdash_{MP} \mathcal{E}_1$. Normally, one should distinguish between the acceptable and not acceptable interactions, depending on a criterion of admissibility of the system states. Each acceptable interaction applies to an admissible state $\mathcal{E}_0$ and yields an admissible state $\mathcal{E}_1$. However, the intermediate state $\mathcal{E}'_1$ may in general be inadmissible, in which case the reaction of MP compensates for the destructive actions of SP . We represent the admissibility criterion by an *integrity constraint (IC)* expressed by a formula Φ over DB states. In terms of the IC the acceptability of the interaction is expressed as follows: the interaction of the form above is *acceptable* if $\mathcal{E}_0 \models \Phi$ and $\mathcal{E}_1 \models \Phi$. Thus, the system $\mathcal{B}$ representing the interactive discrete dynamic system has in fact the form $< MP, SP =< SP_1, ..., SP_n >, \Phi >$, and its local behavior is expressed in terms of acceptable interactions.

Global behavior of the system in current state $\mathcal{E}_0$ is represented by (infinite) sequences of interactions starting in $\mathcal{E}_0$ which we call trajectories

$$\mathcal{E}_0 \vdash_{SP} \mathcal{E}'_1 \vdash_{MP} \mathcal{E}_1 \vdash_{SP} \mathcal{E}'_2 \vdash_{MP} \mathcal{E}_2 ...$$

A trajectory whose all local interactions are acceptable represents the stable behavior of the system: any possible destructive action of the slave programs SP is compensated by some action of the master program MP along all the trajectory. Such the trajectories are called *stable.*

The trajectories of the system $\mathcal{B}$ form a tree $T(\mathcal{E}_0)$ with the root $\mathcal{E}_0$. A number of natural properties of interactive behavior of $\mathcal{B}$ in a given DB state can be formalized in terms of this tree, in particular, different kinds of stability.

Definition 1 *Let* $Q_1, Q_2 \in \{\forall, \exists\}$. *Then* $\mathcal{B}$ *is* Q_1Q_2-stable in DB state $\mathcal{E}_0$ *if in the tree* $T(\mathcal{E}_0)$ *there is a* Q_1Q_2*-subtree in which all infinite branches are stable trajectories.* [1]

One of natural questions connected with these notions is to consider algorithmic decidability of the stability problems. Of course, in general case these problems are undecidable. In [1,2] some classes of systems of logic programs were distinguished for which the stability problem is decidable. But only one slave (which represents an internal control program of a DDDB) was allowed there, and a

[1] We omit here the straighforward definition of Q_1Q_2-subtrees. E.g., $\forall\exists$ -subtree T_1 of T has the following properties: if a node N belongs to an even level of T_1 , then all successors of N in T are also successors of N in T_1 , and any node belonging to an odd level of T_1 has at least one successor (from T).

very simple kind of updates was considered as possible actions of the master (which represents an active environment of the system). Here we consider more general case when SP is represented by a set of working in parallel programs, and MP belongs to the same class as programs of SP. Because of space limitations we present here only results for the case when programs MP and SP belong to the class GPROD of ground productional logic programs with updates. We show that for the cooperative systems of this class the decision problems for stability are decidable and have the same decision complexity as for the corresponding problems in [1,2]. To prove our results we show that the variants of the stability problem which are considered here are reducible to the satisfiability problem for a variant of the propositional logic of branching time. Moreover, for $\exists\exists$ -stability this reduction is simultaneously a reduction to the satisfiability problem for the logic of linear time. As a corollary we obtain that results from [1,2] on the polynomial space and exponential time complexity of the stability problems for GPROD are generalized to the systems of cooperating programs from GPROD (the similar result also holds for the dual notion of homeostaticity: in this case the slaves correct destructive actions of the master). Moreover, we note that some lower bounds in [1,2] can be improved. Namely, the results on EXPTIME-hardness of the stability problem can be complemented by the $2^{n/logn}$ lower bound of the time complexity.

2 Basic Notions and Definitions

2.1 Productional Logic Programs

We consider *productional logic programs* with updates in a signature Σ consisting of a set of constants C and a set of predicate simbols Pr . Let $\mathbf{H}$ denote the Herbrand base over Σ. A productional logic program defines the unique intensional predicate $q \notin Pr$ by a set of clauses which have the form

$$q \ :- \ Con_1, \ldots, Con_k, Act_1, \ldots, Act_m$$

where each Con_i (elementary condition) is either a ground atom of $\mathbf{H}$ or its negation, and each Act_j (*action*) is one of elementary updates $insert(A)$, $delete(A)$ where $A \in \mathbf{H}$. In fact, these rules are equivalent to the productions used in AI, so in further we use for them their usual syntax:

$$Con_1 \& ... \& Con_k \Longrightarrow Act_1, ..., Act_m.$$

We can assume that there are no conflicts in application of actions in productions, i.e. there are simultaneously no $Act_i = insert(A)$ and $Act_j = delete(A)$ in one production π.

A data base (DB) state $\mathcal{E}$ is a finite subset of the Herbrand base $\mathbf{H}$. The production π is *applicable* to a DB state $\mathcal{E}$ iff for every $1 \leq i \leq k$ $Con_i \in \mathcal{E}$ if Con_i is a ground atom and $Con_i \notin \mathcal{E}$ if Con_i is a negated ground atom. We consider here only productinal programs such that for any DB state $\mathcal{E}$ at least one production of the program is applicable to $\mathcal{E}$ (this assumption is inessential and is taken only to make the temporal logic formulas describing below stability properties less cumbersome).

Let $\pi =< \pi_1, ..., \pi_n >$ be a set of productions. We define now the simultaneous application of these productions to a state $\mathcal{E}$. It can be defined in different ways. We choose here the following one. If there is a production π_i not applicable to $\mathcal{E}$ then π is not applicable to $\mathcal{E}$. In other case the result $\pi(\mathcal{E})$ of simultaneous application of productions π to $\mathcal{E}$ is defined as a DB state $\mathcal{E}_1$ obtained from $\mathcal{E}$ by adding all atoms A such that there is a production $\pi_i \in \pi$ whose action includes $insert(A)$ and by deleting all atoms A such that there is a production $\pi_i \in \pi$ whose action includes $delete(A)$. When for some atom A there are two productions in π one of which wants to insert A and the another one wants to delete it, then A does not change, i.e. $A \in \mathcal{E}_1 \leftrightarrow A \in \mathcal{E}$. (Of course, another strategies of conflict resolution are possible as well, e.g. by introducing some kind of priority for programs.) So, the set of productions π defines an update relation $\vdash_\pi$ on the set of all DB states: $\mathcal{E} \vdash_\pi \mathcal{E}_1$ iff $\mathcal{E}_1 = \pi(\mathcal{E})$. The update relation $\vdash_{LP}$ induced by a set of productional logic programs $LP =< LP_1, ..., LP_n >$ is defined as

$$\vdash_{LP} = \cup_{\{\pi | \pi = <\pi_1, ..., \pi_n>, \pi_i \in LP_i\}} \vdash_\pi .$$

We consider as integrity constraints (ICs) quantifier-free first order formulas over Σ. We say that a DB state $\mathcal{E}$ *satisfies* an IC Φ iff $\mathcal{E} \models \Phi$.

2.2 Propositional Temporal Logic

We use the following variant of propositional logic of branching time (BPTL). It differs from the logics CTL and CTL^* considered in the survey [3] by presence of the past temporal operator $\forall Y$ ("in the previous state"), though it is simpler in other respects: it does not contain complex temporal operators of the kind $\forall F$. CTL-like logics with past temporal operators were considered in [4] and [5]. The temporal structure used in BPTL is tree-like (branching forwards and linear backwards). Such variant of the time structure is also considered in [5] among other variants (the time structure used in [4] is branching backwards as well as forwards). Other more general than BPTL systems can be found in the area of the propositional dynamic logics.

The formulas of BPTL are constructed from propositional variables by using the Boolean connectives and the temporal operators $\forall X, \forall Y$ and $\forall G$ (operators $\exists X, \exists Y$ and $\exists F$ are expressed as $\neg\forall X\neg$, $\neg\forall Y\neg$ and $\neg\forall G\neg$, respectively).

Models of BPTL have the form $< T, \pi >$ where T is an infinite tree with branches of the height ω , and π assigns to any node s of T a set of propositional variables satisfied on s (as usual we write $s \models p$ instead of $p \in \pi(s)$). The relation $\models$ is extended to all the formulas of BPTL in the following way:

semantics of boolean connectives is defined as usual;

$s \models \forall X\, p$ iff $s' \models p$ for all sons s' of s;

$s \models \forall Y\, p$ iff $s' \models p$ if s is not the root of T and s' is the predecessor of s (if s is the root we can assume $s \models \forall Y\, p$ for any formula p);

$s \models \forall Gp$ iff $s' \models p$ for all nodes s' of the forward paths beginning with s.

According to the definition above $\exists Yp$ means "there exists the predecessor s' of s such that $s' \models p$ " (the meaning of other operators is also clear).

The given above version of semantics for BPTL supposes that time structure is branching forwards and linear backwards. Another variant of semantics for BPTL assumes that time is linear forwards, too.

3 Reduction of Stability to BPTL

In this section we construct for a system of cooperating logic programs $\mathcal{B} =< MP, SP =< SP_1, ..., SP_n >, \Phi >$ and DB state $\mathcal{E}$ BPTL-formulas representing Q_1Q_2- stability of $\mathcal{B}$ in $\mathcal{E}$. To simplify notations we suppose that $n = 2$. Let MP be the productional logic program

$f_1 \Longrightarrow upd_1$

...

$f_m \Longrightarrow upd_m$,

and let SP_1 be the productional logic program

$f_{11} \Longrightarrow upd_{11}$

...

$f_{1n_1} \Longrightarrow upd_{1n_1}$,

and SP_2 be the productional logic program

$f_{21} \Longrightarrow upd_{21}$

...

$f_{2n_2} \Longrightarrow upd_{2n_2}$,

where f_{ij} are conditions, upd_{ij} are updates.

Any DB state $\mathcal{E}$ can be described statically as conjunction $Conj(\mathcal{E})$ of (positive ground) atoms occurring in $\mathcal{E}$. But to reflect changes of states caused by actions of MP, SP_1 and SP_2 we should in following to take into account also some negative atoms. So, with any DB state $\mathcal{E}$ and logic programs MP, SP_1, SP_2 we connect the formula $s(\mathcal{E})$ which is conjunction of $Conj(\mathcal{E})$ and negations of ground atoms occurring in MP, SP_1 or SP_2 but not in $\mathcal{E}$.

Note that in fact we can consider ground atoms as propositional letters. In what follows Σ will denote the set of propositional letters which occur in MP, SP_1, SP_2.

For any update upd which inserts $a_1, ..., a_k$, deletes $b_1, ..., b_l$ and leaves invariant $c_1, ..., c_m$ we introduce below a formula UPD with the intended meaning:

$s \models UPD$ iff the following is true: for any $\mathcal{E}$ the formula $s(\mathcal{E})$ is satisfied in s iff there exists a DB state $\mathcal{E}'$ such that $\mathcal{E}$ is obtained by applying upd to $\mathcal{E}'$ and $s(\mathcal{E}')$ is satisfied in the state s' of T previous to s.

UPD has the form $\bigwedge_{i=1}^{m} (c_i \equiv \exists Y c_i) \wedge \bigwedge_{i=1}^{k} a_i \wedge \bigwedge_{i=1}^{l} \neg b_i$.

For any $x \in \Sigma$ we introduce new variables x^-, x^+. Using these variables we introduce two variants of UPD :

$UPD' = \bigwedge_{i=1}^{m} (c_i \equiv \exists Y c_i) \wedge \bigwedge_{i=1}^{k}(a_i^+ \wedge a_i) \wedge \bigwedge_{i=1}^{l}(b_i^- \wedge \neg b_i)$.
$UPD'' = \bigwedge_{x \in \Sigma}(\neg x^+ \wedge \neg x^-) \wedge \bigwedge_{i=1}^{m} (c_i \equiv \exists Y c_i)$
$\wedge \bigwedge_{i=1}^{k}((\neg \exists Y a_i^- \rightarrow a_i) \wedge (\exists Y a_i^- \rightarrow (a_i \equiv \exists Y \exists Y a_i)))$
$\wedge \bigwedge_{i=1}^{l}((\neg \exists Y b_i^+ \rightarrow \neg b_i) \wedge (\exists Y b_i^+ \rightarrow (b_i \equiv \exists Y \exists Y b_i)))$.

Formulas UPD' and UPD'' are used below to simulate parallel executions of productions from SP_1 and SP_2 ; the variables x^+ and x^- in them are used to store the information for the conflict resolution.

Let Q be a new propositional variable. Then the formula $EVEN$ of the form

$$Q \wedge \forall G\ (Q \rightarrow (\forall X\ \neg\ Q \wedge \forall X\ \forall X\ Q))$$

expresses the property " Q is true exactly on the states in even levels of T ". A somewhat more complicate formula $THIRD$ (using some auxiliary propositional letter besides Q) expresses the property " Q is true exactly on the states in any third level of T ".

Let $Safety$ denote the formula

$THIRD \wedge \forall G\ (Q \rightarrow \Phi)$.

It is obvious that if this formula is satisfied on the root of T then the integrity constraint Φ is satisfied in all states at any third level of T.

Now we are ready to write out the formulas which show reducibility of the stability problems for the cooperating logic programs to the satisfiability problem for BPTL.

$(\exists\exists)$: $\mathcal{B} =< MP, < SP_1, SP_2 >, \Phi >$ is $\exists\exists$-stable in $\mathcal{E}$
iff the formula
$s(\mathcal{E}) \wedge Safety \wedge \forall G\ (Q \rightarrow \bigvee_{i=1}^{n_1}(f_{1i} \wedge \exists X(UPD'_{1i} \wedge \bigvee_{j=1}^{n_2}(\exists Y f_{2j} \wedge \exists X(UPD''_{2j} \wedge \bigvee_{k=1}^{m}(f_k \wedge \exists X UPD_k))))))$
is satisfiable.

Remark. For this formula the linear and branching time satisfiability coincide.

$(\forall\exists)$: $\mathcal{B} =< MP, < SP_1, SP_2 >, \Phi >$ is $\forall\exists$-stable in $\mathcal{E}$
iff the formula
$s(\mathcal{E}) \wedge Safety \wedge \forall G\ (Q \rightarrow \bigvee_{i=1}^{n_1} f_{1i} \wedge \bigvee_{i=1}^{n_2} f_{2i} \wedge \bigwedge_{i=1}^{n_1}(f_{1i} \rightarrow \exists X(UPD'_{1i} \wedge \bigwedge_{j=1}^{n_2}(\exists Y f_{2j} \rightarrow \exists X(UPD''_{2j} \wedge \bigvee_{k=1}^{m}(f_k \wedge \exists X UPD_k))))))$ is satisfiable.

Similar formulas can be given for the $\forall\forall$ -stability and the $\exists\forall$ -stability. Moreover, it is not difficult to modify these formulas to describe the stability properties for the systems of productional programs defining partial relations and for some other variants of cooperative execution of productional programs.

Remark 1. In fact, using the past operators in these formulas can be avoided. For the $\exists\exists$ -stability it is rather straightforward (using the linear time logic) and does not increase the size of the corresponding formulas. But for the case of $\forall\exists$-stability the branching structure of the time is essential. It seems that in this case the description of updates without using the past operator needs to explicitly consider all the DB states, but it leads to the exponential increasing of the formula size.

Remark 2. The papers [1,2] also contain decidabilty results for the stability problems for systems of more powerful logic programs (with variables and some variants of restricted recursion). Some of these results can be also extended by reduction of corresponding problems to the quantifier-free temporal predicate logic.

Note that all these reductions have polynomial complexity. In general, the reduction formulas have the polynomial size with respect to the size of the original logic programs. So, if we use the exponential time decision algorithm for BPTL (such algorithms can be obtained by easy adapting the known algorithms for different propositional temporal or dynamic logics, e.g. from [6]) we obtain for the stability problems an upper bound of complexity which has the form of an exponential on a polynomial. However, we can obtain some more exact complexity bound since the complexity of the satisfiability problem for BPTL is exponential respectively to the number of subformulas of the formula considered (not to the length of the formula), and it is easy to see that the number of subformulas in the reduction formulas is linear with respect to the size of the original programs. So, we obtain the following

Theorem 1. *(i) The Q_1Q_2-stability problem for cooperating programs in GPROD with quantifier-free integrity constraints is decidable in exponential time for any $Q_1, Q_2 \in \{\exists, \forall\}$;*

(ii) The $\exists\exists$-stability problem for the same classes of programs and integrity constraints is decidable in polynomial space.

The point (ii) is obtained using reduction to the linear time logic (see remark above) for which there exists an algorithm with polynomial space complexity (see [3]).

Acknowledgement. We express our gratitude to anonymous referees for their helpful comments.

References

[1] Dekhtyar M.I., Dikovsky A.Ja. Dynamic deductive data bases with steady behavior. In "Proc. of the 12 Intern. Conf. on Logic Programming", Ed. L.Sterling, The MIT Press, 1995, 183-197.

[2] Dekhtyar M.I., Dikovsky A.Ja. On homeostatic behavior of dynamic deductive data bases. In: D.Bjorner, M.Broy, I.Pottosin (eds.) Proc. 2nd Int. A. P. Ershov Memorial Conference "Perspectives of Systems Informatics", Lect. Notes in Comput. Sci., vol. 1181, 1996, 420-432.

[3] Emerson E.A. Temporal and modal logic. In "Handbook of Theor. Comput. Sci.", Ed. J. van Leeuwen, Elsewier Sci. Publishers, 1990.

[4] Pinter S.S., Wolper P. A temporal logic for reasoning about partially ordered computations. Proc. 3rd ACM Symp. on Principles of Distributed Computing, 1984, 28-37.

[5] Valiev M.K. On axiomatization of logic of discrete branching time. In "Modal and Intensional Logics. Proc. VIII Confer. on Logic and Method. of Science", Palanga, 1982 (in Russian).

[6] Valiev M.K. Decision complexity of variants of propositional dynamic logic. Lect. Notes in Comput. Sci., vol. 88, 1980, 656-664.

On Semantics and Correctness of Reactive Rule-Based Programs

Man Lin[1*], Jacek Malec[2**], and Simin Nadjm-Tehrani[1]

[1] Department of Computer and Information Science
Linköping University
S–581 83 Linköping, Sweden
linma,jam,snt@ida.liu.se

[2] Department of Computer Engineering
Mälardalens Högskola
Box 883, S–721 23 Västerås, Sweden

Abstract. The rule-based paradigm for knowledge representation appears in many disguises within computer science. In this paper we address special issues which arise when the rule-based programming paradigm is employed in the development of reactive systems. We begin by presenting a rule-based language RL which has emerged while developing intelligent cruise control systems. We define a desired declarative semantics and correctness criteria for rule-based programs which respect causality, synchrony assumption and desired determinism. Two alternative approaches are proposed to analyze RL programs. Both approaches build upon static checks of a rule-based program. In the first approach we accept programs which are correct with respect to a constructive semantics while in the second approach, a stratification check is imposed. The combination of rules and reactive behaviour, together with a formal analysis of this behaviour is the main contribution of our work.

1 Overview

The rule-based paradigm for knowledge representation appears in many disguises within computer science. Language issues related to this paradigm appear in production systems [3], parallel program design (e.g. Unity [2]), default reasoning within AI [9], logic programming [1], rewriting [7], active and deductive databases [4], and logics for action and change [15].

Our work combines results from the three areas of rule-based knowledge representation, reactive systems [11,6], and programming language semantics. The combination of rules and reactive behaviour, together with a formal analysis of this behaviour is thus the main contribution of our work. Different approaches

* Man Lin has been supported by TFR (Swedish Research Council for Engineering Sciences) and WITAS (the Wallenberg laboratory for research on Information Technology and Autonomous Systems).

** Jacek Malec has been partially supported by Mälardalens Real-Time Research Center (MRTC).

D. Bjørner, M. Broy, A. Zamulin (Eds.): PSI'99, LNCS 1755, pp. 235–246, 2000.

for specification of real-time and reactive systems range over automata-based, temporal logics, Petri nets, action systems, and process algebras. In our view a rule-based language with a formal semantics shares the benefits of these specification languages. In addition, it has a special appeal: it mimics the natural mode of reasoning by humans in many applications. Therefore, it can be considered as a powerful tool for capturing expert knowledge and formally analyzing it. Moreover, rules can be executed and can therefore be seen as both a specification and a programming language.

The synchronous family of high-level programming languages [5] for real-time systems (Lustre, Esterel, Signal) shares the above characteristic. They too can be used both for capturing high level design and as executable code. Though very different in syntax and style of programming, adding reactiveness to our rules leads to formal semantics which is reminiscent of a couple of the proposed semantics for Statecharts [14], and Esterel [13].

2 Rules and Reactiveness

A reactive rule-based system (illustrated in Figure 1) is a system that reacts to the changes of its environment continuously [12]. Such a system is composed of three entities called *state*, *rules*, and *inference engine*. The state consists of *slots*: state variables, with associated pairs of values indicating the *previous* and the *current* value of the slot, respectively. During a period when no changes happen (*equilibrium period*, EP), the two values of a slot are identical. At a point when there is a change (a stimulus comes from the environment), the current value of some slot becomes updated. We call such a moment an *asynchronous computational point* (ACP). At each ACP, the stimulus triggers one or more rules, producing new changes in the slots, which in turn trigger other rules, and so on. This is continued until no changes are possible, i.e. a steady state is reached. Then the system starts "resting" in its new EP, awaiting new stimuli. The inference engine is in charge of the computations at the ACPs.

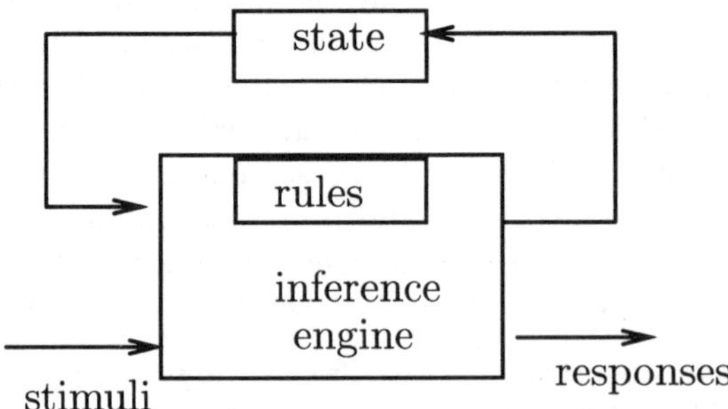

Fig. 1. A reactive rule-based system

The rule language RL (syntax can be found in the appendix) is developed to express responses of the system at each ACP. The language has been successfully used for developing a reactive application: a driver-support system [10].

The rules in an RL program have an event-condition-action form, e.g.:

```
WHEN A *= a IF (B *= b AND NOT E |= e) THEN D := d;
```

read as "When `A` changes to `a` then if `B` changes simultaneously to `b` and `E` has not been `e` then `D` obtains value `d`". The `WHEN` part: `A *= a` is called the *trigger* part of the rule, the `IF` part: `(B *= b AND NOT E |= e)` is called the *condition* part of the rule, and the `THEN` part `D := d` is called the *assignment* part of the rule. The trigger part and the condition part together are called the *precondition* of the rule. The characteristics of this language are:

- The meaning of a reactive program is independent of the ordering of the rules (in case of larger systems rule ordering is a cumbersome and error-prone process; the semantics of such programs is unclear and easy to distort). In our approach a program can be enhanced by simply adding new rules to the existing rule base;
- The language assumes finite domains for variables (c.f. datalog) allowing a finite model;
- The language allows the logical operations, negation and conjunction;
- The language allows for taking account of concurrent events (in the example rule events `A *= a` and `B *= b` occur simultaneously);
- The language models time flow without introducing metric time (`E |= e` checks if "`E` has had value `e` before", while `E *= e` checks if "`E` has changed to value `e`");

A rule responds to external stimuli at a given state by checking whether the rule is enabled at the current state, and firing the rule (performing the assignments) if so is the case.

A stimulus to a system, denoted as I, is a set of *changes* which are (slot, value) pairs. A state of a rule-based system is a pair (S, C) where S contains the values of all the variables (slots), and C contains the set of changes. We use S_x to denote the value of x in the latest EP. During an EP, S is the same and $C = \emptyset$. At an ACP, S is the same as S in the previous EP and C contains the changes occurring at this ACP including the external stimuli and the changes derived as the result of the assignments of the enabled rules.

A rule r being enabled at a state (S, C) is denoted by $(S, C) \vdash r$. A rule r being not enabled at a state (S, C) is denoted by $(S, C) \not\vdash r$. To check whether $(S, C) \vdash r$, we only need to check if all the primitive preconditions of rule r are satisfied at (S, C). By primitive precondition, we mean positive condition including X |= v (was), X *= v (changes to), or negative condition including NOT X |= v (was not), NOT X *= v (does not change to). The trigger part of a rule contains only one primitive condition X *= v , while the condition part of a rule can be a conjunction of primitive conditions. We define $\vdash$ for rules by first defining $\vdash$ for primitive conditions of rules, here delimited by [ ].

- $(S, C) \vdash [x \,|\!= v]$ iff $S_x = v$;
- $(S, C) \vdash [x *= v]$ iff $S_x \neq v$ and $\langle x, v \rangle \in C$;
- negation (NOT) and conjunction (AND) are interpreted as standard logical connectives. That is:
  - $(S, C) \vdash [\text{ NOT } p]$ where p is any positive primitive iff not $(S, C) \vdash p$.
  - $(S, C) \vdash [p_1 \text{ AND } p_2]$ where p_1 and p_2 are primitive preconditions iff $(S, C) \vdash p_1$ and $(S, C) \vdash p_2$.
- $(S, C) \not\vdash r$ iff not $(S, C) \vdash r$.

Let's look at a simple example. Suppose x, y, and z are the three slots of the system. Let $S_x = 0$, $S_y = 0$, $S_z = 0$ and $C = I = \{\langle x, 1 \rangle\}$. Program `P1` contains only one rule `r1`:

```
r1:     WHEN x *= 1 IF y |= 0 THEN z := 1;
```

Rule `r1` is enabled at (S, C) since $\langle x, 1 \rangle \in C$ and $S_y = 0$. The effect of firing this rule is to assign 1 to z. Therefore, the set of changes becomes $C1 = \{\langle x, 1 \rangle, \langle z, 1 \rangle\}$.

Let's consider another program `P2` containing only `r2` with the same (S, C):

```
r2:     WHEN z *= 1 IF y |= 0 THEN y := 1;
```

Rule `r2` is not enabled at (S, C) since $\langle z, 1 \rangle \notin C$. Therefore, the set of changes is still $\{\langle x, 1 \rangle\}$.

If an RL program contains several rules, then the response of the system at each ACP may no longer be only one (or zero) firing of rule. There could be several rule firings some of which are caused by others.

3 Synchrony Assumption and Causality

One might ask why the responses only occur at ACPs. The fundamental assumption taken here is the *synchrony* assumption: each response is assumed to be synchronous with the effects it causes. This assumption is realistic if the responses of the system are fast enough so that the environment does not change during the responses (which should be checked in practice). The effects of the execution of one component are instantly broadcast to all the other components of the system. Therefore, all the components of the system have the same view of the system state.

The smallest component of an RL program is one single rule. If several rules get fired at the same ACP, then all the rule firings are considered to occur at the same time. We don't care how the rule firings are done step by step if only synchrony requirement is considered. What is interesting is only the result of the response. The result of a response at (S, I) is a stable state (S, C') and a set of fired rules R^f where:

- C' is the result of firing all the rules in R^f at the given initial state (S, I). Let $\mathcal{A}_r$ denote the assignments of rule r. Then

  $$C' = \bigcup_{r \in R^f} \mathcal{A}_r \cup I.$$

  (S, C') is seen as the state after the response.

– R^f is the maximal set of rules that are enabled at state (S, C'). First, all the rules in R^f are enabled at (S, C'). Second, no other rules not belonging to R^f are enabled at (S, C').

However, we would like to retain *causality* which is a very important property for a reasoning system. The principle of causality requires that any change issued should have a sequence of (enabled) rule firings leading to it. The following example shows a causal reasoning. By composing earlier programs `P1` and `P2`, we get a new program `P3` which contains two rules: `r1` and `r2`. One can infer that both `r1` and `r2` are fired and the new set of changes becomes $C3 = \{\langle x,1\rangle, \langle y,1\rangle, \langle z,1\rangle\}$. The reasoning is simple. Since `r1` is enabled at (S, I), `r1` is fired and the effect: the change $\langle z,1\rangle$ is instantaneously broadcast. The system state becomes $(S, C1)$ where $C1 = \{\langle x,1\rangle, \langle z,1\rangle\}$. Since `r2` is enabled at $(S, C1)$, `r2` is also fired and results in the final set of changes $C3$.

For the above example, $C' = C3$ and $R^f = \{r1, r2\}$. The synchrony requirement is also satisfied since $C3 = I \cup \mathcal{A}_{r1} \cup \mathcal{A}_{r2}$, and `r1` and `r2` are the only rules enabled at $(S, C3)$.

However, not all the responses respect both synchrony hypothesis and the principle of causality. Let's look at two examples.

Given S where $S_x = 0, S_y = 0, S_z = 0$, $I = \{\langle y,1\rangle\}$ and a program with two rules `r3` and `r4`, what are the final state and the fired rule set?

```
r3: WHEN x *= 1 IF y |= 0 THEN z := 1;
r4: WHEN z *= 1 IF y |= 0 THEN x := 1;
```

There are two solutions which satisfy the synchrony requirement. One is $C' = I$ and $R^f = \emptyset$. The other is $C' = \{\langle y,1\rangle, \langle x,1\rangle, \langle z,1\rangle\}$ and $R^f = \{r3, r4\}$. The problem with the second solution is that without the firing of `r4`, `r3` can not get fired. The same is for `r4`: without the firing of `r3`, `r4` can not get fired. The result is self-triggered. Or, in other words, it is not causal since we can not generate this final result via a causal sequence of rule firings.

The above example shows that not all the responses satisfying synchrony requirement are causal. Next, we show that not all the causal responses satisfy the synchrony requirement either.

Suppose (S, I) be $S_x = 0, S_y = 0, S_z = 0$, $I = \{\langle y,1\rangle\}$, and a program be as follows.

```
r5: WHEN y *= 1 IF NOT x *= 1 THEN z := 1;
r6: WHEN y *= 1 IF x |= 0 THEN x := 1;
```

A causal rule firing sequence is `r5` followed by `r6` which results in $C' = \{\langle y,1\rangle, \langle x,1\rangle, \langle z,1\rangle\}$. The problem is that $r5$ is not enabled at (S, C') which violates the synchrony requirement.

4 Other Requirements

As we deal with variables, one important requirement is not to assign different values to the same variable at the same ACP. Another requirement is that there should be only one final result at each ACP. This requirement is understood as observable determinism.

Next, we provide a desired semantics definition for a response which respects the synchrony hypothesis, the principle of causality and the above requirements.

5 Declarative Semantics

Definition 1. *Suppose R is the set of rules of a program P. The* declarative response *of the program P in a state (S, I) is any sequence of firings*

$$\sigma_0 \sigma_1 \ldots$$

such that

- $\sigma_0 = (C_0, R_0^f) = (I, \emptyset)$,
- $\sigma_{i+1} = (C_{i+1}, R_{i+1}^f)$

$$= \begin{cases} (C_i \cup A_{r_f}, R_i^f \cup \{r_f\}) \text{ where } r_f \in \overline{R} = \{r | r \in R \setminus R_i^f \wedge (S, C_i) \vdash r\} & \text{if } \overline{R} \neq \emptyset \\ \sigma_i & \text{if } \overline{R} = \emptyset \end{cases}$$

□

In the definition, each firing (σ_i) contains a set of changes (C_i) and a set of fired rules (R_i^f).

It can be proved that a declarative response has always a finite length [8].

Definition 2. *Let R be the rule set in a program P. Let a declarative response of the program in a state $(S, \emptyset)$ to a stimulus I be $\sigma_0 \sigma_1 \ldots \sigma_m$. Let $\sigma_m = (C_m, R^f)$ and $R^f = \{r_1, r_2, \ldots, r_m\}$. The declarative response is* correct *if and only if*

- *the response is* **rule-consistent***:*

$$\forall r (r \in R^f \rightarrow (S, C_m) \vdash r)$$

that is, none of the rules fired in this response will become disabled after the final firing;

- *the response is* **slot-consistent***:*

$$\forall x (\langle x, v_1 \rangle \in C_m \wedge \langle x, v_2 \rangle \in C_m \rightarrow v_1 = v_2)$$

that is, no slot can have more than one change of value in this response;

- *the response is* **unambiguous***: for any other declarative response $\sigma_0 \sigma'_1 \ldots \sigma'_k$ with $\sigma'_k = (C'_k, R'^f)$ that is both rule-consistent and slot-consistent, we have $C'_k = C_m$.* □

A correct response is the desired response. This semantics is referred to as declarative semantics. An RL program is **correct** if and only if it has a correct response for any possible combination of state and stimuli. Two natural questions arise:

- Can we construct an operational semantics to implement the desired declarative semantics?
- Can we identify the ill-behaved programs during compile time without having to generate all the responses for each state-and-stimulus combination?

We will devote the next two sections to answering the above questions.

6 Constructive Semantics

6.1 The Semantics

Constructive semantics is an application of the three-valued-logic approach to non-monotonic reasoning in the setting of reactive systems. It also resembles the recently proposed semantics for pure Esterel [13]. The main differences are in the structure of programs (rule-based in our case, imperative in the case of Esterel), and the means of communication (change in slot values in our case, pure signals/events in Esterel). In what follows we present the constructive semantics.

The constructive semantics needs not only positive information about the changes of the system, but also negative information about the lack of changes. In constructive semantics, we deal with extended system state (S, Z) where S records the values of the slots before the ACP and Z contains a set of annotated changes where each (slot, value) pair has a annotation indicating the *status* of this change. The status is an element from the set $\{+, -, \bot\}$. $+$ is read as *positive*, and $\langle x, v\rangle^+$ means that $\langle x, v\rangle$ does occur in this ACP; $-$ is read as *negative*, and $\langle x, v\rangle^-$ means that the change $\langle x, v\rangle$ can not possibly occur in this ACP; $\bot$ is read as *Unknown*, and $\langle x, v\rangle^\bot$ means that the change of x to v is not present yet at this point of the computation, but it is not sure whether it will take place later.

The result of evaluation of a rule is one of the following: *True*, *False* or *Unknown* instead of only *True* or *False* as in 2-valued logic. The evaluation evaluates a rule to be *Unknown* if it is not known whether the rule will evaluate to true or false after this response. More specifically, a primitive condition (NOT x *= v) is evaluated to be *True* at a state (S, C) if $\langle x, v\rangle$ does not belong to C when reasoning under 2-valued logic, but *Unknown* in the case of constructive semantics if $\langle x, v\rangle$ is not explicitly marked with unchangeable status (positive or negative).

The ordering between the status annotations is

$$\preceq = \{(\bot, -), (\bot, +), (\bot, \bot), (-, -), (+, +)\}.$$

Let Z, Z' be two sets of annotated changes. Z is *less informative* than Z', denoted $Z \preceq Z'$ if and only if

$$(\forall \langle x, v\rangle^a \in Z)(\exists a')(\langle x, v\rangle^{a'} \in Z' \wedge a \preceq a').$$

Given C, C^+ is defined as the extension of C where:

$$C^+ = \{\langle x, v\rangle^+ \mid \langle x, v\rangle \in C\} \cup \{\langle x, v'\rangle^- \mid \langle x, v\rangle \in C \wedge v' \neq v\} \cup \\ \cup \{\langle x, v\rangle^\bot \mid \forall v' \langle x, v'\rangle \notin C\}$$

Symmetrically, given Z, Z^- is defined as the reduction of Z where:

$$Z^-=\{\langle x, v\rangle \mid \langle x, v\rangle^+ \in Z\}.$$

A rule being 3-enabled at an extended state (S, Z) is denoted by $(S, Z) \vdash_3 r$. A rule being 3-non-enabled at an extended state (S, Z) is denoted by $(S, Z) \not\vdash_3 r$. $(S, Z) \vdash_3 r$ if and only if all the primitive preconditions are evaluated to be True at (S, Z). $(S, Z) \not\vdash_3 r$ if and only if one of the primitive precondition is evaluated to be False at (S, Z). The evaluation of a primitive condition p at a given extended state (S, Z) is shown as follows:

- $[x\,|\!=\!v]$ is True if $S_x = v$;
  $[x\,|\!=\!v]$ is False if $S_x \neq v$;
- $[x{*}{=}v]$ is True if $\langle x, v\rangle^+ \in Z$ and $S_x \neq v$;
  $[x{*}{=}v]$ is False if $\langle x, v\rangle^- \in Z$ or $S_x = v$;
- [NOT p] is True if p is False; [NOT p] is False if p is True;
- With the exception of [True], all other primitive conditions are evaluated to Unknown.

It should be observed that there are intermediate cases when neither $(S, Z) \vdash_3 r$ nor $(S, Z) \not\vdash_3 r$ is true.

The negative changes are derived by function `never`. Function `never` works iteratively. At each iteration, a negative change is added into the set of annotated changes. The change added has one of the following characteristics:

- No rule in the program can issue such change.
- All the rules that can issue such change are 3-non-enabled at the current extended state.

When we say adding negative changes or positive changes, we mean updating the annotation of the (slot, value) pair in the set of annotated changes. This is done by `update` function. The annotation can only be changed from $\perp$ to $+$ or $-$. An attempt to change the status from $+$ to $-$ or vice versa indicates a symptom of slot-inconsistency. When such situation occurs, the set of annotated changes returned is an empty set to indicate failure. The formal definition for `never` and `update` can be found in [8].

We are now in a position to define an operational semantics.

Definition 3. *Given a program P with a rule set R, an initial system state $(S, \emptyset)$, and a stimulus I, the* constructive response *of the program is a sequence*

$$\gamma_0\gamma_1\cdots$$

such that

- $\gamma_0 = (Z_0, \emptyset)$, *where* $Z_0 = \texttt{never}(S, I^+, R)$,
- $\gamma_{i+1} = (Z_{i+1}, R^f_{i+1})$

$$= \begin{cases} (\emptyset, R^f_i) & \text{if } Z_i = \emptyset, \\ (\texttt{never}(S, \texttt{update}(Z_i, \mathcal{A}^+_{r_f})), R), R^f_i \cup \{r_f\}) & \text{if } Z_i \neq \emptyset \text{ and} \\ & r_f \in \overline{R_i} \neq \emptyset, \\ (Z_i, R^f_i) & \text{if } \overline{R_i} = \emptyset, \end{cases}$$

where $\overline{R_i} = \{r | r \in R \setminus R^f_i \wedge (S, Z_i) \vdash_3 r\}$. □

As we can see, if there exists an unfired rule 3-enabled in the current state, and no slot-inconsistency occurred in the `update` of the previous step ($Z_i \neq \emptyset$), then the current set of annotated changes Z_i is updated with positive changes, and negative changes. The positive changes come either from the external stimulus (step 0) or from the assignments of the selected rule that is 3-enabled at the current extended state (subsequent steps). The negative changes derived by `never` function are those potential negative changes that could be deduced from the current state. If there is no unfired rule 3-enabled by the current state, then the procedure returns the same tuple as in the previous step. Finally, if the state indicates the occurrence of slot-inconsistency ($Z_i = \emptyset$), the procedure returns the empty set as the new set of annotated changes.

We say that the constructive response *terminates* at Z_m if and only if ($Z_m = \emptyset$ and $Z_{m-1} \neq Z_m$)or ($\overline{R_m} = \emptyset$ and $\overline{R_{m-1}} \neq \emptyset$), that is, a slot-inconsistency occurs or there is no rule to be selected.

A terminating constructive response is *accepted* if and only if it terminates at Z_m and $Z_m \neq \emptyset$ and $(\forall \langle x, v\rangle^a \in Z_m)(a \neq \bot)$. That is, an accepted constructive response terminates *normally*, meaning that no slot-inconsistency occurs ($Z_m \neq \emptyset$), and the set of annotated changes of its final state is *complete*, meaning that no change in Z_m is marked with $\bot$.

6.2 Properties

It can be proved that given a program P and (S, I), all the constructive responses reach the same final set of annotated changes (the thereom can be found in [8]).

It can also be proved that any accepted constructive response yields a correct declarative response. In order to prove this, we first define a mapping from an accepted constructive response to a sequence of firings and then prove that this sequence is a construction of a declarative response (see [8]). Then, we prove that this declarative response is a correct one (see theorem 1).

Definition 4. *Let* $CR = \gamma_0\gamma_1 \ldots \gamma_m$ *be an accepted constructive response, where* $\gamma_i = \langle Z_i, R^f_i\rangle, 0 \leq i \leq m$. *Then*

$$\texttt{map}(CR) = \sigma_0, \sigma_1, \ldots, \sigma_m,$$

where $\sigma_i = (Z^-_i, R^f_i)$. □

Theorem 1. *(Soundness) If $DR = \texttt{map}(CR)$ is a declarative response obtained from an accepted constructive response CR, then DR is correct.* □

The proof can be found in [8].

The static checker performs an exhaustive check of acceptability of the responses for all possible states and stimuli. It can be easily proved that that all the programs passing the constructive check procedure are correct ones with respect to the desired declarative semantics.

7 Stratified Program

Stratified program is a well-known notion in logic programming and deductive databases. It was an early attempt to deal with dependencies between relations in presence of negation. The fixpoint computation along strata gives this class of programs a natural semantics. We introduce the idea of stratification into reactive rule-based systems to achieve rule-consistency. An arbitrary declarative response is not necessarily rule-consistent since a condition (NOT x *= v) of a rule r can be disabled by firing other rules after r, which may generate $\langle x, v\rangle$. By firing rules in a *stratified* order, this kind of situation can be avoided. Working with stratified rule sets has the following effect: every time a rule which has a condition part including negation over [s*=v] is tested for being enabled, we can be sure that a rule with an assignment v to s has been fired earlier in the response (if it is included in the final fired rule set of this response at all).

Note, however, that the user needs not explicitly consider these dependencies when introducing rules. The support at compile time is supposed to check whether such a stratification exists. Given a program P and a pair $\langle x, v\rangle$, the *definition* of $\langle x, v\rangle$ is the set of rules in whose assignment part $\langle x, v\rangle$ appears.

A stratified rule-based program consists of a disjoint set of rules $P = P^1 \cup \ldots \cup P^i \cup \ldots \cup P^k$ called *strata*. If a program is stratifiable, its stratification is constructed as follows:

- If a positive pair [x*= v] appears in the trigger part or condition part of a rule from P_i, then its definition is contained within $\bigcup_{j \leq i} P_j$;
- If a negative pair [NOT x*=v] appears in the condition part of a rule from P_i, then its definition is contained within $\bigcup_{j<i} P_j$.

For a given a stratified correct program, the responses generated by such operational semantics are correct if they are slot-consistent. Unfortunately, for a stratified program this operational semantics does not guarantee slot-consistency. Stratification simply provides a sufficient condition for rule-consistency.

8 Summary

The technical results obtained in our research can be summarized as follows:

- We have defined a rule-based language RL that combines asynchronous interaction with an environment with synchronous treatment of a response. Time and concurrency are thus dealt with in a simple manner;

- For this language we have defined a declarative semantics which enables a natural treatment of causality, atomicity, and desired determinism;
- We have defined a correctness criterion for reactive RL programs. A correct program ensures termination of rule firings at each reaction, consistency of the fired rules and a unique reaction for each new set of stimuli to the system;
- We have defined and implemented constructive semantics, based on three-valued evaluation of rules, that guarantees the correct results of computations for correct programs;
- We have developed and implemented a static procedure for checking the correctness of programs;
- We have proven soundness of the obtained results;
- For stratified programs we have developed the computational support which guarantees correctness w.r.t. one particular consistency requirement.

References

1. K. Apt and R. Bol. Logic programming and negation: A survey. *Journal of Logic Programming*, 19/20:9–71, 1994.
2. K. M. Chandy and J. Misra. *Parallel Program Design: A Foundation.* MA: Addison-Wesley, 1988.
3. T. A. Cooper and N. Wogrin. *Rule-based Programming with OPS5.* Morgan Kaufmann Publishers, Inc, 1988.
4. K.R. Dittrich, S. Gatziu, and A. Geppert. The active database management systems manifesto: A rulebase of ADBMS features. In Timos Sellis, editor, *Rules in Database System.* RIDS'95, Springer Verlag, 1995.
5. N. Halbwachs. *Synchronous Programming of Reactive Systems.* Kluwer Academic Publishers, 1993.
6. D. Harel and A. Pnueli. On the development of reactive systems. In K. R. Apt, editor, *Logics and Models of Concurrent Systems*, volume 13 of *NATO ASI Series.* Springer Verlag, 1985.
7. G. Huet. Confluent reductions: Abstract properties and applications to term rewriting systems. *Journal of ACM*, 27(4):797–821, 1980.
8. M. Lin. *Formal Analysis of Reactive Rule-based Programs.* Licentiate thesis, Linköping University, 1997. Linköping Studies in Science and Technology, Thesis No 643, ISBN 91-7219-030-2, ISSN 0280-7971.
9. W. Łukaszewicz. *Non-Monotonic Reasoning.* Ellis Horwood, 1990.
10. J. Malec, M. Morin, and U. Palmqvist. Driver support in intelligent autonomous cruise control. In *Proceedings of the IEEE Intelligent Vehicles Symposium'94*, pages 160–164, Paris, France, October 1994.
11. Z. Manna and A. Pnueli. *The Temporal Logic of Reactive and Concurrent Systems.* Springer-Verlag, 1992.
12. M. Morin, S. Nadjm-Tehrani, P. Österling, and E. Sandewall. Real-time hierarchical control. *IEEE Software*, 9(5):51–57, September 1992.
13. G. Plotkin, C. Stirling, and M. Tofte, editors. *Language and Interaction: Essays in Honour of Robin Milner*, chapter The Foundations of Esterel. MIT Press, 1998. To Appear.
14. A. Pnueli and M. Shalev. What is in a step: On the semantics of Statecharts. *Theoretical Aspects of Computer Software, LNCS*, 526:510–584, 1991.
15. E. Sandewall. *Features and Fluents*, volume 1. Clarendon Press. Oxford, 1994.

A Appendix: Syntax

The syntax for RL is defined as follows.

Definition 5. *A rule is a string*

`WHEN` <r_{trig}> `IF` <r_{cond}> `THEN` <r_{assign}>

fulfilling the requirements of the following grammar:

<r_{trig}> ::= <*slot-name*> `*=` <*slotval*>
<*slotval*> ::= <*ident*>
<r_{cond}> ::= <r_{cond}> `AND` <$r_{literal}$>
  | <$r_{literal}$>
  | `TRUE`
<$r_{literal}$> ::= `NOT` <$r_{literal}$>
  | <*slot-name*> `*=` <*slotval*>
  | <*slot-name*> `|=` <*slotval*>
<r_{assign}> ::= <*assignment*> | `{` <*assignment-list*> `}`
<*assignment-list*> ::= <*assignment*> | <*assignment-list*> `,` <*assignment*>
<*assignment*> ::= <*slot-name*> `:=` <*slotval*>
<*slot-name*> ::= <*ident*>

where <*ident*> denotes an identifier. □

Compositional Verification of CCS Processes

Mads Dam[1] and Dilian Gurov[2]

[1] Dept. of Teleinformatics, Royal Institute of Technology (KTH/IT), Electrum 204, SE-164 40 Kista, Sweden, mfd@sics.se

[2] Swedish Institute of Computer Science, Box 1263, SE-164 29 Kista, Sweden, dilian@sics.se

Abstract. We present a proof system for verifying CCS processes in the modal μ-calculus. Its novelty lies in the generality of the proof judgements allowing parametric and compositional reasoning in this complex setting. This is achieved, in part, by the use of explicit fixed point ordinal approximations, and in part by a complete separation, following an approach by Simpson, of rules concerning the logic from the rules encoding the operational semantics of the process language.

1 Introduction

In a number of recent papers [1,2,3,4,9] proof-theoretical frameworks for compositional verification have been put forward based on Gentzen-style sequents of the shape $\Gamma \vdash \Delta$, where the components of Γ and Δ are correctness assertions $P : \phi$. Several programming or modelling languages have been considered, including CCS [3], the π-calculus [2], CHOCS [1], general GSOS-definable languages [9], and even a significant core fragment of a real programming language, Erlang [4]. An important precursor to the above papers is [10] which used ternary sequents to build compositional proof systems for CCS and SCCS vs. Hennessy-Milner logic [6].

A key idea is that the use of a general sequent format allows correctness properties $P : \phi$ to be stated and proved in a *parametric* fashion. That is, correctness statements ϕ of a composite program $P(Q_1, Q_2)$, say, can be relativized to correctness statements of the components, Q_1, Q_2. A general rule of subterm cut

$$\frac{\Gamma \vdash Q : \psi, \Delta \quad \Gamma, x : \psi \vdash P : \phi, \Delta}{\Gamma \vdash P[Q/x] : \phi, \Delta} \tag{1}$$

allows such subterm assumptions to be introduced and used for compositional verification.

It is, however, difficult to support temporal properties within such a framework. As is well known [12], logics like LTL, CTL, or CTL* are poorly equipped for compositional reasoning without resort to devices like history or prophecy variables. For this reason, our investigations have tended to focus on logics based, in some form, on the modal μ-calculus in which the recursive properties needed

D. Bjørner, M. Broy, A. Zamulin (Eds.): PSI'99, LNCS 1755, pp. 247–256, 2000.

for property decomposition can more adequately be expressed. In [3] the first author showed one way of realizing a proof system using the subterm cut rule, and built, for the first time, a compositional proof system capable of handling general CCS terms, including those that create new processes dynamically. In [4] we used a similar, though considerably improved, approach to address Erlang.

The approach of [3] suffered from two main shortcomings, however:

1. Though systematic, the embedding of the CCS operational semantics into the proof system was indirect, and allowed only rather weak completeness results to be obtained.
2. The handling of recursive formulas was very syntactic and hedged by complicated side conditions, hiding the essence of our proof-theoretical approach from view.

In this paper both these issues are addressed. First, following an idea by Simpson [9] we fully separate the embedding of the transitional semantics for P from the general handling of the logic by employing process variables and transition assertions of the shape $P \xrightarrow{\alpha} Q$. These assertions provide a semantically explicit bridge between the transitions of P and the one-step modalities of the logic. A similar approach is used to handle the second complication. The essential difficulty is that, to be sound, rates of progress for fixed point formulas appearing in different places in a sequent must be related. To achieve this in a simple and semantically explicit way we employ fixed point approximations using ordinal variables, and ordinal constraints of the shape $\kappa_1 < \kappa_2$.

In the paper we first introduce the modal μ-calculus with explicit ordinal approximations, and we introduce the basic form of judgment used in the proof system. In the absence of process structure such as CCS, models are just standard Kripke models. Correspondingly, the proof system in this case can be seen to provide an account of Gentzen-style logical entailment. The novelty, in this case, lies in the use of ordinal approximations. This fragment of the proof system is introduced in Sect. 3. The key ingredient to release the power of this proof system is a rule of discharge, or termination, which recognizes proofs by well-founded induction. In another paper [5] we introduce a game which embodies such a rule, and show completeness of the resulting proof system by reduction to Kozen's well-known axiomatization [7]. A practical rule of discharge, however, must be local which the game condition of [5] is not. Here, instead, we introduce a local version of the discharge rule which is, we believe, a simple and intuitive approximation of the complete global condition. This local discharge rule is introduced (summarily, in this abstract) in Section 4. A full instantiation of our approach to CCS requires in addition an embedding of the CCS operational semantics into the present Gentzen-style format (following Simpson [9]) plus the subterm cut rule (1). This extension is shown in Section 5, and then in Section 6 we give a rough sketch of a correctness proof of a simple infinite state CCS process.

2 Logic

Formulas ϕ are generated by the following grammar, where κ ranges over a set of *ordinal variables*, α over a set of *actions*, and X over a set of *propositional variables.*

$$\phi ::= \phi \vee \phi \mid \neg\phi \mid \langle\alpha\rangle\phi \mid X \mid \mu X.\phi \mid (\mu X.\phi)^{\kappa}$$

An occurrence of a subformula ψ in ϕ is *positive*, if ψ appears in the scope of an even number of negation symbols. Otherwise the occurrence is negative. The formation of least fixed point formulas of one of the shapes $\mu X.\phi$ or $(\mu X.\phi)^{\kappa}$ is subject to the usual formal monotonicity condition that occurrences of X in ϕ are positive. We use the symbols U and V to range over (unindexed) fixed point formulas $\mu X.\phi$. A formula ϕ is *propositionally closed* if ϕ does not have free ocurrences of propositional variables. Standard abbreviations apply:

$$\begin{aligned}
\mathit{false} &= \mu X.X,\\
\mathit{true} &= \neg\mathit{false},\\
\phi \wedge \psi &= \neg(\neg\phi \vee \neg\psi),\\
[\alpha]\phi &= \neg\langle\alpha\rangle\neg\phi,\\
\nu X.\phi &= \neg\mu X.\neg(\phi[\neg X/X])
\end{aligned}$$

We assume the standard modal μ-calculus semantics [7]:

$$\begin{aligned}
\|\phi \vee \psi\|\rho &= \|\phi\|\rho \cup \|\psi\|\rho\\
\|\neg\phi\|\rho &= \mathcal{S}\backslash\|\phi\|\rho\\
\|\langle\alpha\rangle\phi\|\rho &= \{P \mid \exists Q \in \|\phi\|\rho. P \xrightarrow{\alpha} Q\}\\
\|X\|\rho &= \rho(X)\\
\|\mu X.\phi\|\rho &= \bigcap\{S \mid S \subseteq \|\phi\|\rho[S/X]\}
\end{aligned}$$

augmented by the clause:

$$\|(\mu X.\phi)^{\kappa}\|\rho = \begin{cases} \emptyset & \text{if } \rho(\kappa) = 0\\ \|\phi\|\rho[\|(\mu X.\phi)^{\kappa}\|\rho/X, \beta/\kappa] & \text{if } \rho(\kappa) = \beta + 1\\ \bigcup\{\|(\mu X.\phi)^{\kappa}\|\rho[\beta/\kappa] \mid \beta < \rho(\kappa)\} & \text{if } \rho(\kappa) \text{ is a limit ordinal}\end{cases}$$

where ρ is an interpretation function (environment), mapping ordinal variables to ordinals, and propositional variables to sets of closed process terms, or *states*, from a domain $\mathcal{S}$ ranged over by P.

The use of ordinal approximation hinges on the following results (of which (1) is the well-known Knaster-Tarski fixed point theorem).

Theorem 1.

1. $\|\mu X.\phi\|\rho = \bigcup_{\beta} \|(\mu X.\phi)^{\kappa}\|\rho[\beta/\kappa]$
2. $\|(\mu X.\phi)^{\kappa}\|\rho = \bigcup_{\beta<\rho(\kappa)} \|\phi\|\rho[\|(\mu X.\phi)^{\kappa}\|\rho/X, \beta/\kappa]$

Observe how this casts the properties U and U^κ as existential properties: This is useful to motivate the proof rules for fixed point formulas given below. Observe also that, for countable models, quantification over countable ordinals in Theorem 1 suffices. In the definition below, we extend interpretation functions ρ to map process variables x to closed process terms (states).

Definition 1 (Assertions, Judgements).

1. *An* assertion *is an expression of one of the forms* $E : \phi$, $\kappa < \kappa'$, *or* $E \xrightarrow{\alpha} F$, *where* E, F *are a process terms and* ϕ *is a propositionally closed formula.*
2. *The assertion* $E : \phi$ *is* valid for an interpretation function ρ *(written* $E \models_\rho \phi$*), if* $E\rho \in \|\phi\|\rho$. *The assertion* $\kappa < \kappa'$ *is valid for* ρ, *if* $\rho(\kappa) < \rho(\kappa')$. *The assertion* $E \xrightarrow{\alpha} F$ *is valid for* ρ, *if* $E\rho \xrightarrow{\alpha} F\rho$ *is a valid transition.*
3. *A* sequent *is an expression of the form* $\Gamma \vdash \Delta$, *where* Γ *and* Δ *are sets of assertions.*
4. *The sequent* $\Gamma \vdash \Delta$ *is* valid *(written* $\Gamma \models \Delta$*), if for all interpretation functions* ρ, *all assertions in* Γ *are valid for* ρ *only if some assertion in* Δ *is valid for* ρ *as well.*

An assertion of the shape $E : \phi$ is called a *property assertion*, an assertion of the shape $\kappa < \kappa'$ is called an *ordinal constraint*, and an assertion of the shape $E \xrightarrow{\alpha} F$ is called a *transition assertion.*

3 Proof System: Logical Entailment

We first consider the problem of logical entailment. In this case, process terms E in assertions of the shape $E : \phi$ are variables.

Structural Rules. We assume the axiom rule, the rule of cut, and weakening:

$$\text{Ax}\ \frac{\cdot}{\Gamma, A \vdash A, \Delta}$$

$$\text{Cut}\ \frac{\Gamma \vdash A, \Delta \quad \Gamma, A \vdash \Delta}{\Gamma \vdash \Delta}$$

$$\text{W-L}\ \frac{\Gamma \vdash \Delta}{\Gamma, A \vdash \Delta} \qquad \text{W-R}\ \frac{\Gamma \vdash \Delta}{\Gamma \vdash A, \Delta}$$

As in [9], in the axiom rule assertion A needs only be instantiated to transition assertions, and then Δ can be assumed to be empty. Since Γ and Δ are sets, structural rules like permutation and contraction are vacuous. We conjecture that both cut and the weakening rules are admissible.

Logical Rules. In the following listing we assume that $U = \mu X.\phi$.

$$\neg\text{-L}\,\frac{\Gamma \vdash E : \phi, \Delta}{\Gamma, E : \neg\phi \vdash \Delta} \qquad \neg\text{-R}\,\frac{\Gamma, E : \phi \vdash \Delta}{\Gamma \vdash E : \neg\phi, \Delta}$$

$$\vee\text{-L}\,\frac{\Gamma, E : \phi \vdash \Delta \quad \Gamma, E : \psi \vdash \Delta}{\Gamma, E : \phi \vee \psi \vdash \Delta} \qquad \vee\text{-R}\,\frac{\Gamma \vdash E : \phi, E : \psi, \Delta}{\Gamma \vdash E : \phi \vee \psi, \Delta}$$

$$\langle\alpha\rangle\text{-L}\,\frac{\Gamma, E \xrightarrow{\alpha} x, x : \phi \vdash \Delta}{\Gamma, E : \langle\alpha\rangle\phi \vdash \Delta}\,\mathit{fresh}(x)$$

$$\langle\alpha\rangle\text{-R}\,\frac{\Gamma \vdash E \xrightarrow{\alpha} E', \Delta \quad \Gamma \vdash E' : \phi, \Delta}{\Gamma \vdash E : \langle\alpha\rangle\phi, \Delta}$$

$$U\text{-L}\,\frac{\Gamma, E : U^{\kappa} \vdash \Delta}{\Gamma, E : U \vdash \Delta}\,\mathit{fresh}(\kappa) \qquad U\text{-R}\,\frac{\Gamma \vdash E : \phi[U/X], \Delta}{\Gamma \vdash E : U, \Delta}$$

$$U^{\kappa}\text{-L}\,\frac{\Gamma, \kappa' < \kappa, E : \phi[U^{\kappa'}/X] \vdash \Delta}{\Gamma, E : U^{\kappa} \vdash \Delta}\,\mathit{fresh}(\kappa')$$

$$U^{\kappa}\text{-R}\,\frac{\Gamma \vdash \kappa' < \kappa, \Delta \quad \Gamma \vdash E : \phi[U^{\kappa'}/X], \Delta}{\Gamma \vdash E : U^{\kappa}, \Delta}$$

The side condition $\mathit{fresh}(x)$ ($\mathit{fresh}(\kappa)$) is intended to mean that x (κ) does not appear freely in the conclusion of the rule.

The rules for unindexed and indexed fixed point formulas are directly motivated by Theorem 1. The lack of symmetry between rules U-L and U-R is not accidental; their symmetric counterparts are in fact admissable.

Ordinal Constraints. Finally, we need to provide rules for reasoning about ordinal constraints.

$$\mathit{OrdTr}\,\frac{\Gamma, \kappa' < \kappa \vdash \kappa'' < \kappa', \Delta}{\Gamma, \kappa' < \kappa \vdash \kappa'' < \kappa, \Delta}$$

This rule is sufficient provided ordinal variables and constraints are only being introduced during the proof, i.e., do not appear in the root sequent.

Theorem 2 (Local Soundness). *All rules for logical entailment are individually sound: Each rule's conclusion is valid whenever its premises are valid.*

4 Proof System: Rule of Discharge

Processes and formulas can be recursive, allowing for proof trees to grow unboundedly. Intuitively, one would like to terminate an open branch whenever a "repeating" sequent is reached, i.e. a sequent which is an instance, up to some substitution σ, of one of its ancestors, its "companion", in the proof tree. A proof structure, all leaf nodes of which are either axioms or such repeating nodes, serves as the basis for well-founded ordinal induction arguments. A *global discharge condition* is a sufficient condition for such an argument to be valid. In case a global discharge condition applies all leaves which are not axioms can be considered induction hypothesis instances in some, possibly deeply nested, proof by well-founded induction.

The use of ordinal variables and constraints allows global discharge conditions to be phrased in a clear and semantically transparent way. The most general view of discharge is presented in game-based terms elsewhere [5]. In essence, global discharge guarantees well-foundedness of proofs: That along every infinite path in the infinitely unfolded proof tree, ordinal constraints grow downwards in an unbounded manner.

Here we present a discharge condition which is, in contrast to the global condition of [5], more local, and easier to understand and apply. Moreover, even though it is in general incomplete, it is, in our experience, adequate in a great many situations. In particular it is powerful enough to handle the example considered below.

First a single piece of terminology: Two repeat nodes are called *related* if they are in the same strongly connected component in the directed graph obtained from the proof structure by identifying the repeat nodes with their companions.

Definition 2 (Rule of Discharge). *A node labelled $\Gamma \vdash \Delta$ can be* discharged *with U^κ and substitution σ against an ancestor node labelled $\Gamma' \vdash \Delta'$ if:*

(i) *U^κ occurs as subformula in Γ' or Δ';*
(ii) *$\phi\sigma \in \Gamma$ whenever $\phi \in \Gamma'$, and $\phi\sigma \in \Delta$ whenever $\phi \in \Delta'$;*
(iii) *$\Gamma \vdash \kappa\sigma < \kappa$ is derivable;*
(iv) *assuming the related discharge nodes labelled $\Gamma_1 \vdash \Delta_1 \ldots \Gamma_n \vdash \Delta_n$ have been discharged with $U_1^{\kappa_1} \ldots U_n^{\kappa_n}$ and $\sigma_1 \ldots \sigma_n$ against $\Gamma_1' \vdash \Delta_1' \ldots \Gamma_n' \vdash \Delta_n'$, there is a linear ordering $\prec$ on these discharge nodes including the present node, such that whenever $i \prec j$: (a) $U_i^{\kappa_i}$ occurs as subformula in Γ_j' or Δ_j', and (b) either $\kappa_i\sigma_j = \kappa_i$, or $\Gamma_j \vdash \kappa_i\sigma_j < \kappa_i$ is derivable.*

In clause (*iv*), the linear ordering can be chosen differently each time the rule is applied (and a new node is added to the corresponding class of related discharge nodes). The purpose of the clause is to guarantee that along every infinite path in the infinitely unfolded proof tree, ordinal constraints grow downwards in an unbounded manner.

Theorem 3 (Soundness). *The proof system including the rules for logical entailment and the rule of discharge is sound: All sequents derivable in the proof system are valid.*

For finite state labelled transition systems the above proof system reduces to an ordinary model checker like the one presented in [11], and is hence complete for such systems. In general, however, due to undecidability of the model checking problem addressed here, the system is necessarily incomplete.

5 Proof System: Operational Semantics

Having transition assertions allows the transitional semantics of a process language to be embedded directly into the proof system as a separate set of proof rules. This can be done in a straightforward manner for any GSOS-definable language [9]. Here we illustrate this approach on a well-known process language, Milner's Calculus of Communicating Systems [8].

We assume that CCS process terms E are generated by the following grammar, where l ranges over a given set of *labels*, L over subsets of this set of labels, α over *actions* of the shape τ, l or $\overline{l}$, and x over a set of *process variables*.

$$E ::= 0 \;\Big|\; \alpha.E \;\Big|\; E + E \;\Big|\; E|E \;\Big|\; E\backslash L \;\Big|\; x \;\Big|\; \mathit{fix}\, x.E$$

The set of states $\mathcal{S}$ used in Section 2 is the set of all closed process terms. The operational semantics of CCS is given as a closure relation on processes through a set of transition rules [8]: the transitions that a CCS process can perform are exactly those derivable by these rules. Hence, the transition rules can be included directly as right introduction rules into our proof system, while the left introduction rules (stating what transitions are *not* possible), come from the closure assumption.

We present only the most significant of the resulting rules, and in particular the ones used in the Example to follow.

$$\text{0-L}\ \frac{\cdot}{\Gamma, 0 \xrightarrow{\alpha} x \vdash \Delta} \qquad \alpha\text{-R}\ \frac{\cdot}{\Gamma \vdash \alpha.E \xrightarrow{\alpha} E, \Delta}$$

$$\alpha\text{-L-1}\ \frac{\Gamma[E/x] \vdash \Delta[E/x]}{\Gamma, \alpha.E \xrightarrow{\alpha} x \vdash \Delta} \qquad \alpha\text{-L-2}\ \frac{\cdot}{\Gamma, \alpha.E \xrightarrow{\beta} x \vdash \Delta}\ \alpha \neq \beta$$

$$+\text{-L}\ \frac{\Gamma[y/x], E \xrightarrow{\alpha} y \vdash \Delta[y/x] \quad \Gamma[z/x], F \xrightarrow{\alpha} z \vdash \Delta[z/x]}{\Gamma, E + F \xrightarrow{\alpha} x \vdash \Delta}$$

$$+\text{-R}\ \frac{\Gamma \vdash E \xrightarrow{\alpha} E', \Delta}{\Gamma \vdash E + F \xrightarrow{\alpha} E', \Delta}$$

$$|\text{-R-1}\ \frac{\Gamma \vdash E \xrightarrow{\alpha} E', \Delta}{\Gamma \vdash E|F \xrightarrow{\alpha} E'|F, \Delta} \qquad |\text{-R-2}\ \frac{\Gamma \vdash E \xrightarrow{l} E' \quad \Gamma \vdash F \xrightarrow{\overline{l}} F', \Delta}{\Gamma \vdash E|F \xrightarrow{\tau} E'|F', \Delta}$$

$$|\text{-L-1}\ \frac{\Gamma[y|F/x], E \xrightarrow{l} y \vdash \Delta[y|F/x] \quad \Gamma[E|z/x], F \xrightarrow{l} z \vdash \Delta[E|z/x]}{\Gamma, E|F \xrightarrow{l} x \vdash \Delta}$$

$$|\text{-L-2}\ \frac{\begin{array}{c}\Gamma[y_1|F/x], E \xrightarrow{\tau} y_1 \vdash \Delta[y_1|F/x] \\ \Gamma[E|y_2/x], F \xrightarrow{\tau} y_2 \vdash \Delta[E|y_2/x] \\ \Gamma[z_1|z_2/x], l_1 = \overline{l_2}, E \xrightarrow{l_1} z_1, F \xrightarrow{l_2} z_2 \vdash \Delta[z_1|z_2/x]\end{array}}{\Gamma, E|F \xrightarrow{\tau} x \vdash \Delta}$$

$$\textit{fix}\text{-L}\ \frac{\Gamma, E[fix\,x.E/x] \xrightarrow{\alpha} y \vdash \Delta}{\Gamma, fix\,x.E \xrightarrow{\alpha} y \vdash \Delta} \qquad \textit{fix}\text{-R}\ \frac{\Gamma \vdash E[fix\,x.E/x] \xrightarrow{\alpha} E', \Delta}{\Gamma \vdash fix\,x.E \xrightarrow{\alpha} E', \Delta}$$

In addition to these rules, a subterm cut rule is needed to allow for parametric and compositional reasoning:

$$\text{SUBTERMCUT-R}\ \frac{\Gamma \vdash F : \psi, \Delta \quad \Gamma, x : \psi \vdash E : \phi, \Delta}{\Gamma \vdash E[F/x] : \phi, \Delta}\ \textit{fresh}(x)$$

6 Example

Consider a process

$$\textit{Counter} = \textit{fix}\,x.\ \textit{up}.\,(x \mid \textit{down}.x)$$

which can alternatingly engage in *up* and *down* actions, generating a new copy of itself after each *up* action. Clearly, in any point in time, regardless how many counters have already been spawned, this system can engage in finite sequences of consecutive *down* actions only. This propery can be formalised as the negation of the following formula:

$$\phi = \mu X.\neg\,\mu Y.\neg\,(\langle up\rangle X \vee \langle down\rangle \neg\, Y)$$

So, we want to prove validity of the sequent

$$\vdash \textit{Counter} : \neg\,\phi$$

We perform the proof backwards, from this goal sequent towards the axioms, guided by the shape of the formulas and process terms involved. After eliminating the negation and approximating ϕ one obtains

$$\textit{Counter} : \phi^{\kappa} \vdash \tag{2}$$

Continuing in the same straightforward manner we soon arrive at the following two sequents:

$$\kappa' < \kappa,\ \textit{up}.\,(\textit{Counter} \mid \textit{down}.\textit{Counter}) \xrightarrow{down} x \vdash x : \psi$$

$$\kappa' < \kappa,\ \textit{Counter} \mid \textit{down}.\textit{Counter} : \phi^{\kappa'} \vdash$$

the first of which is an axiom. The second sequent is similar to sequent (2), with the important difference of a new *down.Counter* component having appeared. This is the point where one would like to perform an inductive argument on the system structure, and this can be done using subterm cut. The most important question is what the property of the component being cut is that yields the overall system property being verified. A convenient case is when it is the same property, i.e., when the property being verified composes nicely. This is the case in our example, partly because there is no communication between the components. So, after two applications of subterm cut we obtain the following three sequents:

$$\kappa' < \kappa, Counter : \phi^{\kappa'} \vdash$$

$$\kappa' < \kappa, down.Counter : \phi^{\kappa'} \vdash x : \phi^{\kappa'}$$

$$\kappa' < \kappa, x \mid y : \phi^{\kappa'} \vdash x : \phi^{\kappa'}, y : \phi^{\kappa'}$$

the first of which can be discharged with ϕ^{κ} and substitution $[\kappa \mapsto \kappa']$ against (2). Notice that this node has no related discharge nodes (so far), so only clauses (i)–(iii) of the Rule of Discharge have to be checked in this case. The second sequent is easily reduced to an axiom and a discharge node. Handling the remaining sequent is only slightly more involved.

7 Conclusion

We presented a proof system for verifying CCS processes in the modal μ-calculus. Its novelty lies in the generality of the proof judgements allowing parametric and compositional reasoning, in the complex setting of this powerful logic. This is achieved, in part, by the use of explicit fixed point ordinal approximations, and in part by a complete separation, following Simpson [9], in the proof system of the rules concerning the logic from the rules encoding the operational semantics of the process language (here CCS). This makes the proof system easily adaptable to other languages with a clean transitional semantics.

References

1. R. Amadio and M. Dam. Reasoning about higher-order processes. In *Proc. CAAP'95,* Lecture Notes in Computer Science, 915:202–217, 1995.
2. R. Amadio and M. Dam. A modal theory of types for the π-calculus. In *Proc. FTRTFT'96,* Lecture Notes in Computer Science, 1135:347–365, 1996.
3. M. Dam. Proving properties of dynamic process networks. *Information and Computation*, 140:95–114, 1998.
4. M. Dam, L.-å. Fredlund, and D. Gurov. Toward parametric verification of open distributed systems. In *Compositionality: the Significant Difference,* H. Langmaack, A. Pnueli and W.-P. de Roever (eds.), Lecture Notes Notes in Computer Science, Springer-Verlag, 1536:150–185, 1998.
5. M. Dam and D. Gurov. μ-calculus with explicit points and approximations. In preparation, 1999.
6. M. Hennessy and R. Milner. Algebraic laws for nondeterminism and concurrency. *Journal of the ACM*, **32**:137–162, 1985.
7. D. Kozen. Results on the propositional μ-calculus. *Theoretical Computer Science*, **27**:333–354, 1983.
8. R. Milner. *Communication and Concurrency.* Prentice Hall International, 1989.
9. A. Simpson. Compositionality via cut-elimination: Hennessy-Milner logic for an arbitrary GSOS. In *Proceedings, Tenth Annual IEEE Symposium on Logic in Computer Science*, pages 420–430, San Diego, California, 26–29 1995. IEEE Computer Society Press.
10. C. Stirling. Modal logics for communicating systems. *Theoretical Computer Science*, 49:311–347, 1987.

11. C. Stirling and D. Walker. Local model checking in the modal mu-calculus. *Theoretical Computer Science*, 89:161–177, 1991.
12. P. Wolper. Temporal logic can be more expressive. *Information and Control*, **56**:72–99, 1983.

Compositional Style of Programming FPGAs

Elena Trichina

Institute for Computer Systems
ETH Zentrum, Zurich, CH-8092, Switzerland
trichina@inf.ethz.ch

Abstract. We review the use of categories with products as a vehicle for the construction of bit-level functions that correspond to combinational circuits. Further we show that results from the category theory concerning list homomorphisms can help in our search for a computational model that captures the desirable properties of digital circuits, namely locality of communications and simple, repetitive structure of computational components. We demonstrate applications of the theory to some simple problems.

1 Introduction

New reconfigurable computing technology redefines the traditional hardware/ software boundary and enables the rapid realization of algorithm-specific hardware architectures at a low-cost base, such as Field Programmable Gate Arrays (FPGA) [3]. We want to develop a rigorous methodology for creating a range of application-specific high-level languages that can be compiled directly into FPGAs. Two crucial issues should be captured by our approach, namely hardware–independent software development and efficient compilation of programs into digital circuits. Moreover, since applications that profit from reconfigurable computing usually have high degree of parallelism and/or concurrency, and involve additional design decisions regarding decomposition, communication, routing, timing, etc., a rigorous methodology is needed for development of such programs. This suggest that a good level of abstraction must be mathematically based, so that reasoning and formal development are possible.

The categorical data type (CDT) approach [8] is an extension of the abstract data type in a way that appears to be particularly useful for parallel computations [10,5]. CDTs have operations, equations relating them, and a guarantee that all of the required operations and equations are present. A theory of CDTs is a theory of algebraic structures that behave like the constructed data type, and homomorphisms among them. The important property of homomorphic operations is that the pattern of computations follows the structure of the argument. Thus, for homomorphic functions, *locality* of communication, *regularity* and *partitionability* of computation are inherent properties [5,6].

Many polymorphic higher-order functions are homomorphisms or almost homomorphisms. Consider functionals like *map*, that applies some function to all

D. Bjørner, M. Broy, A. Zamulin (Eds.): PSI'99, LNCS 1755, pp. 257–264, 2000.

individual elements of a data aggregate independently, producing a data aggregate with new values of individual elements, or *reduce*, that calculates a "cumulative sum" of all elements in a data aggregate. These functionals can be defined over different data types, such as *cons* [2] and *conc* [7] lists, homogeneous binary trees [7], arrays [1], etc. While data types vary from application to application (i.e., arrays are appropriate for image processing, trees for divide and conquer algorithms, streams for signal processing, etc.), the general patterns of computation on these types are the same.

The main idea is that for any given application a set of appropriate basic data types is defined in terms of categories with products, and operations on these types are compiled directly into blocks of FPGA logic cells. Then higher-order functions, or *operations* for application specific data aggregates are defined within the scope of a CDT and implemented as templates for composition of basic primitives. Having been carefully chosen so as to satisfy constraints of the FPGA technology, these operations ensure an efficient implementation of an application on FPGA-based hardware. In other words, an ability to express an application in terms of a composition of the set of predefined higher-order functions on specific data aggregates is a *test-bed* for an efficient implementation of the application.

2 Categories with Products

To describe and analyse combinational circuits (i.e., circuits without latches and feedbacks) we use a category with products. Let $\mathbf{B} = \{0, 1\}$. Consider category **Circ** [8] with objects $\mathbf{B}^0$, $\mathbf{B}^1$, $\mathbf{B}^2$,... and arrows that represent all functions between these sets. Notice that $\mathbf{B^0} = \{*\}$, or **unit** object, $\mathbf{B^1} = \mathbf{B}$, and $\mathbf{B^n} = \{(x_1, x_2, ..., x_n) : x_i \in \mathbf{B}\}$ for $n > 1$. In a category, each morphism has a designated domain and codomain in objects; any object A has an *identity* morphism

$$1_A : A \to A,$$

and for any given morphisms $f : A \to B$, $g : B \to C$, $h : C \to D$, there is a designated composition of morphisms which satisfies identity and associative laws:

$$g \circ f : A \to C; \qquad 1_B \circ f = f = f \circ 1_A, \qquad h \circ (g \circ f) = (h \circ g) \circ f : A \to D.$$

The product of $\mathbf{B^m}$ and $\mathbf{B^n}$ is $\mathbf{B^{m+n}}$ with the following projections:

$$p_1 : \mathbf{B^{m+n}} \to \mathbf{B^m}, \qquad p_2 : \mathbf{B^{m+n}} \to \mathbf{B^n}$$

such that $(x_1, x_2, ..., x_m, ..., x_{m+n}) \mapsto (x_1, x_2, ..., x_m)$, and $(x_1, x_2, ..., x_m, ..., x_{m+n}) \mapsto (x_{m+1}, ..., x_{m+n})$. Two functions from $\mathbf{B^0}$ to $\mathbf{B^1}$ are constants *true* and *false*. Some further interesting functions in this category are: *negation*, $\neg : \mathbf{B} \longrightarrow \mathbf{B}$, logical *and*, $\& : \mathbf{B^2} \longrightarrow \mathbf{B}$, logical *or*, $OR : \mathbf{B^2} \longrightarrow \mathbf{B}$, and *excluded or*, $XOR : \mathbf{B^2} \longrightarrow \mathbf{B}$. Two useful unary fuctions $=_1$ and $=_0$ check the equality of the argument to 1 and 0 respectively. It is easy to see that $(=_1) = (1_B)$ and $(=_0) = (\neg)$.

- In a category with products, we can define a *parallel composition* of two functions. Given $f : X_1 \longrightarrow Y_1$ and $g : X_2 \longrightarrow Y_2$, a parallel composition is a function $f \times g : X_1 \times X_2 \longrightarrow Y_1 \times Y_2$ which maps (x_1, x_2) into a pair $(f(x_1), g(x_2))$. This function obeys the laws of projection:

$$p_{Y_1} \circ (f \times g) = f \circ p_{X_1}, \qquad p_{Y_2} \circ (f \times g) = f \circ p_{X_2}.$$

- A *diagonal* function Δ which produces two copies of its input can also be defined in a category with products: $\Delta_X : X \longrightarrow X \times X$, suct that $x \mapsto (x, x)$.

$$p_1 \circ \Delta_X = 1_X, \qquad p_2 \circ \Delta_X = 1_X.$$

- Function *twist* : $X \times Y \longrightarrow Y \times X$ interchanges its two inputs : $(x, y) \mapsto (y, x)$. If p_1, p_2 and q_1, q_2 are projections of $X \times Y$ and $Y \times X$ respectedly, then

$$q_1 \circ twist = p_2, \qquad q_2 \circ twist = p_1.$$

It is known [8] that in category **Circ** one can construct any logical function starting with *true, false, not, and, or*, identity maps, and projections using only compositions and the property of products. Moreover, any such function can be implemented using a circuit without latches, consisting of wires and gates. Indeed, the set **B** is the set of possible states of each wire. The functions &, *OR* and *XOR* are implemented directly as gates, as shown in Fig.1. Identity map(s) 1_{B^n}, $n \geq 1$ and $=_1$ correspond to a (group of adjacent) wire(s); $\neg$ and $=_0$ to an inverter.

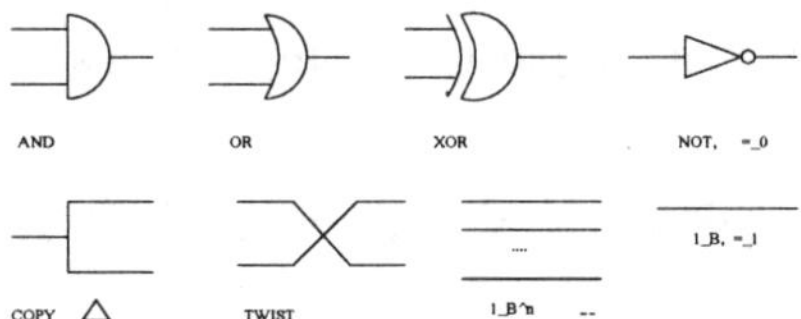

Fig. 1. Implementation of functions in category **Circ**

We can do a number of things with wires and components that correspond to constructions of new functions in category **Circ**:

- Splitting wires corresponds to the diagonal function, $\Delta_B : \mathbf{B} \longrightarrow \mathbf{B^2}$.
- We can twist two wires. This corresponds to function *twist* : $\mathbf{B^2} \longrightarrow \mathbf{B^2}$.
- We can put two components side by side. This corresponds to parallel composition $f \times g : \mathbf{B^n} \times \mathbf{B^m} \longrightarrow \mathbf{B^k} \times \mathbf{B^l}$.
- We can put two components in a series, connecting output wires of one component with the input wires of another. This corresponds to composition $g \circ f : \mathbf{B^n} \longrightarrow \mathbf{B^m}$.

Example. Consider a 1-to-2 decoder function which is defined in category **Circ** as follows. $d : \mathbf{B^2} \longrightarrow \mathbf{B^2}$, where $(x, s) \mapsto (y_1, y_0)$ such that $y_1 = x\&(=_1 s)$, and $y_0 = x\&(=_0 s)$. A decomposition of function d is straightforward: first, copy both inputs x and s, pair them by twisting "middle" elements, apply functions $=_1$ and $=_0$ to each copy of s, and finally compute & of each resulting pair:

$$1-to-2: \qquad \mathbf{B}\times\mathbf{B} \stackrel{\Delta_B\times\Delta_B}{\longrightarrow} \mathbf{B^4} \stackrel{1_B\times twist\times 1_B}{\longrightarrow} \mathbf{B^4} \stackrel{1_B\times 1_B\times 1_B\times\neg}{\longrightarrow} \mathbf{B^4} \stackrel{\&\times\&}{\longrightarrow} \mathbf{B^2}.$$

A circuit which implements a decoder function is drawn in Fig. 2. Notice how the circuit corresponds exactly to the decomposition given above. Suppose now we

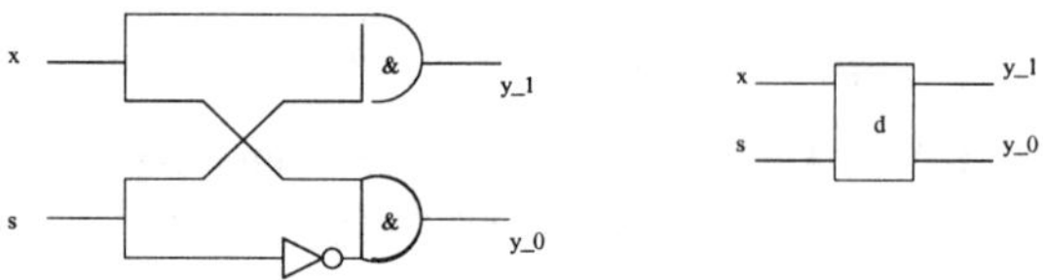

Fig. 2. A 1-to-2 decoder

want to design a 2-to-4 decoder $\mathbf{B^3} \longrightarrow \mathbf{B^4}$, where $(x, s_1, s_0) \mapsto (y_3, y_2, y_1, y_0)$, such that $y_0 = x\&(=_0 s_1)\&(=_0 s_0)$, $y_1 = x\&(=_0 s_1)\&(=_1 s_0)$, $y_2 = x\&(=_1 s_1)\&(=_0 s_0)$, and $y_3 = x\&(=_1 s_1)\&(=_1 s_0)$. A decomposition can use previously defined function d. Indeed, first compute $x\&(=_1 s_1)$ and $x\&(=_0 s_1)$ using a 1-to-2 decoder. Then pair each of the outputs with a copy of signal s_0 using *twist* operation, and give the resulting pairs as inputs to two identical 1-to-2 decoders, each computing the second half of the formulae. Thus a 2-to-4 decoder function is decomposed into a sequence of parallel compositions (a so-called *cascading principle*) as follows:

$$2-to-4: \qquad \mathbf{B^2}\times\mathbf{B} \stackrel{d\times\Delta_B}{\longrightarrow} \mathbf{B^4} \stackrel{1_B\times twist\times 1_B}{\longrightarrow} \mathbf{B^4} \stackrel{d\times d}{\longrightarrow} \mathbf{B^4}.$$

A corresponding circuit is depicted in Fig. 3. However, it is much more tedious to describe and decompose into basic components, say a 4-to-16 decoder, and it

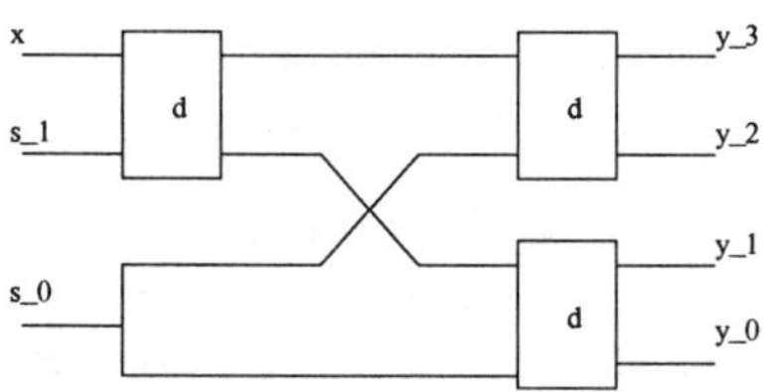

Fig. 3. A 2-to-4 decoder

is impossible to describe a general $n-to-2^n$ $(n \geq 1)$ decoder. In order to be able to manipulate with tuples of bits of any length, *concatenation lists* can be used.

3 Concatenation Lists

Suppose $\alpha, \beta, ...$ are primitive data types with identity functions $id_\alpha : \alpha \to \alpha$, $id_\beta : \beta \to \beta, ...$ defined for every type. If α is a type, we can form the type $\alpha*$; its elements are lists of elements of type α. Using the standard CDT technique, operations on $\alpha, \beta, ...$ can be lifted to operations on $\alpha*$, $\beta*, ...$ [7].

Conc, or join lists [5,7] have three constructors, one that makes an empty list, $[] : \mathbf{unit} \to \alpha*$, another creates a singleton list, $[.] : \alpha \to \alpha*$, and the third concatenates two lists to make a longer one, $+\!\!+ : \alpha * \times \alpha* \to \alpha*$. A table below summarises some of the list operations.

	Combinator Functions
distribute-left	$distl \quad [x_1, ..., x_n] \quad y = [(y, x_1), ..., (y, x_n)]$
shift-left	$\tau \quad e \quad [x_1, ..., x_n] = [e, x_1, ..., x_{n-1}]$
zip	$zip \quad [x_1, ..., x_n][y_1, ..., y_n] = [(x_1, y_1), ..., (x_n, y_n)]$
	Functionals
map	$f* \quad [a_1, a_2, ..., a_n] = [f \quad a_1, f \quad a_2, ..., f \quad a_n]$
reduce	$/\oplus \quad [a_1, a_2, ..., a_n] = a_1 \oplus a_2 \oplus ... \oplus a_n$
directed-reduce	$(/ \to \oplus \quad e) \quad [a_1, a_2, ..., a_n] = (...((e \oplus a_1) \oplus a_2)... \oplus a_n)$

Operations on *conc* lists are known to be homomorphisms [7]. Many of these operations incorporate inherent parallelism and have fixed communication patterns [5,6]. *Map* $f*$ is completely parallel and requires no communication. It can be implemented as a parallel composition of n combinational circuits, each circuit representing function f applied to an individual list element. *Reduce* can be evaluated in an obvious tree-like fashion. *Directed reduce* can be implemented as a *pipeline*, or a sequential composition of combinational circuits, each implementing $\oplus$ on a corresponding list element and the output of a previous circuit. A set of implemetation templates for list operations is given in Fig. 4. An important part of categorical definitions of list operations is that they come with the set of algebraic laws which are used in transformational program derivation [2,4].

3.1 $n - to - 2^n$ Decoder

A general $n - to - 2^n$ decoder function is described as follows. Given an input signal x and a number $s = s_0 * 2^0 + s_1 * 2^1 + ... + s_{n-1} * 2^{n-1}$ represented as a bit list $[s_{n-1}, s_{n-2}, ..., s_0]$, the decoder must produce 2^n outputs $[y_{2^n-1}, \cdots, y_0]$, such that $y_i = x\&(i = s)$, $0 \le n \le 2^n - 1$.

An $n - to - 2^n$ decoder function can be represented as a *directed reduce.* First, bits x and s_{n-1} are used by a $1 - to - 2$ decoder to produce a pair of outputs, $x\&(=_1 s_{n-1})$ and $x\&(=_0 s_{n-1})$. These outputs represent partial results that are to be used in a next cascade, as in a $2 - to - 4$ example, with the element s_{n-2} of the input list distributed among these partial results. This produces 4 new bits which, in their turn, have to be paired with the consecutive element s_{n-3} of the

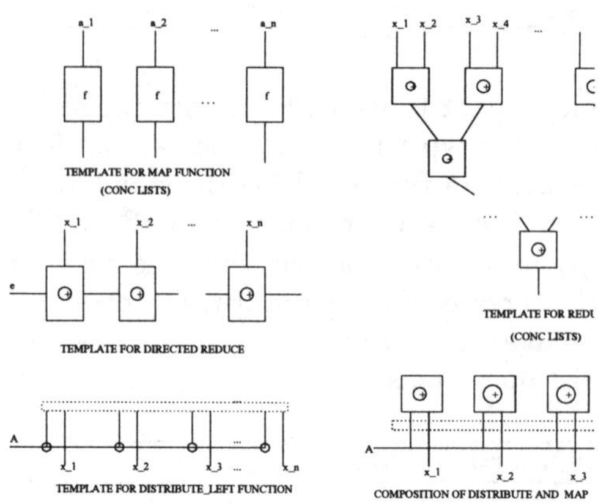

Fig. 4. Implementation templates for list operations

input list, etc. We want to express this method in terms of list operations, hence we will be using lists to represent both, input signal s and intermediate results:

$$n - to - 2^n : \qquad \mathbf{B}* \times \mathbf{B}* \longrightarrow \mathbf{B}*$$

$$n\text{–}to\text{–}2^n([x],[s_{n-1},...,s_0]) = (/ \rightarrow (/ \mathbin{+\!\!+} \circ (MakeList \circ d) * \circ distl)[x])[s_{n-1},...,s_0].$$

Function $MakeList$ makes a list of two elements from a pair: $MakeList(x,y) = [x,y]$ or, more concisely, $MakeList = \mathbin{+\!\!+} \circ ([.] \circ p_1 \times [.] \circ p_2)$, where p_1 and p_2 are projection functions. Function d is a 1-to-2 decoder defined in a previous section. A combinational circuit for an $n - to - 2n$ decoder can be obtained by taking a general template for a directed reduce (see Fig. 4) and substituting every $\oplus$ "box" for operation $(/ \mathbin{+\!\!+} \circ (MakeList \circ d) * \circ distl)$. In the latter composition, $/ \mathbin{+\!\!+}$ and $MakeList$ are "service" operations that only change representation of data; their implementation does not require separate cicuits. Hence, every $\oplus$ box in the directed reduce template is, in its turn, a composition of templates for *distl* and $d*$ (*map*). A straightforward substitution of $\oplus$ boxes for a composition ofcorresponding templates for operations *distl* and $d*$ results in a circuit depicted in Fig. 5.

4 Discussion

A set of basic algebras for bits, characters, short and long integers, etc., can easily be fully specified in terms of categories with products. These primitive data types reflect characteristics of the basic components from which to build a particular application. These basic components are realized in a straightforward compositional way by combinational circuits and implemented by blocks of FPGA logic cells.

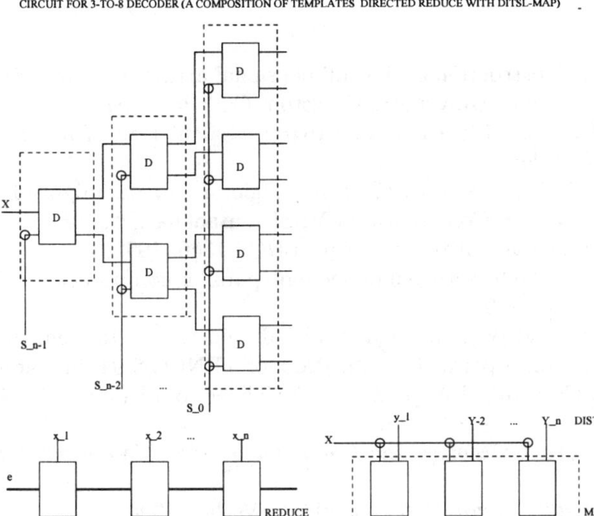

Fig. 5. $n - to - 2^n$ decoder is a composition of templates

Concatenation lists are natural data aggregates for many applications. Lists can be fully defined by a fixed set of (homomorphic) operations, and for each operation from this set we can design one or more *implementation templates* that have desirable properties, such as regular, repetitive structures and local interconnections between components.

However, as soon as we need delays, combinational circuits alone are not enough. To implement a delay, we need a *latch*, i.e., a circuit with a *feedback* loop. To reason about such circuits we have to consider at any moment the state of the whole circuit. Assuming the synchronous model, we need functions which describe the general change of state. Unfortunately, we cannot do it in a category with products only. However, if we follow the advice given by N. Wirth [9], restricting circuit design to combinational circuits, and having latches and registers as complete parts, so that feedback loops exist only within these parts, we can still retain much of the simplicity and expressive power of homomorphisms.

In future, we want to extend our approach to design and analysis of any synchronous, sequential circuit, i.e., circuits that consist of combinational circuits and registers, the latter represent a state. We hope to develop a compositional approach, similar to the one described in this paper, within the scope of the distributive category, so that any state machine can be designed and analysed in a concise stepwise manner.

References

1. C.R. Banger, Construction of multidimensional arrays as Categorical Data Types. PhD Thesis, Queen's University, Kingston, Canada, 1994.
2. R.S. Bird, Algebraic Identities for Program Calculation, *The Computer Journal*, 32(2):122-126, 1989.
3. J.P. Gray, and T.A. Kean, Configurable logic: a new paradigm for computations. In Decennial Caltech Conference on VLSI, Pasadena CA, 1989.
4. B. Möller, Deductive hardware design. LNCS 1546, 1999.
5. D.B. Skillicorn, Architecture-independent parallel computation. *Computer Journal*, 23(12): 38-51, 1990.
6. D.B. Skillicorn, and W. Cai, Equational code generation: Implementing Categorical Data Types for data parallelism. In Proc. of TENCON'94, Singapore, 1994.
7. M. Spivey, A Categorical Approach to the Theory of Lists. LNCS 375, pp. 399-408, 1988.
8. R. F. C. Walters. *Categories and Computer Science.* Cambridge University Press, 1991.
9. N. Wirth. *Digital Circuit Design.* Springer-Verlag, 1995.
10. G. Winskel, Category theory and models of parallel computation, In Proc. Summer Workshop on Category and Computer Programming LNCS 240, pp. 266-281, 1986.

Using Experiments to Build a Body of Knowledge

Victor Basili[1], Forrest Shull[2], and Filippo Lanubile[3]

[1] Fraunhofer Center Maryland and Computer Science Dept.
University of Maryland
College Park, MD 20742, USA
basili@cs.umd.edu

[2] Institute for Advanced Computer Studies Computer Science Dept.
University of Maryland
College Park, MD 20742, USA
fshull@cs.umd.edu

[3] Dipartimento di Informatica Universita' di Bari
Via Orabona, 4
70126 Bari, Italia
lanubile@di.uniba.it

Abstract. Experimentation in software engineering is important but difficult. One reason it is so difficult is that there are a large number of context variables, and so creating a cohesive understanding of experimental results requires a mechanism for motivating studies and integrating results. This paper argues for the necessity of a framework for organizing sets of related studies. With such a framework, experiments can be viewed as part of common families of studies, rather than being isolated events. Common families of studies can contribute to important and relevant hypotheses that may not be suggested by individual experiments. A framework also facilitates building knowledge in an incremental manner through the replication of experiments within families of studies. Building knowledge in this way requires a community of researchers that can replicate studies, vary context variables, and build abstract models that represent the common observations about the discipline. This paper also presents guidelines for lab packages, meant to encourage and support replications, that encapsulate materials, methods, and experiences concerning software engineering experiments.

1 Introduction

Experimentation in software engineering is necessary. Common wisdom, intuition, speculation and proofs of concepts are not reliable sources of credible knowledge. On the contrary, progress in any discipline involves building models that can be tested,through empirical study, to check whether the current under-

D. Bjørner, M. Broy, A. Zamulin (Eds.): PSI'99, LNCS 1755, pp. 265–282, 2000.

standing of the field is correct[1]. Progress comes when what is actually true can be separated from what is only believed to be true. To accomplish this, the scientific method supports the building of knowledge through an iterative process of model building, prediction, observation, and analysis. It requires that no confidence be placed in a theory that has not stood up to rigorous deductive testing [21]. That is, any scientific theory must be (1) falsifiable, (2) logically consistent, (3) at least as predictive as other competing theories, and (4) its predictions have been confirmed by observations during tests for falsification. According to Popper, a theory can only be shown to be false or not yet false; researchers only become confident in a theory when it has survived numerous attempts made at its falsification. This paradigm is a necessary step for ensuring that opinion or desire does not influence knowledge.

Experimentation in software engineering is difficult. Carrying out empirical work is complex and time consuming; this is especially true for software engineering. Unlike manufacturing, we do not build the same product, over and over, to meet a particular set of specifications. Software is developed and each product is different from the last. So, software artifacts do not provide us with a large set of data points permitting sufficient statistical power for confirming or rejecting a hypothesis. Unlike physics, most of the technologies and theories in software engineering are human-based, and so variation in human ability tends to obscure experimental effects. Human factors tend to increase the costs of experimentation while making it more difficult to achieve statistical significance.

Abstracting conclusions from empirical studies in software engineering research is difficult. An important reason why experimentation in software engineering is so hard is that the results of almost any process depend to a large degree on a potentially large number of relevant context variables. Because of this, we cannot *a priori* assume that the results of any study apply outside the specific environment in which it was run. For isolated studies, even if they

[1] For the purpose of this paper, we use the definitions of some key terms from [15] and [1]. An *empirical study*, in a broad sense, is an act or operation for the purpose of discovering something unknown or of testing a hypothesis, involving an investigator gathering data and performing analysis to determine what the data mean. This covers various forms of research strategies, including all forms of experiments, qualitative studies, surveys, and archival analyses. An *experiment* is a form of empirical study where the researcher has control over some of the conditions in which the study takes place and control over the independent variables being studied; an operation carried out under controlled conditions in order to test a hypothesis against observation. This term thus includes quasi-experiments and pre-experimental designs.

A *theory* is a possible explanation of some phenomenon. Any theory is made up of a set of hypotheses. A *hypothesis* is an educated guess that there exists (1) a (causal) relation among constructs of theoretical interest; (2) a relation between a construct and observable indicators (how the construct can be observed). A *model* is a simplified representation of a system or phenomenon; it may or may not be mathematical or even formal; it can be a theory.

are themselves well-run, it is difficult to understand how widely applicable the results are, and thus to assess the true contribution to the field.

As an example, consider the following study:

- **Basili/Reiter.** This study was undertaken in 1976 in order to characterize and evaluate the development processes of development teams using a disciplined methodology. The effects of the team methodology were contrasted with control groups made up of development teams using an "ad hoc" development strategy, and with individual developers (also "ad hoc"). Hypotheses were proposed: that (BR1) a disciplined approach should reduce the average cost and complexity (faults and rework) of the process and (BR2) the disciplined team should behave more like an individual than a team in terms of the resulting product. The study addressed these hypotheses by evaluating particular methods (such as chief programmer teams, top down design, and reviews) as they were applied in a classroom setting. [7]

This study, like any other, required the experimenters to construct models of the processes studied, models of effectiveness, and models of the context in which the study was run. Replications that alter key attributes of these models are then necessary to build up knowledge about whether the results hold under other conditions. Unfortunately, in software engineering, too many studies tend to be isolated and are not replicated, either by the same researchers or by others. Basili/Reiter was a rigorous study, but unfortunately never led to a larger body of work on this subject. The specific experiment was not replicated, and the applicability of the hypotheses in other contexts was not studied. Thus it was never investigated whether the results hold, for example:

- for software developers at different levels of experience (the original experiment used university students);
- if development teams are composed differently (the original experiment used only 3-person teams);
- if another disciplined methodology had been used (i.e., were the benefits observed due to the particular methodology used in the experiment, or would they be observed for any disciplined methodology?).

2 A Motivating Example: Software Reading Techniques

Yet even when replications *are* run, it's hard to know how to abstract important knowledge without a framework for relating the studies. To illustrate, we present our work on reading techniques. Reading techniques are procedural techniques, each aimed at a specific development task, which software developers can follow in order to obtain the information they need to accomplish that task effectively [2, 3]. We were interested in studying reading techniques in order to determine if beneficial experience and work practices could be distilled into procedural form, and used effectively on real projects. We felt that reading techniques were of relevance and value to the software engineering community, since reading software documents (such as requirements, design, code, etc.) is a key technical activity. Developers are often called upon to read software documents in order to extract specific information for important software tasks, e.g. to read a requirements document in order to find defects during an inspection, or an Object-Oriented design in order to identify reusable components. However, while developers are usually taught how to *write* software documents, the skills required for effecting *reading* are rarely taught and must be built up through experience. In fact, we felt that research into reading could provide a model for how to effectively write documents as well: by understanding how readers perform more effectively it may be possible to write documents in a way that facilitates the task.

However, the concept of reading techniques cannot be studied in isolation. Like any other software process, reading techniques must be tailored to the environment in which they are run. Our aim in this research was to generate sets of reading techniques that were procedurally defined, tailorable to the environment, aimed at accomplishing a particular task, and specific to the particular document and notation on which they would be applied. This has led a series of studies in which we evaluated the following types of reading techniques:

- Defect-Based Reading (**DBR**) focused on defect detection in requirements, where the requirements were expressed using a state machine notation called SCR [13, 22].
- Perspective-Based Reading (**PBR**) also focused on defect detection in requirements, but for requirements expressed in natural language [4, 16].
- Use-Based Reading (**UBR**) focused on anomaly detection in user interfaces [27].
- Second Version of PBR (**PBR2**) consisted of new techniques that were more procedurally-oriented versions of the earlier set of PBR techniques. In particular, we made the techniques more specific in all of their steps [24].
- Scope-Based Reading (**SBR**) consisted of two reading techniques that were developed for learning about an Object-Oriented framework in order to reuse it [10, 23].

A framework that makes explicit the different models used in these experiments would have many benefits. Such a framework would document the key choices made during experimental design, along with their rationales. The framework could be used to choose a focus for future studies: i.e., help determine the important attributes of the models used in an experiment, and which should be held constant and which varied in future studies. The ultimate objective is to build up a unifying theory by creating a list of the specific hypotheses investigated in an area, and how similar or different they all are.

Using an organizational framework also allows other experimenters to understand where different choices could have been made in defining models and hypotheses, and raises questions as to their likely outcome. Because these frameworks provide a mechanism by which different studies can be compared, they help to organize related studies and to tease out the true effects of both the process being studied and the environmental variables.

3 The GQM Goal Template as a Tool for Experimentation

Examples of such organizational frameworks do exist in the literature, e.g. [9, 17, 20]. For the purpose of this paper we find the Goal/Question/Metric (GQM) Goal Template [8] useful. The GQM method was defined as a mechanism for defining and interpreting a set of operational goals using measurement. It represents a top-down systematic approach for tailoring and integrating goals with models of software processes, products, and quality perspectives, based upon the specific needs of a project and organization.

The GQM goal template is a tool that can be used to articulate the purpose of any study. It ties together the important models, and provides a basis against which the appropriateness of a study's specific hypotheses, and dependent and independent variables, may be evaluated. There are five parameters in a GQM goal template:

- *object of study*: a process, product or any other experience model
- *purpose*: to characterize (what is it?), evaluate (is it good?), predict (can I estimate something in the future?), control (can I manipulate events?), improve (can I improve events?)
- *focus*: model aimed at viewing the aspect of the object of study that is of interest, e.g., reliability of the product, defect detection/prevention capability of the process, accuracy of the cost model
- *point of view*: e.g., the perspective of the person needing the information, e.g., in theory testing the point of view is usually the researcher trying to gain some knowledge
- *context*: models aimed at describing environment in which the measurement is taken

For example, the goal of the Basili/Reiter study, previously described, might be instantiated as:

To analyze the *development processes of a 1) disciplined-methodology team approach, 2) ad hoc team approach, and 3) ad hoc individual approach*
for the purpose of *characterization and evaluation*
with respect to *cost and complexity (faults and rework) of the process*
from the point of view of the *developer and project manager*
in the context of *an advanced university classroom*

Due to the nature of software engineering research, instantiated goals tend to show certain similarities. The *purpose* of studies is often evaluation; that is, researchers tend to study software technologies in order to assess their effect on development. For our purposes, the *point of view* can be considered to be that of the researcher or knowledge- builder. While studies can be run from the point of view of the project manager, i.e. requiring some immediate feedback as to effects on effort and schedule, published studies have usually undergone additional, post-hoc analysis.

The remaining fields in the template require the construction of more complicated models, but still show some similarities. The *object of study* is often (but not always) a process; researchers are often concerned with evaluating whether or not a particular development process represents an improvement to the way software is built. (E.g.: Does Object-Oriented Analysis lead to an improved implementation? Does an investment in reviews lead to less buggy, more reliable systems? Does reuse allow quality systems to be built more cheaply?) When the object of study is a process, the focus of the evaluation is the process' effect. The experimenter may measure its effect on a product, that is, whether the process leads to some desired attribute in a software work product. Or, the experimenter may attempt to capture its effect on people, e.g. whether practitioners were comfortable executing the process or found it tedious and infeasible. Finally, the *context* field should include a large number of environmental variables and therefore tends to exhibit the most variability. Studies may be run on students or experts; under time constraints, or not; in well-understood application domains, or in cutting-edge areas. There are numerous such variables that may influence the results of applying a technique.

For the remainder of this paper, we will illustrate our conclusions by concentrating on studies that investigate process characteristics with respect to their effects on products. A GQM template for this class of studies is:

> Analyze *processes* to *evaluate* their *effectiveness on a product* from the point of view of the *knowledge builder* in the context of (a particular *variable set*).

For particular studies in this class, constructing a complete GQM template requires making explicit the process (object of study), the effect on the product (focus), and context models in the experiment. Making these models explicit is necessary in order to understand the conditions under which the experimental results hold.

For example, consider the GQM templates for the list of reading technique experiments described in the previous section. There are many ways of classifying processes, but we might first classify processes by scope as:

- Techniques (processes that can be followed to accomplish some specific task),
- Methods[2] (processes augmented with information concerning when and how the process should be applied),
- Life Cycle Models (processes which describe the entire software development process).

Each of these categories could be subdivided in turn. The set of techniques, for example, could be classified based on the specific task as: Reading, Testing, Designing, and so on. We have found it helpful to think of the range of values as organized in a hierarchical fashion, in which more general values are found at the top of the tree, and each level of the tree represents a new level of detail. (Figure 1)

Selecting a particular type of process for study, our GQM template then becomes:

> Analyze *reading techniques* to *evaluate* their *effectiveness on a product* from the point of view of the *knowledge builder* in the context of a particular *variable set*

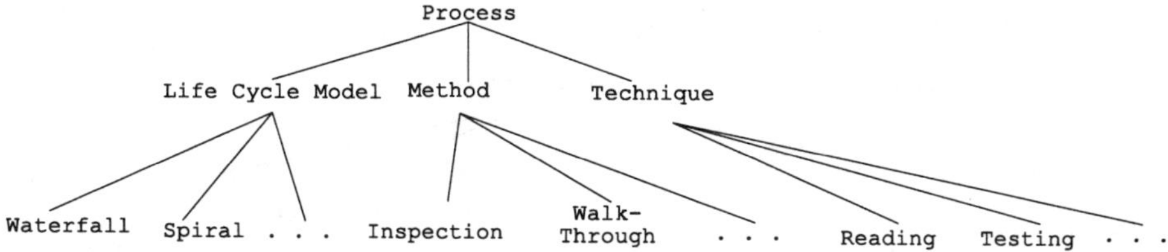

Fig. 1. A portion of the hierarchy of possible values for describing software processes

The reading technique experiments were concerned with studying the effect of the reading technique on a product. So, the model of focus needs to specify both how effectiveness is to be measured and the product on which the evaluation is performed.We find it useful to divide the set of effectiveness measures into analysis and construction measures, based on whether the goal of the process is to analyze intrinsic properties of a document or to use it in building a new system. Each of these categories can be further broken down into more specific types of process goals, for which different effectiveness measures may apply (Fig. 2). For example, the effectiveness of a process for performing maintenance can be evaluated by how that process effects the cost of making a change to the system. The effectiveness of a process for detecting defects in a document can be measured by the number of faults it helps find. Of course, many more measures exist than will fit into Figure 2. For instance, rather than measure the number of faults a defect detection process yields, it might be more appropriate to measure the number of errors[3], or the amount of effort required, among other things.

Similarly, a software document can be classified according to the model of a software system it contains (a relatively well-defined set) and further subdivided into the specific notations that may be used (Fig.3). The main purpose of organizing the possible values hierarchically is to organize a conception of the problem space that can be used by others for classifying their own experiments. The actual criteria used are somewhat subjective; naturally there are multiple criteria for classifying processes, effectiveness measures, and software documents, but we have selected just those that have contributed to our conception of reading techniques.

Thus a GQM template for the PBR experiment could be:

Analyze *reading techniques* to *evaluate* their *ability to detect defects in a Requirements Document written in English* from the point of view of the *knowledge builder* in the context of a particular *variable set.*

---

[2] The definitions of "technique" and "method" are adapted from [5].

[3] Here we are using the terms "faults" and "errors" according to the IEEE standard definitions [14], in which "fault" refers to defects appearing in some artifact while "error" refers to an underlying human misconception that may be translated into faults.

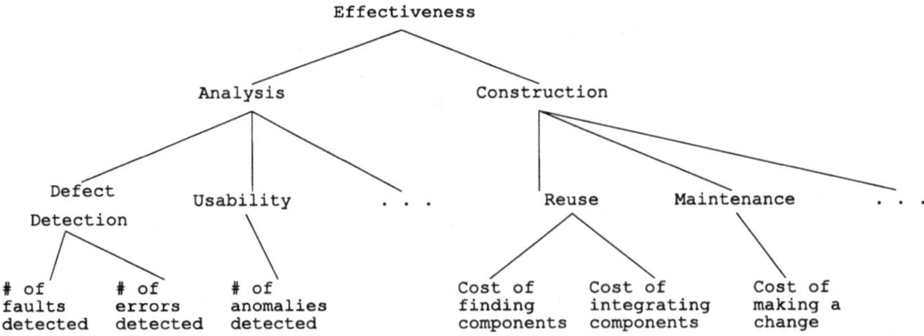

Fig. 2. A portion of the hierarchy of possible values for describing the effectiveness of software processes

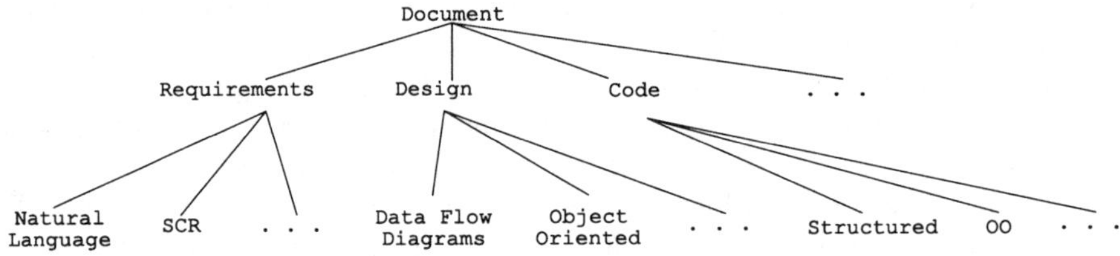

Fig. 3. A portion of the hierarchy of possible values for describing software documents

A GQM goal is not meant to be a definitive description, but reflects the interests and priorities of the experimenter. If we were to study the process model for the reading techniques in each experiment in more detail, we would see that each technique is tailored to a specific task (e.g., analysis or construction, etc.) and to a specific document. This is what characterizes the reading techniques and distinguishes them from one another. Thus the process goals used to classify measures of effectiveness in Figure 2 can be easily adapted to describe the processes themselves (Figure 4). The distinction between analysis and construction process goals can apply directly to processes. That is, we hypothesize that analysis tasks differ sufficiently from construction tasks that, along with differences in the way they may be evaluated for effectiveness, there may also be different guidelines used in their construction. Thus figures 2 and 3 can also be mechanisms for identifying process model attributes. They should be accounted for in the process model as well as the effect on process.

Thus we can say that we are:

analyzing a reading technique *for the purpose of* evaluating its ability to detect defects in a natural language requirements document

or we can say that we are:

analyzing a reading technique *tailored to* defect detection in natural language requirements for the purpose of evaluation.

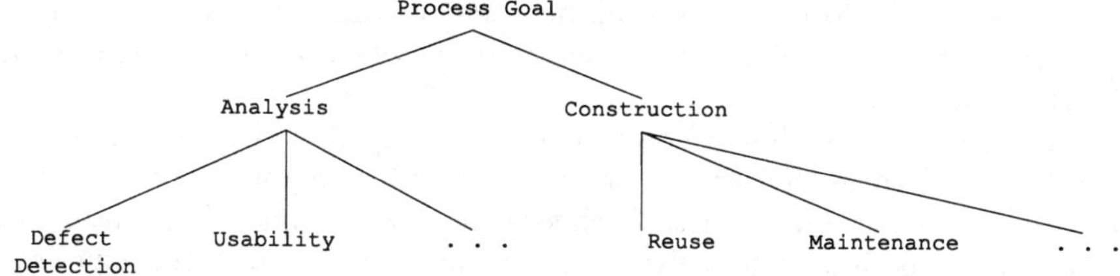

Fig. 4. A portion of the hierarchy of possible values for describing the goal of a software engineering process

It depends on whether we are emphasizing the definition of the process or of its effectiveness.

In linking goal templates to hypotheses, we can think of the process model (object of study) as the independent variable, the effect on product (focus) as the dependent variable, and the context variables as the variables that exist in the environment of the experiment. The differences or similarities between experimental hypotheses can then be described in terms of these hierarchies of possible values. For example, consider the studies of DBR and PBR. In both cases, the process model was focused on the same task (defect detection); although the notation differed, both were also focused on the same document (requirements). If all other attributes for process, product, and context models were held constant, we could begin to think of hypotheses at a higher level of abstraction. That is, instead of the hypothesis:

> **Subjects using a reading technique tailored to defect detection in natural language requirements are more effective than subjects using ad hoc techniques for this task**

The following hypothesis might be more useful:

> **Subjects using reading techniques tailored to defect detection in requirements are more effective than subjects using ad hoc techniques for this task.**

The difference between these hypotheses is that the focus of the study is described at a higher level of abstraction for the second hypothesis (requirements) than for the first (natural language requirements).

This difference in abstraction makes the second hypothesis more difficult to test. In fact, probably no single study could ever give us overwhelming evidence as to its validity, or lack thereof. Testing the second hypothesis would require some idea of what types of requirements notation are of interest to practitioners. Building up a convincing body of evidence requires the combined analysis of multiple studies of specific reading techniques for defect detection in requirements. But the effort required to formulate the hypothesis and begin building a body of evidence helps advance the field of software engineering. At best, the evidence can lead to the growth of a body of knowledge, containing basic and important theories underlying some aspect of the field. At worst, the effort spent in specifying the models forces us to think more deeply about the relevant ways of characterizing software engineering models that we, as researchers, are implicitly constructing anyway.

The above discussion should not be taken to imply that the attributes identified in Figures 1 through 4 are the only ones that are important, or for which hierarchies of possible values exist. To choose another example, in specifying the model of the context it is almost always important to characterize the experience of the subjects of the experiment. The most appropriate way of characterizing experience depends on many things; two possibilities are proposed in Figure 5.

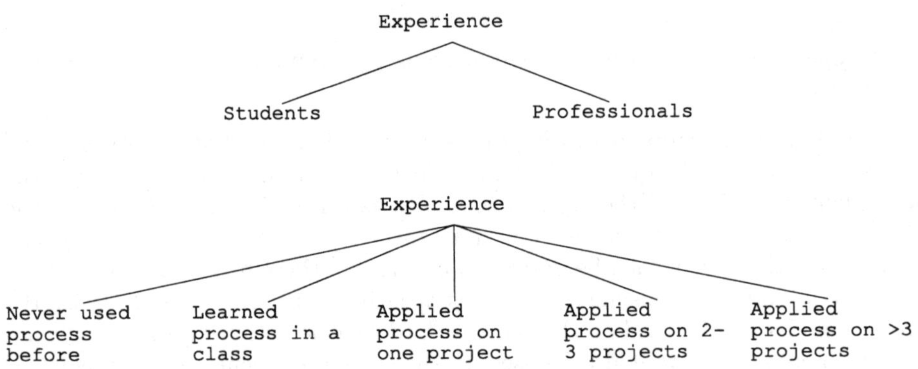

Fig. 5. Two possible value hierarchies for measuring subject experience

The trees shown in Figure 5 present two different ways of characterizing experience. The first is a simpler way of characterizing the attribute that distinguishes only between subjects who are still learning software engineering principles versus those who have applied them on real projects. The second hierarchy attempts to place finer distinctions on the amount of experience a subject has applying a particular process. Each may be appropriate to different circumstances.

4 Replicating Experiments

In preceding sections of this paper, we have tried to raise several reasons why families of replicated experiments are necessary for building up bodies of knowledge about hypotheses. Another reason for running replications is that they can increase the amount of confidence in results by addressing certain threats to validity: Internal validity defines the degree of confidence in a cause-effect relationship between factors of interest and the observed results, while external validity defines the extent to which the conclusions from the experimental context can be generalized to the context specified in the research hypothesis [11]. In this section, we discuss replications in more detail and look at the practical considerations that result.

Our primary strategy for supporting replications in practice has been the creation of lab packages, which collect information on an experiment such as the experimental design, the artifacts and processes used in the experiment, the methods used during the experimental analysis, and the motivation behind the key design decisions. Our hope has been that the existence of such packages would simplify the process of replicating an experiment and hence encourage more replications in the discipline. Several replications have been carried out in this manner and have contributed to a growing body of knowledge on reading techniques.

4.1 Types of Replications

Since we consider that replications may be undertaken for various reasons, we have found it useful to enumerate the various reasons, each of which has its own requirements for the lab package. In our view the types of replications that need to be supported can be grouped into 3 major categories:

1. **Replications that do not vary any research hypothesis.** Replications of this type vary none of the dependent or independent variables of the original experiment.
   - 1.1. **Strict replications** (i.e. replications that duplicate as accurately as possible the original experiment). These replications are necessary to increase confidence in the validity of the experiment. They demonstrate that the results from the original experiment are repeatable, and have been reported accurately by the original experimenters.
   - 1.2. **Replications that vary the manner in which the experiment is run.** These studies seek to increase our confidence in experimental results by addressing the same problem as previous experiments, but altering the details of the experiment so that certain internal threats to validity are addressed. For example, a replication may vary the order of activities to avoid the possibility that results depend not on the process used, but on the order in which activities in the experiment are completed.
     The attempt to compensate for threats to internal validity may also lead to other types of changes. For example, a process may be modified so that the researchers can assess the amount of process conformance of subjects. Although the aim of the change may have been to address internal validity, the new process should be evaluated in order to understand whether unanticipated effects on process effectiveness have resulted. Thus such a replication would fall into the second major category, discussed below.
2. **Replications that vary the research hypotheses.** Replications of this type vary attributes of the process, product, and context models but remain at the same level of specificity as the original experiment.
   - 2.1. **Replications that vary variables intrinsic to the object of study (i.e. independent variables).** These replications investigate what aspects of the process are important by systematically varying intrinsic

properties of the process and examining the results. This type of experiment requires the process to be supplied in sufficient detail that changes can be made. This implies that the original experimenters must provide the rationales for the design decisions made as well as the finished product. For example, researchers may question whether the specificity at which the process is described affects the results of applying the process. In this sense, the study of PBR2 may be seen as a replication of the study of PBR, in which the level of specificity of the process was varied but all other attributes of the process model remained the same.

2.2. Replications that vary variables intrinsic to the focus of the evaluation (i.e. dependent variables). Replications of this type may vary the ways in which effectiveness is measured, in order to understand for what dimensions of a task a process results in the most gain. For example, a replication might choose another effectiveness measure from those listed in Figure 2, investigating whether a defect detection process is more beneficial for finding errors than faults. Other aspects of the focus model might be varied instead, e.g. a process might be evaluated on a document of the same type but different notation to see if it is equally effective (see Figure 3).

2.3. Replications that vary context variables in the environment in which the solution is evaluated. These studies can identify potentially important environmental factors that affect the results of the process under investigation and thus help understand its external validity. For example, replications may be run using the same process and product models as the original experiment but on professionals instead of students (see Figure 5) to see if the same results are obtained.

3. Replications that extend the theory. These replications help determine the limits to the effectiveness of a process, by making large changes to the process, product, and/or context models to see if basic principles still hold. We discussed replications in the previous category as replacing the value of some variable (e.g. document on which the process was applied, Figure 3) with another, equally specific value (e.g. SCR requirements instead of English- language requirements). Replications in this category, however, can be thought of as replacing an attribute of a process, product, or context model with a value at a higher level of abstraction (i.e. from a higher level in the hierarchy). Again using Figure 3, researchers may choose to study whether a type of process is applicable to requirements documents in general, rather than limiting their scope to a specific kind. The type of hypotheses associated with such replications was discussed in section 3.

4.2 Implications for Lab Package Design

In software engineering research, there has been a movement toward the reuse of physical artifacts and concrete processes between experiments. This is indeed a useful beginning. The cost of an experiment is greatly increased if the preparation of multiple artifacts is necessary. Creating artifacts which are representative of those used in real development projects is difficult and time consuming. Reusing artifacts can thus reduce the time and cost needed for experimentation. A more significant benefit is that reuse allows the opportunity to build up knowledge about the actual use of particular, non-trivial artifacts in practice. Thus replications (and experimentation in general) could be facilitated if there were repositories of reusable artifacts of different types (e.g. requirements) which have a history of reuse and which, therefore, are well understood. (A model for such repositories could be the repository of system architectures [12], where the relevant attributes of each design in the repository are known and described.)

A first step towards this goal is the construction of web-based laboratory packages. At the most basic level, these packages allow an independent experimenter to download experimental materials, either for reuse or for better understanding. In this way, these packages support strict replications (as defined in section 4.1), which require that the processes and artifacts used in the original experiment be made available to independent researchers.

However, web-based lab packages should be designed to support more sophisticated types of replications as well. For example, packages should assist other experimenters in understanding and addressing the threats to validity in order to support replications that vary some aspects of the experimental setup. Due to the constraints imposed by the setting in which software engineering research is conducted, it is almost never possible to rule out every single threat to validity. Choosing the "least bad" set of threats given the goal of the experiment is necessary. Lab packages need to acknowledge this fact and make the analysis of the constraints and the threats to validity explicit, so that other studies may use different experimental designs (that may have other threats to validity of their own) to rule out these threats.

Replications that seek to vary the detailed hypotheses have additional requirements if the lab package is to support them as well. For example, in order for other experimenters to effectively vary attributes of the object of study, the original process must be explained in sufficient detail that other researchers can draw their own conclusions about key variables. Since it is unreasonable to expect the original experimenters to determine all of the key variables *a priori*, lab packages must provide rationales for key experimental context decisions so that other experimentalists can determine feasible points of variation of interest to themselves. Similarly, lab packages must specify context variables in sufficient detail that feasible changes to the environment can be identified and hypotheses made about their effects on the results.

Finally, in order to build up a body of knowledge about software engineering theories, researchers should know which experiments have been run that offer related results. Therefore, lab packages for related experiments should be linked, in order to collect different experiments that address different areas of the problem space, and contribute evidence relevant to basic theories. The web is an ideal medium for such packages since links can be added dynamically, pointing to new, related lab packages as they become available. Thus it is to be hoped that lab packages are "living documents" that are changed and updated to reflect our current understanding of the experiments they describe.

Lab packages have been our preferred method for facilitating the abstraction of results and experiences from series of well-designed studies. Interested readers are referred to existing examples of lab packages: [25, 26]. By collecting detailed information and results on specific experiments, they summarize our knowledge about specific processes. They record the design and analysis methods used and may suggest new ones. Additionally, by linking related studies they can help experimenters understand what factors do or do not impact effectiveness.

4.3 The Experimental Community

A group of researchers, from both industry and academia, has been organized since 1993 for the purpose of facilitating the replication of experiments. The group is called ISERN, the International Software Engineering Research Network, and includes members in North America, Europe, Asia, and Australia. ISERN members publish common technical reports, exchange visitors, and organize annual meetings to share experiences on software engineering experimentation[4]. They have begun replicating experiments to better understanding the success factors of inspection and reading.

The *Empirical Software Engineering* journal has also helped build an experimental community by providing a forum for publishing descriptions of empirical studies and their replications. An especially noteworthy aspect of the journal is that it is open to publishing replicated studies that, while rigorously planned and analyzed, yield unexpected results that did not confirm the original study. Although it has traditionally been difficult to publish such "unsuccessful" studies in the software engineering literature, this knowledge must be made available if the community is to build a complete and unbiased body of knowledge concerning software technologies.

5 Conclusions

The above discussion leads us to propose that the following criteria are necessary before we can begin to build up comprehensive bodies of knowledge in areas of software engineering:

1. Hypotheses that are of interest to the software engineering community and are written in a context that allow for a well defined experiment;
2. Context variables, suggested by the hypotheses, that can be changed to allow for variation of the experimental design (to make up for validity threats) and the context of experimentation;
3. A sufficient amount of information so that the experiment can be replicated and built upon; and

[4] More information is available at the URL http://wwwagse.informatik.uni-kl.de/ISERN/isern.html

4. A community of researchers that understand experimentation, the need for replication, and are willing to collaborate and replicate.

With respect to the Basili/Reiter study introduced in section 1, we can note that while it satisfied criteria 1 and 3, it failed with respect to criteria 2 and 4. It was not suggested by the authors that other researchers might vary the design or manipulate the processes or criteria used for evaluation (although the analysis of the data was varied in a later study [6]). Nor was there a community of researchers willing to analyze the hypotheses even if suggestions for replication had been made.

In contrast, the set of experiments on reading, discussed in a working group at the 1997 annual meeting of ISERN [18], is an example that we have built up a body of knowledge by independent researchers working on different parts of the problem and exposing their conclusions to different plausible rival hypotheses. We have shown in this paper that experimental constraints in software engineering research make it very difficult, and even impossible, to design a perfect single study. In order to rule out the threats to validity, it is more realistic to rely on the "parsimony" concept rather than being frustrated because of trying to completely remove them. This appeal to parsimony is based on the assumption that the evidence for an experimental effect is more credible if that effect can be observed in numerous and independent experiments each with different threats to validity [11].

A second conclusion is that empirical research must be a collaborative activity because of the huge number of problems, variables, and issues to consider. This complexity can be faced with extensive brainstorming, carefully designing complementary studies that provide coverage of the problem and solution space, and reciprocal verification.

It is our contention that interesting and relevant hypotheses can be identified and investigated effectively if empirical work is organized in the form of families of related experiments. In this paper, we have raised several reasons why such families are necessary:

- To investigate the effects of alternative values for important attributes of the experimental models;
- To vary the strategy with which detailed hypotheses are investigated;
- To make up for certain threats to validity that often arise in realistically designed experiments.

Discussion within the experimental community is also needed to address other issues, such as what constitutes an "acceptable" level of confidence in the hypotheses that we address as a community. By running carefully designed replications, we can address threats to validity in specific experiments and accumulate evidence about hypotheses. However, we are unaware of any useful and specific guidelines that concern the amount of evidence that must be accumulated before conclusions can confidently be drawn from a set of related experiments, in spite of the existence of specific threats. More discussion within the empirical software engineering community as to what constitutes a sufficient body of credible knowledge would be of benefit.

Building up a body of knowledge from families of experiments has the following benefits for the software engineering researcher:

- It allows the results of several experiments to be combined in order to build up our knowledge about software processes.
- It increases the effectiveness of individual experiments, which can now contribute to answering more general and abstract hypotheses.
- It offers a framework for building relevant practical software engineering knowledge, organized around the GQM goal template or another framework from the literature.
- It provides a way to develop and integrate laboratory manuals, which can facilitate and encourage the types of replications that are necessary to expand our knowledge of basic principles.
- It helps generate a community of experimenters, who understand the value of, and can carry out, the needed replications.

The ability to carry out families of replications has the following benefits for the software engineering practitioner:

- It offers some relevant practical SE knowledge; fully parameterizing process, product, and context models allows a better understanding of the environment in which the experimental results hold.
- It provides a better basis for making judgements about selecting process, since practitioners can match their development context to the ones under which the processes are evaluated.
- It shows the importance of and ability to tailor "best practices", that is, it shows how software processes can be altered by meaningful manipulation of key variables.
- It provides support for defining and documenting processes, since running related experiments assists in determining the important process variables.
- It allows organizations to integrate their experiences by making explicit the ways in which experiences differ (i.e. what the relevant process, product, and context models are) or are similar, and allowing the abstraction of basic principles from this information.

Acknowledgements

This work was supported by NSF grant CCR9706151, NASA grant NCC5170, and UMIACS. The authors would like to thank Michael Fredericks and Shari Lawrence Pfleeger for their valuable comments on earlier drafts of this paper.

References

1. V.R.Basili, "The experimental paradigm in software engineering", Experimental Software Engineering Issues: Critical Assessment and Future Directions, International Workshop, Dagstuhl, Germany, 1992. Appeared in Springer-Verlag, Lecture Notes in Computer Science, Number 706, 1993.

2. V. R. Basili, "Evolving and packaging reading technologies", *Journal of Systems and Software*, vol. 38, no. 1, pp.3–12, July 1997.
3. V. Basili, G. Caldiera, F. Lanubile, and F. Shull, "Studies on reading techniques", *Proc. of the Twenty-First Annual Software Engineering Workshop*, SEL-96-002, Goddard Space Flight Center, Greenbelt, Maryland, pp.59–65, December 1996.
4. V. R. Basili, S. Green, O. Laitenberger, F. Lanubile, F. Shull, S. Soerumgaard, M. Zelkowitz, "The empirical investigation of perspective-based reading"; *Empirical Software Engineering Journal*, vol. 1, no. 2, 1996.
5. V. R. Basili, S. Green , O. Laitenburger, F. Lanubile, F. Shull, S. Sorumgard, and M. Zelkowitz, "Packaging researcher experience to assist replication of experiments", *Proc. of the ISERN meeting 1996*, Sydney, Australia, 1996.
6. V. R. Basili, and D. H. Hutchens, "An empirical study of a syntactic metric family", *IEEE Transactions on Software Engineering*, vol. SE-9, pp.664–672, November 1983.
7. V. R. Basili, and R. W. Reiter, "A controlled experiment quantitatively comparing software development approaches", *IEEE Transactions on Software Engineering*, vol. SE-7, no. 3, pp.299–320, May 1981.
8. V. R. Basili, and H. D. Rombach, "The TAME project: Towards improvement-oriented software environments", *IEEE Transactions on Software Engineering*, vol. SE-14, no. 6, June 1988.
9. V. R. Basili, R. W. Selby, and D. H. Hutchens, "Experimentation in software engineering", *IEEE Transactions on Software Engineering*, vol. SE-12, no. 7, pp. 733–743, July 1986.
10. V. Basili, F. Lanubile, F. Shull, "Investigating maintenance processes in a framework-based environment", *Proc. of the Int. Conf. on Software Maintenance*, Bethesda, Maryland, pp.256-264, 1998.
11. D. T. Campbell, and J. C. Stanley, *Experimental and Quasi-Experimental Designs for Research*, Boston: Houghton Mifflin Co, 1963.
12. Composable Systems Group, "Model Problems", http://www.cs.cmu.edu/ Compose/html/ModProb/, 1995.
13. P. Fusaro, F. Lanubile, and G. Visaggio, "A replicated experiment to assess requirements inspections techniques", *Empirical Software Engineering Journal*, vol.2, no.1, pp.39-57, 1997.
14. IEEE. Software Engineering Standards. *IEEE Computer Society Press*, 1987.
15. C. M. Judd, E. R. Smith, and L. H. Kidder, *Research Methods in Social Relations*, sixth edition, Orlando: Harcourt Brace Jovanovich, Inc., 1991.
16. O. Laitenberger, and J. M. DeBaud, "Perspective-based reading of code documents at Robert Bosch GmbH", *Journal of Information and Software Technology*, 39, pp.781–791, 1997.
17. F. Lanubile, "Empirical evaluation of software maintenance technologies", *Empirical Software Engineering Journal*, vol.2, no.2, pp.95–106, 1997.
18. F. Lanubile, "Report on the results of the parallel project meeting reading techniques", http://seldi2.uniba.it:1025/isern97/readwg/index.htm , October 1997.
19. F. Lanubile, F. Shull, V. Basili, "Experimenting with error abstraction in requirements documents", *Proc. of the 5th Int. Symposium on Software Metrics*, Bethesda, Maryland, pp.114–121, 1998.
20. C. M. Lott, and H. D. Rombach, "Repeatable software engineering experiments for comparing defect-detection techniques", *Empirical Software Engineering Journal*, vol.1, no.3, pp.241–277, 1996.
21. K. Popper, *The Logic of Scientific Discovery*, Harper Torchbooks, New York, NY, 1968.

22. A. Porter, L. Votta, V. Basili, "Comparing detection methods for software requirements inspections: a replicated experiment", *IEEE Transactions on Software Engineering*, vol. 21, no. 6, pp. 563–575, 1995.
23. F. Shull, F. Lanubile, and V. R. Basili, "Investigating Reading Techniques for Framework Learning", Technical Report CS-TR-3896, UMCP Dept. of Computer Science, UMIACS-TR-98-26, UMCP Institute for Advanced Computer Studies, *ISERN-98-16*, International Software Engineering Research Network, May 1998.
24. F. Shull. *Developing Techniques for Using Software Documents: A Series of Empirical Studies.* Ph.D. thesis, University of Maryland, College Park, December 1998.
25. F. Shull, "Reading Techniques for Object-Oriented Frameworks", `http://www.cs.umd.edu/projects/SoftEng/ESEG/manual/sbr_package/manual.html`
26. F. Shull, "Lab Package for the Empirical Investigation of Perspective-Based Reading", `http://www.cs.umd.edu/projects/SoftEng/ESEG/manual/pbr_package/manual.html`
27. Z. Zhang, V. Basili, and B. Shneiderman, "An Empirical Study of Perspective-based Usability Inspection", Human Factors and Ergonomics Society Annual Meeting, Chicago, Oct. 1998.

Patterns in Words versus Patterns in Trees: A Brief Survey and New Results

Gregory Kucherov and Michaël Rusinowitch

INRIA-Lorraine/LORIA
615, rue du Jardin Botanique, BP 101
54602 Villers-lès-Nancy, France
{kucherov,rusi}@loria.fr

Abstract. In this paper we study some natural problems related to specifying sets of words and trees by patterns.

1 Introduction

Patterns are probably the most simple and natural way to specify non-trivial families of combinatorial structures. Abstractly, let $\mathcal{G}$ be a class of combinatorial structures with a substructure relation (such as graphs, trees, strings, etc.). Usually, given $\mathcal{G}$ we can define in a natural way a notion of pattern, interpreted as an *under-specified* structure of $\mathcal{G}$, that is a structure with some "unspecified parts". A pattern defines a set of *instances* which are structures obtained by instantiating the pattern's unspecified parts by other structures. For example, in case of graph structures, patterns could be defined as graphs with some "meta-nodes" which can be instantiated by other graphs.

Using these informal definitions, we now introduce central notions of this paper. For a set S of patterns, we denote by $Inst(S)$ the set of structures which are instances of patterns of S. By $Cont(S)$ we denote the set of structures which have a substructure in $Inst(S)$. In the above example of graphs, if S is a set of patterns (graphs with "meta-nodes"), $Inst(S)$ is the set of instances of patterns from S and $Cont(S)$ could be defined as the set of graphs having a subgraph that is an instance of a pattern of S. We will also study the complements of sets $Inst(S)$ and $Cont(S)$, defined by $\overline{Inst(S)} = \mathcal{G} \setminus Inst(S)$ and $\overline{Cont(S)} = \mathcal{G} \setminus Cont(S)$.

In this paper we consider two structures, which are probably the most widely used data structures in computer science: words and trees. We will define the notion of pattern for each of these structures and we will compare the complexity of different natural problems related to patterns in the cases of words and trees. In this perspective, we survey various known results and give several new ones.

2 Words, Trees, and Patterns

Let us start with basic definitions. Given a finite alphabet A of *letters*, *words* over A are defined in the usual way as finite sequences of letters. A^* stands

D. Bjørner, M. Broy, A. Zamulin (Eds.): PSI'99, LNCS 1755, pp. 283–296, 2000.

for the set of words over A. From algebraic point of view, words over A are elements of the free monoid generated by A. *Word patterns* over A are defined as words over alphabet $A \cup X$, where X is an infinite alphabet of *variables*. For example, $v = abaababaabaab$ is a word over the alphabet $\{a, b\}$ and assuming that $x, y \in X$, $abaxbayb, xabax, xaxxaxax$ are patterns over $\{a, b\}$. A variable occurring more than once in the pattern is called *non-linear*, otherwise it is *linear*. A *subword* of a word is a fragment of its letter sequence. For example, *baab* is a subword of v and *abba* is not. A *substitution* is a morphism $\sigma : (A \cup X)^* \to A^*$ such that $\sigma(a) = a$ for all $a \in A$. A substitution is *non-erasing* if $\sigma(x) \neq \varepsilon$, where ε is the empty word, and *erasing* otherwise. A word $w \in A^*$ is an *instance* of a pattern $p \in (A \cup X)^*$ if $w = \sigma(p)$ for some substitution σ. In this case we say also that p *matches* w. A substitution can be simply seen as a mapping replacing variable occurrences in the pattern by words such that the occurrences of the same variable are replaced by the same word. For example, the word v is an instance of each of the three patterns above.

A *tree* is a well-formed expression over a *signature* Σ of function symbols, where each symbol is indexed by an integer number, called its *arity*. For example, $u = f(f(f(a, a), h(a)), h(a))$ is a tree over the signature $\Sigma = \{f, h, a\}$, where symbols f, h, a have arity 2,1,0 respectively. The set of trees over Σ is denoted by $T(\Sigma)$. From algebraic point of view, $T(\Sigma)$ is a free Σ-algebra generated by Σ. Thus, we are dealing with node-labeled trees representing *first-order terms* over a given signature. We will use the words *tree* and *term* interchangeably. Clearly, we assume that the signature contains at least one 0-arity (constant) symbol, otherwise the set of terms is empty. A *tree pattern* is a tree over $\Sigma \cup X$, where X is an infinite set of 0-arity symbols of *variables*. Thus, $f(x, h(y))$, $f(f(f(y, a), x), x)$ are tree patterns over $\{f, h, a\}$, where x, y are variables. A *subtree* of a tree t is a subexpression of t. In other words, a subtree of t is a tree occurring at some node of t. The subtrees of u are $f(f(f(a, a), h(a)), h(a))$, $f(f(a, a), h(a))$, $f(a, a)$, $h(a)$ and a. Note that $h(a)$ and a have several occurrences in u. A *substitution* is a homomorphism $\sigma : T(\Sigma \cup X) \to T(\Sigma)$ such that $\sigma(a) = a$ for each constant a from Σ. Again, if $t = \sigma(p)$ for some term t, pattern p and substitution σ, then t is said to be an *instance* of p, and p is said to *match* t. Similar to words, a substitution replaces variables in patterns by trees such that the same variable is replaced by the same term. For example, term u is an instance of both patterns $f(x, h(y))$ and $f(f(f(y, a), x), x)$, but is not an instance of $f(f(x, x), h(a))$.

Note that words can be represented as trees in at least two ways. One way is to map each letter to a distinct unary symbol, and to add to the signature one constant symbol. Then a word can be naturally represented by a non-branching tree. However, to represent a pattern consistently, we need to introduce variables at internal nodes (second-order variables) which does not fit to our framework. Another way is to map each letter to a corresponding constant symbol and use one additional binary symbol for concatenation. In this case, however, one word is represented by several trees, due to the associativity property of concatenation. In general, words can be seen as trees over one associative function symbol. We will see in this paper that this associativity property makes many problems on words much more difficult than their counterparts for trees.

3 Problems

We now state the problems we will address in this paper. We assume that we are given a set S of word (resp. tree) patterns. As defined in Introduction, $Inst(S)$ denotes the set of word (resp. tree) instances of patterns of S, and $Cont(S)$ denotes the set of words (trees) having respectively a subword (subtree) that is an instance of a pattern from S. If S consists of a single pattern p, we will write $Inst(p)$ and $Cont(p)$ as a short-hand for $Inst(\{p\})$ and $Cont(\{p\})$.

We are interested in the following problems for both words and trees. Below u is a word (resp. tree), p is a word (resp. tree) pattern, and S is a set of patterns.

P1.1 $u \in Inst(p)$?
P1.2 $u \in \overline{Cont(p)}$?
P2.1 is $\overline{Inst(S)}$ a finite set?
P2.2 is $Inst(S)$ a regular set?
P3 $Inst(p) \subseteq Inst(S)$?
P4 $Inst(p) \subseteq \overline{Cont(S)}$?
P5.1 is $\overline{Cont(S)}$ a finite set?
P5.2 is $Cont(S)$ a regular set?

These questions are standard language-theoretic problems. P1.1 and P1.2 are membership problems for *Inst*- and *Cont*-languages. Since $Inst(S)$ and $Cont(S)$ are generally infinite, it makes sense to ask if these sets are co-finite. This justifies problems P2.1 and P5.1. Problems P2.2 and P5.2 ask whether $Inst(S)$ (respectively $Cont(S)$) is a regular set of words (trees). If the notion of regular word set (language) is well-known, the notion of regular tree language is probably less standard. For readers who are not familiar with regular tree languages, we refer to books [GS84, NP92]. Finally, problems P3 and P4 are also usual language inclusion questions, as $Inst(S) = \cup_{p \in S} Inst(p)$, and $Inst(S) \subseteq L$ iff for all $p \in S$, $Inst(p) \subseteq L$.

4 The Tree Case

We now start with the tree case and survey what is known here about the questions above. This will motivate our study and will allow to compare these results with their counterparts for the word case.

P1.1 is a trivial problem for the tree case. It asks whether a term is an instance of a tree pattern, which can be easily done in linear time. It is sufficient to check if the pattern coincides with the term at all non-variable positions, and check that the subterms of the term corresponding to distinct occurrences of the same variable in the pattern coincide. Clearly, this can be done in time $O(|u| + |p|)$.

P1.2 is the *subterm matching* problem which has numerous applications in functional and logic programming, automated deduction, term rewriting and other areas related to symbolic computation. The problem consists of testing whether a given pattern occurs in a given tree, that is matches one of its subtrees.

Usually, one wants also an algorithm to find all such subtrees, and not only to test if there is one. The restricted version of this problem, when the pattern contains only linear variables, is known under the name *tree matching*. In early 80's, a simple practical solution has been proposed [HO82]. More recently, a series of work has been done to find the most efficient (in the worst-case) algorithm for tree matching. We refer to the latest achievement [CHI99] which proposes an $O(n \log^3 n)$ deterministic algorithm, where n is the size of the tree (assumed to be bigger than the size of the pattern). The algorithm (as well as previously proposed theoretically efficient algorithms) is however rather complicated and difficult to implement, and the problem of designing an efficient and practical tree matching algorithm is still on the agenda. Now, if a pattern contains non-linear variables, we can preprocess the subject tree by indexing its nodes in such a way that if the subtrees rooted in two nodes are the same, then these nodes have the same index. This preprocessing can be done in linear time (under the assumption that the signature has a constant size) by a bottom-up traversal of the tree. Then we can "forget" about repeated variables in the pattern and consider all variable nodes to be labeled by distinct variables. We then run a tree matching algorithm for linear patterns, and check, each time we find an occurrence of the linear pattern, if the subterms corresponding to occurrences of the same variable in the original pattern are equal (by looking at their indexes). This comparison takes time proportional to the maximal number of occurrences in the original pattern ($O(|p|)$ in the worst case), which introduces a $|p|$ factor with respect to the theoretic complexity of linear pattern matching. We refer to [RR92] for a detailed algorithm of subterm matching in presence of non-linear variables.

Let us now turn to problem P2.1, and consider a generalization of it. Instead of asking whether $\overline{Inst(S)}$ is finite, we ask if $\overline{Inst(S)}$ can be itself represented as $Inst(S')$ for some finite set of patterns S'. Such a set S' is called a *complement representation* of S [KP98]. Again, non-linear variables in patterns of S play an important role. Consider the set $S = \{h(x), f(h(x), y)\}$ over the signature $\{f, h, a\}$ as above. Then the set $S' = \{a, f(a, x), f(f(x, y), z)\}$ is a complement representation of S. One can generalize this and prove that if all patterns in the set are linear, a finite complement representation of this set can be constructed. However, one can prove that the set $S = \{f(x, x)\}$ does not have a finite complement representation. The exhaustive analysis of the situation has been given in [LM87]. The main result can be stated as follows.

Theorem 1 ([LM87]). *A set of patterns S has a finite complement representation iff there exists a set of* linear *patterns S_{lin} such that $Inst(S) = Inst(S_{lin})$. Moreover,*

- *if such a set S_{lin} exists, it can be obtained by instantiating the non-linear variables in the patterns of S by terms,*
- *the property of having a finite complement representation is decidable.*

Let us illustrate Theorem 1 by an example. Consider the set $S = \{a, f(x,h(y)), f(x,x), f(x,f(y,z))\}$, still over the signature $\{f,h,a\}$. This set contains a non-linear term $f(x,x)$. However, a simple analysis shows that $f(x,x)$ can be replaced by $f(a,a)$ without changing the set of instances. Thus, $Inst(S) = Inst(S_{lin})$, where S_{lin} is a set of linear patterns obtained from S by substituting a to x in the term $f(x,x)$. Furthermore, as S_{lin} contains only linear patterns, a complement representation of S_{lin} can be constructed: $S'_{lin} = \{h(x), f(h(x),a), f(f(x,y),a)\}$. Theorem 1 asserts that this example is typical: if a finite complement exists, the set is "linearizable", that is non-linear variables can be replaced by terms without changing the set of instances. The decidability of this property, stated in Theorem 1, means that a bound on the size of terms replacing non-linear variables can be effectively computed.

Recently, the study of finite complement representations has received a new impulse [GP99, Pic99], motivated by its applications in different areas, and in particular in logic programming. In [Pic99], it has been proved that testing if a given set has a finite complement representation (see Theorem 1) is co-NP-complete.

Coming back to problem P2.1, to check if $\overline{Inst(S)}$ is finite, we first check, according to Theorem 1, if S has a finite complement representation. If the answer is positive, we compute such a representation. If all patterns in the representation are terms (i.e. do not contain variables), then $\overline{Inst(S)}$ is finite. Otherwise, if at least one pattern has a variable, $\overline{Inst(S)}$ is infinite. This shows that P2.1 is in co-NP. The NP-hardness of P2.1 follows from [KNRZ91], where it was proved that deciding if $\overline{Inst(S)} = \emptyset$, is co-NP-complete. An easy modification of the hardness part of this proof shows that P2.1 is co-NP-hard, and therefore co-NP-complete.

Theorem 1 gives actually an answer to problem P2.2 too. It is an easy exercise to prove that if a set S contains only linear patterns, $Inst(S)$ is a regular tree language [GS84, NP92]. Thus, when a set is "linearizable" in the sense of Theorem 1, the set of instances is regular. On the other hand, if a set is not linearizable, it can be shown using a pumping lemma argument that the set of instances is not regular. This is however not easy to prove, but follows from the work [Kuc91] that we will survey below. We summarize the discussion in the following statement.

Proposition 1. *In the tree case, P2.1 and P2.2 are co-NP-complete problems.*

Now let us skip problem P3 for a moment and turn to problem P4 which has now a more-than-ten-years history. The problem, known under the name of *ground reducibility* problem, has attracted a lot of attention in the area of *term rewriting* [DJ90] because of its application to automated inductive proofs [JK89]. The problem consists of testing if all instances of a given tree pattern p have a subtree matched by one of the patterns of a given set S. Once again, non-linear variables in patterns of S make the problem much more difficult. In the middle and late 80's, several authors observed that the problem is decidable if patterns of S only contain linear variables. The problem was first proved decidable in the general case by Plaisted [Pla85], and later by other authors independently [KNZ87, Com88]. Recently, the problem was shown to be EXPTIME-complete [CJ97].

Problem P3 can be expressed in terms of P4 in the following way. Assume we have a pattern p and a set of patterns S, and we want to test whether $Inst(p) \subseteq Inst(S)$. First delete from S those patterns which do not have the same root symbol as the root symbol of p (obviously, these patterns cover no instance of p). Then choose a new symbol α and replace the root symbol in p and in all remaining patterns in S by α. Let p' and S' be the resulting pattern and set respectively. It can be shown that $Inst(p) \subseteq Inst(S)$ iff $Inst(p') \subseteq Cont(S')$. The latter property, which is a special instance of ground reducibility, can be expressed as the so called *sufficient completeness* property for specifications with free constructors (see [KNRZ91]). Deciding this property has been proved co-NP-complete in [KNRZ91].

Proposition 2. *In the tree case, P3 and P4 are both decidable problems. P3 is co-NP-complete and P4 is EXPTIME-complete.*

Finally, let us turn to problems 5.1 and 5.2. Problem 5.1 has been proved decidable in [Pla85, KNZ87]. Concerning Problem 5.2, the following Theorem has been proved in [Kuc91].

Theorem 2. *For a set of patterns S, $Cont(S)$ is a regular tree language iff there exists a set of* linear *patterns S_{lin} such that $Cont(S) = Cont(S_{lin})$. Moreover,*

- *if such a set S_{lin} exists, it can be obtained by instantiating the non-linear variables in the patterns of S by terms.*

Theorem 2 is a lifting of Theorem 1 from the set of instances $Inst(S)$ to the set $Cont(S)$ of terms containing instances of S as subterms. The latter case is however much more difficult, and the proof of Theorem 2 used a non-constructive combinatorial argument, based on Ramsey Theorem. Therefore, no effective bound on the size of terms to be substituted for the non-linear variables, resulted from the proof, and the decidability of the regularity of $Cont(S)$ remained an open problem. This problem, considered important in the area of rewriting, has appeared in the list of major open problems in rewriting in [DJK91]. Soon after, the regularity of $Cont(S)$ has been proved decidable by three groups of authors [KT92, VG92, HH92]. The results of [KT95] provided also a new proof of the decidability of problem 5.1, and even gave an effective bound on the size of $\overline{Cont(S)}$ in the case it is finite. We then conclude this section with the following

Proposition 3. *In the tree case, P5.1 and P5.2 are both decidable problems.*

5 The Word Case

The overview of the tree case given in the previous section shows that all the problems are decidable, though the complexity of some of them appears to be high. In this section we study these problems in the word case and see that most of them, and even some restricted versions of them, turn out to be undecidable. We also analyze the complexity of these problems in the case of linear patterns.

We first remark that in the tree case, $Cont(S)$ is a "meta-notion" with respect to $Inst(S)$, due to the fact that the notion of subtree cannot be expressed by means of patterns, as only first-order variables are allowed in patterns. In contrast, in the word case $Cont(S)$ can be expressed in terms of $Inst(S)$:

$$Cont(S) = Inst(\{xpy, xp, py, p | p \in S \text{ and } x, y \text{ do not occur in } p\})$$

This implies that, in contrast to the tree case, the problem for $Cont(S)$ is simpler than its counterpart for $Inst(S)$. In particular, if a problem is decidable for $Inst(S)$, it is also decidable for $Cont(S)$. On the other hand, if a problem is undecidable for $Inst(S)$, the undecidability of its counterpart for $Cont(S)$ may be harder to prove. We will face this situation later in this section.

Note another difference with the tree case: in contrast to trees, we may allow variables in word patterns to be substituted by the empty word. This gives rise to two cases depending of whether this possibility is allowed or not. Following Kari et al. [KMPS95], we call these cases *erasing* (*E-case* for short), if substituting by the empty word is allowed, and *non-erasing* (*NE-case*), if it is not allowed. We will generally speak about the NE-case, unless the E-case is explicitly mentioned.

An early result of Angluin [Ang80] asserts that problem P1.1 is NP-complete. This implies that P1.2 is also NP-complete, as $w \in Inst(p)$ iff $\#w\# \in Cont(\#p\#)$ where # is a fresh letter. This NP-completeness result immediately shows that the word case appears to be much more difficult, as P1.1 and P1.2 are polynomial problems in the tree case, of low polynomial degree. However, if pattern p is linear, P1.1 and P1.2 can be solved in linear time, as they actually reduce to the well-known string matching problem, and can be solved, e.g., by the Knuth-Morris-Pratt algorithm [CR95]. In the general case, the naive algorithm solving P1.1 is in $O(|w|^{\Delta})$ (respectively $O(|w|^{\Delta+2})$ for P1.2), where Δ is the number of distinct variables in p. Néraud [Nér95] showed how this complexity can be slightly reduced (roughly, the exponent can be decreased by 2) and obtained some specialized efficient algorithms for P1.2 for the cases of low Δ (1 or 2).

Proposition 4. *In the word case, problems P1.1 and P1.2 are NP-complete. Both problems can be solved in linear time if pattern p is linear.*

The difficulty of matching problems P1.1 in the case of words can be also illustrated by the fact that if a word w is matched by a pattern p, that is $w = \sigma(p)$, then substitution σ does not have to be unique. For example, pattern xy can match a word w in $(|w| - 1)$ different ways, corresponding to the factorizations of w into two parts. It is easy to see that many patterns admit this situation (e.g. all linear patterns), but not all of them – for example, patterns x, xx (and more generally, one-variable patterns) have a unique way to match a word. Formally, a pattern p is called *non-ambiguous* if there is a unique way for p to match each word of $Inst(p)$, and *ambiguous* otherwise. The ambiguity of patterns was studied by Mateescu and Salomaa [MS94]. They introduced the notion of *degree of ambiguity* of a pattern p defined as the maximal number of ways for p to match a word from $Inst(p)$ provided this number is finite; otherwise the degree of ambiguity is ∞. It is easy to exhibit patterns with the degree of ambiguity 1 or ∞, and much more difficult with a finite degree of ambiguity different from 1. In [MS94], it was shown that pattern $p = xabxbcayabcy$ has the degree of ambiguity 2. For example, there are two ways for p to match the word *caabcabcaabcbcabcabcbc*, and any word from $Inst(p)$ is matched by p in at most two ways. The authors also found a pattern of degree of ambiguity 3, and by some composition technique, patterns of any degree 2^m3^n. However, they state it as an open question if *every* finite degree of ambiguity is realizable by some pattern. The decidability status of determining if the degree of ambiguity of a pattern is finite, is also open.

Let us now turn to problem P3. A striking result has been proved in [JSSY93]: inclusion $Inst(p) \subseteq Inst(S)$ is undecidable even if S consists of a single pattern. This contrasts to the fact that the equivalence problem $Inst(p_1) = Inst(p_2)$ is trivial: the equivalence holds iff p_1 and p_2 are equal modulo a variable renaming. The latter is however true only in the NE-case, and for the E-case the decidability status of the equivalence problem $Inst(p_1) = Inst(p_2)$ is open. We also point out to paper [Fil88] for some results about the inclusion problem $Inst(p_1) \subseteq Inst(p_2)$ in the E- and NE-case.

Proposition 5. *In the word case, problem P3 is undecidable even if S consists of a single pattern.*

Formally, the undecidability result of [JSSY93] for problem P3 does not imply the undecidability of problem P4 (see the discussion in the beginning of this section). Problem P4 has been studied in [KR95b], where it has been proved undecidable.

Proposition 6. *In the word case, problem P4 is undecidable.*

An interesting feature of the proof of [KR95b] is that it implies that the problem $Inst(p) \subseteq Cont(S)$ remains undecidable if p has a very simple form, namely the form axa, where a is a letter and x a variable. It seems very difficult (if at all possible) to further simplify p. We will come back to this issue below.

Based on the proof of the result of [KR95b], we now establish a new result.

Theorem 3. *In the word case, problem P2.1 is undecidable.*

Proof. We give a very general idea of the proof. To reconstruct the details, the reader is referred to [KR95b].

First, we review the proof of [KR95b] of Proposition 6. To show that $Inst(axa) \subseteq Inst(S)$ is undecidable, the construction of S is based on the following idea. The instances of $p = axa$ are assumed to encode runs of a given deterministic Minsky (two-register) machine M on a given data d. Patterns of S are designed in such a way that every instance of p which does not encode a correct run of machine M on data d, contains some pattern from S. To put it in another way, an instance of p which does not contain any pattern of S, must encode a correct finite run of machine M on data d. Therefore, there exists an instance of p which does not contain an instance of S iff M halts on d, which is an undecidable property.

To prove Theorem 3, we modify the proof as follows. We modify the set of patterns S in such a way that S encodes only a Minsky machine M, and does not specify any input data d. Assume that S' is the modified set of patterns. Consider now the set of patterns

$$\tilde{S} = \{\alpha x | \alpha \in A,\ \alpha \neq a\} \cup \{x\alpha | \alpha \in A,\ \alpha \neq a\} \cup \{xpy | p \in S' \text{ and } x, y \text{ do not occur in } p\}, \quad (1)$$

where a is the same letter as in the pattern p above. From the previous discussion, it is clear that the words which are in $\overline{Inst(\tilde{S})}$ are words of the form awa, which are not instances of S'. By construction of S', these are words which encode a correct finite run of the machine M on some input data. Since it is undecidable if a machine stops on a finite number of input data, it is undecidable if the set $\overline{Inst(\tilde{S})}$ is finite or not.

The decidability status of Problem P2.2 is open [KMPS95]. The inverse problem, whether a given regular language is expressible as $Inst(S)$ is also not known to be decidable. It is also open if it is decidable for a language $Inst(S)$ to be context-free. However, it was proved in [KMPS95] that it is undecidable if a given context-free language is expressible as $Inst(S)$.

Let us now consider problem P5.1. The proof of Theorem 3 above may suggest that P5.1 is not so much different from P2.1 and must be also undecidable by a similar proof. Indeed, all "important" patterns occur in the third set of (1), and patterns in the first and the second sets are extremely simple – they consists of a single letter followed or preceded by a variable. However, these "extremely simple" patterns play a crucial role as they actually specify the first and last letter in the words of the language, which is necessary for an undecidability proof (see [KR95b]).

The decidability status of Problem 5.1 is open. Actually, it is the most general version of the famous *avoidability* problem. The avoidability problem was studied in the word combinatorics under a very restricted form – when S contains a single pattern p, and moreover, p contains only variables and no letters. However, even in this restricted form the problem turns out to be extremely difficult.

It is not known if testing the finiteness of $\overline{Cont(p)}$ is decidable or not. The author of [Cur93] offered 100 US dollars[1] for a solution of this problem.

A pattern p is called *unavoidable* (*blocking* according to the terminology of [Zim84]) if $\overline{Cont(p)}$ is finite, and *avoidable* otherwise. Clearly, p is avoidable iff there exists an infinite word which does not contain (finite) subwords which are instances of p.

[1] 2278.78 russian rubles as for February 12, 1999

Interestingly, a study of avoidability is historically at the origin of word combinatorics and formal language theory. Back to the beginning of the century, Axel Thue obtained his famous construction of an infinite *square-free* word on the three-letter alphabet and an infinite *cube-free* word on the two-letter alphabet. In the terminology of pattern avoidance, a square-free and cube-free word is a word which does not contain respectively the pattern xx and xxx. Trivially, xx is unavoidable on two letters and xxx is unavoidable on one letter. A pattern which is avoidable on four letters but not on three letters has been described in [BEM79]. No pattern is known which is avoidable on k letters but unavoidable on $k-1$ letters for $k > 4$.

The above discussion shows that the size of the alphabet may be crucial in avoiding patterns. We refer to [Cas94] for a survey of the state-of-the-art in pattern avoidance. A key result in the area is an algorithm proposed independently in [BEM79, Zim84], which decides if *there exists an alphabet* on which a given pattern can be avoided. However, as was mentioned above, it is not known if *for a fixed alphabet* one can decide, given a pattern, if it is avoidable on this alphabet.

The rest of the paper is devoted to analyzing some of our problems in case the set S consists of *linear* patterns. We already mentioned that problems P1.1 and P1.2 can be efficiently solved if p is a linear pattern. For the other problems we will see that although they become decidable in the linear case, they remain untractable.

Note that if S consists of linear patterns, the languages $Inst(S)$ and $Cont(S)$ are regular languages specified by a regular expression of the form

$$\cup_{i=1}^{n} (A^*) w_{i1} A^* w_{i2} \ldots A^* w_{ik_i} (A^*), \tag{2}$$

where w_{ij}'s are words and parenthesis indicate that A^* may or may not occur in the beginning and the end of the expression. Thus, problems P2.2 and P5.2 are always positively answered. Note also that inclusion and equivalence of regular languages specified by general regular expressions is a PSPACE-complete problem (cf [GJ79]).

In [KR95a] problems P4 and P5.1 have been studied under the condition that the patterns of S are linear. As for P4, it has been proved that it is decidable in this case, regardless if p is linear or not. If p is restricted to be linear too, the problem has been proved to be co-NP-complete [KR95a]. The exact complexity of the case when patterns of S are linear but pattern p is not, is not known to us. However, if the maximal number of occurrences of a variable is bounded, the problem remains co-NP-complete.

Proposition 7. *Problem P4 of testing $Inst(p) \subseteq Cont(S)$ is decidable if S consists of linear patterns. If p is linear in addition, the problem is co-NP-complete.*

It was also proved in [KR95a] that if S is restricted to contain linear patterns only, problem P5.1 is co-NP-complete too.

To move on, we need to sketch the co-NP-completeness proofs from paper [KR95a]. Consider problem P4 for the case that pattern p and all patterns of

S are linear. The co-NP-hardness of this problem is easy to show. We refer to [KR95a] for the reduction from MONOTONE-ONE-IN-THREE-SAT. However, proving the membership in co-NP represents a non-trivial part. It amounts to show that if $Inst(p) \not\subseteq Cont(S)$, there is an instance of p *of size polynomial on* $(|S| + |p|)$ which does not contain any pattern from S. Of course, the language $Cont(S)$ and its complement $\overline{Cont(S)}$ are regular, as $Cont(S)$ has form (2). The proof of [KR95a] consisted of defining a compact *deterministic finite automaton* (DFA) for these languages verifying the following key property: although the total size (number of states) of this automaton is exponential in $|S|$, the length of the longest loop-free path from the initial to the finite state is of polynomial length. We refer to [KR95a] for further details.

This property of the automaton allowed to show that in case $Inst(p) \not\subseteq Cont(S)$, the minimal size of an instance of p which is not in $Cont(S)$ has a size polynomial on $|S|$. Similarly, if $\overline{Cont(S)}$ is finite (problem P5.1), we can give a polynomial bound on the length of words in $\overline{Cont(S)}$. This provides a key argument in the co-NP-completeness proof.

Here we use this argument to show the co-NP-completeness of two other problems – P3 (in case p is a linear pattern) and P2.1.

Since P3 is a more general problem than P4 in the word case, P4 is co-NP-hard if p is a linear pattern. Similarly, P2.1 is more general than P5.1 and is then also co-NP-hard. To prove that both of them are in co-NP, we use an adaptation of the deterministic automaton construction from [KR95a] from the language $Cont(S)$ to $Inst(S)$. We skip the details of the construction which would require us too much space, and summarize the results in the following statement.

Theorem 4. *Assuming a linear pattern p and a set of linear patterns S, problems P2.1, P3, P4 and P5.1 are co-NP-complete.*

Finally, for a linear pattern p, following [Shi82], we can build a DFA recognizing $Inst(p)$ in polynomial (linear) time: if $p = (x_0)u_1x_1 \dots x_{n-1}u_n(x_n)$ $(u_i \in A^+, x_i \in X)$, the idea is to build DFA's $D_1, \dots, D_n$ recognizing respectively $Cont(u_1), \dots, Cont(u_n)$, and then to identify the final state of D_i with the initial state of D_{i+1}. This construction implies, in particular, that for the special case of P3 and P4 where p is linear and S consists of a single linear pattern, a solution can be obtained in polynomial time: the question $Inst(p) \subseteq Inst(p')$ is equivalent to the emptiness of the language $Inst(p') \cap \overline{Inst(p)}$ whose DFA is easily derived in polynomial (quadratic) time [HU79].

Proposition 8. *Assuming a linear pattern p and* $S = \{p'\}$ *with* p' *a linear pattern, P3 and P4 can be checked in polynomial time.*

6 Conclusions

In this paper we formulated several language-theoretic problems which are meaningful for any combinatorial structure equipped with a notion of pattern and a substructure relation. We then studied the algorithmic complexity of those problems for two particular structures – trees over a finite signature and words over a finite alphabet. It turns out that the instances of these problems for words and trees cover a large area of research, including seemingly quite unrelated subareas. Some problems on trees have been studied in term rewriting theory, with relation to the theory of tree languages. Some other problems, such as tree matching, have received much attention in the area of algorithm development. Applied to words, those problems have been studied in the area of word combinatorics and formal language theory, including the recent research stream on pattern languages. Again, the matching problem for words has been subject of intensive studies in the algorithmics area. We found it interesting that all these problems can be expressed uniformly as classical problems on languages specified by patterns.

We attempted to give a brief survey of considered problems, putting the stress on comparing the tree and the word case. Moreover, we gave several new results for the word case. We showed that all problems are easier on the tree case than their counterparts for the word case. In particular, except for the matching problem, all problems are decidable in the tree case and undecidable in the word case. For the word case, we gave a special attention to the linear case, where the problems become decidable but, as we have showed, remain of high algorithmic complexity.

References

[Ang80] D. Angluin. Finding patterns common to a set of strings. *J. Comput. System Sci.*, 21:46–62, 1980.

[BEM79] D.R. Bean, A. Ehrenfeucht, and G.F. McNulty. Avoidable patterns in strings of symbols. *Pacific J. Math.*, 85(2):261–294, 1979.

[Cas94] J. Cassaigne. *Motifs évitables et régularités dans les mots.* Thèse de doctorat, Université Paris VI, 1994.

[CHI99] R. Cole, R. Hariharan, and P. Indyk. Tree pattern matching and subset matching in deterministic $o(n \log^3 n)$-time. In *Proceedings of the 10th Annual ACM-SIAM Symposium on Discrete Algorithms, Baltymore, Maryland, January 17-19, 1999*, pages 245–254. ACM, SIAM, 1999.

[CJ97] H. Comon and F. Jacquemard. Ground reducibility is EXPTIME-complete. In *Proceedings, Twelth Annual IEEE Symposium on Logic in Computer Science*, pages 26–34, Warsaw, Poland, 29 June–2 July 1997. IEEE Computer Society Press.

[Com88] H. Comon. *Unification et disunification. Théories et applications.* Thèse de Doctorat d'Université, Institut Polytechnique de Grenoble (France), 1988.

[CR95] M. Crochemore and W. Rytter. Squares, cubes, and time-space efficient string searching. *Algorithmica*, 13:405–425, 1995.

[Cur93] J. Currie. Open problems in pattern avoidance. *American Mathematical Monthly*, 100:790–793, 1993.

[DJ90] N. Dershowitz and J.-P. Jouannaud. *Handbook of Theoretical Computer Science*, volume B, chapter 6: Rewrite Systems, pages 244–320. Elsevier Science Publishers B. V. (North-Holland), 1990. Also as: Research report 478, LRI.

[DJK91] N. Dershowitz, J.-P. Jouannaud, and J. W. Klop. Open problems in rewriting. In R. V. Book, editor, *Proceedings 4th Conference on Rewriting Techniques and Applications, Como (Italy)*, volume 488 of *Lecture Notes in Computer Science*, pages 445–456. Springer-Verlag, 1991.

[Fil88] G. Filè. The relation of two patterns with comparable languages. In R. Cori M. Wirsing, editor, *Proceedings of the 5th Annual Symposium on Theoretical Aspects of Computer Science (STACS '88)*, volume 294 of *Lecture Notes in Computer Science*, pages 184–192, Bordeaux, France, February 1988. Springer.

[GJ79] M. Garey and D. Johnson. *Computers and Intractability. A guide to the theory of NP-completeness.* W. Freeman and Compagny, New York, 1979.

[GP99] G. Gottlob and R. Pichler. Working with ARMs: Complexity results on atomic representations of Herbrand models. In *Proceedings of LICS'99*, 1999. to appear, available from `http://www.dbai.tuwien.ac.at/staff/gottlob/arms.ps`.

[GS84] F. Gécseg and M. Steinby. *Tree automata.* Akadémiai Kiadó, Budapest, Hungary, 1984.

[HH92] D. Hofbauer and M. Huber. Computing linearizations using test sets. In M. Rusinowitch and J.-L. Rémy, editors, *Proceedings 3rd International Workshop on Conditional Term Rewriting Systems, Pont-à-Mousson (France)*, pages 145–149. CRIN and INRIA-Lorraine, 1992.

[HO82] C. M. Hoffmann and M. J. O'Donnell. Pattern matching in trees. *Journal of the ACM*, 29(1):68–95, 1982.

[HU79] J. E. Hopcroft and J. D. Ullman. *Introduction to Automata Theory, Languages and Computation.* Addison-Wesley Publishing Company, Reading, Mass., USA, 1979.

[JK89] J.-P. Jouannaud and E. Kounalis. Automatic proofs by induction in theories without constructors. *Information and Computation*, 82:1–33, 1989.

[JSSY93] T. Jiang, A. Salomaa, K. Salomaa, and S. Yu. Inclusion is undecidable for pattern languages. In Svante Carlsson Andrzej Lingas, Rolf G. Karlsson, editor, *Automata, Languages and Programming, 20th International Colloquium*, volume 700 of *Lecture Notes in Computer Science*, pages 301–312, Lund, Sweden, 5–9 July 1993. Springer-Verlag.

[KMPS95] L. Kari, A. Mateescu, G. Paun, and A. Salomaa. Multi-pattern languages. *Theoretical Computer Science*, 141:253–268, 1995.

[KNRZ91] D. Kapur, P. Narendran, D. J. Rosenkrantz, and H. Zhang. Sufficient completeness, ground-reducibility and their complexity. *Acta Informatica*, 28:311–350, 1991.

[KNZ87] D. Kapur, P. Narendran, and H. Zhang. On sufficient completeness and related properties of term rewriting systems. *Acta Informatica*, 24:395–415, 1987.

[KP98] G. Kucherov and D. Plaisted. The complexity of some complementation problems. submitted, 1998.

[KR95a] G. Kucherov and M. Rusinowitch. Complexity of testing ground reducibility for linear word rewriting systems with variables. In *Proceedings 4th International Workshop on Conditional and Typed Term Rewriting Systems, Jerusalem (Israel)*, volume 968 of *Lecture Notes in Computer Science*, pages 262–275. Springer-Verlag, 1995.

[KR95b] G. Kucherov and M. Rusinowitch. Undecidability of ground reducibility for word rewriting systems with variables. *Information Processing Letters*, 53:209–215, 1995.

[KT92] G. Kucherov and M. Tajine. Decidability of regularity and related properties of ground normal form languages. In M. Rusinowitch and J.-L. Rémy, editors, *Proceedings 3rd International Workshop on Conditional Term Rewriting Systems, Pont-à-Mousson (France)*, pages 150–156. CRIN and INRIA-Lorraine, 1992.

[KT95] G. Kucherov and M. Tajine. Decidability of regularity and related properties of ground normal form languages. *Information and Computation*, 118(1):91–100, April 1995.

[Kuc91] G. A. Kucherov. On relationship between term rewriting systems and regular tree languages. In R. V. Book, editor, *Proceedings 4th Conference on Rewriting Techniques and Applications, Como (Italy)*, volume 488 of *Lecture Notes in Computer Science*, pages 299–311. Springer-Verlag, April 1991.

[LM87] J.-L. Lassez and K. Marriot. Explicit representation of terms defined by counter examples. *Journal of Automated Reasoning*, 3(3):301–318, 1987.

[MS94] A. Mateescu and A. Salomaa. Nondeterminism in patterns. In P. Enjalbert, E.W. Mayr, and K.W. Wagner, editors, *Proceedings of the 11th Annual Symposium on Theoretical Aspects of Computer Science (STACS'94), Caen, France, February 1994*, volume 775 of *Lecture Notes in Computer Science*, pages 661–668. Springer-Verlag, 1994.

[Nér95] J. Néraud. Detecting morphic images of a word: On the rank of a pattern. *Acta Informatica*, 32:477–489, 1995.

[NP92] M. Nivat and A. Podelski, editors. *Tree Automata and Languages.* Studies in Computer Science and Artificial Intelligence 10. North-Holland, 1992.

[Pic99] R. Pichler. The explicit representability of implicit generalizations. submitted, april 1999.

[Pla85] D. Plaisted. Semantic confluence and completion method. *Information and Control*, 65:182–215, 1985.

[RR92] R. Ramesh and I.V. Ramakrishnan. Nonlinear pattern matching in trees. *Journal of the ACM*, 39(2):295–316, April 1992.

[Shi82] T. Shinohara. Polynomial time inference of pattern langages and its applications. In *Proceedings of the 7th IBM Symposium on Mathematical Foundations of Computer Science, Mathematical Theory of Computations/The Complexity of Algorithms*, pages 191–209, 1982.

[VG92] S. Vágvölgyi and R. Gilleron. For a rewriting system it is decidable whether the set of irreducible ground terms is recognizable. *Bulletin of European Association for Theoretical Computer Science*, 48:197–209, 1992.

[Zim84] A.I. Zimin. Blocking sets of terms. *Math. USSR Sbornik*, 47:353–364, 1984. Original version in russian published in 1982, 119 (3), 363–375.

Extensions: A Technique for Structuring Functional-Logic Programs

Rafael Caballero and Francisco J. López-Fraguas*

Departamento de Sistemas Informáticos y Programación
Universidad Complutense de Madrid,
{rafa,fraguas}@sip.ucm.es

Abstract. Monads are a technique widely used in functional programming languages to address many different problems. This paper presents *extensions*, a functional-logic programming technique that constitutes an alternative to monads in several situations. Extensions permit the definition of easily reusable functions in the same way as monads, but are based on simpler concepts taken from logic programming, and hence they lead to more appealing and natural definitions of types and functions. Moreover, extensions are compatible with interesting features typical of logic programming, like multiple modes of use, while monads are not.

1 Introduction

Functional-Logic programming, FLP in short, aims to integrate of functional and logic programming, allowing the use of techniques from both paradigms into the same declarative framework (see [5] for a survey). Moreover, the combination of ideas of the two worlds gives rise to new features specific to FLP. This work should be seen as a contribution in this direction, for it presents a new technique, the *extensions*, that can be used as an alternative to the functional technique of *monads* when programming in a functional-logic language.

The concept of monad comes from category theory, and it has been widely used in functional programming to structure functions, pointing out the essence of the algorithms represented while concealing the data flow and the associated computations [13,14,15].

In several FLP frameworks such as *Escher* [9], *Curry* [6] or our working language, $\mathcal{TOY}$ [3,12], monads can be used directly, yielding the same benefits as in the case of functional programming. However, FLP has a wider range of programming mechanisms, including logical variables, and it should be questioned whether it is possible to define a specific FLP technique to address the same kind of problems from a different point of view. In the rest of the paper we describe such an alternative, the FLP *extensions*. Although lacking the theoretical background and wide range of applications of monads, extensions present some specific advantages, such as:

* Work was partially supported by the Spanish CICYT (project TIC98-0445-C03-02/97 "TREND") and the ESPRIT Working Group 22457 (CCL-II).

D. Bjørner, M. Broy, A. Zamulin (Eds.): PSI'99, LNCS 1755, pp. 297–310, 2000.

• Extensions can replace monads in several different situations, allowing the same expressiveness but using much simpler concepts.

• Multiple modes of use are allowed by extensions, which is not so easy to achieve when defining monads in an FLP context.

• In the case of adding new features to functions, monads enforce the evaluation of both the old and the new values simultaneously. Conversely, extensions can use the new feature only where it is required, thus avoiding unnecessary computations.

2 The FLP Framework: A Succinct Description of $\mathcal{TOY}$

All the programs in the next sections are written in the purely declarative functional-logic language $\mathcal{TOY}$, which is a concrete realization of *CRWL*, a theoretical framework for declarative programming (see [4]). We present here only the subset of the language relevant to this work. A more complete description and a number of representative examples can be found in [3].

A $\mathcal{TOY}$ program consists of *datatype*, *type alias*, *infix operator* definitions, and rules for defining *functions*. Syntax is mostly borrowed from Haskell [7], with the remarkable exception that variables begin with upper-case letters whereas constructor and function symbols use lower-case.

```
infixr 20 :/:
data expr = val real | expr :/: expr

eval:: expr → real
eval (val A) = A
eval (A :/: B) = (eval A)/(eval B)
```

Fig. 1. Monadic variations of the basic evaluator

Our first example of a program written in $\mathcal{TOY}$ may be seen in figure 1. This program is the $\mathcal{TOY}$ version of the evaluator for simple expressions presented by P. Wadler in his article [15], and will be our starting point in order to compare monads and extensions. The evaluator itself is represented by function `eval`, which takes an expression E as the only input parameter, and returns the real number resulting from evaluating E. An expression can be either a real number r, represented as `val r` or a quotient between expressions e_1 and e_2, represented as e_1 :/: e_2.

In general, each function `f` in $\mathcal{TOY}$ is defined by a set of conditional rules of the form

$$\texttt{f}\ t_1\ \ldots t_n\ \texttt{=}\ \texttt{e} \Longleftarrow e_1\ \texttt{==}\ e'_1,\ \ldots,\ e_k\ \texttt{==}\ e'_k$$

where $(t_1 \ldots t_n)$ forms a tuple of linear (i.e. with no repeated variable) constructor terms, and e, e_i, e'_i are *expressions*. No other conditions (except well-typedness) are imposed to function definitions. Rules have a conditional reading: `f` $t_1 \ldots t_n$ can be reduced to `e` if all the conditions $e_1 == e'_1, \ldots, e_k == e'_k$ are satisfied. The condition part is omitted if $k = 0$ (as in our previous example `eval`). The symbol `==` stands for *strict equality*, which is the suitable notion for equality when non-strict functions are considered. With this notion a condition `e == e'` can be read as: `e` and `e'` can be reduced to the same constructor term.

$\mathcal{TOY}$ can introduce non-deterministic computations by different means, but we only need one of them for this discussion, namely the occurrence of *extra* variables in the right side of the rules like in

```
z_list = [0|L]
```

Although in this case `z_list` reduces only to `[0|L]`, the free variable `L` can be later on instantiated to any list. Therefore, any list of integers is a possible value of `z_list`.

Computing in $\mathcal{TOY}$ means solving *goals*, which take the form

$$e_1\ \texttt{==}\ e'_1,\ \ldots,\ e_k\ \texttt{==}\ e'_k$$

giving as its result a substitution for the variables in the goal making it true. Evaluation of expressions (required for solving the conditions) is done by a variant of lazy narrowing based on a sophisticated strategy, called *demand driven strategy* which uses the so-called *definitional trees* [2] to guide unification with patterns in left-hand sides of rules (see [8]). For instance, using the evaluator defined above we may try the goal:

```
eval (val 16 :/: val 4 :/: val 1 :/: val 8) == R
```

which yields `R == 0.5`.

As an aside, we remark that the current version of our language does not incorporate *lambda* abstractions or *let* constructions. However, these syntactic facilities are usual in the functional programming literature, and we have included them in some of our examples in order to fairly represent the monadic approach. For testing the examples in the actual implementation, we have simply needed to 'lift' such constructions using well-known techniques [10].

3 Funcional-Logic Monads

In this section we present two variations of the basic evaluator, following the lines of Wadler's paper [15]. We also recall briefly some of the basic concepts concerned with monads, which will be useful when comparing monads and extensions. However, we will not delay very much at this point, assuming that the definition and usefulness of monads are well-known, and referring to the cited article for a deeper discussion of these issues.

To convert a function *f::A* $\rightarrow$ *B* to monadic form we change its type to *f::A* $\rightarrow$ *m B*, meaning that function *f* accepts a parameter of type *A* and returns a value of type *B*, with an associated computation represented by *m*. The structure of the function will be based on the functions *unit:: A* $\rightarrow$ *m A* (also known as *result*) and *(*)::m A* $\rightarrow$ *(A* $\rightarrow$ *m B)* $\rightarrow$ *m B* (usually called *bind*) and indicates how the value *B* is constructed, avoiding any explicit reference to the computation *m*. Only *unit* and * (and perhaps some auxiliary functions) will 'know' what *m* is actually, and how to deal with it. If we want to add some extra capabilities to the original code of *f* later, we only need to look for an appropriate data constructor *m'* that captures the essence of the modification. Then we redefine the type of the function to *f::A* $\rightarrow$ *m' B*, define the new versions of * and *unit* and, perhaps, make a few local changes in the code of the function itself, but always keeping the same basic structure.

Figure 2 shows two 'classical' variations of the original evaluator.

```
type state = int

type m A = state → (A,state)

unit:: A → m A
unit A X = (A,X)

infixr 30 *
(*)::m A → (A → m B) → m B
(*) M K S = let (A,S2) = M S
            in K A S2

tick :: m ()
tick X = ((),X+1)

eval:: expr → m real
eval (val A) = unit A

eval (A :/: B) =
     eval A * λR1. eval B * λR2.
     tick * λ(). unit (R1/R2)
```

```
type output = string

type m A = (output,A)

unit:: A → m A
unit A = ("",A)

infixr 30 *
(*)::m A → (A → m B) → m B
(X,A) * K = let (Y,B) = K A
            in (X++Y,B)

out::output → m ()
out X = (X,())

eval:: expr → m real
eval (val A) = out(line(val A) A)
               * λ().unit A
eval (A :/: B) =
     eval A * λR1. eval B * λR2.
     out (line (A :/: B) (R1/R2))
      * λ().unit (R1/R2)
```

Fig. 2. Monadic variations of the basic evaluator

The first variation, is based on the very useful *state monad*, taken from [15] and adapted to $\mathcal{TOY}$ syntax, which is used to count the total number of divisions performed while evaluating the expression. The second variation produces a trace of the evaluation. This last variation uses a function `line` which produces a step of the trace and may be defined as:

```
line T R = "eval(" ++  showterm T ++  ")⟸ " ++
                number_to_string R ++  "\n"
```

assuming suitable definitions for `showterm` and `number_to_string`. The infix operator `++` is the standard function for concatenation of lists. It can be seen that the basic structure of `eval` is kept almost unaffected. If we had modified the initial code directly, this would have been more difficult to achieve.

4 Functional-Logic Extensions

In the previous section we have sketched how the monadic approach can be adopted in $\mathcal{TOY}$. Now it is time to present the alternative provided by our FLP extensions.

4.1 An Informal Introduction to Extensions

The idea of FLP extensions is quite simple, and constitutes itself a good example of mixing the resources of logic and functional programming:

Suppose we would like to add a new capability of type C to a given function $f::A \to B$. Then, all we need to do is to *extend* the type of the function to $f::A \to B \to C$, meaning that the old returned value is now an *output parameter*, while the new value is introduced as the *result* of the function.

Consider the initial basic evaluator and suppose we want to enrich the capabilities of the function

```
eval::expr → real
```

by associating a new value of type `C` to the currently returned real number. Then, we extend the function with the new feature, changing its type to

```
eval::expr → real → C
```

Of course the definition of `eval` also needs to be modified, acknowledging that the result of the evaluation is no longer the result of the function, but an output parameter.

In order to hide the way the values of type `C` are composed we define a combinator

```
(*)::C → C → C
```

Hence the second rule for `eval` will have the shape

```
eval (A :/: B) R = eval A R1 * eval B R2 ...
```

with the values `R`, `R1`, `R2` standing for the result of the evaluation of `A :/: B`, `A` and `B` respectively. The problem of constructing the new result of the function seems to be solved: `eval A R1` and `eval B R1` are actual values of type `C` related to the 'old' values `R1` and `R2`, and therefore can be combined by using `*`. If later we change `C` by `C'` we only need to change the definition of `*` but not the basic structure of `eval`.

However, we still need to associate the value `R1/R2` with the result of the evaluation `R`. This will be performed by function `unit`, which must 'identify' `R` and `R1/R2`. In order to generalize the definition to other situations, both values `R` and `R1/R2` will be input parameters of `unit`. The logical way of adding `unit` to the definition of `eval` is simply by using `*`:

```
eval (A :/: B) R = eval A R1 * eval B R2 * unit (R1/R2) R
```

This means that `unit` should return a value of type C and, since we said above that the result of the functions was already properly constructed by `eval A R1 * eval B R2` , the value of `unit` must be a truly *unit value* with respect to the operation `*`. Therefore given a *unit element* `e` of type `C`, we can define `unit` as

```
unit::real → real → C
unit A A = e
```

where the repeated variable is just a 'syntactic sugar' of

```
unit A B = e ⟸ A==B
```

That is, `unit` returns `e` if the strict equality `A==B` succeeds. This produces the desired identification between the result `R` and `R1/R2`.

4.2 Extensions of the Basic Evaluator

The 'extension counterpart' of the monadic variations presented in the previous section may be seen in figure 3. The type `C` of our discussion is represented respectively by the types `trans` and `output`, while the unit elements are `id` and `" "`, where the standard function `id` is defined as usual:

```
id X = X
```

Further details about these examples may be found in section 5.

4.3 Definition of Extension

A *FLP extension* is a tuple *(b, unit, *)* where b is an specific type, *unit* is a function of type $A \to A \to b$ and definition *unit* $A\ A = e,\ e \in b$, and where * is a function of type $b \to b \to b$ such as (e, *) is a monoid.

```
type state = int
type trans = state → state

unit:: A → A → trans
unit A A = id

infixr 30 *
(*)::trans → trans → trans
(*) M K S = K S2 ⇐= M S == S2

tick :: trans
tick = (1+)

eval:: expr → real → trans
eval (val A) R = unit A R

eval (A :/: B) R =
    eval A R1 * eval B R2 *
    unit (R1/R2) R * tick
```

```
type output = string

unit:: A → A → output
unit A A = ""

infixr 30 *
(*)::output → output → output
M * K = M ++ K

out::output
out = id

eval:: expr → real → output
eval (val A) R = unit A R *
    out (line (val A) A)
eval (A :/: B) R =
    eval A R1 * eval B R2 *
    unit (R1 / R2) R *
    out (line (A :/: B) R)
```

Fig. 3. Extensions of the basic evaluator

Now it can be proved easily that the variations of figure 3 are actually extensions. For example, the pair (“”,++) used in the output extension is known to satisfy the properties of monoids. The proof for the other case is quite straightforward. Although this definitions lacks the theoretic background of the definition of monad, the structure of monoid is enough to prove some simple assertions about the functions defined using `*` and `unit` in the same line as that of [15].

5 A Comparative Survey

So far we have presented two ‘classical’ variations of the basic evaluator, using both extensions and monads. Now we can present a first comparative study of the two techniques. In the following points we show some of the advantages of using extensions that can be checked directly in the examples.

• The definitions of types for extensions are simpler than in the case of monads. Indeed, we do not need to worry about how to combine the old and the new value, while monads need to define a suitable type constructor `m`. For example, in order to add the output trace to the basic evaluator, we have defined the type

```
type output = string
```

while the monadic version needs also define

```
m A = (A, output)
```

• As a consequence of the previous point, functions `unit` and `*` admit simpler definitions. For instance

```
(*):: output → output → output
M * K = M ++K
```

indicates that the result of combining two outputs is the concatenation of both of them. Observe, in particular, the symmetrical aspect of the type of `(*)`. This definition seems more readable than the monadic variation:

```
(*):: m A → (A → m B) → m B
(X,A) * K =  let (Y,B) = K A in (X++Y,B)
```

• The symmetrical definition of * also entails some practical consequences, as it allows the programmer to change the order of the combined values. Thus we do not need to end the sequence with a `unit` expression, as in the case of monads. For instance, take the second rule for `eval` in the output monad:

```
eval (A :/: B) = eval A * λR1. eval B *
                 λR2. out (line (A :/: B) (R1/R2)) *
                 λ(). unit (R1/R2)
```

It would better to change the order of `unit` and `out`, writing instead

```
eval (A :/: B) = eval A * λR1. eval B * λR2. unit (R1/R2)
                 *λR. out (line (A :/: B) R)
```

avoiding the unnecessary repeated calculation of $R1/R2$ and separating the *side effect* from the main computation, but this is not possible without changing the definition of `out`. However the definition of * for extensions allows us to write

```
eval (A :/: B) R = eval A R1 * eval B R2 * unit (R1/R2) R
                   * out (line (A :/: B) R)
```

where $R1/R2$ is computed only once.

• The separation between the old and the new values also benefits the definitions of auxiliary functions such as `tick` or `out`. For example, as `tick` must increase the state we need only write

```
tick = (1+)
```

instead of the monadic definition

```
tick X = ((),X+1)
```

These straightforward definitions also avoid the useless dummy variables and values () that appear in the monadic definitions.

Of course, extensions have some disadvantages like any other programming technique. We can point out the following drawbacks:

• Monads are a more abstract technique. They are based upon deep theoretical results and can be applied to a number of different areas beyond programming, such as type inference or semantics, while extensions are hitherto just a specific methodology of FLP.

• Some monads cannot be thought of in terms of extensions, because they are not meant to add new values to a previously given function. For instance, *lists* may be seen as a monad (see [15]), while they cannot be defined in terms of extensions.

Therefore, extensions cannot be applied to the same situations as monads. And, can monads substitute extensions? In Section 6 we will present some applications of extensions that cannot be accomplished by monads, hence showing that neither of both techniques may be subsumed into the other one.

6 Other Features of Extensions

Extensions and monads look quite similar, but actually they can be used to solve different problems. We have pointed out in Section 5 some limitations of extensions. Now we are going to show how extensions can be used in two situations where monads cannot be readily applied.

6.1 Avoiding Unnecessary Computations

Monads (as well as extensions) allow one to increase the capabilities of functions while keeping their basic structures unaffected. Of course, these extra features also entail extra computation time. The efficiency of the two techniques is quite similar (both in time and space) when the extra features are computed. However the situation changes remarkably in the points of the program where still only the old value of the function is required. This may be specially extreme when dealing with the state monad (or extension).

Imagine for example that we need a variation of the evaluator of expressions that not only computes the resulting real number but also maintains an ordered list with the numbers that appear in the expression. Such variation may be seen in figure 4 using monads and extensions
with the function `insert` defined as usual. Functions `*`, `unit` and types `m A` and `trans` have not been included for they are those of the state variations we showed before (figures 2 and 3). Here function `tick` is used to insert an element in the ordered list, while the initial state is the empty list. For example, using extensions we may try

```
eval (val 8 :/: val 4 :/: val 2) R [] == L
```

`type state = [real]`	`type state = [real]`
`tick :: real → m ()` `tick A S = ( (), insert A S)`	`tick :: real → trans` `tick A = insert A`

`eval:: expr → m real`
`eval (val A) = tick A * λ().unit A`
`eval (A :/: B) = eval A *`
`λR1.eval B *`
`λR2. unit (R1/R2)`
	`eval:: expr → real → trans`
	`eval (val A) R = tick A * unit A R`
	`eval (A :/: B) R = eval A R1 *`
	`eval B R2 *`
	`unit (R1/R2) R`

Fig. 4. Evaluator yielding an ordered list, using monads (left) and extensions (right)

which returns the values

```
R == 4
L == [2, 4, 8]
```

However, it is possible that we might still need to evaluate expressions just to get the result, dismissing the list. In this case, the insertion of all the elements in the list is an unnecessary overweight that should be avoided. Using extensions this can be done by simply not providing the initial state [] to the goal. Then the result of evaluating the expression is computed as usual, but the state is returned as a 'chain of actions' not evaluated yet, as is witnessed by the goal

```
eval (val 8 :/: val 4 :/: val 2) R == L
```

that returns

```
R == 4
L == (insert 8 * id) * ((insert 4 *id) * (insert 2 *id) *id) *id
```

Thus the actual insertion in the list is not carried out, and we can define a function `eval'` as

```
eval' Expr = R ⟸ eval Expr R == _
```

Note that this cannot be done by using monads, because the two values, the numeric result and the list are actually parts of a single value. Effectively, if we do not provide the initial state to the monadic variation, a goal like

```
eval (val 8 :/: val 4) == L
```

yields an expression of the shape

```
L == (tick 8 * λ().unit 8) * λR1.(tick 4 * λ().unit 4) *
     λR2.unit(R1/R2)
```

because functions `tick`, `unit` and `*` cannot be reduced until a initial state is provided. Thus we can either compute both the result and the ordered list, or neither.

The use of the function `eval'` whenever the list is not required can speed up the program considerably. Checked with a expression of 300 numbers, we have found out that the differences of time between `eval'` and `eval` using extensions, can vary from $0'38s$ to $5'10s$. And, despite the big chain of `insert` and `id` functions that `eval'` must construct, the space required is also less than in the case of actually performing the insertions with `eval`.

6.2 A Parser for Free

Consider the boolean expressions defined as

```
infixr 20 :/\:
infixr 15 :\/:

data expr = val bool | expr :/\: expr | expr :\/: expr
```

Suppose that we decide to define a evaluator `evalb` for this expressions, returning not only the result of the evaluation, but also a suitable representation of the expression. The code for such function may be seen in the figure 5, using monads (left side) and using extensions (right side), and is a simple application of the `output` feature presented before.

Functions `or` and `and` are defined as usual in functional programming, while function `conv` may be easily defined as

```
conv true  = "T"
conv false = "F"
```

For example, using the monadic variation, we may try

```
evalb (val true :/\: (val false :\/: val true)) == R
```

which returns

```
R == ( "(T and (F or T))" , true )
```

Suppose now that, after evaluating a few expressions using the new variation, we decide that representations like `"(T and (F or T))"` are definitely nicer and more readable than

```
evalb (val true :/\: (val false :\/: val true))
```

```
evalb:: expr → m bool

evalb (val A) = out (conv A) *
     λ _. unit A

evalb (A :\/: B) =
     out "(" * λ(). evalb A *
     λ R1. out " or " * λ().
     evalb B * λR2. out ")" *
     λ(). unit (R1 `or` R2)

evalb (A :/\: B) =
     out "(" * λ(). evalb A *
     λ R1. out " and " * λ().
     evalb B * λR2. out ")" *
     λ(). unit (R1 `and` R2)
```

```
evalb:: expr → bool → output

evalb (val A) R = out (conv A) *
     unit A R

evalb (A :\/: B) R =
     out "(" * evalb A R1 *
     out " or " *
     evalb B R2 *
     unit (R1 `or` R2) R * out ")"

evalb (A :/\: B) R =
     out "(" * evalb A R1 *
     out " and " *
     evalb B R2 *
     unit (R1 `and` R2) R * out ")"
```

Fig. 5. Boolean evaluator with output, using monads and extensions

and that we would like to define a version of `evalb` accepting strings representing expressions as input parameter. Does it mean that now we need to define a parser for boolean expressions? The answer is *no, if we use extensions.* Indeed, the extension of the boolean evaluator showed in the figure 5 can be used as a parser without making any changes, as witnessed by the goal

```
evalb Expr R == "(F and (F or T))"
```

which succeeds with

```
Expr == val false :/\: (val false :\/: val true)
R == false
```

This nice outcome of extensions is an example of the *generate & test* techniques, very usual in logic programming. Therefore, ours is actually a recursive top-down parser of the grammar rules expressed in `evalb` by means of `output` (for terminals) and recursive calls of `evalb` (for non-terminals).

But, why is it not possible to use the monadic variation in this case? It is due to the combination of the string representation and the output value, which is a free variable. For example, the goal

```
evalb Expr == ("(F and T)",R)
```

loops. We must recall that strict equality does a 'careful matching' as we showed before. In the example, this means generating the outer constructor of both `"(F` and T)" and R by means of evalb Expr. But getting an outer constructor for R entails generating a whole expression, and by using the second rule of evalb, infinite expressions may be generated. These expressions, all of which have an or in their representations, when finally compared with (F and T), fail.

7 Conclusions

We have shown throughout this paper that extensions are a suitable mechanism to solve a number of problems when working in a functional-logic language. Although lacking the deep theoretical background of monads, extensions can be used as an alternative to define easily reusable code. The concepts used are simple, and were already known in each declarative paradigm, such as the use of arguments in logic programming to return output values, or the definition of higher order combinators (e.g. *) in order to connect different computations in sequence. The novelty of our approach is that it combines techniques of both main declarative streams, yielding a new mechanism that allows us to address problems, as the addition of new features to functions, in a simple and appealing way. Specifically, extensions avoid the necessity of lambda abstractions, provide a more symmetric definition of the combinator * – from the point of view of types – and lead to nicer and more natural definitions of types and auxiliary functions.

In spite of all the resemblances, extensions and monads are different techniques, each one with its own particularities and limitations. An advantage of extensions is that they provide functions with the possibility of multiple modes of use, therefore defining functions that can be reused in a wider sense than in the case of monads. Another advantage is that the state extension allows one to dismiss the stateful computations whenever they are not interesting, hence saving both time and space.

References

1. S. Antoy , R. Echahed, M. Hanus. *A Needed Narrowing Strategy.* 21st ACM Symp. on Principles of Programming Languages, 268–279, Portland 1994.
2. S. Antoy. *Definitional Trees,* In Proc. ALP'92, Springer LNCS 632, 1992, 143–157.
3. R. Caballero-Roldán, F.J. López-Fraguas and J. Sánchez-Hernández. *User's Manual For TOY* . Technical Report D.I.A. 57/97, Univ. Complutense de Madrid 1997. The system is available at `http://mozart.sip.ucm.es/incoming/toy.html`
4. J.C. González-Moreno, T. Hortalá-González, F.J. López-Fraguas, M. Rodríguez-Artalejo. *An Approach to Declarative Programming Based on a Rewriting Logic.* Journal of Logic Programming, Vol 40(1), July 1999, pp 47–87.
5. M. Hanus. *The Integration of Functions into Logic Programming: A Survey.* J. of Logic Programming 19-20. Special issue "*Ten Years of Logic Programming*", 583–628, 1994.
6. M. Hanus (ed.). *Curry, an Integrated Functional Logic Language*, Draft, February 1998. Available at `http://www-ir.informatik.rwth-aachen.de/ hanus/curry/report.htlm`

7. *Report on the Programming Language Haskell: a Non-strict, Purely Functional Language.* Version 1.4, Peterson J. and Hammond K. (eds.), January 1997.
8. R. Loogen, F.J. López-Fraguas,M. Rodríguez-Artalejo. *A Demand Driven Computation Strategy for Lazy Narrowing.* Procs. of PLILP'93, Springer LNCS 714, 184–200, 1993.
9. Lloyd, J.W. *Declarative Programming in Escher.* Technical Report CSTR-95-013, Departament of Computer Science, University of Bristol, June 1995.
10. S.L. Peyton-Jones. *The implementation of functional languages*, Prentice Hall, 1987.
11. S.L. Peyton-Jones, P. Wadler. *Imperative functional programming*, 20 Annual Symposium on Principles of Programming Languages, Charleston, South Carolina, 1993.
12. F.J. López-Fraguas, J. Sánchez-Hérnandez. *$\mathcal{TOY}$: A Multiparadigm Declarative System.* Proc. RTA'99, Springer LNCS 1631, 244–247, 1999.
13. P. Wadler. *Comprehending Monads*, Proc. ACM Conf. on Lisp and Functional Programming, 1990.
14. P. Wadler. *The essence of functional programming*, Proc. ACM conference on the Principles of Programming Languages, pages 1-14, 1992.
15. P. Wadler. *Monads for functional programming.* In J. Jeuring and E. Meijer editors, Lecture Notes on Advanced Functional Programming Techniques, Springer LNCS 925. 1995

Language Tools and Programming Systems in Educational Informatics

S.S. Kobilov

Samarkand State University
703004, Samarkand-4, University Bl., 15
andrey@bisr.silk.org

Abstract. The present work is oriented on the description of the elementary educational informatics based on the programming support environment. The environment structure and its components developed on national languages are being investigated. The problems of language tools and program development system as well as computer support and informatics systems are being studied.

1 Introduction

Educational informatics provides elementary computer knowledge [1]. This course should be supplied with a special teaching conception (model). Educational informatics can be considered as an elementary subject (such as mathematics, physics, biology), but it has two peculiarities which should be taken into consideration:

1. Methodological and technological basis and methods of teaching are being rapidly changed;
2. It needs constant support with special technical, language and programming means. That's why the chosen teaching model and implementation of its program language support should take into account these peculiarities.

We present one of the educational informatics models and introduce the ways of developing language tools and programming systems aimed to support this model. The paper consists of three parts and a conclusion. The first part deals with the description of informatics teaching model. The peculiarities of development of complex components are introduced in the second and third parts.

2 Informatics Teaching Model

At present different methods are used in conceptual development of informatics teaching. One of them is the usage of the vanguard style directed to the study of logic-mathematical base of algorithmization and elements of programming. Taking this model as the basis, we can offer the informatics teaching model. Its general strategy consists in the following five principles:

D. Bjørner, M. Broy, A. Zamulin (Eds.): PSI'99, LNCS 1755, pp. 311–315, 2000.

1. Subject-tool informatics usage. Informatics is studied via computer means and informatics technology is used to support the universal ways of educational activities [1];
2. Learners' qualification. The main accent is made on teaching algorithmics and programming;
3. Knowledge in algorithms base structures and typical programming methods. Constant interconnection between algorithmization and programming is demonstrated, and "smooth" transition from one level to another is shown;
4. Usage of the native language. Teaching is aimed at the learner's native language with the use of language-program means and technological methods based on national interface;
5. Multinational tools. Language, program and technological means of study are developed with account of their adaptation to various lexicons.

The functional purpose of such a method and language tools and programming systems is to satisfy needs of the informatics teaching model for senior pupils and junior students.

3 Language Tools

Language tools contain a special language used for the description of algorithms and a programming language of higher level.

Algorithmic Language. A special algorithmic language (SAL) [2] has chosen as the algorithmic language. This language has different notations, close to the natural language, algorithms in it can be written and read as a usual text and, what is more, the study of this language will help one to get more profound knowledge of any programming language in the future. Another important aspect of SAL is that its structure is close to algorithmic mentality of a learner, it has no goto command, which satisfies the reguirements of structural construction, and there are no details connected with the computer device.

For easy usage and realization needs, some changes and additions were made to SAL, such as introduction of two new commands (**input** and **output**) which are used for intermediate data input and output; specification of dynamic tables; the usage of key words without underlining and linear notation of expressions, etc., as in modern programming languages (PL).

Programming Language. We have chosen Pascal/R [3] which has the basic Russian notation of Standard Pascal [4]. In general, we can state two main factors having effect on defining the language tools.

The first is the choice of the minimum necessary structures sufficient for initial study of algorithms and programming and traditional for many modern languages. Some data types, as well as statements and special Pascal functions, were excluded. The **label**, data type **set**, variant **record**, **goto** statement, cycle statements of the type **for... downto** and **repeat...until** were reduced and the procedures **get**(f) and **put**(f) of the processing file f were not used. For practical needs data types **string** and **string**[n] were included into the language, as well as two new procedures of file processing (Close and Assign) of the programming language Turbo Pascal.

The second factor is connected with the national lexicons of the language means. That is why they were localized on the other languages (Russian, Uzbek, Tajik) on the basis of Cyrillic and Latin graphics. Thus, algorithmics and programming should be studied on the basis of the native language of the learner, and input languages of the system should have modifiable lexical structure.

4 Programming Systems

The programming complex consists of a specialized system on the basis of SAL and a programming system (PS) with the localized input language Pascal. The first system is used for computer support of the algorithmic course, and PS, for study of fundamentals of programming. Each of these systems are developed in the form of an integrated environment with common components. The environment is initially produced to support a definite style of constructing and debugging of algorithms (programs). Its components are the working window with the main menu, editor, compiler, help subsystem and data base (DB). Let us briefly discuss the peculiarities of the teaching environment and its components.

The Program Construction and Debugging Style. The environment is oriented at the style of structured construction on the basis of structure editing algorithms. It is also supplied with the debugging display and program running [5]. The structural construction in educational informatics gives the following advantages:

a) This type of construction is closer to operation mentality of a man. It gives the possibility of more adequate description of typical processes in the application area of the task with the help of definite integral constructions of the programming language;

b) It combines the "strict" requirements to the structural and usual types of string editing. The first of them puts limitations on the user actions and is useful in training the beginners;

c) The program becomes an active object at the very beginning and within the process of its construction. Partially, it is ready for use even not being completed. This provides the program check out which step by step ensures the programmer in correctness of his choice and actions.

Another important mechanism of the education process is visualization of debugging and running of a program. To display the process of running, the output facilities should be realized in the system so that the text of the original program should be presented on display with its increased detailed block-scheme, with underlined and coloured areas of constructions' domains and keywords of the language, and values of variables being indicated in the control points.

Working Panel and Main Menu Console. It is known that the interactive mode is the basic in the training systems. It provides interconnection with the pupil. The program start is followed by displaying the main menu at the top of the window. Menu contains options: File, Editing, Translation, Lexics — each can have vertical suboptions. In the lower part of the display there is a prompting string showing the coincidence between the functional keyboards and actions. Using the option Lexic[suboption], a learner chooses the notation for writting algorithms on the basis of SAL (Pascal program) and lexicon of the communication system. Further work is fullfilled in this language environment.

Editor. The embedded system editor has two operation modes — textual and structural. The structural mode is the main one, since in the process of studying PL much attention is given to its syntactical constructions and rules. Editor has both traditional and specialized operations with texts in the structural mode, such as call of language constructions which are kept in the form of "ready-made" pictures, transformation of the source program text into an abstract syntactic tree (AST) and vice versa, reorganization of AST, recognition of elementary errors and output information on them, creation and modification of pictures. At first, the pictures (general structure of algorithms in SAL and of Pascal programs, program items, commands, statements, additional algorithms and subprograms) are kept in the data base and called when needed and, after the processing, "loaded" ("hung") in a definite place of the abstract tree.

For example, the construction

$$\textbf{if}\ \langle\text{condition}\rangle\ \textbf{then}\ \langle\text{statement1}\rangle\ \ \textbf{else}\ \langle\text{statement2}\rangle;$$

is entirely produced on display, while the parts put into brackets are easily deleted and their place is taken by real constructions.

Thus, this principle of structural editing gives us the possibility of program check at each step of the process of its development, being useful for the learner and preventing him from "making errors".

Compiler. The specialized translators of the system on the basis of SAL and PS with Pascal input language are developed in the form of an interpreter. This method is used to simplify its implementation and possesses the following peculiarities. The interpreter opens the perspective of easy process-projecting management, debugging and visualization of programs [6]. Using the interactive mode, we can write, check and run programs, within the interpreter. Errors can be easily corrected. We should not go back to editor and compile the program again. Structural construction and editing [7] provides the intermediate representation and interpretation of incompleted programs. Programming systems can be used for educational purpose and are not aimed to solve the tasks which require immediate actions.

Help Subsystem and Database System. DB is developed on the basis of the electronic textbook ideology. It is supposed to keep the structural information: theoretical, practical and methodological materials (glossaries containing the basic notions and terms of input language, the set of type schemes, demonstration algorithms and programs, as well as many tests aimed to control and evaluate the trainer's knowledge).

The database of environment is organized and kept in the form of a hypertext. The data base files contain texts of the main and intermediate representation programs, educational texts and additional information connected with a definite lexicon. The support of construction and functioning of the components of the help subsystem and the data base is fulfilled by a separate tool system. It contains the set of special operations working with the hypertext, information input, processing, and output in the DB system.

5 Conclusion

The educational model for studying informatics is discussed in this work, as well as the questions of the language tools and programming system development intended to support this model. The general strategy of teaching is based on advanced learning of algorithmics and elements of programming on the basis of a native language. The structure of the complex and requirements on its components including the language and program facilities and hardware support has been defined.

References

1. Ershov A. P. Computerization of Schools and Mathematical Education // Proc. of the Sixth Intern. Congress on Mathematical Education. Budapest, 1988. P. 49—65.
2. Ershov A. P. Basic Concepts of Algorithms and Programming to Be Taught in a School Course in Informatics // Proc. of the Intern. Joint Conf. on Theory and Practice of Software Development (Tapsoft). Berlin, 1985. 14 p.
3. Kobilov S. S. Programming system Pascal/R. In: Important Problems of Application Mathematics and Economics, Samarkand: SSU, 1997, pp. 73—79. (in Russian).
4. Jensen K., Wirth N. Pascal. User Guide and Report. Springer-Verlag,1978.
5. Boltaev T. B., Kuzminov T. V., Pottosin I. V. On Structured Construction and Supporting Tools. In: Programming Environments: Methods and Tools, Novosibirsk, 1992, pp. 22—37. (in Russian).
6. Gries D. Compiler Construction for Digital Computers. John Wiley& Sons, Inc., N 4, 1971.
7. Boltaev T. B. Interpreter of Incompleted Programs. In: Programming Environments: Methods and Tools, Novosibirsk, 1992, pp. 38—50. (in Russian).

Current Directions in Hyper-Programming

Ronald Morrison[1], Richard C.H. Connor[2], Quintin I. Cutts[2], Alan Dearle[3], Alex Farkas[4], Graham N.C. Kirby[1], Robert McGettrick[3], and Evangelos Zirintsis[1]

[1] School of Mathematical and Computational Sciences, University of St Andrews, North Haugh, St Andrews, Fife, KY16 9SS, Scotland
{ron, graham, vangelis}@dcs.st-and.ac.uk

[2] Department of Computer Science, University of Glasgow, Glasgow G12 8QQ, Scotland
{richard, quintin}@dcs.gla.ac.uk

[3] Department of Computing Science and Mathematics, University of Stirling, Stirling, FK9 4LA, Scotland
{al, rmc}@cs.stir.ac.uk

[4] Vision Systems Ltd, Adelaide, S.A., Australia
Alex.Farkas@vsl.com.au

Abstract. The traditional representation of a program is as a linear sequence of text. At some stage in the execution sequence the source text is checked for type correctness and its translated form is linked to values in the environment. When this is performed early in the execution process, confidence in the correctness of the program is raised. During program execution, tools such as debuggers are used to inspect the running state of programs. Relating this state to the linear text is often problematical. We have developed a technique, *hyperprogramming*, that allows the representations of source programs to include direct links (hyper-links) to values, including code, that already exist in the environment. Hyper-programming achieves our two objectives of being able to link earlier than before, at program composition time, and to represent sharing and thus closure and through this the run-time state of a program. This paper reviews our work on hyper-programming and proposes some current research areas.

1 Introduction

Fig. 1, taken from [1], shows an example of a Napier88 hyper-program. The program source, which is itself a persistent object, comprises text and hyper-links to other objects in the persistent store.

The first hyper-link is to a persistent first-class procedure value *writeString* which writes a prompt to the user. The program then calls another procedure *readString* to read in a name, and then finds an address corresponding to that name. This is done by calling a procedure *lookup* to find the address in a table data structure linked into the hyper-program. The address is then written out.

D. Bjørner, M. Broy, A. Zamulin (Eds.): PSI'99, LNCS 1755, pp. 316–340, 2000.

Note that the code objects (*readString*, *writeString* and *lookup*) are denoted using exactly the same mechanism as data objects (the table)[1] and all of these are external to the hyper-program but within the persistent environment.

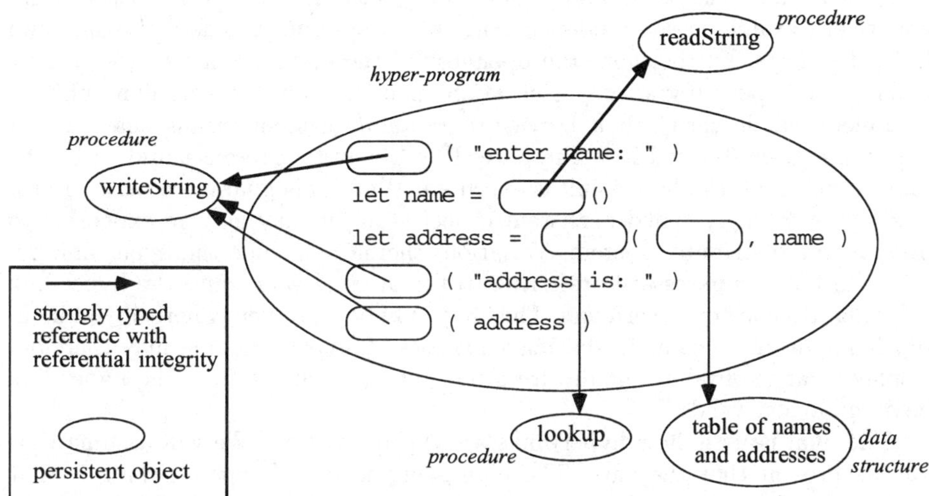

Fig. 1. A Napier88 Hyper-Program

A requirement for hyper-programming is the presence of an external value space to which bindings can be constructed during program composition. The external source may be provided by a persistent store, a file system or any other mechanism such as the WWW. No matter which external source is used, a fundamental change in the nature of the source program has taken place since it now contains both text and hyper-links to values in the environment. This non-flat representation of the program source challenges our traditional notions of what constitutes a computer program. The reason for the name *hyper-program* is the analogy with hyper-text which is also nonflat and contains both text and hyper-links to other hyper-text.

The major issue in building hyper-programming systems concerns the semantics of the hyper-links, such as:

- what can a hyper-link refer to?
- what guarantees can be made about a hyper-links referent data?
- how are hyper-links typed and when does type-checking occur?

The degrees of freedom regarding what a hyper-link can refer to depend upon the programming language semantics and the measure of openness is the

[1] Note also that the names used in this description of the hyper-links have been associated with the objects for clarity only, and are not part of the semantics of the hyper-program.

system. Normally hyper-links will be able to refer to all language first class values. Second class entities, not in the value space such as types, may also be conveniently hyper-linked depending on the flavour of the language. Update may be accommodated through hyper-links by linking to locations, which may or may not be first class values. More interesting is the extent to which hyper-links may refer to values created independently of the system, such as Web pages and DCOM objects. Furthermore the openness of the system can be extended by making the hyper-program representation open for other tools to manipulate.

Referential integrity in a hyper-programming system means that once a hyper-link is established it is guaranteed by the system to exist and to be the same value when the hyper-link is executed. While this guarantee may be provided by a strongly typed persistent object store, it may also be expensive to provide in a distributed system. Variations therefore include the hyper-link being valid but not necessarily referring to the original value, and the hyper-link referring to a copy of the original. This may only be a problem where object identity is important such as in sharing semantics. A hyper-program may therefore display a range of failure modes from not failing to failure from the hyper-link being no longer valid.

The final issue is how hyper-links are typed, if at all. We will assume that for the present that they are. The interesting aspect of type checking is that the contract between the program and the referenced value may now take on a different agreement procedure. Instead of the program asserting the type of the hyper-link and the type checking system ensuring that the hyper-link has the correct type when it is used, the reverse may be used. That is the hyper-link knows its own type and therefore when it is used the program can be made to conform to this type. Statically this removes the need for type specifications for hyper-links in hyper-programs and dynamically it means that the program may be in error rather than the hyper-link.

This paper reviews our work on hyper-programming, discusses the advantages of the technique and proposes some current research areas. These include presenting a single representation of data and code throughout the software process; adapting hyper-programming to persistent contexts that do not enforce referential integrity, such as the WWW; and implementing and using hyper-programming in standardised languages and inter-operability mechanisms.

2 Motivations & Previous Work

Our work on hyper-programming is motivated by a belief that programming language systems could provide better support for the software engineering process than they do at present. In particular, consider the traditional *compose-compile-link-execute* cycle of program development as illustrated in Fig. 2.

In precis, a program is composed using a text-editor; compiled using a compiler, which may also link in other source text; linked with other pre-compiled code; and finally executed where it may link to persistent data such as files. During execution, other tools such as symbolic debuggers and run-time browsers may

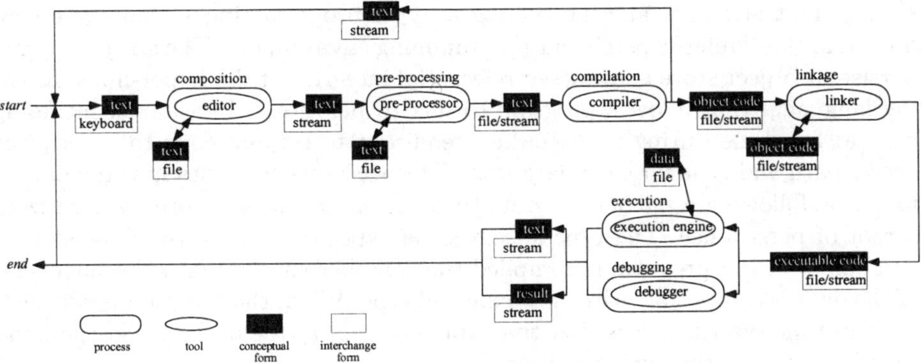

Fig. 2. The Traditional Compose-Compile-Link-Execute Cycle

be used to inspect the running state of the program. Thus there are four main processes: composition, compilation, linking and execution each with their appropriate tools such as text-editors, compilers, linkers, debuggers and browsers. Each tool operates on a particular translated version of the program such as source text, object code or executable code.

There are two obvious questions that may be asked about the compose-compile-link-execute cycle. They are:

- why are there so many processes and translated forms of the program? and
- what level of detail should the user see?

For the systems programmer the processes and translated forms provide the necessary level of control over the cycle. The translated forms allow common tools, such as optimisers, to be used even where the original forms are from disparate sources. The processes are necessary for manipulating the translated forms.

From the applications programmers point of view, the processes and translated forms often constitute noise in the execution cycle and a distraction from the task of constructing the system. Modern programming environments, such as CodeWarrior [2], attempt to hide this level of detail from the applications programmer. Hyper-programming is a further step in this direction and the paper explores how effective the concept can be in different environments.

2.1 Constructing Hyper-Programs

The primary motivation for hyper-programming is to allow the user to compose programs interactively [3, 4], navigating the environment and selecting data items, including code, to be incorporated into the programs. This removes the need to write access specifications for extant data items that are used by a program. For example, in a file system it may be a path name, and in a persistent object store it may be a path to an object from a root of persistence.

Our first attempts at constructing a hyper-programming system were conducted in the Napier88 persistent programming environment. The strongly typed persistent object store guaranteed referential integrity of the hyper-links. Existing languages that allow a program to link to persistent data items, including files, at any time during its execution require it to contain code to specify the access path and type for each data item. The access path defines how the data is found by following a particular route through the persistent store starting from a root of persistence. The type specifies the expected type of the data at that position. When a program is compiled the compiler checks that subsequent use of the data is compatible with this expected type. When the program is executed the run-time system checks that the data is present at the declared position and that it does have the expected type.

This mechanism gives flexibility because a program can link to data in the store at any time during its execution. However in many cases the programmer knows that a particular data item is present in the store at the time the program is written and the programming system could obtain all the information in the access specification by inspecting the data item at that time.

In a hyper-programming system the programmer has the option of linking existing data items into a program by pointing to graphical representations rather than writing access specifications. There are two advantages to this early composition-time linking. Firstly, errors that may occur in programs due to the access specification being invalid at the time of execution are completely avoided. This may occur where the store topology has changed and the access path no longer exists, even if the object does; where the object has been deleted; or where the object has been replaced by one of a different type. In all cases the contract between the program and the persistent store has been broken and the program may not execute safely.

In the hyper-programming system the hyper-link is direct to the object and is guaranteed to be valid, at the time of the program execution, by the persistent stores referential integrity. Thus if the topology of the store changes, the link will still be valid; the object may not be deleted since the hyper-program still has access to it; and it may not change its type.

Fig. 3 shows an example of the user interface that might be presented to the user by a hyper-program editing/browsing tool. The editor window (top-left) contains embedded buttons representing hyper-program links; when a button is pressed the corresponding object is displayed in a browser window (lower region).

The hyper-links to persistent values are placed in the hyper-program by selecting each value with the store browsing tool and then pressing the *Link* button. In Napier88, the system asks the programmer whether to link the program to the value itself or to the store location that currently contains the value. The editor then inserts the link at the current text position, represented by a light-button.

2.2 Safety and Efficiency

Hyper-programming can provide improved safety in several ways. One of these is that it allows some program checks to be performed earlier than normal, sub-

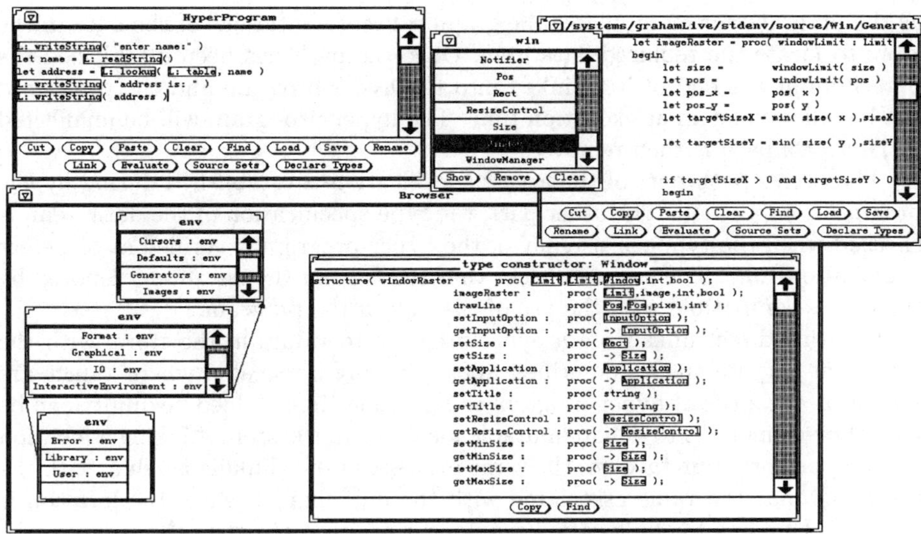

Fig. 3. User Interface to a Hyper-Program Editor

sequently giving increased assurance of program correctness. This is possible because data items accessed by a program may be available for checking before run-time. Referential integrity then ensures that the checked data remains available at run-time.

Checking can be performed at several stages in the program development process in existing systems. The principal opportunities are at compilation-time when a program is translated into an executable program, and at run-time when the executable program is executed. Categories of checking include checking programs for syntactic correctness and type consistency, and checking persistent data access.

Checking Persistent Data Access. In conventional strongly typed persistent systems a program contains an access specification for each persistent data item used. These access specifications are checked at run-time: at that time the system verifies that each data item is present in the store, with the previously declared access path and type.

A program execution will fail if the store does not contain a route to a data item corresponding to the access path specified in the program. Thus even if it is known at the time of writing that a particular program will execute correctly, it cannot be predicted when it may fail on some future execution.

The use of hyper-programs as source representations allows the checking of access specifications to be performed before run-time. Each link in a hyper-program denotes a data item that exists in the store at the time the hyper-program is composed. The process of checking the access path is moved from run-time to program composition time. The access path is established incrementally as the programmer manipulates the graphical representations of the data in the store to locate the required data item. Once the path has been established the data item at the end of it is linked into the hyper-program and the path need not be followed again at execution time. The hyper-pro- gram will be unaffected if the access path is then removed.

The access path part of the access specification is established during hyper-program composition. The other part, the type specification of the data item, is checked when the type consistency of the hyper-program is verified at or before compilation-time. The system checks that the type of the data item denoted by the link is compatible with the use of the link in the program.

Creating direct links from a hyper-program to values in the store, with the attendant safety benefits described above, is only applicable where values are present in the store at hyper-program composition time. Added flexibility can be gained by using links to denote mutable locations in the store. Linking a location into a hyper-program involves the same processes as for linking a value, with the difference that the value associated with the link changes when the location is updated. Updates to the location may occur at any time after the composition of the hyper-program. Strong typing ensures that the type of any value assigned to a location is compatible with the type of its original contents. This allows the type checking of persistent locations to be performed at compilation-time. The values in locations associated with the links in a hyper-program can vary but their types will always remain compatible. Where a link denotes a location, that location is linked directly into the executable program produced from the hyper-program, so that updates to the location also affect the executable program.

2.3 Experience

The benefits of hyper-programming described in [1, 3, 4] may be summarised as:

- being able to perform program checking early
- support for source representations of all object closures
- being able to enforce associations from executable programs to source programs
- availability of an increased range of linking times
- increased program succinctness
- increased ease of program composition

3 Current Work

3.1 Options for Further Development

Hyper-programming as described in the previous section is implemented in Napier88 [5] and using a persistent form of Java, PJama [6]. Both implementations are based on the use of a closed-world, single-language, programming environment. The principle advantage of this is the degree of control that can be exercised over the data and code within the environment. In particular, a type system can be enforced over the entire lifetime of the data and code, and referential integrity can be guaranteed by the environment implementation. Thus, once established, a reference between two components will never become accidentally invalid.

The use of such an environment offers various benefits, as discussed previously, at the cost of limiting flexibility. There are thus two main avenues for further development of the hyper-programming concept:

- to further pursue the benefits of using a closed-world system, accepting the limitations that this implies; and
- to investigate how far the closed-world restrictions may be relaxed to increase flexibility, while retaining at least some of the original benefits of hyper-programming.

Sections 3.2 to 3.4 describe three areas of research based on a closed-world platform: *hyper-code*, in which a single uniform representation of code and data is presented throughout the programming life-cycle; support for application evolution based on tracking relationships between system components using referential integrity; and statically checkable dependant types. Some other areas in which a closed-world could be exploited, although not discussed further here, include:

- version control, configuration management and documentation systems [1]; and
- debugging, profiling and optimisation [7].

Sections 3.5 and 3.6 examine two ways in which the hyper-program platform constraints may be usefully relaxed: constructing programs over an unreliable network such as the World Wide Web; and hyper-programming using commercially significant languages and inter-operability standards, such as C++ [8], CORBA [9], DCOM [10] etc.

3.2 Hyper-Code

One of the original motivations for persistent programming was to remove the conceptually unnecessary distinction between short-term and long-term data [11]. This was followed by the recognition that code and data can usefully be treated in a uniform way [12]. Hyper-programming itself involved a further unifying step in which source programs themselves became persistent data, along with the compilers, editors and other tools with which they were manipulated [4]. There has thus been a progression of attempts to encompass ever more of the disparate entities that comprise a Persistent Application System (PAS) within a unified framework.

Visual interaction with persistent data, such as that provided by generic object browsing systems [13–19], has proved to be a convenient and natural way for database users to address informal queries over the contents of a database. The users of such tools can browse freely around the data structures and values of a database, avoiding the necessity to write down algebraic expressions to perform the equivalent accesses. Where appropriate it is also possible to perform updates or invoke more complex methods over the objects depicted on the screen. Such tools are greatly preferred to a traditional query-based approach for simple queries and updates to persistent data such as held in object-oriented databases.

The advantages of this style of access are comparable to the advantages of a modern iconic operating system interface over a traditional command-line based approach. In addition, however, a more general programming algebra is required so that more complex and longer-running queries may be handled. This rather frustratingly gives rise to two quite separate mechanisms for manipulating the same values within a system, with the choice of mechanism being somewhat arbitrary for tasks in the middle ground between trivial and complex.

Current work on *hyper-code* aims to complete the progressive integration of PAS entities [20], by presenting the programmer with a single representation form for all code and data throughout all stages of the programming process. These stages include at least object store browsing, program construction, execution, debugging and maintenance. The single representation form is based on source code, the argument being that all other forms of code and data are used for pragmatic implementation-driven reasons, rather than being conceptually necessary. Since the representation must be able to accommodate closures, by necessity it is a hyper-program form that can include direct links.

Hyper-code provides the basis for a new style of editor that includes three unifying concepts, the combination of which makes the editor the only mechanism that is required for interaction with the database system. The three important unifying concepts are:

- Data of any type supported by the system may be browsed and edited in a uniform manner. This includes a uniform treatment of procedure closures; a drawback of previous browsers is that they could not adequately handle procedures.
- Source code is treated not as a fundamental building block within the programming system, but instead as a transient text-based view of a value. The source does not have a conceptual permanent existence within the system, but is apparently generated from any value that may be browsed.
- As a further consequence of the generic treatment of procedure values and source code, the artificial distinction between source and executable values within a running system is completely removed.

The major difference between this and other browsers is therefore in the uniform treatment of the executable and source code forms of procedures, and hence programs. Furthermore, the manipulation of code made possible by the unification strategy is sufficiently general to subsume the usual process of program editing, compilation and linking which is normally associated with the manipulation of code bodies within a system. In constructing a program, the programmer writes hyper-code. During execution, during debugging, when a run time error occurs or when browsing existing programs, the programmer is presented with, and only sees, the hyper-code representation. Thus the programmer need never know about those entities that the system may support for reasons of efficiency, such as object code, executable code, compilers and linkers. These are maintained and used by the underlying system but are merely artifacts of how the program is stored and executed, and as such are completely hidden from the programmer.

A consequence of the above is that the hyper-code editor is the only interfacing tool required to perform queries of any complexity against the database, or to introduce new data and program to it. The programmer may thus concentrate on the inherent complexity of the application rather than on that of the support system.

Hyper-Code Operations. The previous hyper-programming implementations in Napier88 [21] and Java [19] approach this ideal, but fall short in two ways. Firstly, the programmer is aware of a distinction between the source and compiled versions of code entities; and secondly, code and data entities are manipulated differently, using an editor and an object browser respectively. Hyper-code removes these distinctions. In the first case, the occurrence of system activities such as compilation and linking is hidden, since they are implementation details — the view presented to the programmer is one of source level interpretation. In the second case, all interaction with the hyper-code system is via a single hyper-code editor that fulfils the functions of both the browser and editor in the previous systems. The hyper-code editor supports only the following operations:

- *evaluate*: this executes a selected fragment of hyper-code and returns the result, if any, as a new hyper-code fragment;
- *explode*: this expands a selected link in a hyper-code fragment to show more detail, which is itself expressed in the form of hyper-code;
- *unexplode*: this contracts an exploded link back to its original form;
- *edit*: this includes all conventional editing facilities;
- *get root*: this returns a selected persistent root, as a hyper-code fragment.

When composed, these operations are sufficient to support all program construction, execution and persistent object browsing activities. Note that various system activities are implicit in the operations. For example, the implementation of the *evaluate* operation involves syntax checking, compilation and invocation of the selected code representation.

The semantics of the hyper-code operations can be defined in terms of four abstract operations, which are *reflect*, *reify*, *execute* and *transform*. As shown in Fig. 4, these operate on two distinct domains: the domain of persistent hyper-code entities and the domain of hyper-code representations. The former domain contains all of the first class values defined by the programming language, together with various non-first-class entities for which it may be useful to have representations, such as types, classes and executable code. Only the latter domain, that of hyper-code representations, is made explicit to the programmer.

The *reflect* and *reify* abstract operations simply map between the hyper-code entities and their representations. The *execute* operation takes place within the hyper-code entities domain: it involves the execution of an executable entity,

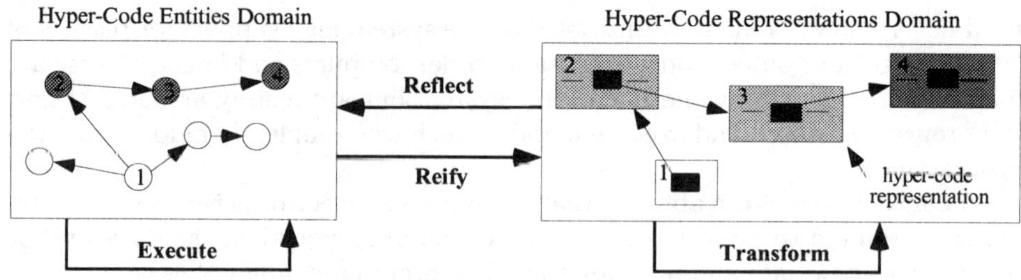

Fig. 4. Hyper-Code Domains and Abstract Operations

potentially with side-effects on the domain. Correspondingly, the *transform* operation takes place within the representation domain, involving the manipulation of hyper-code representations. The hyper-code operations can be understood in terms of the abstract operations as follows:

- *evaluate* first *reflects* a hyper-code representation to a corresponding hyper-code entity. If that entity is executable it is *executed*. If the execution produces a result entity, or if the original entity is non-executable, that entity is *reified* to produce a result representation.
- *explode* and *unexplode* both *reflect* a hyper-code representation to a corresponding hyper-code entity, and then *reify* that entity to produce a more or less detailed result representation, respectively.
- *edit* involves *transformation* of an existing or null hyper-code representation into a new representation.
- *get root* involves *reification* of a hyper-code entity to produce a representation.

It should be stressed that the abstract operations are purely definitional: only the hyper-code representations domain and the hyper-code operations are visible to the programmer.

Hyper-Code Representations. The operations and domains described in the previous section may be applied to an implementation of hyper-code in any suitable language. The precise form of the hyper-code representation (HCR) will vary depending on the syntax of the chosen language, but will be guided by the following criteria that will apply for all languages:

- The HCR must accommodate new programs written in the normal way. This implies that the representation must include pure text as a special case.
- The HCR must support hyper-program links, for the reasons already discussed.
- The HCR must support detailed views of linked entities, to arbitrary levels of detail, in order that the hyper-code editor may subsume the functions of an object browser.
- Since there must only be a single HCR, the detailed views of entities must themselves comprise text and hyper-program links in the same form as could be constructed by the programmer.

- Furthermore, the detailed views should be self-contained and syntactically valid. Thus, for any detailed view of an entity, it should be possible to copy its representation, paste this into a new window, and evaluate it without error. The result of this evaluation will depend on the semantics of the language.

Currently we have designed HCR forms for PJama and ProcessBase[2], and have implemented a prototype in PJama. Fig. 5 shows an example in ProcessBase, in which unexploded links to values are denoted by rounded white rectangles, and unexploded links to types by rounded black rectangles. Exploded links are denoted by shaded rectangles, with the internal details depending on the particular entity. The example shows the definition of a procedure *newPerson*, which takes a name and an age as parameters, and returns a view (record) containing them and a unique id number. The id is obtained by calling another procedure to increment a shared location, and then dereferencing that location.

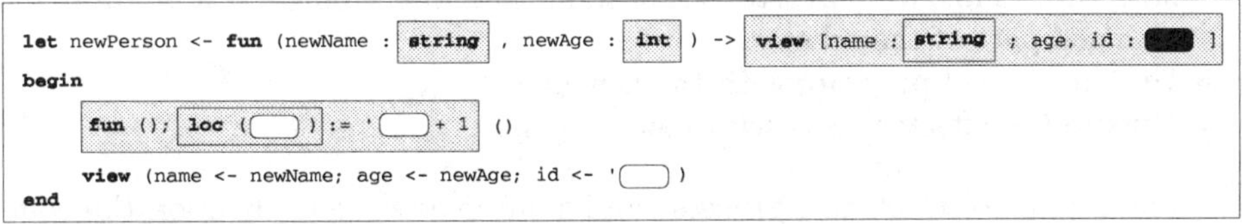

Fig. 5. Example of Hyper-Code Representation in ProcessBase

Our HCR design for PJama, an example of which shown in Fig. 6, is similar to that in Fig. 5, although it is less elegant due to the higher number of non-first-class entities to which it must support linking, and the presence of non-public object fields.

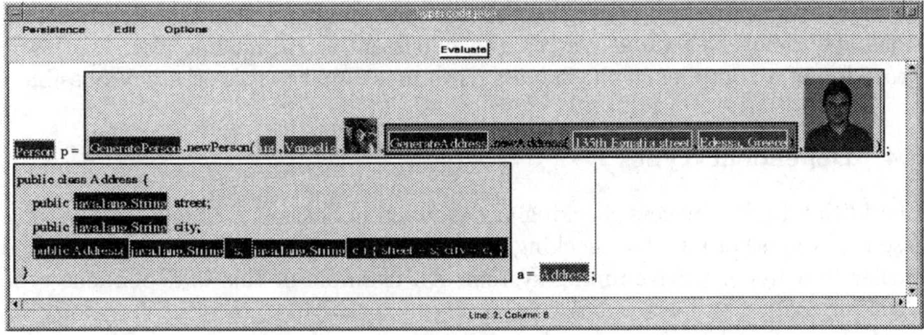

Fig. 6. Example of Hyper-Code Representation in PJama

[2] A simple persistent language being developed as part of the Compliant Systems Architecture project [22, 23].

3.3 System Evolution

Hyper-programming is also the basis for providing new solutions to the problem of schema editing which requires location and translation of affected queries and data [24]. The essential elements are at hand in the hyper-programming system. The schema may keep a record of which programs (queries) and data are associated with particular parts of the schema via secure links. The programs always have hyper-program source and therefore source code and data translation is possible. The schema evolution mechanism transforms the programs and data affected by a schema edit. This is achieved as follows:

- Locate, from the schema, all affected programs and data.
- For each program which may be affected, obtain its hyper-program.
- Locate the points in the hyper-program which access the changed part of the schema and edit the hyper-program to reflect the new logical schema structure. This will involve establishing new links both to and from the changed part of the schema.
- Update the old program with the new one.
- Update the affected data with new versions.

The extent to which this process can be automated depends upon the complexity of the schema change incurred. The essential point is that all interrogation and manipulation of schema, program and data occurs within a single integrated environment, and may therefore be represented as a meta-level program within that environment.

The mechanism relies heavily upon the self-contained nature of the persistent environment. As all the data and code is held in the same environment as the schema, it is possible to keep not only links from the schema to the data it describes but also reverse links from the schema to programs which bind to particular points of it. The hyper-programming concept makes it possible to map between executable and source representations. The fact that these representations are themselves values within the persistent environment, along with the provision of a compiler in the same environment, makes this strategy possible.

3.4 Dependent Types

In addition to data access checking as described in Section 2.2, language systems also perform other kinds of checking at run-time, some of which can be performed earlier in a hyper-programming system. An example of this is dependent type checking [25].

A dependent type is a type that depends on a value. In general this requires dynamic type checking. To determine whether two dependent types are compatible, the languages type checker takes account of the associated values as well as their structure. An example of a dependent type is the generic type *map* [26], instances of which are associations between sets of values. The type of a particular map is dependent on the identity of the procedure that defines equality over the key set. Because of this it is not generally possible to type-check at compilation-time a program that contains map operations, as the map values themselves must be tested.

In a hyper-programming system the value on which a dependent type depends may be linked directly into a program, and may thus be available for checking at compilation-time. This makes it possible for the system to check operations on dependent types at compilation-time rather than planting code in the executable program to perform the checking at run-time. The system may also provide tools that allow the programmer to verify the type compatibility of selected values before they are linked into the hyper-program.

More generally the programmer may perform arbitrary checks on data values before linking them into a hyper-program, by writing and executing other programs that compute over them. If the checks succeed, the code that performs the checking can then be omitted from the main hyper-program, since the links to the original values are guaranteed to remain intact.

3.5 Internet Programming

The potential association between the concept of hyper-programming, and the Web, is obvious. The source format of hyper-programs is similar to hyper-text, and the Web provides a well-known hyper-text system over the global autonomous network. The clear appeal, therefore, is to somehow extend the paradigm to make it work in this context.

This appeal, however, is fraught with serious technical difficulty, and it would be over-ambitious and pre-emptive to attempt to document it fully in this paper. We therefore restrict the discussion to an elaboration of the problems involved, and outline strategies which we believe may eventually provide solutions.

Problems exist in the following categories:

- how can program source be represented?
- how can typed data be integrated with the http protocol?
- how could data deriving from other web sources be integrated in a typed computation?
- how can the potential failure of references be made tolerable?

These topics are currently under investigation within the framework of the Hippo project at the University of Glasgow[3]. Here we describe only the direction taken for further investigation within each category.

Program Source. To be properly compatible with the Web, it is necessary to represent hyper-programs in a standard text-based form. In the hyper-programming prototypes that have been built, program source is represented in a proprietary format, manipulated only by specially written editor/browser software. This allows the presentation of the program source to the programmer to be strongly associated with the programming language definition. However,

[3] www.hippo.org.uk

to move to a standard internet treatment, the program source format must be open, textual, and ideally should be HTML itself.

One of the known (and as yet largely unaddressed) problems associated with hyper-programming is how standard language treatments, such as the definition of typing and semantics, can be adapted to the hypertext domain. Widely used methodologies for formal definitions and proofs invariably rely upon a textual source representation; while we can claim properties for hyper-programs on a purely intuitive level, it is not clear how to proceed with elementary proofs within a derived system, to demonstrate beyond doubt that there is no flaw in the soundness of the derived language.

Our proposed solution to these problems is to use a two-level language representation and definition. At a high level, humans can interact with a hypertext source, whereas at a lower level the program is actually represented in HTML, including a standard use of hypertext anchors to represent hyperlinks within programs. This allows standard HTML tools, such as high-level composition tools and browsers, to be used as a human-readable interface over the low-level representation. The low-level representation, using standard HTML, allows text-based protocols to be used to interpret and transport the HTML.

The difficulty with such an approach is how to define the overall system in a manner which gives a clear and formal definition of its semantics. The overall system will be relatively complex, in comparison with existing hyper-programming systems where an intuitive semantics is relatively acceptable, given that the low-level representation is not patent.

One approach to this problem is based on the definition of the two-level programming algebra using linguistic reflection as a language definition technique. This approach is based upon the use of compile-time reflection, as defined in [27]. A subset of HTML may be defined as the core programming algebra, making it possible to define the semantics of both standard language features and hyperlinks. A hyper-text view of programs, as may be presented by both specialist program editors and standard browsers, can be defined (using the terminology of [28]) as a reflective sublanguage, which is used to generate the HTML-based textual form during static analysis by the programming system implementation.

Using linguistic reflection as a definitional mechanism gives a well-defined formal framework in which hyper-programs can be described using relatively conventional definition techniques. Furthermore, it gives a framework wherein the core definition of hyper-programs is text-based, thus allowing their transportation around the various text-based protocols of the Internet without resorting to ad-hoc translation techniques.

Typed Data. Given a persistent programming language which can be used to program over embedded URLs, the next step is to consider how a URL can be used to refer to typed data, even supposing that the URL refers to data generated by the same programming system. The problem in turn decomposes into three further issues. These are:

- unifying the global persistent namespace with those namespaces used in the Web;

- unifying the representation of the typed persistent data with that commonly used on the Web, namely HTML;
- introducing type system mechanisms which allow the integration of remote, unreliable, and autonomous data with an otherwise static type system.

Each of these presents significant technical challenges, and is not further expanded in this context. Interested readers are referred to [29] for a more detailed exposition of the approach taken; once again, solutions to these problems are still beyond our grasp.

Importing Data. The full potential of a web-based hyper-programming system would only be met if it were possible to include links to data which had been generated by some system other than the particular programming language in use. Once again, this is an enormous issue and can not be addressed in this short space. There are two simple solutions: the first is to read the data as text or MIME, and restrict the typing of such links according to its transmitted classification. This results in a type safe language, assuming the consistent use of the protocol, but does not really address the spirit of the problem. The other simple solution is to publish the format used for the systems own typed data, and ensure it is possible to generate that externally. However any serious uptake of this system then requires the retrospective adoption of a new data standard, which is unlikely to succeed.

The more ambitious goal is to attempt to analyse arbitrary data resulting from an *http* request for appropriate structural content and, if it is suitable, integrate it into a typed computation. The outline of our approach is for the programmer to specify a required type for the binding during the composition process. The URL is duly fetched, and translated into a semi-structured format according to a number of ad-hoc rules[4]. Having achieved a semi-structured representation of the data, the programmers asserted type is used to derive a subset of the data which corresponds to the same structure. This data is extracted and incorporated into the ongoing computation. An estimation of how well the data fits the expected type is also generated, and may be either returned to the user of the program or used within the running program.

Although we have evidence that the outline given above is possible to engineer [30, 31], and furthermore gives a viable and understandable programming system, each of the steps described presents its own major problems and the production of such an integrated programming system is still beyond current understanding.

Internet Hyper-Programming? In summary, there is a clear and easy intuition that an extension of the hyper-programming paradigm to encompass the global hyper-text concepts of the World-Wide Web will result in a powerful distributed programming paradigm. While we believe that this is the case,

[4] The ad-hoc nature of this part of the process can be entirely circumvented when the document is XML, which we perceive to be a rapidly emerging standard for Web information.

on deeper inspection the technical issues underlying such a paradigm shift are profound. A great deal of work remains to be done before we can be convincing that the extended concept is feasible, whilst retaining a sound and disciplined programming system.

3.6 An Open C++/DCOM Hyper-Programming Environment

In this section we report on an attempt to apply the hyper-programming model in the context of an open system. We chose a DCOM/C++ system for the experimentation for a number of reasons. Firstly, both C++ [8] and DCOM [10] are being used by a large number of programmers to build systems in the real world. Secondly, having programmed with DCOM and C++, we felt there was a high degree of accidental complexity associated with this style of programming that was not intrinsic in the problem domain. We hoped that hyper-programming might be used to simplify the construction of DCOM programs. Finally we were influenced by the HIPPO work of Connor [29] and sought to discover if C++/DCOM programs could be written which had the same flavour as Hippo programs. If this was possible, the power of the many C++ libraries and environments could be used cheaply construct Web utilities. In addition to creating a hyper-programming environment for a commercial system, a deliberate attempt was made to maximise the use of freely available software and to avoid writing new software whenever possible.

Hyper-Program Construction. A DCOM/C++ hyper-program is constructed using two tools: a text editor and a binder. These are used to specify the hyper-program text and the hyper links respectively. The output from these tools is fed into a pre-processor which unifies the source and the links into standard C++ prior to presentation to the gnu-C++ compiler. The pre-processor also creates files and directories for cache maintenance and in some circumstances pre-fetches Web pages.

Editing Environment. The first tool requirement was for a text editor capable of incorporating hyperlinks and suitable for editing programs. Web editing tools such as Netscape Composer and FrontPage do not support the editing of programs since they are intended as HTML composition tools. Consequently Emacs [32] was used with a (then) freely available extension called Hyperbole [33]. Hyperbole supports the inclusion of hyperlinks into documents. In particular, these links can refer to Uniform Resource Locators (URLs), i.e. Web pages, and can be clicked on with the mouse. A Hyperbole user works with buttons embedded within textual documents. These buttons may be created, modified, moved or deleted. Each button performs a specific action, such as linking to a file or executing a shell command. Fig. 7 shows a C++ hyper-program being edited with the Emacs/Hyperbole environment.

The Hyper-Program Source Code. The program shown in Fig. 8 contains a C++/DCOM hyper-program that finds the telephone number of a member of the

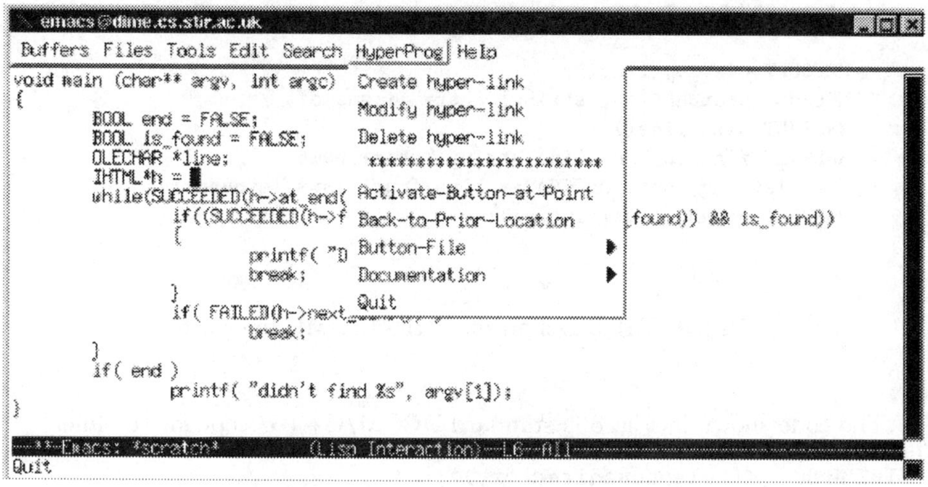

```
emacs@dime.cs.stir.ac.uk
Buffers Files Tools Edit Search HyperProg Help
void main (char** argv, int argc)    Create hyper-link
{                                    Modify hyper-link
        BOOL end = FALSE;            Delete hyper-link
        BOOL is_found = FALSE;       ***********************
        OLECHAR *line;               Activate-Button-at-Point
        IHTML*h = █                  Back-to-Prior-Location     found)) && is_found))
        while(SUCCEEDED(h->at_end(   Button-File          ▶
                if((SUCCEEDED(h->f   Documentation        ▶
                {                    Quit
                        printf( "D
                        break;
                }
                if( FAILED(h->next_
                        break;
        }
        if( end )
                printf( "didn't find %s", argv[1]);
}
---**-Emacs: *scratch*        (Lisp Interaction)--L6--All-------
Quit
```

Fig. 7. Emacs and Hyperbole

Computer Science Department at Glasgow University. It does this by scanning an HTML page denoted by the hyperlink *telephonedirectory*. The program creates a binding denoted by h of type $IHTML*$ to this Web page. The IHTML class shown in Fig. 9 supports a number of operations including the $find\_in\_line$ method which searches lines of the page looking for the sub-string specified in the parameter. If a match is found the line is returned. It also contains a predicate *at_end* indicating that the end of the page has been reached.

```
void main (char** argv, int argc)
{
    BOOL end = FALSE;
    BOOL is_found = FALSE;
    OLECHAR *line;
    IHTML*h = <(telephonedirectory)>;
    while(SUCCEEDED(h->at_end(&end)) && ! end) {
        if((SUCCEEDED(h->find_in_line(
                                argv[1,&line,&is_found)) &&
            is_found)) {
            printf( "Details are %s \n\r", line ); break; }
        if( FAILED(h->next_line()) ) break;
    }
    if( end ) printf( "didnt find %s", argv[1]);
}
```

Fig. 8. A C++/DCOM Hyper-Program

```
interface IHTML : Iunknown
{
    HRESULT display_line();
    HRESULT openURL([in, string] char* filename);
    HRESULT next_line();
    HRESULT find_in_line([in, string] char* name,
         [string, out] OLECHAR** line,[out] int* isfound);
    HRESULT at_end([out] int *i);
}
```

Fig. 9. MIDL Definition of the IHTML Interface

The code shown in Fig. 8 is standard DCOM/C++ except for the line,

```
IHTML*h = <(telephonedirectory)>;
```

which has to be replaced with standard C++, as described above this task is performed by the pre-processor. The code sequence into which this hyper-link is expanded depends on the binding style specified in the binder. This is described the next section.

Creating Bindings. Using the Hyperbole environment, bindings can be made to any Web based data. However, this does not address the need to specify attributes associated with those links such as programming language type, external data type, the location of the data being bound and binding time. To allow hyper-programmers to specify and view bindings, a Web interface to a *binder* has been created and is shown in Fig. 10.

The binder permits users to specify a name for a hyper-link. This is used to match the hyper-links entered in the editor with bindings specified in the binder. The next field is the type of the object in the programming language context. In the current implementation this field contains a string which is used to specify the programming language type of the target object. This field is strictly unnecessary since it could be automatically generated but makes the generated code more readable. The next field, IID, is used to specify the type (interface) of the object being linked to. In the example shown in Fig. 10, the link is to an object of type $IHTML$, shown in Fig. 9. The $CLSID$ field is used to specify a class library containing executable code implementing the class specified in the IID field. For DCOM aficionados, this is used to find by a class moniker to locate the class object. The URL field specifies the location of the data to which the link refers.

The last field is used to specify the time at which the binding is resolved. There are currently two options supported: compile time and run time. These settings change the behaviour of the pre-processor and cause different code to be generated. When the compile-time option is chosen the pre-processor pre-fetches a copy of the target and stores it locally. In this case the code generated contains fewer run-time checks since the data will always be accessible. When run-time binding is employed, failure at runtime is possible and consequently the generated code needs to be more sophisticated. The code generated for the example program shown in Fig. 8 is given in the next section.

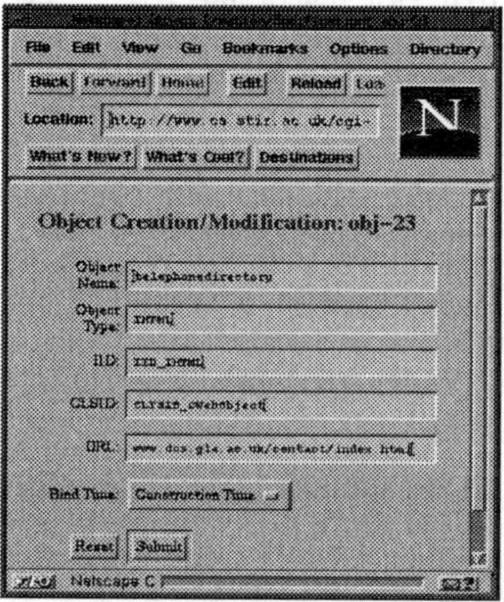

Fig. 10. Entering Details into the Binder

Binding Times and Errors. The code generated depends on the binding time specified in the binder. Fig. 11 shows a slightly simplified version of the code generated for the hyper-program shown in Fig. 8 if construction time (eager) binding is specified. This code assumes that the binder has loaded the Web page into the local cache (home/sag/cache). The dynamic case is similar but requires additional code to fetch the page across the network. The code generated is straightforward DCOM code.

```
void main(int argc, char** argv)
{
    OLECHAR *line = 0;
    IHTML* h = 0;
    IClassFactory *pcf = 0;
    HRESULT res = S_OK;
    IMoniker *pmk = 0;
    IBindCtx *pbc = 0;
    Check(CreateBindCtx(0,&pbc), "CreateBindCtx failed");
    Check(CreateClassMoniker (CLSID_CWebObject, &pmk),
          "CreateClassMoniker failed");
    Check(BindToObject(pbc,0,IID_IClassFactory,
          (void**)&pcf), "BindToObject failed");
    Check(pcf->CreateInstance(0, IID_IHTML, (void**)&h),
          "Create Instance failed");
```

```
    Check(h->openURL("/home/sag/cache/www.dcs.gla.ac.uk/
             contact/index.html"), "Open URL failed");
    BOOL end = FALSE;
    BOOL is_found = FALSE;
    while(SUCCEEDED(h->at_end(&end)) && ! end) {
        if((SUCCEEDED(h->find_in_line(




        argv[1,&line,&is_found)) && is_found)) {
            printf( "Details are %s \n\r", line ); break; }
        if( FAILED(h->next_line()) ) break;
    }
    if( end ) printf( "didnt find %s", argv[1]);
    h->Release();
    pcf->Release();
}
```

Fig. 11. Simplified DCOM Code Generated for Fig. 8

Future Directions. All the examples and screen shots discussed this far describe a system that has been implemented at the University of Stirling. However, this code represents the start rather than the end-point of what we are trying to achieve. We stated earlier that we were seeking an integration of C++/DCOM with hyper-programming and the ideas embodied in the Hippo system. We now describe how we can use what we have implemented to date to achieve this.

```
void main (char** argv, int argc)
{
    BOOL end;
    IPersonSet *s = <(telephonedirectory)>;

    while(SUCCEEDED(s->at_end(&end)) && !end) {

        Person person;
        if(SUCCEEDED(s->next_person(&person) &&
        !strcmp(person.name,argv[1]))) {
            printf("Telephone number of %s is %s\n",
               argv[1],person.phone_no);
            break;
        }
    }

    if (end) printf("didn't find %s\n",argv[1]);
}
```

Fig. 12. A Strongly Typed C++ Hyper-Program

The program shown in Fig. 8 treats the Web data as an HTML file not as a typed entity. We would like to be able to re-write the hyper-program as shown in Fig. 12. In this example, rather than treating the data as HTML text, we have typed it as a set of objects of type *Person*. This requires a number of refinements to the mechanisms already implemented. First the HTML file must be typed as a set of *Person*. To achieve this, a MIDL interface definition of a set of *Person* is created as shown in Fig. 13. This type is structurally similar to the $IHTML$ interface given earlier with the line type being replaced with records of type *Person*. Since the *IPersonSet* interface inherits from $IHTML$, it may use the $IHTML$ interface to assist in the extraction of records of type *Person* from the text file.

```
typedef struct { OLECHAR *name; OLECHAR *phone_no;
                 OLECHAR *nickname; } Person;

interface IPersonSet : IHTML
{
    HRESULT next_person([out] Person* current );
}
```

Fig. 13. MIDL Definition of Person Set Interface

Some mechanism must be provided to convert the textual data retrieved over the Web into typed objects (in this case of type *Person*). This task is encoded in the library providing the implementation of *IPersonSet*. Whilst this implementation could be hand coded, a more desirable approach would be to generate it automatically from a specification. There are two basic approaches to this: (i) use the MIDL as a specification for the Web format and (ii) use the Web format as a specification to generate the MIDL.

If the first approach were employed, a tool could be engineered which took the MIDL interface and a URL as parameters and attempted to find records of the appropriate type in the file. In the case of the URL used in the examples in this Section, the fields are all comma separated making this task easy. This is similar to the construction of indices in database systems and the importation of records using Wizards in Microsoft Excel and Access. Once the index was created, generic code could be used to traverse the data and return records each time $next\_person$ was called. An alternative approach is to generate the IDL from the Web source. This approach is particularly attractive if the Web source is encoded in a structured or semi-structured manner, for example, using XML [34]. In both cases, generic code needs to exist which may be specialised to operate over records of an appropriate type. This may be achieved using the parametric polymorphism provided by the implementation language or using tools such as those suggested by Sheard and Stemple [35] or Kirby [36].

4 Conclusions

Our original motivation for hyper-programming was to allow the user to compose programs interactively, navigating the environment and selecting data items, including code, to be incorporated into the programs. We further believed that programming language systems could provide better support for the software engineering process than they do at present, in particular, with regard to the traditional *compose-compilelink-execute* cycle of program development. From our early implementations of hyper-programming we summarised that the attendant benefits of the concept are:

- being able to perform program checking early
- support for source representations of all object closures
- being able to enforce associations from executable programs to source programs
- availability of an increased range of linking times
- increased program succinctness
- increased ease of program composition

Here we have developed the hyper-programming notion to presenting a single representation of data and code throughout the software process using hyper-code. Furthermore we have explored techniques for adapting hyper-programming to persistent contexts that do not enforce referential integrity, such as the WWW; and implementing and using hyper-programming in standardised languages and inter-operability mechanisms, such as C++ and DCOM.

5 Acknowledgements

We wish to acknowledge the work of Vivienne Dunstan on hyper-code and her contribution to the concepts presented here. The outline of the global hyper-programming challenges described in Section 3.5 relies heavily upon work done within the Hippo project by: David Lievens, Paolo Manghi, Steve Neely, Keith Sibson, Fabio Simeoni and Anna Stavrianou. We also acknowledge the support of EPSRC under grant GR/L32699 Compliant Systems Architecture and the EC Working Group Pastel EC22552.

References

1. Morrison R., Connor R.C.H., Cutts Q.I., Dunstan V.S., Kirby G.N.C. Exploiting Persistent Linkage in Software Engineering Environments. Comp. J. 1995; 38,1:1-16
2. Metrowerks Inc. CodeWarrior Pro 5, 1999
3. Farkas A.M., Dearle A., Kirby G.N.C., Cutts Q.I., Morrison R., Connor R.C.H. Persistent Program Construction through Browsing and User Gesture with some Typing. In: A. Albano and R. Morrison (ed) Persistent Object Systems, Proc. 5th International Workshop on Persistent Object Systems (POS5), San Miniato, Italy. Springer-Verlag, 1992, pp 376- 393

4. Kirby G.N.C., Connor R.C.H., Cutts Q.I., Dearle A., Farkas A.M., Morrison R. Persistent Hyper-Programs. In: A. Albano and R. Morrison (ed) Persistent Object Systems, Proc. 5th International Workshop on Persistent Object Systems (POS5), San Miniato, Italy. Springer-Verlag, 1992, pp 86-106
5. Morrison R., Brown A.L., Connor R.C.H., Cutts Q.I., Dearle A., Kirby G.N.C., Munro D.S. Napier88 Reference Manual (Release 2.2.1). University of St Andrews, 1996
6. Atkinson M.P., Daynes L., Jordan M.J., Printezis T., Spence S. An Orthogonally Persistent Java. ACM SIGMOD Record 1996; 25,4:68-75
7. Cutts Q.I., Connor R.C.H., Kirby G.N.C., Morrison R. An Execution Driven Approach to Code Optimisation. In: Proc. 17th Australasian Computer Science Conference (ACSC'94), Christchurch, New Zealand, 1994, pp 83-92
8. Stroustrup B. The C++ Programming Language. Addison-Wesley, 1986
9. The Common Object Request Broker: Architecture and Specification, Revision 2.2. Object Management Group (OMG), 1998
10. Microsoft Corporation. DCOM Technical Overview. , 1996
11. Atkinson M.P., Bailey P.J., Chisholm K.J., Cockshott W.P., Morrison R. An Approach to Persistent Programming. Comp. J. 1983; 26,4:360-365
12. Atkinson M.P., Morrison R. Procedures as Persistent Data Objects. ACM ToPLaS 1985; 7,4:539-559
13. Goldberg A., Robson D. Smalltalk-80: The Language and its Implementation. Addison Wesley, Reading, Massachusetts, 1983
14. OBrien P.D., Halbert D.C., Kilian M.F. The Trellis Programming Environment. ACM SIGPLAN Notices 1987; 22,12:91-102
15. Dearle A., Brown A.L. Safe Browsing in a Strongly Typed Persistent Environment. Comp. J. 1988; 31,6:540-544
16. Bretl B., Maier D., Otis A., Penney J., Schuchardt B., Stein J., Williams E.H., Williams M. The GemStone Data Management System. In: W. Kim and F. Lochovsky (ed) Object- Oriented Concepts, Databases and Applications. ACM Press and Addison Wesley, 1989, pp 283-308
17. Cooper R.L. On The Utilisation of Persistent Programming Environments. Ph.D. thesis, University of University of Glasgow, 1990
18. Kirby G.N.C., Dearle A. An Adaptive Graphical Browser for Napier88. University of St Andrews Report CS/90/16, 1990
19. Zirintsis E., Dunstan V.S., Kirby G.N.C., Morrison R. Hyper-Programming in Java. In: R. Morrison, M. Jordan and M. P. Atkinson (ed) Advances in Persistent Object Systems, Proc. 8th International Workshop on Persistent Object Systems (POS8) and 3rd International Workshop on Persistence and Java (PJW3), Tiburon, California, 1998. Morgan Kaufmann, 1999
20. Connor R.C.H., Cutts Q.I., Kirby G.N.C., Moore V.S., Morrison R. Unifying Interaction with Persistent Data and Program. In: P. Sawyer (ed) Interfaces to Database Systems, Proc. 2nd International Workshop on User Interfaces to Databases, Ambleside, Cumbria, 1994. Springer-Verlag, 1994, pp 197-212
21. Kirby G.N.C. Reflection and Hyper-Programming in Persistent Programming Systems. Ph.D. thesis, University of University of St Andrews, 1992
22. Morrison R., Balasubramaniam D., Greenwood M., Kirby G.N.C., Mayes K., Munro D.S., Warboys B.C. ProcessBase Reference Manual (Version 1.0.4). Universities of St Andrews and Manchester, 1999
23. Morrison R., Balasubramaniam D., Greenwood M., Kirby G.N.C., Mayes K., Munro D.S., Warboys B.C. A Compliant Persistent Architecture. To Appear: Proc. SoftwarePractice and Experience, 1999

24. Connor R.C.H., Cutts Q.I., Kirby G.N.C., Morrison R. Using Persistence Technology to Control Schema Evolution. In: Proc. 9th ACM Symposium on Applied Computing, Phoenix, Arizona, 1994, pp 441-446
25. Connor R.C.H., Atkinson M.P., Berman S., Cutts Q.I., Kirby G.N.C., Morrison R. The Joy of Sets. In: C. Beeri, A. Ohori and D. E. Shasha (ed) Database Programming Languages, Proc. 4th International Conference on Database Programming Languages (DBPL4), New York City. Springer-Verlag, 1993, pp 417-433
26. Atkinson M.P., Lecluse C., Philbrow P., Richard P. Design Issues in a Map Language. In: P. Kanellakis and J. W. Schmidt (ed) Bulk Types & Persistent Data. Morgan Kaufmann, 1991, pp 20-32
27. Stemple D., Fegaras L., Sheard T., Socorro A. Exceeding the Limits of Polymorphism in Database Programming Languages. In: F. Bancilhon, C. Thanos and D. Tsichritzis (ed) Lecture Notes in Computer Science 416, Proc. 2nd International Conference on Extending Database Technology (EDBT'90), Venice, Italy. Springer-Verlag, 1990, pp 269-285
28. Stemple D., Stanton R.B., Sheard T., Philbrow P., Morrison R., Kirby G.N.C., Fegaras L., Cooper R.L., Connor R.C.H., Atkinson M.P., Alagic S. Type-Safe Linguistic Reflection: A Generator Technology. To Appear: Proc. The FIDE Book, 1999
29. Connor R.C.H., Sibson K., Manghi P. On the Unification of Persistent Programming and the World-Wide Web (LNCS). In: Lecture Notes in Computer Science, Proc. Workshop on the Web and Databases (WebDB'98), Valencia, Spain. Springer-Verlag, 1998
30. Simeoni F. Extracting Typed Data from Semi-Structured Collections. MSc thesis, University of University of Glasgow, 1998
31. Connor R.C.H., Manghi P., Simeoni F. A Kinded Approach to Extracting Typed Subsets from Semi-Structured Data. in preparation. Please contact the authors.
32. Stallman R.M. EMACS: The Extensible, Customizable Self-Documenting Display Editor. ACM SIGPLAN Notices 1981; 16,6:147-156
33. Altrasoft. Hyperbole , 1998
34. Bray T., Paoli J., Sperberg-McQueen C.M. Extensible Markup Language (XML) 1.0. W3C, 1998
35. Stemple D., Sheard T., Fegaras L. Linguistic Reflection: A Bridge from Programming to Database Languages. In: Proc. 25th International Conference on Systems Sciences, Hawaii, 1992, pp 844-855
36. Kirby G.N.C., Connor R.C.H., Morrison R. START: A Linguistic Reflection Tool Using Hyper-Program Technology. In: M. P. Atkinson, D. Maier and V. Benzaken (ed) Persistent Object Systems, Proc. 6th International Workshop on Persistent Object Systems (POS6), Tarascon, France. Springer-Verlag, 1994, pp 355-373

Integration of Different Commit/Isolation Protocols in CSCW Systems with Shared Data*

Lars Frank

Department of Informatics, Copenhagen Business School,
Howitzvej 60, DK-2000 Frederiksberg, Denmark
Phone: +45 38 15 2400, Fax: +45 38152401,
frank@CBS.DK

Abstract. Traditional database systems use ACID properties (Atomicity, Consistency, Isolation and Durability) to implement recovery and concurrency control. However, this implementation is not always appropriate in distributed real time systems and in systems with long-lived transactions. For example, long-lived transactions may be active for days, and at the same time other transactions may need access to data, locked by the long-lived transactions. Therefore, extended transaction models have been developed. These transaction models only implement semantic ACID properties. That is, from an application point of view the system should function as if the traditional ACID properties were implemented. Multi user word processing, CAD and CASE systems may both be distributed and have long-lived transactions. Therefore, extended transaction models may be useful in Computer Supported Cooperative Work (CSCW), where users work with shared data. In this paper we will try to integrate the research in extended transaction models with the CSCW research, which for many years have been aware of the shortcomings of the traditional ACID properties. In the transaction model in this paper the global atomicity property is implemented by combining the possibilities of either forcing the remaining updatings of a transaction to be executed or compensating the already executed updatings of the transaction. The global consistency property may be managed by the CSCW system and/or by human beings supported by tools. The global isolation property is implemented by using countermeasures to the missing isolation of the updating transactions. The global durability property is implemented by using the durability property of the local CSCW/DBMS systems. In the extended transaction model described above we will incorporate some of the most promising CSCW commit/isolation features known from the scientific CSCW literature.

Keywords: CSCW, distributed groupware, collaborative writing, semantic ACID properties, concurrency control, long-lived transactions

* This work was supported in part by The Danish Social Science Research Council, Project No. 9701783.

D. Bjørner, M. Broy, A. Zamulin (Eds.): PSI'99, LNCS 1755, pp. 341–351, 2000.

1 Introduction

CSCW systems may be grouped in synchronous and asynchronous groupware systems.

In *synchronous groupware systems* all modifications can be observed real-time by all members of the collaboration. These WYSIWIS (What You See Is What I See) systems (Stefik et al., 1987) do not have a well-defined transaction concept, and, therefore, the ACID properties of such systems are not will defined either. Anyway, synchronous systems do have consistency problems, and, therefore, the tools of our transaction model may improve the situation.

In *asynchronous groupware systems* (e.g. Koch, 1995 and Jones, 1995) a user may first modify his/her local version of the database/document. When the modifications of the user are ready to be published to the other users, a global updating transaction is executed, and in this situation the semantic ACID properties of our transaction model may be important.

In synchronous groupware systems traditional locks can normally not be recommended as they slow down the real time interaction of the users. In asynchronous systems locking cannot be recommended either, when some of the transactions are long-lived (Gray and Reuter, 1993). The problem is that locking long-lived transactions exclude other users from making updatings, and this may not be acceptable. Therefore, traditional locking is normally not used in CSCW systems, which for many years have used different countermeasures that can reduce the problems occurring when traditional locking cannot be used for concurrency control.

The objective of this paper is to illustrate how to integrate different commit/isolation protocols to facilitate the selection of the right combinations of properties/tools for a CSCW system in a specific application area.

The paper is organized as follows: Section 2 will describe the transaction model used in this paper, i.e. we will give an overview of how the global semantic ACID properties can be implemented. In section 3 we will illustrate how to integrate different commit/isolation protocols for CSCW systems. Concluding remarks are presented in section 4.

Related work: The systematic analysis of countermeasures, described in Frank and Zahle (1998), was not possible until the isolation property was decomposed into disjunctive isolation anomalies by Gray and Reuter (1993) and Berenson et al. (1995).

For many years, extensive research has been made in CSCW systems with shared data in order to bypass the problems of traditional concurrency control. (For example Ellis and Gibbs, 1989; Pacull et al., 1994; Koch, 1995; Jones, 1995 and Salcedo et al., 1997). This paper may be viewed as a supplement to this field of research, where we use the disjunctive consistency problems of Gray and Reuter (1993) to describe in more detail the properties of the different commit/isolation protocols.

The commit/isolation protocols may be described by rules. Therefore, the commit/isolation protocols may be implemented by using the flexible CSCW systems as described in e.g. Georgakopoulos et al. (1994) and Rusinkiewitz et al. (1995), where the rules of the transactions are defined by there activity type. In other words, it is possible to change the commit/isolation protocol by changing the activity type of the transactions.

2 The Transaction Model

In the following, we will give an overview of how the global semantic ACID properties are implemented in our transaction model.

2.1 The Atomicity Property

An updating transaction has the *atomicity property* and is called *atomic* if either all or none of its updatings are executed. In this paper we use *the single pivot transaction model* (Mehrotra et al., 1992; Zhang et al., 1994 and Frank, 1999) for atomicity implementation. In this transaction model the global transaction is partitioned into the following types of subtransactions that are executed at different locations:

1. The *pivot subtransaction* that manages the atomicity of the global transaction, i.e. the global transaction is committed globally when the pivot subtransaction is committed locally. If the pivot subtransaction aborts, all the updatings of the other subtransactions must be compensated or not executed.

2. The *compensatable subtransactions* that all may be compensated. Compensatable subtransactions must always be executed before the pivot subtransaction is executed in order to allow them to be compensated if the pivot subtransaction cannot be committed. Compensation is achieved by executing a *compensating subtransaction.*

3. The *retriable subtransactions* that are designed in such a way that the execution is guaranteed to commit locally (sooner or later). Retriable subtransactions are executed after the local commit of the pivot subtransaction, because they have the pivot subtransaction as parent and are initiated by the pivot subtransaction.

Example

When a primary copy of an object is updated, created or deleted, the secondary copies may be updated with global atomicity by using retriable subtransactions. Suppose all users in a CSCW system have their own local workspace copy of a database, where a primary copy of the database is used to serialize and distribute the updating transactions. In this situation an updating user can send compensatable subtransactions to the other users via the primary copy location. All the updatings of the compensatable subtransactions must be marked as compensatable. If the other users can accept the updatings from the compensatable subtransaction, they send an accept message to the primary copy location. If the primary copy location receives accept messages from all the involved users, a pivot subtransaction can commit the updatings globally by committing the updatings in the primary copy location. After this, retriable subtransactions initiated by the pivot subtransaction are sent to all the users to de-mark the compensatable mark of the updatings committed at the primary copy. The same retriable subtransactions may also try to upgrade any other compensatable marked updatings to the new object version.

2.2 The Consistency Property

A database is *consistent* if the data in the database obeys the consistency rules of the database. *Consistency rules* may be implemented as a control program that rejects transactions, which do not obey the consistency rules.

In CSCW systems consistency rules may be managed by the CSCW system if they are described and initiated by a user (See e.g. Decouchant et al., 1996).

2.3 The Isolation Property

A database where all the transactions have the consistency property may still be inconsistent, if the isolation property is missing. A transaction is executed with the *isolation property* if the updatings of the transaction only are seen by other transactions after the updatings of the transaction have been committed.

In our transaction model the global semantic isolation property is managed by using countermeasures against the isolation anomalies that occur when transactions are executed without the isolation property. In designing countermeasures it is possible to use local locking, but all locks should be released immediately after a subtransaction has been committed/aborted locally in order to avoid blocked data (Data is *blocked* if it is locked by a subtransaction that loses the connection to the parent transaction).

If the isolation property is not implemented, four different types of isolation anomalies may occur. And if none of these isolation anomalies can occur, the execution of the transactions is serializable (Gray and Reuter, 1993 and Berenson et. al., 1995). In the following we will describe the tree isolation anomalies that are important in CSCW systems:

1. *The lost update anomaly* is by definition a situation where a first transaction reads an object for update without using locks. Subsequently, the object is updated by another transaction. Later, the first transaction (based on its earlier read value) updates the object and commits.

   In our transaction model all the local users have there own copy of the database and reading/updating the local database copy functions as reads for update without locks. In such a situation it is possible for conflicting transactions to update the same object, and only the updating of the last transaction will survive.

2. *The dirty read anomaly* is by definition a situation where a first transaction updates an object without locking the object or committing the update. After this, a second transaction reads the object. Later, the first update is aborted (or compensated). In other words, the second transaction has read a version of the object that was never committed and therefore never really did exist.

In our transaction model the dirty read anomaly may happen when the first transaction updates an object by using a compensatable subtransaction that is distributed to all the local databases of the users. Later, these distributed updatings are removed by using compensating subtransactions. If a local user reads the object before it is compensated, the data read will be dirty and may result in a wrong decision.

3. *The non-repeatable read anomaly or fuzzy read* is by definition a situation where a first transaction reads an object without using locks. This object is later updated and committed by a second transaction before the first transaction has been committed. That is, if the first transaction rereads the object, the attributes of the object are changed. In other words, the second transaction may read something that is not true when the transaction commits, and this may result in a wrong decision.

In our transaction model this may happen when the first transaction reads an object in the local copy of the database. Later the same object may be updated by a retriable subtransaction without the local user noticing the update, which may cause the local user to make wrong decisions.

2.4 The Durability Property

Transactions have the *durability property* if the updatings of the transactions cannot be lost after they have been committed. For global atomic transactions the global durability property will automatically be implemented, as it is ensured by the durability of the local databases (Breibart et. al., 1992).

3 Integration of the Commit/Isolation Protocols

In major projects group structures, roles, and activities may change during a project. Therefore, according to e.g. Koch (1995) and Jones (1995), it should be possible to change the commit/isolation procedure while the project is running.

All the commit/isolation protocols described in this section have a precisely defined commit time, after which an update decision cannot be annulled automatically. This is practical from an implementation point of view, and it also suits most structured working situations. However, working groups (and individuals) do not always work in a structured way, and, therefore, it may be important to be able to undo already committed updatings. In this situation it is practical to have a common transaction model (like our transaction model) to manage the transaction back out independent of the commit/isolation protocols used by the transaction that should be backed out.

In this section we will illustrate how to integrate our transaction model with some of the existing commit/isolation protocols described in the scientific literature.

3.1 The Reread Countermeasure

Transactions that use this countermeasure (Frank and Zahle, 1998) read an object twice by using short duration locks for each reading. If a second transaction has changed the object between the two readings, the transaction must abort itself after the second read. In asynchronous CSCW systems the reread countermeasure may be used to protect against the lost update anomaly in the following way: After a user has updated his/her local workspace, both the old version (or the version id.) and the new version of the changed objects are sent to the primary copy location, where the primary copy of these objects are read. If the primary copies of the objects are the same versions as the user's old versions, then the primary copy objects are modified to the user's new versions. Otherwise, the updatings of the user are rejected, and the committed primary copy version of the objects may be displayed for the user in a special color as a "non-repeatable read" warning. Later, the user may upgrade his/her updatings to the new object versions and retry to submit the updating transaction. In real time WYSIWIS systems it may be very confusing if different users delete, change and/or move the same sentence/figure element independently (Greenberg and Marwood, 1994). In this situation the reread countermeasure can prevent the problem in the following way: At first, new updatings are executed at the location of the updating user as compensatable updatings. Later, a pivot subtransaction updates the primary copy if it is unchanged. Finally, the committed updatings of the pivot subtransaction are propagated to the other users. However, if the primary copy vas changed by another user, the pivot updatings are rejected and compensated in the location of the updating user.

3.2 The Version Tree Protocol

If different parallel versions of an object exist, they may be implemented by a version tree (Koch, 1995), where the different parallel versions are children of the same parent object. The following example illustrates how version trees may be integrated in our transaction model.

Example

Insertion of a new subtext (character string) into an object is implemented as a new object, which is a child of the original object. In other words, different transactions can create different versions of the same parent object by storing different child objects related to the same parent object. The child objects are identified by the id of the parent object in combination with the id of the updating transaction (and possibly a sequence number, if the updating transaction creates many child objects). A field value in the child object marks the insertion as "compensatable" if the insertion is not committed globally. A compensatable insertion can easily be committed globally by de-marking the corresponding "compensatable" mark. However, in this situation other compensatable marked updatings to the same object must be upgraded to the new version of the object as described in the next subsection. A computer program can do this, but the upgraded transactions should be marked with "non-repeatable read anomaly" until a human brain has accepted the upgraded insertion as a semantic correct insertion to the new version of the object. If a human cannot accept the upgraded insertion, the corresponding transaction must be compensated.

3.3 The Operational Transformation Protocol

The objective of the *distributed OPperational Transformation (dOPT) Algorithm* described in Ellis and Gibbs (1989) is to implement concurrency control in real time groupware systems. The algorithm was first implemented in the GROVE system (Group Outline Viewing Editor) described in Ellis et al., 1990 and 1991. Later, the method of operational transformation has been improved in Nichols et al. (1995); Ressel et al. (1996); Sun et al. (1998) and Sun and Ellis (1998). Operational transformation prevents lost updatings by transforming a second conflicting updating to another type of updating that cannot overwrite the first updating. The GROVE system uses a conflict matrix that describes how each type of conflict in text updatings may be transformed. By using operational transformation the dirty read anomaly cannot occur either, because an aborted object is only known to the user who made the aborted updating. After a compensatable subtransaction has been committed globally, operational transformation may be used to upgrade automatically other compensatable subtransactions to the new version of the object. Other upgrading techniques are described in e.g. Neuwirth et al. (1992). Operational transformation does not deal with the non-repeatable read anomaly. Therefore, other countermeasures may be used to prevent these anomalies (see e.g. subsection 3.6).

3.4 The Linearization Protocol

Linearization (Herlihy and Wing, 1990, and Pacull and Sandoz, 1993) is both a commit and an isolation protocol. The main idea of the protocol is that the possibility to read, update or annotate the central copy of a document is passed along from one to another on requests. When a user has his/her turn, it is possible to read new updated versions of requested central copy objects, and/or it is possible to overwrite the central copies of the objects with the user's modified object versions. In the main version of this protocol the user only uses short duration locks. By integrating the reread countermeasure it is possible to prevent lost updatings. If another user has changed the central copy of an object, it should be possible to upgrade updatings to the new version. The dirty read anomaly cannot occur. The problems of the non-repeatable read anomaly may be prevented by rereading and control of all the data that has been changed since the last time the user had exclusive update rights. If this is done, the protocol may produce serializable executions. However, this is not realistic, and, therefore, it is also important to integrate countermeasures against the non-repeatable read anomaly in the protocol. This protocol may be integrated in our transaction model in the following way: At first, new updatings are executed at the location of the updating user as compensatable updatings. Later, when the user has access to the primary copy, the pivot subtransaction is executed. Finally, the copies of the other users are updated by using retriable subtransactions. Altogether, we evaluate the Linearization Protocol and its possibilities for integration with other isolation countermeasures to be good. In our view, the main problem of this protocol is how to get the users to collaborate in such a way that they do not spoil each other's updatings, when they have the updating rights. In DUPLEX (Pacull et al., 1994), an implementation of the Linearization Protocol has solved the problem in the following way:

- The document is decomposed into independently editable parts.
- The decomposition is dynamic and based on document structure; it reflects both document state and each author's current responsibility and involvement on different parts.
- Authors are allowed to choose the type of control (exclusive, pessimistic, optimistic, etc.,) that they wish on the document parts they are concerned with.

We believe that these rules are very important in order to manage most asynchronous groupware systems in a consistent way. Therefore, we recommend integrating these rules into the previous described asynchronous protocols wherever it is possible.

3.5 The Read Uncommitted Protocol

In this protocol we will use our transaction model in the following way: At first, new updatings are executed at the location of the updating user as compensatable updatings. Later, a pivot subtransaction updates the corresponding primary copy, and if the primary copy is changed by another user, the pivot updatings are rejected and compensated in the location of the updating user. The primary copy of the database is used to serialize the updating transactions in order to prevent the lost update anomaly. However, this protocols accept both the dirty read anomaly and the non-repeatable read anomaly. The reason is that in CSCW systems with shared data it may be best to have access to "dirty" and "non-repeatable read" data as early as possible, because the alternative only allows access to "old information", and old information may be very old if the updating transactions are long-lived. This protocol has very poor write availability if different long-lived transactions want to update the same data. The protocol almost corresponds to the "read uncommitted" isolation level (ANSI, 1992), where write locks do not exclude reading transactions. However, the ANSI protocol does not deal with primary and secondary copies. The protocol has resemblance to the commit/isolation protocol of the SEPIA hypertext authoring system described in Haake and Wilson (1992), because this system uses the real "read uncommitted" isolation level of the relational DBMS SYBASE. The main difference is that the users of SEPIA do not have their own database copy, but this is not a major difference when the users normally can read what they want as write locks do not exclude readings. By using SEPIA it is possible to use the "SEPIA Activity Spaces" for content, planning, argumentation, etc. as countermeasures against the other consistency problems.

3.6 The Group Awareness Countermeasure

The *group awareness* interaction and cooperation rules suggested in Koch (1995) may prevent the dirty read anomaly and the non-repeatable read anomaly. However, group awareness may also have more social and innovative purposes than countermeasures against consistency problems.

In *tightly coupled* WYSIWIS systems (e.g. Haake and Wilson, 1992), where the users share the same view, an additional communication channel (e.g. audio/video links) is almost necessary in order to prevent consistency problems. In some situations Greenberg and Marwood (1994) recommend using the additional communication channel to both prevent lost updatings and if a warning comes too late the additional channel may be used to repair the lost data.

3.7 Conclusions

This paper has illustrated how distributed semantic ACID properties can be implemented in distributed CSCW systems by using the single pivot transaction model and countermeasures against the different consistency problems that occur when only semantic ACID properties are implemented.

It is not possible to select one protocol as the best, because some protocols are more suitable for large projects and others for small projects, etc. However, our analyzes of the different commit/isolation protocols have illustrated that countermeasures against lost updatings, and the rest of the isolation anomalies may be integrated in such a way that it is possible to tailor commit/isolation protocols for the different phases of a given project. We have also illustrated that it may be important to use a common transaction model for all the commit/isolation protocols supported by a CSCW software product, because this model allows the upgrade- and back out tools for transactions to be designed in such a way that they can accept changes in the commit/isolation protocol used in the different phases of a CSCW project.

References

ANSI X3.135 (1992), American National Standard for Information Systems — Database Language-SQL.

Berenson, H., Phil Bernstein, Jim Gray, Jim Melton, Elizabeth O'Neil and Patrick O'Neil (1995), A Critique of ANSI SQL Isolation Levels, *Proc ACM SIGMOD Conf*, pp. 1–10.

Breibart, Y., H. Garcia-Molina and A. Silberschatz, 'Overview of Multidatabase Transaction Management' (1992), *VLDB Journal*, 2, pp. 181–239.

Decouchant, D., V. Quint and M. R. Salcedo (1996), Structured and Distributed Cooperative Editing in a Large Scale Network, In Rada, 1996.

Ellis, C. and S. Gibbs (1989), Concurrency Control in Groupware Systems, SIGMOD Record. Vol. 18, no. 2, ACM Press, New York, pp. 399–407.

Ellis, C., S. Gibbs and G. Rein (1990), Design and Use of a Group Editor, Engineering for Human Computer Interaction, G. Cockton (ed.), North-Holland, Amsterdam, pp. 13–25.

Ellis, C., S. Gibbs and G. Rein (1991), Groupware- Some Issues and Experiences, Communications of the ACM. Vol. 34, no. 1, pp. 38–58.

Frank, L. (1999a), 'Evaluation of the Basic Remote Backup and Replication Methods for High Availability Databases, *Technical Report*, Department of Informatics, Copenhagen Business School, Accepted for publication in Software — Practice & Experience.

Frank, L. (1999b), 'Atomicity Implementation in Multidatabases with High Performance and Availability', *Proc of the 2nd International Symposium on Cooperative Database Systems (CODAS'99)*, Springer-Verlag, pp 103–114.

Frank, L. and Torben Zahle (1998). Semantic ACID Properties in Multidatabases Using Remote Procedure Calls and Update Propagations, *Software-Practice & Experience*, Vol.28 (1), pp. 77–98.

Georgakopoulos, D., M. Hornick, P. Krychniak, F. Manola (1994), Specification and Management of Extended Transactions in a Programmable Transaction Environment, *Proc. of the 10th IEEE Int. Conference on Data Engineering.*

Gray, J. and Andreas Reuter (1993), Transaction Processing, Morgan Kaufman.

Greenberg, Saul and David Marwood (1994), Real Time Groupware as a Distributed System: Concurrency Control and its Effect on the Interface, *Proceedings of International Conference on Computer Supported Cooperative Work*, pp. 207–217. ACM Press.

Haake, J. and B. Wilson (1992), Supporting Collaborative Writing of Hyperdocuments in SEPIA, *Proceedings of International Conference on Computer Supported Cooperative Work*, pp. 138–146. ACM Press.

Herlihy, M. and J. Wing (1990), A correctness condition for concurrent objects, *ACM Transactions on Programming Languages and Systems*, 12, pp. 463–492.

Koch, M., (1995), Design Issues and Model for a Distributed Multi-User Editor, *Computer Supported Cooperative Work (CSCW)* 3, pp. 359–378.

Jones, S., (1995), Identification and use of guidelines for the design of computer collaborative writing tools, *Computer Supported Cooperative Work (CSCW)* 3, pp. 379–404.

Neuwirth, C., Ravinder Chandhok, David S. Kaufer, P. Erion, James H. Morris and D. Miller (1992), Flexible Diff-ing in a Collaborative Writing System, *Proceedings of 4th International Conference on Computer Supported Cooperative Work*, ACM Press. pp. 147–154.

Nichols, A., P. Curtis, M. Dixon and J. Lamping (1995), High-Latency, Low Bandwidth Windowing in the Jupiter Collaboration System. In *Proceedings of UIST'95*, 1/10.

Pacull, F. and Alain Sandroz Andre Schiper (1993), R-linearizability: An extension of linearizability to replicated objects, *Proceedings of the 4th IEEE Workshop of Future Trends of Computing Systems.*

Pacull, F., Alain Sandroz and Andre Schiper (1994), Duplex: A Distributed Collaborative Editing Environment in Large Scale, *Proceedings of International Conference on Computer Supported Cooperative Work*, pp. 165–173. ACM Press.

Rada, R. (Editor) (1996), Groupware and Authoring, *Academic Press.*

Ressel, M., D. Nitche-Ruhland and R. Guzenbauser (1996), An Integrating Transformation-Oriented Approach to Concurrency Control and Undo in Group Editors. In *Proceedings of ACM Conference on Computer supported Cooperative Work*, pp. 288–297.

Rusinkiewiecz, M., W. Klas, T. Tesch, J. Wasch and P. Muth (1995), Towards a Cooperative Transaction Model — The Cooperative Activity Model, *Proceedings of the 21st VLDB Conference.*

Salcedo, M. and Dominique Decouchant, (1997), Structured Cooperative Authoring for the World Wide Web, *Computer Supported Cooperative Work (CSCW)* 6, pp. 157–174.

Stefik, M., D. G. Bobrow, G. Foster, S. Lanning and D. Tatar (1987), WYSIWIS revised: Early experiences with multiuser interfaces, *ACM Transactions on Office Information Systems*, 5(2), pp. 147–167.

Sun, C. and C. Ellis (1998), Operational Transformation in Real-Time Group Editors: Issues, Algorithms, and Achievements, In *Proceedings of ACM Conference on Computer Supported Cooperative Work.*

Sun, C., X. Jia, Y. Zang, Y. Yang and D. Chen (1998), Achieving Convergence Causality-Preservation in Real-time Cooperative Editing Systems, *ACM Transactions on Computer-Human Integration*, 5/1, pp. 63–108.

Zhang, A., M. Nodine, B. Bhargava and O. Bukhres (1994), 'Ensuring Relaxed Atomicity for Flexible Transactions in Multidatabase Systems', *Proc ACM SIGMOD Conf*, pp 67–78.

A General Object-Oriented Model for Spatial Data

Sima Asgari and Naoki Yonezaki

Department of Computer Science
Graduate School of Information Science and Engineering
Tokyo Institute of Technology
{sima,yonezaki}@cs.titech.ac.jp
http://yonezaki-www.cs.titech.ac.jp/yonezaki-home-e.html

Abstract. Spatial data models have been extensively studied during the last decade. However, requirements of a spatial database system regardless of any specific application, have not received much attention. In this paper, a general Object-Oriented spatial data model is introduced. This model considers a spatial database system in general, without focusing on specific features or applications, and presents a new method for classification of spatial objects into maps. The concept of map as defined here, is an appropriate definition for objects with arbitrary set of spatial components. This concept is similar to the one of a map in the real world. Map definition is followed by the definition of map hierarchy and operations on maps which can be used to answer queries that might be too complicated otherwise.

1 Introduction

Topics such as urban planning, land use, city and road planning have recently received much attention. The spatial data related to these applications have specific features such as high volume and complex structure. Modeling spatial data is a basic step in designing a spatial database system.

Research which has been carried out so far, mostly consider specific features of a spatial database system [6,9], or discuss spatial data modeling from the point of view of a specific application [3]. Furthermore, most of the database systems which have been designed for spatial purposes have been built above the relational approach [7,8]. However, this approach is not powerful enough to be used as a basis for spatial database systems.

A recent approach is to build a spatial database system around an Object-Oriented paradigm [11,4,10]. Object-Oriented benefits comply with the requirements of spatial systems. In the literature, the only object categorization that has been considered is the classification of objects into classes and arbitrary categorization of spatial properties has received no attention.

This paper presents a general Object-Oriented spatial data model without considering any particular features or requirements of a specific application. It introduces the concept of map as an arbitrary class of spatial objects and defines

D. Bjørner, M. Broy, A. Zamulin (Eds.): PSI'99, LNCS 1755, pp. 352–357, 2000.

operations on map. The categorization of objects into maps allows us to create a structure of data in an efficient hierarchical way, define operations such as Join and Zoom on maps which have significant effect on the usability of the database system, and reply a wide range of queries. The benefits of Object-Oriented paradigm provide high flexibility for the data model. Furthermore, the data model is general enough to be used as the basis for a multipurpose spatial database system.

This paper is divided into 5 sections. The following section introduces spatial objects and object hierarchy. Section 3 explains concept of map and the partial order between maps. Operations on maps are given in section 4. Section 5 summarizes and concludes the paper.

2 Spatial Objects and Their Hierarchy

Objects in a spatial database system have spatial and descriptive(non-spatial) attributes. Descriptive attributes might be numbers, character strings or booleans. Various types of spatial attributes have been defined in the literature[6,11]. We employ the main types *point*, *line* and *region*.

The smallest definable spatial attribute is a *point* which can be represented by its coordinates in the Euclidean plane. Given two distinct *points* p_1 and p_2, a *line segment* is defined which connects the two points. A connected graph consisting of a set of *line segments* is defined as a *line*. A *region* is defined as a set of continuous *Points*.

The order relation on spatial data is defined as follows.

Definition 1. *Let P,L and R be spatial attributes with types Point, Line and Region,* $P \lhd L$ *and* $L \lhd R$

We assume that a spatial object is an object with only one spatial attribute. This assumption simplifies the definition of spatial operations. For more complicated cases where various spatial attributes have to be assumed, the concept of map will be considered.

Definition 2. *An object is a spatial object if it has one and only one spatial attribute from types point, line or region.*

Various operations on spatial data have been defined in the literature [11,6]. We have defined a set of spatial operations that could be found in the full paper.

Definition 3. *Two spatial objects* O_1 *and* O_2 *are identical* ($O_1 \approx O_2$) *if and only if their spatial attributes have the same value.*

The following function returns as a result, the spatial attribute of a spatial object.

Definition 4. *Let O be a spatial object and S be its spatial attribute, SA(O)=S.*

2.1 PART-OF Hierarchy

Part-whole relation has already been studied in detail[2,12]. We study this relation from the point of view of a spatial data model. PART-OF relation between spatial objects is defined as follows:

Definition 5. *Let O_1 and O_2 be spatial objects with R_1 and R_2 as their spatial attributes, O_1 PART-OF O_2 iff $R_1 \subset R_2$.*

We recognize four various interpretations for PART-OF relation:

- We say object O_1 is a part of object O_2 such that whole requires part and we write O_1 $WRP-PO$ O_2 if O_2 can not exist without O_1 (e.g. Water-Storage is $WRP-PO$ City).
- Object O_1 is a $PRW-PO$ (part requires whole) part of object O_2 if O_1 can not exist without being part of O_2 (e.g. a Movie-Theater is $PRW-PO$ City).
- A $PART-OF$ relation is called strong $S-PO$ if it is $WRP-PO$ and $PRW-PO$ (e.g. City-Government is $S-PO$ City).
- A $PART-OF$ relation is called weak $W-PO$ if it is neither $WRP-PO$ nor $PRW-PO$ (e.g. Gold-Mine is $W-PO$ City).

2.2 IS-A, PART-OF Interrelationship

Figure 1 displays the general form of interrelationship between IS-A and PART-OF relations. However this interrelationship does not hold for all types of PART-OF.

The following cases of interrelationship between IS-A and PART-OF relations can be derived from Figure 1. In what follows ':' represents class membership and '::' denotes subclass relation.

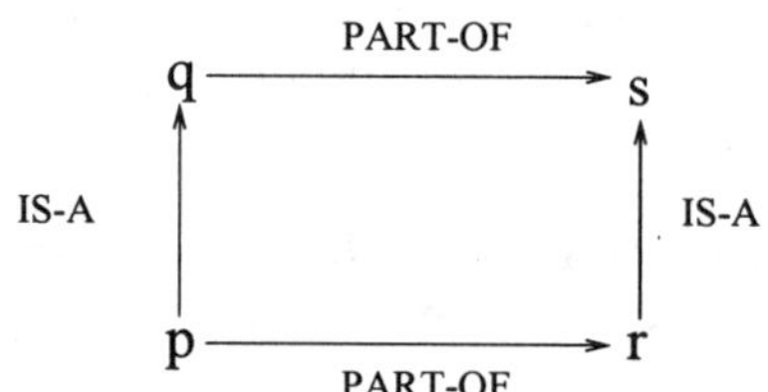

Fig.1. IS-A, PART-OF interrelationship

1. $\forall q, s, r\ (r :: s \vee r : s) \wedge (q\ WRP-PO\ s) \rightarrow$ $\exists p\ ((p :: q \vee p : q) \wedge (p\ WRP-PO\ r))$.
2. $\forall p, q, s\ (p :: q \vee p : q) \wedge (q\ PRW-PO\ s) \rightarrow$ $\exists r(\ (r :: s \vee r : s) \wedge (p\ PRW-PO\ r))$.
3. Cases 1 and 2 also hold for strong part of $(S-PO)$.

3 Object Categorization

A hierarchy of objects is produced by defining spatial objects and relations IS-A and PART-OF on them. Object Country, for instance, can have objects City, River, Road, Lake, Sea and Mountain as its parts. The PART-OF hierarchy, arranges the above set of objects in a hierarchical order.

A map is defined as a specific type of spatial object which might have other spatial objects as its components.

Definition 6. *A map is a spatial object such that there is at least one other spatial object related to it by a PART-OF relation.*

Map m consisted of PARTs $O_1, ..., O_n$ is represented as m$(O_1, ..., O_n)$.

Definition 7. *A spatial object that is not a map(has no parts) is called a simple spatial object.*

3.1 Partial Order of Spatial Objects

The set of all spatial objects is partially ordered and the relation $\leq$ is defined based on level of detailed information that is contained in each object. Partial order is defined recursively. In the following, CR is correspondence relation between two objects.

Definition 8. *Let A and B be spatial objects*
$A \leq B$ *iff*
$(A \approx B) \rightarrow$
(A is a simple spatial object $\vee$ $\forall O$ *PART-OF A* $\exists O'$ *PART-OF B,*
CR(O,O') $\wedge$ $O \leq O'$*)*
$(A \not\approx B) \rightarrow$
(A is a simple spatial object $\wedge$ $SA(A) \lhd SA(B)$*)*

Figure 2 displays partial order between maps.
Partial equality of spatial objects is defined as follows,

Definition 9. *Let A and B be spatial objects,*
$A = B$ *iff* $A \leq B \;\wedge\; B \leq A$.

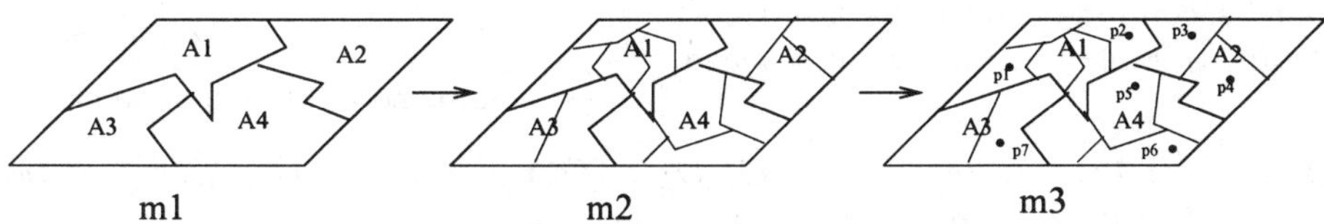

Fig.2. Partial ordering of maps

4 Operations on Maps

Once the concept of map is defined, operations can be introduced to manipulate maps. Some of the operations which have been already defined on objects can be expanded to maps and some new operations can be introduced as well. A set of map operations has been formally defined and will appear in the full paper. Zoom and Join operations will be discussed here in brief.

Join operation creates a new map by joining two adjacent maps. The operation may accept specific conditions to determine if adjacent ($\|$) objects from the same type must be unified into one or may remain separate.

Definition 10. *(Join): Let* $m_1(O_1, O_2, ..., O_n)$ *and* $m_2(O'_1, O'_2, ..., O'_k)$ *be two maps such that* $O_1 : T_1, O_2 : T_2, ..., O_n : T_n$ *and* $O'_1 : T'_1, O'_2 : T'_2, ..., O'_k : T'_k$ *and* $\exists O_i (1 \leq i \leq n)\ \exists O'_j (1 \leq j \leq k),\ T_i = T'_j\ \wedge\ O_i \parallel O'_j,$
Unconditional Join: $m_1\ +\ m_2 = m(O_1, ..., O_n, O'_1, ..., O'_k).$
Conditional Join: $(m_1 \oplus m_2)_{O_i, O'_j} =$
$m_c(O_1, ..., O_{i-1}, O_{i+1}, ..., O_n, O'_1, ..., O'_{j-1}, O'_{j+1}, ..., O'_k, O_c)$ *where* $O_c = O_i \oplus O'_j$.

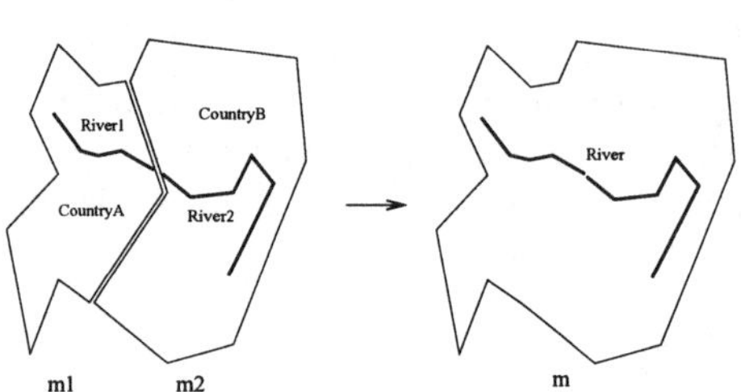

Fig.3. Join maps m1 and m2 on River1 and River2

For instance, two maps West-Germany and East-Germany can be joined into one map called Germany. If no conditions are considered, city objects West-Berlin and East-Berlin will remain as separate objects in the new map, however by the condition to join the two country maps over the two city objects, they will also be joined into one city. Figure 3 displays an example of conditional Join.

Zooming operation on maps is defined based on our definition of partial order of maps. Since maps can be recursively defined, a map can be consisted of other maps. Zooming a map on one of its components will return as a result the next detailed level of that component from the hierarchy of partial order. The zoom can be continued until the last (most detailed) level of hierarchy has reached.

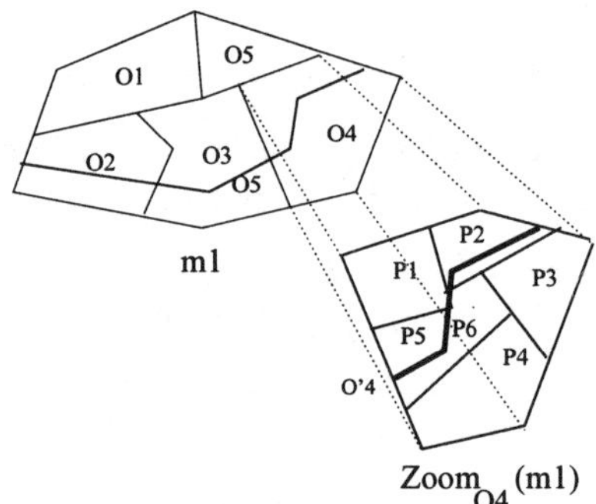

Fig.4. Zoom of map m on o4

Definition 11. *(Zoom): Let* $m_1(O_1, O_2, ..., O_n)$ *and* $m_2(O'_1, O'_2, ..., O'_m)$ *be two map such that* $m_1 \leq m_2$, $Zoom(m_1)_{O_i} = O'_i$.

Figure 4 illustrates zoom operation.

5 Conclusion

A general Object-Oriented spatial data model was presented that has the potential to model various types of data related to a spatial database system. Object hierarchy PART-OF and the interrelationship between PART-OF and IS-A hierarchies were defined. Considering spatial objects with more than one spatial attributes has drawbacks such as complicated process and flat(non hierarchical) structure of objects. Therefore, we assumed a spatial object with only one spatial attribute and defined the concept of map for arbitrary classification of objects with spatial attributes of various types. Definition of map and PART-OF relation between maps create a hierarchy of data similar to the hierarchy between objects in the real world. This hierarchy is introduced as partial order. Another benefit of using maps is the possibility to reuse basic spatial objects in forming maps. Partial order between maps provides the basis for a formal definition for zooming process. Zoom is one of the specific and crucial features of a spatial database system that up to now has not been formally defined. However, introducing a formalism for zoom in modeling phase enables us to specifically determine the portion of data that should be displayed in every step of zooming. Data security in spatial database systems is a very important concern. To build a secure spatial database system, data must be carefully structured in a hierarchical way. The formalisms presented in this paper for map hierarchy and partial order are rich enough to handle issues related to data security.

Join operation on maps was defined. Map operations such as join are applied on maps and act on the map and its components at the same time. In another words, an operation on a map will be recursively applied on its components. The designed data model is a rich collection of database formalisms, conventions and operations.

References

1. S. Abiteboul and R. Hull. IFO: A Formal Semantic Database Model. *ACM Transactions on Database Systems*, 12(4), 12 1987.
2. A. Artale, E. Franconi, N. Guarino, and L. Pazzi. Part-whole relations in object-centered systems: An overview. *Data and Knowledge Engineering*, (20), 1996.
3. A. Car and A. U.Frank. Modelling a Hierarchy of Space Applied to Large Road Networks. *International Workshop on Advanced Research in Geographic Information Systems IGIS'94 (Lecture Notes in Computer Science)*, 884, 1994.
4. A. Chance, R. Newel, and D. Theriault. An object-oriented GIS - Issue and solution. *EGIS'90, Amesterdam*, 1990.
5. M. Hammer and D. Mcleod. Database Description with SDM: A semantic Database Model. *ACM Transactions on Database Systems*, 6(3), 9 1981.
6. R. H. Guting. spatial Relational Algebra: A Model and Query Language for Spatial Database Systems. *International Conference on Extending Database Technology EDBT'88(Lecture Notes in Computer Science)*, 303, 1988.
7. T. Larue, D. Pastre, and Y. Viemont. Strong integration of spatial domains and operators in relational database systems. *SSD'93, Singapore.*
8. S. Morehouse. The Architecture of ARC/INFO. *Auto-Carto 9 Conference, Baltimore*, 19, 1989.
9. J.A. Orenstein. Spatial Query Processing in an Object-Oriented Database System. *Proc. of the ACM SIGMOD Conference*, 1986.
10. J.A. Orenstein. An object-oriented approach to spatial data processing. *Symposium on Spatial Data Handling, Zurich*, 2, 1990.
11. M. Scholl and A. Voisard. Object-Oriented Database Systems for Geographic Applications: an Experiment with O2. *Geographic Database Management Systems (Workshop Proceedings)*, 1991.
12. M. Snoeck and G. Dedene. Generalization/specialization and role in object oriented conceptual modeling. *Data and Knowledge Engineering*, (19), 1996.

Twin — A Design Pattern for Modeling Multiple Inheritance

Hanspeter Mössenböck

University of Linz, Institute of Practical Computer Science, A-4040 Linz
moessenboeck@ssw.uni-linz.ac.at

Abstract. We introduce an object-oriented design pattern called Twin that allows us to model multiple inheritance in programming languages that do not support this feature (e.g. Java, Modula-3, Oberon-2). The pattern avoids many of the problems of multiple inheritance while keeping most of its benefits. The structure of this paper corresponds to the form of the design pattern catalogue in [GHJV95].

1 Motivation

Design patterns are schematic standard solutions to recurring software design problems. They encapsulate a designer's experience and makes it reusable in similar contexts. Recently, a great number of design patterns has been discovered and published ([GHJV95], [Pree95], [BMRSS96]). Some of them are directly supported in a programming language (e.g. the *Prototype* pattern in Self or the *Iterator* pattern CLU), some are not. In this paper we describe a design pattern, which allows a programmer to simulate multiple inheritance in languages which do not support this feature directly.

Multiple inheritance allows one to inherit data and code from more than one base class. It is a controversial feature that is claimed to be indispensable by some programmers, but also blamed for problems by others, since it can lead to name clashes, complexity and inefficiency. In most cases, software architectures become cleaner and simpler when multiple inheritance is avoided, but there are also situations where this feature is really needed. If one is programming in a language that does not support multiple inheritance (e.g. in Java, Modula-3 oder Oberon-2), but if one really needs this feature, one has to find a work-around. The *Twin* pattern — introduced in this paper — provides a standard solution for such cases. It gives one most of the benefits of multiple inheritance while avoiding many of its problems.

The rest of this paper is structured according to the pattern catalogue in [GHJV95] so that the Twin pattern could in principle be incorporated into this catalogue.

1.1 Example

As a motivating example for a situation that requires multiple inheritance, consider a computer ball game consisting of active and passive game objects. The

D. Bjørner, M. Broy, A. Zamulin (Eds.): PSI'99, LNCS 1755, pp. 358–369, 2000.

active objects are balls that move across the screen at a certain speed. The passive objects are paddles, walls and other obstacles that are either fixed at a certain screen position or can be moved under the control of the user.

The design of such a game is shown in Fig. 1. All game items (paddles, walls, balls, etc.) are derived from a common base class *GameItem* from which they inherit methods for drawing or collision checking. Methods such as *draw()* and *intersects()* are abstract and have to be refined in subclasses. *check()* is a template method, i.e. it consists of calls to other abstract methods that must be implemented by concrete game item classes later. It tests if an item intersects with some other and calls the other item's *collideWith()* method in that case. In addition to being game items, active objects (i.e. balls) are also derived from class *Thread*. All threads are controlled by a scheduler using preemptive multitasking.

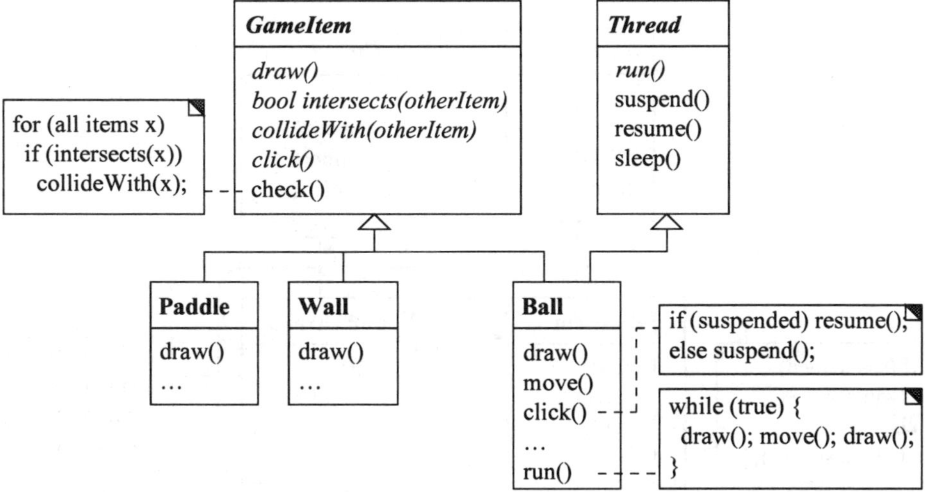

Fig. 1. Class hierarchy of a computer ball game

The body of a ball thread is implemented in its *run()* method. When a ball thread is running, it repeatedly moves and draws the ball. If the user clicks on a ball, the ball sends itself a *suspend()* message to stop its movement. Clicking on the ball again sends a *resume()* message to make the ball moving again.

The important thing about this example is that balls are *both game items and threads* (i.e. they are compatible with both). They can be linked into a list of game items, for example, so that they can be sent *draw()* and *intersects()* messages. But they can also be linked into a list of threads from which the scheduler selects the next thread to run. Thus, balls have to be compatible with both base classes. This is a typical case where multiple inheritance is useful.

Languages like Java don't support multiple inheritance, so how can we implement this design in Java? In Java, a class can extend only one base class but it can implement several interfaces. Let's see, if we can get along with multiple interface inheritance here. *Ball* could extend *Thread* and thus inherit the code of *suspend()* and *resume()*. However, it is not possible to treat *GameItem* just as an interface because *GameItem* is not fully abstract. It has a method *check()*, which contains code. *Ball* would like to inherit this code from *GameItem* and should therefore extend it as well. Thus *Ball* really has to extend two base classes.

This is the place where the Twin pattern comes in. The basic idea is as follows: Instead of having a single class *Ball* that is derived from both *GameItem* and *Thread*, we have two separate classes *BallItem* and *BallThread*, which are derived from *GameItem* and *Thread*, respectively (Fig. 2). *BallItem* and *BallThread* are closely coupled via fields so that we can view them as a Twin object having two ends: The *BallItem* end is compatible with *GameItem* and can be linked into a list of game items; the *BallThread* end is compatible with *Thread* and can be linked into a list of threads.

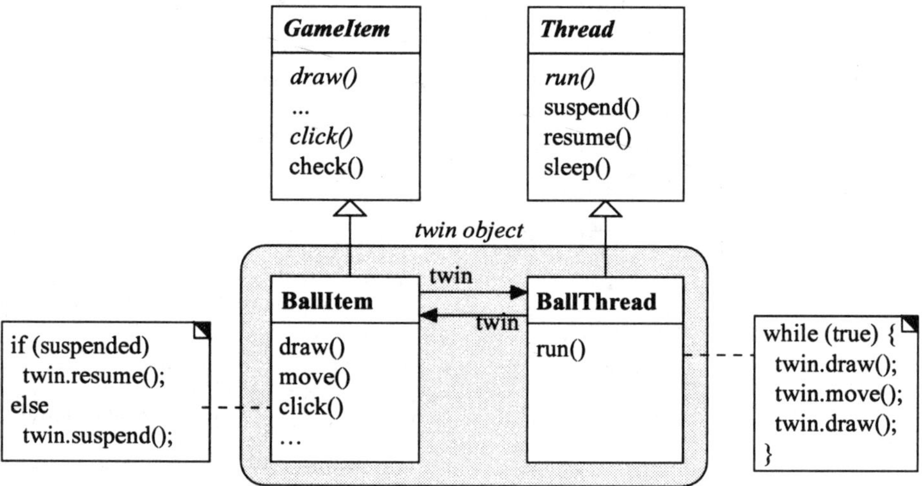

Fig. 2. The class *Ball* from Fig.1 was split into two classes, which make up a twin object

Twin objects are always created in pairs. When the scheduler activates a *BallThread* object by calling its method *run()*, the object moves the ball by sending its twin the messages *move()* and *draw()*. On the other hand, when the user clicks on a ball with the mouse, the *BallItem* object reacts to the click and sends its twin the messages *suspend()* and *resume()* as appropriate.

Using only single inheritance, we have obtained most of the benefits of multiple inheritance: Active game objects inherit code from both *GameItem* and *Thread*. They are also compatible with both, i.e. they can be treated both as game items (*draw, click*) and as threads (*run*). As a pleasant side effect, we have avoided a major problem of multiple inheritance, namely name clashes. If *GameItem* and *Thread* had fields or methods with the same name, they would be inherited by *BallItem* and *BallThread* independently. No name clash would occur. Similarly, if *GameItem* and *Thread* had a common base class *B*, the fields and methods of *B* would be handed down to *BallItem* and to *BallThread* separately — again without name clashes.

2 Applicability

The Twin pattern can be used

- to simulate multiple inheritance in a language that does not support this feature.
- to avoid certain problems of multiple inheritance such as name clashes.

3 Structure

The typical structure of multiple inheritance is described in Fig.3.

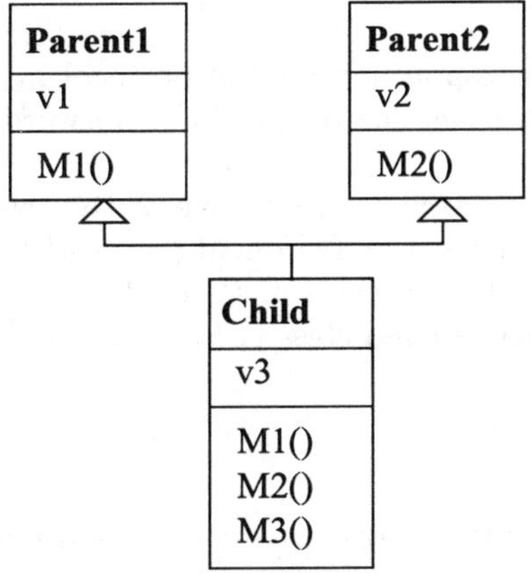

Fig. 3. Typical structure of multiple inheritance

It can be replaced by the Twin pattern structure described in Fig.4.

4 Participants

Parent1 (*GameItem*) and **Parent2** (*Thread*)

- The classes from which you want to inherit.

Child1 (*BallItem*) and **Child2** (*BallThread*)

- The subclasses of *Parent1* and *Parent2*. They are mutually linked via fields. Each subclass may override methods inherited from its parent. New methods and fields are usually declared just in one of the subclasses (e.g. in *Child1*).

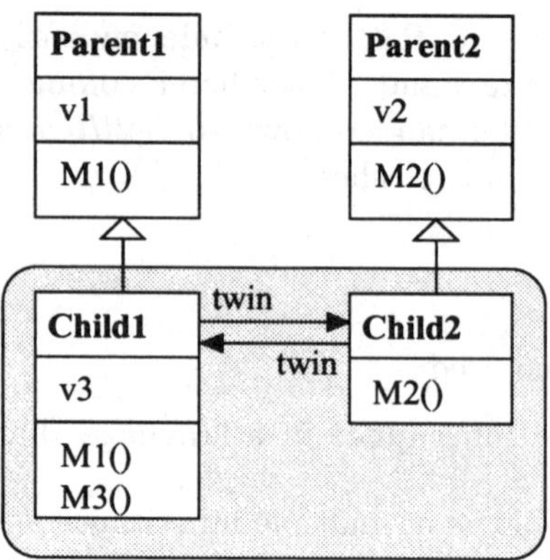

Fig. 4. Typical structure of the Twin pattern

5 Collaborations

- Every child class is responsible for the protocol inherited from its parent. It handles messages from this protocol and forwards other messages to its partner class.
- Clients of the twin pattern reference one of the twin objects directly (e.g. *ballItem*) and the other via its twin field (e.g. *ballItem.twin*).
- Clients that rely on the protocols of *Parent1* or *Parent2* communicate with objects of the respective child class (*Child1* or *Child2*).

6 Consequences

Although the Twin pattern is able to simulate multiple inheritance, it is not identical to it. There are several problems that one has to be aware of:

1. *Subclassing the Twin pattern.* If the twin pattern should again be subclassed, it is often sufficient to subclass just one of the partners, for example *Child1*. In order to pass the interface of both partner classes down to the subclass, it is convenient to collect the methods of both partners in one class. One can add the methods of *Child2* also to *Child1* and let them forward requests to the other partner (Fig.5).
   This solution has the problem that *Sub* is only compatible with *Child1* but not with *Child2*. If one wants to make the subclass compatible with both *Child1* and *Child2* one has to model it according to the Twin pattern again (Fig.6).

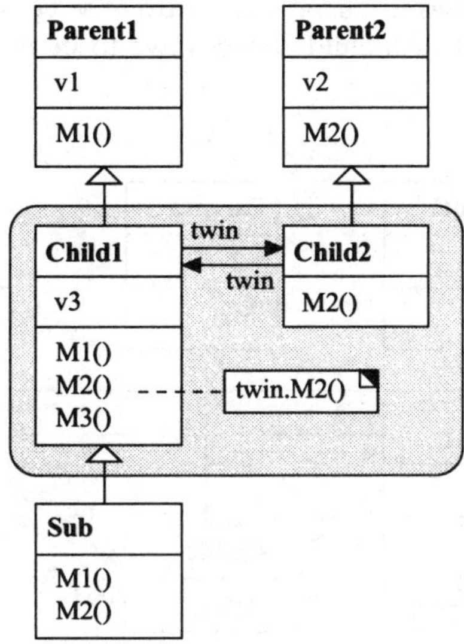

Fig. 5. Subclassing a twin class. *Child1.M2()* forwards the message to *Child2.M2()*

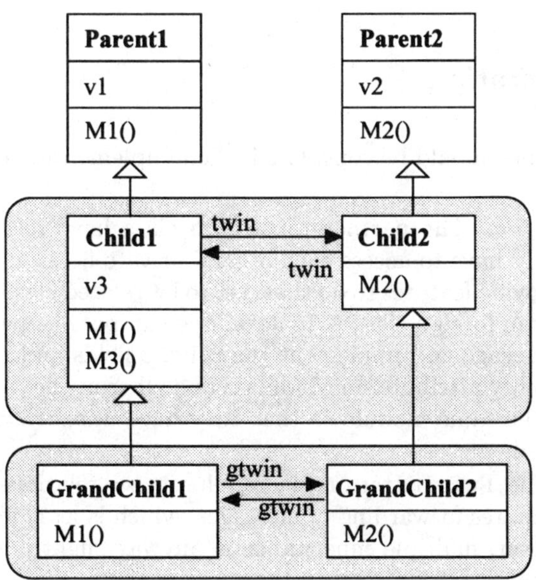

Fig. 6. The subclass of *Child1* and *Child2* is again a Twin class

2. *More than two parent classes.* The Twin pattern can be extended to more than two parent classes in a straightforward way. For every parent class there must be a child class. All child classes have to be mutually linked via fields (Fig.7).

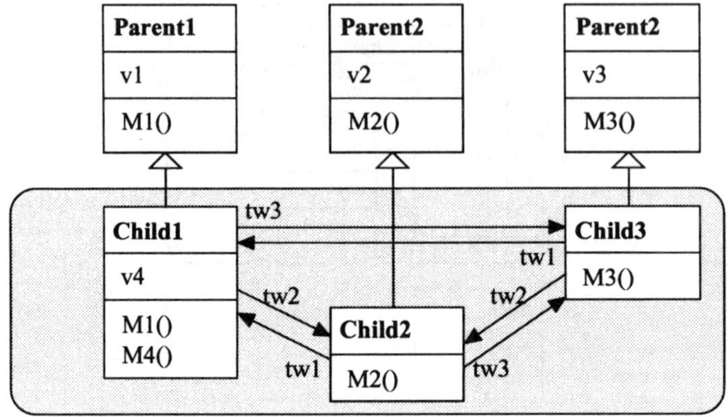

Fig. 7. A Twin class derived from three parent classes

Although this is considerably more complex than multiple inheritance, it is rare that a class inherits from more than two parent classes.

7 Implementation

The following issues should be considered when implementing the Twin pattern:

1. *Data abstraction.* The partners of a twin class have to cooperate closely. They probably have to access each others' private fields and methods. Most languages provide features to do that, i.e. to let related classes see more about each other than foreign classes. In Java, one can put the partner classes into a common package and implement the private fields and methods with the *package* visibility attribute. In Modula-3 and Oberon one can put the partner classes into the same module so that they have unrestricted access to each others' components.
2. *Efficiency.* The Twin pattern replaces inheritance relationships by composition. This requires forwarding of messages, which is less efficient than inheritance. However, multiple inheritance is anyway slightly less efficient than single inheritance [Str89] so that the additional run time costs of the Twin pattern are not a major problem.

8 Sample Code

We sketch the implementation of the motivating example (a computer game board with moving balls) in Java. The board is represented by a class *Game-Board*. It has a certain width and height and a reference to a list of game items.

```
public class Gameboard extends Canvas {
  public int width, height;
  public GameItem firstItem;
  ...
}
```

The game items are derived from an abstract class *GameItem*. Every item has a reference to the game board, a position on this board and a reference to the next game item. It has abstract methods to draw itself, to react on mouse clicks, to check whether it intersects with some other game item and to take measures for a collision with other game items.

```
public abstract class GameItem {
  Gameboard board;
  int posX, posY;
  GameItem next;
  public abstract void draw();
  public abstract void click (MouseEvent e);
  public abstract boolean intersects (GameItem other);
  public abstract void collideWith (GameItem other);
  public void check() { ... }
}
```

The method *check()* is a template method, which checks if this object intersects with any other object on the board. If so, it does whatever it has to do for a collision.

```
public void check() {
  GameItem x;
  for (x = board.firstItem; x != null; x = x.next)
    if (intersects(x)) collideWith(x);
}
```

Balls are twin objects derived from *GameItem* and *Thread*. As shown in Fig. 2 we implement the twin group as *BallItem* (a subclass of *GameItem*) and *BallThread* (a subclass of *Thread*). Ball items move at a certain speed (dx, dy) and have to override the inherited methods *draw*, *click*, *intersects* and *collide-With*.

```
public class BallItem extends GameItem {
  BallThread twin;
```

```
    int radius;
    int dx, dy;
    boolean suspended;
    public void draw() {
      board.getGraphics().drawOval(posX-radius,
      posY-radius, 2*radius, 2*radius); }
    public void move() { posX += dx; posY += dy; }
    public void click() {...}
    public boolean intersects (GameItem other) {...}
    public void collideWith (GameItem other) {...}
  }
```

In order to simplify things, we assume that balls can only collide with walls, which are another kind of game items. The *intersects* method of a *BallItem* can then be implemented as

```
  public boolean intersects (GameItem other) {
    if (other instanceof Wall)
      return posX - radius <= other.posX
        && other.posX <= posX + radius
      || posY - radius <= other.posY
        && other.posY <= posY + radius;
    else return false;
  }
```

A collision with a wall changes the direction of the ball, which can be implemented as

```
  public void collideWith (GameItem other) {
    Wall wall = (Wall) other;
    if (wall.isVertical) dx = - dx; else dy = - dy;
  }
```

When the user clicks on a moving ball it stops; when he clicks on a stopped ball it starts to move again. This is implemented by suspending and resuming the corresponding ball thread (the twin object).

```
  public void click() {
    if (suspended) twin.resume(); else twin.suspend();
    suspended = ! suspended;
  }
```

The class *BallThread* is derived from the standard class *java.lang.Thread*. It has a reference to its twin class *BallItem*. The only method that has to be implemented is *run()*. The implementation of other methods such as *suspend()* and *resume()* is inherited from *Thread*.

```
public class BallThread extends Thread {
  BallItem twin;
  public void run() {
    while (true) {
      twin.draw(); /*erase*/ twin.move(); twin.draw();
    }
  }
}
```

When a new ball is needed, the program has to create both a *BallItem* and a *BallThread* object and link them together, for example:

```
public static BallItem newBall
(int posX, int posY, int radius) {//method of GameBoard
  BallItem ballItem = new BallItem(posX, posY, radius);
  BallThread ballThread = new BallThread();
  ballItem.twin = ballThread;
  ballThread.twin = ballItem;
  return ballItem;
}
```

The returned ball item can be linked into the list of game items in the game board. The corresponding ball thread can be started to make the ball move.

9 Known Uses

The motivating example of a ball game (Section 1) was implemented as a teaching exercise in Oberon-2, a language that does not support multiple inheritance. The Oberon system uses cooperative multitasking. It maintains a list of user processes that are activated whenever the system is idle. A ball is a special instance of a process and at the same time a game object.

Another example can be found in the context of Java applets. Applets are active objects that live on Web pages and react on user input such as mouse clicks. When a user clicks on an applet, the applet notifies all registered mouse listeners to react on the event. If an applet wants to react on the click itself, it has to implement the *MouseListener* interface, so that it can be registered as an appropriate listener with itself. It must also extend the class Applet. The following code shows the declaration of a class *MyApplet*:

```
class MyApplet extends Applet implements MouseListener{
  ...
}
```

The *MouseListener* interface (a standard interface of the Java libraries) specifies 5 methods that have to be implemented in *MyApplet*:

```
interface MouseListener extends EventListener {
    public void mousePressed (MouseEvent event);
    public void mouseClicked (MouseEvent event);
    public void mouseReleased (MouseEvent event);
    public void mouseEntered (MouseEvent event);
    public void mouseExited (MouseEvent event);
}
```

Some of these methods are often identical in different listener implementations. For example, several listeners change the shape of the cursor in the same way when it enters or exits the applet area on the screen. Therefore, we would like to have a prefabricated mouse listener class (*StdMouseListener*), which already provides standard implementations for the methods *mouseEntered* and *mouseExited*. Other listeners could then inherit these standard implementations.

We are now in a situation where we would like to inherit code from two classes, namely from *Applet* and *StdMouseListener*, but this is not possible in Java. We can only inherit from one class. We can, however, apply the Twin pattern, which results in the following architecture (Fig.8).

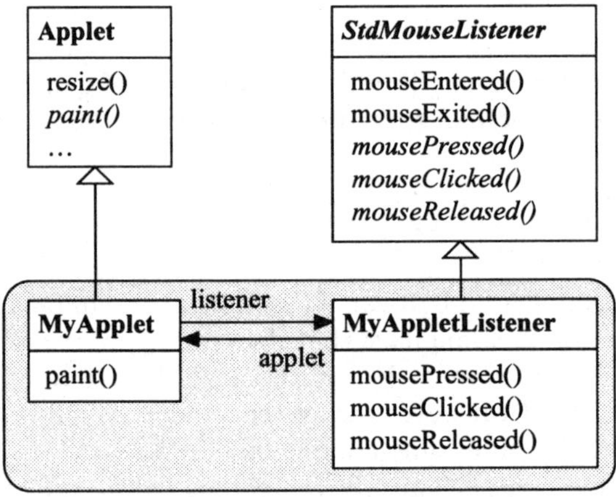

Fig. 8. A twin applet that inherits code both from *Applet* and from *StdMouseListener*

MyApplet inherits code from *Applet*; *MyAppletListener* inherits code from *StdMouseListener*. A *MyAppletListener* object will be registered as a mouse listener for *MyApplet*. When it is notified about a mouse click it accesses its applet to perform an appropriate action.

In [CaW98] a similar solution is presented using inner classes. *MyAppletListener* is implemented there as an inner class of *MyApplet*. This allows *MyAppletListener* to access all private instance variables of *MyApplet*. No explicit link between the classes is necessary. However, this solution is asymmetric. *MyApplet* cannot access the private instance variables of *MyAppletListener*.

10 Related Patterns

The Twin pattern is related to the Adapter pattern, especially to the *Two-Way-Adapter* described in [GHJV95], which is recommended when two different clients need to view an object differently. However, the *Two-Way-Adapter* is implemented with multiple inheritance while the Twin avoids this feature.

Acknowledgements

The technique described in this paper was discovered by Robert Griesemer in the implementation of a game program in Oberon. It was also described — although not as a design pattern — in [Tem93] and [Moe93].

References

[BMRSS96] Buschmann F., Meunier R., Rohnert H., Sommerlad P., Stal M.: Pattern-oriented Software Architecture: A System of Patterns. Wiley 1996.

[CaW98] Campione M., Walrath K.: The Java Tutorial, 2nd edition, Addison-Wesley, 1998.

[GHJV95] Gamma E., Helm R., Johnson R., Vlissides J.: Design Patterns — Elements of Reusable Object-Oriented Software. Addison-Wesley 1995.

[Moe93] Mössenböck H.: Objektorientierte Programmierung in Oberon-2. Springer-Verlag 1993.

[Pree95] Pree W.: Design Patterns for Object-Oriented Software Development. Addison-Wesley 1995.

[Str89] Stroustrup B.: Multiple Inheritance for C++. Proceedings EUUG Spring Conference, Helsinki, May 1989.

[Tem93] Templ J.: A Systematic Approach to Multiple Inheritance Implementation. SIGPLAN Notices 28 (4): 61-66

A Partial Semantics for Object Data Models with Static Binding

Kazem Lellahi[1] and Rachid Souah[2]

[1] LIPN, UPRES-A 7030 C.N.R.S, Université Paris 13, 93430 Villetaneuse France.
Fax:(33) 1 48 26 07 12, kl@lipn.univ-paris13.fr
[2] LRI, U.R.A. 410 C.N.R.S, Université Paris 11, 91405 Orsay cedex France.
Fax:(33) 1 69 15 65 86, souah@lri.fr

Abstract. We propose a formal semantics for object data models. Our approach may be seen as a semantic approach to object-relational models. It is *object-oriented* because it captures the main concepts of object-oriented models namely : class, method, object identity, inheritance, collection types and persistence; it is *relational* because it maintain the main characteristics of the relational model, especially the clear separation between schema, instance and querying. Moreover, it is *functional* in the sense that it is based on a simple algebra of partial functions whose main role is to perform arithmetic computations, similar to commercial languages. Another important aspect of our approach is that it provides a rigorous mathematical treatment of null value.

1 Introduction

A database can be usually seen as a collection of records. The type of a record's field is either a basic type as in the pure relational model [3], or a set of record types as in the nested relational model [17], or any combination of set and record types as in complex object models [2,9]. Some of these models also support null values [19]. But none of these models reflects the semantics of real world objects. On the other hand, object-oriented models claim to overcome this semantics problem.

In object oriented models [1,11] records, called objects in the trade, have a special field and may have other additional fields. The value of the special field is assumed to give a unique identification of the object in a context. The context of an object is its class which is a named collection of objects with the same type. Classes are organized in an inheritance hierarchy. Other additional fields of records are computations (or methods).

In the absence of a standard formal object data model, various models and various query languages have been proposed [4,10,8,5]. The ODMG group carried out an effort of standardization and proposed an object data language `ODL`, and an object query language `OQL` [7]. However, no formal model has emerged with the same authority as the relational model, and no algebraic query language with the same elegance as the relational algebra. We think that existing proposals contain enough material for defining a formal model and an algebraic query

D. Bjørner, M. Broy, A. Zamulin (Eds.): PSI'99, LNCS 1755, pp. 370–382, 2000.

language. In this paper we intend to go towards such a definition, and to a provide rigorous mathematical treatment for all concepts of object-oriented models, namely attributes, methods, classes, inheritance, object identity, persistence and other related concepts. Thus, we don't claim to introduce yet another model, but simply to give formal semantics for most common object concepts in different existing object models. In doing so, we follow the relational database tradition; namely the clear separation between schema, domain, instance and query.
To carry through this objective we consider a class as a named collection of partial functions with the same domain. The result of each function on an object is a calculation or a value which is an element of some type. Type expressions are obtained from basic types and class names, using two constructors *set* and $\otimes$. However, the semantics of $\otimes$ in this paper is not the usual cartesian product of types but a semantics more suitable for dealing with partial functions and null values. Our semantics for $\otimes$ provides a nice and rigorous treatment of null values in the object paradigm. This apparently slightly different way of seeing objects, however, leads to a different philosophy for their design and their manipulation. For example, our approach allows us

- to provide a uniform representation of attributes, methods and inheritance;
- to resolve neatly delicate problems of inheritance, namely multiple inheritance, overloading and renaming;
- to deal with null values, a subject that most object data models do not treat explicitly; and
- to define an algebraic semantics, based on a simple algebra of functions with few simple operations.

In fact, the algebra of functions that we are using, can also serve for defining an algebraic query language. This subject however, is not treated in this paper due to space limitation. The interested reader is referred to [13] for a simple version of this query language.

2 The Data Model

2.1 Database Schema

In what follows, by an *inheritance relation* over a set X, we mean a finite binary relation which is *irreflexive* and has no *cycle.* Clearly the transitive and reflexive closure of any inheritance relation is a partial order. An inheritance relation is represented either (1) as a finite subset R of $X \times X$ or (2) as a set-valued function $\overline{R}\colon X \to \mathcal{P}_f(X)$, where $\mathcal{P}_f(X)$ is the set of finite subsets of X. The correspondence between the two representation is $x \; R \; y \Longleftrightarrow y \in \overline{R}(x)$. We use the same symbol, say R, for both representations, and we denote by $R(x)$ the elements related to x via R. Similarly, given three sets X,Y and Z, we consider a finite ternary relation over (X, Y, Z) alternatively (1) as a finite subset R of $X \times Y \times Z$, or (2) as a function $\overline{R}\colon X \to \mathcal{P}_f(Y \times Z)$.

Definition 1 *A ternary relation R over* (X, Y, Z) *is said to be* XY*-functional to* Z *if it satisfies:* $\forall x \in X\ \forall y \in Y\ \forall z \in Z\ \forall z' \in Z\ \ (R(x,y,z) \wedge R(x,y,z') \Longrightarrow z = z')$.

We begin with three enumerable non empty and pairwise disjoint sets $\mathcal{A}, \mathcal{M}$ and $\mathcal{C}$. Elements of these sets are called *attribute names*, *method names*, and *class names* respectively. Now, let C be a non empty finite set of class names, and β a non empty finite set of type names, that we shall call *basic*. We consider a type system in which types are built from β and C using two constructors $\otimes$ and *set*. That is, the set $\mathcal{T}_C$ of types is defined as follows:

$$\mathcal{T}_C ::= \beta \mid C \mid \mathcal{T}_C \otimes \mathcal{T}_C \mid set\ \mathcal{T}_C$$

Elements of $\mathcal{T}_C$ are called *object-types* (or *types* for simplicity). We omit the subscript C whenever there is no possibility of confusion. In the sequel, $\mathcal{T}_C^+$ will denote the set of non empty sequences of elements of $\mathcal{T}_C$, and inheritance relations will commonly be denoted by *isa*.

Definition 2 *We say* $\mathcal{S} = (C, isa, att, meth)$ *is an object-oriented database schema (or a schema for short) if:*

- *C is a finite non empty subset of class names,*
- *isa is an inheritance relation over C,*
- *att is a finite ternary relation over $(C, \mathcal{A}, \mathcal{T}_C)$, which is $C\mathcal{A}$-functional to $\mathcal{T}_C$,*
- *meth is a finite ternary relation over $(C, \mathcal{M}, \mathcal{T}_C^+)$, which is $C\mathcal{M}$-functional to $\mathcal{T}_C^+$,*

such that for every c in C, one of the three sets $isa(c)$, $att(c)$ or $meth(c)$ is not empty (i.e. $\forall c \in C\ att(c) \cup meth(c) \cup isa(c) \neq \emptyset$). ■

For each c in C, $\mathbf{c} = (c, isa(c), att(c), meth(c))$ is called a *class* of $\mathcal{S}$ with *name* c. Each (a, t) in $att(c)$ is called an *attribute* of $\mathbf{c}$ with *name* a and *type* t; each $(m, t_1 t_2 \ldots t_k)$ in $meth(c)$ is called a method of $\mathbf{c}$ with *name* m and *profile* $t_1 t_2 \ldots t_k$. The above definition implies that classes of a schema have distinct names. Thus, a class can be recognized by its name. We read $c\ isa\ c'$ also as c *inherits* c'. The transitive and reflexive closure of *isa* is denoted by $\leq_{isa}$. We read $c <_{isa} c'$ as c *is a subclass of* c' or c' *is a superclass of* c.
Following definitions 1 and 2, the functionality of *att* and *meth* means that overloading of attributes or methods is not allowed within a class. However, this does not prevent overloading attributes or methods which are in distinct classes. Therefore, an attribute or a method is completely determined only in the context of a class and not intrinsically in the whole schema. In fact in the whole schema, an attribute (a, t) of c should be seen as (c, a, t) and a method $(m, t_1 t_2 \ldots t_k)$ of c should be seen as $(c, m, t_1 t_2 \ldots t_k)$.
Our definition of schema does not impose any restrictions on inheritance. Single inheritance as well as multiple inheritance are allowed. The last condition of Definition 2 says that if a class has no attributes and no methods, it must at least inherit another class, and if a class does not inherit any other class and has no methods (or attributes) it must have at least one attribute (or method).

According to the usual notation of the object-oriented paradigm, we shall denote an attribute (a, t) of a class by $a : t$ and a method $(m, t_1...t_k)$ by $m : t_1...t_{k-1} \longrightarrow t_k$. Since $t_1...t_k$ is a non empty sequence, some methods have the form $m :\longrightarrow t$ (methods without parameters). Such a method can be regarded as a *computed attribute.*

Our definition of schema and class is similar to the standard schema and class declarations of most object-oriented data models. Thus the standard declarations of the opposite Figure correspond in our setting to

$$isa(c) = \{c_1, \ldots, c_m\}$$
$$att(c) = \{(a_1, t_1), \ldots, (a_n, t_n)\}$$
$$meth(c) = \{(m_1, t_1^1...t_{k_1}^1), ..., (m_p, t_1^p...t_{k_p}^p)\}$$

A finite set of such declarations forms a schema iff the resulting functions *isa*, *att* and *meth* satisfy the conditions of Definition 2.

```
class c inherit c1 ... cm
  attributes :
    a1 : t1
    ⋮
    an : tn
  methods :
    m1: t1^1, ... , t^1_{k1-1} → t^1_{k1}
    ⋮
    mp: t1^p, ... , t^p_{kp-1} → t^p_{kp}
```

The schema of Figure 1 will be our running example throughout the paper. In this example, the method *bonus* in class *Prof* needs an argument of type *int* (for example the number of students that he supervises), but the same method in *Emp* has no arguments.

```
class Pers
  attributes :
    name : string
    ssn : int

class Emp inherit Pers
  attributes :
    charge : string
    hired_date : int
    salary : int
  methods :
    bonus: → int
    seniority: int → int

class Dir inherit Emp
  attributes :
    appoint_date : int
  methods :
    seniority: int → int

class Prof inherit Emp
  attributes :
    supervise : set Stud
    teaches : set Course
    charge : set Proj
  methods :
    bonus: int → int

class Stud inherit Pers
  attributes :
    supervisor : Prof
    takes : set Course

class Tutor inherit Stud, Emp
  methods :
    bonus: → int

class Proj
  attributes :
    name : string
    budget : int

class Course
  attributes :
    name : string
    level : string ⊗ int
    preq : set Course
```

Fig. 1. An example of schema

2.2 Inheritance and the Overloading Problem

The inheritance hierarchy of the schema provides a mechanism allowing us to relate together properties of classes. More precisely, when $c <_{isa} c'$, each object of c may be seen as an object of c', thus properties of c' may be considered also as properties of c. But this consideration can cause a name conflict in c. For instance, in our example, the attribute *charge* : *string* in *Emp* gives the assignment of an employee, whereas the same attribute name in the class *Prof* corresponds to the attribute *charge* : *set Proj*, which gives the set of projects that a professor is in charge of. A similar name conflict will happen for methods *seniority* in *Emp* and *seniority* in *Dir* even if they have the same type. In fact the seniority of a person as a director may differ from his/her seniority as an employee.
One way to avoid such name conflicts is to rename inherited attributes or inherited methods whenever conflict may arise. Since our next discussion will not vary if we talk about attributes or methods, we shall do the discussion for attributes only. The same results will be valid for methods.

Definition 3 *Let c and c_1 two classes of a schema of $\mathcal{S}$ such that $c \leq_{isa} c_1$. We say (c_1, a_1, t_1) does not conflict with the class c if for every attribute (c_2, a_2, t_2) of $\mathcal{S}$, we have $c_1 \leq_{isa} c_2$ whenever $c \leq_{isa} c_2$ and $a_1 = a_2$.* ■

In particular, the reflexivity of $\leq_{isa}$ implies readily that an attribute of a class c does not conflict with c itself. In our example no attribute of the class *Pers* conflicts with the classes *Emp* and *Prof*. The attribute *charge* of *Emp* conflicts with *Prof* but does not conflict with *Dir*. Similarly, the method *seniority* of *Emp* conflicts with the class *Dir*. But the method *bonus* in *Tutor* does not create any conflict. Now, we can express our renaming procedure as follows:

Renaming procedure: *For every class c and every superclass c_1 of c, if a property (i.e. attribute or method) p of c_1 conflicts with c then rename p in c.*

Our formal way for renaming will be prefixing. For example if $c \leq_{isa} c_1$ and if an attribute $a_1 : t_1$ (a method $m_1 : t_1 ... t_{k-1} \to t_k$) of c_1 conflicts with c then as an attribute (a method) of c it will be denoted $(c_1)a_1 : t_1$ ($(c_1)m_1 : t_1 ... t_{k-1} \to t_k$) respectively. In practice, instead of prefixing names, new names may be introduced. We stress that our renaming procedure does not depend on the type of the property we have to rename; and the renamed property has the same type as the original one. As a consequence, our notion of inheritance does not impose any covariance or contravariance conditions. This is in contrast to the sub-typing in object programming languages in which the covariance or contravariance constraints enforce the type of a redefined attribute (method) in a subclass, to decrease or to increase respectively [1,6]. For more detail see Section 4.3.

3 The Type System

3.1 Concrete Types

For defining schema we have used types syntactically. Now, we need to know what is the meaning of a type. Let us add to our type system a new special type with one element, called *unit*. Thus:

$$\mathcal{T}_C ::= \beta \mid C \mid \mathcal{T} \otimes \mathcal{T} \mid set\ \mathcal{T} \qquad\qquad \mathcal{T} ::= \mathcal{T}_C \mid unit$$

Each basic type name t is assumed to denote at most one denumerable set $[\![t]\!]$ that we will call *concrete type* of t. The concrete type of each class name is supposed to be a special denumerable set `oid`, which is disjoint from all other basic concrete types. The elements of `oid` are called *object identities.* Now, we consider a symbol $\perp$ and we assume that it denotes an element outside the concrete basic types and the concrete type `oid`. The concrete types of all other types are defined recursively as follows:

- $[\![unit]\!] = \{\perp\}$,
- $[\![t_1 \otimes t_2]\!] = ([\![t_1]\!] \times [\![t_2]\!]) \ + \ ([\![t_1]\!] \times [\![unit]\!]) \ + \ ([\![unit]\!] \times [\![t_2]\!])$
- $[\![set\ t]\!] = \mathcal{P}_f([\![t]\!])$

where $\times$ and $+$ are the usual cartesian product and the usual cartesian coproduct of sets. Every element of a concrete type $[\![t]\!]$ is called a *value* of t. Values will serve to define the stored part of a database. It is important to note that the semantics of $\otimes$ is not the usual cartesian product semantics. However, since $[\![t_1 \otimes t_2]\!]$ is a disjoint union of products, we write an element of $[\![t_1 \otimes t_2]\!]$ as (v_1, v_2) where v_1 or v_2 (but not both) may be the symbol $\perp$. This special semantics of $\otimes$ will allow us to deal with null values and later on with partial functions. Indeed, in the context of databases the special symbol $\perp$ can be seen as the value *null*. Then the above semantics of $\otimes$ expresses that some component of a tuple value can be *null*. Later on we shall see another role of the symbol $\perp$ which will express the undefinedness of functions. If we denote $[\![t]\!]_\perp = [\![t]\!] + [\![unit]\!]$ then we can write down readily the following theorem which relates $\otimes$ to the cartesian product:

Theorem 1 *For all types t_1 and t_2, $[\![t_1]\!]_\perp \times [\![t_2]\!]_\perp$ and $[\![t_1 \otimes t_2]\!]_\perp$ are isomorphic.*■

3.2 Classes as Types

In any type system, basic types come with operations. Usually, an *abstract type* is a named user-defined type. In our setting if $\mathcal{S} = (C, isa, att, meth)$ is a database schema then every class $(c, isa(c), att(c), meth(c))$ can be seen as a special abstract type. The name c of the class is the name and also a *sort* of this abstract type. Operations of c are then defined as follows:

- if (c, a, t) is an attribute then $a \colon c \to t$ is an *operation* over c;
- if $c <_{isa} c'$ and (c', a, t) is an attribute that does not conflict with c, then $a \colon c \to t$ is an *inherited operation* over c;

- if $c <_{isa} c'$ and (c', a, t) is an attribute which conflicts with c, then $(c')a\colon c \to t$ is a *renamed operation* over c;
- if $(c, m, t_1 \dots t_k)$ is a method then $m\colon c \otimes t_1 \otimes \dots \otimes t_{k-1} \to t_k$ is an operation over c;
- if $c <_{isa} c'$ and $(c', m, t_1 \dots t_{k-1} t_k)$ is a method that does not conflict with c then $m\colon c \otimes t_1 \otimes t_2 \dots \otimes t_{k-1} \to t_k$ is an inherited operation over c;
- if $c <_{isa} c'$ and $(c', m, t_1 \dots t_{k-1} t_k)$ is a method which conflicts with c then the renamed method $(c')m\colon c \otimes t_1 \otimes t_2 \dots \otimes t_{k-1} \to t_k$ is an operation over c;
- if $c <_{isa} c'$ then $isa^{c,c'}: c \to c'$ is an operation over c.

The above considerations reflects actually the semantics that we have in mind for a class (see Section 4). Thus, we can see a schema as a set of types and abstract type specifications. When the data model is embedded in a type system, a schema can be seen as a set of types and abstract types specifications. For instance, in O2 [12] and in CPL [5] schemas are defined in this way.

3.3 Functional Terms

In an object data model, calculations appear in two ways. On the one hand they serve to define the dynamic part (i.e. methods) of the database, and on the other hand they perform arithmetical computation. For instance adding or pairing attribute values, accessing a value by a path expression, or calling a method on an object. In our approach each calculation is a term of an algebra. This algebra acts on partial functions and is defined by the following rules:

$$\frac{}{id^*: t \to t} \qquad \frac{f\colon t_1 \to t_2 \qquad g\colon t_2 \to t_3}{f.g\colon t_1 \to t_3}$$

$$\frac{}{fst\colon t_1 \otimes t_2 \to t_1} \qquad \frac{}{snd\colon t_1 \otimes t_2 \to t_2} \qquad \frac{f_1: t \to t_1 \qquad f_2: t \to t_2}{<\!f_1, f_2\!>: t \to t_1 \otimes t_2}$$

$$\frac{}{ter^*: t \to unit} \qquad \frac{}{undef^*: unit \to t}$$

Functional terms of a given schema are outputs of these rules whenever inputs are operations of the schema or operations of basic types.
Note: The superscripte * stresses partiality and will be motivated in semantic level.

Definition 4 *Functional terms of a schema S are defined recursively as follows:*

- *if v is a value of a basic type t then $v^*: unit \to t$ is a functional term, called a constant;*
- *each basic type operation or class operation is a functional term;*
- *if inputs of a rule are functional terms then so is its output.* ∎

Note that the signature of a binary operation on a type t is no more $t \times t \rightarrow t$ but $t \otimes t \rightarrow t$.

Example 1 Suppose *bool*, *int* and *string* are basic types. Let *add**, and *mul** denote, respectively, the prefix notations of the usual operations $+, *$. The following are functional terms in our example.

- $name\colon Pers \rightarrow string,\quad name\colon Stud \rightarrow int,\quad name\colon Prof \rightarrow string$
- $<name, supervisor.name>\colon Stud \rightarrow string \otimes string,$
- $<salary, ter^*.12^*>.mul^*\colon Emp \rightarrow int$
- $bonus : Emp \longrightarrow int,\quad bonus : Prof \otimes int \longrightarrow int,\quad (Emp)bonus : Prof \longrightarrow int$
- $<fst.(Emp)bonus, <snd, ter^*.100^*>>.add^* : Prof \otimes int \longrightarrow int.$ ■

4 The Semantics

4.1 Database Instance

Roughly speaking, we see an instance of a database as a finite set of *persistent objects* and a code for each method. As usual an object is a pair (i, v) where i is an object identity and v is a value of a concrete type $[\![t]\!]$. According to our recursive construction of $[\![t]\!]$, such a value may have a complex structure. Thus, v may refer itself to other object identities. The value v referring to an object identity j is an indication for saying that the type expression t has used a class name in its construction. But, since we have interpreted every class name by the same set `oid`, we are now unable to say what class name has caused the appearance of j in v. However, we need this lost information. The reason is the following natural principle which is supported in most object-oriented systems: *If a persistent object refers to another object the later is also persistent.*

Definition 5 *For every type expression t, every value v of $[\![t]\!]$ and every class name c of the schema $\mathcal{S}$, the set $ref(v : t, c)$ is defined recursively as follows:*

- $ref(v : t, c) = \emptyset$, *for every basic type t;*
- $ref(v : c', c) = \emptyset$, *if $c' \neq c$ and $ref(v : c, c) = \{v\}$;*
- $ref(v : set\ t, c) = ref(v_1 : t, c) \cup \ldots \cup ref(v_n : t, c)$, *where $v = \{v_1, \ldots, v_n\}$;*
- $ref(v : t_1 \otimes t_2, c) = ref(v_1 : t_1, c)\ \cup\ ref(v_2 : t_2, c)$, *where $v = (v_1, v_2)$.* ■

The set $ref(v : t, c)$ is the set of all object identities which appear in v because of the presence of c somewhere in the type expression t.
In our approach a functional term $e : t_1 \longrightarrow t_2$ does not denote a function from $[\![t_1]\!]$ to $[\![t_2]\!]$ but a program which corresponds to a partial function $\hat{e} : [\![t_1]\!] \longrightarrow [\![t_2]\!]$. But we see such a partial function as a function $[\![e]\!] : [\![t_1]\!] \longrightarrow [\![t_2]\!]_\perp$ such that "$\hat{e}$ is *undefined* on x" means that $\hat{e}(x) \in [\![unit]\!] = \{\perp\}$ (recall that $[\![t]\!]_\perp = [\![t]\!] + [\![unit]\!]$). Thus the symbol $\perp$ expresses the undefinedness of functions. Expressing $\perp$ as the undefined value coupled with the semantics of $\otimes$, seen so far, allows a rigorous treatment of the *null* value in the database paradigm. Note that, the symbol $\perp$ appears only in the codomain of $[\![e]\!]$.

Definition 6 *A database instance over a schema $\mathcal{S} = (C, isa, att, meth)$ is a function δ that associates*

1. *with every class name c of C a finite subset $\delta(c)$ of* `oid`*, such that:*
   - *if $c <_{isa} c'$ then $\delta(c) \subseteq \delta(c')$,*
   - *if c and c' have no common subclass and no common superclass then $\delta(c) \cap \delta(c') = \emptyset$;*
2. *with every attribute (c, a, t) of $\mathcal{S}$, a finite function $a^c_\delta : [\![c]\!] \longrightarrow [\![t]\!]_\perp$ such that:*
   - *$def(a^c_\delta) \subseteq \delta(c)$,*
   - *for all $i \in \delta(c)$ and $c' \in C$, $ref(a^c_\delta(i) : t, c') \subseteq \delta(c')$;*
3. *with every method $(c, m, t_1 \dots t_{k-1} t_k)$ of $\mathcal{S}$, a functional term*
   $m^c_\delta \colon c \otimes t_1 \otimes \dots \otimes t_{k-1} \to t_k$. ■

Note that in this definition each class name is seen as a persistent root. There is an explicit distinction between the stored and the computed part of the database. The stored part is defined by clauses 1 and 2 and the computed part by clause 3. The stored part is finite, and consists of a finite set of objects and a set of finite functions, one for each attribute. The computed part is "infinite" and consists of a set of codes, one for each method. A code is an abstract syntax (i.e a functional term). The second part of the second clause of Definition 6 says that: a persistent object cannot refer another object unless that object is persistent. This is actually the principle of persistence seen earlier. The first clause of Definition 6 requires that $\delta(c) \subseteq \delta(c')$ whenever $c <_{isa} c'$. This means that: *the semantics of inheritance is set inclusion.*

4.2 Semantics of Rules

In order to define the semantics of the rules we recall some practical notations:

- For two sets T_1, T_2, $\Pi_i^{T_1 T_2} \colon T_1 \times T_2 \to T_i$ $(i = 1, 2)$ will be the usual projections and $in_i^{T_1 T_2} \colon T_i \to T_1 + T_2$ the usual coprojections. When $T_2 = \{\perp\}$ we write $def^{T_1} \colon T_1 \to T_1 + \{\perp\}$ and $undef^{T_1} \colon \{\perp\} \to T_1 + \{\perp\}$ instead of $in_1^{T_1 \{\perp\}}$ and $in_2^{T_1 \{\perp\}}$. We omit superscripts when there is no risk of confusion.
- For $f_i \colon A \to A_i$ $(i = 1, 2)$, the function $< f_1, f_2 >\colon A \to A_1 \times A_2$ is defined by $< f_1, f_2 > (x) = (f_1(x), f_2(x))$. Similarly for $g_i \colon A_i \to A$ $(i = 1, 2)$ the function $[g_1, g_2] : A_1 + A_2 \longrightarrow A$ is defined by:
  $[g_1, g_2](x) \;=\; if\ (x = in_1 y)\ then\ g_1(y)\ else\ if\ (x = in_2 z)\ then\ g_2(z)$.
- If $f_i \colon A_i \to B_i$ $(i = 1, 2)$ then $f_1 + f_2 \colon A_1 + A_2 \to A_1 + A_2$ is an abbreviation for $[in_1^{B_1 B_2} \circ f_1, in_2^{B_1 B_2} \circ f_2]$.
- For every set T the function $ter \colon T \to \{\perp\}$ is the unique function from T to $\{\perp\}$, $id \colon T \to T$ is the identity function. An element a of T is seen as a function $a \colon \{\perp\} \to T$, where $a(\perp) = a$.

Now, we define the semantics of the rules as follows:

$$[\![id^*]\!] = def \circ id = def \qquad [\![f.g]\!] = [[\![g]\!], undef] \circ [\![f]\!] \qquad [\![<f,g>]\!] = <[\![f]\!], [\![g]\!]>$$

$$[\![fst]\!] = [\Pi_1^{[\![t_1]\!][\![t_2]\!]}, \Pi_1^{[\![t_1]\!][\![unit]\!]}] + \Pi_1^{[\![unit]\!][\![t_1]\!]}$$

$$[\![snd]\!] = [\Pi_2^{[\![t_1]\!][\![t_2]\!]}, \Pi_2^{[\![unit]\!][\![t_2]\!]}] + \Pi_2^{[\![t_1]\!][\![unit]\!]}$$

$$[\![ter^*]\!] = def \circ ter \qquad [\![undef^*]\!] = undef$$

Note that, at the syntax level we compose functions in left-to-right order which corresponds to program chaining; whereas at the semantics level we are using the classical right-to left order's composition of functions. The apparent complexity of the above semantics is due to our concern for treating null values and undefinedness rigorously. This semantics says that: the operation $[\![fst]\!]$ ($[\![snd]\!]$) is undefined whenever its first (second) argument is *null*. Note the introduction of $[[\![g]\!], undef]$ for defining $[\![f.g]\!]$. Indeed, $[\![g]\!] \circ [\![f]\!]$ is ill-typed whereas $[[\![g]\!], undef] \circ [\![f]\!]$ is well-typed.

4.3 Semantics of Functional Terms

According to Definition 4, functional terms are obtained recursively from a schema $\mathcal{S}$ using rules. The basis of the recursion consists of constants, basic type operations and class operations.

Semantics of basic operations: In our type system a binary operation of a basic type looks like $op^* : t \otimes t \longrightarrow t$. Thus, its semantics is $[\![op^*]\!] : [\![t \otimes t]\!] \longrightarrow [\![t]\!]_\perp$. Since the semantics of $t \otimes t$ is $[\![t]\!] \times [\![t]\!] + \{\perp\} \times [\![t]\!] + [\![t]\!] \times \{\perp\}$, one of the two arguments of $[\![op^*]\!]$ may be undefined (i.e. equal to $\perp$). We assume that the result of $[\![op^*]\!]$ is $\perp$ whenever one of its arguments is $\perp$. Formally,

$$[\![op^*]\!] = op + [\Pi_1^{[\![unit]\!][\![t]\!]}, \Pi_2^{[\![t]\!][\![unit]\!]}],$$

where $op : [\![t]\!] \times [\![t]\!] \longrightarrow [\![t]\!]$ is a usual binary operation on $[\![t]\!]$. For a unary or a 0-ary operation f^* of basic types we have $[\![f^*]\!] = def \circ f$. Similarly, if a is a value of a basic concrete type $[\![t]\!]$ then $[\![a^*]\!] = def \circ a$.
The rest of the semantics will be generated from a database instance δ.

Semantics of inheritance relationships: We have expressed $c <_{isa} c'$ syntactically as the operation $isa^{c,c'} : c \rightarrow c'$ of c (Section 3.2). According to Definition 6, $\delta(c) \subseteq \delta(c')$ thus, there is a partial function $isa_\delta^{c,c'} : [\![c]\!] \longrightarrow [\![c']\!]_\perp$ corresponding to this inclusion. Therefore we define: $[\![isa^{c,c'}]\!] = isa_\delta^{c,c'}$.

Semantics of attributes: The attributes of a class act on objects of that class. More precisely,

- For every attribute (c, a, t) in $\mathcal{S}$, $[\![a]\!]^c = a_\delta^c$.
- For all classes c, c', if $c <_{isa} c'$ then for every attribute (c', a, t) which does not conflict with c, $[\![a]\!]^c = [\![isa^{c,c'}.a]\!]$ $(= [[\![a]\!]^{c'}, undef] \circ [\![isa^{c,c'}]\!])$.

- For all classes c, c', if $c <_{isa} c'$ then for every attribute (c', a, t) which conflicts with c, $[\![(c')a]\!]^c = [\![isa^{c,c'}.a]\!]$.

The second (third) of the above clauses says: the semantics of a as an inherited (renamed) attribute of c is the semantics of a as an attribute of c' but restricted to objects in c.

Semantics of methods: Contrary to attributes, methods operate on objects according to the designer's/ user's choice for *static* or *late binding.* In static binding a method operates in the same way on all objects of a class, but in late binding the operation on an object, depends on the way that the object is shared by other classes. The following are the semantics of methods that suit only for static binding (late binding needs a sub-typing and some constraints on schema, and will be treated in a forthcoming paper):

- For every method $(c, m, t_1 \dots t_k)$ in $\mathcal{S}$, $[\![m]\!]^c = [\![m^c_\delta]\!]$.
- For all classes c, c', if $c <_{isa} c'$ then for every method $(c', m, t_1 \dots t_k)$ which does not conflict with c,

$$[\![m]\!]^c = \begin{cases} [\![isa^{c,c'}.m]\!] \ (= [[\![m]\!]^{c'}, undef] \circ [\![isa^{c,c'}]\!]), & if \ \ k = 1 \\ [\![\lessdot fst.isa^{c,c'}, snd \gtrdot .m]\!], & if \ \ k > 1 \end{cases}$$

- For all classes c, c', if $c <_{isa} c'$ then for every method $(c', m, t_1 \dots t_k)$, which conflicts with c,

$$[\![(c')m]\!]^c = \begin{cases} [\![isa^{c,c'}.m]\!], & if \ \ k = 1 \\ [\![\lessdot fst.isa^{c,c'}, snd \gtrdot .m]\!], & if \ \ k > 1 \end{cases}$$

5 Concluding Remarks

We have introduced a formal object-oriented data model with partial semantics. Partiality has been used in the model oriented approach of computation theory for representing the possibility of failure during program execution. In this theory a partial map f from X to Y is seen as a pair $D_f \longrightarrow X$, $D_f \longrightarrow Y$ of total maps such that $D_f \longrightarrow X$ is an inclusion [16]. We have considered a partial map as a total map $X \longrightarrow Y \cup \{\bot\}$, where $\bot$ is supposed to be outside Y. This point of view suits better to database theory in which failure corresponds to undefinedness.

We have considered a database as a set of partial functions. Each function represents an attribute or a method, and $\bot$ represents null value (or value undefined). A similar approach have been proposed in [14,15] with a categorical point of view, but without considering methods and binding modes. This paper investigates with methods and static binding, and improved deeply their concept of inheritance. However, we restrict our study to methods without side-effects.

According to [18] the objective of object-relational model is to extend the relational model by providing a richer type system including object orientation.

In this sense our model can be seen as an object-relational model. We have endowed the type system with an algebra of functions by means of rules. These rules are similar (but, not equivalent) to those presented in [5]. The similarity comes from the fact that they both contain a common mathematical structure. But our semantics for this structure is the universe of sets and partial maps whereas their semantics is based on collection types and total functions. For this reason we have introduced a particular semantics for $\otimes$, whereas they use the usual cartesian product $\times$. Several aspects of particular interest have not been presented here, especially dynamic binding, query language and some interesting developments that concern category theory. These aspects will be reported in a forthcoming work.

References

1. M. Abadi and L. Cardelli. *A Theory of Objects.* Springer-Verlag, 1996.
2. S. Abiteboul and C. Beeri. On the power of languages for the manipulation of complex values. *VLDB Journal*, 4(4):717–794, 1995.
3. S. Abiteboul, R. Hull, and V. Vianu. *Foundation of Databases.* Addison-Wesley, 1995.
4. F. Bancilhon, S. Cluet, and C. Delobel. A query language for o2. *In F. Bancilhon, C. Delobel and P. Kanellakis editors. Building an Object-Oriented Database System, The Story of O2. Morgan Kaufmann*, 1992.
5. P. Buneman, S. Naqvi, V. Tannen, and Limsoon Wong. Principle of programming with complex objects and collection types. *T.C.S.*, 149:3–48, 1995.
6. G. Castagna. *Object-Oriented Programming. A Unified Foundation.* Birkhäuser, 1997.
7. R. Cattel. *The Object Databases Standard: ODMG-93, Release 1.2.* Morgan Kaufmann, 1996.
8. J. Frohn, G. Lausen, and H. Uphoff. Access to objects by path expressions and rules. *VLDB Conference, Santiago*, pages 273–284, 1994.
9. R. Hull. A survey of theoretical research on typed complexe database objects. *J. Pareadens, Ed., Academic Press*, pages 193–256, 1987.
10. M. Kifer, W. Kim, and Y. Sagiv. Querying object-oriented databases. *SIGMOD Conference*, pages 393–402, 1992.
11. W. Kim. *Modern Database Systems. The Object Model, Interoperability, and Beyond.* Addison-Wesley, 1995.
12. C. Lecluse and P. Richard. The o2 data model. *In François Bancilhon, Claude Delobel, and Paris Kanellakis, editors, Building an Object-Oriented Data-base System, The Story of O_2. Morgan Kaufmann*, 1992.
13. S.K. Lellahi, R. Souah, and N. Spyratos. An algebraic query language for object-oriented data models. *DEXA'97, LNCS 1308*, pages 519–528, 1997.
14. S.K. Lellahi and N. Spyratos. Towards a categorical data model supporting structural object and inheritance. *LNCS NO 504*, pages 86–105, 1991.
15. S.K. Lellahi and N. Spyratos. Categorical modelling of database concept. Technical report, FIDE/92/38, University of Glasgow, Dept. of Computer Science, 1992.
16. Morizio Proietti. Connection between partial maps categories and tripos theory. *Proceedings of Category Theory and Computer Science, LNCS 283*, pages 254–269, 1987.

17. H.J. Schek and M.H. Sholl. The relational model with relational valued attributes. *Information Systems*, 11(2):137–147, 1986.
18. M. Stonebraker. *Object-Relational DBMS's.* Morgan Kauffman Publishers, 1996.
19. C. Zaniolo. Database relations with null values. *Journal of Computer and System Sciences*, 28:142–166, 1984.

Heterogeneous, Nested STL Containers in C++

Volker Simonis and Roland Weiss

Wilhelm-Schickard-Institut für Informatik, Universität Tübingen
Sand 13, 72076 Tübingen, Germany
{simonis,weissr}@informatik.uni-tuebingen.de

1 Motivation

The incentive to write a nested, heterogeneous container in C++ surfaced in the SuchThat project [11]. Therein we are working on the implementation of a SuchThat compiler. The first prototype's back-end [14], as well as many of the other components, were implemented in Scheme [8]. One of Scheme's main advantages is the powerful list data structure, which can hold arbitrary data types[1]. This allows the user to build nested lists, e.g. to represent a parse tree or symbol table.

Our current focus is on merging Tecton [7] with SuchThat. Due to severe performance problems with our first prototype we have switched to C++ as implementation language. The STL provides basic containers that suit most simple needs and exhibit very good runtime behavior. The containers' major drawback for our purposes is the inability to hold objects of different types and that they do not support nesting.

We will show that exploitation of C++'s newest technologies, like templates and run-time type information (RTTI), leads to a powerful data structure based on the STL. We think that the different paradigms of generic, object oriented and functional programming, which often are seen as adversaries, can instead complement each other.

2 Approaches

We observed a trade off between syntactic elegance and runtime performance. This made us come up with two fundamentally distinct approaches.

The first one, the more conservative, relies on an abstract base class that provides polymorphic behavior with easy to use parameterized standard elements. The `nseq` class uses template template arguments (see [1], 14.3.3) for maximal flexibility.

The second approach builds on the semantics of chameleon objects [12]. It is outperformed by the first one regarding runtime but excels in usability.

[1] Of course, this holds true for any untyped language.

D. Bjørner, M. Broy, A. Zamulin (Eds.): PSI'99, LNCS 1755, pp. 383–388, 2000.

2.1 Specification of the Problem

We informally state with the following three requirements what we call a *heterogeneous, nested sequence S*.

1. Every STL sequence container should be applicable as underlying implementation container of S (flexibility property).
2. S should be able to hold arbitrary objects (heterogeneity property).
3. Any nested sequence S should be able to hold other nested sequences recursively (nesting property).

2.2 Classical Polymorphism

The well established way in C++ to provide polymorphic behavior uses inheritance. The heterogeneous container holds pointers to a base class and the C++ runtime system will dispatch methods based on the polymorphic type. Our base class `BaseElem` declares the virtual functions `BaseElem* clone()` and `BaseElem* create()` to support the virtual constructor idiom (see [2], 20.5).

Instead of letting the user write wrapper objects for every type he uses, we deliver the template class `Elem<>` that inherits from `BaseElem`. The signature is `template <class valT> class Elem : public BaseElem`. This wrapper class does all the tedious work a user usually has to do on his own: define constructors and destructors, as well as various auxiliary methods (e.g. I/O functions). She must only instantiate the template class. This works for basic types and classes, e.g. `Elem<int> i` or `Elem<string> s("test")`.

Let us examine the class `nseq`, which should fulfill the problem specification given in section 2.1. The heterogeneity property can be obtained by keeping pointers to the base class `BaseElem` in the sequence. If we want to comply to the nesting property, `nseq` must be derived from `BaseElem` itself. Furthermore, in order to use STL containers, `nseq` must also be a subclass of such a container. These considerations lead to this signature of a nested list:

```
class nlist : public list<BaseElem*>, public BaseElem
```

This works fine, but it does not fulfill the flexibility property, because the implementation container is hard-coded. You cannot provide different containers, as the class `nlist` is a subclass of the STL container instantiation `list<BaseElem*>`. To gain the desired additional level of abstaction, we use template template arguments, a very novel C++ feature. `nseq` becomes a template class, whose template argument is a container, which is a template class itself. Therefore, a simple template would not suffice. The final class header for `nseq` reads:

```
template <template <class valT> class containerT>
class nseq : public containerT<BaseElem*>, public BaseElem
```

The `clone()`-function has a boolean parameter `shallow`, which is of importance for nested sequences only. It controls if either a shallow or a deep copy of the container is made. A shallow copy creates a new container with pointers to all top-level elements. A deep copy creates a new container, recursively holding copies of the containers and atoms in the source sequence.

Working with our `nseq` class is quite simple. An instance of a nested deque is created with `nseq<deque> nd`. We can use all of `deque`'s member functions to add elements to our container, e.g. `nd.push_back(new Elem<int>(4711))`. The sequence can be walked with the STL container's iterators, but only at the top-most level. You can recursively descend into nesting layers, if the member function `bool is_atom()` returns false, which is the case for elements that are nested sequences. When you walk a `nseq` and want to operate on the elements, you have to perform a dynamic cast on `BaseElem`. The following code example shows how the first level of a nested sequence is walked with the container provided iterator and every integer entry is replaced by its square power.

```
for (nseq<list>::iterator iter = nl.begin()); iter != nl.end(); ++iter)
  if (intp = dynamic_cast<Elem<int>*>(*iter))
    *intp = intp->getValue() * intp->getValue();
```

Figure 1 compares the layout of `nseq<vector>` and `vector<int>`[2]. It shows that we get a memory overhead of two pointers (eight bytes) for every element, regardless of the wrapped object's type. The first one points to `BaseElem`. This indirection is needed to use C++'s polymorphic mechanism. The second pointer holds the address of the element's virtual table.

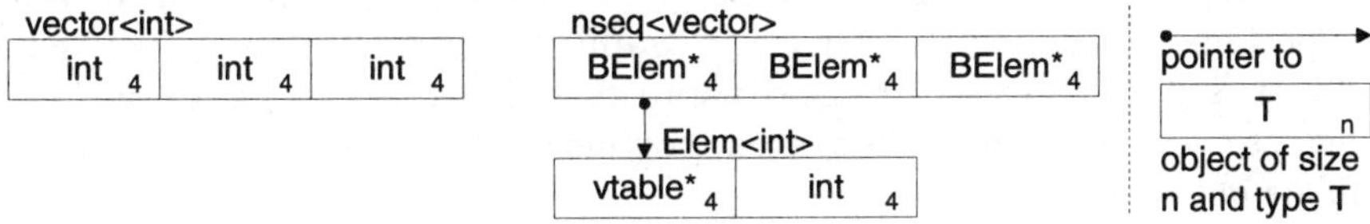

Fig. 1. Layout comparison of a standard STL container and a nested sequence

2.3 Chameleon Objects

In [12] a new technique for providing a generic, type-safe wrapper class is presented. This goal is achieved through the unparameterized class `Value`. Contrary to the class itself, all its methods, like the constructor and a set of overloaded operators, are parametrized, i.e. template functions. Thus, any object of arbitrary type can be assigned to a `Value` object due to the parameterized assignment operator `template<class T> T operator=(const T&)`. In turn, a `Value` object can easily be reassigned to an object of its initial type because of the parameterized conversion operator `template<class T> T& operator T()`.

The `Value` class guarantees strict type safety by signaling any attempt to assign a `Value` object to another object of incorrect type by throwing an exception[3]. To achieve this functionality, the `Value` class keeps all information about the wrapped object in a private, static data member inside a member function, parameterized with the same type.

[2] We assume that sizeof(int) = 4 and sizeof(pointer) = 4, which is true for most contemporary 32bit architectures.

[3] Type identity is defined as name identity here.

Since all used data types are known at compile time, the compiler can instantiate the corresponding methods and data objects. In fact, for every data type used in conjunction with a Value object, a full set of operators and methods is instantiated by the compiler. The type checking of any operation concerning a Value object is performed by these methods at run time. Because of their ability to change their internal type at any time, Value class instances are called *chameleon objects*.

Given this Value class, we can now construct heterogeneous containers based on the standard STL containers by instantiating such a container for Value with list<Value> polyCont. Thereafter, objects of arbitrary type can be inserted into the container, e.g. polyCont.push_back(12), polyCont.push_back(0.9) and polyCont.push_back(string("hello")). Because, as stated above, Value objects can hold objects of any type, even containers can be inserted as elements into a Value parameterized container, thus obtaining nested containers.

The extraction of elements from the container is straightforward, too. If we know the the desired element's type, we can simply query it. Given the list polyCont from the previuos example, we can write int i=polyCont.front() to get the first element of the list. More care must be taken if the type of the desired element is unknown. Since overloading the typeid() operator is not allowed in C^{++} (see [1], 13.5), the Value class defines a method typeId(), which returns the type information for the currently wrapped object. With this information and Value's parameterized method template<class T> T& getValue(), one can access every element of the nested, polymorphic container. This is shown in the following sample code:

```
// double sin(double); a function with this signature must exist
void apply(list<Value> &cont) {
  for (list<Value>::iterator it = cont.begin(); it != cont.end(); ++it) {
    if (it->typeId() == typeid(list<Value>)) apply((list<Value>)*it);
    else if (it->typeId() == typeid(int)) *it = (int)*it * (int)*it;
    else if (it->typeId() == typeid(double)) *it = sin(*it);
  }
}
```

3 Performance Tests

The results of the performance tests are presented in Figure 2. We compared the original STL list and vector containers against their nested counterparts based on our implementations. The tests consisted of two parts, container creation and element access. They were all performed for int and std::string data types. The containers were filled in a loop using push_back(T&). Access was measured by iterating over the created container and mutating its elements.

The charts show the overhead introduced by our containers for the flat, homogeneous case, where of course their additional features are not used. The price you have to pay for nesting and heterogeneity is a runtime penalty ranging from 1.3 to 1.9 for complex objects (std::string in our tests) and 2.9 to 13 for built in types (int).

Furthermore, we want to note that due to the extensive use of the new operator in our element classes, the tests depend heavily on the applied memory allocation scheme. Therefore our source code includes the smart memory allocator presented in [5], which speeds up the tests significantly compared to the default new operator.

Our classes make heavy use of new C++ language features like RTTI and templates. We were able to compile our code at the time of this writing with egcs 1.1 [3], the EDG front-end [4] and IBM VisualAge C++ 4.0 [6].

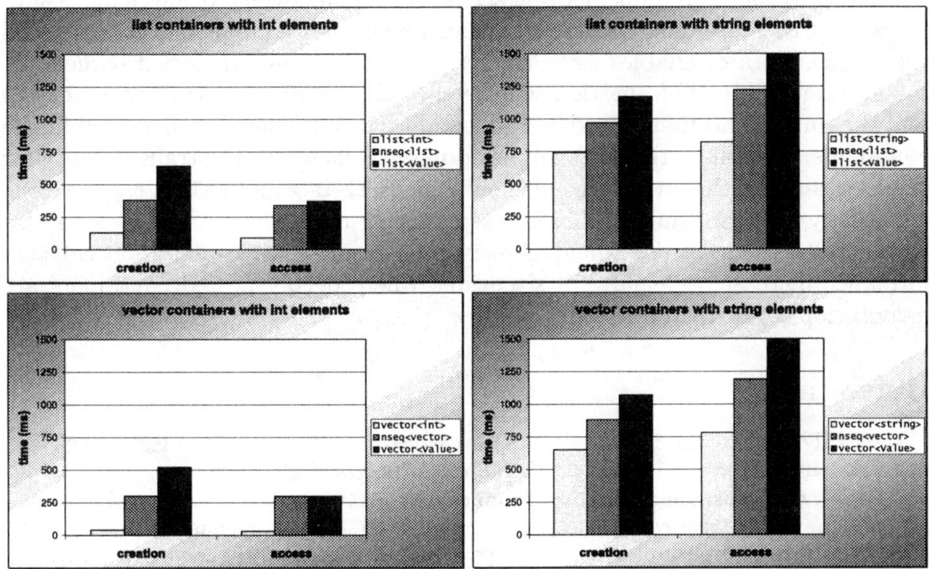

Fig. 2. All tests ran on a Pentium II, 333 MHz, 128MB machine under Windows NT 4 and were compiled with egcs 1.1.1. The container size is 400000 elements

4 Results

We presented two distinct approaches to the problem of implementing a nested, heterogeneous container in C++. The classical one shows better runtime performance. Its overhead, compared to a standard STL container, arises from the pointer indirection, which is necessary for the polymorphic approach, and the virtual table pointer in the Elem<> class (see Figure1). This generic wrapper frees the user of boring work. One drawback is the pointer semantics, uncommon in the value semantics of STL containers. It also forces the user to handle most aspects of memory management.

The container based on chameleon objects offers syntactic elegance that equals untyped data structures, like those present in Scheme. Operations on elements are inherently type-safe, type violations are signalled by exceptions. All this is made possible by the seamless integration of STL containers with the Value class. It hides much of the details of casting and type checking from the user, which is still visible in our classical approach. No efforts must be taken by the user to adapt objects for storage in the nested container. The beauty of this approach is bought at the cost of increased runtime.

Our classes leave it up to the programmer to choose either faster executing code or more elegant source code.

5 Future Work

We currently focus on implementing a `flat_iterator`, which behaves like a simple sequence iterator and traverses all elements in a nested sequence in depth first order. This iterator enables us to use STL algorithms on our nested sequences.

Another interesting question will be the use of different memory allocators and the implementation of garbage collection ([10]) for the objects stored in the containers. We believe this task can be addressed efficiently and transparently for the user through the introduced element classes `Elem<>` and `Value`, respectively.

Finally, one can think of a reference counting mechanism, implemented also through the mentioned element classes, which can lead to a dramatical performance increase, especially in situations where deeply nested containers are heavily copied for read only purposes.

References

1. ANSI/ISO Standard: *Programming languages - C++*, ISO/IEC 14882, 1998.
2. Marshall Cline: *C++ FAQ LITE – Frequently Asked Questions*, `http://www.cerfnet.com/~mpcline/c++-faq-lite`.
3. Cygnus Solutions: *egcs project home page*, `http://egcs.cygnus.com`.
4. Edison Design Group: *The C++ Front End*, `http://www.edg.com/cpp.html`.
5. Sasha Gontmakher and Ilan Horn: *Efficient Memory Allocation*, Dr. Dobbs Journal, p. 116-119, January 1999.
6. IBM: *IBM VisualAge C++*, `http://www.software.ibm.com/ad/visualage_c++`.
7. D. Kapur and David R. Musser: *Tecton: a framework for specifying and verifying generic system components*, Rensselaer Polytechnic Institute Computer Science Technical Report 92-20, 1992.
8. Richard Kelsey, William Clinger, and Jonathan Rees (editors): *Revised^5 Report on the Algorithmic Language Scheme*, 1998.
9. David R. Musser, Atul Saini: *STL Tutorial and Reference Guide*, Addison-Wesley Publishing Company, 1996.
10. Gor V. Nishanov, Sibylle Schupp: *Garbage Collection in Generic Libraries*, Proceedings of the International Symposium on Memory Management 1998, p. 86-97, Richard Jones (editor), 1998.
11. Sibylle Schupp: *Generic programming — SuchThat one can build an algebraic library*, Ph.D. thesis at the Wilhelm-Schickard-Institut für Informatik, Eberhard-Karls-Universität Tübingen, 1996.
12. Volker Simonis: *Chameleon Objects, or how to write a generic type safe wrapper class*, accepted for publication in C++ Report, SIGS Publications, 1999.
13. David Vandevoorde: *C++ Solutions*, Addison-Wesley Publishing Company, 1998.
14. Roland Weiss: *ScmToCpp: a configurable, intelligent back-end for SuchThat*, Internal Report at the WSI für Informatik, Universität Tübingen, 1998.

Data Flow Analysis of Java Programs in the Presence of Exceptions*

Vladimir I. Shelekhov and Sergey V. Kuksenko

A. P. Ershov Institute of Informatics Systems, Siberian Division,
Russian Academy of Sciences,
Acad. Lavrentjev pr. 6, Novosibirsk 630090, Russia
vshel@iis.nsk.su, sergic@iis.nsk.su

Abstract. For data flow analysis of Java program to be correct and precise, the flows induced by exceptions must be properly analysed. In our data flow analysis, the implicit control flow for a raised exception is represented explicitly. Exception branches, exception plateaus, and exception exits for methods and method calls are introduced as additional control flow structures for analysis of exception handling. These structures are constructed dynamically under control of data flow analysis.

Introduction

Java [7] is a new programming language that integrates many useful features of modern languages such as C++ and Oberon-2. In Java, exceptions are elaborated as a quite natural mechanism highly integrated with other parts of the language. Exceptions may be thrown by methods of the standard Java classes, and a user program may catch and handle them. Obviously, exceptions are widely used in Java programs.

Exceptions pose new challenge to developers of data flow analyses. An exception, raised in a method body, induces a control flow other than the main control flow from the method call. So, at the end of the method body, a proper analysis must separate the data flow calculated for the raised exception from the main data flow. Now, a typical data flow analyser either ignores exceptions or, in the best case, roughly mixes data flow for the raised exception with the main data flow. The only known approach of proper analysis of programs with exceptions is described in [1].

Data flow analysis implemented in the static error checker OSA (Oberon-2/Modula-2 Static Analyser) [2] ignores exceptions in Modula-2 programs. Of course, OSA analysis is not correct for exceptions. Nevertheless, there was almost no problem with it so far because exceptions are rarely used in real Modula-2 programs. For the OSA analysis of Java programs to be correct, proper analysis of the exception handling is needed. There exists an additional motivation. In Java programs, **catch** clauses are rarely executed and therefore are

* This research was supported by the Russian Foundation for Basic Research, RFFI 97-01-00724

D. Bjørner, M. Broy, A. Zamulin (Eds.): PSI'99, LNCS 1755, pp. 389–395, 2000.

difficult for testing. So for non-trivial exception handling, it is highly probable for our static analyser to find errors induced by exception handling.

In our data flow analysis, the implicit control flow for a raised exception is represented explicitly. Exception branches, exception plateaus, and exception exits for methods and method calls are introduced as additional control flow structures for analysis of exception handling. These structures are constructed dynamically under control of data flow analysis. The hypergraph representation, previously applied for statements of Oberon-2/Modula-2 programs, is used for method bodies and method calls of analysed Java programs.

The rest of this paper is organized as follows. First, we present the overview of the basic data flow analysis applied in the static analyser OSA. In the second section we describe the Java subset implemented. Our analysis of exception handling is described in next two sections. In the third section we introduce the new notions and new structures applied in the analysis. Next, we present the analysis of all exception-related Java constructs. In the fifth section we outline other approaches in analysis of exception handling in the related work section. In the conclusion, we give some remarks on the implementation.

1 Data Flow Analysis Overview

The static error checker OSA (http://www.xds.ru/osa/) checks programs for run-time errors by analysing the source code. The powerful data flow analysis used in OSA is able to detect various kinds of Modula-2 and Oberon-2 dynamic semantics violations, which are usually found during debugging and testing stages of program development.

All known to us source code checkers (e.g. for the C/C++ languages) that detect run-time errors may produce only long lists of warnings due to weakness of analysis they perform. In order for a source code checker to be useful in practice, it must be able to recognize definite errors for really complicated erroneous situations. It was shown [2] that at least the context-sensitive data flow analysis with approximation of definite def-use relations must be done in such a static error checker.

OSA includes the following analyses:

- context-sensitive and context-insensitive data flow analyses;
- approximation of the definite def-use relations along with the possible ones;
- calculation of variable values: points-to must- and may-aliasing analyses for reference variables and propagation of value ranges for variables of scalar types;
- calculation of branch reachability for conditional statements;
- refinement of variable definitions through conditions for branches of conditional statements;
- approximation of previous instances of heap variables and local variables of recursive procedures.

OSA analysis is structured as a sequence of the following analysis phases:

- context-insensitive analysis phase;
- context-sensitive analysis phase;
- variable value calculation phase;
- backward analysis of unused values of variables (*);
- error analysis phase.

Except the fourth phase (*), all analyses are forward. Data flow analysis is implemented as abstract interpretation of a program [5]. Data flow representation is based on the SSA form [3]. At every program point, a Def context is calculated as a result of the interpretation. A Def context is the set of variable definitions that are valid at the program point. The Def context produced by the first phase for the entry of each method is used as upper approximation in the second analysis phase.

In data flow analysis, the control flow is represented by a structure different from the traditional control flow graph. A program statement is a hyperleg that is a construct with one entry and possibly more than one exit. For example, a loop body with break and return statements is represented as a hyperleg with at least three exits:

- for normal loop body end;
- via break statement;
- via return statement.

The whole program is represented as a hierarchical hypergraph [4]. The control structures of statements of the program source code are preserved in the hypergraph representation.

2 Java Subset Implemented

There are Java language features which implementation in data flow analysis is impossible or highly ineffective. In the current implementation, finalize methods are ignored. The order of the static class initialization of in the OSA analysis may be other than declared by Java semantics. OSA cannot analyse programs with classes that are loaded dynamically during execution. Threads are processed in the OSA analysis as sequential programs; proper implementation of thread analysis is now under development. Runtime exceptions (null dereference, division by zero, etc.) are handled by the OSA analysis only if they were recognized as definite; possible exceptions are ignored because their implementation would be ineffective and as a rule useless. The Java subset currently implemented in the OSA is almost the same as in [1].

3 Structures for Exception Handling Analysis

Unlike the approach [1], the implicit control flow for raised exceptions is represented explicitly in our data flow analysis. The difficulty is that the additional control flow structures have to be constructed dynamically in the process of data flow analysis.

For each **throw** statement, an exception branch is introduced. An exception branch has a label and a Def context at the point of the **throw** statement. A label is the set of types of exceptions that raised by this exception branch. When a **throw** statement is interpreted in data flow analysis, the exception branch associated with that **throw** statement is attached to the current exception plateau. A plateau is the place where exception branches are collected for further processing. There are three kinds of exception plateaus:

- **catch plateau**, inserted after the **try** block and before the first **catch** clause;
- **finally plateau**, inserted before the **finally** block;
- **end method plateau**, placed at the end of the method body.

An exception branch that reached the end of the method body is placed into the end method plateau. When interpretation of the method body has completed, that exception branch is connected with some additional exception exit of the method. So a method body is represented in data flow analysis by the following hyperleg:

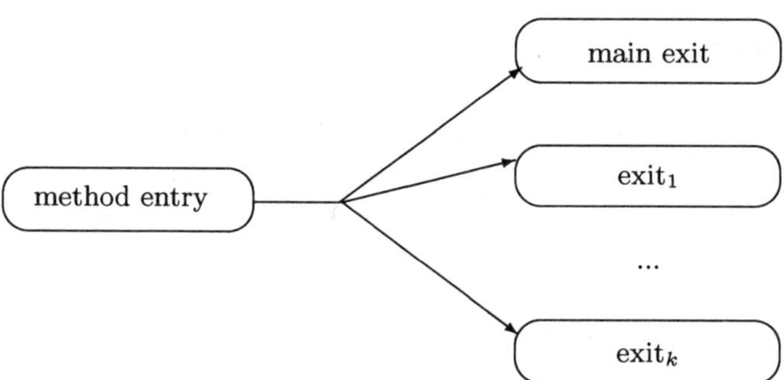

Fig. 1. Hyperleg for a method body. Here exit_1, ..., exit_k are exception exits

An exception exit has a label (the same as for exception branch) and a Def context.

A method call is represented by a hyperleg of the same structure as for method body. Each call exit begins some branch of a program. An exception exit of a method call begins some exception branch, which label is the same as for the exit. At the end of interpretaion of a method call, the exception branch associated with an exception exit of the call is attached to the current exception plateau.

New structures and their interrelation in the analysis of exception handling are shown on the example program in Fig. 2.

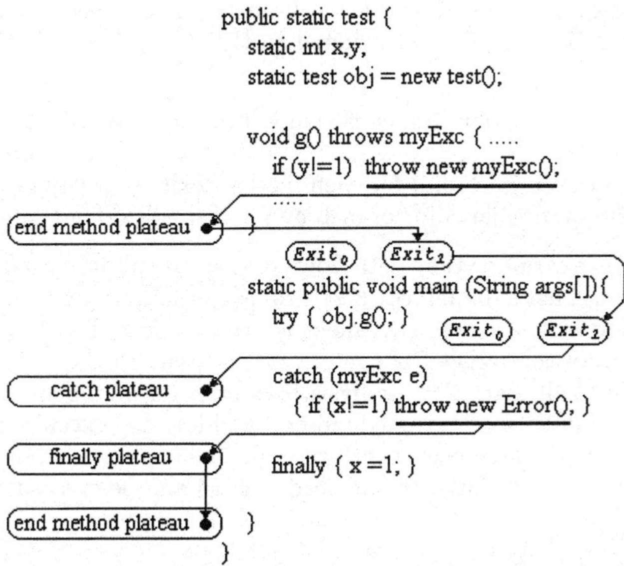

Fig. 2. Processing of exception flows for the program example

4 Implementation of Exception Handling

When interpretation of a **try** block has completed, the **catch plateau** of the **try** statement is interpreted. For each exception branch included in the plateau, the branch label is matched to parameters of catch clauses, according to the Java language semantics. As a result, the exception branch is attached either to some **catch** clause or to the plateau of the innermost enclosing construct. If more than one exception branch is attached to some **catch** clause, the merge statement for the entering Def contexts would be inserted before the **catch** clause. If the branch label is partially matched to the parameter of any **catch** clause, the branch label is splitted, and the new exception branch is created with the part of the label that did not match to the catch clause parameter. That exception branch would be matched to the remaining catch clauses.

In the inner program representation, a **finally** block is represented as an independent procedure whose calls are inserted into all appropriate places of the **try** statement. Such decision guarantees that different data flows in the **try** statement would never be mixed. For each exception branch of the **finally** plateau, a call of the finally block is dynamically inserted; in accordance with the Java language semantics, the main exit of this call is labelled with the exception branch label.

When interpretation of a method body has completed, the **end method plateau** is interpreted. For all exception branches of the end method plateau, method exits are dynamically constructed so that the following conditions are met:

- the label of each exception branch is a subset of the union of labels of method exits;
- for each exception branch and for each method exit, either the exit label is a subset of the branch label, or branch and exit labels do not intersect.

These conditions guarantee that data flows of two exception branches with different labels would never be mixed. If several exception branches are connected with one method exit, a merge statement for the entering Def contexts will be inserted to produce the target Def context for the exit.

For a method call, data flow analysis calculates all methods which may be invoked by this call. For each invoked method and for each exception exit in this method, the call must include exit with the same label as for the method exit. If this is not true, the new exit with the needed label will be created for the call.

5 Related Work

The only known approach of data flow analysis that properly handles exceptions is described in [1]. In this article, data flow information (the conditional points-tos) may be additionally labelled with exceptions. This is a natural but not trivial extension of the context-sensitive Landi-Ryder pointer aliasing algorithm [6].

The problem of fast static calculation of possible uncaught exceptions in SML programs was solved [8]. A program call graph and exception flows are estimated from sets of equations and constraints. As for Java language, a Java compiler must guarantee that each raised checked exception will be caught. For unchecked exceptions, the analyser OSA produces a warning message for each uncaught exception.

6 Conclusion

Unlike the approach [1], the implicit control flow for raised exceptions is represented explicitly in our data flow analysis. Method bodies and method calls are presented as constructs with one entry and possibly more than one exit. In previous works, control flow structures of the analysed program are constructed before data flow analysis. In our approach, new control flow structures for exception flows are constructed dynamically under control of data flow analysis.

Our implementation of the exception handling by means of the extension of the control flow mechanism appears to be considerably less complicated than that one described in [1].

Data flow analysis with the presence of exceptions was implemented in the static analyser OSA for Java language. Beta version of the analyser OSA is available at http://www.xds.ru/osa/. In the process of OSA debugging, many real Java programs were passed through OSA. The number of different exits in a method body was always less than six. According to our estimations, the size of memory and processor time required for exception exits, not exceed 20% of memory and time required for all analysis. As for errors found by the analyser OSA in Java programs, not trivial catch clauses proved to be the most error prone.

Authors are grateful to Dmitry Leskov of XDS for many useful critical notes concerning this paper.

References

1. R. Chatterjee, B.G. Ryder, and W.A. Landi. Complexity of Concrete Type-Inference in the Presence of Exceptions. LNCS 1381, Proceedings of European Symposium on Programming, April, 1998.
2. S.V. Kuksenko, V.I. Shelekhov. The Static Source Code Checker of Run-time Errors, Programmirovanie, 1998, no. 6. (in Russian)
3. R. Cytron, J. Ferrante, B.K. Rosen, M.N. Wegman, and F.K. Zadek. Efficient Computing Static Single Assignment Form and the Control Dependence Graph, ACM Trans. Prog. Lang. Sys., 1991, vol. 13, no. 4, pp. 451–490.
4. Shelekhov, V.I., Invariant of the Programming Language, in Sredstva i instrumenty programmirovaniya (Programming Tools), Novosibirsk: Institute of Informatics Systems, Siberian Division, Russian Academy of Sciences, 1995, pp. 6–22. (in Russian)
5. Cousot, P. and Cousot, R., Abstract Interpretation: A Unified Lattice Model for Static Analysis of Programs by Construction or Approximation of Fixpoints, Rec. 18th ACM Symp. on Principles of Programming Languages, ACM, 1977, pp. 55-56.
6. Landi, W. and Rider, B.G., A Safe Approximate Algorithm for Interprocedural Pointer Aliasing, Proc. ACM SIGPLAN'92 Conf. on Prog. Lang. Design and Implem., SIGPLAN Notices, 1992, vol. 27, no. 7, pp. 235–248.
7. J. Gosling, B. Joy, G. Steele. The Java Language Specification. Pre-Release Version 1.0, Draft 5.2 - July 3, 1996
8. Kwangkeun Yi, Sukyoung Ryu. Toward a Cost-Effective Estimation of Uncaught Exceptions in SML Programs. LNCS 1302, Static Analysis, 4th International Symposium, SAS'97. Proceedings. 1997. pp. 98–113.

Late Adaptation of Method Invocation Semantics

Markus Hof

Department of Computer Science (System Software)
Johannes Kepler University Linz, Austria
hof@ssw.uni-linz.ac.at

Abstract. In distributed object systems, one has the possibility to make method invocations on objects located on other host. During such an invocation, data is sent to another host and back. However, the system tries to hide this and simulate a standcard method invocation as close as possible. Some systems [Voyager] try to offer other invocation semantics, e.g. asynchronous method invocation.
We try to go a step further and offer the actual invocation as first class abstractions. The programmer can build his own abstractions by either implementing his own or by combining existing abstractions. With this system, he can build arbitrary invocations semantics, e.g. synchronous method invocation with transactional semantics, which also logs all method invocations.

1 Overview

Today's highly interconnected systems put more and more emphasis on the exploitation of the advantages inherent to a network, i.e. increased fault tolerance, better availability, and easier scalability. However, network systems have their disadvantages as well, and it is not easy to actually exploit their advantages. Independent failure modes, which have to be handled when dealing with several computers, increase the complexity of software development. Additionally, networked systems are often heterogeneous and highly dynamic. The configuration of available computation resources may change on a moments notice. To cope with these problems different approaches have been proposed. A common approach is to put part of the additional complexity into the object system, i.e., to hide it from the developer, by extending the notion of objects and classes.

However, distributed object systems, e.g. Object Management Group's OMG [OMG], Microsoft's DCOM [Micro], or JavaSoft's Remote Method Invocation [RMI98] use a fix scheme of a point-to-point request/response communication model. While appropriate for a subset of applications using distributed objects, this model inhibits exploiting the advantages of distributed objects for other domains. Other work has been done to widen the application domain for distributed objects by introducing new kinds of method invocation semantics, e.g. Voyager [Voyager] which introduces asynchronous method invocation.

D. Bjørner, M. Broy, A. Zamulin (Eds.): PSI'99, LNCS 1755, pp. 396–401, 2000.

This paper describes a novel approach to widen the application domain for distributed objects even further. We claim that introducing new special cases as done e.g. in Voyager is not sufficient. There is an infinite number of possible desirable kinds of method invocation, e.g. asynchronous vs. synchronous, unicast vs. multicast, replicated, transactional, logged, or atomic. We claim that just as any other aspect of a distributed system, the "invocation style" should be a first class abstraction. One should be able to compose abstractions and use the most adequate ones according to the application needs.

1.1 Distributed Object Methodology

A client sees an object as a reference into memory, some data fields, and a set of type bound procedures (methods). An application does not have to distinguish between local and remote objects.

The application has transparent access to all objects regardless of their actual location. For every accessed remote object, the system automatically generates a so-called *stub object*. A stub object is the local representative (placeholder) of an object located on another site. It offers exactly the same interface as its associated actual object, but redirects incoming requests to the actual object. The request (object ID, invoked method, and actual parameters) is transformed (marshalled) to a byte stream, which is sent from the stub to the skeleton. This stream includes all information needed to reconstruct the receiver object, the called method, and the actual parameters. This mechanism is similar to the RPC mechanism [BiNe84, Tan95], except that a receiver object is passed along with each new invocation.

1.2 Code Generation for Stub and Skeleton

Stub and skeleton code is generated automatically from the interface definition of the given class. Typical stub and skeleton code consists of three parts:

1. Marshalling of all input parameters
2. Activation of the transport mechanism in order to signal the actual object the intercepted method invocation.
3. Unmarshalling of output parameters and the return value

Logically seen we introduce one new additional layer (see Fig. 1). A method invocation, which is not handled locally, is intercepted by its corresponding stub method. Each stub method is tailored to its method and is mainly concerned with marshalling. After the marshalling is done, the stub code calls, regardless of the invocation mode, the global invocation handler. This handler chooses and activates the previously assigned invocation mode. The structure of the invocation modes is explained in the next section.

In our current prototype implementation, we achieve this behaviour without introducing a new layer by using an array of invocation abstractions. Each stub knows the method to be used and chooses the correct one through an index into an invocation array. With help of this mechanism we avoid the additional layer and achieve a faster dispatch.

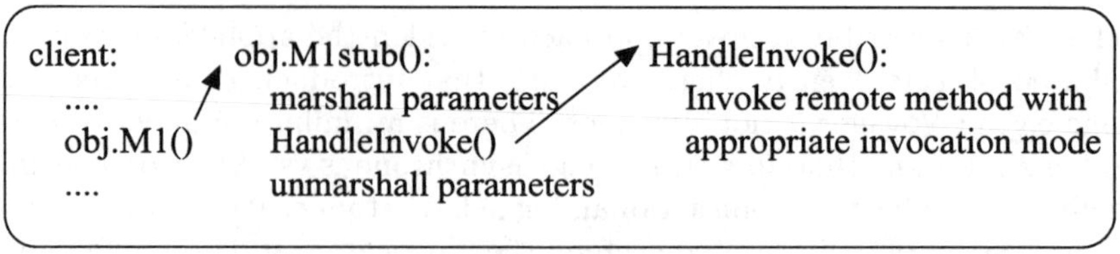

```
client:        obj.M1stub():              HandleInvoke():
  ....           marshall parameters        Invoke remote method with
  obj.M1()       HandleInvoke()             appropriate invocation mode
  ....           unmarshall parameters
```

Fig. 1. Control flow on method invocation

2 Generating Invocation Modes

We offer the programmer a class hierarchy of invocation abstractions. *Invocation* is the abstract base class. Whenever an object is to be exported (made public to other hosts), the programmer must specify the desired invocation modes for every method of the object he exports. One can have an individual invocation configuration for each object of a class or reuse a configuration for all objects of the same class.

To export an object one has to call the procedure Export that is part of a library. One has to specify the host on which the given object is exported, the name of the object and the desired invocation abstractions. As a result of this operation, the system generates 'on-the-fly' the necessary skeleton code to access this object (see example below).

```
invoke := Invocations.GetClassInfo("className");
// ... modify abstractions to current needs
Export(object1, host, name1, invoke);
// ... modify abstractions if necessary
Export(object2, host, name2, invoke);
```

When a client imports an object, it calls the procedure *Import*. One has to specify the name the object and the host where it resides. An appropriate request is sent to the server host. The server host sends back two kinds of information. First, the invocation abstractions of the exported object and second, the actual object data. With help of the received invocation abstractions the necessary stub code is generated and the actual object is generated.

```
Import(obj, host, name);
```

The necessary invocation information is generated with a call to *GetClass-Info*, which uses meta-programming facilities to collect it. It returns the default invocation information for a class. If an object is exported with this information, one gets the following default behaviour:

1. Methods are called synchronous with the standard semantics of method calls.
2. Parameters of a pointer type are copied using deep-copy semantics.

3. If a method returns a pointer value, the referenced object is copied to the caller.

These three standard behaviours can be changed as described in the following three sections.

2.1 Changing the Invocation Mode

By default, all method invocations are handled as standard method invocations, i.e. synchronous. However, one can change the behaviour as needed by composing your own invocation abstractions. Either one can create a new abstraction that suits the current necessities, or one can compose one with help of existing abstractions using the decorator pattern [Gam95]. Let us look at some examples:

1. An asynchronous invocation abstraction, which uses replication and logs the invocations:

```
VAR
  myInvoke: Invocation;
myInvoke := LogMode(ReplicationMode(ASyncInvocation()));
```

2. A synchronous invocation with transaction semantics:

```
VAR
  myInvoke: Invocation;
myInvoke := TransactionMode(SyncInvocation());
```

3. After generation of the desired invocation abstraction one can assign it to the desired method(s) and assign it to an exported object:

```
invoke.Method("name of method", myInvoke);
Export(obj, host, name, invoke);
```

If one wants to implement an own transaction invocation one has to create a new subclass of the class *Invocation* and overwrite the method

```
PROCEDURE (i:Invocation) Invoke(obj:PTR; id:LONGINT; s:Stream):Stream;
```

The method will be called whenever a method that uses this invocation abstraction is activated. *obj* is the invoked method, *id* contains a unique number defining the called method and *s* contains the marshalled parameters. The method has to return the linearized return value and output parameters.

2.2 Changing the Copy-Mode for Individual Parameters

Method can have pointer parameters. This implies, if the method is executed remotely, that the referenced objects have to be transferred from the client to the server and back. Either one can make a deep copy, actually generating a copy of the referenced object on the other host, or one can make a shallow copy. A pointer parameter copied in shallow copy mode is not transferred to the server. Instead, the object is automatically exported with an anonymous name. On the server side, before the server method is invoked, a corresponding import statement is executed automatically (see Fig. 2).

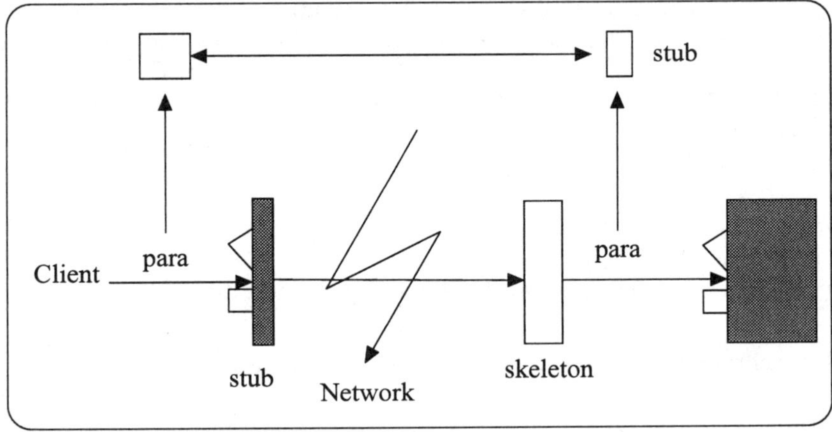

Fig. 2. Shallow copy of parameter

2.3 Changing the Copy Mode of the Return Value

Methods can return pointer values. This implies, if the method is executed remotely, that the referenced object has to be transferred from the server to the client host. As with pointer parameter (section 2.2) one has the possibility to make a deep or a shallow copy, i.e. the procedure returns either the actual object (deep copy) or another stub object (shallow copy).

3 Conclusions

A method invocation that is not handled locally is intercepted by its corresponding stub method. Each stub method is tailored to its method. The stub is concerned mainly with marshalling. The actual invocation is delegated to the procedure *HandleInvocation* (see Fig. 1). When called, *HandleInvocation* decides on the actually used invocation mode:

```
HandleInvocation (rec: PTR; id: LONGINT; data: Stream) : Stream;
info := ... Invocation information for the object rec
invoke := invoke mode for method id in info
data := invoke.Invoke(rec, id, data)
RETURN data
```

An actual implementation of Invoke will do some invocation specific statements (open/close transaction...) and delegate the invocation to the decorated invocation mode, e.g. for the invocation mode resulting from the statement

```
invoke := LogMode(TransactionMode(SyncInvocation()));
```

the actual sequence of invocation modes is as shown in Fig. 3.

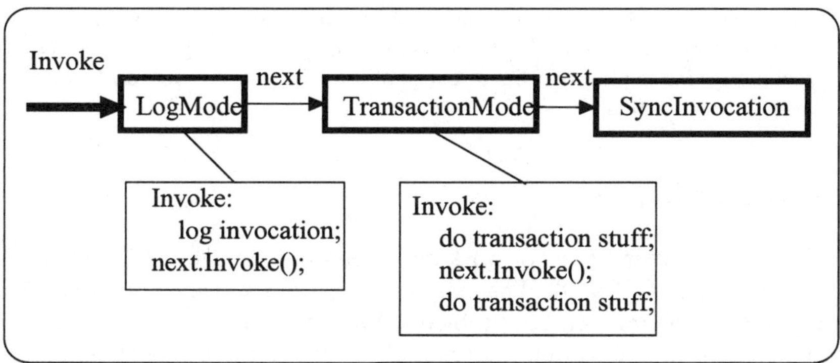

Fig. 3. Example abstraction sequence

The invocation mode is defined only at runtime when an object is exported. Each time one exports an object, one can choose other invocation abstractions.

References

[BiNe84] Birrell A., Nelson B.: Implementing Remote Procedure Calls. ACM Transactions on Computer Systems, vol. 2, Feb. 1984

[Tan95] Tanenbaum A.: Distributed Operating Systems. Prentice Hall 1995

[Micro] Windows DNA http://www.microsoft.com/dna/default.asp

[OMG] Object Management Architecture http://www.omg.org/library/oma1.htm

[Voyager] Objectspace Voyager http://www.objectspace.com/voyager

[RMI98] Remote Method Invocation specification http://java.sun.com/products/jdk/1.1/docs/guide/rmi

[Gam95] Eric Gamma, Richard Helm, Ralph Johnson, John Vlissides: Design Patterns Elements of Reusable Object-Oriented Software. Addison Wesley, 1995

A Control Language for Designing Constraint Solvers

Carlos Castro[1] and Eric Monfroy[2]

[1] LORIA-INRIA, BP 101, F-54602 Villers-lès-Nancy Cedex, France
Carlos.Castro@loria.fr
[2] CWI, P.O. Box 94079, NL-1090 GB Amsterdam, The Netherlands
Eric.Monfroy@cwi.nl

Abstract. We propose a strategy language for designing single constraint solvers as well as their collaborations. Based on the notions of constraint filter, separator, and sorter, we define basic strategy operators that allow us to specify single solvers and their collaboration in a uniform way. We exemplify the use of this language by specifying some techniques for solving non-linear constraints over real numbers and CSPs over finite domains.

1 Introduction

In the last twenty years, a lot of work has been done on solving Constraint Satisfaction Problems (CSPs) [8]. The existing constraint solvers have been successfully applied for solving real-life problems. We could say that constraint solving over a particular domain is well-understood. In the case of solvers based on propagation, either the control is left at the implementation level, or the strategy is fixed. For example, to be completely formal when adding strategies to *Chaotic Iteration*, we must prove that the algorithm and the strategy really compute the same fixed-point as Chaotic Iteration alone [1]. Arc-consistency algorithms, originally developed just for binary constraints, use fixed strategies and fixed data structures, thus, it is not possible to change the strategy [10,4]. Solvers based on other techniques, such as Gröbner bases and the simplex method, use a dedicated strategy. Finally, the deductive approach used in COLETTE allows a fine control of the computation, the strategy being a parameter, but there is no solver collaboration and some features are hidden in the implementation language (such as associative-commutative properties and term manipulation) [6].

Given that the development of constraint solvers is, in general, an expensive and tedious task, the interest for reusing existing solvers is obvious [17]. Even more important, when dealing with problems that cannot be tackled or efficiently solved with a single solver, we definitively realize the interest of integrating several solvers, working, in general, over different domains [15,3,9,16,14]. This is called Collaboration of Solvers [11]. In order to make solvers collaborate, the need for powerful strategy languages to control their integration has been

D. Bjørner, M. Broy, A. Zamulin (Eds.): PSI'99, LNCS 1755, pp. 402–415, 2000.

well recognized [12,13,2]. The existing approaches consider a fixed domain (linear constraints [3], non-linear constraints over real numbers [14,9,7]), a fixed strategy, and a fixed scheme of collaboration (sequential [14,7], asynchronous [9]). In the language Bali, the collaboration is specified using control primitives. The constraint system is a parameter, but the control capabilities for specifying strategies are not fine enough [13].

In this paper, we propose a control language for specifying single constraint solvers and their collaborations. Based on [5], a solver is viewed as a strategy that specifies the order of application of elementary operations expressed by transformation rules. In this framework, different domains mainly mean the definition of different transformation rules, and different heuristics mean different strategies. Extending this idea, we consider the collaboration of solvers as a strategy that specifies the order of application of single, or component solvers.

Our main motivation is to provide a general framework for defining single constraint solvers in a formalism that allows to specify high level operations on constraints as well as syntactical transformations normally hidden in the current implementations of constraint solvers. Our interest is to define this framework in a way that allows its natural extension for specifying the collaboration of solvers, since the design of constraint solvers and the design of collaboration of solvers require similar methods (strategies are often the same: *don't-care*, *fixed point*, *iteration*, *parallel*, *concurrent*, ...). In other words, we propose a language for writing single solvers and collaboration of solvers at the same level, making explicit things that are generally hidden in the implementations: strategies, properties of the operators (such as AC property), term manipulation, ...

We have already used our control language to design several solvers with several strategies: A Simplex algorithm, Gröbner bases computation and some propagation based solvers for finite domains and real numbers. However, for lack of space, we only present in this paper examples over two domains: some solvers for constraints over real numbers, and some solvers for finite domains.

This paper is organized as follows: Section 2 presents some standard definitions. In Section 3, we introduce the basic components of our control language which is later presented in Section 4, and illustrated in Section 5 with the design of solvers for constraints over real numbers and over finite domains. In Section 6, we conclude the paper.

2 Definitions

Definition 1 (Constraint System).
A constraint system is a 4-tuple $(\Sigma, \mathcal{D}, \mathcal{V}, \mathcal{L})$ *where:*

- Σ *is a first-order signature given by a set of function symbols* $\mathcal{F}_\Sigma$*, and a set of predicate symbols* $\mathcal{P}_\Sigma$*,*
- $\mathcal{D}$ *is a* Σ*-structure (its domain being denoted by* $|\mathcal{D}|$*),*
- $\mathcal{V}$ *is an infinite denumerable set of variables, and*

– *$\mathcal{L}$ is a set of constraints: a non-empty set of $(\Sigma, \mathcal{V})$-atomic formulae, called* atomic constraints, *closed under conjunction and disjunction. The* unsatisfiable *constraint is denoted by $\bot$ and the* true *constraint is denoted by $\top$. The set of atomic constraints is denoted by $\mathcal{L}_{At}$.*

An assignment is a mapping $\alpha : \mathcal{V} \to |\mathcal{D}|$. The set of all assignments is denoted by $ASS_{\mathcal{D}}^{\mathcal{V}}$. An assignment α extends uniquely to an homomorphism $\underline{\alpha} : T(\Sigma, \mathcal{V}) \to |\mathcal{D}|$. The set of solutions of a constraint $c \in \mathcal{L}$ is the set $Sol_{\mathcal{D}}(c)$ of assignments $\alpha \in ASS_{\mathcal{D}}^{\mathcal{V}}$ such that $\underline{\alpha}(c)$ holds. A constraint c is valid in $\mathcal{D}$ (denoted by $\mathcal{D} \models c$) if $Sol_{\mathcal{D}}(c) = ASS_{\mathcal{D}}^{\mathcal{V}}$. We denote by $\mathcal{V}ar(c)$ the set of variables from $\mathcal{V}$ occurring in the constraint c. Finally, we introduce the notion of solver.

Definition 2 (Solver). *A* solver *for a constraint system $(\Sigma, \mathcal{D}, \mathcal{V}, \mathcal{L})$ is a computable function $S : \mathcal{L} \to \mathcal{L}$ such that*

1. *$\forall C \in \mathcal{L},\ Sol_{\mathcal{D}}(S(C)) \subseteq Sol_{\mathcal{D}}(C)$ (correctness property)*
2. *$\forall C \in \mathcal{L},\ Sol_{\mathcal{D}}(C) \subseteq Sol_{\mathcal{D}}(S(C))$ (completeness property)*

A constraint C is in solved form with respect to S if $S(C) = C$.

Given a constraint system $(\Sigma, \mathcal{D}, \mathcal{V}, \mathcal{L})$ and a solver S over $(\Sigma, \mathcal{D}, \mathcal{V}, \mathcal{L}')$, such that $\mathcal{L}' \subseteq \mathcal{L}$, we extend S to $(\Sigma, \mathcal{D}, \mathcal{V}, \mathcal{L})$ in the following way: $\forall\ C \in \mathcal{L} \setminus \mathcal{L}'$, $S(C) = C$.

3 Filters and Sorters

We now define the basic components of our strategy language: filters to select specific parts of a constraint, and sorters to classify the elements of a list w.r.t. a given ordering.

We introduce the notion of filter for two main reasons. A solver can, in general, be tried on several parts of a constraint [5]. Second, when dealing with solver collaborations, in general, a single solver is not able to treat the complete constraint [12]. In both cases, we want to identify the sub-parts of the constraint that the solver is actually able to handle. Once we have identified these parts, we generally want to choose some of them based on a given criterion[1]. Thus, we introduce the notion of sorter that is associated to a notion of strategy.

We consider that the equality $=$ is purely syntactic. Thus, we say that C' is a *syntactical form* of C, denoted by $C' \approx C$, if $C' = C$ modulo the associativity and commutativity of $\wedge$ and $\vee$, and the distributivity of $\wedge$ on $\vee$ and of $\vee$ on $\wedge$. In other words, a filter returns an equivalent constraint when we block the associative, commutative, and distributive properties of the operators.

We denote by $\mathcal{SF}(C)$ the finite set of all the syntactical forms of a constraint C: $\mathcal{SF}(C) = \{C' |\ C' \approx C\}$[2]. We say that $C' \in \mathcal{L}$ is a *sub-constraint* of C, denoted by $C_{[C']}$, if:

[1] Minimum Domain criterion, for example, when dealing with finite domains.

[2] The ACD theory defines a finite set of quotient classes that we can effectively filter.

- $\exists C_1, C_2 \in \mathcal{L}$, $\omega_1, \omega_2 \in \{\wedge, \vee\}$, $C = C_1\omega_1C'\omega_2C_2$
- or $\exists C_1 \in \mathcal{L}$, $\omega \in \{\wedge, \vee\}$, $C = C_1\omega C'$
- or $\exists C_1 \in \mathcal{L}$, $\omega \in \{\wedge, \vee\}$, $C = C'\omega C_1$
- or $C = C'$

A couple (C'', C') such that C'' is a sub-constraint of C' and $C' \approx C$ is called an *applicant* of C. We denote by $\mathcal{LA}$ the set of all the lists of applicants, and by $\mathcal{LC}$ the set of all the lists of constraints. Generally, we will use LA to denote a list of applicants, and LC to denote a list of constraints. We denote by $\mathcal{P}(\mathcal{L} \times \mathcal{L})$ the power-set of all the sets of couples of constraints. Finally, $\mathcal{A}tom(C)$ denotes the set of atomic constraints that occur in C: $\{c | c \in \mathcal{L}_{At} \text{and} C_{[c]}\}$.

Definition 3 (Filter). *Let $(\Sigma, \mathcal{D}, \mathcal{V}, \mathcal{L})$ be a constraint system. Then, a filter ϕ on $(\Sigma, \mathcal{D}, \mathcal{V}, \mathcal{L})$ is a computable function $\phi : \mathcal{L} \rightarrow \mathcal{P}(\mathcal{L} \times \mathcal{L})$ such that:*

$$\forall C \in \mathcal{L},\ \phi(C) = \{(Cf^i, C^i), \ldots, (Cf^n, C^n)\}$$

where:

- $\forall i \in [1, n]$, $C \approx C^i$ *(C^i is a syntactical form of C),*
- $\forall i \in [1, n]$, $C^i_{[Cf^i]}$

The elements of $\phi(C)$ are called *candidates*. Given the filters ϕ and ϕ' on $(\Sigma, \mathcal{D}, \mathcal{V}, \mathcal{L})$, we say that:

- ϕ is *selective* if $\forall C \in \mathcal{L}$, $\phi(C) = \{(Cf_1, C_1), \ldots, (Cf_n, C_n)\}$ such that $\forall i, j \in [1, \ldots, n] \times [1, \ldots, n], i \neq j$, $\mathcal{A}tom(Cf_i) \cap \mathcal{A}tom(Cf_j) = \emptyset$.
- ϕ is *stable* if $\forall C \in \mathcal{L}$, $\phi(C) = \{(Cf_1, C'), \ldots, (Cf_n, C')\}$
- ϕ and ϕ' are *disjoint* if $\forall C \in \mathcal{L}$, $\phi(C) = \{(Cf_1, C_1), \ldots, (Cf_n, C_n)\}$, and $\phi'(C) = \{(Cf'_1, C'_1), \ldots, (Cf'_m, C'_m)\}$, s.t. $\forall (i, j) \in [1, \ldots, n] \times [1, \ldots, m]$, $\mathcal{A}tom(Cf_i) \cap \mathcal{A}tom(Cf'_j) = \emptyset$.

Property 1. Let ϕ_1 and ϕ_2 be two filters on $(\Sigma, \mathcal{D}, \mathcal{V}, \mathcal{L})$. Then, $\phi_1; \phi_2$ defined by

$$\forall C \in \mathcal{L}, \phi_1; \phi_2(C) = \phi_1(C) \cap \phi_2(C)$$

is a filter on $(\Sigma, \mathcal{D}, \mathcal{V}, \mathcal{L})$.

Example 1. Consider the constraint system $(\Sigma, \mathcal{D}, \mathcal{V}, \mathcal{L})$ s.t. the predicate $\in$ is in Σ, and that $\mathcal{L}$ contains some *domain constraints*, i.e. $X \in D_X$, where D_X (the *domain* of X) specifies the values that the variable X can take. We now define a filter for these domain constraints:

$$\forall C \in \mathcal{L},\ \phi_D(C) = \{(c, C) | C_{[c]} \text{ and } \exists X \in \mathcal{V},\ c = (X \in D_X)\}$$

The filter ϕ_D is stable and selective. We denote by $\mathcal{L}_{Dom}$ the elements of $\mathcal{L}_{At}$ resulting of the application of this filter. We will re-use this notation in other examples.

Example 2. We now consider patterns of constraints. The utility of this filter will be clarified in Section 5. We want to filter sub-constraints that are the conjunction of a domain constraint, an atomic constraint, and a conjunction of domain constraints, i.e. , an atomic constraint, and all the domain constraints of the variables occurring in it.
$\forall C \in \mathcal{L}$, $\phi_{D\wedge c\wedge Ds}(C) \subseteq \mathcal{L}^2$ and $\phi_{D\wedge c\wedge Ds}(C)$ is defined as follows:

1. Patterns:
$$(C'', C') \in \phi_{D\wedge c\wedge Ds}(C) \Rightarrow \begin{array}{l} C'' = (X \in D_X) \\ \wedge c \bigwedge_{Y \in \mathcal{V}ar(c)\setminus\{X\}} Y \in D_Y \\ \wedge c \in \mathcal{L}_{At} \setminus \mathcal{L}_{Dom} \\ \wedge C' \in SF(C) \\ \wedge C'_{[C'']} \\ \wedge X \in \mathcal{V}ar(c) \end{array}$$
2. Context-free:
$$((C', C_1) \in \phi_{D\wedge c\wedge Ds}(C) \wedge (C', C_2) \in \phi_{D\wedge c\wedge Ds}(C)) \Rightarrow C_1 = C_2$$
3. Commutative-free:
$$\left.\begin{array}{l} (X \in D_X \wedge c \wedge C''_1, C_1) \in \phi_{D\wedge c\wedge Ds}(C) \\ \wedge (X \in D_X \wedge c \wedge C''_2, C_2) \in \phi_{D\wedge c\wedge Ds}(C) \end{array}\right\} \Rightarrow C''_1 \approx C''_2$$

Item 1 requires that elements of $\phi_{D\wedge c\wedge Ds}(C)$ have some syntactical properties; in Item 2, we do not want to consider several times the same sub-constraints issued from different syntactical forms of C; and finally, in Item 3, we specify that the ordering of the conjunction of domain constraints is not relevant.

Item 2 and 3 are not mandatory, but they reduce the number of applicants. This definition does not provide uniqueness of the filter. Depending on our needs, we can consider (1) adding requirements to define one set of applicants per constraint, (2) removing Item 2 and 3, or (3) selecting one of the set corresponding to the definition.

For example, consider the problem of solving CSPs, and S has being a function (or a rewrite rule) which reduces the domain of one variable using one constraint. Then, for each constraint of the CSP, and each variable of this constraint, we can consider a possible application of S.

Definition 4 (Sorter). *A* sorter *Sorter, w.r.t. a partial ordering* $\preceq$, *for a constraint system* $(\Sigma, \mathcal{D}, \mathcal{V}, \mathcal{L})$ *is a computable function* $Sorter : \preceq \times \mathcal{P}(\mathcal{L}\times\mathcal{L}) \rightarrow \mathcal{LA}$ *such that* $\forall\{(Cf_{i_1}, C_{i_1}), \ldots, (Cf_{i_n}, C_{i_n})\} \in \mathcal{P}(\mathcal{L} \times \mathcal{L})$:

1. $Sorter(\preceq, \{(Cf_{i_1}, C_{i_1}), \ldots, (Cf_{i_n}, C_{i_n})\}) = [(Cf_1, C_1), \ldots, (Cf_n, C_n)]$
2. $\forall k \in [1, \ldots, n], \exists j \in [1, \ldots, n]$, $Cf_{i_j} = Cf_k$ *and* $C_{i_j} = C_k$
3. $\forall j \in [1, \ldots, n-1], Cf_j \preceq Cf_{j+1}$

Remark 1. We consider that a sorter is determinist, i.e., if L is a set of applicants, each application of Sorter on L will always return the same list of applicants.

Example 3 (MaxDom and MinDom sorters). $\preceq_{Dom}$ is an ordering based on the width of the domain of domain constraints. For atomic domain constraints, MaxDom and MinDom are straight-forward, but we may need to consider these orderings for more complex constraints (e.g., patterns of constraints issued from filters). MaxDom and MinDom use the width of domains of variables. Let $X \in D_X$ be a domain constraint, we consider the generic function ω which gives the width of a domain [3]. We define the function *width* as follows:

- if $c \in \mathcal{L}_{Dom}$ and $c = X \in D_X$, then $W(c) = \omega(D_X)$,
- if $c \in \mathcal{L}_{At} \setminus \mathcal{L}_{Dom}$, then $W(c) = -1$,
- if $C = c \wedge C'$ or $C = c \vee C'$ and $c \in \mathcal{L}_{At}$, then $W(C) = W(c)$.

$\preceq_{Dom}$ is now defined by:

$$\forall C, C' \in \mathcal{L},\ C \preceq_{Dom} C' \ \text{ if } \ W(C) \leq W(C').$$

The sorter MinDom (respectively MaxDom) is defined using the $\preceq_{Dom}$ ordering (respectively $\succeq_{Dom}$, the reverse ordering of $\preceq_{Dom}$).

4 The Strategy Language

Given a solver S, a filter ϕ and a partial order $\preceq$, we now define several *application mechanisms* for applying solvers to constraints. We assume that a solver is applied only once on a given set of constraints. In the following, we consider given a constraint system $CS = (\Sigma, \mathcal{D}, \mathcal{V}, \mathcal{L})$. Most of the application mechanisms are based on the same technique when applied to a constraint C:

1. A set SC of candidates is built using the filter ϕ on C.
2. The set SC is sorted using $\preceq$. We obtain

$$LC = [(Cf_1, C_1), \ldots, (Cf_n, C_n)],$$

   a sorted list of candidates, where (Cf_1, C_1) is the "best" constraint w.r.t. $\preceq$.
3. The solver S is applied on one/several element of LC.
4. Sub-constraints modified by S are replaced in their corresponding syntactical form of C.

4.1 Basic Solver Compositions

The following operators are standard and analogous to function compositions. They are used to design solvers with "basic" functions, or create solver collaborations with "complex" solvers. Let R and S be two solvers on $(\Sigma, \mathcal{D}, \mathcal{V}, \mathcal{L})$. Then, $\forall C \in \mathcal{L}$ we define:

[3] For interval domains, *width*(D_X) can be the difference between the upper and the lower bound. On the other hand, for domains that are sets of elements, the width can be defined as the cardinality of the set. In every case, width is a numeric value.

- $S^0(C) = C$ (*Identity*),
- $S;R(C) = R(S(C))$ (*solver concatenation*),
- $S^n(C) = S^{n-1};S(C)$ if $n > 0$ (*solver iteration*),
- $S^\star(C) = S^n(C)$ such that $S^{n+1}(C) = S^n(C)$ (*solver fixed-point*),
- $(S,R)(C) = S(C)$ or $R(C)$ (*solver don't-care*).

Property 2. $S;R$, S^n, $S^\star$, and (S,R) are solvers.

4.2 Filtered and Random Applications of a Solver

We first define two operators to apply a solver on specific components of a constraint. The first one takes the component randomly whereas the second one selects it with respect to a given criterion.

Don't Care Application of a Solver Given a solver S, a filter ϕ, and a constraint C, $\mathbf{dc}(S,\phi)$ restricts the use of the solver S to one randomly chosen sub-constraint of a syntactical form of C (obtained using the filter ϕ):

$$\forall C \in \mathcal{L}, \mathbf{dc}(S,\phi)(C) = C'$$

where:

- $[(Cf_1, C_1), \ldots, (Cf_n, C_n)] = \phi(C)$,
- if there exists $i \in [1, \ldots, n]$ such that $S(Cf_i) \neq Cf_i$, then $C' = C_i\{Cf_i \mapsto S(Cf_i)\}$, otherwise $C' = C$.

Best Application of a Solver Given a solver S, a partial order $\preceq$ on $\mathcal{L}$, a filter ϕ, and a constraint C, $\mathbf{best}(S,\preceq,\phi)$ restricts the use of the solver S to the best (w.r.t. the partial order $\preceq$) sub-constraint of a syntactical form of C (obtained using the filter ϕ) that S is able to modify:

$$\forall C \in \mathcal{L}, \mathbf{best}(S,\preceq,\phi)(C) = C'$$

where:

- $[(Cf_1, C_1), \ldots, (Cf_n, C_n)] = Sorter(\preceq, \phi(C))$,
- if there exists $i \in [1, \ldots, n]$, such that $S(Cf_i) \neq Cf_i$, and $\forall j \in [1, \ldots, n]$ $(S(Cf_j) \neq Cf_j \Rightarrow i \leq j)$, then $C' = C_i\{Cf_i \mapsto S(Cf_i)\}$, otherwise $C' = C$.

4.3 Concurrent and Parallel Applications of Solvers

We now define two operators to apply several solvers on a constraint. The first one chooses only one result depending on a given criteria. The second one composes the final result using each application.

Concurrent Application of Solvers The operator **pcc** provides a non-deterministic choice upon which we act by introducing methods: we do not care about which solver actually solved the constraint, but we want the result to verify some property.

A constraint property p on a constraint system $(\Sigma, \mathcal{D}, \mathcal{V}, \mathcal{L})$ is a function from constraints to Booleans (i.e., $p : \mathcal{L} \to \mathcal{B}oolean$).

Given a list of solvers $[S_1, \ldots, S_n]$, a list of orders on constraints $[\preceq_1, \ldots, \preceq_n]$, a list of filters $[\phi_1, \ldots, \phi_n]$, and a property p, $\mathbf{pcc}(p, [S_1, \ldots, S_n], [\preceq_1, \ldots, \preceq_n], [\phi_1, \ldots, \phi_n])$ applies once one of the solvers S_i and returns a constraint that verifies the property p:

$$\forall C \in \mathcal{L}, \mathbf{pcc}(p, [S_1, \ldots, S_n], [\preceq_1, \ldots, \preceq_n], [\phi_1, \ldots, \phi_n])(C) = C'$$

where:

- for all $i \in [1, \ldots, n]$ $[(Cf_{i,1}, C_{i,1}), \ldots, (Cf_{i,m_i}, C_{i,m_i})] = Sorter(\preceq_i, \phi_i(C))$,
- if there exists $(i,j) \in [1, \ldots, n] \times [1, \ldots, m_i]$ such that $p(S_i(Cf_{i,j}))$, and $S_i(Cf_{i,j}) \neq Cf_{i,j}$, then $C' = C_{i,j}\{Cf_{i,j} \mapsto S_i(Cf_{i,j})\}$, otherwise $C' = C$.

Parallel Best Applications of Solvers Given a list of solvers $[S_1, \ldots, S_n]$, a list of orders on constraints $[\preceq_1, \ldots, \preceq_n]$, and a list of stable filters $[\phi_1, \ldots, \phi_n]$ that are pairwise disjoint, $\mathbf{bp}([S_1, \ldots, S_n], [\preceq_1, \ldots, \preceq_n], [\phi_1, \ldots, \phi_n])$ applies n solvers $S_1, \ldots, S_n$ on n sub-parts of one syntactical form of the constraint:

$$\forall C \in \mathcal{L},\ \mathbf{bp}([S_1, \ldots, S_n], [\preceq_1, \ldots, \preceq_n], [\phi_1, \ldots, \phi_n])(C) = C'$$

where:

- for all $i \in [1, \ldots, n]$ $[(Cf_{i,1}, C''), \ldots, (Cf_{i,m_i}, C'')] = Sorter(\preceq_i, \phi_i(C))$,
- for all $i \in [1, \ldots, n]$, if there exists $j \in [1, \ldots, m_i]$, s.t. $S_i(Cf_{i_j}) \neq Cf_{i_j}$, and for all $k < j$, $S_i(Cf_{i_k}) = Cf_{i_k}$, then $\sigma_i = \{Cf_{i,i_j} \mapsto S_i(Cf_{i,i_j})\}$, else $\sigma_i = \emptyset$,
- $C' = C''\sigma$ where $\sigma = \bigcup_{i \in [1, \ldots, n]} \sigma_i$.

4.4 Managing Sub-problems

Finally, we define two operators to apply a solver on each component of a conjunction or disjunction of constraints. The result of the application of these operators is obtained by the conjunction or the disjunction of the resulting constraints, respectively. These operators enable parallel computation, and standard OR_parallel computation.

To this end, we introduce the notion of *separator* that can be seen as a pre-processing for parallel computation. Separators are mainly defined to manipulate the elements of conjunctions and disjunctions of constraints as elements of lists. Each element of the list will then be treated separately but in parallel before gathering together (conjunction or disjunction) all the results.

We define the notion of separator using lists so we can sort and explore the search tree in a deterministic way. This is particularly important when we consider sequential implementations, i.e., we process the branches sequentially. In such cases, the use of sets leads to non deterministic search.

Definition 5 (Separators). *A* **$\wedge$_separator** *δ is a function $\delta : \mathcal{L} \rightarrow \mathcal{LC}$ s.t.:*

$$\forall\, C \in \mathcal{L},\, \exists n \in \mathbb{N},\, \delta(C) = [C_1, \ldots, C_n] \text{ where } C \approx C_1 \wedge \ldots \wedge C_n.$$

Similarly, a **$\vee$_separator** *δ is a function $\delta : \mathcal{L} \rightarrow \mathcal{LC}$ such that:*

$$\forall\, C \in \mathcal{L},\, \exists n \in \mathbb{N},\, \delta(C) = [C_1, \ldots, C_n] \text{ where } C \approx C_1 \vee \ldots \vee C_n.$$

Conjunctive Sub-problems Consider a solver S, and a **$\wedge$_separator** δ. Then, **$\wedge$_p**$(S, \delta)(C)$ applies (in parallel) the solver S to several conjuncts (determined by δ) of the constraint C and the final result is obtained by conjunction of the results computed in parallel:

$$\forall C \in \mathcal{L}, \wedge\_\mathbf{p}(S, \delta)(C) = C'$$

where $[C_1, \ldots, C_n] = \delta(C)$ and $C' = S(C_1) \wedge \ldots \wedge S(C_n)$.

Disjunctive Sub-problems: $\vee$_**p** is analogous to $\wedge$_**p** but δ determines disjuncts, and the final result is the disjunction of the results computed in parallel. Given a solver S and a **$\vee$_separator** δ:

$$\forall C \in \mathcal{L}, \vee\_\mathbf{p}(S, \delta)(C) = C'$$

where $[C_1, \ldots, C_n] = \delta(C)$ and $C' = S(C_1) \vee \ldots \vee S(C_n)$.

4.5 Properties of the Component Functions

In spite of its simplicity, the following property is essential: it allows one to manipulate component functions and solvers at the same level, and thus to create solver collaboration with the same strategy language.

Property 3. **best**, **dc**, **pcc**, **bp**, $\wedge$_**p**, and $\vee$_**p** are solvers.

5 Examples

In order to clarify the use of our strategy language, we now specify some well-known techniques for dealing with constraints over finite and real domains.

5.1 Solvers for Constraints over Real Numbers

We now design solvers for non-linear real constraints using real interval arithmetic. In the following, a CSP P is any conjunction of formulae of the form

$$\bigwedge_{x_i \in \mathcal{X}} (x_i \in D_{xi}) \wedge C$$

where a domain constraint $x_i \in D_{xi}$ is created for each variable x_i occurring in the set of constraints C, D_{xi} being an interval of real numbers. Constraints are equalities of non-linear polynomials.

MaxDom Partial Ordering We instanciate the MaxDom sorter of Example 3: for all interval $I = [a, b]$, $\omega(I) = b - a$.

The *Split* Solver We consider the *split* solver which transforms a domain constraint into a disjunction of two domain constraints if the width of the domain is greater than or equal to a "minimal" width ϵ [4]: $split : \mathcal{L} \to \mathcal{L}$. For all $c = X \in D_X$ from $\mathcal{L}$,

- if $c \in \mathcal{L}_{Dom}$ such that $width(c) \geq \epsilon$, then
$$split(c) = X \in D'_X \vee X \in D''_X$$
where $D_X = D'_X \cup D''_X$ [5],
- otherwise, $split(c) = c$.

A Domain Reduction Function Consider the function b_c which given a non-linear constraint $c \in \mathcal{L}_{At} \setminus \mathcal{L}_{Dom}$, the domain D_X of a variable $X \in \mathcal{V}ar(c)$, and the domains of the other variables of $\mathcal{V}ar(c)$, returns a smaller domain for X such that c is box-consistent [18] with respect to X. Computing b_c generally consists in applying the interval Newton method combined with a "local" splitting mechanism to push the left and right bounds of the interval.

We now define the solver $drf : \mathcal{L} \to \mathcal{L}$. For all $C \in \mathcal{L}$, we compute $drf(C)$ depending on the syntactical form of C:

- if $C = X \in D_X \wedge c \wedge \bigwedge_{Y \in \mathcal{V}ar(c) \setminus \{X\}} Y \in D_Y$ where $c \in \mathcal{L}_{At} \setminus \mathcal{L}_{Dom}$, then
$$drf(C) = X \in D'_X \wedge c \wedge \bigwedge_{Y \in \mathcal{V}ar(c) \setminus \{X\}} Y \in D_Y$$
where $D'_X = b\_c(c, D_X, \{D_Y | Y \in \mathcal{V}ar(c) \setminus \{X\}\})$,
- otherwise, $drf(C) = C$.

Solvers for Non-linear Constraints We now consider the solver *box* defined as follows:
$$box = \mathbf{best}(drf, \succeq_{Dom}, \phi_{D \wedge c \wedge Ds}).$$
When applied to a CSP C, *box* executes one step of reduction: one atomic constraint of C becomes box-consistent with respect to the largest variable of the CSP. Let us now consider the following solver:
$$Box = box^{\star}.$$
Box is the least fixed-point of *box*. When applied to a CSP *Box* returns an equivalent CSP that is box-consistent (i.e., each constraint is box-consistent

[4] For continuous domains, ϵ generally represents the smallest difference that can be computed between two numbers. For discrete domains, ϵ is set to 1.

[5] We generally also enforce that $D'_X \cap D''_X = \emptyset$.

w.r.t. each of its variables). The strategy of this solver is to always reduce the variable with the largest domain, i.e., a well-known and commonly used strategy for interval arithmetic.

Solving CSPs is generally the iteration of two mechanisms: consistency (described above) and splitting. We now describe the splitting mechanism (using the ϕ_D filter defined in Example 1) which enables to extract the isolated solutions:

$$Split = \mathbf{best}(split, \succeq_{Dom}, \phi_D).$$

Applied to a CSP C, *Split* creates a disjunction of two sub-CSPs. We can now give the solver for solving CSPs over non-linear constraints:

$$S_{FullLookAhead} = (Box; Split)^{\star}.$$

The strategy is a full look ahead: each time a domain is splitted, the consistency of the CSP is recomputed. At a lower level, the strategy for applying basic solvers is a Max-Dom. The solving process is neither depth-first nor breadth-first but Max-Dom first, i.e., we make one reduction step on one branch, and then, we eventually choose to explore an other branch.

We are now concerned with a homogeneous exploration of the branches. We consider a $\vee$**_separator** named $CSP_\vee$. For all $C \in \mathcal{L}$,

$$CSP_\vee(C) = [C_1, \ldots, C_n]$$

such that $C \approx C_1 \vee \ldots \vee C_n$ and $\begin{cases} C_1 &= X \in D_X^1 \wedge C' \\ C_2 &= X \in D_X^2 \wedge C' \\ \vdots & \vdots \; \vdots \\ C_n &= X \in D_X^n \wedge C'. \end{cases}$

We now get another solver for non-linear CSPs:

$$S'_{FullLookAhead} = \vee\_\mathbf{p}(Box; Split, CSP_\vee)^{\star}.$$

Depending on the implementation of the $\vee$**_p** operator, we will obtain a depth-first (sequential implementation) or a parallel (parallel implementation) solving process.

5.2 Solvers for Constraints over Finite Domains

We exemplify here the use of the strategy language by simulating some heuristics widely used for solving CSP over finite domains. The skeleton of the solvers that we propose is similar to the one used in the previous example. In the following, a CSP P over finite domains is any conjunction of formulae of the form:

$$\bigwedge_{x_i \in \mathcal{X}} (x_i \in D_{xi}) \wedge C$$

where a domain constraint $x_i \in D_{xi}$ is created for each variable x_i occurring in the set of constraints C, D_{xi} being a finite set of values. Solving this kind of problem can be seen as an interleaving process between local consistency verification and enumeration.

A Domain Reduction Function The most widely used level of consistency verification, *Arc-Consistency*, can be expressed as the repeated application of the following transformation rule that reduces the set of possible values that the variables can take.

$$x_i \in D_{x_i} \land c \land C \Rightarrow x_i \in RD(x_i \in D_{x_i}, c) \land c \land C$$
$$\textbf{if } RD(x_i \in D_{x_i}, c) \neq D_{x_i}$$

where $RD(x_i \in D_{x_i}, c)$ stands for the set $D'_{x_i} = \{v_i \in D_{x_i} \mid (\exists v_1 \in D_{x_1}, \ldots, v_{i-1} \in D_{x_{i-1}}, v_{i+1} \in D_{x_{i+1}}, \ldots, v_n \in D_{x_n}) : c(v_1, \ldots, v_i, \ldots, v_n)\}$.

Let us define it more precisely in the same way we did it for the previous example. For all $C \in \mathcal{L}$, we compute $LocalConsistency(C)$ depending on the syntactical form of C:

- if $C = X \in D_X \land c \land \bigwedge_{Y \in \mathcal{V}ar(c) \setminus \{X\}} Y \in D_Y$ where $c \in \mathcal{L}_{At} \setminus \mathcal{L}_{Dom}$, then
$$LocalConsistency(C) = X \in D'_X \land c \land \bigwedge_{Y \in \mathcal{V}ar(c) \setminus \{X\}} Y \in D_Y$$
where $D'_X = RD(X \in D_X, c)$,
- otherwise, $LocalConsistency(C) = C$.

The *SplitDomain* Solver In order to carry out enumeration, we consider a solver for splitting domains. We re-use the *split* solver defined in the previous sub-section. This time, ϵ is set to 1, and we enforce $D'_X \cap D''_X = \emptyset$.

MaxDom Partial Ordering Finally, we define the MinDom sorter that returns the domain constraint occurring in the set of constraints C with the minimum set of values. To this end, we just need to instanciate the MinDom sorter presented in Example 3: ω is instanciated by the cardinality operator $|\ |$.

Solvers with Usual Strategies In the following paragraphs, we also use the filters ϕ_D already defined in Example 1 and $\phi_{D \land c \land Ds}$ defined in Example 2.

FullLookahead This heuristic firstly enforces local consistency and then carries out an enumeration step followed by local consistency verification. Local consistency verification is always carried out on the whole set of constraints:

$$\begin{aligned} FullLookahead = \ & \mathbf{dc}(LocalConsistency, \phi_{D \land c \land Ds})^{\star}; \\ & (\mathbf{dc}(SplitDomain, \phi_D); \mathbf{dc}(LocalConsistency, \phi_{D \land c \land Ds})^{\star})^{*} \end{aligned}$$

FullLookahead with Minimum Domain This is a simple modification of the first heuristic: the enumeration is carried out based on the variable with the minimum set of remaining values:

$$\begin{aligned} FullLookahead_{MinDom} = \ & \mathbf{dc}(LocalConsistency, \phi_{D \land c \land Ds})^{\star}; \\ & (\mathbf{best}(SplitDomain, \preceq_{Dom}, \phi_D); \\ & \quad \mathbf{dc}(LocalConsistency, \phi_{D \land c \land Ds})^{\star})^{*} \end{aligned}$$

Forward Checking This heuristic, when enforcing local consistency, takes into account just the constraints that are directly related to the enumeration variable. We consider another filter $\phi_{D \wedge c \wedge C \wedge Ds}$: this filter returns a domain constraint D over a variable X, a constraint c that contains X, all the constraints (the conjunction C) that contain X (except c), and all the domain constraints of the variables that appear in $c \wedge C$. We also consider an extension *SplitDomain'* of the solver *SplitDomain* that applies on the result of the filter $\phi_{D \wedge c \wedge C \wedge Ds}$. When applied to a constraint $D \wedge c \wedge C \wedge Ds$, *SplitDomain'* returns $SplitDomain(D) \wedge c \wedge C \wedge Ds$. We can formulate Forward Checking as follows:

$$
\begin{aligned}
&ForwardChecking = \\
&\quad \mathbf{dc}(LocalConsistency, \phi_{D \wedge c \wedge Ds})^\star; \\
&\quad (\mathbf{dc}(SplitDomain'; \mathbf{dc}(LocalConsistency, \phi_{D \wedge c \wedge Ds})^\star, \phi_{D \wedge c \wedge C \wedge Ds}))^*
\end{aligned}
$$

The enumeration carried out by these strategies applies the solver *SplitDomain* which adds a disjunction once it is applied. We can imagine that the repeated application of this solver could generate a number of disjunctions too difficult to deal with. In order to avoid this situation we could use the $\vee$_**p** construction defined in Section 4.4. In this way, when we are carrying out an enumeration we can really decompose a CSP into two subproblems. The obvious advantage is to deal with a simpler problem. The solution to the original problem will be in the union of the solutions to all subproblems.

The modified version of the **Full Lookahead** heuristics is the following:

$$
\begin{aligned}
&\mathbf{dc}(LocalConsistency, \phi_{D \wedge c \wedge Ds})^\star; \\
&\quad (\mathbf{dc}(SplitDomain, \phi_D); \vee\_\mathbf{p}(\mathbf{dc}(LocalConsistency, \phi_{D \wedge c \wedge Ds})^\star, \delta))^*
\end{aligned}
$$

6 Conclusions

We have presented the definition of a strategy language for solving CSPs. A key point in this work is the introduction of the concepts of constraint filter, separator, and sorter. These operators allow us to show in the strategy language the syntactical transformations generally hidden in the current solvers. Then, using these operators we have defined a set of constructors that allow to define single solvers as well as the collaboration of solvers.

We have exemplified the use of this language by the simulation of well-known techniques for solving non-linear constraints over real domains and CSPs over finite domains.

To show the broad scope of our control language potential applications, we have already designed several solvers that are considered of different nature (such as Simplex algorithm, propagation based solvers, and Gröbner bases computation). We are currently working on the implementation of this language in order to evaluate the real applicability of this framework.

References

1. K. R. Apt. The Essence of Constraint Propagation. *Theoretical Computer Science*, 221(1–2):179–210, 1999.
2. F. Arbab and E. Monfroy. Heterogeneous distributed cooperative constraint solving using coordination. *ACM Applied Computing Review*, 6:4–17, 1999.
3. H. Beringer and B. DeBacker. Combinatorial Problem Solving in Constraint Logic Programming with Cooperative Solvers. In C. Beierle and L. Plümer, editors, *Logic Programming: Formal Methods and Practical Applications*, Studies in Computer Science and Artificial Intelligence. North Holland, 1995.
4. C. Bessière and J.-C. Régin. An arc-consistency algorithm optimal in the number of constraint checks. In *Proceedings of the Workshop on Constraint Processing, ECAI'94*, pages 9–16, Amsterdam, The Netherlands, 1994.
5. C. Castro. Building Constraint Satisfaction Problem Solvers Using Rewrite Rules and Strategies. *Fundamenta Informaticae*, 34(3):263–293, June 1998.
6. C. Castro. COLETTE, Prototyping CSP Solvers Using a Rule-Based Language. In J. Calmet and J. Plaza, editors, *Proc. of AISC'98*, volume 1476 of *LNCS*, pages 107–119, Plattsburgh, NY, USA, September 1998.
7. L. Granvilliers. *Consistances locales et transformations symboliques de contraintes d'intervalles.* Phd thesis, University of Orlans, France, 1998. In French.
8. A. K. Mackworth. Constraint Satisfaction. In S. C. Shapiro, editor, *Encyclopedia of Artificial Intelligence*, volume 1. Addison-Wesley Publishing Company, 1992.
9. P. Marti and M. Rueher. A Distributed Cooperating Constraints Solving System. *International Journal of Artificial Intelligence Tools*, 4(1-2):93–113, 1995.
10. R. Mohr and T. C. Henderson. Arc and Path Consistency Revisited. *Artificial Intelligence*, 28:225–233, 1986.
11. E. Monfroy. *Collaboration de solveurs pour la programmation logique à contraintes.* Thèse de Doctorat d'Université, Université Henri Poincaré - Nancy 1, France, November 1996. Also available in english. Available on-line at: http://www.cwi.nl/~eric/Private/Publications/index.html.
12. E. Monfroy. An environment for designing/executing constraint solver collaborations. *ENTCS*, 16(1), 1998.
13. E. Monfroy. The Constraint Solver Collaboration Language of BALI. In *Proc. of FroCoS'98*, Amsterdam, The Netherlands, 1998. To appear in Logic and Computation Series, Research Studies Press Ltd.
14. E. Monfroy, M. Rusinowitch, and R. Schott. Implementing Non-Linear Constraints with Cooperative Solvers. In *Proc. of ACM SAC'96*, pages 63–72, Philadelphia, PA, USA, 1996. ACM Press.
15. G. Nelson and D. C. Oppen. Simplifications by Cooperating Decision Procedures. *ACM Transactions on Programming Languages and Systems*, 1(2):245–257, 1979.
16. C. Ringeissen. Cooperation of decision procedures for the satisfiability problem. In F. Baader and K. Schulz, editors, *Proc. of FroCoS'96*, pages 121–139. Kluwer Academic Publishers, 1996.
17. G. Smolka. Problem Solving with Constraints and Programming. *ACM Computing Surveys*, 28(4es), December 1996. Electronic Section.
18. P. Van Hentenryck, D. McAllester, and D. Kapur. Solving polynomial systems using a branch and prune approach. *SIAM Journ. on Num. Analysis*, 34(2), 1997.

An Algorithm to Compute Inner Approximations of Relations for Interval Constraints

Frédéric Benhamou, Frédéric Goualard, Éric Languénou, and Marc Christie

Institut de Recherche en Informatique de Nantes
2, rue de la Houssinière
B.P. 92208
F-44322 Nantes Cedex 3
{benhamou,goualard,langueno,christie}@irin.univ-nantes.fr

Abstract. Interval constraint-based solvers are valuable tools to scientists and engineers since they ensure many useful properties such as completeness of the result. However, their lack of soundness is sometimes a major flaw. This paper presents an algorithm ensuring soundness by computing inner approximations of real relations using only "traditional" numerical methods. A slight modification of the algorithm permits handling constraint systems with one universally quantified variable. An application to declarative modelling of camera movements is also described.

1 Introduction

Expressiveness, efficiency, and reliability of interval constraint-based tools [16, 2, 4] make them a solution of choice for solving non-linear systems of equations such as the ones arising in robotics [13], chemistry [11], or electronics [14]. Relying on *interval arithmetic* [12, 1], these tools ensure completeness (all solutions present in the input are retained), and permit bracketing solutions with an "arbitrary" accuracy. On the other hand, soundness is not guaranteed, while it is sometimes a strong requirement. For example, consider a civil engineering problem [15] such as floor design where retaining non-solution points may lead to a physically unrealizable structure.

This paper presents an algorithm whose output is a set of sound boxes of variable domains for some constraint system. Soundness is achieved by computing inner approximations of real relations using *box consistency* [3] — a well-known, efficient, *local consistency* [10] — on the negation of the involved constraints. Next, a slight modification of the algorithm is described, which permits solving constraint systems where one variable is universally quantified. Its application to temporal constraints describing camera movements (*virtual cameraman problem* [9]) is then presented along with some preliminary results.

The organization of the paper is as follows: Section 2 introduces the basics related to interval constraint solving; Section 3 presents an extension of the

D. Bjørner, M. Broy, A. Zamulin (Eds.): PSI'99, LNCS 1755, pp. 416–423, 2000.

theoretical framework given in Section 2 to support the notion of *inner approximation*, along with the corresponding new algorithms; Section 4 describes modifications of the algorithms of Section 3 permitting to consider constraint systems with one universally quantified variable; Section 5 discusses the use of the algorithms for the "virtual cameraman problem"; finally, Section 6 synthesizes the contribution of the paper, and points out future directions for improvement of the methods described hereinafter.

2 Interval Constraint Solving

Finite representation of numbers by computers hinders exact solving of real constraints. Underlying real relations must be approximated by considering one of their computer-representable superset or subset. This section presents the basics related to the approximation of real relations the conservative way. Approximation by a subset is deferred until the next section. The shift from reals to floating-point intervals is first described; the notion of *outer approximation* of a real set based on intervals is then presented.

2.1 Preliminary Notions

Let $\mathbb{R}$ be the set of reals and $\mathbb{F} \subset \mathbb{R}$ a finite countable subset of reals corresponding to *floating-point numbers* in a given format [8]. Symbol ∞ is introduced to represent infinity, that is: $\forall \mathsf{g} \in \mathbb{F}$: $-\infty < \mathsf{g} < +\infty$, and $\mathbb{R} \subset (-\infty \mathinner{..} +\infty)$. Let $\mathbb{F}^{\infty} = \mathbb{F} \cup \{-\infty, +\infty\}$. Hereafter, r and s (resp. g and h), possibly subscripted, are assumed to be elements of $\mathbb{R}$ (resp. $\mathbb{F}^{\infty}$).

Let $\mathcal{L} = \{(, [\}$ (resp. $\mathcal{U} = \{),]\}$) be the set of left (resp. right) *brackets*. Let $\mathcal{B} = \mathcal{L} \cup \mathcal{U}$ be the *set of brackets* totally ordered by the ordering $\prec$ [6]: $) \prec [\prec] \prec ($.

The set of *floating-point bounds* $\mathbb{F}^{\diamond}$ is defined from $\mathcal{B}$ and $\mathbb{F}$ as follows:

$$\mathbb{F}^{\diamond} = \mathbb{F}^{\triangleleft} \cup \mathbb{F}^{\triangleright} \quad \text{where} \quad \begin{cases} \mathbb{F}^{\triangleleft} = (\mathbb{F} \times \mathcal{L} \cup \{\langle -\infty, (\rangle, \langle +\infty, (\rangle\}) \\ \mathbb{F}^{\triangleright} = (\mathbb{F} \times \mathcal{U} \cup \{\langle -\infty,) \rangle, \langle +\infty,) \rangle\}) \end{cases}$$

Real bounds set $\mathbb{R}^{\diamond}$ is defined likewise. Floating-point bounds are totally ordered by the ordering $\lhd$: $\forall \beta_1 = \langle \mathsf{g}, \alpha_1 \rangle, \beta_2 = \langle \mathsf{h}, \alpha_2 \rangle \in \mathbb{F}^{\diamond} : \beta_1 \lhd \beta_2 \iff (\mathsf{g} < \mathsf{h}) \vee (\mathsf{g} = \mathsf{h} \wedge \alpha_1 \prec \alpha_2)$. A similar ordering may be defined over $\mathbb{R}^{\diamond}$.

Rounding operations mapping real bounds to float bounds are defined as follows:

Bound downward rounding	*Bound upward rounding*
$\llbracket\,\rrbracket : \mathbb{R}^{\triangleleft} \longrightarrow \mathbb{F}^{\triangleleft}$ $\beta \longmapsto \max\{\gamma \in \mathbb{F}^{\triangleleft} \mid \gamma \unlhd \beta\}$	$\llbracket\,\rrbracket : \mathbb{R}^{\triangleright} \longrightarrow \mathbb{F}^{\triangleright}$ $\beta \longmapsto \min\{\gamma \in \mathbb{F}^{\triangleright} \mid \gamma \unrhd \beta\}$

Bounds are used to construct intervals as follows: $\mathbb{I}_{\circ} = \mathbb{F}^{\triangleleft} \times \mathbb{F}^{\triangleright}$ is the set of *closed/open floating-point intervals* (henceforth referred as *intervals*), with the following notations used as shorthands $((\langle \mathsf{g}, [\rangle, \langle \mathsf{h},] \rangle) \equiv [\mathsf{g} \mathinner{..} \mathsf{h}] \equiv \{\mathsf{r} \in \mathbb{R} \mid \mathsf{g} \leqslant$

$\mathsf{r} \leqslant \mathsf{h}\}$, etc.). For the sake of simplicity, the empty set $\varnothing$ is uniquely represented in $\mathbb{I}_\circ$ by the interval $(+\infty \,..\, -\infty)$.

In the rest of the paper, a Cartesian product of n intervals $\boldsymbol{B} = I_1 \times \cdots \times I_n$ is called a *box*. A non-empty interval $I = (\beta_1, \beta_2)$ with $\beta_1 \in \mathbb{F}^{\triangleleft}$ and $\beta_2 \in \mathbb{F}^{\triangleright}$ is said *canonical* whenever $\beta_2|_v \leqslant (\beta_1|_v)^+$, where $\beta|_v$ is the numerical part of bound β, and g^+ is the smallest float greater than g. A n-ary box $\boldsymbol{B}$ is canonical whenever the intervals $I_1, \ldots, I_n$ are canonical. Given a variable v, an interval I, and boxes $\boldsymbol{B}$ and $\boldsymbol{D}$, let $\mathsf{Dom}_{\boldsymbol{B}}(v) \in \mathbb{I}_\circ$ be the domain of v in box $\boldsymbol{B}$, and $\boldsymbol{B}|_{v,\boldsymbol{D}}$ the box obtained by replacing v domain in box $\boldsymbol{B}$ by its domain in box $\boldsymbol{D}$. The power set of a set $\mathcal{S}$ is written $\mathcal{P}(\mathcal{S})$.

2.2 Approximating a Relation by a Box

A *constraint* is an atomic formula involving variables of $\mathcal{V}_{\mathbb{R}} = \{x_1, x_2, \ldots\}$. Given a constraint $c(x_1, \ldots, x_n)$, ρ_c denotes the underlying real relation. For the sake of readability, relation ρ_{c_i} for some constraint c_i is written ρ_i whenever that notation is non-ambiguous. Let $\bar{c}$ be $\neg c$, that is: $\rho_{\bar{c}} = \mathbb{R}^n \setminus \rho_c$.

A real relation ρ may be approximated conservatively by the smallest box (w.r.t. set inclusion) $\mathsf{Outer}_\circ(\rho)$ containing it.

Discarding values of the variable domains for which a constraint c does not hold is done by *contracting operators*, whose main properties are *contractance*, *completeness*, and *monotonicity*.

The *outer-approximation* operator $\mathsf{OC1}_c$ is a contracting operator for c that tightens variable domains using the $\mathsf{Outer}_\circ$ approximation:

Definition 1 (Outer-approximation operator). *Let c be a n-ary constraint, ρ_c its underlying relation, and $\boldsymbol{B}$ a box. An* outer-approximation operator *of c is a function $\mathsf{OC1}_c \colon \mathbb{I}_\circ^n \longrightarrow \mathbb{I}_\circ^n$ defined by:* $\mathsf{OC1}_c(\boldsymbol{B}) = \mathsf{Outer}_\circ(\boldsymbol{B} \cap \rho_c)$

Proposition 1 (Completeness of OC1). *Given a constraint c, the following relation holds for every box $\boldsymbol{B}$:* $(\boldsymbol{B} \cap \rho_c) \subseteq \mathsf{OC1}_c(\boldsymbol{B})$

The implementation of outer-approximation operators is easily done only for a limited class of constraints (*primitives*). The other constraints are solved by decomposing them into conjunctions of primitives. In order to overcome the loss of domain tightening due to the introduction of new variables by the decomposition process, Benhamou et al. [3] defined a new kind of operator (*outer-box approximation operator* OCb) which considers constraints globally. The following relation between OCb and OC1 does hold:

Proposition 2 (Completeness of OCb). *Given a constraint c, and a box $\boldsymbol{B}$:* $(\boldsymbol{B} \cap \rho_c) \subseteq \mathsf{Outer}_\circ(\boldsymbol{B} \cap \rho_c) \subseteq \mathsf{OCb}_c(\boldsymbol{B})$.

Operators OC1 and OCb narrow the domains of variables occurring in one constraint. Solving constraint systems is done by an algorithm (OC2) which computes the greatest common fixed-point included in the initial domains of all the contracting operators associated to each constraint (see details in [5]).

3 Inner Approximations

In order to compute only solution sets, the outer-approximation of a relation $\rho \subset \mathbb{R}^n$ is replaced by the *inner approximation* of ρ which is the subset of all the elements $\mathsf{r} \in \mathbb{R}^n$ for which the statement $\mathsf{r} \in \rho$ may be checked using only floating-point numbers.

Definition 2 (Inner approximation of a relation). *Given a n-ary relation ρ, the* inner approximation *of ρ is defined by:*

$$\mathsf{Inner}_\circ(\rho) = \{\mathbf{r} \in \mathbb{R}^n \mid \mathsf{Outer}_\circ(\{\mathbf{r}\}) \subseteq \rho\}$$

Proposition 3 (Properties of the Inner approximation). *The* Inner *approximation is monotone, idempotent, and distributive w.r.t. the union and intersection of subsets of $\mathbb{R}^n$.*

The narrowing of variable domains occurring in a constraint is done in the same way as in the outer-approximation case: an *inner-approximation operator* associated to each constraint discards from the initial box all the inconsistent values. The result is a set of boxes.

Definition 3 (Inner-approximation operator). *Let c be a n-ary constraint, and $\boldsymbol{B}$ a box. A* inner-approximation operator *of c is a function $\mathsf{IC1}_c\colon \mathbb{I}_\circ^n \rightarrow \mathcal{P}(\mathbb{I}_\circ^n)$ defined by:*

$$\mathsf{IC1}_c(\boldsymbol{B}) \subseteq \mathsf{Inner}_\circ(\boldsymbol{B} \cap \rho_c)$$

Proposition 4 (Soundness of $\mathsf{IC1}$). *Given a constraint c and a box $\boldsymbol{B}$, a inner-approximation operator $\mathsf{IC1}_c$ for c is such that $\mathsf{IC1}_c(\boldsymbol{B}) \subseteq (\boldsymbol{B} \cap \rho_c)$*

Proposition 4 is an immediate consequence of Inner and Outer definitions.

Inner-approximation operators with stronger properties may be defined, provided some assumptions — namely the ability to compute the "Outer" for constraint expressions —, are fulfilled. These operators are *optimal* in the sense defined below.

Definition 4 (Optimal inner-approximation operator). *Let c be a n-ary constraint, $\boldsymbol{B}$ a box, and $\mathsf{IC1}_c$ an inner-approximation operator for c. $\mathsf{IC1}_c$ is said* optimal *if and only if $\mathsf{IC1}_c(\boldsymbol{B}) = \mathsf{Inner}_\circ(\boldsymbol{B} \cap \rho_c)$*

Devising an inner-approximation operator for a constraint is not as easy as devising an outer-approximation operator since interval techniques only permit to enforce some partial consistencies, that is, values which are discarded are guaranteed to be non-solutions while no information is known about those which are kept. Algorithm 1 ($\mathsf{ICA1}_c$) implements an optimal inner-approximation operator for every n-ary constraint c by using $\mathsf{OC1}_{\overline{c}}$. Since values discarded by this operator are guaranteed to be non-solution of $\overline{c}$ — by completeness of $\mathsf{OC1}$—, they are guaranteed solutions for c.

Algorithm 1. $\mathsf{ICA1}_c$ – Inner contracting algorithm for a constraint c

$\mathsf{ICA1}_c(\mathbf{in}\colon \boldsymbol{B} \in \mathbb{I}_\circ^n; \mathbf{out}\colon \mathcal{U} \in \mathcal{P}(\mathbb{I}_\circ^n))$
begin
    $\boldsymbol{D} \leftarrow \mathsf{OC1}_{\overline{c}}(\boldsymbol{B})$
    $\mathcal{U} \leftarrow \boldsymbol{B} \setminus \boldsymbol{D}$
    if $(\boldsymbol{D} \neq \varnothing$ **and** $\neg\mathsf{Canonical}(\boldsymbol{D}))$ **then**
        $(\boldsymbol{D_1}, \boldsymbol{D_2}) \leftarrow \mathsf{PlainSplit}(\boldsymbol{D})$
        $\mathcal{U} \leftarrow \mathcal{U} \cup \mathsf{ICA1}_c(\boldsymbol{D_1}) \cup \mathsf{ICA1}_c(\boldsymbol{D_2})$
    endif
    return $(\mathcal{U})$
end

The PlainSplit function used in the algorithm splits in two intervals one of the non-canonical domains of $\boldsymbol{D}$. In a typical implementation, each non-canonical domain is chosen in turn in a round-robin fashion at each call of PlainSplit.

Handling constraint systems using inner-approximation operators is done by Algorithm ICA2 (see Algorithm 2): each constraint of the system is considered in turn together with the sets of elements verifying all the previously considered constraints so far. The main difference between OC2 and ICA2 lies in that each constraint needs only be considered once, since after having been considered for the first time, the elements remaining in the variable domains are all solutions of the constraint. As a consequence, narrowing some domain later does not require additional work.

Proposition 5 (Property of ICA2). *Let $\mathcal{S} = \{c_1, \ldots, c_m\}$ be a set of constraints, and $\boldsymbol{B}$ a box. Then,* $\mathsf{ICA2}(\mathcal{S}, \{\boldsymbol{B}\}) \subseteq \mathsf{Inner}_\circ(\boldsymbol{B} \cap \rho_1 \cap \cdots \cap \rho_m)$.

Inclusion in Proposition 5 may be replaced by an equality provided the operators IC1 used are all optimal.

Algorithm 2. ICA2 – Inner contracting algorithm for $c_1 \wedge \cdots \wedge c_m$

$\mathsf{ICA2}(\mathbf{in}\colon \mathcal{S} = \{c_1, \ldots, c_m\} \subset \mathcal{C}, \mathcal{A} \in \mathcal{P}(\mathbb{I}_\circ^n); \mathbf{out}\colon \mathcal{U} \in \mathcal{P}(\mathbb{I}_\circ^n))$
begin
    if $(\mathcal{S} \neq \varnothing)$ **then**
        $\mathcal{B} \leftarrow \varnothing$
        foreach $\boldsymbol{D} \in \mathcal{A}$ **do**
            $\mathcal{B} \leftarrow \mathcal{B} \cup \mathsf{IC1}_{c_1}(\boldsymbol{D})$
        endforeach
        return $(\mathsf{ICA2}(\mathcal{S} \setminus \{c_1\}, \mathcal{B}))$
    else
        return $(\mathcal{A})$
    endif
end

4 Introducing Quantifiers

Given a n-ary constraint $c(x_1, \ldots, x_n)$ and a box $\boldsymbol{B} = I_1 \times \cdots \times I_n$, applying the inner-contracting operator $\mathsf{IC1}_c$ to $\boldsymbol{B}$ gives a set of boxes $\mathcal{U} = \{\boldsymbol{B'_1}, \ldots, \boldsymbol{B'_p}\}$ where each $\boldsymbol{B'_j} = D_1 \times \cdots \times D_n$ is a sub-box of $\boldsymbol{B}$ such that: $\forall \mathsf{r}_1 \in D_1, \ldots, \forall \mathsf{r}_n \in D_n \colon c(\mathsf{r}_1, \ldots, \mathsf{r}_n)$ does hold.

Therefore, solving a constraint of the form $\forall x_k \colon c(x_1, \ldots, x_n)$ consists in retaining only boxes $\boldsymbol{B'} = (D_1 \times \cdots \times D_n)$ of $\mathcal{U}$ such that $D_k = I_k$.

Given v the universally quantified variable, Algorithm $\mathsf{ICA3}_c$ described by Algorithm 3 narrows domains of all variables occurring in a constraint c but v, and is an optimal inner-approximation operator for the constraint $\forall v \colon c$.

An efficient algorithm ($\mathsf{ICAb3}_c$) computing an inner-approximation operator for constraint c may be derived from Algorithm 3 by replacing $\mathsf{OC1}_{\overline{c}}$ by the outer-box approximation operator $\mathsf{OCb}_{\overline{c}}$. Note that optimality is then lost. In the same way, replacing $\mathsf{IC1}_{c_1}$ by $\mathsf{ICAb3}_{c_1}$ in $\mathsf{ICA2}$ leads to Algorithm $\mathsf{ICAb4}$ computing an inner approximation for the constraint $\forall v \colon c_1 \wedge \cdots \wedge c_m$.

Algorithm 3. $\mathsf{ICA3}_c$ – Inner contracting algorithm for $\forall v \colon c$

$\mathsf{ICA3}_c$(**in**: $\boldsymbol{B} \in \mathbb{I}_\circ^n, v \in \mathcal{V}_\mathbb{R}$; **out**: $\mathcal{U} \in \mathcal{P}(\mathbb{I}_\circ^n)$)
begin
  $\boldsymbol{D} \leftarrow \mathsf{OC1}_{\overline{c}}(\boldsymbol{B})$
  $\mathcal{U} \leftarrow \boldsymbol{B} \setminus \boldsymbol{D}|_{v,\boldsymbol{B}}$
  if ($\boldsymbol{D} \neq \varnothing$ **and** $\neg\mathsf{Canonical}_v(\boldsymbol{D})$) **then**
    $(\boldsymbol{D_1}, \boldsymbol{D_2}) \leftarrow \mathsf{Split}_v(\boldsymbol{D}|_{v,\boldsymbol{B}})$
    $\mathcal{U} \leftarrow \mathcal{U} \cup \mathsf{ICA3}_c(\boldsymbol{D_1}, v) \cup \mathsf{ICA3}_c(\boldsymbol{D_2}, v)$
  endif
  return ($\mathcal{U}$)
end

The Split_v function used in the algorithm splits in two intervals one of the non-canonical domains of $\boldsymbol{D}$. Domain $\mathsf{Dom}_{\boldsymbol{D}}(v)$ is never considered for splitting. In the same way, $\mathsf{Canonical}_v$ tests canonicity for all domains but the one of variable v.

5 An Application to the "Virtual Cameraman Problem"

Jardillier and Languénou [9] devised the prototype of a declarative modeller allowing an artist to specify the movements of a camera using the vocabulary proper to the field (*panoramic shot*, *travelling*, ...). The movements description is translated into a constraint system where the time t is a universally quantified variable. To solve a system of the form $\forall t \colon c_1 \wedge \cdots \wedge c_m$, they use Algorithm $\mathsf{EIA4}$ which computes an inner approximation by decomposing the initial domain I_t of t into canonical intervals I_t^1, ... ,I_t^p, and testing whether $c_1 \wedge \cdots \wedge c_m$ does hold for the boxes $I_1 \times \cdots \times I_t^1 \times \cdots \times I_n$, ... , $I_1 \times \cdots \times I_t^p \times \cdots \times I_n$. These evaluations give them results in a three-valued logic, namely (*true*, *false*, *unknown*). Boxes labeled *true* contain only solutions, boxes labeled *false* contain no solution at all, and boxes labeled *unknown* are split recursively and re-tested until they may be asserted true or false, or canonicity is reached. Retained boxes are those verifying: $\forall j \in \{1, \ldots, p\}$: $\mathsf{eval}_{\{c_1 \wedge \cdots \wedge c_m\}}(I_1 \times \cdots \times I_t^j \times \cdots \times I_n) = \mathit{true}$.

We have devised a new modeller, replacing EIA4 by ICAb4. Experimental evidences show that it is up to 40 times faster than the prototype described in [9] on a set of benchmarks. Moreover, ICAb4 splits the explored space in bigger consistent chunks than EIA4, and avoids losing time splitting extensively non-solution areas. Figure 1 compares graphically the splitting sequence for the explored space of $circle_{2,2}$, a collision problem: given points B_1 and B_2 moving along circles of radius r_1 and r_2, find all the possible locations of a point A such that B_1 (resp. B_2) is always at a distance greater than d_1 (resp. d_2) from A. Constraints to solve are then of the form: $\forall \theta \in [-\pi, +\pi]$: $\sqrt{(r_i \sin(\theta) - x)^2 + (r_i \cos(\theta) - y)^2} \geqslant d_i$. In the figure, the darker the area, the later its exploration was achieved. White areas stand for non-solution sets.

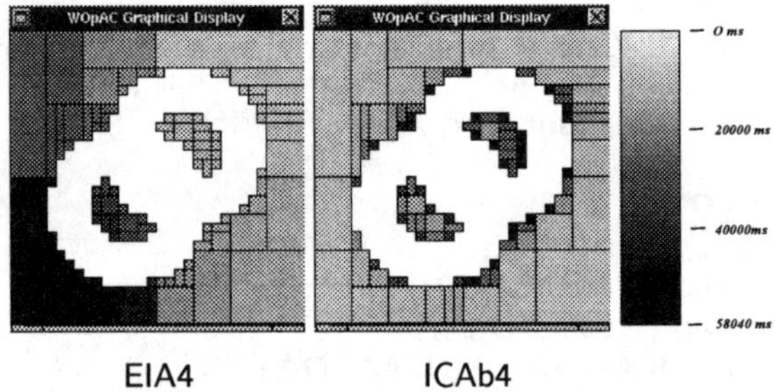

Fig. 1. Comparison of the solutions generation order for $circle_{2,2}$

6 Conclusion

Unlike the methods used to deal with universally quantified variables described in [7], the algorithms presented in this paper are purely numerical ones (except for the negation of constraints). Since they rely on "traditional" techniques used by most of the interval constraint-based solvers, they may benefit from the active researches led to speed-up these tools. However, they are for the moment limited to only one universally quantified variable while the methods of [7] deal with many variables and quantifiers (existential and/or universal). To achieve such a generalization is a major direction for future researches.

References

[1] Götz Alefeld and Jürgen Herzberger. *Introduction to Interval Computations.* Academic Press Inc., New York, USA, 1983.

[2] Applied Logic Systems, Inc. *CLP(BNR) user guide and reference*, 1996. Available at `http://www.als.com`.

[3] Frédéric Benhamou, David McAllester, and Pascal Van Hentenryck. CLP(Intervals) revisited. In *Proceedings of the International Symposium on Logic Programming (ILPS'94)*, pages 124–138, Ithaca, NY, November 1994. MIT Press.

[4] Frédéric Benhamou and Touraïvane. Prolog IV: langage et algorithmes. In *JFPL'95: IVèmes Journées Francophones de Programmation en Logique*, pages 51–65, Dijon, France, 1995. Teknea.

[5] Frédéric Benhamou. Interval constraint logic programming. In Andreas Podelski, editor, *Constraint programming: basics and trends: 1994 Châtillon Spring School, Châtillon-sur-Seine, France, May 16–20, 1994*, volume 910 of *Lecture notes in computer science*, pages 1–21. Springer-Verlag, 1995.

[6] John G. Cleary. Logical arithmetic. *Future Generation Computing Systems*, 2(2):125–149, 1987.

[7] Hoon Hong. Collision problems by an improved CAD-based quantifier elimination algorithm. Technical Report 91-05, RISC-Linz, Johannes Kepler University, Linz, Austria, 1991.

[8] IEEE. IEEE standard for binary floating-point arithmetic. Technical Report IEEE Std 754-1985, Institute of Electrical and Electronics Engineers, 1985. Reaffirmed 1990.

[9] Franck Jardillier and Éric Languénou. Screen-space constraints for camera movements: the virtual cameraman. In N. Ferreira and M. Göbel, editors, *Eurographics'98 proceedings*, volume 17, pages 175–186. Blackwell Publishers, 1998.

[10] Alan K. Mackworth. Consistency in networks of relations. *Artificial Intelligence*, 1(8):99–118, 1977.

[11] Keith Meintjes and Alexander P. Morgan. Chemical equilibrium systems as numerical test problems. *ACM Transactions on Mathematical Software*, 16(2):143–151, June 1990.

[12] Ramon Edgar Moore. *Interval Analysis.* Prentice-Hall, Englewood Cliffs, N.J., 1966.

[13] Bernard Mourrain. The 40 generic positions of a parallel robot. In M. Bronstein, editor, *Proceedings of ISSAC'93*, pages 173–182, Kiev (Ukraine), July 1993. ACM Press.

[14] Jean-François Puget and Pascal Van Hentenryck. A constraint satisfaction approach to a circuit design problem. Research Report CS-96-34, Brown University, December 1996.

[15] Jamila Sam. *Constraint Consistency Techniques for Continuous Domains.* PhD thesis, École polytechnique fédérale de Lausanne, 1995.

[16] Pascal Van Hentenryck, Laurent Michel, and Yves Deville. *Numerica: A Modeling Language for Global Optimization.* The MIT Press, 1997.

Constraint Programming Techniques for Solving Problems on Graphs

Vladimir Sidorov[1], Vitaly Telerman[1], and Dmitry Ushakov[2]

[1] A. P. Ershov Institute of Informatics Systems,
6, Acad. Lavrentjev pr., Novosibirsk, 630090, Russia,
{sidorov,telerman}@iis.nsk.su,
[2] Russian Research Institute of Artificial Intelligence,
6, Acad. Lavrentjev pr., Novosibirsk, 630090, Russia,
ushakov@iis.nsk.su,
http://www.rriai.org.ru/~ushakov

Abstract. In this paper we examine a technology for solving problems on graphs in the constraint programming framework called *Subdefinite Models.* We describe in brief the mechanism of constraint propagation underlying it. We present in detail the facilities for specification of graph problems as subdefinite models. We discuss a class of graph problems with emphasizing on ones having not discussed before.

1 Introduction

Constraint programming, a popular paradigm in computer science, allows one to solve a large class of problems from different fields stated as *Constraint Satisfaction Problems* [1]. Subdefinite models apparatus, proposed by Narin'yani [2] and developed in our works [3], is a powerful constraint programming framework. In the paper we discuss the extension of this framework for solving problems on graphs. In section 2 we describe the mechanism of constraint propagation in subdefinite models enriched with facilities for representation and processing of compound objects like graphs. The third section describes the specification of some graph problems in this framework.

2 Constraint Propagation Based on Subdefinite Models

In this section we define the notions of constraint satisfaction problem, subdefinite extension of a domain, filtering of a relation, and describe the algorithm of constraint propagation.

2.1 Constraint Satisfaction Problem

Definition 1. *A* Constraint Satisfaction Problem (CSP) *is a pair* (V, C), *where*

– V *is a (finite) set of* variables, *each variable* $v \in V$ *has its* domain D_v,

D. Bjørner, M. Broy, A. Zamulin (Eds.): PSI'99, LNCS 1755, pp. 424–433, 2000.

– $C = \bigcup_{m=1}^{M} C_m$ *is a (finite) set of* constraints, *each constraint* $c \in C_m$ *has* m *arguments* $Arg_c : \{1, \ldots, m\} \to V$ *and an* m*-ary relation over the arguments domains:* $R_c \subseteq D_{Arg_c(1)} \times \ldots \times D_{Arg_c(m)}$.

A solution *of CSP* (V, C) *is an assignment of a value* $a_v \in D_v$ *to each variable* $v \in V$ *such that for all* $c \in C$ *(let* $c \in C_m$*)* $(a_{Arg_c(1)}, \ldots, a_{Arg_c(m)}) \in R_c$.

Clearly, we do not have a universal algorithm for finding of all solutions of given CSP. (In the case of finite domains we deal with an NP-hard problem and there are universal algorithms, like "generate-and-test" or "backtracking", for solving CSPs over such domains.) However, there are universal algorithms for finding of an "approximation" of the set of all solutions of the CSP. The algorithms are known as "constraint propagation" algorithms. To describe our variant of one of such algorithms, firstly, we should define some additional notions.

2.2 Subdefinite Extensions

Definition 2. *Given a domain D, its* subdefinite extension (SD-extension) *is a domain (denoted by* $^*D$*) with the following properties:*

– $^*D$ *is a finite set of subsets of* D,
– $\emptyset$ *and* D *are elements of* $^*D$,
– *if* $\mathbf{d}'$ *and* $\mathbf{d}''$ *belongs to* $^*D$*, then* $\mathbf{d}' \cap \mathbf{d}'' \in {}^*D$.

Elements of an SD-extension will be denoted by bold letters. Any subset D' *of* D *can be* approximated *in SD-extension* $^*D$ *as follows:*

$$app_{^*D}(D') = \bigcap_{D' \subseteq \mathbf{d} \in {}^*D} \mathbf{d}.$$

Example 1. Let D be a finite domain. Then we consider $^*D = 2^D$, the set of all subsets of D, as a subdefinite extension of the domain D.

The notion of the SD-extension allows one to apply a single constraint propagation algorithm not just to finite domains, but also to infinite or continuous ones.

Example 2. Let $\mathcal{R}$ be the set of all real numbers. Consider its finite subset R_0. An R_0*-bounded interval* $\mathbf{x} = [\underline{\mathbf{x}}, \overline{\mathbf{x}}]$ (where $\underline{\mathbf{x}}, \overline{\mathbf{x}} \in R_0 \cup \{-\infty, +\infty\}$) is defined as a set $\{x \in \mathcal{R} \mid \underline{\mathbf{x}} \le x \le \overline{\mathbf{x}}\}$. The set of all R_0-bounded intervals will be denoted by $\mathcal{IR}(R_0)$. It is easy to see that $\mathcal{IR}(R_0)$ is an SD-extension of $\mathcal{R}$.

Example 3. Let $\mathcal{Z}$ be the set of all integer numbers. Then one can build a subdefinite extension of $\mathcal{Z}$ either as in example 1 (for a finite subset of $\mathcal{Z}$), or as in example 2.

Example 4. Let $D_1, \ldots, D_n$ be a set of domains, and let $^*D_1, \ldots, {}^*D_n$ be their SD-extensions. Consider a compound domain $D = D_1 \times \ldots \times D_n$. One can build an SD-extension $^*D$ of the domain D as follows:

$$^*D = {}^*D_1 \times \ldots \times {}^*D_n.$$

It satisfies all the conditions from definition 2. Since elements of a subdefinite extension are sets, any element $\mathbf{d} \in {}^*D$ will be considered hereinafter both as a tuple, $\mathbf{d} = (\mathbf{d}_1, \ldots, \mathbf{d}_n)$, and as a set, $\mathbf{d} = \mathbf{d}_1 \times \ldots \times \mathbf{d}_n$. We hope that this notation will not confuse the reader.

Other examples of subdefinite extensions of different domains can be found in [4].

2.3 Filtering

Definition 3. *Let $D_1, \ldots, D_n$ be domains, $^*D_1, \ldots, {}^*D_n$ be their SD-extensions, and R be a relation over them (i. e. $R \subseteq D_1 \times \ldots \times D_n$). The* filtering function,

$$\mathcal{F}_R : {}^*D_1 \times \ldots \times {}^*D_n \to {}^*D_1 \times \ldots \times {}^*D_n,$$

of the relation R in SD-extensions of the domains is defined as follows:

$$\mathcal{F}_R(\mathbf{d}_1, \ldots, \mathbf{d}_n) = app_{^*D_1 \times \ldots \times {}^*D_n}(R \cap \mathbf{d}_1 \times \ldots \times \mathbf{d}_n).$$

The meaning of the filtering function of the relation R is the following. Let $\mathbf{d}_i$ be the set of admissible values of variable x_i (for $i = 1, \ldots, n$) and the values of the $x_1, \ldots, x_n$ are connected by the relation R. The filtering function $\mathcal{F}_R$ "filters" the set of admissible values for each variable, excluding the values, which are known to be incompatible in the sense of the relation R with the values of other variables.

Example 5. Let $D_1, \ldots, D_n$ be finite domains, $^*D_i = 2^{D_i}$ $(i = 1, \ldots, n)$ be their SD-extensions, and $R \subseteq D_1 \times \ldots \times D_n$ be a relation over domains. Then

$$\mathcal{F}_R(\mathbf{d}_1, \ldots, \mathbf{d}_n) = (\pi_1(R \cap \mathbf{d}_1 \times \ldots \times \mathbf{d}_n), \ldots, \pi_n(R \cap \mathbf{d}_1 \times \ldots \times \mathbf{d}_n)),$$

where $\pi_i(X)$ is the i-th projection of a relation X.

Example 6. Let $\mathcal{R}$ be the set of all real numbers, and $\mathcal{IR}(R_0)$ be the set of all R_0-bounded intervals (see example 2) for some finite $R_0 \subseteq \mathcal{R}$. Consider the relation add $\subseteq \mathcal{R}^3$, where $(x, y, z) \in$ add iff $x + y = z$. The filtering function of add, $\mathcal{F}_{\text{add}}$, is defined according to definition 3 as follows:

$$\begin{aligned}\mathcal{F}_{\text{add}}(\mathbf{x}, \mathbf{y}, \mathbf{z}) = (&[\max\{\underline{\mathbf{x}}, (\underline{\mathbf{z}} - \overline{\mathbf{y}})^-\}, \min\{\overline{\mathbf{x}}, (\overline{\mathbf{z}} - \underline{\mathbf{y}})^+\}], \\ &[\max\{\underline{\mathbf{y}}, (\underline{\mathbf{z}} - \overline{\mathbf{x}})^-\}, \min\{\overline{\mathbf{y}}, (\overline{\mathbf{z}} - \underline{\mathbf{x}})^+\}], \\ &[\max\{\underline{\mathbf{z}}, (\underline{\mathbf{x}} + \underline{\mathbf{y}})^-\}, \min\{\overline{\mathbf{z}}, (\overline{\mathbf{x}} + \overline{\mathbf{y}})^+\}]).\end{aligned}$$

Here

$$x^+ = \min\{y \in R_0 \cup \{-\infty, +\infty\} \mid x \le y\},$$
$$x^- = \max\{y \in R_0 \cup \{-\infty, +\infty\} \mid x \ge y\}.$$

It is easy to see that there are effective algorithms for the filtering functions of other relations over real numbers (like $\mathcal{F}_{\text{mul}}$ for "$x * y = z$", or $\mathcal{F}_{\sin}$ for "$\sin(x) = y$", etc.) in interval subdefinite extension $\mathcal{IR}(R_0)$ of $\mathcal{R}$.

Example 7. Consider an arbitrary domain D, and its vector-domain A,

$$A = \underbrace{D \times \ldots \times D}_{n} = D^n$$

for some positive integer n, and the domain of all integer numbers $\mathcal{Z}$. Let $^*D$ be an SD-extension of the domain D, $^*A$ be the following SD-extension of the compound domain A (the same as in example 4):

$$^*A = \underbrace{^*D \times \ldots \times {}^*D}_{n} = (^*D)^n,$$

and $^*\mathcal{Z}$ be an SD-extension of $\mathcal{Z}$. Consider the following relation

$$\text{index} \subseteq A \times \mathcal{Z} \times D,$$

where $(a, i, e) \in \text{index}$ iff the i-th element of a vector a is e, i. e. $a = (e_1, \ldots, e_n)$, and $e_i = e$. The filtering function $\mathcal{F}_{\text{index}}$ of the relation index is defined according to definition 3 as follows. For $\mathbf{a} = (\mathbf{a}_1, \ldots, \mathbf{a}_n) \in {}^*A$, $\mathbf{i} \in {}^*\mathcal{Z}$, and $\mathbf{e} \in {}^*D$,

$$\mathcal{F}_{\text{index}}(\mathbf{a}, \mathbf{i}, \mathbf{e}) = (\mathbf{a}', \mathbf{i}', \mathbf{e}'),$$

where

$$\mathbf{a}' = \begin{cases} (\mathbf{a}_1, \ldots, \mathbf{a}_{i-1}, \mathbf{a}_i \cap \mathbf{e}, \mathbf{a}_{i+1}, \ldots, \mathbf{a}_n), \text{ if } \mathbf{i} \cap \{1, \ldots, n\} = \{i\}, \\ \emptyset, \text{ if } \mathbf{i} \cap \{1, \ldots, n\} = \emptyset, \\ \mathbf{a}, \text{ otherwise} \end{cases},$$
$$\mathbf{i}' = \mathbf{i} \cap \text{app}_{^*\mathcal{Z}}(\{i \mid \mathbf{a}_i \cap \mathbf{e} \neq \emptyset\}),$$
$$\mathbf{e}' = \mathbf{e} \cap \text{app}_{^*D}(\bigcup_{i \in \mathbf{i}} \mathbf{a}_i).$$

One can easily extend the previous example to an indexation of a matrix. The following example demonstrates this.

Example 8. Given a domain D, consider its matrix-domain $M = D^{k \times l}$ for two positive integer numbers k and l. Let $\mathcal{Z}$ be a domain of all integer numbers, $^*D$ be an SD-extension of D, $^*\mathcal{Z}$ be an SD-extension of $\mathcal{Z}$, and $^*M = (^*D)^{k \times l}$ be an SD-extension of domain M. If we regard matrix-domain M as a vector-domain with dimension $n = kl$, we can define relation index as in previous example. Consider another relation *index*2 $\subseteq M \times \mathcal{Z} \times \mathcal{Z} \times D$, where $(m, i, j, e) \in \text{index2}$ iff the element at position (i, j) of a matrix m is equal to e. Therefore, a constraint index2(m, i, j, e) is equivalent to three constraints

$$\begin{cases} \text{index}(m, p, e), \\ \text{add}(q, j, p), \\ \text{mul}(i, l, q). \end{cases}$$

2.4 Subdefinite Models

Definition 4. *Let (V, C) be a CSP. A* subdefinite model *of CSP (V, C) (where $V = \{v_1, \ldots, v_n\}$) is defined as follows:*

- *for the domain D_v of each variable $v \in V$, its SD-extension $^*D_v$ is built; denote the compound domain $D_{v_1} \times \ldots \times D_{v_n}$ by D_V, and its SD-extension $^*D_{v_1} \times \ldots \times {}^*D_{v_n}$ by $^*D_V$;*
- *for each constraint $c \in C$ (let $c \in C_m$), a filtering function*

$$\mathcal{F}_{R_c} : {}^*D_{Arg_c(1)} \times \ldots \times {}^*D_{Arg_c(m)} \to {}^*D_{Arg_c(1)} \times \ldots \times {}^*D_{Arg_c(m)}$$

of its relation R_c is constructed.

To simplify the notation, instead of $\mathcal{F}_{R_c}$ we consider the function

$$\mathcal{F}_c^+ : {}^*D_V \to {}^*D_V$$

defined as follows. Let $Arg_c(j) = v_{i_j}$ for $j = 1, \ldots m$, and $\mathcal{F}_{R_c}(\mathbf{d}_{i_1}, \ldots, \mathbf{d}_{i_m}) = (\mathbf{e}_{i_1}, \ldots, \mathbf{e}_{i_m})$. Then $\mathcal{F}_c^+(\mathbf{d}_1, \ldots, \mathbf{d}_n) = (\mathbf{f}_1, \ldots, \mathbf{f}_n)$, where

$$\mathbf{f}_i = \begin{cases} \mathbf{d}_i, & \text{if } i \notin \{i_1, \ldots, i_m\}, \\ \bigcap_{j: i_j = i} \mathbf{e}_{i_j}, & \text{otherwise.} \end{cases}$$

The algorithm of constraint propagation in a subdefinite model of CSP (V, C) (where $V = \{v_1, \ldots, v_n\}$) is defined as follows.

Definition 5 (Constraint Propagation Algorithm).
At the t-th step, denote

$$\mathbf{d}^{(t)} \in {}^*D_V \text{ – the vector of subdefinite values of variables } V,$$
$$Q^{(t)} \subseteq C \text{ – the set of active constraints.}$$

Step 0. *Let*

$$\mathbf{d}^{(0)} = (D_{v_1}, \ldots, D_{v_n}),$$
$$Q^{(0)} = C.$$

Step $t+1$. *If $Q^{(t)} = \emptyset$, then STOP. Otherwise, choose $c \in Q^{(t)}$ and let*

$$\mathbf{d}^{(t+1)} = \mathcal{F}_c^+(\mathbf{d}^{(t)}),$$
$$Q^{(t+1)} = Q^{(t)} \setminus \{c\} \cup \{c' \in C \mid (\exists i) \quad Arg_c(i) = v_j \quad \text{and} \quad \mathbf{d}_j^{(t)} \neq \mathbf{d}_j^{(t+1)}\}.$$

The properties of the constraint propagation algorithm are summarized in the following proposition (see [3] for proof).

Proposition 1. *In terms of the previous definition, the following assertions are valid:*

1. *Constraint propagation algorithm in subdefinite models always terminates. The number of its steps is less than* $|C| \sum_{v \in V} L({}^*D_v)$, *where* $L({}^*D_v)$ *is the length of the maximal decreasing (with respect to "$\subseteq$") chain of different elements of* ${}^*D_v$.
2. *If* $a = (a_{v_1}, \ldots, a_{v_n})$ *is a solution of CSP* (V, C), *then* $a \in \mathbf{d}^*$, *where* $\mathbf{d}^*$ *is the vector of subdefinite values of variables* V *at the last step of the algorithm.*

3 Graph Problems as CSPs

For considering various kinds of problems on graphs we will discuss the representation of a graph structure in a CSP. Below we briefly redefine the common notions of graph theory.

Definition 6. A directed weighted graph *is a pair* (V, E), *where* V *is a finite set of* vertices *of the graph, and* $E \subseteq V \times V \times \mathcal{R}^+$ *(where* $\mathcal{R}^+$ *is the set of all positive real numbers) is a set of* edges *of the graph. An element* $(i, j, w) \in E$ *denotes an edge from the vertex* i *to the vertex* j *with the* weight $w > 0$. *We suppose that there exists at most one edge between two vertices, i. e. if* $(i, j, w) \in E$, $(i', j', w') \in E$, $i = i'$, *and* $j = j'$, *then* $w = w'$. *For simplicity, we will suppose that* V *is a subset of natural numbers:* $V = \{1, 2, \ldots, m\}$.

An undirected weighted graph *will be considered here as a kind of directed weighted graph* $G = (V, E)$, *where the relation* E *is irreflexive and symmetric for the first and the second arguments, i. e. if* $(i, j, w) \in E$, *then* $(j, i, w) \in E$, *and the edge* (i, i, w) *does not belong to* E *for any* i *and* w.

The adjacency matrix *of the graph* G *is a real non-negative matrix* $M \in \mathcal{R}^{m \times m}$. *An element* m_{ij} *of the matrix* M *is the weight of the edge from the vertex* i *to the vertex* j. *If* $m_{ij} = 0$ *then there is no edge from the vertex* i *to the vertex* j *in the graph* G. *Clearly, the adjacency matrix of an undirected graph is a symmetric matrix with zeros on the main diagonal.*

A vector of edges *of the graph* G *is a vector of triplets* $B \in (V \times V \times \mathcal{R}^+)^n$, *where* n *is the cardinal number of the set* E. *An element* $b_k = (i_k, j_k, w_k)$ *of the vector* B *denotes an edge of the graph* G *from the vertex* i_k *to the vertex* j_k *with the weight* $w_k > 0$.

3.1 Subdefinite Graph

Since we deal with subdefinite values in a CSP, consider the advantages of applying the subdefiniteness to the graph representation.

Let a graph $G = (V, E)$ be represented in a CSP by its adjacency matrix M. For this reason, we define an SD-extension of the domain $\mathcal{R}^{m \times m}$ as

$(\mathcal{IR}(R_0))^{m\times m}$ (see example 2) for some finite real subset R_0. In this case, we can use subdefinite values (R_0-bounded intervals) for the representation of weights of edges. This means that we deal with a graph, which has subdefinite edges. If the subdefinite weight of an edge contains 0, then this edge can be absent in the graph. Otherwise, the edge exists in the graph, but its weight is subdefinite, i. e. only partially known.

Let a graph $G = (V, E)$ be represented in a CSP by its vector of edges. A subdefinite domain for the representation of this vector is $({}^*V \times {}^*V \times \mathcal{IR}^+(R_0))^n$, where $\mathcal{IR}^+(R_0)$ is the set of all R_0-bounded intervals with lower bounds greater than 0. Each edge in the vector has its start and finish vertices that are subdefinite. This means that we know only partial information about an edge: we don't know precisely the vertices connected by the edge. Moreover, the weights of edges are subdefinite too.

One can use only defined (precise) values in an adjacency matrix and in a vector of edges, of course, and therefore one can deal with fully defined graph. However, the possibility of the representation of subdefinite graphs allows one to specify and solve a much more broad class of graph problems. Below we consider various problems on graphs and their representations as CSPs. Also we emphasize problems, which have not been discussed previously in graph theory.

3.2 A Path in a Graph

Definition 7. *Given a directed weighted graph $G = (V, E)$ and two of its vertices $i, j \in V$, a* path *between i and j, $p(i, j)$, is a sequence of vertices $i_1, i_2, \ldots, i_l$, where $i_1 = i$, $i_k = j$, and for all $k = 1, \ldots, l-1$ there exists an edge in the graph G between the vertices i_k and i_{k+1}, i. e. there exists $w > 0$ such that $(i_k, i_{k+1}, w) \in E$. The* weight *of the path $p(i, j) = i_1, i_2, \ldots, i_l$ is the sum of weights of its edges.*

Consider the specification of a CSP for searching a path in a graph. Let a graph $G = (V, E)$ be represented by its adjacency matrix $M \in \mathcal{R}^{m\times m}$. We can represent a path from a vertex i to a vertex j as a vector of vertices $P \in V^m$. The size of the vector is equal to m (the number of vertices of the graph), but only first l elements are meaningful. The specification of the problem for searching a path in a graph is performed with the use of index and index2 relations discussed in the previous section of the paper. The first element of the vector P is equal to i:

$$\text{index}(P, 1, i).$$

Each next element of P should be connected with the previous one by an edge. This condition is represented by the following set of constraints. Let

$$\text{index}(P, k, u)$$

for some k ($1 \le k < m$), then

$$u = j \quad \text{or} \quad \begin{cases} \text{index}(P, k+1, v), \\ \text{index2}(M, u, v, w), \\ w > 0. \end{cases}$$

The specification of a path in the graph G represented by its vector of edges $B \in (V \times V \times \mathcal{R}^+)^n$ is performed similarly, except instead of

$$\text{index2}(M, u, v, w)$$

we specify the constraint

$$\text{index}(B, r, (u, v, w))$$

with an integer variable r.

The constraints above are used to specify a CSP for searching a path in a graph. One can easily add to this CSP other constraints expressing the weight of a path and find the path with minimal weight (see [5] to learn about the constraint propagation algorithm for searching an optimal solution of a CSP). Here we want to emphasize that one can solve problem of searching an optimal path in a graph with subdefinite (partially known) edges or edges with subdefinite weights. For example, we have specified and solved *the Travelling Salesman Problem* with subdefinite data using the tools described above.

3.3 A Spanning Tree of a Graph

Definition 8. *Given an undirected weighted graph $G = (V, E)$, its* spanning tree *is a graph $S(G) = (V, E')$, where $E' \subseteq E$, and $S(G)$ is* a tree *(a connected acyclic graph).*

There is an equivalent definition of a tree in graph theory. In our terms it sounds as follows: an undirected weighted graph $G = (V, E)$ is a tree iff it is connected (i. e. there exists a path between each pair of its different vertices), and $|E| = 2(|V| - 1)$.

We need two groups of constraints to specify a spanning tree. The first one is the condition $E' \subseteq E$. Let graphs $G = (V, E)$ and $S(G) = (V, E')$ be represented by their adjacency matrices M and M' respectively. Then the condition may be specified as follows:

$$m'_{ij} = 0 \quad \text{or} \quad m'_{ij} = m_{ij}$$

for all $i, j = 1, \ldots, m$.

The second group of constraints is the condition that $S(G)$ has to be a tree. Since a tree is a connected graph, we specify the existence of a path between each pair of different vertices in $S(G)$. The corresponding group of constraints was discussed in the previous subsection. The only we need to specify else is the condition $|E'| = 2(m - 1)$. Clearly, $|E'|$ is equal to the number of positive elements of matrix M'.

One of the popular graph problems is a building of a spanning tree of a given undirected weighted graph with minimal sum of the weights of its edges. We can easily specify and solve such problem as a CSP using constraints defined above. Moreover, we can solve this problem with additional constraints on degrees of vertices of the spanning tree. In our terms, the degree of a vertex i in the graph G represented by its adjacency matrix M is equal to the number of positive elements in the i-th row (or, equivalently, in i-th column) of matrix M. Since we can deal with subdefinite values, these degrees can be given as integer intervals. As far as we know, such kind of graph problems has not been discussed before in graph theory.

4 Experimental Results

Consider a graph G with the following adjacency matrix M:

$$\begin{array}{cccccccccccc}
- & 3 & 5 & 48 & 48 & 8 & 8 & 5 & 5 & 3 & 3 & 0 \\
3 & - & 3 & 48 & 48 & 8 & 8 & 5 & 5 & 0 & 0 & 3 \\
5 & 3 & - & 72 & 72 & 48 & 48 & 24 & 24 & 3 & 3 & 5 \\
48 & 48 & 74 & - & 0 & 6 & 6 & 12 & 12 & 48 & 48 & 48 \\
48 & 48 & 74 & 0 & - & 6 & 6 & 12 & 12 & 48 & 48 & 48 \\
8 & 8 & 50 & 6 & 6 & - & 0 & 8 & 8 & 8 & 8 & 8 \\
8 & 8 & 50 & 6 & 6 & 0 & - & 8 & 8 & 8 & 8 & 8 \\
5 & 5 & 26 & 12 & 12 & 8 & 8 & - & 0 & 5 & 5 & 5 \\
5 & 5 & 26 & 12 & 12 & 8 & 8 & 0 & - & 5 & 5 & 5 \\
3 & 0 & 3 & 48 & 48 & 8 & 8 & 5 & 5 & - & 0 & 3 \\
3 & 0 & 3 & 48 & 48 & 8 & 8 & 5 & 5 & 0 & - & 3 \\
0 & 3 & 5 & 48 & 48 & 8 & 8 & 5 & 5 & 3 & 3 & -
\end{array}$$

We have tried to solve a travelling salesman problem for this graph (searching a path with minimal weight containing all the vertices of the graph which start and finish vertices are the same). To show the performance we have considered a set of graphs with sizes less or equal to 12 (by excluding from the adjacency matrix last rows and columns). For the same set of graphs we have solved a problem of a building of a spanning tree.

The table below summarizes the performance characteristics measured on PC with AMD K6 200 MHz processor and 64 MBytes RAM.

Problem	Size	Time (in sec.)	Backtracks
TSP with adjacency matrix	10	123	16479
	11	932	108809
	12	6232	601248
TSP with vector of edges	10	108	2025
	11	618	11014
	12	3011	47078
Spanning Tree	7	161	222
	8	2538	1882

5 Conclusion

We have solved all the problems on graphs discussed in this paper using constraint programming environment *NeMo+* [6] developed in our Institutes. The obtained results allow us to hope on successful application of proposed techniques for solving a large class of graph problems.

Our future work will aim to extend the class of graph problems and to propose new constraint programming techniques for its solving.

The authors are indebted to Sergei Sannikov and Eugene Rukoleev, who have taken part in the coding of some of these problems in *NeMo+*, and to the referees for helpful comments on the paper.

References

1. Mayoh, B.: Constraint Programming and Artificial Intelligence: In: Mayoh, B., Tyugu, E., Penjaam, J. (eds.): Constraint Programming: Proceedings 1993 NATO ASI Parnu, Estonia. Springer-Verlag, Berlin Heidelberg New York (1993) 18–53
2. Narin'yani, A. S.: Subdefiniteness and Basic Means of Knowledge Representation. Computers and Artificial Intelligence, Bratislawa **2**, No.5 (1983) 443–452
3. Ushakov, D.: Some Formal Aspects of Subdefinite Models. Preprint Institute of Informatics Systems, Novosibirsk **49** (1998)
4. Telerman, V., Ushakov, D.: Data Types in Subdefinite Models. In: Calmet, J., Campbell, J. A., Pfalzgraf, J. (eds.): Artificial Intelligence and Symbolic Mathematical Computation: Proceedings. Lecture Notes in Computer Science, Vol. 1138. Springer-Verlag, Berlin Heidelberg New York (1996) 305–319
5. Telerman, V., Ushakov, D.: Constraint Satisfaction Techniques for Mathematical Programming Problems. In: Proceedings of International Conference on Interval Methods and their Application in Global Optimization, INTERVAL'98. Nanjing, China (1998)
6. Telerman, V., Sidorov, V., Ushakov, D.: Problem Solving in the Object-Oriented Technological Environment *NeMo+*. In: Bjørner, D., Broy, M., Pottosin, I. V. (eds.): Perspectives of System Informatics: Proceedings. Lecture Notes in Computer Science, Vol. 1181. Springer-Verlag, Berlin Heidelberg New York (1996) 91–100

Extensional Set Library for ECL^{i}PS^{e*}

Tatyana Yakhno and Evgueni Petrov

A. P. Ershov Institute of Informatics Systems,
6, Acad. Lavrentjev pr., Novosibirsk, 630090, Russia,
{yakhno,pes}@iis.nsk.su

Abstract. Extensional Set (XS) library is an extension of ECL^{i}PS^e which solves set-theoretical constraints over extensional sets containing variables with numeric domains. To efficiently process such a class of set domains, XS library employs a constraint programming method called Subdefinite Computations. Within that framework, a domain representation and an approximate unification algorithm are proposed. The abilities of the library are illustrated by a geometric application.

1 Introduction

Because people usually express their knowledge in an implicit way employing partial information, computers need a special knowledge representation in order to "understand" such partial specifications. Few years ago in the field of Constraint Programming (CP), it has been proposed to simply add a control mechanism to these specifications provided they are sufficiently formal.

During recent twenty years Constraint (Logic) Programming has developed a number of methods and tools processing numeric data and ranging from arc-consistency for finite domains [10] to box-consistency for interval domains [13]. However, constraint programming systems which process sets are not very numerous [14,9,7,4,5,15]. A related research area is program analysis which employs sets for automatic inference of various properties of programs [6,2,1]. Finally, in the imperative environment, sets are most significantly supported in a language SETL [12].

With respect to CP classification, Subdefinite (SD) Computations are a consistency technique [11]. Given a set of constraints, it produces a compact description of a set which contains all the solutions to the constraints. In Section 3 SD computations are described in more details.

ECL^{i}PS^e is a CLP system. It allows users to program constraint satisfaction techniques directly at the language level. Our paper discusses these facilities (Section 2) and a technique of implementation of SD computations in ECL^{i}PS^e (Section 1). Section 4 describes how this technique is employed in XS library for resolution of constraints over finite extensional sets. Section 7 compares XS library against a powerful library for resolution of set constraints within ECL^{i}PS^e. Section 8 describes a geometric application of XS library.

* This project is supported by grant 98–06 from Institut Franco-Russe A. M. Liapunov d'informatique et de mathématiques appliquées.

D. Bjørner, M. Broy, A. Zamulin (Eds.): PSI'99, LNCS 1755, pp. 434–444, 2000.

2 ECL^{i}PS^e

ECL^{i}PS^e is an abbreviation for *ECRC Common Logic Programming System*. It is a Prolog-based system whose aim is to serve as a platform for creating various extensions of logic programming. ECL^{i}PS^e offers two data types, *meta-term* and *delayed goal*, which significantly simplify this process. Using meta-attributes and delayed goals, an application can organize additional information and control flows in its own way, independently of Prolog standards.

A meta-term consists of two or more terms, the first term visible to "everyone", called *Prolog value* of the meta-term, and the others, called *meta-attributes*, visible only to few tools which convert meta-terms to standard Prolog data and vice versa. A meta-term is written like `T{name1:T1,...}` where `T` is its Prolog value, `T1` is its meta-attribute `name1`, etc.

Formally, a delayed goal is a Prolog goal whose execution has been delayed. A delayed goal represents an action that should be done in the future. There are three major operations with delayed goals: creation, scheduling for execution, and execution of all scheduled goals. A delayed goal is written like `'GOAL'(G)` where `G` is the goal that has been delayed and `'GOAL'` is a label indicating that fact.

3 SD Computations

SD computations have been introduced by A. S. Narinyani in early 1980's and are intensely studied by our colleagues from A. P. Ershov Institute of Informatics Systems and Russian Research Institute of Artificial Intelligence.

Let us take some signature without function symbols, with predicate symbols $\{Q, \ldots\}$, variables $\{x, y, \ldots\}$, constants $\{a, \ldots\}$, and some interpretation of this signature. A symbol and its interpretation are typed identically.

A *constraint* is an atomic formula. A *constraint satisfaction problem* (CSP) is a finite set of constraints. A *solution* to a CSP C is a valuation of the variables under which each constraint in C holds. The value a of a variable x is *extensible to a solution* of CSP C, if there is a solution to C which maps x to a.

Given a CSP C, SD computations produce for each variable x a set of values which contains all the values of x extensible to a solution of C. Observing the traditions of CP, such a set of values is called a domain of x. A variable and its domain are denoted by the same small latin letter.

SD computations pay much attention to domain representation because it is, in fact, a question of effectiveness. Simpler domains are less informative, but on the other hand they are processed faster. A domain representation is a function $(\cdot)^\star$ which widens an arbitrary domain up to the closest representable one.

A constraint $Q(x\,y\ldots)$ defines the following transformations of x, y, ... [1]

$$x \leftarrow \mathrm{Pr}_1(Q \cap x \times y \times \ldots)^\star, \tag{1}$$

$$y \leftarrow \mathrm{Pr}_2(Q \cap x \times y \times \ldots)^\star, \ldots. \tag{2}$$

[1] In the Cartesian products, a constant a is replaced with $\{a\}^\star$. If a is not finitely representable, then $\{a\}^\star$ is larger than $\{a\}$.

which are called *calculation functions* (Pr_i is projection on i-th coordinate, $\times$ is Cartesian product). The calculation function (1) *reads* x, y, ... and *writes* x, the calculation function (2) *reads* x, y, ... and *writes* y, etc.

Each CSP defines a network of calculation functions which is similar to networks of constraints proposed by other authors [10]. The network contains nodes of two types, variables and calculation functions, and naturally splits into star-like segments. The center of each star is a calculation function, and its rays reach the variables it reads and writes.

If the domain of a variable x changes, then the calculation functions that read x propagate this change to the neighbours of x. Using the data-driven control mechanism, SD computations propagate this wave of domain updates through the network of calculation functions until the wave expires.

Implementation in ECL^{i}PS^e. In what follows we briefly describe how data types from Section 2 are applied to implementation of SD computations. Let $C \ni Q(x\,y\ldots)$ denote the CSP to which SD computations are applied. Each variable x occurring in C is turned into a meta-term $x\{\mathtt{sd:var(T}_x\mathtt{,\ Fs)}\}$ whose meta-attribute `sd` stores the domain of x (the term $\mathtt{T}_x$) and a list of calculation functions reading x (the list `Fs`).

Each predicate symbol Q of arity n is associated with an $(n+1)$-ary Prolog predicate `compute_q` whose intended meaning is

$$\mathtt{q(1,T}_x\mathtt{,T}_y\mathtt{,\ldots)} \iff x = \mathrm{Pr}_1(Q \cap x \times y \times \ldots)^\star,$$
$$\mathtt{q(2,T}_x\mathtt{,T}_y\mathtt{,\ldots)} \iff y = \mathrm{Pr}_2(Q \cap x \times y \times \ldots)^\star, \quad \ldots$$

where the terms $\mathtt{T}_x$, $\mathtt{T}_y$, etc. denote the domains of x, y, etc.

Calculation functions of the form (1), (2), etc. are turned into delayed goals `'GOAL'(comput_q(1,`x`,`y`,...))`, `'GOAL'(comput_q(2,`x`,`y`,...))`, etc. Figure 1 shows an encoding for a calculation function.

```
q(1, X, Y, ...):-
  make_suspension(q(1, X, Y, ...), 3, F),         % [1]
  extract(Y, Y_dom, Y_goals),                     % [2]
  assign(Y, Y_dom, [F|Y_goals]),                  % [3]
  ...                                               ...
  extract(X, X_dom, X_goals),                     % [2*n]
  compute_q(1, X_dom, Y_dom, ..., Changed),       % [2*n+1]
  ( var(Changed) -> true ;                        % [2*n+2]
    assign(X, X_dom, []),                         % [2*n+3]
    schedule_woken(X_goals),                      % [2*n+4]
    wake                                          % [2*n+5]
  ).
```

Fig. 1. A simplified code of a calculation function

4 Brief Introduction to XS Library

Extensional Set (XS) library is an extension of ECL^{i}PS^e which solves set-theoretical constraints over extensional sets containing variables with numeric domains. The particular constraint solver for numeric data (at present, Interval Domain library [16]) is a parameter to XS library. The only requirement of such a solver is that it offer access to the bounds of numeric domains and creation of numeric domain variables.

Generally speaking, XS library computes sets of ground *tuples*. A tuple is a term constructed of numbers and numeric domain variables with the help of functors ($\mathtt{x}/n$) ($n \geq 1$). Each set variable is associated with a set domain. A set domain consists of two ground sets of tuples $l \subseteq u$. If this domain is associated with a variable x, then $l \subseteq x \subseteq u$.

Each constraint over sets is enclosed in curly braces and states either equality or inclusion (for two sets), or membership (for a tuple and a set). A set inside such a constraint is specified either by a set domain variable, or by a list of (not necessarily ground) tuples, or by an expression built of such variables and lists. Besides that, cardinality of a set can occur in constraints over numeric data.

Equality. Keeping two sets equal, XS library modifies set domains (if at least one of the sets is specified by a set domain) and numeric domains (if at least one of the sets is specified by a list of non-ground tuples containing numeric domain variables).

Equality of a set domain variable and a list of tuples is maintained by two delayed goals which transfer information between the set domain and numeric domains inside the tuples (if any). Enforcing equality of two set domain variables, XS library intersects their domains and unifies the variables themselves; no delayed goals are generated.

The following example shows the effect of stating equality of two sets:

```
[eclipse 17]:
        { [x(0,1),x(1,2),x(2,4)] = [x(0,X0),x(N,XN),x(2,X2)] }.
N = 1
X0 = 1
XN = 2
X2 = 4
yes.
```

Enforcing equality constraint between two sets fails, if XS library is able to determine that the sets are different. For example, the following query fails:

```
[eclipse 18]: A setdom []..[x(0,1),x(1,2)], { A = [x(N,N),x(A,B)] }.
no (more) solution.
```

Inclusion. Likewise keeping two sets equal, keeping set `A` included into set `B` updates set and numeric domains involved into specification of `A`, `B`. For example:

```
[eclipse 21]: A setdom []..[x(0,1),x(1,2),x(2,4)],
        { [x(0,1),x(1,X1)] subseteq A }.
A = A{[x(0,1),x(1,2)]..[x(0,1),x(1,2),x(2,4)]}
X1 = 2
yes.
```

Set Expressions. A set can be specified by a set expression, e.g.

```
[eclipse 22]: { A\/[0,N] = [0,1,2] }, { A /\ [0,1] = [] }.
N = 1
A = A{[2]}
yes.
```

Membership. The fact of presence (absence) of a particular element in a set is stated by membership constraint. The constraint { `X in A` } ({ `not X in A` }) tells XS library "not to let the tuple `X` out of (into) the set `A`".

Relating a tuple and a set of tuples by membership constraint, one is able to model application of a function to an argument as follows:

```
app(F, I, FI):- { x(I, FI) in F }.
```

The typical usage of (app/3) is illustrated by the following problem taken from [8]): given integer $m \leq n$, find such a function f that $f(i) = i - 1$, if $i \in [m+1, n]$, and $f(i) = f(f(i+2))$, if $i \in [0, m]$. The specification is as follows:

```
findall(x(I, FI), (between(0, N, I), FI ** 0 .. N), Up),
{ F = Up },
forall(I:  0..M, app(F, I) *== app(F, app(F, I+2))) ),
forall(I:M+1..N, app(F, I) *== I-1 ).
```

For example, if `M = 6` and `N = 9`, then the solution is `F{[x(0, 6), x(1, 6), x(2, 6), x(3, 6), x(4, 6), x(5, 6), x(6, 6), x(7, 6), x(8, 7), x(9, 8)]}`. In the general case, XS library spends approximately $O(m^2 + n)$ units of time on each instance of this problem.

5 Representation of Set Domains

Sets are so-called content addressable structures. In an imperative environment, data of that kind are usually represented by hash tables which make data having specified content accessible in nearly constant time. However, in logic programming, this approach is likely to be hard to stick to.

XS library transforms lower and upper bounds of set domains to balanced binary trees of ground tuples. Tuples in such a tree are arranged with respect to $\prec$ defined recursively as follows:

1. $t \prec u$, if t, u are numbers, and $t < u$,
2. $t \prec u$, if t is a number, u is a tuple,
3. $t \prec u$, if t, u are tuples, and t is shorter than u,

4. $t \prec u$, if $t = \mathtt{x}(\ldots t_i \ldots)$, $u = \mathtt{x}(\ldots u_i \ldots)$ are of the same length, and $t_i = u_i$ for $i \in [1, k-1]$, $t_k \prec u_k$.

The order $\prec$ agrees well with unification in the following sense. Let t be a non-ground tuple. Let l (respectively u) be the ground tuple obtained from t by replacing each variable v in t with the lower (respectively upper) bound of the domain of v. It is easy to see that, if $a \prec l$ or $u \prec a$ for some tuple a, then unification of a and t will fail.

Such a representation of set domains is advantageous twofold. First, because lower and upper bounds of domains are sorted, all operations on set domains take linear amount of time (with respect to the sum of sizes of involved upper bounds). Second, because $\prec$ and unification agree, retrieving from a set all the instances of a non-ground tuple usually requires scanning only small part of the set. For example, if `X` is a constant, `Y` is a variable and `S` is the rectangle [0,`N`] $\times$ [0, 7], then XS library enforces the constraint { `x(X, Y) in S`} in 0.03, 0.05, and 0.07 seconds for `N`=400, 800, and 1600.

6 Approximate Set Unification

The Set Unification problem is stated as follows: given two sets of terms (of some signature), find a substitution which makes the sets identical. The Set Unification problem has been proved NP-complete. Besides that, even if two sets are unifyable, their most general unifier sometimes is not enough "informative", e.g, the most general unifier of $\{0, 1\}$ and $\{x, y\}$ is the identity substitution $\{x/x, y/y\}$ which bypasses the fact of unification. In order to be efficient, (constraint) logic programming systems usually restrict the class of processed sets [14,9,7,5].

XS library reduces unification of sets, each specified by a list of tuples, to unification of set domain variables which are related to these lists by special predicates (`st/2`) and (`ts/2`). The predicates approximate calculation functions of the following relation σ between finite sets and lists:

$$\sigma = \{(s, l) |\ s = \{t_1, \ldots, t_n\}, l = [t_1, \ldots, t_n], t_i \text{ are ground tuples} \, (i \in [1, n])\}.$$

Though precisely computing the calculation functions of σ seems to be intractable, some larger domains can be computed efficiently. Suppose, the lower and upper bounds of the set domain are l, u, and for each $i \in [1, n]$ the tuple t_i is ground iff $i \leq k$. In the notation each non-ground tuple is treated as the set of its ground instances.

Current version of XS library recomputes the lower and upper bounds l, u of the set domain as follows (the predicate (`ts/2`)):

- $l \leftarrow l \cup \{t_1, \ldots, t_k\}$,
- $u \leftarrow u \cap (\{t_1, \ldots, t_k\} \cup \bigcup_{i=k+1}^{n} t_i)$,
- if $|l| = n$, then $u \leftarrow l$.

That procedure may compute a larger set domain than the corresponding calculation function would do. For example, if $n = 4$, $t_1 = 1$, $t_2 = 99$, $t_3 = 99$, t_4 is a variable with the domain $[0,9]$, $l = \{9\}$, $u = [0,9] \cup \{99\}$, then, after a call to (ts/2), l will be $\{1,9,99\}$ and u will be unchanged. It is easy to check, that the true calculation function will set l and u to $\{1,9,99\}$.

The non-ground tuples t_i ($i \in [k+1,n]$) are iteratively recomputed according to the following rules (the predicate (st/2)):

- if $a \in l$, $a \in t_{i_a}$ for a unique $i_a \in [k+1,n]$, then $t_{i_a} \leftarrow a$,
- $t_i \leftarrow t_i \cap u$,
- if $|l| = n$, $i \in [1,n]$, $i \neq j$, t_i is ground, then $t_j \leftarrow t_j \setminus \{t_i\}$.

The computations stop when the tuples stop changing. And again, the above procedure may compute, for some variable, a larger numeric domain than the corresponding calculation function would do. This is a reasonable price for efficiency of the procedure.

7 Comparison to a Library Conjunto

Conjunto is a powerful library for resolution of set-related problems within ECL^{i}PS^e. Conjunto processes finite set domains and constraints stating inclusion, disjointness, equality for sets, membership for sets and arbitrary terms, cardinality for sets and integers. The basic algorithm employed by Conjunto is constraint propagation adjusted for set domains represented by lower and upper bounds w.r.t. inclusion.

If speaking of purely set-theoretical problems, XS library and Conjunto offer basically the same facilities and performance. However, XS library solves large instances of some problems several times faster than Conjunto. For example, computing the set P_N of all prime numbers between 1 and N takes (in seconds, on Pentium, 100MHz, under Linux):

N	500	1000	2000	4000	8000
Conjunto	1.27	3.71	11.42	39.80	152.47
increase		2.92	3.07	3.48	3.83
XS	1.80	4.43	10.53	23.89	55.81
increase		2.46	2.37	2.26	2.33

The constraints specifying P_N are as follows (π_N is 96, 169, 304, 551, 1008 for N=500, 1000, 2000, 4000, 8000):

$$P_N \subseteq [1,N], \quad \mathrm{card}(P_N) = \pi_N, \quad \bigwedge_{i=2}^{\sqrt{N}} \bigwedge_{j=i}^{N/i} (ij \notin P_N).$$

XS library works faster and time it consumes grows slower because it sorts the elements of each set domain it processes. The following example with exclusion shows how remarkably this effort is rewarded. Conjunto spends 0.08, 0.15, 0.30 seconds on exclusion of an element from the set $[1,N]$ for N =8000, 16000, 32000. XS library spends 0.01 seconds on each exclusion independently of N.

XS library and Conjunto cooperate with numerical solvers, but XS library does it more intensely. For example, both libraries allow specifying the cardinality of a set by a numeric domain variable and then update the set domain accordingly to updates to the numeric domain.

In general, XS library cooperates with a numerical solver in a more complicated way than Conjunto. For example, given a set S, the following mixture of constraints states that A, B, C belong to S and are sorted.

$$A \in S, \quad B \in S, \quad C \in S, \quad A < B, \quad B < C.$$

For each set S made up of three integers, these constraints have a unique solution.

If $S \subseteq \{1, 9, 99\}$, A, B, C are between 1 and 99, then Conjunto and Finite Domains library output $\{\} \mathinner{..} \{1, 9, 99\}$ for S, $1 \mathinner{..} 97$ for A, $2 \mathinner{..} 98$ for B, $3 \mathinner{..} 99$ for C. Unlike that, XS and Interval Domain library jointly produce $S = \{1, 9, 99\}$, $A = 1$, $B = 9$, $C = 99$.

XS library behaves wiser because it accesses not only set domains. For example, if the calculation function of $A \in S$ computing $A^\star$ is invoked for $A^\star = [1, 97]$, $S^\star = [\emptyset, \{1, 9, 99\}]$, then it outputs $A^\star = [1, 9]$. Clearly, that is correct, because in no case 10, 11, and other large numbers from $A^\star$ belong to S. By analogy, $B^\star = [2, 98]$ and $C^\star = [3, 99]$ shrink to a singleton $\{9\}$ and an interval [9,99].

Because the domain of B is a singleton $\{9\}$, the calculation function of $B \in S$ computing S adds 9 to the lower bound of S, and $S^\star$ becomes $[\{9\}, \{1, 9, 99\}]$. Continuing this process, we arrive to the results output by XS library. Sorting n integral numbers in the worst case, XS library spends $O(n^2)$ units of time.

8 Full Minimum Steiner Trees

We turn to Minimum Steiner Tree (MST) problem because it consists of non-trivial numeric and combinatorial parts. The problem is stated as follows. Given a set R of required vertices, find the shortest tree among trees spanning $R \cup S$, S being any set of (Steiner) vertices. The sets R, S are subsets of Euclidean plane, R is finite. Finding the MST is an NP-complete problem [3].

We focus on finding the MST among trees spanning $R \cup S$, S having cardinality $|R| - 2$, and call it a full MST. Let R and S be sets of required and Steiner vertices. The leaves and inner vertices of the full MST form respectively R and S. Each inner vertex is incident to 3 edges which meet at the angle of $\pi/3$. Thus a full MST is a binary tree with an extra vertex attached to its root.

Let $R = \{p_1, \dots, p_k\}$, $S = \{p_{k+1}, \dots, p_{2k-2}\}$, $p_i = (x_i, y_i)$. The topology of the full MST is specified by finite sets $\{(i, l_i)\}_{i=k+1}^{2k-2}$ and $\{(i, r_i)\}_{i=k+1}^{2k-2}$ of arcs mapping each inner vertex to its left and right children. Because trees are acyclic, the sets $\{l_i\}_{i=k+1}^{2k-2}$ and $\{r_i\}_{i=k+1}^{2k-2}$ of left and right children are disjoint, each containing exactly $k - 2$ elements. Note that points in S can be numbered so that, for all i, $l_i < i$, $r_i < i$.

The topology of the full MST meets the following mixture of constraints over set-theoretical and numeric data.

```
findall(x(I, _), between(K+1, 2*K-2, I), L),
findall(x(I, _), between(K+1, 2*K-2, I), R),
term_variables(L, Lchilds),
term_variables(R, Rchilds),
forall(I:K+1..2*K-2, app(L, I) *=< I-1),
forall(I:K+1..2*K-2, app(R, I) *=< I-1),
{ Lchilds /\ Rchilds = [] },
# Lchilds *== K-2, # Rchilds *== K-2,
```

Functions `L`, `R` map a vertex to its children. Lists `Lchilds`, `Rchilds` specify the sets of respective children.

For each arc (i, j), let (α_j, ρ_j) be the polar coordinates of p_j w.r.t p_i. Then, for each inner vertex, there hold the following constraints.

```
forall(I:K+1..2*K-2, (
  app(X, app(L,I)) *== app(X,I)+app(Rh,app(L,I))*cos(app(Al,app(L,I))),
  app(Y, app(L,I)) *== app(Y,I)+app(Rh,app(L,I))*sin(app(Al,app(L,I))),
  app(X, app(R,I)) *== app(X,I)+app(Rh,app(R,I))*cos(app(Al,app(R,I))),
  app(Y, app(R,I)) *== app(Y,I)+app(Rh,app(R,I))*sin(app(Al,app(R,I))),
  app(Al,app(L,I)) *== app(Al,I)+pi/3,
  app(Al,app(R,I)) *== app(Al,I)-pi/3
))
```

Functions `X`, `Y` map a vertex to its coordinates; functions `Al`, `Rh` map a vertex to its polar coordinates w.r.t. its ancestor. Choose p_{2k-2} and p_1 to be the root and the extra vertex attached to it. That gives the last two constraints.

```
app(X, 2*K-2) *== app(X,1)+app(Rh,2*K-2)*cos(app(Al,2*K-2)),
app(Y, 2*K-2) *== app(Y,1)+app(Rh,2*K-2)*sin(app(Al,2*K-2))
```

The constraints describing the topology and coordinates of Steiner vertices define a space of feasible trees which can be explored by some search algorithm in order to find the full MST. Figure 2 shows an example of the full MST computed by XS library for $|R| = 16$.

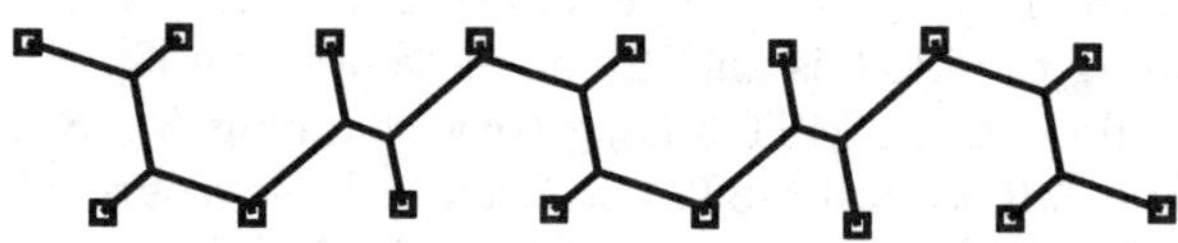

Fig. 2. A Full Minimum Steiner Tree

9 Conclusion

Our paper is an introduction to Extensional Set (XS) library for logic programming system ECL^{i}PS^e. XS solves set-theoretical constraints over extensional sets containing numeric domain variables within a framework of Subdefinite Computations by A. Narin'yani.

Because, processing numeric data in set specifications, XS library cooperates with an external solver, it is, to a certain degree, a generic constraint solver. Such an approach seems more advantageous and reasonable than equipping XS with its own solver for numeric constraint satisfaction problems.

Intrinsic complexity of Set Unification is the reason that restricts the class of tractable sets in many constraint logic programming systems. Compared against Conjunto, Gődel, $\{log\}$, XS library efficiently manages a reacher class of extensional specifications, allowing for numeric domain variables. Instead of "thorough" algorithm of set unification, XS library uses a fast approximate one.

In the future, XS library will develop toward efficient low-level implementation of operations on set domains and implementation of higher-level operartions oriented to resolution of problems from combinatorial geometry.

We are cordially grateful to Natalya Cheremnykh and Olga Drobyshevich, Alexander Zamulin, Yury Zagorul'ko from A. P. Ershov Institute of Informatics Systems, Tamara Kashevarova, Alexander Narin'yani from Russian Research Institute of Artificial Intelligence for invaluable comments and discussion.

References

1. Alexander Aiken and Edward L. Wimmers. Solving systems of set constraints. In *IEEE Symp. on Logic in Comput. Sci.*, June 1992.
2. L. Bachmair, H. Ganzinger, and U. Waldmann. Set constraints are the monadic class. In *Proc. of the LICS'93*, 1993.
3. Nicolos Christofides. *Graph theory: an Algorithmic Approach.* Management Science. Academic Press, Imperial College, London, 1975.
4. Agustino Dovier and G. Rossi. Embedding extensional finite sets in CLP. In *Proc. 3rd Int. Logic Programming Symp.*, Vancouver, Canada, 1993.
5. Carmen Gervet. Conjunto: Constraint logic programming with finite set domains. In M. Bruynooghe, editor, *ILPS'94: Proc. 4th Int. Logic Programming Symp.*, pages 339–358, 1994.
6. N. Heintze and J. Jaffar. A decision procedure for a class of set constraints. In *IEEE Symp. on Logic in Comput. Sci.*, July 1991.
7. P. M. Hill and J. W. LLoyd. *The Gődel programming language (CSTR 92-27).* Bristol University, 1992.
8. S. V. Konyagin, G. A. Tonoyan, I. F. Sharygin, I. A. Kopylov, M. B. Cevryuk, M. L. Sitnikov, O. A. Baiborodin, V. P. Burichenko, G. V. Golovin, D. O. Orlov, L. B. Parnovski, T. A. Sokova, I. V. Stetsenko, V. V. Titenko, and S. A. Filippov. *International Mathematical Contests.* Moskva: Nauka, 1987.
9. Bruno Legeard and E. Legros. Short overview of the CLPS system. In *Proc. PLILP'91*, Passau, Germany, August 1991.
10. Alan K. Mackworth. Consistency in networks of relations. *Artificial Intelligence*, 8(1):99–118, 1977.
11. Alexander S. Narinyani. Subdefiniteness and basic means of knowledge representation. *Computers and Artificial Intelligence*, 2(5):443–452, 1983.

12. J.T. Schwartz, R.B.K. Dewar, E. Dubinsky, and E. Schonberg. *Programming with Sets. An Introduction to SETL.* Texts and Monographs in Computer Science. Springer-Verlag, 1986.
13. Pascal Van Hentenryck, Laurent Michel, and Yves Deville. *Numerica: a Modelling Language for Global Optimization.* The MIT Press, Cambridge, MA, 1997.
14. Clifford Walinsky. CLP(Σ^*): Constraint logic programming with regular sets. In Giorgio Levi and Maurizio Martelli, editors, *Proc.6th Int.Conf. on Logic Programming*, pages 181–196, Lisbon, Portugal, June 1989. The MIT Press.
15. Tatyana M. Yakhno and Evgueni S. Petrov. LogiCalc: integrating constraint programming and subdefinite models. In *Practical Application of Constraint Technology*, pages 357–372, Westminster Central Hall, London, UK, April 1996.
16. Tatyana M. Yakhno, Vyatcheslav Z. Zilberfaine, and Evgueni S. Petrov. Applications of ECL^{i}PS^e: Interval Domain library. *The ICL Systems Journal*, pages 35–50, November 1997.

Introducing Mutual Exclusion in Esterel*

Klaus Schneider and Viktor Sabelfeld

University of Karlsruhe, Department of Computer Science
Institute for Computer Design and Fault Tolerance (Prof. Dr.-Ing. D. Schmid)
P.O. Box 6980, 76128 Karlsruhe, Germany
{Klaus.Schneider,Viktor.Sabelfeld}@informatik.uni-karlsruhe.de
http://goethe.ira.uka.de/

Abstract. We show how the synchronous programming language Esterel can be extended by a new statement to implement mutual exclusive code sections. We also show how the thereby extended Esterel language can be translated back to standard Esterel and we prove the correctness of this transformation. Additionally, we show that the translation fits well into different verification approaches.

1 Introduction

Synchronous languages like Esterel [1,3] allow to describe multithreaded systems where the threads run in a synchronous manner. The synchronization of threads is for free since it is achieved directly by the semantics of the language: Most of the statements of synchronous languages do not consume time. Instead, consumption of time must be explicitely enforced by special statements, as e.g. the **pause** statement of Esterel. As it is only possible to consume a multiple of a logical unit of time, all threads of a system run synchronously to each other[1].

There exist techniques to translate a multithreaded Esterel program into a single-threaded program [2] such that it can be translated into standard sequential programming languages like C. Therefore, Esterel designs can be conveniently translated to software parts of embedded systems. Moreover, there are techniques to directly map Esterel designs to register-transfer circuits [2]. It has been shown that the results of this hardware synthesis are almost optimal [8,9] such that additional optimizations are usually not necessary. For this reason, Esterel can also be used as a good basis for hardware synthesis.

To summarize, Esterel can be used as basis for hardware-software codesign where Esterel allows to describe the system independent of the later realization in hardware or software. Hence, Esterel is a good language for designing the digital part of embedded systems. However, from the viewpoint of software engineers, the communication mechanisms provided by Esterel are rather poor: the only

* This work has been financed by the DFG priority program 'Design and Design Methodology of Embedded Systems'.

[1] Note however that the real amount between different synchronization points of time may differ, i.e. the synchronization points need not be equidistant.

D. Bjørner, M. Broy, A. Zamulin (Eds.): PSI'99, LNCS 1755, pp. 445–459, 2000.

way for threads to communicate with each other is to broadcast globally visible signals. Instead, software engineers are often used to implement communication via shared memory. Clearly, this presupposes that we have critical sections of code that are executed in a mutually exclusive manner.

It is not surprising that a lot of different communication principles can be implemented with the basic broadcasting principle provided by Esterel. In particular, the communication over shared variables is, of course, possible. The problem is, however, that the mutual access to these variables must be guaranteed by the programmer, since there are no semaphore constructs in Esterel. Nevertheless, these can be implemented in Esterel, but we feel that especially the imitation of mutual exclusion is an error prone task.

The mutual exclusion problem was first formulated by Dijkstra [4]: One considers n ($n \geq 2$) processes that communicate with each other through shared variables. The processes have *critical* and *noncritical* code sections. The solution of the 'mutual exclusion problem' must satisfy the *mutual exclusion property*: avoid simultaneous execution of critical sections in two or more processes. Therefore, at any time one or more processes wish to execute their critical sections, one of them is selected. While all others are suspended, the chosen one executes its critical section. In addition, the following *fairness condition* must be satisfied: each critical section that can be executed will not be ignored infinitely many times. We say a solution of the 'critical section problem' is safe iff it fulfills the mutual exclusion property, and it is called to be fair iff it fulfills the fairness property.

In 1968, Dijkstra described [5] a safe and fair solution for two processes. Lamport [6] presented in 1974 the correct solution for n processes, called the *bakery algorithm*. This algorithm uses unbounded counters, and can therefore not be implemented by a finite state machine. The first finite state solution for n processes was described by Peterson [7] in 1983.

In principle, we could choose Peterson's algorithm for the solution of our problem. We preferred however another solution since this allowed us to separate the mutual exclusion problem from the remaining program statements: To implement the mutual exclusion, we introduce an explicit arbitration process that schedules the different critical sections that could be executed next. It is important that the arbitration is safe, i.e. at each point of time, at most one process is granted access to the critical section, and fair. As it is not straightforward to implement such an arbitration process, we have extended the Esterel language by a new region statement for establishing critical sections.

To implement the arbitration process, we use a modification of the DMA arbitration controller given by Martin [10]. This modification is finite state: For n processes, we obtain $4n+2$ boolean valued signals, where only $2n$ of these signals are state variables. The state number grows proportional to $O(n2^n)$, but what is more important: The representation by OBDDs for symbolic model checking is polynomial [10], so that this implementation lends itself well for verifying such programs by symbolic model checking. We show in this paper how programs with the new region statement can be translated to standard Esterel programs and we prove the correctness of this translation. The translation involves mainly the parallel execution of a fair arbitration process and interfacing the critical sections with a simple protocol. It is our aim to develop a translation that leads to a simple verification afterwards. In terms of model checking, this means that the arbitration process should have a good BDD representation. Hence, we avoid the usage of queues or other higher order data types.

The paper is organized as follows: in the next section, we present the syntax and the intuitive semantics of our new statement for establishing critical sections. We also present the basics of the translation of these programs back to standard Esterel. After that, we prove the correctness of the translation. This is done twofold: on the one hand, we prove the correctness by means of model checking techniques. This shows that our arbitration process has a good BDD representation such that Esterel programs with critical sections can be directly verified by model checking techniques. On the other hand, we prove the correctness by a paper-and-pencil proof that leads to an interactive proof rule that can be used to eliminate region statements for proving a given specification. Finally, we discuss a syntactic strategy for avoiding deadlocks in our extended Esterel programs.

2 Extending Esterel by Mutual Exclusion

To express mutual exclusion, we extend the Esterel language by a *region* statement designed for declaring critical program sections that can only be executed exclusively from each other. The syntax of the region statement is as follows, where *ident* is a name and *statement* is an arbitrary (extended) Esterel statement:

region *ident statement* **end region**

We say that the region statement **region** A S **end region** belongs to the region A and consists of the *body* S. A program can contain many region statements belonging to the same region. The meaning of the statement is as follows: If some region statements **region** A S_i **end region** for $i = 1, \ldots, k$ are to be executed in parallel, only one body S_j of the region statements is chosen for execution while the remaining statements have to wait. The body S_j of this selected region statement is then executed, while all other region statements are suspended until the execution of S_j terminates. After termination of S_j a new choice among the remaining region statements is made and so on.[2] Hence, at each point of time, at most one body $S_j, 1 \leq j \leq n$ of a region statement belonging to the region A can be active (mutual exclusion). Note that execution of the body S_j of the selected region statement starts at the same point of time where the region statement is executed, i.e., entering the region statement and the arbitration do not consume time.

[2] To avoid obvious deadlocks, we forbid nested region statements that belong to the same region.

It is important that the access to the region A is fair, i.e. if a region statement **region** A S_j **end region** is started, then we guarantee that its body S_j will be executed after some time. In other words, we avoid that one of the region statements must wait forever and is never allowed to execute its body. Clearly, to assure this, we must assume that all bodies S_j of the region statements terminate in each case. For example, suppose we have k stores $store_i$, for $i = 1, \ldots, k$, three modules $Produce_i$, $Consume_i$, and $Duplicate_i$ for all $i = 1, \ldots, k$, and wish to implement the mutual excluded access to the stores $store_i, i = 1, \ldots, k$. To this end, we can use now the following region statements with identifiers $A_1, \ldots, A_k$ and run them in parallel:

- **region** A_i $Produce_i$ **end region**
- **region** A_i $Consume_i$ **end region**
- **region** A_i $Duplicate_i$ **end region**

Although Esterel does not directly provide statements for mutual exclusive execution of threads, the Esterel statements are powerful enough to implement such a behavior. To see this, we show now how our region statements can be translated to standard Esterel: Let R_i=**region** A S_i **end region** for $i = 1, \ldots, n$ are all the region statements belonging to the region A in an extended Esterel program $\mathcal{S}(R_1, \ldots, R_n)$. Then, we replace $\mathcal{S}(R_1, \ldots, R_n)$ by the following statement:

$$\left[\begin{array}{l}\textbf{trap}\ trm\ \textbf{in}\\ \quad\textbf{signal}\ \varrho_1,\ldots,\varrho_n,f_A,\alpha_1,\ldots,\alpha_n\ \textbf{in}\\ \quad\quad\mathcal{S}(P_1,\ldots,P_n);\textbf{exit}\ trm\\ \quad\|\\ \quad\quad arbitrate_A(\varrho_1,\ldots,\varrho_n,f_A,\alpha_1,\ldots,\alpha_n)\\ \quad\textbf{end signal}\\ \textbf{end trap}\end{array}\right] \text{ where } P_i = \left[\begin{array}{l}\textbf{weak abort}\\ \quad\textbf{sustain}\ \varrho_i\\ \textbf{when immediate}\ \alpha_i;\\ S_i;\\ \textbf{emit}\ f_A\end{array}\right]$$

The statement **exit** trm is used to leave the entire statement in case $\mathcal{S}$ terminates. The statement P_i behaves as follows: Firstly, the wish of '**region** A S_i **end region**' to access the critical region A is signaled by emitting the request signal ϱ_i. The additional Esterel thread $arbitrate_A(\varrho_1, \ldots, \varrho_n, f_A, \alpha_1, \ldots, \alpha_n)$ collects all these requests and decides which one of the region statements is allowed to enter the critical section. This decision is broadcasted via the signal α_i which allows the statement R_i to enter the critical section. After that, S_i is executed and no further grants are given by the arbitration thread before S_i terminates. The termination of S_i is signaled in P_i by emitting the release signal f_A of region A which indicates that R_i currently leaves the region A. This instructs the arbitration thread to make new choices and emit new access signals α_j.

The arbitration thread can immediately select one of the regions and hence, the emission of ϱ_i can be immediately aborted in P_i. The abortion is however weak which means that even if P_i is immediately selected, there will be an emission of ϱ_i for at least one point of time. Note further that the request signal ϱ_i is emitted as long as P_i is not allowed to enter its critical section S_i.

The above replacement of the region statements by standard Esterel statements is straightforward and the code size remains more or less the same. However, the correctness of the replacement is based on a correct Esterel implementation of the arbitration process. Hence, the correctness of the translation depends clearly on a sound implementation of the arbitration process that is given in the next section.

3 Esterel Implementation of the Arbitration Process

In this section, we present a possible implementation of the arbitration process that can be used for a translation of our extended Esterel language back to standard Esterel. The basic idea of this arbitration process goes back to a DMA controller given by Martin [10]. However, the circuit given by Martin makes arbitration decisions at any point of time since it assumes that a single unit of time is sufficient for accessing the shared resource. However, this does not hold in our case and therefore, we need to adapt the arbitration.

Now, what does the arbitration process have to do? It has to choose one of all requesting threads, i.e. one of the indices i where the corresponding request signal ϱ_i is present at the current instant. The decision is then signaled via emitting a grant signal α_i. After getting access, the region statement i executes its critical section, and hence the arbitration thread must await the termination of S_i (signaled by f_A). The next arbitration decision can be made when the release signal f_A is emitted by P_i.

The Esterel implementation of the arbitration process for a region A with n region statements is given in Figure 1. There are n inputs $\varrho_1, \ldots, \varrho_n$ that are emitted by the region statements for requesting access to the shared resource. The arbitration process emits one of the n outputs $\alpha_1, \ldots, \alpha_n$ for allowing access to one of the processes.

We will now explain how the arbitration process works without going into details of the Esterel language. For this reason, we translate the Esterel program to a finite state machine by means of the Esterel semantics [2]. It is however reasonable to present an intermediate result of the translation and not the final one. In particular, we consider a combination of parallel running interacting finite state machines for the subsequent Esterel threads of the arbitration process given in Figure 1. These finite state machines are given in Figure 2. Moreover, we define for $i \in \{1, \ldots, n\}$ the output signals α_i as $\alpha_i := \mathit{arb} \wedge \varrho_i \wedge (t_i \wedge p_i \vee \mathit{static} \wedge \bigwedge_{j=1}^{i-1} \neg\varrho_j)$, where $\mathit{static} := \bigwedge_{j=1}^{n}(t_j \rightarrow \neg p_j)$.

It is to be noted that this translation is based on the formal semantics of Esterel and is therefore sound wrt. the semantics of Esterel. To see the principle of the translation, we list the translation of a subsequent thread that sets the persistence flag p_k.

```
module arbitrate_A(ϱ_1,...,ϱ_n, f_A, α_1,...,α_n):
  signal t_1,...,t_n, p_1,...,p_n, arb in
    [ loop
        abort sustain t_1 when arb;
        ⋮
        abort sustain t_n when arb
      end loop ]                                  //rotating tokens for daisy chain
  ||
    [ loop
        await ϱ_1 ∧ t_1;                          //setting persistence
        weak abort sustain p_1 when ¬ϱ_1          //for process 1
      end loop ]
  ||
    ⋮
  ||
    [ loop
        await ϱ_n ∧ t_n;                          //setting persistence
        weak abort sustain p_n when ¬ϱ_n          //for process n
      end loop ]
  ||
    [ loop
       await immediate ⋁_{i=1}^{n} ϱ_i;
       emit arb;
         present ⋁_{i=1}^{n}(t_i ∧ p_i)
         then present
                case ϱ_1 ∧ t_1 ∧ p_1 do emit α_1;
                ⋮
                case ϱ_n ∧ t_n ∧ p_n do emit α_n;   //give acknowledge
             end present                           //when arbitration is
         else present                              //required
                case ϱ_1 do emit α_1;
                ⋮
                case ϱ_n do emit α_n;
             end present
         end present;
       await f_A
      end loop ]
  end signal
end module
```

Fig. 1. Implementation of the arbitration process in Esterel

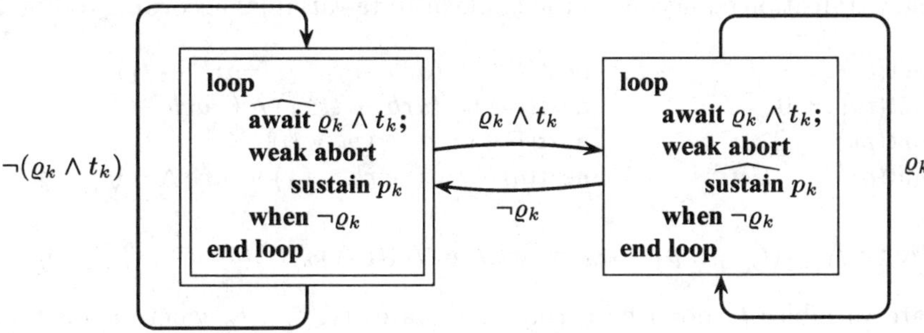

In the thread for setting the persistence flag p_k, there are two program locations where the control flow rests for the next point of time. These locations are indicated by a hat in the above finite state machine. It is easy to see that the above finite state machine matches with the corresponding one given in Fig. 2. The others are obtained similarly.

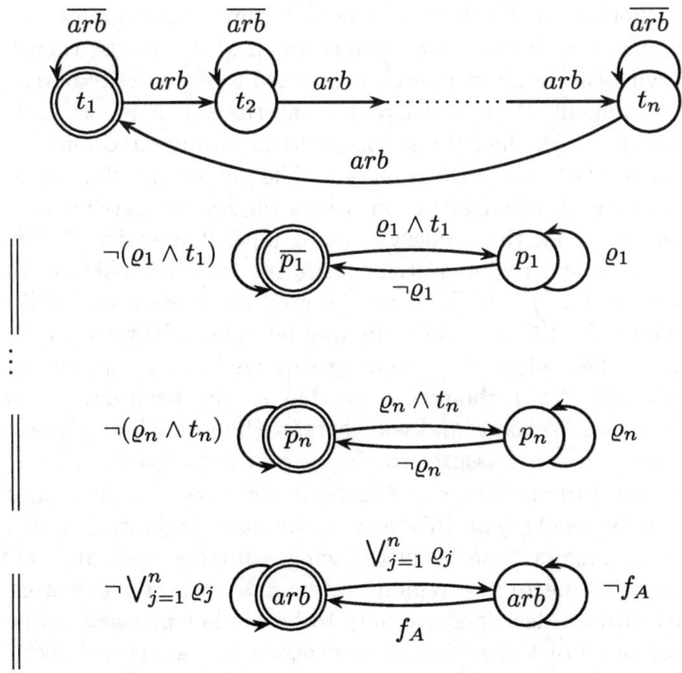

Fig. 2. Transition diagram for the finite state machine of the arbitration process

To formally reason about the function of the entire arbitration thread, we derive now transition equations of the boolean state variables according to Fig. 2:

$$\begin{array}{ll} \mathsf{init}(t_1) := 1 & \mathsf{next}(t_1) := (arb \rightarrow t_n) \wedge (\neg arb \rightarrow t_1) \\ \mathsf{init}(t_k) := 0 & \mathsf{next}(t_k) := (arb \rightarrow t_{k-1}) \wedge (\neg arb \rightarrow t_k) \\ \mathsf{init}(p_k) := 0 & \mathsf{next}(p_k) := \varrho_k \wedge (p_k \vee t_k) \\ \mathsf{init}(arb) := 1 & \mathsf{next}(arb) := (\neg arb \wedge f_A) \vee (arb \wedge \neg \bigvee_{j=1}^{n} \varrho_j) \end{array}$$

$$static := \bigwedge_{j=1}^{n}(t_j \rightarrow \neg p_j) \quad \alpha_k := arb \wedge \varrho_k \wedge (t_k \wedge p_k \vee static \wedge \bigwedge_{j=1}^{k-1} \neg \varrho_j)$$

The state variables t_k describe a ring of n states $t_1, \ldots, t_n$ where transitions are made from t_k to $t_{(k \bmod n)+1}$ whenever an arbitration decision can be made. This models a round robin schema, i.e. there is a rotating token associated with the region statements: we say a region statement R_k 'has the token' whenever we are in state t_k. *Note that at each point of time, exactly one of the boolean state variables* $t_1, \ldots, t_n$ *is present.*

There are two reasons why a statement R_k may be granted access to their critical section: If α_k holds, then we have $arb \wedge \varrho_k \wedge t_k \wedge p_k$ or $arb \wedge \varrho_k \wedge static \wedge \bigwedge_{j=1}^{k-1} \neg \varrho_j$. Both cases exclude each other: First assume $arb \wedge \varrho_k \wedge t_k \wedge p_k$ holds. This means that in particular, $t_k \wedge p_k$ holds, and hence *static* can not hold, so that the second case can not hold either. On the other hand, assume $arb \wedge \varrho_k \wedge static \wedge \bigwedge_{j=1}^{k-1} \neg \varrho_j$ holds. Then, *static* holds, that implies $t_k \rightarrow \neg p_k$. Thus $t_k \wedge p_k$ can not hold which would be necessary to satisfy the first case.

Therefore, there are two different reasons for an arbitration decision: firstly, the access may be granted by *static priorities*. If *static* holds, then the region statement R_i with the smallest index i is granted to execute its body. Secondly, if the region statement R_k that currently has the token ($t_k = 1$) has set its persistence flag ($p_k = 1$), then the static priorities are ignored and R_k is immediately granted access to the critical section. The persistence flags p_k are used to establish the fairness of the arbitration: whenever R_k requests for accessing the critical section ($\varrho_k = 1$), the request remains until it is satisfied. Hence, there will be some time where region statement R_k receives the token and this event sets the persistence flag p_k. If R_k is not granted to access its critical section at this point of time, the token will rotate another round. However, if the request has not been satisfied when the token returns again (this implies $static = 0$, since we then have $t_k \wedge p_k$), then we know that R_k has been ignored at least for the last n arbitration decisions and will therefore be immediately granted access to the critical section. This assures the fairness of the arbiter.

While a region statement executes its body statement, no further arbitration decisions are to be made. For this reason, we stop the rotation of the token during this time. This is done by introducing a further boolean state variable *arb* that is false iff one of the region statements currently executes its body statement. Arbitration decisions are only to be made when *arb* holds. Initially, *arb* holds since none of the region statements is in the critical section. Then, we are waiting until one of the processes requests for the access. If this is the case, one of these region statements is immediately allowed to execute its body (cf. specification 'Immediate Grant' below). Therefore, arb is unset and remains false until the termination signal f_A is emitted by the region statement that has been granted access to the critical section.

4 Verifying the Arbitration Process

Note that the implementation given in Figure 1 is only a particular choice of an arbitration process that can be replaced by any other that satisfies the following requirements that we present in temporal logic [11]:

Exclusive: At each point of time, at most one R_k may enter the critical section:

$$\bigwedge_{k=1}^{n} \mathsf{G}\left(\alpha_k \rightarrow \bigwedge_{j=1,j\neq k}^{n} \neg\alpha_j\right)$$

Only Requested: Only statements are granted to enter the critical section that request for an access:

$$\bigwedge_{k=1}^{n} \mathsf{G}\,(\alpha_k \rightarrow arb \wedge \varrho_k)$$

Immediate Grant: Whenever arbitration decisions can be made, i.e. no process is currently in its critical section, and there are requests, then there will immediately be a grant:

$$\underbrace{\mathsf{G}\left[\bigwedge_{j=1}^{n} \varrho_j \rightarrow [\varrho_j\ \mathsf{U}\ \alpha_j]\right]}_{\text{persistent requests}} \rightarrow \underbrace{\mathsf{G}\left[arb \wedge \left(\bigvee_{k=1}^{n} \varrho_k\right) \rightarrow \left(\bigvee_{k=1}^{n} \alpha_k\right)\right]}_{\text{immediate decision}}$$

Fairness: The arbitration is fair, if we assume that all bodies S_i terminate and if all entering requests persist either until they are granted (or forever):

$$\underbrace{\mathsf{G}\left[\left(\bigvee_{j=1}^{n} \alpha_j\right) \rightarrow \mathsf{XF}f_A\right]}_{\text{termination}} \wedge \underbrace{\mathsf{G}\left[\bigwedge_{j=1}^{n} \varrho_j \rightarrow [\varrho_j\ \mathsf{U}\ \alpha_j]\right]}_{\text{persistent requests}} \rightarrow \underbrace{\bigwedge_{j=1}^{n} \neg\mathsf{FG}\,[\varrho_j \wedge \neg\alpha_j]}_{\text{fairness}}$$

The latter condition is very subtle and is therefore explained in more detail. The first assumption is that each body S_i of each region statement $R_i =$ **region** $A\ S_i$ **end region** terminates in any case. Clearly, if this would not hold, we would not be able to guarantee the fairness. The second assumption is that once a region statement requests for accessing the critical section, it insists on requesting until it receives a grant to enter the critical section.[3] Note that the assumption uses

[3] It is easy to see that the P_i's of Section 2 implement this.

a *weak until* operator which means that the assumption does also hold if the region statement is never granted access to their critical section (i.e. α_i remains false from a certain point of time). The fairness condition proves however that this can never happen.

To verify the above specification for an arbitration process for n region statements, we used the linear time temporal model checker implemented at our institute [12,13]. The *Exclusive* and *Only Requested* conditions of our specification above have been checked within a second even for large n, so that we do not list detailed runtimes for them. The experimental results that we obtained for the *Immediate Grant* and *Fairness* conditions are given in Figure 3 (SUN Sparc 10, 300 MHz, Solaris 5.7, 640 MByte main memory).

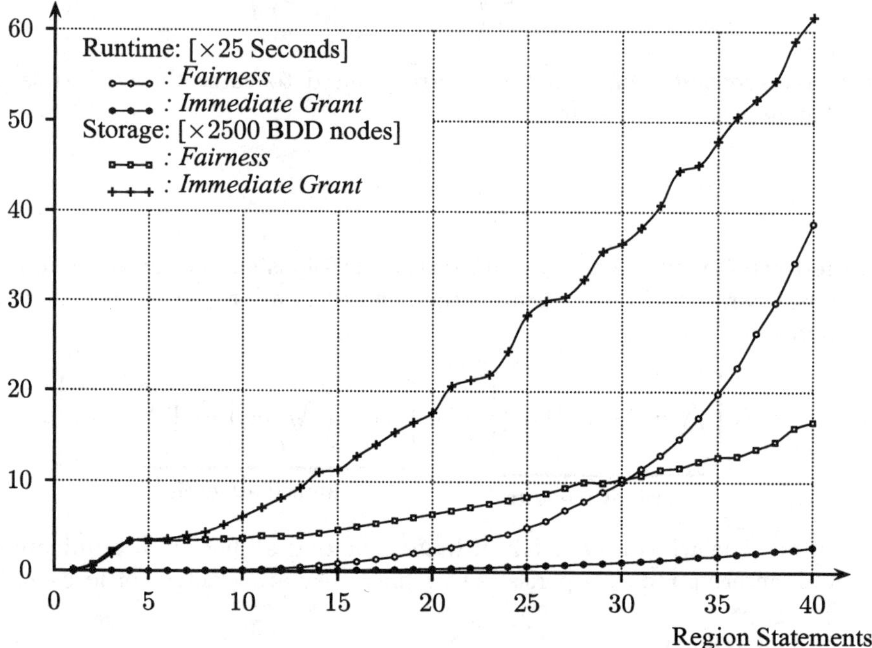

Fig. 3. Runtimes for the verification of the arbitration process

The automatic verification is in this case completely sufficient: we are able to verify the fairness of more than 40 region statements in less than one third of an hour. Therefore, we see that the implementation of our arbitration process lends itself well for model checking techniques. We therefore believe that also Esterel programs with mutual exclusive sections can be verified efficiently with model checking techniques.

5 Interactive Proofs

The correctness can also be proven by means of a theorem prover such as the HOL system [14]. Again, the most complicated condition to prove is the fairness condition. The proof of the fairness runs in the following lines: First of all, it follows from the termination of the body statements that for any k, the region statement R_k will receive the token infinitely often, i.e. we have (1) $\mathsf{GF}t_k$ for any k. Now, assume there exists some k such that (2) $\mathsf{FG}(\varrho_k \wedge \neg\alpha_k)$ holds, i.e., after some point of time t_0, it holds forever that the region statement R_k requests for their critical section, but is never allowed to enter it. As R_k will receive the token infinitely often (as any region statement does according to (1)), it will also receive the token after t_0. Let t_0+t_1 be the first point of time after t_0 when R_k receives the token. Then, it follows that the persistence flag p_k of this region statement R_k is set at t_0+t_1. As ϱ_k holds always after t_0 by (2), p_k remains true after t_0+t_1 by definition of p_k. However, by (1), R_k will receive the token also infinitely often after t_0+t_1, so let $t_0+t_1+t_2$ be the first time after t_0+t_1 when R_k receives the token again. By definition of the grant signals, this will immediately grant R_k access to their section (as now $arb \wedge \varrho_k \wedge t_k \wedge p_k$ holds). Therefore, we obtain a contradiction, so that (2) must be false and the arbitration is fair for any number of threads. The other properties are easily proved by a simple consideration of the implementation of the thread $arbitrate_A$: The **present** statements allow only one grant at a time.

As a result, we can now establish a proof rule for the verification of Esterel programs with region statements. This rule can be used interactively to transform verification goals with Esterel statements with region statements into other goals that do no longer contain these region statements. The rule is obtained by the correctness of the arbiter in that we use the following proof rule:

$$\frac{\mathcal{S} \parallel \mathcal{A} \models \Phi \qquad \mathcal{A} \models \Psi}{\mathcal{S} \models \Psi \rightarrow \Phi}$$

The above rule eliminates a thread $\mathcal{A}$ in that it is replaced by a property Ψ that is already known to hold for $\mathcal{A}$. We use this rule to eliminate the arbitration thread $arbitrate_A$ after replacing the region statement as outlined in Section 2.

As a result, we obtain the following proof rule, where $\varrho_1, \ldots, \varrho_n, f_A, \alpha_1, \ldots, \alpha_n$ are disjoint signals that do neither occur in $\mathcal{S}(R_1, \ldots, R_n)$ nor in Φ:

$$\frac{\mathcal{S}(R_1, \ldots, R_n) \models \Phi}{\mathcal{S}(P_1, \ldots, P_n) \models \left(\begin{array}{l} \bigwedge_{k=1}^{n} \mathsf{G}\left(\alpha_k \rightarrow \bigwedge_{j=1, j\neq k}^{n} \neg\alpha_j\right) \wedge \\ \bigwedge_{k=1}^{n} \mathsf{G}\left(\alpha_k \rightarrow \varrho_k\right) \wedge \\ \mathsf{G}\left[\left(\bigvee_{k=1}^{n} \alpha_k\right) \rightarrow \mathsf{X}\left[\left(\bigwedge_{j=1}^{n} \neg\alpha_j\right) \mathsf{U}\, f_A\right]\right] \wedge \\ \left(\mathsf{G}\left[\left(\bigvee_{j=1}^{n} \alpha_j\right) \rightarrow \mathsf{XF} f_A\right]\right) \rightarrow \bigwedge_{j=1}^{n} \neg\mathsf{FG}\left[\varrho_j \wedge \neg\alpha_j\right] \\ \rightarrow \Phi \end{array}\right)}$$

The rule is to be read as follows: Given that our task is to prove that an Esterel program $\mathcal{S}(R_1,\ldots,R_n)$ that contains the region statements $R_1,\ldots,R_n$ belonging to the same region A satisfies the property Φ which may be given in a first-order temporal logic formula as described in [15]. Then, it is sufficient to prove that the Esterel program $\mathcal{S}(P_1,\ldots,P_n)$ satisfies the property Φ, where we can use as additional assumptions the above listed properties. The rule simplifies the proof task since it encodes the semantics of the **region** statements by replacing them with corresponding specifications. Note further that in the reduced goal, no arbitration process occurs, since we already know that it is correct. In fact, the arbitration process has been replaced with the new assumptions that can therefore be viewed as an declarative form of our arbiter.

6 Avoiding Deadlocks

We have already proved that the translation of our region constructs to standard Esterel is safe, i.e., at any point of time any critical section is executed by at most one thread, and fair, i.e., no thread must wait infinitely long for accessing the critical section (provided that any thread leaves the critical section after a finite amount of time).

Of course, this does not mean that there are no deadlocks. Clearly, when we only have one region, i.e., if all region statements refer to the same region name, then we can state that the program is free of deadlocks. In this case, according to the syntactic restriction there are no nested region statements, and the deadlock-freedom property follows from the fairness of the arbitration process. In the case, we have more than one region name, it is however obvious, that deadlocks may occur, as given by the following simple program P_{dead}:

```
region A                 ||   region B
   pause;                ||      pause;
   region B              ||      region A
      ⋮                  ||         ⋮
   end region            ||      end region
end region               ||   end region
```

In a first step, the left hand thread requests for an access to the region A, while the right hand thread request for an access to the region B. If there are no other requests, the arbitration thread for region A will grant the left hand thread above the access region A, and analogously, will the right hand thread receive a grant to access region B. At the next point of time, however, the left hand thread above requests for region B, while the right hand thread requests for region A. Both requests can not be granted since both arbitration threads are now not in the arbitration mode since both critical sections for regions A and B are already accessed.

There are well-known strategies for avoiding deadlocks [16] and we can also use such strategies in our case. In the remainder of this section, we briefly describe further syntactic restrictions that assure the absence of deadlocks. We emphasize that these restrictions can be easily checked at compile time. However, there are programs that do not fulfill these restrictions, but are nevertheless free of deadlocks. However, as deadlock-freedom is in general undecidable, decidable criteria like our ones are necessary.

Our restrictions are based on the dependency relation $\preceq_P$ on regions in a given program P that is defined as follows: we say that a region A *depends* on a region B, denoted as $A \preceq_P B$, if P contains a region statement **region** B S **end region**, such that S contains a region statement **region** $A \ldots$ **end region**. Hence, some region A statement is nested in a region B statement. We denote the reflexive-transitive hull of $\preceq_P$ by $\preceq_P^*$.

As the example P_{dead} above shows, we can not guarantee the deadlock-freedom property if the region dependence relation $\preceq_P$ is cyclic. We therefore impose now the syntactic restriction that $\preceq_P$ must be acyclic. It is easily seen that this is equivalent to the property that $\preceq_P^*$ is antisymmetric which means that $\preceq_P^*$ is a partial order. Hence, we can extend the partial order $\preceq_P^*$ to a linear order $\leq_P$ of all regions occurring in P:

$$A_0 \leq_P \ldots \leq_P A_m$$

Note that $A_i \leq_P A_j$ with $i \neq j$ implies either $A_i \preceq_P^* A_j$ or that there is no dependency ($\preceq_P^*$) between A_i and A_j. In any case, it follows that $A_i \leq_P A_j$ with $i \neq j$ implies $A_j \not\preceq_P^* A_i$. We eliminate all region statements **region** $A_i \ldots$ **end region** successively for $i = m, \ldots, 0$ applying the described transformation to standard Esterel using the new thread $arbitrate_{A_i}$.

The restriction that $\preceq_P$ must be acyclic implies deadlock freedom. To see this note that the acyclicity of $\preceq_P$ means that if some region A statement is somewhere nested in the body of a region B statement, then there must be no region A statement in the program P whose body contains some region B statement. Hence, at any time of the execution, if a thread S_i has already accessed regions $M_i = \{A_{k_{i,1}}, \ldots, A_{k_{i,n_i}}\}$ and requests for another region A_k, then it follows that $k < \min\{k_{i,1}, \ldots, k_{i,n_i}\}$. This is a simple consequence of the construction of $\leq_P$: the regions that are requested from one thread are requested in descending order $\leq_P$.

Suppose now the execution of the modified program would come to a deadlock. Then there are threads S_0, ..., $S_{\ell-1}$ so that S_i requests for some region A_{k_i} and has already accessed regions $M_i = \{A_{k_{i,1}}, \ldots, A_{k_{i,n_i}}\}$. Define $m_i := \min\{k_{i,1}, \ldots, k_{i,n_i}\}$. By the above explanation, it follows that $k_i < m_i$ holds. Suppose now without loss of generality that A_{k_i} belongs to $M_{(i+1) \bmod \ell}$. Now, it follows that $m_{(i+1) \bmod \ell} \leq k_i$, and therefore $m_{(i+1) \bmod \ell} < m_i$. But then, we have $m_0 < m_1 < \ldots m_{\ell-1} < m_0$, a contradiction. For this reason, a deadlock can not occur.

Surely, there exist deadlock-free programs with a cyclic region dependence relation $\preceq_P$: For example, take the program P_{nodead} that results from the program P_{dead} by replacing the parallel statement '$\|$' by the sequential statement ';'. The region dependence relation $\preceq_P$ of that program is cyclic, since $A \preceq_P B$ and $B \preceq_P A$ holds, but the program is deadlock free.

This could be handled by introducing the 'dynamic region dependence relation' $\preceq_P^d$, which relates accessed regions and currently requested regions (in the above example, where we considered the threads S_0, ..., $S_{\ell-1}$, we would only have $A_{k_i} \preceq_P^d A_{k_{i,j}}$). Of course, $\preceq_P^d$ changes during the execution of the program. A deadlock occurs iff $\preceq_P^d$ becomes cyclic. Hence, the region management aims at keeping $\preceq_P^d$ acyclic. Consider again the program P_{nodead}, it is easily seen that all dynamic region dependence relations arising in the execution of P_{nodead} are acyclic.

However, it can not be recognized whether all dynamic region dependence relations arising in the execution of an arbitrary program are acyclic: this problem is undecidable since the undecidable reachability problem can be reduced to this problem. That is why our restriction on 'static region dependence relations' can be considered as a reasonable restriction guaranteeing deadlock freedom of extended Esterel programs.

Our syntactic, static check for deadlock-freedom is motivated by hierarchic resource managements in operating systems [16]: Usually, interrupts coming from the main memory are served before interrupts coming from hard disk, so that an acyclic relation between the resources is established. This is quite similar to our approach, but at another abstraction level.

7 Conclusions

We have shown how the synchronous language Esterel can be extended by a new statement so that mutually exclusive sections are provided by the syntax. We have moreover shown how the thereby extended Esterel language can be translated back to standard Esterel by surrounding the critical code sections by a simple protocol, and adding a separate arbitration thread for each region. Also, we have proved the correctness of this arbitration thread by means of model checking the temporal logic specifications for some numbers of threads, and also by a paper-and-pencil proof for arbitrary numbers of threads. In particular, we have proved that the solution is safe, i.e., at any point of time any critical section is executed by at most one thread, and fair, i.e., no thread must wait infinitely long for accessing the critical section (provided that any thread releases the critical section after a finite amount of time). Moreover, we have given syntactic restrictions that guarantee freedom of deadlocks.

Acknowledgement. We thank our collegue M. Baldamus for carefully reading the paper and giving useful comments.

References

1. G. Berry and G. Gonthier. The Esterel synchronous programming language: Design, semantics, implementation. *Science of Computer Programming*, 19(2):87–152, 1992.
2. G. Berry. The constructive semantics of pure Esterel, May 1996.
3. G. Berry. The foundations of Esterel. In G. Plotkin, C. Stirling, and M. Tofte, editors, *Proof, Language and Interaction: Essays in Honour of Robin Milner*. MIT Press, 1998.

4. E. W. Dijkstra. Solution of a problem in concurrent programming control. *Comm. ACM*, 8(9):569, 1965.
5. E. W. Dijkstra. Cooperating sequential processes. In F. Genuys, editor, *Programming Languages*, Academic Press, New York, p.43-112, 1968.
6. L. Lamport. A new solution of Dijkstra's concurrent programming problem. *Comm. ACM*, 17(8):453-455, 1974.
7. G. L. Peterson. A new solution to Lamport's concurrent programming problem. *ACM Transactions on Progr. Lang. and Systems*, 5(1):56-65, 1983.
8. H. Touati and G. Berry. Optimized controller synthesis using Esterel. In *International Workshop on Logic Synthesis*, Lake Tahoe, 1993. IEEE Computer Society Press.
9. H. Toma, E. Sentovitch, and G. Berry. Latch optimization in circuits generated from high-level descriptions. In *IEEE/ACM International Conference on Computer Aided Design (ICCAD)*. ACM/IEEE, IEEE Computer Society Press, 1996.
10. K.L. McMillan. *Symbolic Model Checking.* Kluwer Academic Publishers, Norwell Massachusetts, 1993.
11. E.A. Emerson. Temporal and Modal Logic. In J. van Leeuwen, editor, *Handbook of Theoretical Computer Science*, volume B, pages 996–1072, Amsterdam, 1990. Elsevier Science Publishers.
12. K. Schneider. CTL and equivalent sublanguages of CTL*. In C. Delgado Kloos, editor, *IFIP Conference on Computer Hardware Description Languages and their Applications (CHDL)*, pages 40–59, Toledo,Spain, April 1997. IFIP, Chapman and Hall.
13. K. Schneider. Model checking on product structures. In G.C. Gopalakrishnan and P.J. Windley, editors, *Formal Methods in Computer-Aided Design*, vol.1522 of *Lecture Notes in Computer Scienc*, pages 483–500, Palo Alto, CA, November 1998. Springer Verlag.
14. M.J.C. Gordon and T.F. Melham. *Introduction to HOL: A Theorem Proving Environment for Higher Order Logic.* Cambridge University Press, 1993.
15. K. Schneider and T. Kropf. The C@S system: Combining proof strategies for system verification. In T. Kropf, editor, *Formal Hardware Verification – Methods and Systems in Comparison*, volume 1287 of *Lecture Notes in Computer Science*, pages 248–329. Springer Verlag, state of the art report edition, August 1997.
16. K.M. Chandry and J. Misra. *Parallel Program Design: A Foundation.* Addison-Wesley, 1988.

Experiences with the Application of Symbolic Model Checking to the Analysis of Software Specifications

Richard J. Anderson, Paul Beame, William Chan, and David Notkin

Department of Computer Science and Engineering,
University of Washington
Box 352350, Seattle, Washington 98195-2350, USA, +1-206-543-1695
{anderson, beame, wchan, notkin}@cs.washington.edu

Abstract. Symbolic model checking is a powerful formal-verification technique which has been used to analyze many hardware systems. In this paper we present our experiences in applying symbolic model checking to software specifications of reactive systems. We have conducted two in depth case studies: one, using the specification of TCAS II (Traffic Alert and Collision Avoidance System II), and the other using a model of an aircraft electrical system. Based on these case studies, we have gained significant experience in how model checking can be used in to analyze software specifications, and have also overcome a number of performance bottlenecks to make the analysis tractable.
The emphasis of this paper is the uses of model checking in the analysis of specifications. We will discuss the types of properties which we were able to evaluate in our case studies. These include specific errors we were able to identify, as well as general properties we were able to establish for the systems. We will also discuss, in more general terms, the potential uses of symbolic model checking in the development process of software specifications.

Keywords. Formal methods, formal verification, symbolic model checking, binary decision diagrams, software specification, finite state representations.

1 Specification of Reactive Systems

Reactive systems are central to modern technology. Examples of their deployment range from air traffic control systems to advanced medical devices. Since they are often deployed in safety critical applications where their malfunctioning could cause significant injury or loss of life, their correct implementation is of great importance.

In studying the problem of how to better design these systems, we concentrate on the specification level. Correct specification is particularly important, since it is widely recognized that errors introduced early in system design are the most difficult and expensive to fix. We restrict attention to specifications which

D. Bjørner, M. Broy, A. Zamulin (Eds.): PSI'99, LNCS 1755, pp. 460–469, 2000.

are represented as finite state machines, using languages such as statecharts or RSML.

The broad goal of the work is to develop techniques that allow us to increase our confidence in specification. This includes being able to show that specifications obey general design rules, as well as satisfy particular domain dependent properties. We are interested in incorporating these techniques into the development process of the specification — using them to debug the specification as it is being created, as opposed to just using them in a validation phase to verify the specification when it is complete.

2 Model Checking Technology

Model checking is a formal verification technique based on state space exploration. Given a state transition system and a property, model checking algorithms exhaustively explore the state space to determine whether the system satisfies the property. Properties are often expressed in a temporal logic such as CTL (Computation Tree Logic) [9]. An important aspect of model checking is that when a formula is discovered to be false, a counter example is provided. This helps with the understanding of the source of the error, which could be in the model, the translation, or even in the formula being evaluated.

A natural concern about model checking, is that since the entire state space must be explored, the run time of algorithms is at least proportional to the size of the state space, which is potentially enormous. The breakthrough, which has allowed model checking to be applied to systems with much larger state spaces, was to use an implicit representation of that that space, and to use symbolic techniques for exploration [4,16]. Instead of visiting states one at a time, symbolic model checkers visit sets of states in each step. The underlying representation which is generally used is the Binary Decision Diagram (BDD) [2]. In many practical cases, the size of the BDDs needed to represent the sets of states used in the model checking algorithm is small. The size of the BDDs used generally determine the performance of the algorithms. Much of the technical model checking literature deals with the issue of managing BDD size.

Model checking was first used in the analysis of hardware designs, and is now recognized as an important formal tool to use when building hardware systems. When we started our work on applying model checking to software, it was an open question whether or not model checking would yield interesting results on software. There was a belief by some researchers that software specifications lacked the requisite structure to allow model checking to succeed. However, there have been a series of case studies by ourselves [5,6] and other researchers [1,10,14,19] reporting positive results for applying model checking to software. The impetus for the work was to determine *if* model checking could be used to analyze software specifications, but now the issue has shifted to determining *how* to get the most leverage in using model checking the design process.

3 Application of Model Checking to Software

The question of the feasibility of model checking can be phrased in a number of ways. We distinguish between these to emphasize that the issue is not "does it work or not", but "how can the technology be most effective."

Modeling the system. The first step in model checking is to translate from the specification language (in our case RSML [15] or Statecharts [11]) to the representation of the model checker (we used SMV [16]). When this is done, the basic model can be constructed, and a reachable state space is computed. It is possible that the initial step could fail because of BDD size explosion, so a negative result could be reached prior to evaluating any formula. In our case studies, we had to do a substantial amount of work to reach the point where the initial construction of the model was feasible.

Evaluation of Properties. The second step in establishing feasibility of model checking is to show that there are non-trivial properties which can be evaluated. The standard test (to claim a positive result for model checking), is to find previously undiscovered bugs in the specification under analysis. Note that this changes the emphasis to falsification – the desire is to show the specification does not work. The absence of falsifying examples is not verification. We believe that this will be one of the major uses of model checking: as a debugging tool for identifying errors. This will be an important tool to improving overall quality by augmenting the ways that errors can be found. We discuss below various types of properties which can be evaluated.

Range of Properties. The next question is what range of properties can be evaluated. There are limitations on BBD based symbolic model checking which have ramifications on the types of properties which can be checked. For example, BDDs do a poor job of representing multiplication, which limits our ability to check properties which involve complicated arithmetic.

Performance. The performance question is often the issue between a check being feasible and infeasible. For example, our first successful check (of a trivial property) took 13 hours. This was later reduced to just minutes by modifying the algorithm. In many situations, the tolerable wait for a result is probably measured in minutes (because of interactive use, or because of a group of checks being performed at once. The performance of the algorithm is directly correlated with the size of the intermediate structures which are generated.

Ease of use. The long range goal is to develop model checking technology so that it can be used by engineers who are not experts in model checking. Our work has not reached the stage where this can be assessed. Our success in the case studies required modifying the underlying model checking algorithms.

Development process. Our view is that the critical question is how to use model checking while developing specifications. One can imagine a development methodology where a set of invariants are maintained as components of a system are designed. Components can initially be modeled at a high level of abstraction — either by specifying their desired behavior, or by using non-deterministic devices.

4 Case Studies

We have conducted two major case studies where we applied symbolic model checking to software specifications. The first study was our TCAS study [5], and the second involved a model of an aircraft electrical system [6]. The second study was done in collaboration with engineers from the Boeing Corporation. These studies both involved large, real world specifications, written by other people. Size was an important issue, since we wanted to validate the technique on specifications of commercial scale, as opposed to just on toy problems.

4.1 TCAS

TCAS II is an airborne collision avoidance system required by the United States Federal Aviation Administration (FAA) on most commercial aircraft that enter U.S. airspace. The TCAS-equipped aircraft is surrounded by a protected volume of airspace. When another aircraft intrudes into this volume, TCAS II generates warnings (traffic advisories) and suggests possible escape maneuvers (resolution advisories, or RAs) in the vertical direction to the pilot.

The system requirements specification of TCAS II, a 400-page document, was written in RSML. The first obstacle to analysis was its sheer size. As a first attempt we decided to try to verify a portion of it, namely a state machine called Own-Aircraft , which occupies about 30% of the specification. Own-Aircraft has close interactions with another state machine called Other-Aircraft , which tracks the state of other aircraft in the vicinity and possibly generates RAs. Up to thirty other aircraft can be tracked. From the RAs given by all the instances of Other-Aircraft , Own-Aircraft derives a composite RA and generates visual and audio outputs to the pilot.

We were able to evaluate various properties of the specification, including some which revealed errors in the specification[1]. One example was testing the following:

```
AG ((Composite-RA = Climb
     & Composite-RA-Evaluated-Event)
    -> Displayed-Model-Goal >= 1500)
```

A pilot receives two different outputs from TCAS when being given instructions on avoiding another aircraft: an action (Climb or Descend), and a desired altitude rate of change. The query is checking that when the pilot is instructed to climb, the rate of altitude change is positive. There was a fairly complicated counterexample to this, which involved an intruder aircraft changing its climb rate in adjacent time intervals. Further discussion of the properties we were able to check is given below.

We now mention a few of the major steps in the analysis. We made significant use of non-determinism in our analysis. This means that some of the state

[1] We were working with a preliminary version of the specification (Version 6.00, March 1993). We do not know if the issues are present in later versions of the specification.

machines were represented as machines which could make arbitrary transitions, instead of the transitions made in the specification. Using non-deterministic machines means that the analysis is conservative with respect to safety properties. Using non-determinism allowed us to apply model checking in an incremental fashion: we only needed to have portions of the system translated in order to check properties, and we could refine our translation in response to results of the model checker. (This was important, since it allowed us to catch errors in our translation). There were portions of the system, involving multiplication and division in the transition relation which we were not able to model. We replaced these by non-deterministic operators, which gave a superset of possible transition. Again, this was done so that we could evaluate properties without having a complete model of the system.

State machines are a natural model for reactive systems which interact with the outside world. The inputs to the system are external events. In TCAS, an example of an external event is a transponder signal received from another aircraft. State machines also generate internal events which are used to communicate between different submachines. There has been much discussion of the semantics of these different types of events [13,18,12]. One issue is whether the internal events can be active when there are external events received. The TCAS model (using RSML) uses the synchrony hypothesis, which is that all internal events are processed between external events. One way of viewing this is that internal events are infinitely faster than external events. (This is reasonable for systems such as TCAS, where the separation of external events is measured in seconds). To model synchronization, a state variable `stable` is introduced to keep track of when there are active internal events. The handling of synchronization has a major impact on the performance of the model checking algorithms.

A major difference between the TCAS specification and many hardware specification is that some of the transition rules in TCAS depend on arithmetic operations. Examples include comparing altitudes to determine separation, and estimating positions based upon velocities and accelerations. Arithmetic involving addition and comparison can be handled, provided that it is represented at the bit-wise level, and the bits are interleaved appropriately. However, multiplication operations are not amenable to BDD representation [3], and this did limit the portions of the specification that we could analyze. Proper handling of multiplication is an open problem. In other work, we have attempted to integrate constraint solving and model checking to handle transitions based on multiplications [7].

4.2 Aircraft Electrical System

Our second case study was an analysis of a statecharts model of the electrical power distribution (EPD) system on the Boeing 777 aircraft. We stress that the statecharts model was developed for research purposes and does not represent the actual requirements used to develop the on-board system. As such the model by intent did not include all the logic necessary for a complete specification. The model was intended as a high-level abstraction of the electrical system, which included only the logic necessary to accomplish the goals of a wider airplane system analysis [17].

The purpose of the EPD system is to distribute AC and DC power to other airplane systems. It comprises separate interconnected distribution systems including main AC power, backup AC power, DC power, standby power, and flight controls power. Electrical power is distributed from power sources to power busses via a number of relayed circuit breakers. Failures of the power sources or circuit breakers are automatically detected and isolated. We focus on the portion of the statecharts that models the main and backup AC distribution subsystems.

One of the requirements of the electrical system was that it supports a degree of redundancy – components should remain powered in spite of several failures. Checks contingent on a number of failures could easily be represented in the logic, so we were able to evaluate various fault tolerant properties.

Two properties we checked were "Not only should the busses be powered when there are no failures, they should be powered by different sources" and "The main busses should in fact tolerate one failure in the power sources or circuit breakers using the formulas

```
AG ((Stable & No-Failures)
        -> Separate-Sources)
```

and

```
AG ((Stable & At-Most-1-Failure) -> main)
```

respectively. Both of these properties failed for essentially, the same reason: there was a subtle modeling flaw in specifying the circuit breaker. The failure of a circuit breaker and its subsequent recovering were represented as boolean variables, and not as events, so a transistion was not made inside the circuit breaker after its recovery, and it was left in an incorrect state. The scenerios to trigger the error were moderately involved. For example, in the second example it involves a failure in a circuit breaker, a change in inputs to induce a state change in its controller, the circuit breaker's recovery, and a subsequent failure in one of the power sources.

5 Uses of Model Checking

The prime use of model checking is as a debugging tool. Specific properties are tested, and when a violation is found, a counter example is given. In contrast to verification, model checking is used to find errors, not prove correctness. Model checking can be used in conjunction with other testing methods (such as simulation) to gain confidence that errors have been found and eliminated.

A fundamental question in applying model checking is "What to check?". Our experience is that the properties of interest divide into two broad classes: domain dependent, which require understanding of the domain, and domain independent, which can be considered as "design rules" for specifications.

5.1 Domain Dependent Properties

A key to our success in the two case studies was access to experts on the systems that we were working with. We would not have been able to identify the properties to evaluate for the TCAS study without this expertise. Issues such as looking checking the consistency of the outputs to the pilot (advisor and climb rate) would not have occurred to us. The understanding of counterexamples also required significant domain knowledge. It was necessary to thoroughly understand the counterexamples in order to determine the type of the error. We do not believe that it will be possible to reduce the role of the domain expert in the model checking process.

In our study of the aircraft electrical system, we also worked with domain experts (the designers of the model). In this study, the properties to test were more accessible. We had a document which outlined a set of fault tolerance requirements. These were phrased in terms of probability of failure, but there was a correspondance between this and bounding the number of simultaneous failures. Expertise was still necessary in order to clarify several of the properties that had to be tested. Model checking turned out to be an excellent tool to use for the evaluation of fault tolerance, since the number of failures could be included in the precondition of the property being checked.

5.2 Domain Independent Properties

Domain independent properties can be viewed as design rules that specifications should satisfy. An example of a property that is quite easy to check is whether the state transitions are deterministic: is it the case that every state can have at most one transistion enabled at a time. This can be tested by defining a property which tests for simultaneoulsy active transitions in reachable states. The reason why it is generally argued that deterministic transitions are important is that if there is a choice in the behavior, then different implementations may behave differently. A related property is "function consistency". If a function is defined in terms of cases, it is natural require that the cases are mutually disjoint. Discussions of other domain independent properties can be found in our papers [5,6].

6 Performance

Both of our case studies involved large specifications which generated models which were close to the maximum size which could be evaluated with a model checker. In the TCAS study, the model had a global state space with 227 Boolean variables, 10 of which are for events, 36 for the states of Own-Aircraft , 19 for the states of Other-Aircraft , 134 for altitude and altitude rates, 22 for inputs other than altitude and altitude rates, and 6 for other purposes. The size of the state space is about 1.4×10^{65}. The size of the *reachable* state space is at least 9.6×10^{56}. In the electrical system study, there are 33 two-state machines, 23 Boolean inputs, and 34 events, for a total of 90 Boolean state variables, or about 10^{27} global states, of which at least 10^{15} are reachable.

Our general experience is that the performance question is between feasibility and infeasibility as opposed to optimizing performance. Most of our successful checks ran in under 10 minutes using about 10 megabytes of memory. Unsuccessful checks were usually terminated after several hours. Failing computations generally had excessively large internal (BDD) representations.

Our initial attempts to check formulas in both the TCAS and the EPD studies were unsuccessful. In both cases we were forced to make significant changes to model checking algorithm, and to our methods of translating from the state machine model to the representation for the model checker. More detailed descriptions of our performance enhancements can be found in our papers: [5,8,6]. Our methods for addressing the performance problems have included:

Bitwise arithmetic. The order of variables in a BDD can influence it's size. We needed to interleave the variables corresponding to the bits of binary data. This was done by a transformation which was applied when compiling to the source language of SMV.

Search Order. We found it necessary to modify the search algorithms used by SMV. One modification involved storing information during a forward search to make generation of counter examples more efficient. The choice between forward search and backwards search was often important.

Short circuiting. This technique reduced the number of BBD's generated by stopping the iterations before a fixed point was reached.

Making exclusive events explicit. This allowed backwards search to be performed much more efficiently reducing the size of BDD's.

Partitioning strategies. One of the ways to reduce the size of the BDD for the transition relation is to decompose it several BBD's with disjunctive or conjunctive partitioning [4].

Abstraction One abstraction technique that we applied was to identify portions of the system the were not relevent to a check (with a conservative analysis), and remove that part of the system to reduce the size of the model. One of the keys to making this work well is to be able to identify false dependencies.

Synchronization. Our representation of state machines distinguihed between macrosteps (for outside events) and microsteps (for internal events). Inside a macrostep, all internal events would be executed, so the next macrostep could not start until no more internal events could be generated. We discovered that performance could be greatly improved if we made the synchronization process as regular as possible, even at the expense of increasing the number of states, or the lengths of event chains.

7 Conclusions

The goal of our work has been to show that symbolic model checking can be used in the analysis of software specifications. We have conducted case studies on real specifications, and have had success in identifying errors in the specifications that were not previously known. We have also developed techniques improve the performance of the model checking algorithms, and allow checks to be made which were previously intractable. We are optiministic about the future of model checking in the software development process. There is still much work to do in refining the algorithms and developing tool support for software model checking, but there is a growing body of evidence that model checking is applicable in the software domain as well as in the hardware domain.

References

1. J. M. Atlee and J. Gannon. State-based model checking of event-driven system requirements. *IEEE Transactions on Software Engineering*, 19(1):24–40, January 1993.
2. R. E. Bryant. Graph-based algorithms for boolean function manipulation. *IEEE Transactions on Computers*, 35(6):677–691, August 1986.
3. R. E. Bryant. On the complexity of VLSI implementations and graph representation of boolean functions with applications to integer multiplication. *IEEE Transactions on Computers*, 40(2):205–213, February 1991.
4. J. R. Burch, E. M. Clarke, D. E. Long, K. L. McMillan, and D. L. Dill. Symbolic model checking for sequential circuit verification. *IEEE Transactions on Computer-Aided Design of Integrated Circuits*, 13(4):401–424, April 1994.
5. W. Chan, R. J. Anderson, P. Beame, S. Burns, F. Modugno, D. Notkin, and J. D. Reese. Model checking large software specifications. *IEEE Transactions on Software Engineering*, 24(7):498–520, July 1998.
6. W. Chan, R. J. Anderson, P. Beame, D. H. Jones, D. Notkin, and W. E. Warner. Decoupling synchronization from logic for efficient symbolic model checking of statecharts. In *Proceedings of the 1999 International Conference on Software Engineering: ICSE 99*, Los Angeles, USA, May 1999. To appear.
7. W. Chan, R. J. Anderson, P. Beame, and D. Notkin. Combining constraint solving and symbolic model checking for a class of systems with non-linear constraints. In O. Grumberg, editor, *Computer Aided Verification, 9th International Conference, CAV'97 Proceedings*, volume 1254 of *Lecture Notes in Computer Science*, pages 316–327, Haifa, Israel, June 1997. Springer-Verlag.
8. W. Chan, R. J. Anderson, P. Beame, and D. Notkin. Improving efficiency of symbolic model checking for state-based system requirements. In M. Young, editor, *ISSTA 98: Proceedings of the ACM SIGSOFT International Symposium on Software Testing and Analysis*, pages 102–112, Clearwater Beach, Florida, USA, March 1998. Published as *Software Engineering Notes*, 23(2).
9. E. M. Clarke, E. A. Emerson, and A. P. Sistla. Automatic verification of finite-state concurrent systems using temporal logic specifications. *ACM Transactions on Programming Languages and Systems*, 8(2):244–263, April 1986.
10. J. Crow and B. L. Di Vito. Formalizing space shuttle software requirements. In *Proceedings of the ACM SIGSOFT Workshop on Formal Methods in Software Practice*, pages 40–48, January 1996.
11. D. Harel. Statecharts: A visual formalism for complex systems. *Science of Computer Programming*, 8(3):231–274, June 1987.
12. D. Harel and A. Naamad. The STATEMATE semantics of statecharts. *ACM Transactions on Software Engineering and Methodology*, 5(4):293–333, October 1996.

13. D. Harel, A. Pnueli, J. P. Schmidt, and R. Sherman. On the formal semantics of statecharts (extended abstract). In *Proceedings: Symposium on Logic in Computer Science*, pages 54–64, Ithaca, New York, USA, June 1987. IEEE.
14. J. Helbig and P. Kelb. An OBDD-representation of statecharts. In *Proceedings: The European Design and Test Conference. EDAC, The European Conference on Design Automation. ETC, European Test Conference. EUROASIC, The European Event in ASIC Design*, pages 142–149, Paris, France, February/March 1994. IEEE.
15. M. S. Jaffe, N. G. Leveson, M. P. E. Heimdahl, and B. E. Melhart. Software requirements analysis for real-time process-control systems. *IEEE Transactions on Software Engineering*, 17(3):241–258, March 1991.
16. K. L. McMillan. *Symbolic Model Checking.* Kluwer Academic Publishers, 1993.
17. C. R. Nobe and W. E. Warner. Lessons learned from a trial application of requirements modeling using statecharts. In *Proceedings of the 2nd International Conference on Requirements Engineering*, pages 86–93, Colorado Springs, USA, April 1996. IEEE.
18. A. Pnueli and M. Shalev. What is in a step: On the semantics of statecharts. In T. Ito and A. R. Meyer, editors, *Theoretical Aspects of Computer Software, International Conference TACS'91*, volume 526 of *Lecture Notes in Computer Science*, pages 244–264, Sendai, Japan, September 1991. Springer-Verlag.
19. J. M. Wing and M. Vaziri-Farahani. A case study in model checking software systems. *Science of Computer Programming*, 28(2/3):273–299, April 1997.

Formal Verification of a Compiler Back-End Generic Checker Program*

Axel Dold and Vincent Vialard

Universität Ulm
Fakultät für Informatik
D-89069 Ulm, Germany
fax: ++49 +731 50-24119
{dold|vialard}@ki.informatik.uni-ulm.de

Abstract. This paper reports on a non-trivial case-study carried out in the context on the German correct compiler construction project *Verifix*. The PVS system is here used as a vehicle to formally represent and verify a generic checker routine (run-time result verification) used in compiler back-ends. The checker verifies the results of a sophisticated labeling process of intermediate language expression trees with instances of compilation rule schemata. Starting from an operational specification (i.e. a set of recursive PVS functions), necessary declarative properties of the checker are formally stated and proved correct.

Keywords: formal verification, checker-based program verification, generic specification

1 Introduction

The German project *Verifix* on compiler verification aims at developing innovative methods for the construction of correct realistic compilers for practically relevant source languages and concrete target architectures. Correct execution of source programs depends on the correctness of the binary machine code executable, thus either the final executable has to be verified or the compiler used is to be shown correct [3].

A realistic state-of-the-art compiler is a large and complex program system consisting of many hard, highly optimizing algorithms which are difficult to verify since mathematical inductive arguments often fail. For example, the code generation phase of a compiler often uses clever routines for register allocation, instruction scheduling or pipeline optimizations. For this reason, a more practical modular approach is taken: we use a checker-based approach to program verification, which works if partial correctness suffices (i.e. rather no result than a wrong result). It is often much easier to check the correctness of a given result at run time than to verify the generating algorithm and its implementation. In

* This work has been supported by the Deutsche Forschungsgemeinschaft (DFG) project *Verifix*

D. Bjørner, M. Broy, A. Zamulin (Eds.): PSI'99, LNCS 1755, pp. 470–480, 2000.

our case, for instance, we would rather check that every assigned register is free and available than totally verify the sophisticated register allocation algorithm. Thus, one can concentrate on the verification of (in general) small checking (filter) routines built into the code in order to establish partial correctness of the entire program. Of course, this only makes sense if the verification of the checker is indeed easier than the verification of the program whose results are checked [4,6]. Checkers have been used to ensure type correctness properties of a C subset compiler [7] and to verify the compilation of synchronous languages to C [9], but not yet to "verify" totally a machine code generation procedure.

In this paper the PVS specification and verification system is utilized to formally verify the specification of such a checker program to be used in the back-end part of a compiler. The back-end translates linear intermediate code (i.e. sequence of assignments of expressions) into linear assembly code. This back-end is to be generated from a set of local translation rule schemata and additional components such as optimized register allocators and schedulers. The rule schemata were independently verified with respect to source and target language semantics [1].

The part of the compiler we are to check gets as input an intermediate language expression tree and outputs a labeled expression tree. The labels consist of the rule used to compute the node, assignments of the register and numerical variables to actual registers and values respectively, as well as the schedule number of the rule.

Our formalization is generic with respect to the languages and translation rules. It is realized as a parameterized PVS theory. The specification being written in an operational style is executable within the prover. It has been applied to a small realistic example of translation from the intermediate language MIS to DEC Alpha assembly code.

We present these results as follows: the next section gives a brief introduction to PVS. Sect. 3 outlines the principle of generator-based back-end generation. In Sect. 4 the PVS formalization of the checker is presented and declarative correctness properties are stated, formalized and proved correct. All PVS theories and proof scripts are available from the authors upon request.

2 A Brief Introduction to PVS

The PVS system [8] combines an expressive specification language with an interactive prover/proof checker. The PVS specification language builds on classical typed higher-order logic with the usual base types, `bool`, `nat`, among others, the product type constructor `[A,B]` and the function type constructor `[A->B]`. The type system of PVS is augmented with *dependent types* and *abstract data types*. The special type `TYPE` designates an unspecified type, and `TYPE+` an unspecified non empty type. A distinctive feature of the PVS specification language are *predicate subtypes*: the subtype `{x:A | P(x)}` consists of exactly those elements of type `A` satisfying predicate `P`. Predicate subtypes are used, for instance, for explicitly constraining the domains and ranges of operations in a specification and to define partial functions. Sets are identified with their characteristic predicates, and thus the expressions `pred[A]` and `set[A]` are interchangeable. For a predicate `P` of type `pred[A]`, the notation `(P)` is just an abbreviation for the predicate subtype `{x:A | P(x)}`.

In general, type-checking with predicate subtypes is undecidable; the type-checker generates proof obligations, so-called *type correctness conditions* (TCCs) in cases where type conflicts cannot immediately be resolved. A PVS expression is not considered to be fully type-checked unless all generated TCCs have been proved. PVS only allows total functions, hence it must be ensured that all (recursive) functions terminate. For this purpose, a well-founded ordering or a *measure function* is used. The definition of a recursive function `f` generates a TCC which states that the measure function applied to the recursive arguments decreases with respect to a well-founded ordering. A built-in *prelude* and loadable *libraries* provide standard specifications and proved facts for a large number of theories (we use for instance the `finite_set` type, the `upto` and `subrange` subtypes of `nat`, the `empty?` predicate over sets, the `choose` function to extract an element from a set, etc...). Specifications are realized as possibly parameterized PVS theories and theory parameters can be constrained by means of *assumptions.* When instantiating a parameterized theory, TCC's are automatically generated according to the assumptions.

Proofs in PVS are presented in a sequent calculus. There exists a large number of atomic commands (for quantifier instantiation, automatic conditional rewriting, induction, etc...) and built-in strategies generating proofs for the easiest subgoals automatically.

3 Back-End Generation by Term Rewriting

The back-end of a compiler is the part of the program in charge of the final translation from a low-level intermediate language to assembly or machine code (this phase is usually called code generation). Its main task is to generate sequences of target level instructions to compute the value of intermediate language expressions. The state-of-the-art code generators are themselves generated from a set of optimized translation rules schemata and include complex mechanisms for optimal rule selection, register allocation and operation scheduling.

The rule schemata are local translation rules associating a sequence of assembly code to an expression subtree, the latter being arbitrarily complex depending on the level of resource and time optimization. They are parameterized by use of variables in place of registers and constants, and the set of registers or register variables used in input, output and temporary storage (in the generated code) are given. These rules are mechanically proved correct with respect to the semantics of the intermediate and target languages independently from the whole process in PVS using a user defined strategy [1].

As already stated, we want to avoid the verification of the specification, let alone the implementation, of the rule selector/allocator/scheduler taking care of the labeling of the expression trees. This is possible by verifying the output of the procedure at run time, aborting the compilation if ever an error occurs (giving the available elements for the correction of the bug). The checking procedure must however be proven to detect any case where the code that will further be generated from the labeled tree will not exactly implement the computation of the translated expression.

Figure 1 gives an overview of the compilation process. As illustrated, the back-end generator must be partly verified to make sure that the verified code it uses is not altered in any way, and that the components on the correctness critical path are correctly connected. The generated back-end contains non verified code whose results will be checked at run time by the verified checker.

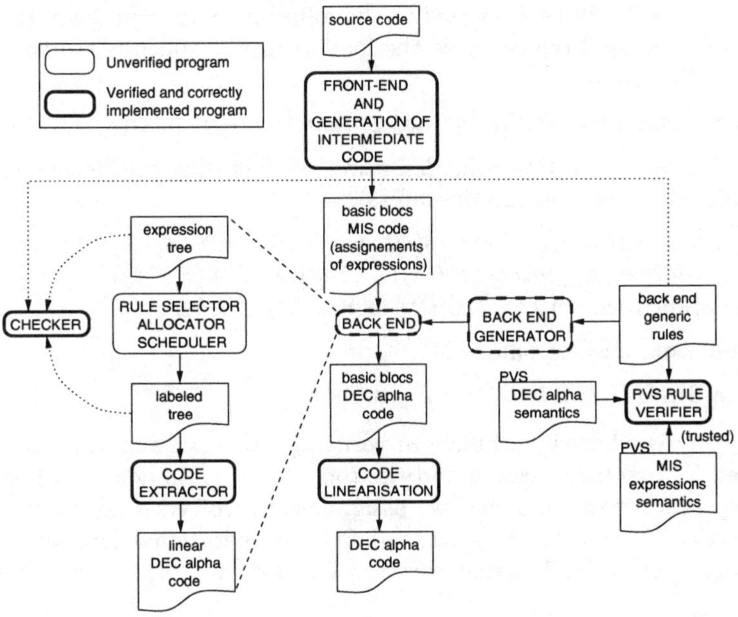

Fig. 1. Overview of the compilation with detailed back-end principle

The straightforward way to make sure that the labeling was correctly done is to extract the code of the labeled tree according to the schedule, and show that this code implements the computation of the initial expression. This is clearly unpracticable at runtime, as we would have to deal with the semantics of the languages. But the rule schemata were already proved correct, and thus the translation will be correct if the rules are "properly" used. The proper use of a rule being hard to define formally, we will verify properties that are intuitively needed and give elements to show that these properties actually imply a correct resulting code given a correct implementation of the code extractor.

The labeling process actually represents a covering of the expression tree with instances of the expression trees of the translation rules used, each of the rule trees being rooted at the node for which the rule is applied (as the expression part of the rules may be a single unary operator as well as a complex expression).

The correctness requirements of this process are to make sure the covering is correct (every expression node is covered with a rule node with a correct operator), to verify the schedule (subterms must computed before their use), to verify the value passing from children to parent rule (output register of the child rule is the same as the corresponding input register of the parent rule - via assignment of register variables) and to verify that the values computed are not overwritten before their use.

Let us continue with an example exposed in [10]. The source language statement $V := V + 1$ will be compiled to the following MIS expression (the storage address of V being 8 relatively to the local pointer - which is stored in register 1 on the DEC-Alpha):

$$intassign(local(intconst(8)), intadd(content(local(intconst(8))), intconst(1)))$$

and this expression will be compiled using the following rule schemata (remark the encoding size of constant operators):

$$rule1 : intassign(local(intconst16(i)), reg(X)) \rightarrow \bullet; STQ(X, i, 1)$$
$$rule2 : intadd(reg(X), intconst16(i)) \rightarrow Y; ADDI(X, i, Y, Q)$$
$$rule3 : content(local(intconst16(i))) \rightarrow Y; LDQ(1, i, Y)$$

to the following DEC-Alpha code:

$$LDQ(1, 8, 3); ADDI(3, 1, 3, Q); STQ(3, 8, 1)$$

Figure 2 sketches the problem of verifying value passing between the codes generated for a sub-expression and the top operator. As one would expect, the three expression trees and the two assignments involved make this verification somewhat complex. This lead us to define an operational formulation of this verification process, and similar specifications for the others properties.

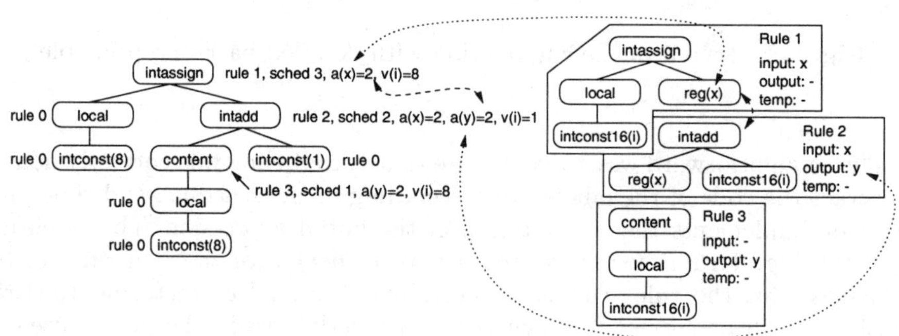

Fig. 2. Verification of value passing

These specifications are hardly usable as is in a proof context, thus more declarative properties have been stated and proved to hold for any labeled tree successfully checked. These properties shall be the basis for all future proofs.

4 Formalization of the Checker

We tried to keep the specification as generic as possible by abstracting over the syntax and structures. We had though to select a proper structure for the expression trees in order to be able to use induction in the proofs. We defined the abstract datatype `Tree` (nodes have a value, a left and a right son, leaves are terminal) parameterized by the type of the values of the nodes and PVS generated the induction theorems for this structure. We used this type for both the labeled trees and rule trees encoding. The parameterization of our PVS theory is presented in Fig. 3.

The four verifications described in the previous section are undertaken by four independent predicates (functions of type `[Node->bool]`): `covercheck?`, `schedulecheck?`, `valuecheck?` and `overwritecheck?`. Some of these predicates have a straightforward formulation with mutually recursive functions. Unfortunately, the PVS system does not support mutual recursive functions due to termination problems. We therefore wrote them using a single recursive function with a flag indicating which of the bodies is to be evaluated. Termination of these functions is ensured by a measure function using a lexicographical ordering of the flag and the measure functions of the bodies. Figure 4 presents the PVS code for the `valuecheck?` predicate.

As stated before, these operational formulations of the checkers with their flagged recursion schemes are hardly usable in a proof context, and is therefore not very helpful to establish the correctness of the back-end. To prove that the code to be generated from the labeled tree will actually implement the expression compiled, we will have to induct on the number of code extraction steps and therefore need more usable declarative properties about the resulting machine code. As these properties are not easily expressed, we identified the situations that do cause an error:

- covering problem: the root of a rule tree does not match the operator of the referencing labeled node, or a node from a rule rooted somewhere in the labeled tree does not match the operator of the labeled node it covers (except if the rule node is a register and covered node is labeled with a rule)
- schedule problem: there is a node, labeled with a rule, having a schedule number smaller than the one of its child node also labeled with a rule.
- input problem: there is a register node from a rule rooted somewhere in the labeled tree covering a node not labeled with a rule, or covering a node with a rule whose output register variable is not assigned to the same instance as the covering register.
- overwrite problem: there is a node, labeled with a rule and with a schedule number comprised between the schedule numbers of two "communicating" rules using the value passing register as output or temporary node.

```
checker [

  R       :TYPE+,                          % registers

% Operator type and accessors
  Op      :TYPE+,                          % operators in expressions
  RegVar  :TYPE+,                          % register variables
  NumVar  :TYPE+,                          % numerical variables
  val?    :pred[Op],                       % value operator
  val     :[(val?)->int],                  % accessor for value
  reg?    :pred[Op],                       % register variable operator
  reg     :[(reg?)->RegVar],               % accessor for register variables
  num?    :pred[Op],                       % numerical variable operator
  num     :[(num?)->NumVar],               % accessor for numerical variables
  cbits   :[(num?)->nat],                  % size of the numerical variable

  nrule   :nat,                            % number of translation rules

% Labeled node type and accessors
  Node    :TYPE+,                           % labeled nodes
  oper    :[Node->Op],                      % operator
  rnum    :[Node->upto(nrule)],             % rule number
  areg    :[Node->[RegVar->R]],             % assignment of register vars
  anum    :[Node->[NumVar->nat]],           % assignment of numerical vars
  sched   :[Node->nat],                     % schedule number

% Rule type and accessors
  Rule    :TYPE+,                           % translation rules
  rtree   :[Rule->Tree[Op]],                % operators tree of the rule
  inp     :[Rule->finite_set[RegVar]],      % input register vars of the rule
  out     :[Rule->at_most_one[RegVar]],     % output register of the rule
  tmp     :[Rule->finite_set[RegVar]],      % temporary register variables

  rulemap : [subrange(1,nrule)->{r:Rule | node?(rtree(r))}] % rule list

  ] : THEORY

  :
  LTree : TYPE = Tree[Node]                 % labeled trees
  RTree : TYPE = Tree[Op]                   % rule trees
  Asg   : TYPE = [RegVar->R]                % register assignments
  :
```

Fig. 3. Parameterization of the PVS theory

If none of these situations is encountered, the values of the sub-expressions should be computed correctly, in time, stored and retrieved in the proper registers, and the temporary storages should be made in a secure manner. This should imply the correctness of the code generated. It will have to be established formally by an induction proof on the structure of the initial expression with help of the correctness property of the rule schemata.

To express these properties we need a function that retrieves the rule node covering a subnode of the expression tree. The subset of nodes covered by a rule is defined by the predicate `rule_covers_subtree?` and the function `covering_op` retrieves the operator from the rule tree covering a given node.

The PVS predicate `wrong_input` presented in Fig. 5 encodes the input problem property for the rule rooted at `t`. It will be usable in place of the corresponding checker function (Fig. 4) in the proof thanks to the lemma presented in Fig. 6. We proceeded in a similar manner for the three other checkers.

The proofs were done by structural induction on the expression tree. The induction hypothesis being implications, we had to write the checker functions in such a way that it is provable that the successful check of a tree implies the same for its subtrees (in order to "trigger" the consequence part of the implication of the hypothesis). These properties were themselves established by structural induction and sometimes needed other inductive lemmas (i.e. nested induction).

The proofs are not trivial (a few weeks were invested into specification, correction, and proofs) but relatively short (1000 interactive steps for the whole theory, including TCCs). They could be further automated, using eventually user-defined strategies, but once established, thanks to the parameterization of the theory, it will not be necessary to re-work them.

We encoded in PVS a subset of rule schemata for the translation from the MIS intermediate language to DEC-Alpha and instantiated the checker theory for such verifications. The small example presented in the previous section was successfully processed.

The proof of the global process will be achieved by induction over the schedule number of the successfully checked labeled tree. We will consider a pair (*code*, *tree*) constituted of an assembly code sequence and an intermediate language expression tree. The assembly code is considered to be evaluated prior to the expression, bringing the machine in a state (values stored in registers and/or memory) in which the expression will then be evaluated. We start with an empty code sequence and the initial labeled expression tree, and the pair will be updated at each step to a new pair ($code +\!\!+ code'$, $tree'$) as follows:

- in the expression tree the selected node is replaced by a node labeled with its output register (according to the substitution) with two leaves as sons.
- the assembly code part of the rule associated to the selected node (with its variables instantiated accordingly to the assignments) is appended to the existing code sequence.

The equivalence between the two pairs will be established using the declarative properties that were shown to be implied by a successful check along with the

```
valcheck?(newrule?:bool,t:LTree,r:RTree,a:Asg) : RECURSIVE bool =
  IF newrule? THEN
    CASES r OF                      % new rule
      leaf: ⊥,                      % - shouldn't be empty
      node(vr,lr,rr):
        CASES t OF
          leaf: ⊥,                  % - shouldn't cover a leaf
          node(vt,lt,rt):           %   nor a register (continue verifying)
            ¬reg?(vr) ∧ valcheck?(⊥,lt,lr,a) ∧ valcheck?(⊥,rt,rr,a)
        ENDCASES
    ENDCASES
  ELSE                              % old rule
    CASES r OF
      leaf :                        % - is a leaf
        CASES t OF
          leaf : ⊤,                 % -- and covers a leaf (ok, over)
          node(vt,lt,rt) :          % -- or covers a node (continue verifying)
            IF rnum(vt) = 0
            THEN valcheck?(⊥,lt,r,a) ∧ valcheck?(⊥,rt,r,a)
            ELSE valcheck?(⊤,t,rtree(rulemap(rnum(vt))),areg(vt))
            ENDIF
        ENDCASES,
      node(vr,lr,rr) :              % - is a node
        CASES t OF
          leaf : ⊥,                 % -- shouldn't cover a leaf
          node(vt,lt,rt) :          % -- covers a node, verify if a value is
            IF rnum(vt) = 0         %    required, and passed if necessary
              THEN ¬Reg?(vr)
              ELSE Reg?(vr) ∧ ¬empty?(out(rulemap(rnum(vt))))
                ∧ a(Reg(vr)) = areg(vt)(choose(out(rulemap(rnum(vt)))))
                ∧ valcheck?(⊤,t,rtree(rulemap(rnum(vt))),areg(vt))
              ENDIF                 %    ... and continue verifying
            ∧ valcheck?(⊥,lt,lr,a) ∧ valcheck?(⊥,rt,rr,a)
        ENDCASES
    ENDCASES
  ENDIF
MEASURE lex2(depth(t), bool2nat(¬newrule?)) % either t decreases
                                            % or newrule? becomes true
valuecheck?(t:LTree) : RECURSIVE bool =
  CASES t OF
    leaf: ⊤,   % real verification starts at the first node with a rule
    node(v,lt,rt): IF rnum(v) = 0
                   THEN valuecheck?(lt) ∧ valuecheck?(rt)
                   ELSE valcheck?(⊤,t,tree(rulemap(rnum(v))),areg(v))
                   ENDIF
  ENDCASES
MEASURE t by <<    % t is structurally decreasing
```

Fig. 4. Operational specification of the value passing checker

```
% t is labeled with a rule that covers a subtree t1 with a register node
% but t1 doesn't store a value in the proper register

wrong_input(t:LTree) : bool =
  CASES t OF
    leaf : ⊥,
    node(vt,lt,rt) :
      rnum(vt) /= 0
      ∧∃(t1:(rule_covers_subtree?(rtree(rulemap(rnum(vt))),t))) :
          Reg?(covering_op(rtree(rulemap(rnum(vt))),t)(t1))
          ∧ (leaf?(t1)
             ∨ rnum(val(t1)) = 0
             ∨ empty?(out(rulemap(rnum(val(t1)))))
             ∨ areg(vt)(Reg(covering_op(rtree(rulemap(rnum(vt))),t)(t1)))
                ≠ areg(val(t1))(choose(out(rulemap(rnum(val(t1))))))))
  ENDCASES
```

Fig. 5. Declarative characterization of the input problem

```
% If t is valuechecked then it does not have a subtree with an input
% problem

valuecheck_correct : LEMMA
  ∀(t:LTree) :
    valuecheck?(t) ⇒ ¬(∃(t1:(subtree?(t))) : wrong_input(t1))
```

Fig. 6. Link between operational specification and declarative property

correctness properties of the translation rules. Intuitively, the properties implied by `covercheck?(t)` will be used to show the correct use of the rules and the others the proper storage and retrieval of the subterms values.

5 Conclusion

We described in this paper our approach to the problem of formally specifying a validation procedure of the results of a compiler back-end. We defined a generic operational PVS specification for such a program and proved declarative properties more usable for the global correction proof. The genericity of the specification should allow an easy use of the theory for various intermediate languages and target machines.

The specification can be refined step by step into a PVS function close enough to the actual encoding of the checker in order to prove its implementation correct (it is the approach taken in [2]). If the checker is to be implemented in a higher level language, there must exist a correctly implemented compiler for it (this initial compiler is part of the Verifix project [5]).

References

1. A.Dold, T.Gaul, V.Vialard, and W.Zimmermann. ASM-Based Mechanized Verification of Compiler Backends. In Uwe Glässer and Peter H. Schmitt, editors, *5th International Workshop on ASM*, pages 50–67, 1998.
2. Axel Dold. Software Development in PVS using Generic Development Steps. In *Dagstuhl Seminar on Generic Programming (April 98)*, LNCS, 1998.
3. W. Goerigk, A. Dold, T. Gaul, G. Goos, A. Heberle, F.W. von Henke, U. Hoffmann, H.Langmaack, H. Pfeifer, H. Ruess, and W. Zimmermann. Compiler Correctness and Implementation Verification: The *Verifix* Approach. In P. Fritzson, editor, *Poster Session of CC '96*, IDA Technical Report LiTH-IDA-R-96-12, Linkøping, Sweden, 1996.
4. W. Goerigk, T. Gaul, and W. Zimmermann. Correct Programs without Proof? On Checker-Based Program Verification. In *ATOOLS'98 Workshop on "Tool Support for System Specification, Development, and Verification"*, ACS, Malente, 1998. Springer Verlag.
5. W. Goerigk and U. Hoffmann. Rigorous Compiler Implementation Correctness: How to Prove the Real Thing Correct. In *FM-TRENDS'98*, LNCS, Boppard, 1998.
6. A. Heberle, T. Gaul, W. Goerigk, G. Goos, and W. Zimmermann. Construction of Verified Compiler Front-Ends with Program-Checking. PSI'99 (this volume), 1998.
7. G.C. Necula and P. Lee. The Design and Implementation of a Certifying Compiler. In *ACM SIGPLAN'98 PLDI*, pages 333–344, Montreal, Canada, 17–19 June 1998.
8. S. Owre, J. M. Rushby, and N. Shankar. PVS: A Prototype Verification System. In Deepak Kapur, editor, *CADE'11*, volume 607 of *LNAI*, pages 748–752, Saratoga NY, 1992. Springer-Verlag.
9. A. Pnuelli, M. Siegel, and E. Singermann. Translation Validation for Synchronous Languages. In S. Skyum K.G. Larsen and G. Winskel, editors, *ICALP 98*, pages 235–246.
10. W. Zimmermann and T. Gaul. On the Construction of Correct Compiler Back-Ends: An ASM Approach. *Journal of Universal Computer Science*, 3(5):504–567, 1997.

Construction of Verified Compiler Front-Ends with Program-Checking

Andreas Heberle[1], Thilo Gaul[1], Wolfgang Goerigk[2], Gerhard Goos[1], and Wolf Zimmermann[1]

[1] Institut für Programmstrukturen und Datenorganisation
Universität Karlsruhe
Zirkel 2, D-76128 Karlsruhe, Germany
{gaul,goos,heberle,zimmer}@ipd.info.uni-karlsruhe.de
[2] Institut für Informatik und Praktische Mathematik
Christian-Albrechts-Universität zu Kiel
Preußerstr.1–9, D-24105 Kiel
wg@informatik.uni-kiel.de

Abstract. This paper describes how program-checking can be used to establish the correctness of a compiler front-end which was generated by unverified compiler construction tools. The basic idea of program-checking is to use an unverified algorithm whose results are checked by a verified component at run time. The approach not only simplifies the construction of a verified compiler front-end because checking the result of the analysis is much simpler to verify than the verification of a high sophisticated compiler front-end. It even allows to define a notion of front-end correctness. Furthermore, we are still able to use existing generators tools without major modifications. Additionally, this work points out the tasks which still have to be verified and it discusses the flexibility of the approach.

1 Introduction

In order to construct a verified compiler we have to consider not only the transformation and code generation phase which can be verified with respect to the source and target language semantics but also the analysis of programs. Usually, work on constructing correct compilers ignores this analysis phase. All semantic definitions of the source language are based on attributed structure trees obtained after semantic analysis, see e. g. [3,15,6,1].

However, in order to construct a correct compiler, the correctness of the analysis phase must not be ignored. This paper bridges the gap, i. e., we show how to construct a correct front-end. In fact, it is not trivial to define the correctness of the analysis phase. Basically it maps a character sequence to attributed syntax trees. But how to define correctness of this mapping?

It is common to define semantics of programming languages on abstract and/or attributed syntax trees. Hence, in order to have a complete language definition, the relation between the source text and the attributed syntax tree

D. Bjørner, M. Broy, A. Zamulin (Eds.): PSI'99, LNCS 1755, pp. 481–492, 2000.

has to be specified. We expect this relation ϕ to be available. Usually, compiler writers prefer to use their own representation of attributed syntax trees and base the dynamic semantics on them. For a correct compiler, it must be proven that the programming language semantics used in the compiler preserves the programming language semantics as defined by the language definition. In this paper, we assume that this is already being done. Hence, we have to ensure that the relation between source text and attributed syntax trees is implemented correctly.

Instead of proving the correctness of the analysis phase, we check the correctness of the results produced during the analysis dynamically. For simplicity, we assume that the static semantics is specified by an attribute grammar AG, and the relation ϕ between source text and attributed syntax trees is specified inductively over the structure of the syntax trees. The basic idea of front-end checking is first to check the semantic analysis where it is sufficient to check that for every attribution rule $n_i.a \leftarrow f(m_1, \ldots, m_k)$ in AG the corresponding attributes of the attributed structure tree define an equality. Second, if the result of the semantic analysis was accepted, we check scanner and parser by checking whether the source text is related by ϕ to the abstract syntax tree. Our approach allows the use of front-ends generated by unverified tools or front-ends implemented by hand. We do not assume anything about the implementation language of the front-end. Especially we do not assume that it is implemented in a language for which there exists a verified compiler. Of course, the checker itself has to be verified.

In our case study we use the cocktail tool box [8] which generates C programs. Our implementation language for the checker part is SATHER-K [11], a type-safe object-oriented language with generic classes (similar to templates in C++). The benefit of our approach is illustrated by the number of lines of codes which have to be verified in order to prove the front-end implementation correct. The generated front-end of our case study is implemented by 22.000 lines of C code while the checker consists of 1.300 lines of SATHER code.

The following section introduces the idea of program checking in general and discusses related work. In Section 3 we present an architecture for front-end checking and describe the particular components of the checker in more detail. We examine the checking of semantic analysis, we describe the checker for scanner and parser, and we discuss correctness properties of each component of the checker. In Section 4 we present an example and draw conclusions in Section 5.

2 Basics and Related Work

The idea of program checking shows how to construct partially correct programs without direct verification of the program. Instead, it uses a verified checker as a filter. Consider a program π with input x and output y. Let $P(x)$ be a precondition of π and $Q(x, y)$ a postcondition. A program π is *partially correct*, iff for every x satisfying $P(x)$ either π refuses x or π computes an output y such that $Q(x, y)$ (i.e. $\{P(x)\}\ y := \pi(x)\ \{Q(x, y)\}$ in Hoare-Triple notation). The idea of program checking can be summarized by the following function π':

fun $\pi'(x : T) : T'$ **is**
  $y := \pi(x)$;
  if $check\_\pi(x, y)$ **then return** y;
  else abort
end

The boolean function $check\_\pi$ must imply the postcondition Q. The following theorem shows the validity of the approach.

Theorem 1 (Program Checking). *Let $\pi(x : T) : T'$ be an unverified program without side-effects, $check\_\pi(x : T, y : T')$:* **bool** *be a side-effect free function satisfying $\{P(x)\}\ z := check\_\pi(x, y)\ \{z = true \Rightarrow Q(x, y)\}$. Then, it holds $\{P(x)\}\ y := \pi'(x)\ \{Q(x, y)\}$*

Proof. We sketch the proof. It can be formal using standard Hoare calculus. Since π is side-effect free, the input x remains unchanged. If π' does not abort, it returns y. The y returned is the same as the input in $check\_\pi(x, y)$, because $check\_\pi(x, y)$ is side-effect free. Furthermore, when y is returned it must hold $check\_\pi(x, y) = true$. Hence, it holds $Q(x, y)$.

Hence, the only assumption on π is the side-effect freeness. No further assumptions on π are made. The function π' therefore provides a bootstrapping approach to construct partial correct programs. It is useful to apply the approach if the formal verification of $check\_\pi$ is much easier than that of π or the size of π is much larger than the size of $check\_\pi$. However, the difficulty is the assumption on the side-effect freeness of π. We will call this property of a program being side-effect free "wrap"-property.

Related Work. Our checker approach is closely related to the work of M. Blum on result-checking [2,16] and the ideas of [9]. A more detailed discussion of the theoretical aspects of our approach can be found in [10].

Program checking is already used in compiler construction for checking properties necessary to establish correctness of a transformation. Necula and Lee [14] describe a compiler which contains a certifier that automatically checks the type safety and the memory safety of any assembler program produced by the compiler. The certification process detects statically compilation errors of a certain kind but it does not establish full correctness of the compilation. Nevertheless, this work shows that program checking can be used to produce efficient implementations with consideration of safety requirements.

3 The General Approach

Figure 1 describes our architecture for compiler front-end checking. white boxes denote components which can be used without verification while grey boxes denote parts which have to be verified in order to construct a correct front-end.

The architecture of the analyzer is the typical architecture of a compiler front-end. It accepts the program Π represented as a character sequences and produces an attributed abstract syntax tree. The *scanner* produces a sequence of tokens, i.e. the internal representation of key-words, identifiers, constants, special symbols such as ":=", ":" etc. We use the word *symbol* to denotes this character sequence. The scanner may be generated by regular expressions RE' describing the symbols. It removes white spaces and comments. The *parser* produces an abstract syntax tree. It may be generated by a context-free grammar G'. Finally, the *semantic analysis* enriches the abstract syntax tree by attributes. Again, the semantic analysis may be generated by an attribute grammar AG'. The attribute grammar AG' used for the generation of semantic analysis needs not to be the same than AG, because semantic analysis generators may require special classes of attribute grammars.

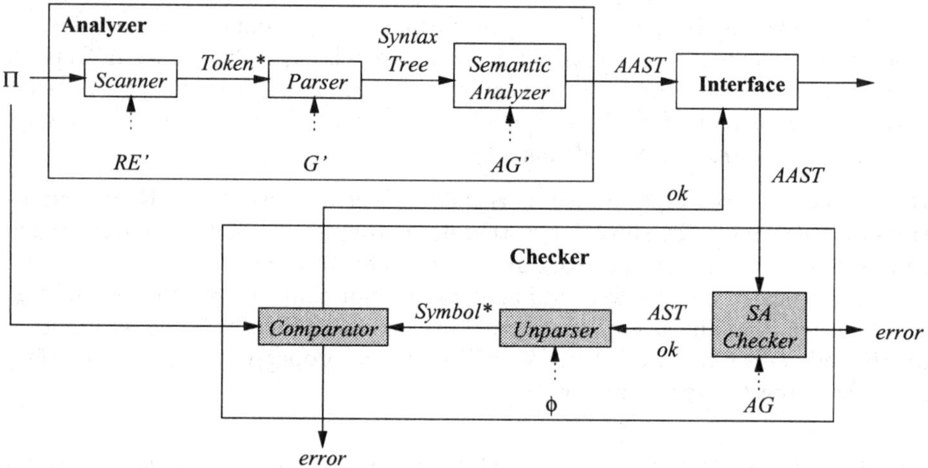

Fig. 1. A general architecture for checking compiler front-ends

The checker accepts the program Π and the attributed abstract syntax tree $AAST$ as inputs. The *SA Checker* verifies the validity of attribute values w.r.t. the attribute grammar AG from the language specification. If the check does not reveal an error then the abstract syntax tree is passed to the *Unparser* which uses the relation ϕ to compute a sequence of symbols. This sequence of symbols is taken as a reference the original file is compared with. Of course the comparison has to ignore white spaces and comments. If the comparison succeeds the program was parsed correctly. Otherwise the program is rejected. In fact, this does not mean that the program was compiled faulty. It just means that the checker was not able to establish the correctness of the compilation. Of course it is our goal to build a checker which is able to check the correctness of all compiled programs. The *interface* basically implements the functionality of the function π'. It ensures the requirements of Theorem 1. Thus, the checker implements the following function:

fun $check\_frontend(\Pi : Char^*, AAST : AG) : BOOL$ **is**
  if $\neg check\_semantic\_analysis(AAST)$ **then return** *false*; **fi**;
  $s := unparse(AAST)$;
  return $compare(\Pi, s)$;
end;

In Section 3.1 we discuss different implementations of the interface, Section 3.2 describes how to implement the checker for semantic analysis, and Section 3.3 describes the implementation of the checker for the scanner and parser.

3.1 Safe Communication of Checker and Front-End

As Theorem 1 shows that the function π to be checked - in our case the compiler front-end - must be free of side-effects. This can be ensured by strictly separating the memory spaces of the compiler and its checker. If the operating system is assumed to be correct[1] there are several alternatives to make sure that it is impossible for the front-end to write in the memory of the checker.

- If the implementation language does not allow pointers to the memory, we are able to prove that the compiler behaves safe.
- If checking and compiling are two parallel processes with different memory spaces the operating system assures that memory of one process can not be altered by another process. Nevertheless, we have to verify and implement the protocol on which the two processes communicate. In our implementation of this protocol, compiler and checker communicate by mutual file access. The attributed structure tree is written to a file in a general interchange format which is then translated to an internal representation. This representation of the AST is reliable when the check has succeeded. The interchange format is defined in [12].

3.2 Checking Semantic Analysis

The general idea of checking semantic analysis is to interpret the attribute definition rules R of the language specification AG as equations on the corresponding attributes. Instantiating these equations with the attribute values computed by the compiler (using AG') leads to a set of equations. Semantic analysis worked correctly if all these equations together with the conditions C on attribute values are fulfilled.

The definition of static programming language semantic is specified by an attribute grammar AG. An *attribute grammar* is a quadruple $AG = (G, A, R, C)$

[1] Compiler verification does not deal with hardware verification or verification of the operating system. Though correctness of the base system is essential for the correctness of the global system this is beyond the scope of our work.

where $G = (N, T, P, Z)$ is a context-free grammar describing the abstract syntax, $A = \bigcup_{X \in T \cup N} A_X$, A_X is the set of attributs belonging to X, $R = \bigcup_{p \in P} R(p)$, $R(p)$ is a set of attribution rules for the production $p \in P$, $C = \bigcup_{p \in P} C(p)$, $C(p)$ is the set of conditions for the production $p \in P$. We write $X.a$ to indicate that $a \in A_X$. The *attribution rules* for production $p : X_0 ::= X_1 \ldots X_n$ have the form $X_{i_0}.a_0 \leftarrow f(X_{i_1}.a_1, \ldots, X_{i_k}.a_k)$, $0 \le i_1, \ldots, i_k \le n$. A *condition* for p has the form $c(X_{j_1}.b_1, \ldots, X_{j_l}.b_l)$, $0 \le j_1, \ldots, j_l \le n$.

An attributed abstract syntax tree t is *correctly attributed* iff for each node ν_0 of t with children $\nu_1, \ldots, \nu_n$ obtained by production $p : X_0 ::= X_1 \cdots X_n$, the following properties are satisfied:

1. $\nu_{i_0}.a_{i_0} = f(\nu_{i_1}.a_{i_1}, \ldots, \nu_{i_k}.a_{i_k})$ for each attribution rule $X_{i_0}.a_0 \leftarrow f(X_{i_1}.a_1, \ldots, X_{i_k}.a_k) \in R(p)$.
2. $c(\nu_{j_1}.b_1, \ldots, \nu_{j_l}.b_l) = true$ for each $c(X_{j_1}.b_1, \ldots, X_{j_l}.b_l) \in C(p)$

Here $\nu.a$ denotes the value of attribute a of node ν. It must be $a \in A_X$ if ν corresponds to non-terminal X.

Therefore, a checker for semantic analysis must check whether all attributes of AG are computed, and whether (i) and (ii) are satisfied. This simply can be done by traversing the attributed abstract syntax tree (in any order) and perform the checks. Thus:

fun *check_semantic_analysis*$(AAST : AG) : BOOL$ **is**
    for each instance node ν_0 of $AAST$ **do**
        let X_0 be the non-terminal corresponding to ν_0;
        for $a \in A_{X_0}$ **do**
            if $\nu_0.a$ has no value **then return** *false*; **fi**
        let $\nu_1, \ldots, \nu_n$ be the children of ν_0 produced
        according to production $X_0 ::= X_1 \cdots X_n$;
        for each attribution rule $X_{i_0}.a_0 \leftarrow f(X_{i_1}.a_1, \ldots, X_{i_k}.a_k) \in R(p)$ **do**
            if $\nu_{i_0}.a_0 \neq f(\nu_{i_1}.a_{i_1}, \ldots, \nu_{i_k}.a_{i_k})$ **then return** *false*; **fi**;
        for each condition $c(X_{j_1}.b_1, \ldots, X_{j_l}.b_l) \in C(p)$ **do**
            if $c(\nu_{j_1}.b_1, \ldots, \nu_{j_l}.b_l) = $ *false* **then return** *false*; **fi**;
    od;
    return *true*;
end;

Remark 1. The checking of the attribution is much simpler than computing the attributes according to a special evaluation order. Thus, the attribute grammar AG defined by the language designer may be different from the attribute grammar AG' used for constructing the semantic analysis. While AG' has to have properties useful for generation, e. g. AG' has to be ordered, AG needs only to be well-defined.

3.3 Checking the Correctness of Scanner and Parser

Semantic analysis together with scanning and parsing implements a function from character sequences to attributed structure trees. It yields a unique AST for a particular program. After the checking of the attributed structure tree it is safe that the computed attributes are consistent with the language specification.

We ignore the attributes of the AAST. The *Unparser* implements the relation ϕ defined by the language designer. It produces a sequence of symbols, i. e. a sequence of character sequences representing the relevant units of a program. The symbols of the reference sequence have to occur in the same order in the original program. Therefore the unparser is *correct* iff $\phi(t, \mathit{unparse}(t))$ for each attributed abstract syntax tree t. The correctness of an unparser might be ensured by a checker.

The *Comparator* processes the sequence of symbols produced by the *Unparser* and compares it with the original file. Informally spoken, the comparator shifts a kind of window over the character sequence. The information about the context of this window is used to determine the actions of the *Comparator*: ignore white spaces, add white spaces, over read comments, report an error etc.

Some properties of existing programming languages require additional checking capabilities:

- Valid symbols which are prefix of other valid symbols require consideration of significant white spaces in order to check the principle of the longest match.
- Priorities of operators are usually defined informally and are not represented in the abstract syntax. Thus they have to be checked separately.
- Different notations of the same numbers have to deal with in any case since the actual values of constants are processed during compilation[2].
- Superfluous symbols, e. g.E ';' or the number of parentheses, can be ignored during the comparison.

Remark 2. This approach checks also implicit rules such as the principle of longest match and operator priorities. Both are mandatory for the correctness of the front-end. However, the checker might reject legal attributed abstract syntax trees. For example, if the unparser just includes the semantically necessary parantheses in expressions and the symbol sequence contains more paranthesis, the comparator returns *false*. In order to improve the quality, the unparser has also to produce semantically superfluous symbols. This information can be obtained from the derivation tree of the syntactic analysis. For example we could save the number of reductions performed to accept a parenthesized expression in an attribute. During the unparsing we create paranthesis according to the number saved in the tree.

With such extensions, it is possible to define correct checkers for many of the existing programming languages. Though the checkers are not complete, we can improve them using more sophisticated comparison strategies. The trick of generating a programming language instead of parsing it eliminates a lot of problems, e. g. ambiguities of the grammar or special properties of the acception mechanism (LL or LR), which make scanning and parsing quite complicated.

---

[2] In order to preserve simplicity of our checker we decided to check correctness of the transformation of numbers separately.

The *Comparator* is allowed to ignore characters which do not carry information. Which characters carry information depends on the actual programming language. Even white spaces may carry information in some special cases. This has to be considered to establish correctness. In general, one has to prove that the comparator accepts the same AST with or without this additional information. The comparator is implemented by the following algorithm:

fun $compare(\Pi : Char^*, s : Symbol^*) : BOOL$
  while $\neg empty(s) \vee \neg empty(\Pi)$ **do**
    $remove\_white\_spaces(\Pi)$;
    if $\neg match(head(s), \Pi)$ **then return** *false*; **fi**;
    if $\neg is\_delimiter(last)head(s))) \wedge \neg is\_delimiter(head(\Pi))$
    then return *false* **fi**;
    $s := tail(s)$;
  od;
  $remove\_white\_spaces(\Pi)$;
  return $empty(s) \wedge empty(\Pi)$;
end

Compare considers in turn each symbol of s. Such a symbol is compared with the first characters of Π. For this purpose, first all superfluous characters are removed from Π, e.g. white spaces, newline characters, and comments. This is implemented by the function *remove_white_spaces* which implements a finite automaton specified by the language definition. Then, the function *match* compares the symbol with the characters at the front of Π. Again, *match* implements a finite automaton defined by the language report. The function *match* removes the accepted characters from Π. Numbers may require a special treatment since different character sequences may represent the same number, e.g. leading zeroes are superfluous, leading zeroes or the plus sign in the exponent of a floating point number may be superfluous, or trailing zeroes in the mantissa of a floating point number are superfluous. *match* must take into account these properties. As a side-effect, the function *match* removes the accepted characters from Π. After each match of $head(s)$, the first character of Π must be a delimiter, provided $head(s)$ is not a delimiter, because each non-delimiter symbol be followed by a delimiter. Delimiters are specified by the language definition; characters like white spaces, newlines, paranthesis, semicolons etc. are typical delimiters. After termination of the while-loop and removing all leading superfluous characters from Π, the symbol sequence must be empty and the character sequence must be empty.

4 Example

Our example language defines simple expressions with variables, constants, addition, and multiplication. The attribute grammar *AG* in Fig. 2 describes the abstract syntax of a simple language for expressions. The attribution computes the "expression is constant" attribute ($b = 1$ or $b = 0$). Multiplication has higher precedence than addition. Addition is left-associative. The mapping ϕ specifies the concrete syntax for the example language. For simplicity, we omitted the parantheses in the specification of ϕ. Additionally, it must be specified that if a multiplication has a subtree representing an addition, the addition must be enclosed by "("... ")" and that any other expression or subexpression may have an arbitrary number of enclosing paranthesis.

$$
\begin{array}{rl}
E ::= & Ident\ \{b \leftarrow false, id \leftarrow STRING\} \\
\mid & IntConst\ \{b \leftarrow true, value \leftarrow INT\} \\
\mid & +(E_1, E_2)\ \{b \leftarrow b_1 \wedge b_2\} \\
\mid & *(E_1, E_2)\ \{b \leftarrow b_1 \wedge b_2\}
\end{array}
\qquad
\begin{array}{r}
\phi(Var) = Var.id \\
\phi(Value) = Val.value \\
\phi(+(E_1, E_2)) = \phi(E_1)\ '+'\ \phi(E_2) \\
\phi(*(E_1, E_2)) = \phi(E_1)\ '*'\ \phi(E_2)
\end{array}
$$

Fig. 2. Attribute grammar and mapping ϕ from abstract to concrete syntax

The left-hand side of Fig. 3 shows the AST representation of the expression $a * (3 + 4) + b$, the right-hand side shows the set of equations derived from the attribution of the AST. The superscript of an AST node describes the attribute values computed by the semantic analysis. The subscript is a unique number which relates the AST node with an equation on the right. The function *correctly_attributed* instantiates the equations corresponding to attribution rules of the abstract syntax with the attributes computed by the semantic analysis and then checks the consistency of the formulae. The equations in our example are consistent, cf. 3. Thus, semantic analysis worked correctly and the function *unparse*, derived from ϕ, is invoked. It traverses the AST and produces the

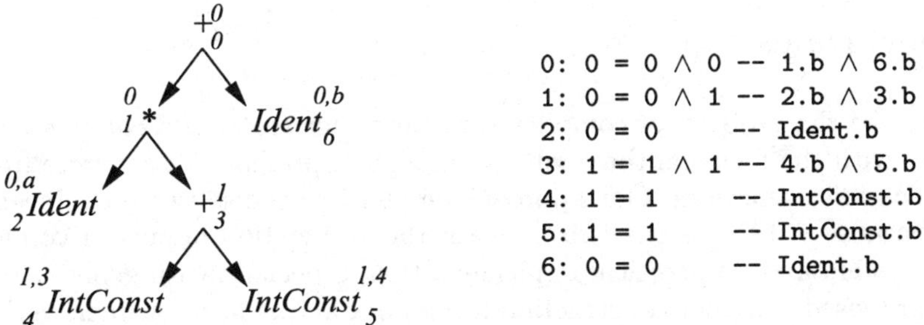

Fig. 3. AIF representation and attribute equations for $a * (3 + 4) + b$

stream "a", "*", "(", "3", "+", "4", ")", "+", "b". Since *unparse* considers operator precedences the parentheses were inserted. Thus, the original expression is produced which establishes the correctness of syntactic analysis.

We show how the checker reacts on erroneous parsers. Suppose, the parser had accidently ignored the parantheses (or the scanner removed accidently the tokens), i.e the syntax tree in Fig. 4(a) would be produced by the erroneous parser. The unparser produces the stream "a", "*", "3", "+", "4", "+", "b". In contrast to the above example, parantheses are not included because of the priorities. The comparator recognizes that this stream differs from the input text.

Assume now, the parser accidently exchanged priorities of "*" and "+". Then, it produces the syntax tree in Fig. 4(b). The unparser produces the stream "a", "*", "(", "3", "+", "4", "+", "b", ")" which also differs from the source text.

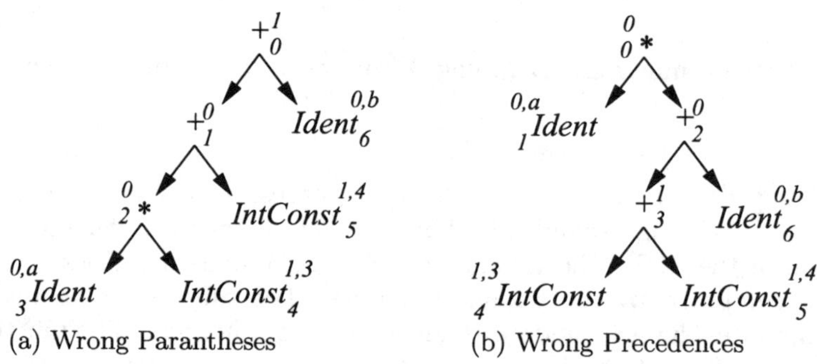

(a) Wrong Parantheses
(b) Wrong Precedences

Fig. 4. Erroneous Syntax Trees

5 Conclusions

We addressed the problem of compiler verification for real-world compilers and languages with the focus on the analysis phase, and presented a concrete front-end verification framework. Our approach emphasizes the software engineering aspect, because it bridges the gap between the verification of such a complex software system and its practical implementation, especially with generators.

The proposed compiler construction framework allows to implement verified front-ends down to correct machine implementation. The main idea is to assure correctness of the implementation by introducing runtime program-checkers that check the result of syntactic and semantic analysis. The result of such a 'checked' analysis-phase is an attributed abstract syntax tree, that carries all the information needed for the transformation phase. We want to stress here again, that this checking is independent of the interleaving of semantic and syntactic analysis. Even if the syntactical structure is determined only after the semantic analysis, the checking can be performed independently. Measurements in our case-study

	C/Sather-K		Binary Prog.
	Lines	Byte	Byte
Generators COCKTAIL	110.000	2.4 MB	1.2 MB
Generated C Code Impl. IS-Front-End	22.000	600 KB	300 KB
Checker (Sather-K)	500 (Parser) +100 (Compare) +700 (AST)	14 KB 3 KB 30 KB	200 KB

The first line shows the amount of C code of the compiler toolbox COCKTAIL used to generate the unverified front-end. This includes the involved generators for scanner, parser and abstract tree construction. The second line shows the same information for the herewith generated front-end (C code) in lines and bytes, and the size of the compiled program. To obtain a verified implementation without checking one would have to verify the generated C code or the generators. The 'Checker' line shows the amount of code (Sather-K) needed to construct the fully functional program checker.

Table 1. Case study: Lines of program code to verify for a program-checked front-end

(see table 1) show the practicability of our approach. The number of lines to verify is decreased by a factor of 80 compared to the generator source and 1:17 compared to generated C code. In our case-study we compile a C-subset language *IS* [4,13] to DEC-alpha machine code.

Though we did not discuss the correctness of the transformation and code generation phase, this is part of our work in the *Verifix* project. *Verifix* is a large scale case study in program verification with the major goal to verify not only specification and high level implementation of compilers, but also to guarantee the correctness of their final binary executables on hardware, cf. [7]. State of the art compiler construction uses complex and high sophisticated algorithms in order to achieve efficient code. Assuring correctness by checking their results enables us to use these algorithms in our verified compiler implementation and even to generate them with available unverified compiler generators [5].

Acknowledgements This work is supported by the *Deutsche Forschungsgemeinschaft* project Go 323/3-1 *Verifix* (Construction of Correct Compilers). We are grateful to our colleagues in *Verifix*.

References

1. E. Börger and I. Durdanovic. Correctness of Compiling Occam to Transputer code. *The Computer Journal*, 39:52–93, 1996.

2. Manuel Blum and Sampath Kannan. Designing programs that check their work. *Journal of the Association for Computing Machinery*, 42(1):269–291, January 1995.
3. D. F. Brown, H. Moura, and D. A. Watt. Actress: an action semantics directed compiler generator. In *Compiler Compilers 92*, volume 641 of *LNCS*, 1992.
4. A. Dold, T. Gaul, W. Goerigk, G. Goos, A. Heberle, F. von Henke, U. Hoffmann, H. Langmaack, H. Pfeifer, H. Ruess, and W. Zimmermann. Definition of the Language IS. Verifix Working Paper [Verifix/UKA/1], University of Karlsruhe/Kiel/Ulm, 1995.
5. A. Dold, T. Gaul, V. Vialard, and W. Zimmermann. ASM-Based Mechanized Verification of Compiler Backends. In Uwe Glässer and Peter H. Schmitt, editors, *Proceedings of the 5th International Workshop on Abstract State Machines*, pages 50–67, 1998.
6. Stephan Diehl. *Semantics-Directed Generation of Compilers and Abstract Machines.* PhD thesis, University of the Saarland, Germany, 1996.
7. W. Goerigk, A. Dold, T. Gaul, G. Goos, A. Heberle, F. von Henke, U. Hoffmann, H. Langmaack, H. Pfeifer, H. Ruess, and W. Zimmermann. Compiler Correctness and Implementation Verification: The Verifix Approach. In P. Fritzson, editor, *Proceedings of the Poster Session of CC'96 - International Conference on Compiler Construction*, pages 65 – 73. ida, 1996. TR-Nr.: R-96-12.
8. J. Grosch and H. Emmelmann. A tool box for compiler construction. In *Compiler Compilers, Third International Workshop, CC'90; Schwerin, FRG; Proceedings*, volume 477 of *LNCS*. Springer-Verlag, 1990.
9. J.B. Goodenough and S.L. Gerhart. Toward a Theory of Test Data Selection. *SIGPLAN Notices*, 10(6):493–510, June 1975.
10. W. Goerigk, T.S. Gaul, and W. Zimmermann. Correct Programs without Proof? On Checker-Based Program Verification. In *Proceedings ATOOLS'98 Workshop on "Tool Support for System Specification, Development, and Verification"*, Advances in Computing Science, Malente, 1998. Springer Verlag.
11. Gerhard Goos. Sather-K — The Language. *Software — Concepts and Tools*, 18:91–109, 1997.
12. A. Heberle and T. Gaul. Syntax einer Sprache zur textuellen Repräsentation von Graphen. Interner Bericht, 1998.
13. Andreas Heberle and Dirk Heuzeroth. The formal specification of IS. Technical Report [Verifix/UKA/2 revised], IPD, Universität Karlsruhe, January 1998.
14. G. C. Necula and P. Lee. The design and implementation of a certifying compiler. In *Proceedings of the 1998 ACM SIGPLAN Conference on Programming Language Design and Implementation (PLDI)*, pages 333–344, 1998.
15. M. Pettersson. *Compiling Natural Semantics.* PhD thesis, Linkoeping University, 1995.
16. Hal Wasserman and Manuel Blum. Software reliability via run-time result-checking. *Journal of the ACM*, 44(6):826–849, November 1997.

Translating SA/RT Models to Synchronous Reactive Systems: An Approximation to Modular Verification Using the SMV Model Checker*

Claudio de la Riva, Javier Tuya, and José R. de Diego

Computer Science Department
University of Oviedo
Campus of Viesques, E-33203 Gijón (Spain)
[claudio|tuya|dediego]@lsi.uniovi.es

Abstract. Integration of non formal methods, notations and tools with formal ones is a promising way of linking scientific results to the daily work of practitioners. In this paper, we present a formal notation based in a synchronous reactive execution semantics (Synchronous Reactive System) for graphical specifications (SA/RT models). We use the Synchronous Reactive System as intermediate format to formally verify graphical specifications using the SMV model checker. We deal with the state space explosion problem using modular verification.

1 Introduction

Structured Methods [19], also known as Structured Analysis for Real-Time (SA/RT) are a widespread graphical formalism that is adequate to model Reactive System and it is supported by a high number of commercial CASE tools. But most of them lack analytical capabilities (usually limited to syntax checks such as balancing or simulation).

The original (informal) definition of the semantics as proposed by Ward and Mellor is inspired in the execution rules of Petri nets. In this paper, we will use a more up-to-date, deterministic and causal semantics, similar to the one implemented in STATEMATE [10] or RSML [12]. The essential difference with regard to Ward's approach is that more than one transition can be executed in parallel at each step.

Little work has been made in the model checking of this type of graphical specifications. In a previous work [18] we have used SA/RT methods in conjunction with SMV [15], in which the model is executed as a set of interleaved processes. In [7] and [8] Statecharts are used, but the semantics is not based on the concept of *micro* and *macro − steps* and not use modular verification. Anderson et al. [2] [3] have used SMV to verify requirements written in RSML.

* This work has been funded by the "Comisión Interministerial de Ciencia y Tecnología" (Spain) under project EDIC (TIC96-0652)

D. Bjørner, M. Broy, A. Zamulin (Eds.): PSI'99, LNCS 1755, pp. 493–502, 2000.

They perform a manual translation and verify some interesting properties (safety, transition and function consistency).

Most of the current approaches to verification of synchronous systems (see e.g. [11]) perform a first step in which a global transition graph is elaborated and verification is performed on this global graph (the same as the one that is produced by the compilation process in Esterel programs [5]). But the verification using a precompiled transition graph does not resolve the state explosion problem, because if the system is composed of different subsystems that are not tightly coupled, the total number of states increases exponentially. In such cases, it is very important to partition the model and to perform separate verifications on each part of the model (modular verification).

In the Section 2 we describe the computational model of Synchronous Reactive Systems which we use as intermediate format to compile the graphical specification. In the Section 3 we sketch the procedure of translation from Synchronous Reactive System into the language accepted by a model checker (SMV [15]), and show how we can perform the modular verification. Finally, in Section 4 some conclusions and future work are presented.

2 The Framework of Synchronous Reactive Systems

In this section, we present a brief introduction to the SA/RT models and we show the underlying computational model that we denoted *Synchronous Reactive System* (SRS).

2.1 SA/RT Methods

SA/RT is a short name for Structured Analysis methods with extensions for Real Time. Using Structured Methods we can view the model of the system as a leveled set of diagrams that include concurrent processes and the communication between them. Each process communicates with others and with the environment using data and control flows (in our model only control flows are needed and we will denote them events). Each process is decomposed into a diagram showing a more detailed view. The primitive control processes (processes which not decompose in other) are specified using State Transition Diagrams (STDs).

2.2 State Transitions Diagrams

In the SA/RT methods [19], the behaviour of a primitive control process is defined using a State Transition Diagram or STD. An STD contains all states that the process may reaches and all transitions that it may performs. In the rest of this paper, we use the term "process" and "STD" indistinctly, due to there is a mapping between a process and its STD.

Definition 1. *An STD is a 5-tuple* $< \Sigma, s_0, I, O, \delta >$ *where*

- Σ *is the set of states,*
- s_0 *is the initial state of STD,* $s_o \in \Sigma$*,*

- *I is the set of input events that the STD receives,*
- *O is the set of output events that the STD produces, $I \cap O = \oslash$,*
- *δ is the transition relation, $\delta \subseteq \Sigma \times I \times O \times \Sigma$.*

Usually, we denote the transition $\tau = (s, c, a, s') \in \delta$ using the notation $s \longrightarrow_a^c s'$, which means that STD executes the transition τ when it receives the input event c (see Remark 1), changing to state s' and producing the set of output events $a \subseteq O$. In the context of individual transitions, we will refer to the pair (c, a) like *label* of transition and we will refer to c like *condition* and a like *action*. All STD implicitly has a *control variable* or *control state* π, which denotes the local state of process (initially $\pi = s_0$). A transition $\tau = (s, c, a, s')$ is *enabled* if $(\pi = s)$ and the evaluation of c is true. The set of enabled transitions in a state s is denoted as $enabled(s)$.

Remark 1. The original syntax from Ward [19] specifies that a condition in an STD must be composed only of control flows (individual events). In order to achieve a higher expressiveness of the specification, we allow the conditions to be formed by logical expressions of events of I, values of the states of other processes and the proposition *true* (equivalent to the "blank" condition in the graphical model).

2.3 Synchronous Reactive Systems

An SRS consists of a set of STDs interacting over a set of input events and a set of output events. The events that communicate STDs we denote them *internal events* due to this events are not observable out of the SRS.

The semantics adopted to describe the behaviour of a SRS is related with the concepts of *Berry's synchronous hypothesis* [5] (the system reacts instantaneously to external events) and the semantics of Micro/Macro Step in STATEMATE [10] and RSML [12]. Basically, we can view the execution of the SRS as infinite series of $macro-steps$ that produce sequences of output events in response to input events, and internally, the execution can be viewed as a chain of $micro-steps$. At each one, the system will reacts to the input events producing output events and internal events that initiate other $micro-step$ until no more $micro-step$ can be taken.

Definition 2. *A Synchronous Reactive System (SRS) Φ is a 5-tuple $< \Delta, GE, IE, OE, \longrightarrow^{\mu} >$ where*

- *$\Delta = \{M_1, M_2, \ldots, M_n\}$ is the set of STDs that compound Φ*
- *GE is the set of internal events that communicate the STDs in Δ,*

$$GE = (\bigcup_{i=1}^{n} I_i) \cap (\bigcup_{i=1}^{n} O_i)$$

- *IE is the set of input events that Φ receives of the environment,*

$$IE = \bigcup_{i=1}^{n} I_i - GE$$

– *OE is the set of output events that Φ produces to the environment,*

$$OE = \bigcup_{i=1}^{n} O_i - GE$$

– $\longrightarrow^{\mu}$ *is the transition relation of Φ which describes the semantics outline above and we will define next.*

The initial state of Φ is formed by the set of the initial states of the STDs in Δ, $S_0 = \{s_o, s_1, \ldots, s_n\}$. An state (global state) S of Φ is composed by the control states of the STDs in Δ, $S = (\pi_1, \ldots, \pi_n)$. We denoted by $C = (S, IE, OE, GE)$ as the *configuration* of Φ. The set of all possible configurations of Φ is denoted by $Global(\Phi)$. We will describe the transition relation $\longrightarrow^{\mu} \subseteq Global(\Phi) \times Global(\Phi)$ in basis to the following inference rules (similar to [13]):

Advance Rules: Applies to an STD M_i if it has an enabled transition in a state of the current configuration. If the STD have multiples enabled transitions in the configuration, one of them is taken non-deterministically:

$$\frac{(\pi_i = s_i) \wedge (\exists \tau_i : s_i \longrightarrow_{a_i}^{c_i} s_i' \in \delta_i / \tau_i \in enabled(s_i))}{((\pi_1, \ldots, s_i, \ldots, \pi_n), IE, OE, GE) \longrightarrow^{\mu} ((\pi_1, \ldots, s_i', \ldots, \pi_n), \oslash, OE \cup A_i, A_i')} \quad (1)$$

where $A_i = \{e \in a_i / e \in OE\}$ and $A_i' = \{e \in a_i / e \in GE\}$.

If various STDs of SRS have enabled transitions, then each of them execute simultaneously:

$$\frac{\begin{array}{c}(\pi_i = s_i) \wedge (\exists \tau_i : s_i \longrightarrow_{a_i}^{c_i} s_i' \in \delta_i / \tau_i \in enabled(s_i)) \\ (\pi_j = s_j) \wedge (\exists \tau_j : s_j \longrightarrow_{a_j}^{c_j} s_j' \in \delta_j / \tau_j \in enabled(s_j))\end{array}}{\begin{array}{c}((\pi_1, \ldots, s_i, \ldots, s_j, \ldots, \pi_n), IE, OE, GE) \longrightarrow^{\mu} \\ ((\pi_1, \ldots, s_i', \ldots, s_j', \ldots, \pi_n), \oslash, OE \cup A_i \cup A_j, A_i' \cup A_j')\end{array}} \quad (2)$$

Stuttering Rule: If an STD M_i is in a state in the current configuration and it does not have any enabled transition, then it consumes events but it does not produce events. This notation is adequate to represent the concept of *reactivity* (in any state, there exists at least one transition to execute):

$$\frac{(\pi_i = s_i) \wedge (\exists \tau_i : s_i \longrightarrow_{a_i}^{c_i} s_i' \in \delta_i / \tau_i \notin enabled(s_i))}{((\pi_1, \ldots, s_i, \ldots, \pi_n), IE, OE, GE) \longrightarrow^{\mu} ((\pi_1, \ldots, s_i, \ldots, \pi_n), \oslash, OE, \oslash)} \quad (3)$$

The above rules show the execution of the SRS at level of $micro-step$. When all STDs $M_1, \ldots, M_n$ in the SRS only can to advance executing the rule 3, the SRS has reached to an *stable configuration* (no more transitions can be taken).

At level of $macro-step$, the execution of SRS can be viewed like a sequence of stable configurations, where at each one, the SRS receives input events IE and produces output events OE:

$$C = (S, IE, \oslash, \oslash) \longrightarrow^{\eta} C' = (S', \oslash, OE, \oslash) \quad (4)$$

where S and S' represent the global states of SRS before and after of the *macro–step*, C' is an stable configuration and $\longrightarrow^{\eta}$ represents a chain of *micro – steps*:

$$C \longrightarrow^{\eta} C' \equiv C \longrightarrow^{\mu} C_1 \longrightarrow^{\mu} \ldots \longrightarrow^{\mu} C_n \longrightarrow^{\mu} C' \tag{5}$$

3 Verification of SRS

The intermediate format presented in the later section is translated into the language accepted by the SMV [15] model checker. In the SMV language, we can specify the operational model and check its desired properties written in CTL Temporal Logic [6]. The execution of an SMV specification can be viewed as a sequence of steps that change the values of variables according to the transition relation of the automata represented by the SMV code. We will outline the translation procedure of the semantics ($\longrightarrow^{\eta}$ and $\longrightarrow^{\mu}$) to SMV and how we include support for performing modular verifications.

3.1 Translating SRS into SMV

The execution of each *macro – step* consists of a first step, in which the changes produced in the environment are perceived, and a sequence of *micro – steps*, until a stable configuration is reached. Since SMV executes step by step, without any difference between steps, we must differentiate the first step from the others using a special variable named `MicroStep`. The following pseudo-code reproduces the behavior of $\longrightarrow^{\eta}$:

if MicroStep = 0 **then**
  Allow changes in external inputs and set MicroStep = 1
else
  if some transition can be executed **then**
    Perform a micro-step by executing transitions
  else
    Set MicroStep = 0
  end if
end if

We use a boolean variable for each event and a variable for representing the state of process (namely, π). Changes of each variable representing an external input event $in1 \in IE$ are performed by sentences that set the event to a random value only when the value of `MicroStep` is 0. Otherwise its value will be set to 0 (external input events can influence only the first *micro – step*):

```
next(in1) := case
  MicroStep=0 : {0,1}:
  1 : 0;
esac;
```

The execution of each *micro−step* ($\longrightarrow^{\mu}$) follows a similar schema, but, since we need to know if some transitions where enabled or not in order to decide whether to continue the chain of *micro − steps* or not, we use an additional variable TP for each process, that represents the transition that will be executed. For instance, if two transitions τ_1 and τ_2 leave the state S0 towards S1 and S2, having conditions C1 and C2 respectively, we first select the transition to be executed with a direct assignment (if no transition can be executed, then TP is set to 0):

```
TP := case
  MicroStep=1 & pi=S0 & C1 : 1;
  MicroStep=1 & pi=S0 & C2 : 2;
  1 : 0;
esac;
```

The SMV case sentence is deterministic: it selects the first row that has the condition true. If we want the selection to be non-deterministic, we can do as shown in [18].

Output events and next states are set according to the value of this variable. For instance, if event $out1 \in OE$ is sent as a consequence of the execution of transition τ_1 and also as a consequence of another transition τ_3, the next value for out1 will be:

```
next(out1) := case
  TP=1 | TP=3 : 1;
  1 : 0;
esac;
```

The last term sets the value to zero for the same reason as in external input events.

The next state (assuming that variable pi holds its value) will be coded as:

```
next(pi) := case
  TP = 1 : S1;
  TP = 2 : S2;
  1 : pi;
esac;
```

The chain of *micro − steps* finishes when no transition can be executed. For instance, if we have two processes in the SRS, each one having its own variable (TP1 and TP2) which indicates the transition executed, we will have:

```
next(MicroStep) := case
  MicroStep=0 : 1;   -- environment has changed
  TP1=0 & TP2=0 : 0;   -- end of macro-step
  1 : MicroStep;
esac;
```

3.2 Approach for Modular Verification

Due to the state explosion problem, when the size of the system grows, it is desirable to be able to perform local verifications in separate components and deduce some global property for the whole model. This procedure can be called Modular Verification and is based on the Abadi and Lamport composition theorem [1], also known as rely-guarantee or assumption-commitment rules. If a model Φ can be decomposed into the parallel composition of two (or more) components (SRSs) $[\Phi_1||\Phi_2]$, we can perform the verification of local properties (ϕ_1, ϕ_2) for each component (Φ_1 or Φ_2, respectively) assuming some kind of behavior for the other (abstracted) component. For instance, we can prove that ϕ_2 is true for the component Φ_2 assuming certain behavior ϕ_{E1} of the abstracted model Φ_1, and symmetrically for Φ_1. If we also prove that ϕ_{E1} is true for Φ_1 (discharge the assumption) and its symmetric (ϕ_{E2} is true on Φ_2), then property $\phi_1 \wedge \phi_2$ will be true for the whole model Φ provided that assumptions are safety properties [1].

When we divide the model into different SRSs (each one groups several processes in the SA/RT model), internal events that communicate them must be treated differently to the others. We name these *Ghost Events* and at each $micro-step$ we set their values to random ones. A safety property which is true in the component will also be true in the whole model (the converse is not true, since this simplification introduces additional computations that may not be present in the whole model).

When including ghost events, the termination of each $macro-step$ (determined by the portion of code that gives a value to the variable `MicroStep`) must be modified to take into account the fact that if at some step no transition is enabled, the abstracted model may still be executing a transition that will send a ghost event at the next $micro-step$. The end of the $macro-step$ must include additional conditions to avoid finishing when the next value of some ghost event has been sent. For instance, assuming that we have two variables (`g1` and `g2`) representing ghost events, the above fragment will be:

```
next(MicroStep) := case
  0 : 1;  -- environment has changed
  next(g1)=0 & next(g2)=0
    & TP1=0 & TP2=0 : 0;  -- end of macro-step
  1 : MicroStep;
esac;
```

When we wish to specify some kind of assumption, we use a set of simple rules coded as sentences like: $ASSUME(cond, g, v)$, which states that if condition *cond* is true, then variable g must have the value v. Assumptions are included in the portion of code that sets a value to the ghost event as shown below (recall that the `case` sentence selects the first condition that is true):

```
next(g) := case
  MicroStep=1 & cond : v;
```

```
    -- other assumptions ...
    MicroStep=1 : {0,1};  -- possible change
    1 : 0;
  esac;
```

3.3 Specification of Properties

System properties must be checked at the end of each *macro – step*. It suffices to transform a formula $AG(\phi)$, where ϕ is another CTL formula or proposition, into

$$AG(MicroStep = 0 \rightarrow \phi)$$

Due to a high number of properties of interest being input/output responses, which relate input with output events, and the values of input events are maintained only at the first *micro–step*, we also provide a predicate $WAS0(f)$ which is true if f was true at some *micro – step* of the current *macro – step*. Using an additional variable for each one, the translation is straightforward.

When we discharge an assumption (commitment) in the form $ASSUME(cond, g, v)$, we use a CTL formula that is checked at each *micro–step* like:

$$AG(MicroStep = 1 \rightarrow (cond \rightarrow g = v))$$

An essential property of this type of model is the absence of a kind of livelock situation in which the system is executing an infinite chain of *micro–steps* (step termination). This situation is checked with the following CTL formula:

$$AG(MicroStep = 1 \rightarrow AF(MicroStep = 0))$$

When we try to prove this property in a component that has some ghost events as input, an important risk is that of falling into false infinite loops caused by an infinite sequence of these events. In that case, a common assumption is to prevent a ghost event from appearing more than once (or more) in a *macro–step*: it suffices to use assumptions like $ASSUME(WAS0(g), g, 0)$.

4 Conclusions

The approach taken for modular verification of synchronous reactive system allows mitigate the effects of the state explosion. Although a compilation of the synchronous model previous to its model checking (as in [11]) is more efficient due to the elimination of all *micro – steps* and so, its corresponding states), the explicit representation of all *micro – steps* allows us to state the adequate assumptions and prove them without any distortion of the semantics of the whole model. The assumptions used are composed by a number of simple rules whose translation into code is straightforward. Nevertheless, they must be obtained manually, which can be a difficult task if the interface is complex. So, our present work is addressed to attaining these constraints in a more automatic way.

We think that the use of modular verification might be essential when the model is composed of relatively independent devices. The result in [16] and [9] confirm our idea that it is possible to (nearly) interactively perform verifications of interesting properties of a system as we describe in [17], thus making model checking a powerful tool for detecting bugs and for debugging the specification.

References

[1] Martin Abadi and Leslie Lamport. Conjoining specifications. *ACM Transactions on Programming Languages and Systems*, 17(3):507-534, 1995.

[2] Richard J. Anderson, Paul Beame, Steve Burns, William Chan, Francesmary Modugno, David Notkin and Jon D. Reese. Model checking large software specifications. In *Proceedings of the 4th ACM SIGSOFT Symposium on the Foundation of Software Engineering*, pages 156–166, 1996.

[3] Richard J. Anderson, Paul Beame, William Chan and David Notkin. Experiences with Application of Symbolic Model Checking to the Analysis of Software Specifications. In *Proceedings of the Third International Conference Perspectives of System Informatics (PSI'99)*, pages 355–361, Akademgorodok, Novosibirsk, Russia, 1999.

[4] Albert Benveniste and Gérard Berry. The synchronous approach to reactive and real-time systems. *Proceedings of the IEEE*, 79(9):1270–1282, 1991.

[5] Gérard Berry and Georges Gonthier. The esterel synchronous programming language: Design, semantics, implementation. *Science of Computer Programming*, 19(2):83–152, 1992.

[6] Edmund C. Clarke, E. Emerson and A. Sistla. Automatic verification of finite-state concurrent systems using temporal logic specifications. *ACM Transactions on Programming Languages and Systems*, 8(2):244–63, 1986.

[7] Werner Damm, Hardi Hungar, Peter Kelb and Rainer Schlör. Using graphical specifiction languages and symbolic model checking in the verification of a production cell. In Lewerentz and Lindner [14], pages 89–107.

[8] N. Day. A model checker for Statecharts (linking CASE tools with formal methods). Master's thesis, University of British Columbia, Dept. of Computer Science, 1993. also published as Tech. Report 93-35.

[9] Jose R. de Diego, Claudio de la Riva and Javier Tuya. Analisis empirico de SMV en la verificacion de Sistemas Reactivos. In *Jornadas Iberoamericanas de Ingenieria de Requisitos y Ambientes Software (IDEAS'98)* pp. 145-156. 1998

[10] David Harel and Amnon Naamad. The STATEMATE semantics of Statecharts. *ACM Transactions on Software Engineering and Methodology*, 5(4):293–333, 1996.

[11] Lalita J. Jagadeesan, Carlos Puchol and James E. Von Olnhausen. A formal approach to reactive systems software: A telecommunications application in ESTEREL. In *Proceedings of the Workshop on Industrial-Strength Formal Specification Techniques*, 1995.

[12] Nancy G. Leveson, Mats P. E. Heimdahl, Holly Hildreth and Jon D. Reese. Requirements specification for process control systems. *IEEE Transactions on Software Engineering*, 20(9):684–707, 1994.

[13] Erich Mikk, Yassine Lakhnech and Michael Siegel. Hierarchical automata as model of statecharts. In *Asian Computing Science Conference (ASIAN'97)* volume 1345 of *Lecture Notes in Computer Science*. Springer-Verlag. 1987.

[14] Claus Lewerentz and Thomas Lindner, editors. *Case Study "Production Cell"*, volume 1/94. Forschungszentrum Informatik, Karlsruhe University, 1994.

[15] Kenneth L. McMillan. *Symbolic Model Checking.* Kluwer Academic Publishers, 1993.

[16] Javier Tuya, José R. de Diego, Claudio de la Riva and José A. Corrales. Dynamic analysis of SA/RT models using SPIN and modular verification. In J. C. Grégoire, G. J. Holzmann, and D. A. Peled, editors, *The Spin Verification System*, volume 32 of *DIMACS*, pages 165–183. American Mathematical Society, 1997.

[17] Javier Tuya, Claudio de la Riva, José R. de Diego and José A. Corrales. CASE support for modular verification of syncronous reactive systems. In S. Gnesi and D. Latella, editors, *2nd International Workshop on Formal Methods for Industrial Critical Systems*, pages 125–137, Cesena, Italy, 1997.

[18] Javier Tuya, Luciano Sánchez and J. A. Corrales. Using a symbolic model checker for verify safety properties in SA/RT models. In *5th European Software Engineering Conference*, volume 989 of *Lecture Notes in Computer Science*, pages 59–75. Springer Verlag, 1995.

[19] Paul T. Ward. The transformation schema: An extension of the data flow diagram to represent control and timing. *IEEE Transactions on Software Engineering*, 12(2):198–210, 1986.

Multi-agent Optimal Path Planning for Mobile Robots in Environment with Obstacles

Fedor A. Kolushev and Alexander A. Bogdanov

St. Petersburg Institute for Informatics and Automation of Russian Academy of Science, St. Petersburg, Russia,
glot@mail.convey.ru, alexb@homepage.ru

Abstract. The paper describes a problem of multi-agent path planning in environment with obstacles. Novel approach to multi-agent optimal path planning, using graph representation of environment models is described. When planning the path of each robot, the graph model of environment is dynamically changed for path correction and collision avoidance. New algorithm applies changes of robots' paths and speeds to avoid collisions in multi-agent environment.

1 Introduction

Problems of multi-agent robot systems control have got significant importance. Each multi-agent robot system has some transport subsystem, which consists of several mobile robots. The problem of controlling such mobile robot group can be divided into two main parts:

- Optimal global (general) task decomposition into subtasks, and their optimal distribution between separate robots in the group.
- Path planning, control and movement correction for each mobile robot.

New approach to path planning and motion programming for mobile robots is proposed. The method is based on graph optimization algorithms. Novelty of the developed multi-agent path planning algorithm is as follows:

- All mobile robots are considered as dynamic obstacles.
- Graph representation of common environment models is used for path planning.
- Each edge of the graph has two weights: distance and motion time (speed).
- Weights of edges can be modified during path planning.
- The quickest path is planned (time optimization).
- Expert rules for speed and path correction are synthesized to provide collision avoidance.

The algorithm is formulated in terms of the optimal find-path problem on a graph, where the graph edges are labelled with some values. It is usually possible to transform common environment models (e.g. vector or grid model) to the corresponding graph representation. Thus, the algorithm can be applied, for example, on visibility graphs and grid environment models.

D. Bjørner, M. Broy, A. Zamulin (Eds.): PSI'99, LNCS 1755, pp. 503–510, 2000.

2 Background

The problem of path planning for various types of mobile robots was widely investigated by many researchers [5,8,9,10,11], but almost all of them consider the problem of path planning for a single mobile robot. The problem of path planning for a group of mobile robots was investigated in [10,11], but the proposed algorithms did not provide path optimality in any sense. In [6] there was introduced an approach to control a group of mobile robots by means of the global task decomposition into several subtasks, with non-intersected paths of the robots. This is not possible for many practical tasks, like manufacturing, traffic control, etc. Therefore, a problem of adaptation of known optimal path planning algorithms for multi-agent robot systems exists [1,2].

Planning mobile robot motions in a multi-agent robot system has a number of peculiarities and some additional difficulties. They are related to necessity of taking into account not only possible obstacles (including unknown ones) in a working space, but also movement of other robots, while planning the path of each agent-robot. It seems logical to divide the problem of path planning and control of mobile robots-agents in a working zone into two subproblems.

- Path planning and optimization for each agent-robot individually, taking into account other robots movement. This problem can be solved by modifying algorithms of path planning and optimization in an environment with obstacles. At this stage, full knowledge of the environment is supposed (i.e. the environment does not contain unknown obstacles).
- Unforeseen collisions avoidance and the planned paths correction in case, when information about the environment is incomplete, or robot paths deviate from the planned ones. There are two basic alternatives to solve this problem. First is to correct the paths by means of various path local correction algorithms. Shortage of this approach is non-optimal agent-robot motions. The second method is complete or local-optimal path re-planning, when new obstacles discovered or collisions occurred.

It should be mentioned, that cooperation between individual agent-robots is necessary to solve the path planning and optimization problem. Each agent-robot has to share information about its planned path and actual motions with other agent-robots. Maintaining the planned paths database and motion coordination could be performed by the special agent-supervisor. The agent-supervisor maintains information about environment and each agent-robot motions. Information about environment is collected by agent-robots, equipped with sensors. The path planning system of each agent-robot can use information from the agent-supervisor. In some cases the agent-supervisor plans paths for all the agents-robots and transmits the planned paths to them.

Solution of the second problem would be more reasonable to be assigned to local control systems of agents-robots, thus the accident-free realization of the robots tasks is ensured even in case of malfunctioning communication of the agents. To solve this problem, an agent-robot should have its own sensor system, which must be able to provide distinguishing static obstacles and moving robots.

Besides, sensor systems of robots can be applied to correction of the environment model for more accurate path planning.

3 Environment Models

There are a lot of widely known environment models, for example, grid (occupancy cell), vector (obstacles are represented by polygons), graph (visibility graph, Voronoi diagram, etc.) [3] and their modifications. Special types of environment model, for example, analytic-predicate, semantic, etc., exist as well [1,12].

Each environment model has certain advantages and disadvantages for path planning purposes, for instance:

Grid model is simple to be used, corrected and updated with data, gathered by different robots. But it requires high memory expenses, it also has high data redundancy and lack of accuracy. Some of these drawbacks can be eliminated by using more comprehensive grid model [8].

Vector models feature high precision, low memory expenses, but it is difficult to plan a path, using this type of models, it is also difficult to update the environment model with data from robots' sensor systems, since sensor information is usually presented in discrete form and, hence, needs to be transformed into the vector form.

Graph models are more suitable for path and motion planning problems. As a rule, graph model only consists of possible paths, i.e. information about obstacles is excluded during the graph constructing. Grid and Vector models can be mapped onto the graph model. There are known various algorithms for solving optimization problem on the graph, for example, Dijkstra algorithm, A*, D*–algorithm [5], etc. The possible paths in vector environment model can be represented by a visibility graph. The visibility graph is a graph, which nodes represent vertices of polygonal obstacles, and its edges represent straight possible paths, connecting the obstacle vertices, i.e. lines of "visibility". Once the static graph is constructed, target and starting points are added and the visible edges, connecting them with other graph nodes, are computed. To plan paths, graph model will be further used. Graph of possible paths can be obtained from both vector and grid environment models. Moreover, graph of admissible paths can be constructed on the base of agent-robots' experience of motion. Information about agent-robots' motions can be stored separately, or in the graph nodes.

In summary, the advantages of using a visibility graph, or graph of possible paths for motion-planning are in fact that it is a simple, well-understood method which yields optimal paths in 2D, or 3D configuration space.

4 Graph Environment Model

The graph environment model used for multi-agent optimal path planning is described below. Points (places) in the environment and admissible (possible) paths between them are represented by the graph, nodes of which represent certain places in the environment and edges represent admissible paths. Each edge of the graph has a weight, that is adequate to path length, travel time, or difficulty of traveling, etc. between corresponding nodes. Note that the graph by creation only consists of admissible paths.

Let us consider a graph $G\langle V, E\rangle$ with M nodes. All nodes are numbered. Each node i has $M_i \geq 1$ adjacent nodes (vertices) $i_1, i_2, \ldots, i_{M_i}$. Besides, all graph nodes are characterized with a weight W_i. Weight W_i of a node i ($i = 1, 2, \ldots, M$) corresponds to the value of minimized functional (for example, distance, or motion time). To each edge of the graph, connecting nodes i and j, there are assigned two characteristics: S_{ij} — distance in space between these two nodes and l_{ij} — motion time, depending also on motion speed. In summary, any such graph possesses the properties, as follows:

Each Node of graph is characterized by:

1. Coordinates of a point in the environment space.
2. Value W_i of functional to be minimized (distance, time, etc.).
3. Set of adjacent nodes $i_1, i_2, \ldots, i_{M_i}$.
4. Additional characteristics needed for multi-agent path planning, such as set of agent-robots, moving through the node, and the corresponding set of time moments.

Each Edge of graph is characterized by:

1. Distance S_{ij} between nodes i and j.
2. Weight of the edge l_{ij} corresponds to time of motion from node i to j. This value is variable and may be changed while planning the path.
3. Additional characteristics. For example, the edge may have two different weights l_{ij} and l_{ji}, that depend on direction of motion between i and j. It allows to simulate 3-D environment or bi-directional roads.

5 Multi-agent Path Planning Algorithm

Let us introduce some definitions: the shortest path is a path of minimal length, the quickest path is a path of minimum motion time.

Let there is required to find a node sequence, which denotes the shortest path from the start point to the target point. Before the path planning, all weights l_{ij} of the graph edges have to be initialized as follows:

$$l_{ij} = \frac{S_{ij}}{V}, \tag{1}$$

where V is an average speed of the agent-robot. This is done, assuming that robots move along the paths with some average (economy) speed, and to take into account possibility of braking and acceleration as well.

The weights of the graph nodes must be initialized with a maximum possible value ∞. The start node must be initialized by the start time value $W_0 = t_0$. According to known edge weights, and using one of optimization algorithms, for example Dijkstra's algorithm, the shortest path is found then. During path planning, weights of nodes change and get equal to the moments of time, at which the agent-robot passes through these nodes. Note, that in fact, taking into account the above described initialization method, the algorithm finds the quickest path, but in case of one path planning, the shortest and the quickest paths are the same.

When planning paths of several robots, let us consider the path of each robot not only in environment Cartesian space (as it was done for a single robot path planning). Let us plan the path in the time-space continuum in order to take into account other robots movement. Such approach allows to avoid collision of separate agent-robots, simultaneously moving in the time-space continuum. Hence, paths are planned not in 2D planar environment, but in 3D time-space environment, taking into account movement of all other agents-robots. Let us note here, that if one-agent path planning is performed in 3D Cartesian environment, the multi-agent path planning is performed in 4D space — with concern of time (schedule of robots movement). The described below algorithm uses this approach and plans agents-robots paths sequentially (path by path), and when planning the next robot path, all already planned paths are taken into account to eliminate collisions.

According to the described approach, the main differences of the developed multi-agent optimal path planning algorithm from the one-agent one are as follows:

- to each graph node i $(i = 1, 2, \ldots, M)$ there is assigned not only its weight W_i, but the node additionally stores two sets: moments of time, when other agents-robots move through this node i (let t_{ji} is a time when robot j passes through node i), and IDs of these agents-robots as well.
- The graph (in particular, weights of the edges) can be changed, when planning a path of each robot to avoid collisions.

For multi-agent path planning the one-agent path planning algorithm must be supplied with a number of expert rules, which provide collision-free planning. Collision avoidance is performed by means of the graph correction — changing edge weights. This results either in path correction (a robot is forbidden to move on the edge, occupied by another robot), or change of robot's speed (robot is forced to move faster, or slower on some edges in order to free up the way for others, the paths of which are planned earlier and, hence, already known). Besides, if D*–algorithm is used as a basic path optimization algorithm, the distance between two nodes can be changed. Changing the distance corresponds to environment model correction.

Initialization of graph node weights W_i $(i = 1, 2, \ldots, M)$ is the same as in the one-agent path planning algorithm, and it is performed before each robot path planning. When planning a path for any robot, graph node weights are changed just as in the one-agent path planning algorithm:

$$W_{i_j} = \begin{cases} W_i + l_{ii_j}, if(W_i + l_{ii_j}) < W_{i_j} \\ W_{i_j}, if(W_i + l_{ii_j}) \geq W_{i_j} \end{cases} \tag{2}$$

The only difference is that this rule is supplied with expert rules of avoiding collisions in the graph nodes, which correspond to crossroads, and expert rules of avoiding collisions on the graph edges, which correspond to the straight roads (we assume one-way simultaneous movement, i.e. no two robots can move simultaneously on the same graph edge in different directions).

5.1 The Expert Rules

1. Avoiding collisions in the graph nodes (crossroads)
if $W_i + l_{ii_j} = t_{ki_j}$, $(k = 1, 2, \ldots, n)$, where n is a number of robots,
then $l_{ii_j} = l_{ii_j} + \varepsilon$, where ε is a value, that defines minimum time interval between different robots passing the same crossroads. This value must provide safe crossroads passage. Hence, it depends on robot sizes and speeds. Weight W_{i_j} of node i_j is computed then according to formulae (2). This means the increase of time of the robot motion on the graph edge from node i to i_j by ε time units, and corresponds to the robot speed change. The speed is piece-wise constant on the path, and is computed for each edge, connecting nodes i and j as

$$V_{ij} = \frac{S_{ij}}{l_{ij}} \ . \tag{3}$$

2. Avoiding collisions on the graph edges (straight roads)
if $(W_i < t_{ki}) \wedge [(W_i + l_{ii_j}) < t_{ki_j}]$, $(k = 1, 2, \ldots, n)$, **then**
if $t_{ki} > t_{ki_j}$, **then** this is a case, when two robots will move in opposite directions, and the robot, which path is being planned, will pass through the edge before robot k. No collision happens, hence, change of the edge weight is not necessary. The weight of the next node W_{i_j} is computed as (2).
else if $(t_{ki} < t_{ki_j}) \wedge \left[t_{ki} \le \frac{W_i(t_{ki_j} - t_{ki}) - t_{ki} \cdot l_{ii_j}}{t_{ki_j} - t_{ki} - l_{ii_j}} \le t_{ki_j}\right]$, **then** collision is possible: robot k will follow the robot, which path is being planned, and hit it on the edge. To avoid collision, it is necessary to change the edge weight for the current robot (i.e. to change the motion time by increasing speed):

$$l_{ii_j} = \frac{(W_i - t_{ki_j} - \varepsilon)(t_{ki_j} - t_{ki})}{t_{ki} - t_{ki_j} - \varepsilon} \ , \tag{4}$$

Then the node weight W_{i_j} is computed according to (2).
else robot k will follow the robot, which path is being planned, but its speed is insufficient to hit the currently computed robot on the edge. Then the edge weight is not to be changed, and the node weight W_{i_j} is computed as (2)
if $(W_i > t_{ki}) \wedge [(W_i + l_{ii_j}) > t_{ki_j}]$, $(k = 1, 2, \ldots, n)$, **then**
if $t_{ki} > t_{ki_j}$, **then** this is a case, when two robots move in opposite directions, and robot k will pass through the edge earlier, than the robot, path of which is being planned, drives onto the edge. There is no need in this case to change the edge weight, since no collision is to occur. Then the node weight W_{i_j} is computed as (2).

else if $(t_{ki} < t_{ki_j}) \wedge \left[t_{ki} \leq \frac{W_i(t_{ki_j}-t_{ki})-t_{ki}\cdot l_{ii_j}}{t_{ki_j}-t_{ki}-l_{ii_j}} \leq t_{ki_j}\right]$, **then** collision is to happen: the robot, which path is being planned, will follow robot k on the edge, and hit it due to high speed. To avoid the collision, it is necessary to decrease speed of the robot, which is being computed, i.e. to increase its time of motion on this edge according to (4), then the node weight is determined as (2).

else the robot, which path is being planned has insufficient speed to catch and hit robot k before the crossroads. The node weight W_{i_j} then is computed as (2).

if $(W_i < t_{ki}) \wedge [(W_i + l_{ii_j}) > t_{ki_j}]$, $(k = 1, 2, \ldots, n)$, **then**

if $t_{ki} < t_{ki_j}$, **then** collision is possible: robot k will follow and hit the robot, which path is being planned, before the crossroads. To avoid the collision, the speed of the current robot obviously should be increased. For this to be achieved, the edge weight is to be changed according to (4), then the node weight is computed as (2).

else if $t_{ki} > t_{ki_j}$, **then** collision can not be avoided: robot k will have been moving on the edge in the opposite direction, when the robot, which path is being planned, drives onto the edge. To avoid collision, the motion through the edge from node i to node i_j must be forbidden for the current robot. To reach this goal, let us change the weight of the edge as follows:

$$l_{ii_j} = \infty \ . \tag{5}$$

Then the node weight W_{i_j} is computed according to (2). Let us note, that at further path constructing this edge will not be included into the path due to its infinite weight. Therefore this type of collisions is also avoided.

if $(W_i > t_{ki}) \wedge [(W_i + l_{ii_j}) < t_{ki_j}]$, $(k = 1, 2, \ldots, n)$, **then** $t_{ki} < t_{ki_j}$ and the collision is possible (it is the only possible case, since $l_{ii_j} \geq 0$): the robot, which path is being planned, will follow and hit robot k before the crossroads. To avoid the collision, it is necessary to change the edge weight according to (4), and then the node weight is computed as (2).

6 Summary

Using graph of possible paths makes developed algorithms of robot path planning abstract to environment model, thus improving their application capacity.

These algorithms provide global optimality while path planning according to various given optimum criteria: least motion time, least path length, etc.

Multi-agent path planning algorithm also provides robots collision avoidance. That algorithm automatically plans safe robot paths, which do not intersect each other in time-space continuum. Simulation results approve effectiveness of synthesized algorithms.

Finally, let us note that the described multi-agent algorithm implies sequential path planning for each of robots (path by path), and when planning the next robot path, all already planned paths are taken into account to eliminate collisions. Therefore, path of the first robot in the sequence is planned with the one-agent algorithm, path of the second robot is planned with concern of the first robot's path, when planning path of the third robot, paths of first two are taken into account, etc. And the described algorithm provides optimality of all planned paths. It means, that currently planned path is optimal of all possible at this stage. However, the paths (and, hence, their lengths and motion times) depend on the order of planning, i.e. there is a question, which robot path should be planned first, which is to be second, etc. This problem is not significant, if relation of possible paths quantity on the graph to the number of robots is big enough. But if the described expert rules correct the graph (edge weights) too frequently while path planning, then the choice of the right sequence of robots for path planning may have significant influence on the general robot team performance. This problem is still open, and it is a question of a separate research to investigate it.

References

1. Bogdanov, A. A., Kolushev, F. A., Optimal Path Planning and Adaptive Neural Control of Robots. Proc. of Int. Conf. on Informatics and Control, St.-Petersburg, June 9-13, 1997, pp. 600-605.
2. Kolushev, F. A., Bogdanov, A. A., Timofeev, A.V., Path Planning and Correction of Mobile Robots Motions in Multi-Agent Robotics Systems. Int. Scientific Issue "Intelligent Autonomous Systems", Ufa State Aviation Technical Univ, 1998, pp.132-139
3. Maron O., Lozano-Perez T., Visible Decomposition: Real-Time Path Planning in Large Planar Environments. AI Memo 1638, January 1996
4. Stenz A., Map-Based strategies for Robot Navigation in Unknown Environments Proc. AAAI 96 Planning with incomplete information for Robot Problems.
5. Stenz A., The focussed D* algorithm for real-time replanning. Proceedings of the International Joint Conference on Artificial Intelligence, August 1995.
6. Brummit, B. L., Stenz, A., Dinamic Mission Planning for Multiplay Mobile Robots, Proc. IEEE International Conference on Robotics and Automation, May, 1996
7. Saffiotti A., Ruspini, E. H., Konolige, K., Robust Execution of Robot Plans Using Fuzzy Logic. Fuzzy Logic in Artificial Intelligence IJCAI 93, pp. 24-37
8. Yahja, A., Stenz, A., Singh, S., Brumitt, B. L., Framed-Quadtree Path Planning for Mobile Robots Operating in Sparse Environments. Proc. IEEE Conference on Robotics and Automation, May 1998.
9. Bugman, G., Denham, M. J., Taylor, J. G., Sensor and memory based path planning in the egocentric reference frame of an autonomous mobile robot. Reserch Report NRG-94-01, January, 1994.
10. Harinarayan, V. J. Lumelsky, Sensor-based motion planning for multiplerobots in an uncertain environment. IEEE International conference on intelligent robots and systems, pp 1485-1492, 1994
11. Kant, A., Zucker, S., Towards efficient planning: the path-velocity decomposition. International Journal of Robotics Research, 5: 72-89, 1986.
12. Kasinski, A., Skrzypczynski, P., Cooperative Perception and World- Model Maintenance in Mobile Navigation Tasks. DARS III, pp173-182, 1998

Approach to Understanding Weather Forecast Telegrams with Agent-Based Technique*

Irina S. Kononenko, Ivan G. Popov, and Yury A. Zagorulko

Russian Research Institute of Artificial Intelligence
and A.P. Ershov Institute of Informatics Systems
Acad. Lavrentjev pr., 6, Novosibirsk, 630090, Russia
irina@mail.nsk.ru, {popov,zagor}@iis.nsk.su

Abstract. The paper describes an experimental system for understanding short texts from a limited problem domain (weather forecast telegrams written in Russian). A semantics-oriented and text type specific approach to analysis is proposed which gives preference to lexical-semantic and topical coherence mechanisms in their relation to the domain structure. The system is implemented with both classical means for knowledge representation and processing and methods of object-oriented and agent-based technique.

1 Introduction

The paper describes an experimental system for understanding real short texts from a limited problem domain, cf. previous work in [1,2]. The goal of the analysis is to explicate the informational content of the input text by a semantic network (tree), which is used as a basic knowledge representation language suitable for further transforming to represent information in any other terms. The choice of formal means and the underlying linguistic approach are based upon the following principles: a) the understanding system is both the domain and genre (text type) specific; b) the analysis procedure is semantics-oriented; c) information of different linguistic levels (lexical, syntactic, semantic, pragmatic) is processed simultaneously due to the object-oriented paradigm using class hierarchy with multiple inheritance; d) special means to represent linguistic indeterminate units are utilized; e) the declarative descriptions with a system of agents provide a local bottom-up parsing procedure.

The presented experimental system is implemented with the help of the software environment SemP-A that is an advanced version of SemP-TAO system [3]. SemP-A is based on an integrated knowledge representation model which combines both classical means for knowledge representation and processing (such as frames, semantic networks with binary relations etc.) and methods of object-oriented and constraint programming. Important features of the environment are the ability to operate with objects, that can have attributes with imprecisely

* This work is supported by Russian Foundation for Basic Research (grant N 99-01-00495)

D. Bjørner, M. Broy, A. Zamulin (Eds.): PSI'99, LNCS 1755, pp. 511–516, 2000.

defined values, and the utilization of the agent-based technique as a main means for definition of logical inference and data processing.

Each agent reacts only to related events (e.g. appearance of new objects of certain class or changing values of their attributes or setting new relations between objects). Actuation of the agent can lead to creating new objects or changing state of the existing ones. This, in turn, causes activation of other agents associated with the new or modified objects and so on. Unlike the production systems that use an expensive pattern-matching routine, the activation of agents is based on the associative event-driven mechanism that significantly increases efficiency of the inference and control processes.

2 Text Corpus and Problem Domain

The texts under consideration are weather forecast telegrams sent by local forecasters to the central meteorological offices (*M-texts*). An example of M-text is given below in literal translation from Russian:

> *weather tomsk region 19/08/98=*
> *variable cloudiness in morning local fogs over south parts locally small short rains thunderstorms wind south south-west 7-12 m/s temp at night 8-13 at day time 8-23 tomsk night 10-12 day 21-23=*

An M-text contains a sequence of prognostic statements with parametric semantics (an "object — parameter — value" scheme). The estimations are given in terms of parametric Features grouped around meteorological Elements (Precipitation, Cloudiness, WeatherPhenomena, Wind, Temperature, Inflamability) within topically coherent text fragments. Each topical fragment contains a sequence of estimations for the same Element. The correspondence between Elements and their Features is represented by the Element-Feature relation, the third argument of the relation presenting basic parameters of the Element: *Element-Feature(Element: "Wind", Features: {"WindDirection", "WindVariation", "WindSpeed", "WindGust"}, DefaultFeatures: "WindDirection", "WindSpeed").*

Estimations are time- and site-specific, i.e. they are made with respect to certain Temporal and Locative objects. The territory and the date mentioned in the heading part of the text are basic Loc and Temp objects of the domain. The objects of estimation in elementary statements are related to the basic Loc and Temp objects as their parts: e.g. LocValue *local* and TempValue *in morning* in the fragment *in morning local fogs.* Circumstantial Values may be implicit in the fragment and are in this case recovered from the previous context: e.g. ***over south parts locally*** *small short rains | thunderstorms.*

The output semantic representation of the topical fragment *wind south south-west 7-12 m/s* from the example above is given in section 5, Fig. 4.

3 Approach to Text Understanding

Our approach to text understanding takes into account not only the domain structure but the text pragmatics as well. The telegram genre causes main peculiarities of the text corpus. Texts are extremely concise — they are written in "telegraphic style". On the one hand, the semantic units (Elements, Features, Loc and Temp Values) are reduced as they can be easily recovered due to the strong semantic and topical coherence and regular word order. On the other hand, grammatical and syntactic elements are regularly omitted (lack of prepositions, conjunctions, or even inflexions). Means of text segmentation are absent (there are no punctuation marks and capital letters). Abbreviations are widely used. Texts bear a lot of mistakes as a result of their spontaneous production.

Previously, our experiments in different problem domains [1] involved local morphological and syntactic processing. The specificity of the M-text corpus results in a strong semantic bias of our approach to analysis. According to it, lexical semantics of words and word collocations is defined in terms of "orientations" as pointers to the domain system of concepts. The semantic orientation indicates a set of Features that can be represented by a lexeme on the surface level. The topic orientation relates a lexeme to the set of Elements whose description admits this lexeme. For example, the vocabulary unit *variable* is the Value of "CloudAmount" or "WindDirection" Features and topically corresponds to "Cloudiness" or "Wind" Elements. This information is stored in the slots Orientation and TopicOrientation of the vocabulary entry of the lexeme.

The semantics-oriented approach admits processing syntactic non-regularities resulting in proper output semantic structures. Several types of semantic units (features, values, locations, etc.) that appear in text fragment under analysis are combined into topical and semantic structures using orientations and word order information. Topical mechanisms provide the recovery of reduced semantic objects.

4 Class Hierarchy

Fig. 1 shows a part of our class hierarchy and illustrates interaction between lexical units and concepts of the problem domain. The hierarchy takes into account the peculiarities of the text corpus: it lacks classic grammar classes (no verbs, nouns, etc. and no morphological characteristics). The base class Object has the only slot State with two possible values: "working" means that object is to be processed and "worked_out" means that the object is no longer subject to any further processing.

The **lexical hierarchy** includes classes for words, numbers and signs. The base class LexObject contains common lexical information for the vocabulary look-up. A chain of LexObjects is produced by a special **LexSequence relation**.

The **text hierarchy** is also reduced, as there are no paragraphs, sentences and clauses. The only text-structure class is Topic used in the process of decomposition of the input chain into the sequence of topically coherent fragments. SemWord objects are related to Topic by a special **Topical relation**.

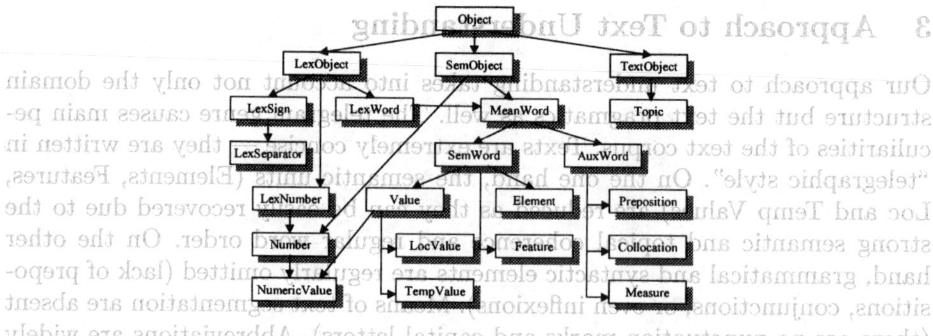

Fig. 1. Class hierarchy

The **semantic hierarchy** corresponds to lexical level of the domain concepts. SemObjects are characterized with orientation slots. SemWords are elements of the future semantic tree bound with **SemTree relations**. The auxiliary words (AuxWord) are opposed to the SemWord class as they serve to modify meanings or even to refine classes of SemWords but are never present in the resulting structure.

5 Agents and Analysis Procedure

The analysis procedure is performed by a set of agents, which may be classified according to their functions in the process.

The first group of agents interacts with the input chain to execute the **lexical processing**. Agents react to the current portion of the chain, delimit and create LexObject nodes, refine their classes (LexSigns, LexNumbers and LexWords), fill their slots and insert them into the network. A special agent performs the vocabulary look-up for class and slot values information. The LexSequence relation joins the node being inserted into the network to the previous one.

The agents of the second group perform the **presemantic processing**. They react to the appearance of instances of Number or AuxWord classes. The AuxWord subclasses require different types of processing and their contribution may be different. For example, Preposition with locative orientation serves to disambiguate words like *west* and to refine its class as a LocValue (*over west regions* vs. *wind west*). Fig. 2 presents the results of lexical and presemantic analysis for the fragment *wind south south-west 7-12 m/s*. The collocations have been assembled, Number orientation specified, interval composed and refined as NumericValue.

The third group of agents realizes the **topical analysis**. Agents simulate the left-to-right "reading" of the lexical chain, interact with nodes of the SemWord class , the AuxWord nodes being simply passed by in case their states are "worked_out" (otherwise the topical processing stops and waits until the nodes are presemantically processed). The topical relation is created between

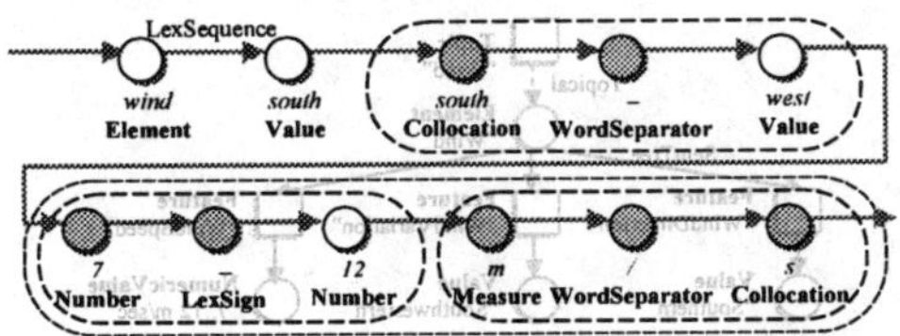

Fig. 2. Lexical and presemantic processing

the "working" Topic and a SemWord node provided that their TopicOrientation values conform. The topical shift (creation of a new Topic node) may be provoked by a new SemWord if its TopicOrientation does not agree with that of the "working" Topic, e.g. *thunderstorms* | *wind south south-west 7-12 m/s*. Circumstantial SemWords provoke a subtopic hypothesis (text fragment with a more precise description of the same Element) that may be later rejected. Fig. 3 demonstrates the results of topical analysis for our example: the new Topic node has been generated on meeting the Element node and further bound with SemWord nodes by Topical relations.

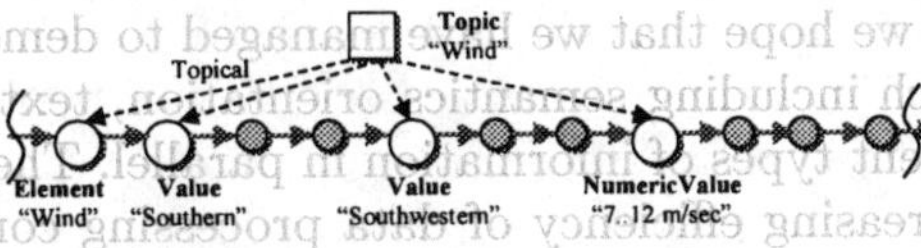

Fig. 3. Topical analysis

The fourth group of agents performs the **semantic analysis**, which involves three types of actions. Several agents deal with specification of semantic orientations of Values and Features. Special agents react to situations of semantic reduction in order to recover missing units. A few agents are intended to realize the bottom-up process of constructing the semantic tree by finding out the semantically dominant counterpart for any SemWord node and creating SemTree relation between them. All the semantic agents are able to work under the condition that Topic related to the SemWord nodes under analysis is "worked_out", i.e. the topical fragment construction is completed. Consider our example *wind south south-west 7-12 m/s* and its resulting semantic structure presented in Fig. 4. The indeterminate Values *south*, *south-west* ("WindDirection" vs. "WindVariation") and *7-12 m/s* ("WindSpeed" vs. "WindGust") have been disambiguated. The basic Features ("WindDirection" and "WindSpeed") have been recovered due to the DefaultFeatures information of Element-Feature relation and the corresponding SemTree relations set up. Of the two competing Values to be attached to the recovered "WindDirection" Feature node the first one has been chosen by a special condition on the word order. Note that semantic trees of all the topical fragments of the text will be further connected to the basic Locative and Temporal units immediately or via their local circumstantial units (if any).

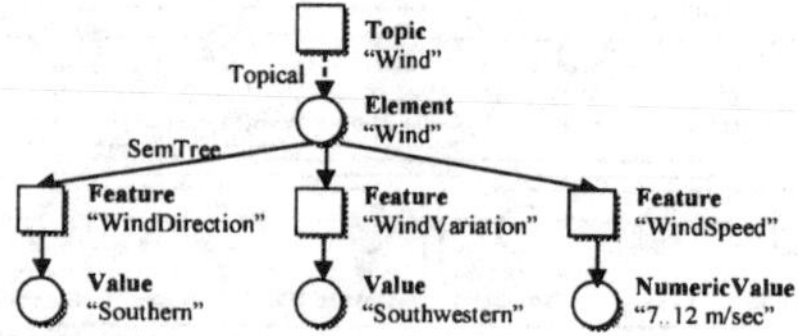

Fig. 4. Semantic analysis

It is necessary to emphasize that all agents work simultaneously. While lexical agents are processing the input chain and creating lexical nodes, topical agents are assembling them in coherent text fragments. The progress of topical analysis is being provided by presemantic agents that are creating the required conditions in the lexical chain. At the same time the completely analyzed topical fragments are subject to semantic processing.

6 Conclusion

Several questions of M-texts processing have been left out of the scope of this paper. Nevertheless, we hope that we have managed to demonstrate basic principles of our approach including semantics orientation, text type consideration and processing different types of information in parallel. The use of agent-based technique allows increasing efficiency of data processing control in comparison to production systems. This is achieved by using the associative event-driven mechanism instead of an expensive pattern matching routine.

Meteorological telegrams, with their text specificity and lucidity of structure of underlying problem domain, appeared to be a good testing ground for experiments and development of the agents mechanism. The most interesting perspective seems to be the analysis of abbreviations and mistakes. Disambiguation of deviating lexical units implies local multivariant processing that can be efficiently realized within the framework of event-driven approach.

References

1. Kononenko I., Sharoff S. Understanding Short Texts with Integration of Knowledge Representation Methods. In: Perspectives of Sysem Informatics, Lecture Notes in Computer Science; Vol. 1181, Springer, (1996), pp.111–121.
2. Narin'yani A.S. Automatic Text Understanding — New Perspective. In: Dialogue'97. Computational Linguistics and its Applications. Moscow, 1997, pp. 203–208.
3. Zagorulko Yu.A., Popov I.G. Object-Oriented Language for Knowledge Representation Using Dynamic Set of Constraints. In: Knowledge-Based Software Engineering. (Proc. 3rd Joint Conf., Smolenice, Slovakia), Amsterdam: IOSPess, 1998, pp.124–131.

Approach to Development of a System for Speech Interaction with an Intelligent Robot

George B. Cheblakov, Farida G. Dinenberg, David Ya. Levin, Ivan G. Popov, and Yury A. Zagorulko

Russian Research Institute of Artificial Intelligence
and A.P. Ershov Institute of Informatics Systems
Acad. Lavrentjev pr., 6, Novosibirsk, 630090, Russia
zagor@iis.nsk.su

Abstract. We consider an approach to the development of a speech control system for a robot. The robot is working in an environment containing several rooms; it can perform user commands and answer questions of the following types: *Where are you?* or *What do you see in the room?* The system includes the following components: speech input subsystem, linguistic processor to translate English commands into a formal representation, the robot (simulated by a program) and a speech synthesizer to voice the robot's messages. The speech input and output subsystems are based on standard commercially available software packages. The linguistic processor and robot simulator are implemented with the help of two original instrumental systems – Lingua-F and SemP-TAO. An outline of the Lingua-Voice project is also given.

Introduction

Although the problem of controlling technical devices by means of speech is not new, it is still important. It has become of particular importance recently, as speech recognition systems have become available.

Modern projects have demonstrated a trend to use natural language (NL) in all aspects of interaction with the robot. At the specification stage, NL is used to state instructions to the robot or a qualitative description of the desired situation, while during execution of a command the robot produces detailed messages about its current actions. As stated in [1], the main advantage of using the natural language for robot control is its ability to express information with varying degree of detail and at different abstraction levels, which is difficult to achieve with a formal language.

One of the first programs understanding natural language was the famous system of Winograd [2]. Another well-known system, SHAKEY [3], was a mobile robot without a manipulator; it could understand simple natural-language commands. The paper [4] proposed a system to control a remote robot with the help of a limited vocabulary of words in a natural language.

The purpose of project KANTRA [1,5] is to create a system for speech communication with an autonomous mobile robot that has two manipulators and is designed to perform complex assembly work.

D. Bjørner, M. Broy, A. Zamulin (Eds.): PSI'99, LNCS 1755, pp. 517–529, 2000.

An approach to the development of an NL interface for a system controlling a mobile service robot working in a room was examined in [6]. Another similar system [7] includes a well-developed NL interface that enables the human operator to use NL to describe scenes (e.g., rooms in a building, objects in the rooms, spatial relationships between objects, etc.) as well as commands and scenarios of robot's actions in the environment (e.g., go to a room, carry an object from one place to another, clean the room).

The Russian Research Institute of Artificial Intelligence (RRIAI, Moscow-Novosibirsk) and the Institute of Informatics Systems (Novosibirsk), together with the Institute of Applied Knowledge Processing Systems (FAW, Ulm), are working on a speech control system for an intelligent robot.

The robot controlled by the system is working in a building containing several rooms. It executes user commands expressed in English, e.g., *Go to room 5* or *Transfer the computer from the first room to the second room.* In addition, it can answer some questions, e.g., *Where are you?* or *What is located in the room?*

This paper presents the architecture and scheme of operation of a system for speech control of an intelligent robot. We give a detailed description of the world in which the robot is working, the robot's abilities and the control language. Implementation characteristics of the main components of the system are presented; the paper contains numerous examples.

1 Architecture and Operation of the System

The problem of robot control with spoken natural-language commands is divided into the following subtasks:

- speech recognition;
- translation of command text into a formal representation;
- execution of the command and the corresponding modification of the robot's world;
- visualization of command execution results;
- generation of the robot's response and its transformation into a voice message.

It is important also to ensure a closed loop in the operation of the speech control system: reception of a command, its analysis, execution, and return to the reception of the next command.

To perform these functions, the system includes the following components:

- a speech entry subsystem containing a microphone, a sound card, and a software speech recognizer;
- a linguistic processor that receives the text of command in a natural language (English) from the speech recognizer and translates it into a formal representation;
- a command execution subsystem (the robot simulator);
- a speech synthesizer that voices the robot's messages.

The speech entry subsystem is based on a commercially available package, ViaVoice by IBM, which produced quite satisfactory results after some necessary adjustment. Speech synthesis uses a standard software component, Microsoft Concatenated Text-to-speech Engine.

The linguistic processor is constructed with the Lingua-F [8] instrumental system that uses a semantics-oriented approach to the analysis of NL texts that was proposed by A. S. Narin'yani [9].

The subsystem of command execution and the environment emulating the robot's world were implemented with the help of SemP-TAO [10]. SemP-TAO is an integrated software environment for knowledge representation and processing that was developed for the construction of intelligent systems requiring description of subject domains with complex structure and semantics, as well as a combination of logical inference and calculations over imprecise values.

The functional overview of the system in Fig. 1 demonstrates the complete cycle of execution of a command given to the robot.

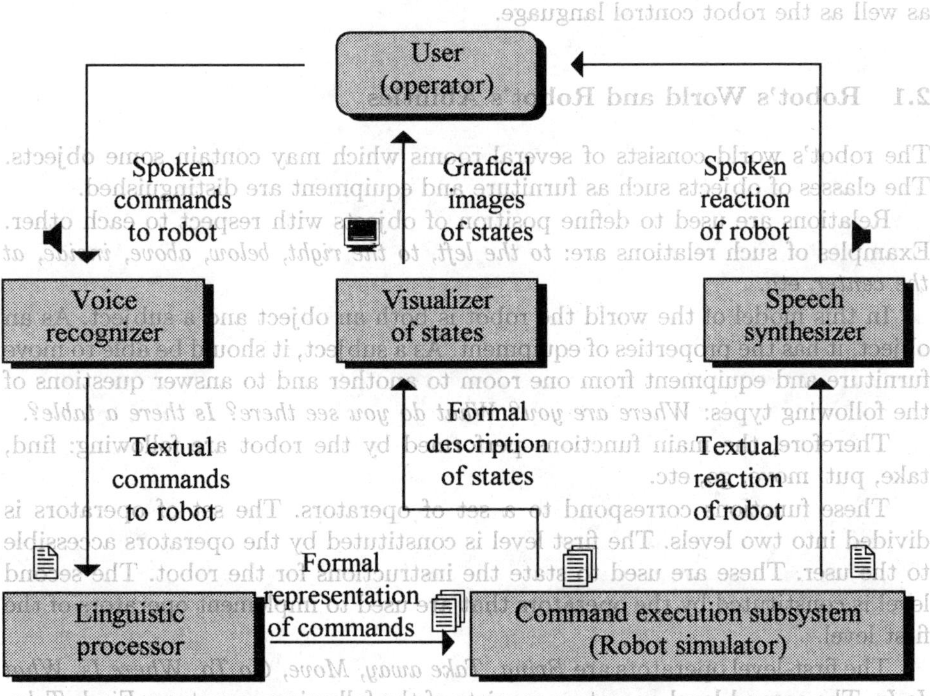

Fig. 1. The functional overview of the system

A command pronounced by the operator is transmitted to the voice recognition system that transforms a phonetic representation into the textual sentence. Then, this text is processed by a linguistic processor that translates the sentence into certain sequence of formal commands. For interpretation, formal commands are transported to the simulator – a subsystem which simulates the robot's behavior. According to the commands, the simulator performs all prescribed actions which generally results in a transformation of the simulated environment – the world of robot. Such transformations are visualized on the screen of computer by special program that enables an operator to check robot actions and states of its environment. If a command assumes certain explicit answer, then a subsystem of command interpretation generates an appropriate text; this text is then transformed into speech form and is pronounced.

When processing of a command is completed, the operator can input the next command.

2 Intelligent Robot and Its Control Language

In this section we consider the robot's world, the robot's features and abilities as well as the robot control language.

2.1 Robot's World and Robot's Abilities

The robot's world consists of several rooms which may contain some objects. The classes of objects such as furniture and equipment are distinguished.

Relations are used to define position of objects with respect to each other. Examples of such relations are: *to the left*, *to the right*, *below*, *above*, *inside*, *at the center*, etc.

In this model of the world the robot is both an object and a subject. As an object, it has the properties of equipment. As a subject, it should be able to move furniture and equipment from one room to another and to answer questions of the following types: *Where are you? What do you see there? Is there a table?*.

Therefore, the main functions performed by the robot are following: find, take, put, move, go, etc.

These functions correspond to a set of operators. The set of operators is divided into two levels. The first level is constituted by the operators accessible to the user. These are used to state the instructions for the robot. The second level is constituted by the operators that are used to implement operators of the first level.

The first-level operators are *Bring, Take away, Move, Go To, Where Is, What Is In.* The second-level operators consists of the following operators: *Find, Take, Free, Put, Say.*

There is a separate operator scheme for each operator; it determines the conditions, the order (plan) and the results of execution of the operator. In contrast to the systems STRIPS and ABSTRIPS [11,12] that use linear operator schemes, in our system recursive operator schemes are utilized.

For example, the following scheme corresponds to the second-level operator *Find*:

```
Find ($this) {
  if locations of $this and the robot are identical, then
    save current location of the robot in variable $location;
    return $location as a result;
  else
    mark current room as already examined;
    if the next room has not been examined yet, then
      save location of the next room in variable $new_location;
      Go to ($new_location);
      Find ($this);
    else
      Say ($this, "not found");
}
```

Now we describe the scheme for the first-level operator *Bring*:

```
Bring ($this){
  save current location of the robot in variable $here;
  $location:=Find ($this);
  Move ($this, $location, $here);
}
```

2.2 Formal Language for Robot Control

Formal language for robot control is developed on the base of the operator schemes described above. It was called FOROL (the FOrmal RObot Language).

This language includes the operators *WhereIs*, *GO*, and *MOVE*. Arguments of these operators may be objects and rooms.

The description of an object has the following form:

OBJECT(name: name_of_object, color: color_of_object),

here *name_of_object* is the name of the object, and *color_of_object* is the color (may be not given).

The description of a room in FOROL has the following form:

ROOM(number: number_of_room),

here *number_of_room* is an integer which denotes the number of room.

We now give a description of the syntax and semantics of the operators of the language.

The operators *WhereIs* has the following form:

WhereIs(what: object, where: room).

Here *object* is the description of an object whose location must be determined or confirmed, and *room* describes a room.

Note that one or both arguments in the operator *WhereIs* can be omitted. The semantics of the operator *WhereIs* depends on which arguments are given, and which are omitted. Consider each case separately.

If only first argument is given, then execution of the operator results in searching for an object with given characteristics and issuing a written or spoken message on its location. If several objects satisfy the description, then the information on the first object is output. In case of failure, the corresponding message is issued.

If only second argument is given, then the characteristics of all objects found in room are output.

If both parameters are omitted, then the characteristics of all objects found in the current room are output.

The operators *GO* has the following form:

GO(to: room),

here *room* describes a room to which the robot should go.

In according to this operator the robot must go to the specified room. If this is impossible, the corresponding message is output.

The operators *MOVE* has the following form:

MOVE(what: thing, from: room1, to: room2)

Here *thing* is the description of the object that should be moved from *room1* to *room2*. The values of the characteristics of the object are identical to those in the operator *WhereIs*, with the exception that *Robot* should not be used for the name of the object.

We note that only the first argument of the operator *MOVE* is required always. All the other arguments are optional. The semantics of the operator *MOVE* as well as *WhereIs* depends on which arguments are given.

So, if all of three arguments are given, then the object *thing* must be moved from *room1* to *room2*.

If only two arguments *what* and *from* are given, then the object *thing* should be moved from *room1* to the room where the robot is.

If two arguments *what* and *to* are given, then *thing* should be found and moved to *room2*.

Finally, if only argument *what* is given, then the object *thing* should be found and moved to the room where the robot is situated.

In all versions of *MOVE*, a suitable message is issued in the case of failure. For example: *Green chair is not found, Room 200 does not exist, Computer is already in room 5*, etc.

Note that the FOROL language includes a small set of operators, but due to a great power of the operators, this set suffices to describe all the tasks which should be performed by the robot.

3 Linguistic Processor

The linguistic processor (LP) was constructed with the help of a current modification of the Lingua-F software environment that was developed in the 80's [8]. Lingua-F supports construction of an LP that translates the text of an NL communication into a formal representation using the FOROL language. Lingua-F supports all stages of LP construction:

- forming a vocabulary;
- writing production rules for lexical and base analysis of the input text and rules for generation of the output representation;

– compilation of the rules and the vocabulary;
– debugging and testing of the linguistic processor on a comprehensive data bank of various NL messages to the robot.

Lingua-F has a facility for saving a stand-alone LP that can exist on its own and can be used in other software packages.

The LP thus constructed is included in the speech control system of the robot as a component. A natural-language text is placed at the input of the LP, and the corresponding formal representation is generated at the input. The transformation of the text into a formal form is based on a semantics-oriented approach that enables one to analyse the input text based on the semantics and pragmatics of the subject domain in which the communication with the robot occurs.

The linguistic processor consists of two components: the vocabulary containing the lexicon of NL requests to the robot and the production component. Consider the two components in more detail.

3.1 The Vocabulary and Types of NL Requests

In the current version of the system an operator uses two types of NL requests to the robot: a directive (command) and an inquiry (question). At the semantics-oriented approach, the words that are included in the requests are subdivided into significant words which are reflected in a formal representation, and insignificant ones ignored at an analysis.

We distinguish the following types of significant words used when addressing to the robot:

– verbs which define moving of objects, e.g., *bring, transfer, move*;
– verbs which initiate movement of robot, e.g. *go*;
– verbs and interrogative words and collocations which define search of an object, e.g. *where, find, search, what room*;
– objects, e.g., *chair, box, table, computer*;
– numerals which can be used in requests, e.g., *one, first*;
– adjectives which define colours, e.g., *red, white, brown, green*;
– locations, e.g., *room*;
– prepositions, e.g., *from, to*;

In addition, requests can include insignificant words, like: *number, a, an, the, situated.*

Using the above mentioned words one can compose directives: *Go to ..., Move something from ... to ...* and inquiries: *Where* or *What room is located ...*, etc. An order and a number of components of a request as well as word order within each component is generally not fixed. The word order is defined by a grammar of the particular natural language. The rules of analysis and synthesis are constructed so that to minimise a feeling of language restrictions for an operator.

We give below several examples of NL requests with corresponding formal representations. These examples demonstrate some degrees of a lingual flexibility, one of which in particular is a defining of a room number. Having either digital or literal spelling, a room number can be defined by both quantitative and ordinal numeral and, accordingly, located in a postposition or preposition to the word *room*.

First, we consider the directives that are divided into types *MOVE* and *GO*:

a) In a directive of the type *MOVE*: *Transfer the blue armchair from the first room to room number 4!* a transposition of the locative components is admitted: *... to room number 4 from the first room.* In addition, a similar command will be analysed correctly when formulated with an ellipsis: *Transfer the blue armchair from the first room to 4!* In all cases the directive will be translated into:

MOVE(what: THING(name: armchair, color: blue), from: ROOM(number: 1), to: ROOM(number: 4));

b) A directive like *Go to the second room!* has completely transparent translation:

GO(to: ROOM(number: 2)).

The system distinguishes questions that meet the user informational needs of both the location of various objects and the presence of objects in the specified place:

a) A question *Where is the robot?* can also be formulated as to a partner in communication: *Where are you?* Its formal representation is:

WhereIs(what: OBJECT(name: robot));

b) In addition to a question on the robot it is possible to ask about any object *Where is the red box?* or *What place is the red box located in?* The directive *Find / Search the red box!* is interpreted as an indirect question on the location of the object:

WhereIs(what: OBJECT(name: box, color: red));

c) Questions on the presence of any objects in the room where the robot is *What is (located) here / there / in this room?* are translated into:

WhereIs(what: ?, where: ?);

d) Questions intended to detect any objects in the specified place *Is something in room 5?*, *What is located / situated in room 5?* are formally represented as:

WhereIs(what: ?, where: ROOM(number: 5));

e) Alternative question *Is computer in the room number 2?* corresponds to:

WhereIs(what: OBJECT(name: computer), where: ROOM(number: 2)).

3.2 Production Component

The production component of the linguistic processor translates the incoming NL phrase in several steps: lexical analysis, base analysis, and generation.

The rules of lexical analysis divide the entry string into lexical tokens which, after accessing the dictionary, are replaced by the corresponding dictionary entries. Multiple components that are elements of a composite entry are combined into a single component. Such a composite entry often serves to resolve ambiguities. Defining a usage context of a word, i.e., creating a composite entry, makes it possible to link several meanings to a single word.

For instance, consider the word *room* in several contexts: a) *room 1* (or *the first room*), b) *in what room*. In the first case, the word *room* is a locating component, while in the second it denotes a question of type *WhereIs*. Creation of the composite entry *what room*, synonymous with the word *where*, ensures correct parsing.

In the base analysis stage, the parsing tree reflecting the predicate-actant structure of the phrase is constructed. First, we construct the second actant, which is the object group consisting of a noun (the object) and an adjective, e.g., *green armchair*. Next, we construct actants of two types, *from* and *to*, which are the locative components represented by nouns with prepositions, e.g., *from room number two*. Finally, the predicate is concatenated with the second actant (e.g., *bring* is concatenated with *green armchair*) and all locative groups, if any. If the parsing succeeds, the whole phrase is reduced to a single component.

The generation rules transform the tree representation of the phrase resulting from the base analysis into the output representation in FOROL.

4 The Lingua-Voice System: Towards a Cooperative Processor for Spoken Language Understanding

In this section, we shortly summarize the presented results and outline our next project related to a voice recognition field.

The speech control system described in the paper has been fully implemented and tested, demonstrating stable operation in a large number of tests.

The integrated object-oriented environment SemP-TAO enabled us to represent the robot's world in a natural manner, specify and implement an extensible formal language for robot control, support visualization of the states of the world, and provide a convenient user interface.

It should be noted that the system is not just a prototype version of the speech control system that will be connected to the real device. The integrated model of the robot is a good base for experiments and extensions directed at the study of a broad range of knowledge representation and processing problems. The FOROL language, for example, served as a base for more powerful robot control language, including additional tools to work with spatial relationships and advanced facilities for description of rooms and objects. Implementation of this language will make it possible to work on the development of a robot control system using both formal communication means and a richer natural language.

The system described in this paper can also be used as a solid testing ground for research of the use of a spoken language for communication with a wide spectrum of applications. In this respect, it has given a rise to a new project called Lingua-Voice which we outline below.

The idea of the Lingua-Voice project is to technologically fulfill a gap between an output of a standard voice recognition system and an input of an application.

Today, industrial speech processors produce rather raw output which, in the best case, can include a simple post-processing based on a user-defined context-free grammar. In fact, a voice recognition system itself supports only a small part of job needed to provide a really comprehensive communication with applications. In particular, voice processing systems presented today in the software market are responsible for selection (from a dozen of phonetic hypotheses) of "the most probable" word, taking into account some universal phonetic and statistic data, not the information related somehow to the world of application or to linguistics.

We are certain that the approach described in [8] for automatic text processing based on orientation to a restricted subject domain and simultaneous processing of many variants is especially adequate for spoken language (SL) understanding.

Our new project called Lingua-Voice concerns the following principles:

- Multi-variant processing,
- Automated specification and adjustment of a SL-processor to application,
- Specialized agents for SL-processing,
- Closer integration of voice and linguistic processing.

This development leads us to a construction of a software architecture and environment which are shortly characterized below. Their general structure is presented at Fig. 2 (where "Voice recognizer" and "Linguistic processor" functionally correspond to similar components shown at Fig. 1).

The Lingua-Voice system is based on a version of the Lingua-F support environment which has recently been implemented by M.Zhigalov and D.Shishkin.

The Lingua-Voice system starts with initiation of a certain voice recognition engine: ViaVoice, Dragon or whatever. After the engine has completed its work, the whole set of phonetic variants is "extracted" from its inner memory and transmitted to further processing modules. This data has the following structure:

$$W = <w_1 = \{h_{1,1}; h_{1,2}; ...; h_{1,n_1}\}, ..., w_s = \{h_{s,1}; h_{s,2}; ...; h_{s,n_s}\}>$$

where w_i is a cluster of words detected for the i-th potential word. (This picture is obviously simplified for continuous speech.) We call clusters *subdefinite words* and W-structures *subdefinite phrases* to note a relationship between the issues considered here and classical works of A.Narin'ani on processing of non-complete information.

In the general case, the purpose of a concrete Lingua-Voice processor is to organize the application of specialized processing agents to such a vector W. If no correct variants are found, the process is considered to be failed; if a unique variant is found, it is passed over to the application; if the result is ambiguous, then, in order to refine it, a kind of a dialog is initiated.

To exemplify these agents, we mention here

- statistical corrector,
- syntactical filter,
- semantic filter and
- multi-variant analyzer.

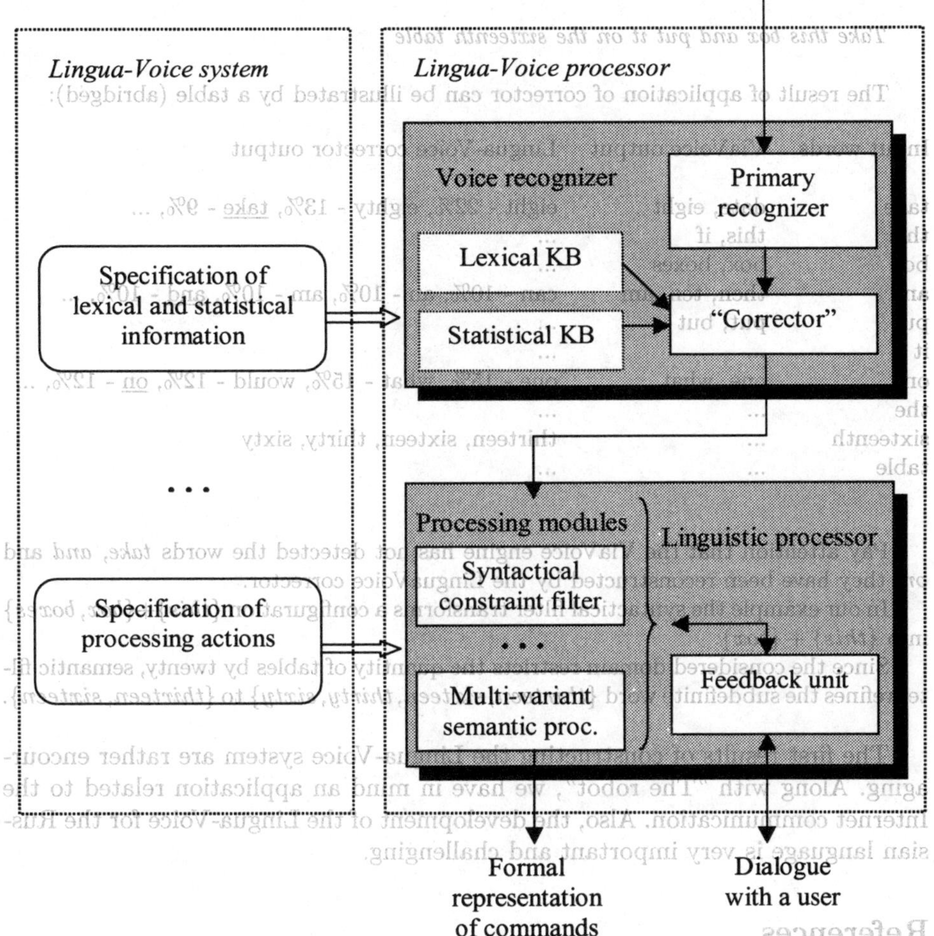

Fig. 2. General structure of the Lingua-Voice

Thus, statistical corrector uses lexical and statistical knowledge entered through the special user-friendly environment of the Lingua-Voice system during an adjustment of a concrete processor. These data enables us to efficiently rearrange and refine too universal "probability estimations" elaborated by a voice recognition engine; in some cases, corrector is able to extend the set of hypotheses by additional words due to a priori defined contextual statistical associations.

The work of the above mentioned components can be illustrated by an artificially simplified example of processing a phrase:

Take this box and put it on the sixteenth table

The result of application of corrector can be illustrated by a table (abridged):

Input words	ViaVoice output	Lingua-Voice corrector output
take	date, eight	eight - 22%, eighty - 13%, take - 9%, ...
this	this, if	...
box	box, boxes	...
and	then, ten, am	can - 10%, an - 10%, am - 10%, and - 10%, ...
put	put, but	...
it	...	...
on	one, what	one - 15%, what - 15%, would - 12%, on - 12%, ...
the	...	...
sixteenth	...	thirteen, sixteen, thirty, sixty
table	...	...

Pay attention that the ViaVoice engine has not detected the words *take*, *and* and *on*: they have been reconstructed by the LinguaVoice corrector.

In our example the syntactical filter transforms a configuration $\{this\}+\{box, boxes\}$ into $\{this\} + \{box\}$.

Since the considered domain restricts the quantity of tables by twenty, semantic filter refines the subdefinite word $\{thirteen, sixteen, thirty, sixty\}$ to $\{thirteen, sixteen\}$.

The first results of constructing the Lingua-Voice system are rather encouraging. Along with "The robot", we have in mind an application related to the Internet communication. Also, the development of the Lingua-Voice for the Russian language is very important and challenging.

References

1. Stopp, E., Gapp, K.-P., Herzog, G., Laengle, T., Lueth, T.C.: Utilizing Spatial Relations for Natural Language Access to an Autonomous Mobile Robot. KI-94: Advances in Artificial Intelligence, (Proc. of 18th German Conf. on Art. Int., Berlin), Heidelberg: Springer, 1994, pp.39-50.
2. Winograd T. Understanding natural language. New York: Acad. Press , 1972.
3. Nilsson N.J. Shakey the Robot. Technical Note 323, Artificial Intelligence Center, SRI International, Menlo Park, CA, 1984.
4. Sato T. and Hirai S. Language-Aided Robotic Teleoperation System (LARTS) for Advanced Teleoperation. IEEE Journal on Robotics and Automation (RA), 3(5), 1987, pp. 476-480.
5. Luth T.C., Langle Th., Herzog G., Stopp E., and Rembold V.. KANTRA: Human-Machine Interaction for Intelligent Robots using Natural Language. 3rd IEEE Int. Workshop on Robot and Human Communication, RO-MAN'94, Nagoya, Japan, 1994, pp.106-111.

6. Torrance M.C. Natural Communication with Robots. Master's thesis, MIT, Dep. of Electr. Eng. and Comp. Science, Cambridge, MA, 1994.
7. Tanaka T., Yamafuji K., Miyagava W., Watanabe H., Takahashi H. and Ulyanov S.V. Intelligent Locomotion control system of the Mobile Robot for Service Use, 2nd Int. Conf. on Mechatronics and Machine Vision, Hong Kong, 1995, pp. 107-112.
8. Trapeznikov S.P. The System for the Development of Linguistic Processors // Artificial Intelligence ll: Methology, systems, applications. (Amsterdam: North Holland, 1987, pp.332-339.
9. Narin'yani A.S. Interaction with a limited object domain – ZAPSIB project. // Proc. of Int. Conf. Computational Linguistics-1980, Tokyo, 1980.
10. Yu.A.Zagorulko, I.G.Popov. Object-Oriented Language for Knowledge Representation Using Dynamic Set of Constraints // Knowledge-Based Software Engineering, (Proc. 3rd Joint Conf., Smolenice, Slovakia), Amsterdam: IOSPess, 1998, pp.124-131.
11. Fikes R., Nilson N. STRIPS: A new approach to the application of the theorem proving to problem solving // Proc. 2nd Joint Inter. Conf. on Artificial Intelligence, London, 1971, pp.608-619.
12. Sacerdoti E.D. Planing in a hierarchy of abstraction spaces. – Artificial Intelligence, v. 5, pp.115-135.

Analysis of Sign Languages: A Step Towards Multi-lingual Machine Translation for Sign Languages

Susantha Herath[1], Chie Saito[1], and Ajantha Herath[2]

[1] Aizu University, Aizu-Wakamatsu 965-80, Japan
[2] Gifu University, Gifu 500, Japan

Abstract. Many different sign languages are in use to communicate, especially among the hearing impaired people. Translation of one sign language to another is a difficult problem that need efficient solution. Processing of signs is different from the processing of words in natural languages. Sign languages use shapes and movements to express meaning. The objective of our research project is to develop a multi-lingual machine translation system for sign languages. As a first step towards achieving this objective we analyzed three sign languages. This paper outlines the current research results.

1 Introduction

Many different sign languages are in use in many different parts of the world. People who are using different sign languages communicate with the help of a translator. People with no hearing disability and unfamilier with the sign language may need interpreters of sign languages to communicate with hearing impaired people. With the recent advances in communication and transportation technologies, there is an increasing demand for such interpreters and translators for the disabled. The problem of translation of sign languages can be eliminated by using a universally accepted standard sign language. Developing a machine translation system for sign languages is another solution. This paper presents the results of the later approach.

1.1 Sign Languages

Sign Language (SL) is one of the methods used by the hearing impaired people to communicate with others. SL is not unique. The formation of a SL is influenced by the environment, customs, regions of a country and the natural language used in that country. Thus, the signs can be different in from one SL to another. Signs express meaning through shapes and movements. This way of communication is different from the words and sentences used in natural languages. It is observed that different sign languages share common signs between them. For example, the signs for *victory* and *failure* are the same in any SL [1]. A sign can have a

D. Bjørner, M. Broy, A. Zamulin (Eds.): PSI'99, LNCS 1755, pp. 530–537, 2000.

different meaning in a different SL; for example, the *promise* sign in Japan is the same as the *friend* sign in Sri Lanka.

There were attempts to develop a standard universal sign language for all. However, these attempts were not successful enough to develop a universally accepted or truly international SL. In 1971, the international sign form called *Gestuno* was developed by the World Federation of the Deaf [2]. Its vocabulary is based on the European SLs and some European countries have adopted *Gestuno*. It is mainly used at international meetings. However, *Gestuno* is not widely accepted in the world for day to day use. Translators perform the much needed help to establish communication between different SL users [3].

Until the 1960s, SL was not considered to be a language, and it was used only for educating for hearing impaired. In the 1980s, the *Sign Linguistics* was born and SL began to be researched from a linguistics point of view [4].

The term signs include gestures in its general meaning. When used in SL linguistics, the term signs mean the components of SL which are equivalent to a word in a natural language.

Three SLs, American Sign Language (ASL), Sri Lankan Sign Language (SSL) and Japanese Sign Language (JSL) are analyzed in this paper. Section 2 of this paper discusses the methodology used to compare sign languages. Section 3 outlines the implementation and experimental results. Section 4 gives the conclusion.

2 Methodology

2.1 The Basic Idea

Analysis of SLs is a basic requirement in developing a SL machine translation system. To discover the rules for translating a sign from one SL into another enables the development of the translation system. Also, it is necessary to analyze the relationships between SLs for developing the system. Some of these rules and relationships between SLs will be discussed in this section.

In natural language processing, the basic unit is a word in analysis. Similarly, the analysis of a sign leads to the analysis of a SL. The structure of a sign can be defined by morpheme and phoneme. These morphological and the phonological analysis are the objects of mainstream research [4]. Following section focuses on the phonological analysis.

2.2 Phonological Analysis

In phonological analysis, the parameters of a sign are defined. It is considered that four parameters correspond to the phoneme of a sign language [4]. William C. Stokoe introduced composition parameters, DEZ (designator), TAB (tabulations) and SIG (signation). DEZ represents hand shapes, TAB represents locations on the body and SIG represents hand movements. Battison [4] added the fourth one, ORI (the orientation of the palm). These four parameters are considered to be the components of a sign. We analyze the signs according to these four articulatory parameters.

3 Implementation

3.1 Vocabulary

Signs common to all three SLs are picked up from existing books [5][6][7]. Table 1 shows the total number of signs for the SLs.

Table 1. Number of signs

	in books	*selected*	comparable		
			verbs	nouns	no.
ASL	1167	650			
SSL	1051	441	25	81	10
JSL	15293	3941	(Total:116)		

Selected vocabulary in Table 1 shows the number of signs after eliminating the signs representing strong religious meaning, or unique cultural characteristics, country names and signs with complex movement. The vocabulary of SSL is the smallest of three, and it is picked up as the basic SL. Among selected signs, only 116 signs are comparable among 3 SLs. They are divided into three categories, verbs, nouns and numbers.

3.2 Computerizing Signs

For computers to recognize signs, they must be coded for parameters. Figure 1 shows the code form, mainly divided into two, the right hand and the left hand. The right hand part begins from r and the left hand part begins from l. Same components are applied to both hands.

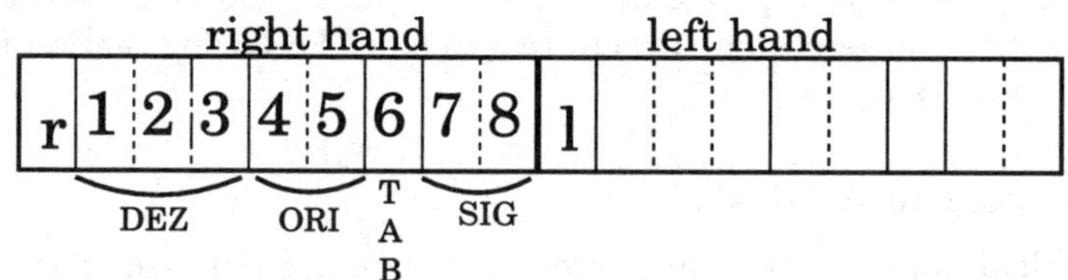

Fig. 1. Code Form

By default, the right hand is considered as the preferred hand and the fingers are open. The complete code is given in the Lab. report [8].

1. DEZ (Hand shape)
   There are 20 hand shapes and 8 shape aspects. In Figure 1, the columns 1 to 3 represent a code for DEZ parameter. The first half, a pair of 1 and 2, represents a hand shape, and the second half, 3, represents a shape aspect. The column 1 shows the number of standing fingers, and the column 2 represents the code identity. For example, code *23* means two fingers are standing (*2*) and belongs to third hand shape (*3*) (the V shape, the index and the middle fingers are standing).
2. ORI (Orientation of the palm in relationship to the body)
   The columns 4 and 5 represent a code for ORI parameter. There are 6 orientations of the palm in relation to the body; up, down, front, back, inside and outside. The column 5 shows direction of the fingertips.
3. TAB (Initial location)
   The column 6 shows a code for TAB parameter. Signing space in relation to the body is divided horizontally into six positions from *above the head* to *below the waist*.
4. SIG (Movement)
   The columns 7 and 8 are for SIG parameter. In column 7, seven hand movements are identified, one static and six dynamic movements where the oblique movements are also includes. Column 8 for representing 11 movement aspects. These were selected carefully according to Stokoe's classification [4].

For an example, according to the above process, the ASL sign for *read* is coded as `r233rr42w l512ur50n`.

3.3 Automatic Code Generator

The automatic code generator is developed on SunOS 4.1.4. for efficient data input. Figure 2 shows the basic screen of generator. The screen is divided into two, information part and coding part. At information part, user selects the target SL from ASL, SSL or JSL and inputs a meaning of sign from the keyboard. Result of coding appears in this part. At coding part, 14 lists correspond to the columns of Figure 1. Figure 2 shows only the right hand part. A sign is coded by clicking twice in one of the each list. This work makes three code databases for each SL, like

```
go : r120ru55w l120ru55w
look : r233rr25n
read : r233rr42w l512ur50n
```

3.4 Structured Comparison

Using the database described in section 3.3, coded signs are compared for parameters, DEZ, ORI, TAB and SIG on *commonality*, *similarity* and *difference* of SLs. In *commonality*, all numbers or characters of a code are completely the same. In *similarity*, only the first half code is the same. In *difference* codes are completely different. Table 2 shows examples in DEZ parameter.

Out of all 116 signs are compared, only 50 signs involve both hands.

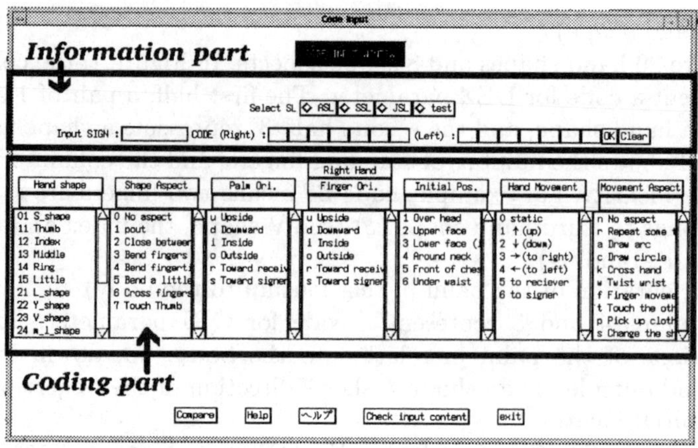

Fig. 2. Automatic code generator

Table 2. Examples

	Commonality (adopt)	*Similarity* (bread)	*Difference* (wear)
ASL	510	512	232
SSL	510	510	510
JSL	510	515	110

4 Experimental Results

4.1 Commonality

Figure 3 shows the percentage of commonality in the SLs. In the graph of the right hand, the range of values is 10% to 60%. About 10% of the signs are common to three SLs in any parameter. DEZ, ORI and SIG parameters show a low rate of commonality. TAB is by far the highest about 35%. With respect to two SLs, in any SL combination, its rate is higher about 5% to 20% than that of three SLs. The graph of the left hand shows a similar tendency to the right hand.

4.2 Similarity

Figure 4 shows the percentage of similarity between SLs. Commonality value also a subset of similarity. In the right hand, 12% of the signs are judged to be similar, in all three SLs, in all parameters. DEZ rate is high as well as TAB, except between SSL and JSL. However, the rate of commonality between them is high. DEZ and ORI rates increase 20% compared to the rate of commonality,

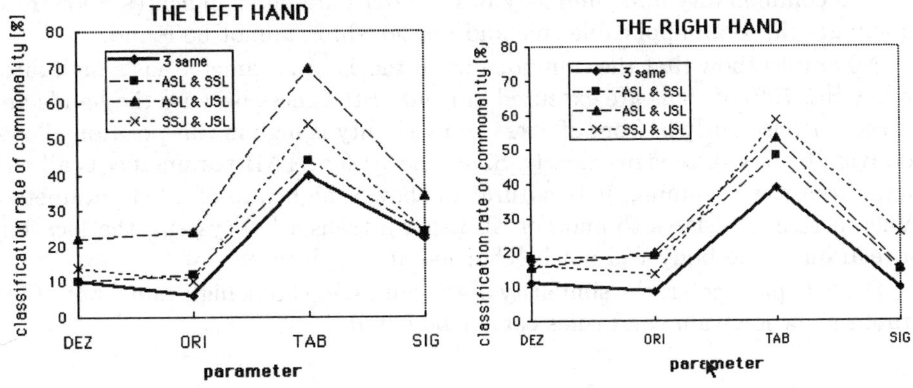

Fig. 3. Classification rate of commonality

while TAB and SIG rates increase only about 5%. The rate of SIG is the lowest, and it is a little different from the commonality rate.

The left hand is almost the same as the right hand, but in the SIG parameter, the value shows high comparatively.

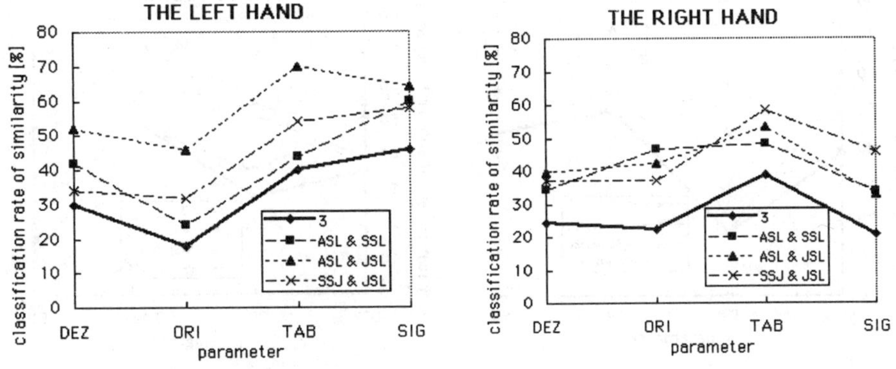

Fig. 4. Classification rate of similarity

4.3 Consideration

For the DEZ parameter, there is a 55% of similarity between ASL and JSL, so it can be applied to a SL translation system that the hand shapes of sign are the same between these two SLs.

The commonality and similarity of the ORI parameter indicates a low rate in any graph, so an applicable rule and relationships cannot be found.

All graphs show that the commonality of the TAB parameter has a high rate. In any SL, 70% of signs are executed in front of the chest because the hands are placed unconsciously in front of chest and visibility is high in this position allows receivers to recognize signs clearly. Since the 70% of TAB parameters is all the same from the beginning, it is natural to show a high rate of TAB parameter. When a sign translates to another SL using a translation system, the location in relation to the body will not be changed at a high rate.

For SIG parameter, the similarity of the left hand shows high value, but other graphs show low value and rules cannot be found.

4.4 The Verb Category

The above analysis applied to all the signs. Now, the analysis turns to a comparison by parts of speech and the four parameters. One hundred and sixteen signs are classified into three categories, verbs, nouns and numbers. Only verbs are considered here. The verb category has 25 signs out of which 18 signs use the both hands.

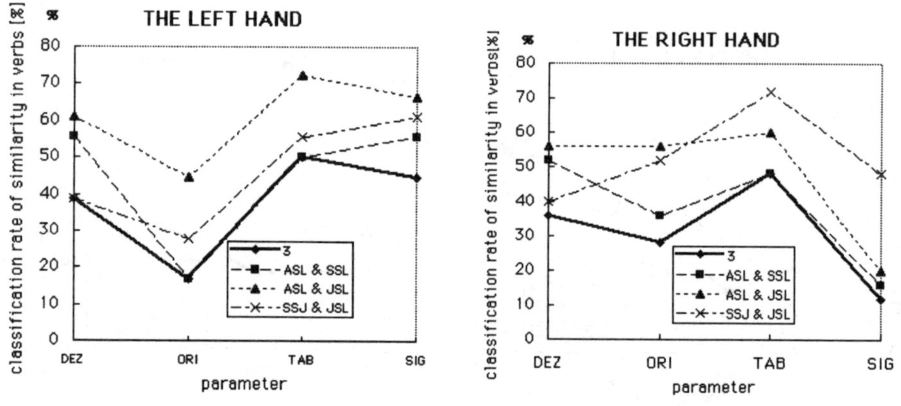

Fig. 5. Classification rate of similarity in the verb category

Figure 5 shows the result of the comparison of verbs by the four parameters. It is similar to the results for similarity and commonality, except the similarity rate of SIG is higher than the others. The reason for this result is that verbs involve movement in natural language and their concepts are almost the same in any language. The description of a sign for verb also has a similar concept and this is reflected in the similarity of SIG parameter.

5 Conclusions

The relationships between SLs are found by comparing SLs according to parameters and categories. 40% of signs show a common location on the body in three SLs. 60% of hand shapes are similar in ASL and JSL. The orientation of the palm needs more research to find some rules. The hand movement also needs further research, but in the verb category, 25% are similar in the three SLs. Analysis of the verb category proves that more rules can be found in the specified categories. It is effective to find the rules and relationships between SLs by category. Classifying categories correctly, and comparing categories is meaningful.

There was no special relationship or similarity between any pair of SLs among 3 SLs investigated. This implies a SL is unique. Each country, U.S., Sri Lanka or Japan, has own unique culture and, so a high rate of similarity may not exist.

The vocabulary of a SL is said over 20,000, and only 0.05% are analyzed in this paper. More vocabulary to be investigated for better conclusions. Some sign descriptions in books are difficult to interpret, so practical knowledge of 3 SLs are needed. Expanding the analysis of other SLs is also necessary.

References

1. Masao Itou, Shigeru Takemura, sekainoshuwa nyumon-hen, 1997.
2. World Federation of the Deaf, GESTUNO, Zen-nihon roua renmei, 1995
3. O.Van Itallie and C.G.Draper, *Computer Aided Learning of Sign Language,* http://science.cqu.edu.au/mc/Staff/Owen_Van_Itallie/Research/Multimedia/Sign_Language/default.HTM 1997
4. Kazuyuki Kanda, shuwa-gaku kougi, hukumura press, 1994
5. Tom Hunphires and Carol Padden, *Learning American Sign Language,* Prentice-Hall, Inc. 1992
6. National Institute of Education, *Sri Lankan Sign Dictionary 1-5.* 1989-1996
7. Shuwa komyunikeisoun kenkyu-kai, Shin shuwa jiten, chuou houki, 1998
8. Chie Saitou, *GR report of s1021028*, Human Interface Lab. of University of Aizu. 1998
9. Shigeru Takemura, shuwa Koseido, 1996

Conclusion

Author Index

Lecture Notes in Computer Science

For information about Vols. 1–1684
please contact your bookseller or Springer-Verlag

Vol. 1685: P. Amestoy, P. Berger, M. Daydé, I. Duff, V. Frayssé, L. Giraud, D. Ruiz (Eds.), Euro-Par'99. Parallel Processing. Proceedings, 1999. XXXII, 1503 pages. 1999.

Vol. 1686: H.E. Bal, B. Belkhouche, L. Cardelli (Eds.), Internet Programming Languages. Proceedings, 1998. IX, 143 pages. 1999.

Vol. 1687: O. Nierstrasz, M. Lemoine (Eds.), Software Engineering – ESEC/FSE '99. Proceedings, 1999. XII, 529 pages. 1999.

Vol. 1688: P. Bouquet, L. Serafini, P. Brézillon, M. Benerecetti, F. Castellani (Eds.), Modeling and Using Context. Proceedings, 1999. XII, 528 pages. 1999. (Subseries LNAI).

Vol. 1689: F. Solina, A. Leonardis (Eds.), Computer Analysis of Images and Patterns. Proceedings, 1999. XIV, 650 pages. 1999.

Vol. 1690: Y. Bertot, G. Dowek, A. Hirschowitz, C. Paulin, L. Théry (Eds.), Theorem Proving in Higher Order Logics. Proceedings, 1999. VIII, 359 pages. 1999.

Vol. 1691: J. Eder, I. Rozman, T. Welzer (Eds.), Advances in Databases and Information Systems. Proceedings, 1999. XIII, 383 pages. 1999.

Vol. 1692: V. Matoušek, P. Mautner, J. Ocelíková, P. Sojka (Eds.), Text, Speech and Dialogue. Proceedings, 1999. XI, 396 pages. 1999. (Subseries LNAI).

Vol. 1693: P. Jayanti (Ed.), Distributed Computing. Proceedings, 1999. X, 357 pages. 1999.

Vol. 1694: A. Cortesi, G. Filé (Eds.), Static Analysis. Proceedings, 1999. VIII, 357 pages. 1999.

Vol. 1695: P. Barahona, J.J. Alferes (Eds.), Progress in Artificial Intelligence. Proceedings, 1999. XI, 385 pages. 1999. (Subseries LNAI).

Vol. 1696: S. Abiteboul, A.-M. Vercoustre (Eds.), Research and Advanced Technology for Digital Libraries. Proceedings, 1999. XII, 497 pages. 1999.

Vol. 1697: J. Dongarra, E. Luque, T. Margalef (Eds.), Recent Advances in Parallel Virtual Machine and Message Passing Interface. Proceedings, 1999. XVII, 551 pages. 1999.

Vol. 1698: M. Felici, K. Kanoun, A. Pasquini (Eds.), Computer Safety, Reliability and Security. Proceedings, 1999. XVIII, 482 pages. 1999.

Vol. 1699: S. Albayrak (Ed.), Intelligent Agents for Telecommunication Applications. Proceedings, 1999. IX, 191 pages. 1999. (Subseries LNAI).

Vol. 1700: R. Stadler, B. Stiller (Eds.), Active Technologies for Network and Service Management. Proceedings, 1999. XII, 299 pages. 1999.

Vol. 1701: W. Burgard, T. Christaller, A.B. Cremers (Eds.), KI-99: Advances in Artificial Intelligence. Proceedings, 1999. XI, 311 pages. 1999. (Subseries LNAI).

Vol. 1702: G. Nadathur (Ed.), Principles and Practice of Declarative Programming. Proceedings, 1999. X, 434 pages. 1999.

Vol. 1703: L. Pierre, T. Kropf (Eds.), Correct Hardware Design and Verification Methods. Proceedings, 1999. XI, 366 pages. 1999.

Vol. 1704: Jan M. Żytkow, J. Rauch (Eds.), Principles of Data Mining and Knowledge Discovery. Proceedings, 1999. XIV, 593 pages. 1999. (Subseries LNAI).

Vol. 1705: H. Ganzinger, D. McAllester, A. Voronkov (Eds.), Logic for Programming and Automated Reasoning. Proceedings, 1999. XII, 397 pages. 1999. (Subseries LNAI).

Vol. 1706: J. Hatcliff, T. Æ. Mogensen, P. Thiemann (Eds.), Partial Evaluation – Practice and Theory. 1998. IX, 433 pages. 1999.

Vol. 1707: H.-W. Gellersen (Ed.), Handheld and Ubiquitous Computing. Proceedings, 1999. XII, 390 pages. 1999.

Vol. 1708: J.M. Wing, J. Woodcock, J. Davies (Eds.), FM'99 – Formal Methods. Proceedings Vol. I, 1999. XVIII, 937 pages. 1999.

Vol. 1709: J.M. Wing, J. Woodcock, J. Davies (Eds.), FM'99 – Formal Methods. Proceedings Vol. II, 1999. XVIII, 937 pages. 1999.

Vol. 1710: E.-R. Olderog, B. Steffen (Eds.), Correct System Design. XIV, 417 pages. 1999.

Vol. 1711: N. Zhong, A. Skowron, S. Ohsuga (Eds.), New Directions in Rough Sets, Data Mining, and Granular-Soft Computing. Proceedings, 1999. XIV, 558 pages. 1999. (Subseries LNAI).

Vol. 1712: H. Boley, A Tight, Practical Integration of Relations and Functions. XI, 169 pages. 1999. (Subseries LNAI).

Vol. 1713: J. Jaffar (Ed.), Principles and Practice of Constraint Programming – CP'99. Proceedings, 1999. XII, 493 pages. 1999.

Vol. 1714: M.T. Pazienza (Eds.), Information Extraction. IX, 165 pages. 1999. (Subseries LNAI).

Vol. 1715: P. Perner, M. Petrou (Eds.), Machine Learning and Data Mining in Pattern Recognition. Proceedings, 1999. VIII, 217 pages. 1999. (Subseries LNAI).

Vol. 1716: K.Y. Lam, E. Okamoto, C. Xing (Eds.), Advances in Cryptology – ASIACRYPT'99. Proceedings, 1999. XI, 414 pages. 1999.

Vol. 1717: Ç. K. Koç, C. Paar (Eds.), Cryptographic Hardware and Embedded Systems. Proceedings, 1999. XI, 353 pages. 1999.

Vol. 1718: M. Diaz, P. Owezarski, P. Sénac (Eds.), Interactive Distributed Multimedia Systems and Telecommunication Services. Proceedings, 1999. XI, 386 pages. 1999.

Vol. 1719: M. Fossorier, H. Imai, S. Lin, A. Poli (Eds.), Applied Algebra, Algebraic Algorithms and Error-Correcting Codes. Proceedings, 1999. XIII, 510 pages. 1999.

Vol. 1720: O. Watanabe, T. Yokomori (Eds.), Algorithmic Learning Theory. Proceedings, 1999. XI, 365 pages. 1999. (Subseries LNAI).

Vol. 1721: S. Arikawa, K. Furukawa (Eds.), Discovery Science. Proceedings, 1999. XI, 374 pages. 1999. (Subseries LNAI).

Vol. 1722: A. Middeldorp, T. Sato (Eds.), Functional and Logic Programming. Proceedings, 1999. X, 369 pages. 1999.

Vol. 1723: R. France, B. Rumpe (Eds.), UML'99 – The Unified Modeling Language. XVII, 724 pages. 1999.

Vol. 1724: H. I. Christensen, H. Bunke, H. Noltemeier (Eds.), Sensor Based Intelligent Robots. Proceedings, 1998. VIII, 327 pages. 1999 (Subseries LNAI).

Vol. 1725: J. Pavelka, G. Tel, M. Bartošek (Eds.), SOFSEM'99: Theory and Practice of Informatics. Proceedings, 1999. XIII, 498 pages. 1999.

Vol. 1726: V. Varadharajan, Y. Mu (Eds.), Information and Communication Security. Proceedings, 1999. XI, 325 pages. 1999.

Vol. 1727: P.P. Chen, D.W. Embley, J. Kouloumdjian, S.W. Liddle, J.F. Roddick (Eds.), Advances in Conceptual Modeling. Proceedings, 1999. XI, 389 pages. 1999.

Vol. 1728: J. Akoka, M. Bouzeghoub, I. Comyn-Wattiau, E. Métais (Eds.), Conceptual Modeling – ER '99. Proceedings, 1999. XIV, 540 pages. 1999.

Vol. 1729: M. Mambo, Y. Zheng (Eds.), Information Security. Proceedings, 1999. IX, 277 pages. 1999.

Vol. 1730: M. Gelfond, N. Leone, G. Pfeifer (Eds.), Logic Programming and Nonmonotonic Reasoning. Proceedings, 1999. XI, 391 pages. 1999. (Subseries LNAI).

Vol. 1731: J. Kratochvíl (Ed.), Graph Drawing. Proceedings, 1999. XIII, 422 pages. 1999.

Vol. 1732: S. Matsuoka, R.R. Oldehoeft, M. Tholburn (Eds.), Computing in Object-Oriented Parallel Environments. Proceedings, 1999. VIII, 205 pages. 1999.

Vol. 1733: H. Nakashima, C. Zhang (Eds.), Approaches to Intelligent Agents. Proceedings, 1999. XII, 241 pages. 1999. (Subseries LNAI).

Vol. 1734: H. Hellwagner, A. Reinefeld (Eds.), SCI: Scalable Coherent Interface. XXI, 490 pages. 1999.

Vol. 1564: M. Vazirgiannis, Interactive Multimedia Documents. XIII, 161 pages. 1999.

Vol. 1591: D.J. Duke, I. Herman, M.S. Marshall, PREMO: A Framework for Multimedia Middleware. XII, 254 pages. 1999.

Vol. 1624: J. A. Padget (Ed.), Collaboration between Human and Artificial Societies. XIV, 301 pages. 1999. (Subseries LNAI).

Vol. 1635: X. Tu, Artificial Animals for Computer Animation. XIV, 172 pages. 1999.

Vol. 1646: B. Westfechtel, Models and Tools for Managing Development Processes. XIV, 418 pages. 1999.

Vol. 1735: J.W. Amtrup, Incremental Speech Translation. XV, 200 pages. 1999. (Subseries LNAI).

Vol. 1736: L. Rizzo, S. Fdida (Eds.): Networked Group Communication. Proceedings, 1999. XIII, 339 pages. 1999.

Vol. 1737: P. Agouris, A. Stefanidis (Eds.), Integrated Spatial Databases. Proceedings, 1999. X, 317 pages. 1999.

Vol. 1738: C. Pandu Rangan, V. Raman, R. Ramanujam (Eds.), Foundations of Software Technology and Theoretical Computer Science. Proceedings, 1999. XII, 452 pages. 1999.

Vol. 1739: A. Braffort, R. Gherbi, S. Gibet, J. Richardson, D. Teil (Eds.), Gesture-Based Communication in Human-Computer Interaction. Proceedings, 1999. XI, 333 pages. 1999. (Subseries LNAI).

Vol. 1740: R. Baumgart (Ed.): Secure Networking – CQRE [Secure] '99. Proceedings, 1999. IX, 261 pages. 1999.

Vol. 1741: A. Aggarwal, C. Pandu Rangan (Eds.), Algorithms and Computation. Proceedings, 1999. XIII, 448 pages. 1999.

Vol. 1742: P.S. Thiagarajan, R. Yap (Eds.), Advances in Computing Science – ASIAN'99. Proceedings, 1999. XI, 397 pages. 1999.

Vol. 1743: A. Moreira, S. Demeyer (Eds.), Object-Oriented Technology. Proceedings, 1999. XVII, 389 pages. 1999.

Vol. 1744: S. Staab, Extracting Degree Information from Texts. X; 187 pages. 1999. (Subseries LNAI).

Vol. 1745: P. Banerjee, V.K. Prasanna, B.P. Sinha (Eds.), High Performance Computing – HiPC'99. Proceedings, 1999. XXII, 412 pages. 1999.

Vol. 1746: M. Walker (Ed.), Cryptography and Coding. Proceedings, 1999. IX, 313 pages. 1999.

Vol. 1747: N. Foo (Ed.), Adavanced Topics in Artificial Intelligence. Proceedings, 1999. XV, 500 pages. 1999. (Subseries LNAI).

Vol. 1748: H.V. Leong, W.-C. Lee, B. Li, L. Yin (Eds.), Mobile Data Access. Proceedings, 1999. X, 245 pages. 1999.

Vol. 1749: L. C.-K. Hui, D.L. Lee (Eds.), Internet Applications. Proceedings, 1999. XX, 518 pages. 1999.

Vol. 1750: D.E. Knuth, MMIXware. VIII, 550 pages. 1999.

Vol. 1751: H. Imai, Y. Zheng (Eds.), Public Key Cryptography. Proceedings, 2000. XI, 485 pages. 2000.

Vol. 1753: E. Pontelli, V. Santos Costa (Eds.), Practical Aspects of Declarative Languages. Proceedings, 2000. X, 327 pages. 2000.

Vol. 1754: J. Väänänen (Ed.), Generalized Quantifiers and Computation. Proceedings, 1997. VII, 139 pages. 1999.

Vol. 1755: D. Bjørner, M. Broy, A.V. Zamulin (Eds.), Perspectives of System Informatics. Proceedings, 1999. XII, 540 pages. 2000.

Vol. 1760: J.-J. Ch. Meyer, P.-Y. Schobbens (Eds.), Formal Models of Agents. Poceedings. VIII, 253 pages. 1999. (Subseries LNAI).

Vol. 1762: K.-D. Schewe, B. Thalheim (Eds.), Foundations of Information and Knowledge Systems. Proceedings, 2000. X, 305 pages. 2000.